ELECTRIC AND HYBRID ELECTRIC VEHICLES

James Halderman

Curt Ward

Pearson

Content Management: Tara Warrens
Content Production: Isha Sachdeva
Product Management: Derril Trakalo
Rights and Permissions: Jenell Forschler

Please contact https://support.pearson.com/getsupport/s/ with any queries on this content

Cover Image by Herr Loeffler/Shutterstock; fanjianhua/Shutterstock

Copyright © 2023 by Pearson Education, Inc. or its affiliates, 221 River Street, Hoboken, NJ 07030. All Rights Reserved. Manufactured in the United States of America. This publication is protected by copyright, and permission should be obtained from the publisher prior to any prohibited reproduction, storage in a retrieval system, or transmission in any form or by any means, electronic, mechanical, photocopying, recording, or otherwise. For information regarding permissions, request forms, and the appropriate contacts within the Pearson Education Global Rights and Permissions department, please visit www.pearsoned.com/permissions/.

Acknowledgments of third-party content appear on the appropriate page within the text.

PEARSON and ALWAYS LEARNING are exclusive trademarks owned by Pearson Education, Inc. or its affiliates in the U.S. and/or other countries.

Unless otherwise indicated herein, any third-party trademarks, logos, or icons that may appear in this work are the property of their respective owners, and any references to third-party trademarks, logos, icons, or other trade dress are for demonstrative or descriptive purposes only. Such references are not intended to imply any sponsorship, endorsement, authorization, or promotion of Pearson's products by the owners of such marks, or any relationship between the owner and Pearson Education, Inc., or its affiliates, authors, licensees, or distributors.

Library of Congress Cataloging-in-Publication Data

Names: Halderman, James D.
Title: Electric and hybrid electric vehicles / James D. Halderman.
Description: First edition. | Hoboken, NJ : Pearson Education, Inc., [2023] | Includes index.
Identifiers: LCCN 2021056834 (print) | LCCN 2021056835 (ebook) | ISBN 9780137532124 (paperback) |
  ISBN 0137532121 (paperback) | ISBN 9780137532193 (ebook)
Subjects: LCSH: Electric vehicles—Maintenance and repair—Textbooks. | Hybrid electric vehicles—Maintenance and
  repair—Textbooks.
Classification: LCC TL220 .H345 2023 (print) | LCC TL220 (ebook) | DDC 629.22/93—dc23/eng/20220105
LC record available at https://lccn.loc.gov/2021056834
LC ebook record available at https://lccn.loc.gov/2021056835

2 2022

ISBN 10: 0-13-753212-1
ISBN 13: 978-0-13-753212-4

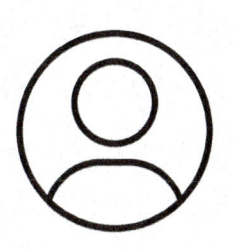

Pearson's Commitment to Diversity, Equity, and Inclusion

Pearson is dedicated to creating bias-free content that reflects the diversity of all learners.

We embrace the many dimensions of diversity, including but not limited to race, ethnicity, gender, socioeconomic status, ability, age, sexual orientation, and religious or political beliefs.

Education is a powerful force for equity and change in our world. It has the potential to deliver opportunities that improve lives and enable economic mobility. As we work with authors to create content for every product and service, we acknowledge our responsibility to demonstrate inclusivity and incorporate diverse scholarship so that everyone can achieve their potential through learning. As the world's leading learning company, we have a duty to help drive change and live up to our purpose to help more people create a better life for themselves and to create a better world.

Our ambition is to purposefully contribute to a world where:

- Everyone has an equitable and lifelong opportunity to succeed through learning.
- Our educational content accurately reflects the histories and lived experiences of the learners we serve.
- Our educational products and services are inclusive and represent the rich diversity of learners.
- Our educational content prompts deeper discussions with students and motivates them to expand their own learning (and worldview).

Accessibility

We are also committed to providing products that are fully accessible to all learners. As per Pearson's guidelines for accessible educational Web media, we test and retest the capabilities of our products against the highest standards for every release, following the WCAG guidelines in developing new products for copyright year 2022 and beyond.

You can learn more about Pearson's commitment to accessibility at
https://www.pearson.com/us/accessibility.html

Contact Us

While we work hard to present unbiased, fully accessible content, we want to hear from you about any concerns or needs with this Pearson product so that we can investigate and address them.

Please contact us with concerns about any potential bias at
https://www.pearson.com/report-bias.html

For accessibility-related issues, such as using assistive technology with Pearson products, alternative text requests, or accessibility documentation, email the Pearson Disability Support team at **disability.support@pearson.com**

PREFACE

Introducing an innovative first edition in electric and hybrid electric vehicles! Designed to meet the needs of a third or fourth semester course in electrical systems, *Electric and Hybrid Electric Vehicles* is also designed for a special topic or certificate course in electric and hybrid electric vehicles or for an introductory course in connected and autonomous vehicles. It features all of the advanced technology of on-board diagnosis and up-to-date electrified vehicles technology, plus the same organization, flow, and features of the renowned Professional Technician series by Pearson!

DEPTH OF CONTENT AND FORMAT

Scope: Based on input and suggestions from automotive instructors, this title is aligned with ASE standards and includes comprehensive coverage as follows:

- The first four chapters are designed to introduce electric and hybrid electric vehicles including safety (chapter 1), introduction (chapter 2) and background information on the importance of the need for electrified vehicles (chapter 3), and hybrid ICE information (chapter 4).
- Chapter 5 (Hybrid and Electric Vehicle Preventative Maintenance) covers the routine maintenance required to be performed on electric and hybrid electric vehicles.
- Chapters 6 (Digital Storage Oscilloscope Testing) covers the uses of digital storage oscilloscopes (DSOs) with the emphasis on detailed analysis to locate the root cause of a customer concern.
- Chapter 7 (Energy and Power) includes the terms and definitions used throughout the rest of the text regarding energy and power including electrical units of measure commonly used when discussing electric and hybrid electric vehicles.
- Chapter 8 (Advanced AC and DC Electricity) is designed to prepare the reader for the circuits and testing of electric and hybrid electric vehicles.
- Chapter 9 (Low-Voltage Batteries and Stop-Start Micro Hybrids) includes useful information for the technician when dealing with currently available electric and hybrid electric vehicles.
- Chapter 10 (High-Voltage Batteries) includes the types and designs of high-voltage batteries used in both electric and hybrid electric vehicles.
- Chapter 11 (EV and HEV Motors, Converters, and Inverters) introduces the reader to the electronics involved in the electrified vehicle propulsion system.
- Chapters 12 (EV and PHEV Charging) and 13 (Electric Vehicle Charging Equipment) include all the details that are needed to know about levels 1, 2, and 3 charging.
- Chapters 14 (Regenerative Brakes), 15 (Electric Power Steering), 16 (EV and HEV HVAC System), 17 (EV and HEV Transmissions), and 18 (EV and HEV Driver Assist Systems) each round out the details that service technicians need to know to understand and service electric and hybrid electric vehicles.
- Chapter 19 (Fuel Cells and Advanced Technologies) covers advanced systems that are currently on the market and likely to be expanded in the future.
- Chapter 20 (First Responder Procedures) includes important procedures for identifying and mitigating potentially dangerous situations when working with electric and hybrid electric vehicles.
- The appendix provides a Sample ASE-type L3 Certification Test.

Organization: The content includes the basics needed by all service technicians and covers the following organization for most systems:

- Purpose and function of the system
- Parts involved and operational description
- Diagnosis and service

HALLMARK IN-TEXT FEATURES

The following highlights the unique core features that set the Professional Technician Series book apart from other automotive textbooks.

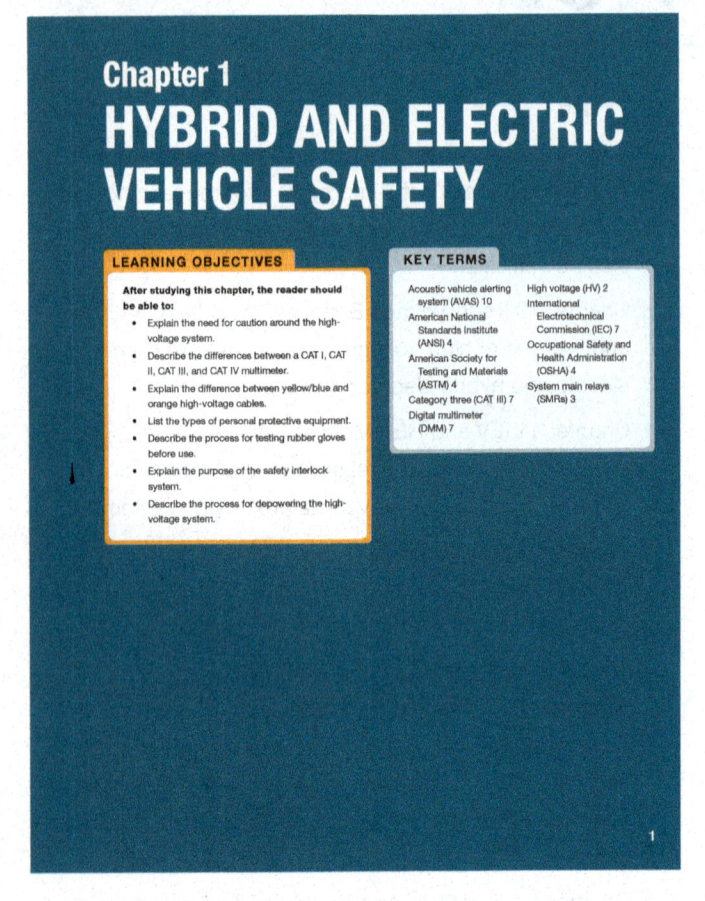

Chapter 1
HYBRID AND ELECTRIC VEHICLE SAFETY

LEARNING OBJECTIVES

After studying this chapter, the reader should be able to:
- Explain the need for caution around the high-voltage system.
- Describe the differences between a CAT I, CAT II, CAT III, and CAT IV multimeter.
- Explain the difference between yellow/blue and orange high-voltage cables.
- List the types of personal protective equipment.
- Describe the process for testing rubber gloves before use.
- Explain the purpose of the safety interlock system.
- Describe the process for depowering the high-voltage system.

KEY TERMS

Acoustic vehicle alerting system (AVAS) 10
American National Standards Institute (ANSI) 4
American Society for Testing and Materials (ASTM) 4
Category three (CAT III) 7
Digital multimeter (DMM) 7
High voltage (HV) 2
International Electrotechnical Commission (IEC) 7
Occupational Safety and Health Administration (OSHA) 4
System main relays (SMRs) 3

OBJECTIVES AND KEY TERMS appear at the beginning of each chapter to help students and instructors focus on the most important material in each chapter. The chapter objectives are based on specific ASE tasks.

TECH TIP

Test Motor Before Replacing the Inverter

Before replacing a failed inverter, test the electric motor for any defects. It is relatively common for shorted electric motor windings to cause a failure of the inverter. The new inverter is likely to fail upon installation if the electric motor failure is not resolved first.

TECH TIPS feature real-world advice and "tricks of the trade" from ASE-certified master technicians.

PHOTO SEQUENCE

1. A Mustang Mach E electric SUV is showing 66 miles (27%) of charge remaining.
2. Using a smartphone app, Plug Share in this case, the driver located a Level 3 charging station.
3. After using a credit card to gain access, the driver removed the SAE CCS charge plug from the charging station.
4. The charge post on the Mustang Mach E is located on the left front fender.
5. During charging, the Mach E lights a series of lights around the charge receptible to let the driver know the level of charge. When all lights are on, the vehicle has been fully charged.
6. The charging station also shows the state-of-charge on the display. Most experts recommend only charging to 80% unless traveling when the extra range is required to help protect the HV battery.

STEP-BY-STEP PHOTO SEQUENCES show in detail the steps involved in performing a specific task or service procedure.

Case Study

The Case of the Vibrating Tesla

An owner of a Tesla Model Y visited a tire shop complaining of a vibration in the steering wheel at highway speeds. A local tire shop balanced both front tires. The right front only needed a quarter ounce whereas the left front required over four ounces to balance. After leaving the shop, the owner immediately noticed that the vibration was much worse. The owner returned to the shop and this time the tire was removed from the rim. It became apparent that the vibration issue was caused by the foam inside the tire. This foam that generally played the role of reducing noise had separated and was loose inside the tire. The shop removed the foam and did not try to reinstall it. The wheel was balanced, which solved the vibration concern. The driver did not notice any increase in noise. ● **SEE FIGURE 2-6.**

Summary:
- **Complaint**—A Tesla owner complained of a vibration in the steering wheel at highway speeds.
- **Cause**—The acoustical foam inside a tire that is supposed to reduce noise had separated from the inner liner of the left front tire.
- **Correction**—The foam was removed from the tire and the tire/wheel assembly was balanced which corrected the vibration concern.

CASE STUDIES present students with actual automotive scenarios and shows how these common (and sometimes uncommon) problems were diagnosed and repaired. Uses the Three Cs approach (Complaint, Cause, Correction).

> **NOTE:** These numbers originally referred to the metric dimensions of the graticule in centimeters. Therefore, an 8 × 10 display would be 8 centimeters (80 millimeters or 3.14 inches) high and 10 centimeters (100 millimeters or 3.90 inches) wide.

NOTES provide students with additional technical information to give them a greater understanding of a specific task or procedure.

FREQUENTLY ASKED QUESTION

How Do You Reboot the Digital Display?

For most electric vehicles, pull the first responder loop under the hood, then disconnect the negative battery terminal by the fuse box. Wait 5 minutes, reconnect the battery terminal and then the first responder loop.

On the Tesla Model 3, hold down both scroll wheels on the steering wheel until the display reboots. Press and hold both scroll wheels on either side of the steering wheel for up to 10 seconds and the main/central screen will reboot. A soft reboot is performed by holding in both scroll wheels until the touchscreen turns off. A hard reboot is allegedly doing the same thing, but pressing and holding the brake pedal until the Tesla logo appears on the touchscreen. Another variation of a "reboot" is to power off the car from the touchscreen and leave it off for a few minutes (you have to stay in the car).

On a Mustang Mach E, to reboot the SYNC 4 system, push Volume Down button and Forward seek button. Hold them both down at the same time until the screen reboots.

FREQUENTLY ASKED QUESTIONS are based on the author's own experience and provide answers to many of the most common questions asked by students and beginning service technicians.

> **CAUTION:** Check the instructions for the scope being used before attempting to scope household AC circuits. Some scopes are not designed to measure high-voltage AC circuits.

CAUTIONS alert students about potential damage to personal property that can occur during a specific task or service procedure.

HALLMARK IN-TEXT FEATURES

> **WARNING**
>
> To avoid an electrical shock, any capacitor should be treated as if it were charged until it is proven to be discharged.

WARNINGS alert students to the potential dangers of personal injury during a specific task or service procedure.

THE SUMMARY, REVIEW QUESTIONS, AND CHAPTER QUIZ at the end of each chapter help students review the material presented in the chapter and test themselves to see how much they have learned.

AFFORDABLE PURCHASE OPTIONS FOR STUDENTS

Print: This first edition is available as an affordable, rent-to-own option.

eBooks: This text is also available in multiple eBook formats. These are a great choice for busy students that are looking to save money. As an alternative to renting/purchasing the printed textbook, students can purchase an electronic version of the same content. Pearson eText is an easy-to-use digital textbook. It lets students customize how they study and learn with enhanced search and the ability to create flashcards, highlight, add notes, and listen to the audio version all in one place. The mobile app lets students learn wherever life takes them, offline or online. Additionally, the Pearson eText features approximately 20 minutes of simulated, instructive animations providing students with an enhanced visual reference for essential automotive concepts and skills. For more information on Pearson eText, visit www.pearson.com/learner.

SUPPLEMENTS

All Pearson Automotive Series textbooks are accompanied by a full set of instructor and student supplements.

- Instructor's Resource Manual
- PowerPoint Presentation
- TestGen Computerized Testbank
- ASE Correlated Task Sheets (Download Only by instructors) for *Electric and Hybrid Electric Vehicles*
- Instructor Resources can be downloaded at www.pearsonhighered.com/irc. If you don't already have a username and password for access, you can request access at www.pearsonhighered.com/irc. Within 48 hours of registering, you will receive a confirming email including an instructor access code. Once you have received your code, locate your text in the online catalog and click on the Instructor Resources button on the left side of the catalog product page. Select a supplement and a login page will appear. Once you have logged in, you can access instructor material for all Pearson textbooks.

Student Supplements (for purchase):
ASE Correlated Task Sheets for *Electric and Hybrid Electric Vehicles*, ISBN: 9780137532155

ACKNOWLEDGMENTS

Many people and organizations have cooperated in providing the reference material and technical information used in this text. The authors wish to express their sincere thanks to the following persons for their special contributions:

- Carl Borsani—Graphic Home Design & Marketing, LLC
- Stephen Ellis—Honda Motor Company, Ltd.
- Ford Motor Company
- Tom Freels—Sinclair Community College
- General Motors Corporation
- Tim Jones—Honda Training Center
- Chris Karr—Ford Motor Company
- Andy Knevel—Toyota Motor Corporation
- Lloyd Koppes—Toyota Motor Corporation
- Toyota Motor Sales—USA, Inc.
- Dick Krieger—Michigan Institute of Technology
- Jeff Rehkopf
- Dan Avery
- Dr. John Kershaw
- Steve Cartwright—Federal Mogul Training Center
- Chuck Taylor—Sinclair Community College
- Tom Birch
- David Norman—San Jacinto College
- Joe Palazzolo—GKN Driveline
- Glen Plants

TECHNICAL AND CONTENT REVIEWERS The following people reviewed the manuscript before production and checked it for technical accuracy and clarity of presentation. Their suggestions and recommendations were included in the final draft of the manuscript. Their input helped make this textbook clear and technically accurate while maintaining the easy-to-read style that has made other books from the same authors so popular.

- Jim Anderson—Greenville High School
- Rankin E. Barnes—Guilford Technical Community College
- Kevin Murphy—Stark State College of Technology
- Teresa L. Noto, M.S.—Farmingdale State College
- Paul Pate—College of Southern Nevada
- Fritz Peacock—Indiana Vocational Technical College
- Dennis Peter—NAIT (Canada)
- Eric Pruden—Pennsylvania College of Technology
- Jeff Rehkopf—Florida State College
- Kenneth Redick—Hudson Valley Community College
- Matt Roda—Mott Community College
- Mitchell Walker—St. Louis Community College at Forest Park

SPECIAL THANKS Special thanks to instructional designer Alexis I. Skriloff James.

The authors wish to thank Mike Mills and Adam Fullam; The Lexus of Dayton dealership; and Chuck Taylor of Sinclair Community College in Dayton, Ohio, who helped with many of the photos. A special thanks to Ron Morris, Jeff Rehkopf, and Tom Birch for their detailed and thorough reviews of the manuscript before publication. Most of all, we wish to thank Michelle Halderman for her assistance in all phases of manuscript preparation.

—Jim Halderman
—Curt Ward

ABOUT THE AUTHORS

JIM HALDERMAN brings a world of experience, knowledge, and talent to his work. His automotive service experience includes working as a flat-rate technician, a business owner, and a professor of automotive technology at a leading U.S. community college.

He has a Bachelor of Science degree from Ohio Northern University and a master's degree from Miami University in Oxford, Ohio. Jim also holds a U.S. patent for an electronic transmission control device. He is an ASE certified Master Automotive Technician and is also Advanced Engine Performance (L1) ASE certified. Jim is the author of many automotive textbooks, all published by Pearson Education. Jim has presented numerous technical seminars to national audiences, including the California Automotive Teachers (CAT) and the Illinois College Automotive Instructor Association (ICAIA). He is also a member and presenter at the North American Council of Automotive Teachers (NACAT). Jim was also named Regional Teacher of the Year by General Motors Corporation and a member of the advisory committee for the department of technology at Ohio Northern University. Jim and his wife, Michelle, live in Dayton, Ohio. They have two children. You can reach Jim at: jim@jameshalderman.com

CURT WARD Prior to his years at Chrysler, Curt has worked as a technician, shop foreman, and service manager in the retail sector of the automotive industry for 13 years. During this time, he became a Chrysler Master Technician. Curt has an Associates of Applied Science in Automotive Service Technology from Southern Illinois University. He has a Bachelor of Fine Arts in Organizational Communications from North Central College. He earned his master's degree in Adult Education at the University of Phoenix.

Curt is an ASE Master Automotive Technician. He has presented technical seminars at numerous conferences around the country. He has presented for the Illinois College Automotive Instructor Association (ICAIA), the California Automotive Teachers (CAT), and the North American Council of Automotive Teachers (NACAT). Curt is an active member in the ICAIA and the NACAT. He has served as the secretary and president of the NACAT organization and was the conference host for the 2015 NACAT Conference. In 2015, Curt was named the NACAT MVP award winner for his outstanding contribution to the NACAT organization. Curt and his wife Tammy have five children and five grandchildren. Together they enjoy traveling and exploring historical sites. In his spare time, Curt enjoys modeling 3-rail O-gauge railroads. You can reach Curt at: curt@curtward.net

BRIEF CONTENTS

chapter 1	Hybrid and Electric Vehicle Safety	1
chapter 2	Introduction to Electric and Hybrid Electric Vehicles	14
chapter 3	Health and Environmental Concerns	27
chapter 4	Hybrid Engine Systems	36
chapter 5	Hybrid and Electric Vehicle Preventative Maintenance	56
chapter 6	Digital Storage Oscilloscope Testing	65
chapter 7	Energy and Power	78
chapter 8	Advanced AC and DC Electricity	89
chapter 9	Low-Voltage Batteries and Stop-Start Micro Hybrids	102
chapter 10	High-Voltage Batteries	119
chapter 11	EV and HEV Motors, Converters, and Inverters	141
chapter 12	EV and PHEV Charging	163
chapter 13	Electric Vehicle Charging Equipment	178
chapter 14	Regenerative Brakes	188
chapter 15	Electric Power Steering	199
chapter 16	EV and HEV HVAC System	207
chapter 17	EV and HEV Transmissions	228
chapter 18	EV and HEV Driver Assist Systems	250
chapter 19	Fuel Cells and Advanced Technologies	268
chapter 20	First Responder Procedures	282
appendix	Sample Hybrid/Electric Vehicle Specialist (L3) ASE-Type Certification Test	291
	Glossary	295
	Index	303

CONTENTS

chapter 1
HYBRID AND ELECTRIC VEHICLE SAFETY   1

- Learning Objectives   1
- Key Terms   1
- High-Voltage Safety   2
- Electric Shock Potential   3
- Electric Vehicles in the Service Area   3
- Personal Protective Equipment (PPE)   4
- High-Voltage Tools and Equipment   7
- Safety Interlock System   8
- Depowering the High-Voltage System   9
- Hoisting a Hybrid or Electric Vehicle   9
- Moving a Hybrid or Electric Vehicle Around the Shop   10

SUMMARY   10
- High-Voltage Glove Photo Sequence   11

REVIEW QUESTIONS   13
CHAPTER QUIZ   13

chapter 2
INTRODUCTION TO ELECTRIC AND HYBRID ELECTRIC VEHICLES   14

- Learning Objectives   14
- Key Terms   14
- Hybrid Electric Vehicles   15
- Electric Vehicle   15
- History   15
- Efficiencies of Electric Motors and ICEs   16
- Driving a Hybrid or Electric Vehicle   16
- Levels of Hybrid Vehicles   20
- Classifications of Hybrid Vehicle Powertrain   20
- One-, Two-, and Three-Motor Hybrid System   22
- Advantages and Disadvantages of an Electric Vehicle   23

SUMMARY   25
REVIEW QUESTIONS   25
CHAPTER QUIZ   26

chapter 3
HEALTH AND ENVIRONMENTAL CONCERNS   27

- Learning Objectives   27
- Key Terms   27
- Need for Electric Vehicles (EV) and Hybrid Electric Vehicles (HEV)   28
- Ozone   30
- Ultraviolet Radiation absorption   31
- Health Effects of Air Pollution   32
- Acid Rain   32
- Carbon Footprint   33

SUMMARY   35
REVIEW QUESTIONS   35
CHAPTER QUIZ   35

chapter 4
HYBRID ENGINE SYSTEMS   36

- Learning Objectives   36
- Key Terms   36
- Hybrid Internal Combustion Engines (ICE)   37
- Engine Fundamentals   37
- Atkinson Cycle   38
- Hybrid Engine Design Features   40
- Variable Valve Timing   42
- Diagnosis of Variable Valve Timing Systems   45
- HEV ICE Cooling System   46
- Cooling System Testing   47
- Coolant Heat Storage System   49
- Hybrid Engine Run Mode   50
- Hybrid Engine Testing   52

SUMMARY   54
REVIEW QUESTIONS   54
CHAPTER QUIZ   55

chapter 5
HYBRID AND ELECTRIC VEHICLE PREVENTATIVE MAINTENANCE 56

- Learning Objectives 56
- Key Terms 56
- Routine Service Procedures 57

SUMMARY 63
REVIEW QUESTIONS 63
CHAPTER QUIZ 64

chapter 6
DIGITAL STORAGE OSCILLOSCOPE TESTING 65

- Learning Objectives 65
- Key Terms 65
- Types of Oscilloscopes 66
- Scope Setup and Adjustment 67
- DC and AC Coupling 68
- Pulse Trains 68
- Number of Channels 70
- Triggers 70
- Using a Scope 71
- Using DSO Accessories 71
- Waveform Analysis 72
- Scope Setup Photo Sequence 74

SUMMARY 76
REVIEW QUESTIONS 76
CHAPTER QUIZ 76

chapter 7
ENERGY AND POWER 78

- Learning Objectives 78
- Key Terms 78
- Energy 79
- Torque, Work, and Power 80
- Electrical Power 81
- Solar Electric Generation 82
- Wind Energy Generation 83
- Hydroelectric Generation 85
- Geothermal Energy 85

SUMMARY 87
REVIEW QUESTIONS 87
CHAPTER QUIZ 87

chapter 8
ADVANCED AC AND DC ELECTRICITY 89

- Learning Objectives 89
- Key Terms 89
- DC Electricity 90
- AC Electricity 91
- Power Output (Watts) 92
- Capacitors 92
- Magnetic Force 94
- Motor Control 94
- EV and HEV Electrical Measurements 96
- EV and HEV Module Communications 97
- Module Reprogramming 98

SUMMARY 100
REVIEW QUESTIONS 101
CHAPTER QUIZ 101

chapter 9
LOW-VOLTAGE BATTERIES AND STOP-START MICRO HYBRIDS 102

- Learning Objectives 102
- Key Terms 102
- Introduction to the 12-Volt Battery 103
- How a Battery Works 103
- Valve-Regulated Lead-Acid Batteries 104
- 12-Volt Battery Ratings 105
- Battery Service Safety Precautions 105
- 12-Volt Battery Voltage Test 106
- 12-Volt Battery Load Testing 107
- 12-Volt Battery Conductance Testing 108
- 12-Volt Battery Charging 108
- The 36-48-Volt Battery 109
- Stop-Start Defined 110
- Stop-Start Systems 110
- Micro Hybrids 112
- Diagnosis 114
- Mild Hybrids 115

SUMMARY 117
REVIEW QUESTIONS 118
CHAPTER QUIZ 118

chapter 10
HIGH-VOLTAGE BATTERIES 119

- Learning Objectives 119
- Key Terms 119
- Hybrid and Electric Vehicle High-Voltage Batteries 120
- Nickel-Metal Hydride Batteries 120
- Lithium-Ion High-Voltage Batteries 123
- Designs of Lithium-Ion Cells 124
- Types of Lithium-Ion Batteries 125
- HEV/EV Electronics Cooling 126
- High-Voltage Battery Cooling and Heating 128
- Battery Capacity vs Vehicle Range 129
- High-Voltage Battery Control Components 130
- Battery Management System (BMS) 131
- Electrical Distribution System (EDS) 131
- HEV High-Voltage Battery Monitor 133
- Lithium-Ion Battery Repair 134
- Alternative Out-of-Vehicle HV Battery Service 134
- Battery Degradation and Balancing 136
- Photo Sequence HEV-HV Battery Inspection and Testing 137

SUMMARY 139
REVIEW QUESTIONS 139
CHAPTER QUIZ 139

chapter 11
EV AND HEV MOTORS, CONVERTERS, AND INVERTERS 141

- Learning Objectives 141
- Key Terms 141
- Electromagnetism 142
- Electromagnetic Induction 143
- Electric Motors 144
- Brushless Motors 146
- Electric Motor Control 148
- Capacitors in Converters 151
- Converters and Inverters 153
- Electronic System Cooling System 156
- Motor–Converter–Inverter Diagnostics 157
- Photo Sequence—Inverter/Converter Replacement 159

SUMMARY 162
REVIEW QUESTIONS 162
CHAPTER QUIZ 162

chapter 12
EV AND PHEV CHARGING 163

- Learning Objectives 163
- Key Terms 163
- Plug-In Hybrid Electric Vehicles 164
- Electric Vehicles 166
- Level 1 Charging 167
- Level 2 Charging 168
- Level 3 Charging 169
- Owning and Charging an EV 172
- Photo Sequence 175

SUMMARY 176
REVIEW QUESTIONS 176
CHAPTER QUIZ 176

chapter 13
ELECTRIC VEHICLE CHARGING EQUIPMENT 178

- Learning Objectives 178
- Key Terms 178
- Electric Vehicle Supply Equipment 179
- Wireless Charging 184
- Installing a Home Charging Station Photo Sequence 186

SUMMARY 187
REVIEW QUESTIONS 187
CHAPTER QUIZ 187

chapter 14
REGENERATIVE BRAKES 188

- Learning Objective 188
- Key Terms 188
- Regenerative Braking in Vehicles 189
- Types of Regenerative Brake Systems 191
- One-Pedal Driving 194
- Deceleration Rates 195
- Servicing Regenerative Brakes 195

SUMMARY 197
REVIEW QUESTIONS 197
CHAPTER QUIZ 198

chapter 15
ELECTRIC POWER STEERING 199

- Learning Objectives 199
- Key Terms 199
- Electric Power Steering 200
- Parts and Operation 201
- Electric Power Steering Diagnosis 204

SUMMARY 205
REVIEW QUESTIONS 206
CHAPTER QUIZ 206

chapter 16
EV AND HEV HVAC SYSTEM 207

- Learning Objectives 207
- Key Terms 207
- HEV ICE Cooling System 208
- HEV Cabin Heating Systems 209
- Coolant Heat Storage System 212
- PTC Heaters 213
- HEV Cabin Cooling 213
- HEV A/C Components 215
- EV Heating 220
- Heat Pump 222

SUMMARY 226
REVIEW QUESTIONS 226
CHAPTER QUIZ 226

chapter 17
EV AND HEV TRANSMISSIONS 228

- Learning Objectives 228
- Key Terms 228
- Transmissions and Transaxles 229
- Principles Involved 230
- HEV Transmissions 230
- GM Parallel Hybrid Truck (PHT) 231
- GM Two-Mode Hybrid Transmission 232
- Ford/Lincoln 10R80 MHT 234
- Toyota/Lexus Power-Split System 236
- Toyota Hybrid eCVT Transmission 243
- Hybrid Electric Rear Axle 244
- Hybrid Transmission Diagnosis 244
- Electric Vehicle Transmissions 245

SUMMARY 248
REVIEW QUESTIONS 248
CHAPTER QUIZ 248

chapter 18
EV AND HEV DRIVER ASSIST SYSTEMS 250

- Learning Objectives 250
- Key Terms 250
- Advanced Driver Assist Systems 251
- Human–Machine Interface (HMI) 251
- Blind Spot Monitor 252
- Parking-Assist Systems 253
- Lane Departure Warning 254
- Lane Keep Assist 255
- Adaptive Cruise Control 255
- Rear Cross-Traffic Warning (RCTW) 257
- Automatic Emergency Braking 258
- Pre-Collision System 258
- Cameras 259
- Lidar Systems 260
- Driver Assist Diagnosis 261
- Camera and Radar Sensor Calibration 261
- Autonomous Vehicle Operation 263
- Levels of Automation 263
- Artificial Intelligence (AI) 265
- Dedicated Short-Range Communication (DSRC) 265

SUMMARY 266
REVIEW QUESTIONS 266
CHAPTER QUIZ 267

chapter 19
FUEL CELLS AND ADVANCED TECHNOLOGIES 268

- Learning Objectives 268
- Key Terms 268
- Fuel-Cell Technology 269
- Refueling with Hydrogen 272
- Direct Methanol Fuel Cells 272
- Fuel-Cell Vehicle Systems 273
- Fuel-Cell Hybrid Vehicles 275
- Hydrogen Storage 275
- Ultracapacitors 277
- Fuel-Cell Vehicle Transaxles 277
- HCCI 279

SUMMARY 280
REVIEW QUESTIONS 280
CHAPTER QUIZ 281

chapter 20
FIRST RESPONDER PROCEDURES 282

- Learning Objectives 282
- Key Terms 282
- EV and HEV First Responder Procedures 283
- EV and HEV Items to Check 284
- First Responder Safety 285
- Electric Shock Potential 287
- Emergency Response 287
- Fire 288
- Hazmat Issues 288
- Submerged Vehicles 289

SUMMARY 289
REVIEW QUESTIONS 290
CHAPTER QUIZ 290

appendix
SAMPLE HYBRID/ELECTRIC VEHICLE SPECIALIST (L3) ASE-TYPE CERTIFICATION TEST 291

GLOSSARY 295

INDEX 303

Chapter 1
HYBRID AND ELECTRIC VEHICLE SAFETY

LEARNING OBJECTIVES

After studying this chapter, the reader should be able to:

- Explain the need for caution around the high-voltage system.
- Describe the differences between a CAT I, CAT II, CAT III, and CAT IV multimeter.
- Explain the difference between yellow/blue and orange high-voltage cables.
- List the types of personal protective equipment.
- Describe the process for testing rubber gloves before use.
- Explain the purpose of the safety interlock system.
- Describe the process for depowering the high-voltage system.

KEY TERMS

Acoustic vehicle alerting system (AVAS) 10
American National Standards Institute (ANSI) 4
American Society for Testing and Materials (ASTM) 4
Category three (CAT III) 7
Digital multimeter (DMM) 7
High voltage (HV) 2
International Electrotechnical Commission (IEC) 7
Occupational Safety and Health Administration (OSHA) 4
System main relays (SMRs) 3

HIGH-VOLTAGE SAFETY

NEED FOR CAUTION Electrical systems have been used on vehicles for more than a century. Technicians have been repairing vehicle electrical systems without fear of serious injury or electrocution. However, when working with electric or hybrid electric vehicles, this is no longer true. It is now possible to be seriously injured or electrocuted (killed) if proper safety procedures are not followed.

Electric and hybrid electric vehicles use **high-voltage (HV)** circuits that if touched with an unprotected hand could cause serious burns or even death.

PRECAUTIONS FOR ELECTRONIC MEDICAL DEVICES

- Electronic medical devices include cardiac pacemakers and cardioverter defibrillators.

- Technicians who rely on cardiac pacemakers should not service or repair electric or hybrid electric vehicles because of strong magnetic fields.
- Technicians who rely on implanted cardiac pacemakers or implanted cardioverter defibrillators should check with the manufacturer of the device before being in or around a charging vehicle.

IDENTIFYING HIGH-VOLTAGE CIRCUITS HV components are identified with warning labels. HV cables are identified by color of the plastic conduit and are indicated by the following colors:

- **Blue or yellow**—Up to 60 volts (not a shock hazard, but an arc will be maintained if a circuit is opened). ● SEE FIGURE 1-1a and 1-1b.

? FREQUENTLY ASKED QUESTION

How Much Current Is Too Much?

Low voltage, such as the 12–14 volts used in conventional vehicles, does not represent a shock hazard and it is safe to handle. The only concern would be a possible burn could occur if a 12-volt wire were to touch ground causing the wiring to overheat. Voltages between 14 and 60 volts do not present a shock hazard, but an arc can occur if a connector carrying current is opened. High voltage, over 60 volts, does create a shock hazard and all precautions must be adhered to prevent personal injury. Typical current and how it affects the body are given as follows:

- 1 milliamp—May be noticeable as a slight tingle.
- 2–5 milliamps—May be noticeable as a light shock forcing the technician to let go.
- 6–25 milliamps—Noticed by pain and the technician cannot let go of the wires or component.
- 26–150 milliamps—Severe pain and possibly fatal.
- 1,000 milliamps—One ampere across the heart can stop the heart (fatal).

Also, always wear HV gloves for protection whenever working on or near a potential HV circuit or component. To help prevent an electric current from flowing through the body, always place one hand in a pocket and use only one hand when measuring a potential HV circuit or disconnecting a potential HV circuit.

FIGURE 1-1a When the belt starter alternator assembly is installed, the three blue cables run between the inverter assembly and the alternator.

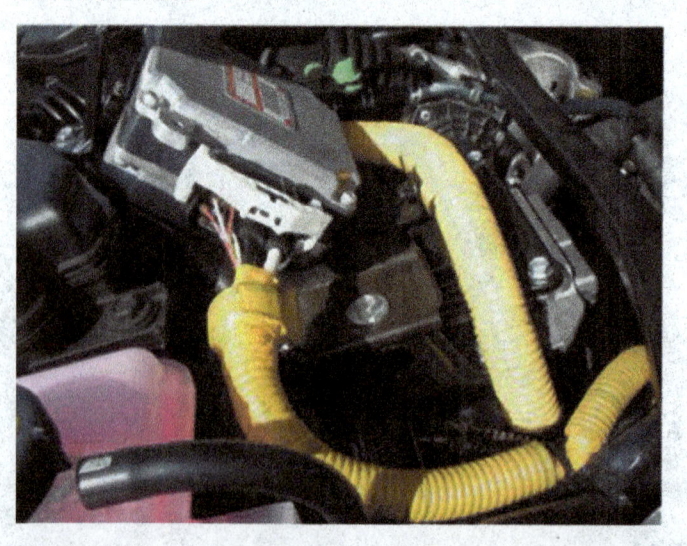

FIGURE 1-1b The yellow cable is part of the electric power steering system on a Toyota/Lexus vehicle.

FIGURE 1-2 The orange cables connect to the high power distribution module (HPDM) on the Chevrolet Bolt.

- **Orange**—Above 60 volts. ● **SEE FIGURE 1-2.**

Follow all precautions when working on or near HV wiring or components.

ELECTRIC SHOCK POTENTIAL

LOCATIONS WHERE SHOCK CAN OCCUR Accidental and unprotected contact with any electrically charged ("hot" or "live") HV component can cause serious injury or death. However, receiving an electric shock from a hybrid vehicle is highly unlikely because of the following:

1. Contact with the battery module or other components inside the battery box can occur only if the box is damaged and the contents are exposed, or the box is opened without following proper precautions.
2. Contact with the electric motor can occur only after one or more components are removed.
3. The HV cables can be easily identified by their distinctive orange color, and contact with them can be avoided.
4. The **system main relays (SMRs)** or contactors disconnect power from the cables the moment the ignition is turned off.

ELECTRIC VEHICLES IN THE SERVICE AREA

For a safe working environment:

- Be sure the work area is clean and dry.
- Care should be taken that HV warnings and safety cones are posted.
- Additional precautions, such as a roof cone or warning tape, are also recommended.

They are used to establish a safety zone around the vehicles so that other technicians will know that a possible shock hazard may be present. ● **SEE FIGURE 1-3**.

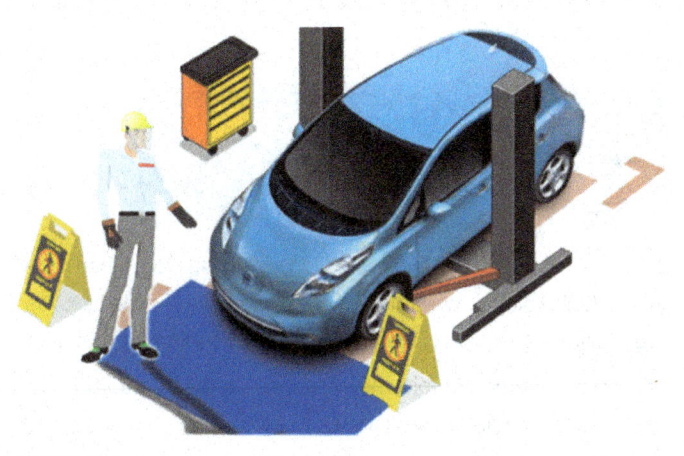

FIGURE 1-3 A clearly defined safety zone needs to be established in the area where a hybrid or electric vehicle is being repaired.

> ### TECH TIP
>
> **Silence Is NOT Golden**
>
> Never assume the vehicle is shut off just because the engine is off. When working with a hybrid electric vehicle, always look for the READY indicator status on the dash display. The vehicle is shut off when the READY indicator is off.
>
> The vehicle may be powered by:
>
> 1. The electric motor only.
> 2. The gasoline engine only.
> 3. A combination of both the electric motor and the gasoline engine.
>
> The vehicle computer determines the mode in which the vehicle operates to improve fuel economy and reduce emissions. The driver cannot manually select the mode.
> ● **SEE FIGURE 1-4.**

FIGURE 1-4 The Ford Escape Hybrid instrument panel showing the vehicle in park and the tachometer on "EV" instead of 0 RPM. This means the gasoline engine could start at any time depending on the state of charge of the HV battery and other factors.

PERSONAL PROTECTIVE EQUIPMENT (PPE)

EYE PROTECTION Eye protection should be worn when testing for high voltage, which is considered by many experts to be over 60 volts. Eye protection should include the following features:

1. Plastic frames (Avoid metal frames as these are conductive and could cause a shock hazard.)
2. Side shields
3. Meet the standard ANSI Z87.1

NOTE: Some vehicle manufacturers specify that full-face shields be worn instead of safety glasses when working with HV circuits or components. SEE FIGURE 1-5.

HIGH-VOLTAGE GLOVES Before working on the HV system of a hybrid electric vehicle, ensure that HV lineman's gloves are available. Be sure that the gloves are rated at least 1,000 volts and class "0" by ANSI/ASTM. ● **SEE FIGURE 1-6.** The **American National Standards Institute (ANSI)** is a private, nonprofit organization that administers and coordinates the U.S. voluntary standardization and conformity assessment system. ANSI International, originally known as the **American Society for Testing and Materials (ASTM)**, was formed over a century ago to address the need for component testing in industry. The **Occupational Safety and Health Administration (OSHA)** requirements specify that the HV gloves get inspected every six months by a qualified glove inspection laboratory. Do not use gloves on which the expiration date has expired. Inspect the gloves carefully before each use. High voltage and current (amperes) in combination are fatal.

Before using the rubber gloves, they should be tested for leaks using the following procedure:

1. Roll the glove up from the open end until the lower portion of the glove begins to balloon from the resulting air pressure. Make sure to "lean" into the sealed glove to raise the internal

FIGURE 1-5 Safety glasses or a full-face shield similar to the items depicted must be worn when testing for the presence of high voltage.

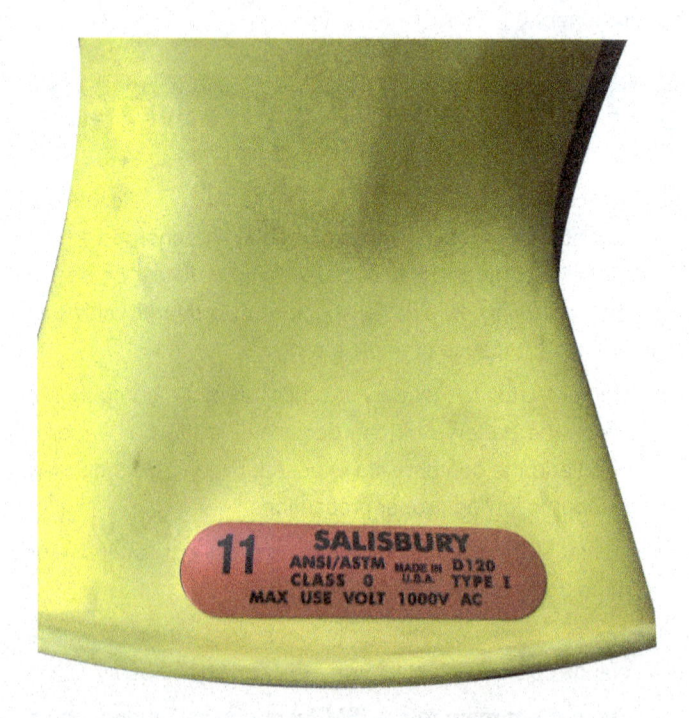

FIGURE 1-6 The gloves should be clearly marked indicating that they are class "0" and rated for 1,000 volts.

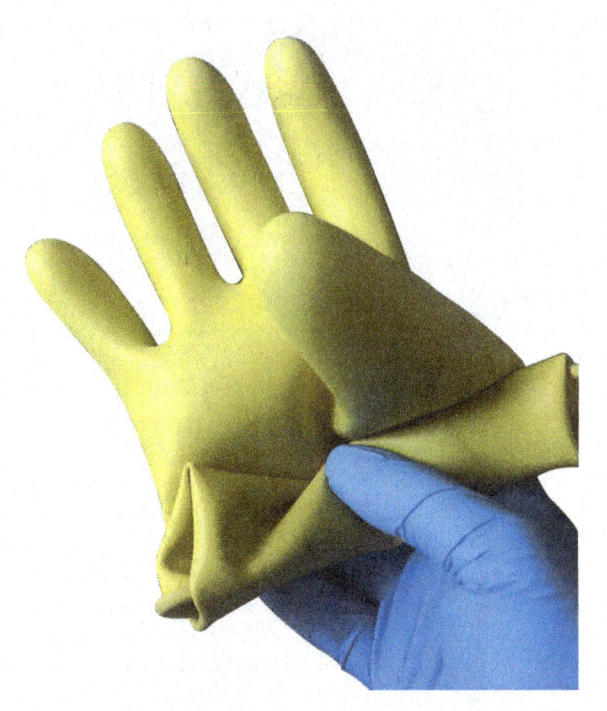

FIGURE 1-7 The glove is rolled up on the open end to check for air pressure and any air leakage.

WARNING

Do not use shop air to test HV gloves. The high air pressure will damage the gloves and lead to a lack of personal protection against high voltage.

air pressure. If the glove leaks any air, discard the gloves.
● SEE FIGURE 1-7.

2. An approved electric glove inflator can also be used to test the gloves before use. ● SEE FIGURE 1-8.

3. The gloves should not be used if they show any signs of wear and tear.

LEATHER PROTECTORS Use an outer leather glove to protect the HV rubber gloves. Be sure the rubber lineman's glove extends at least 50 mm beyond the leather protector. The leather

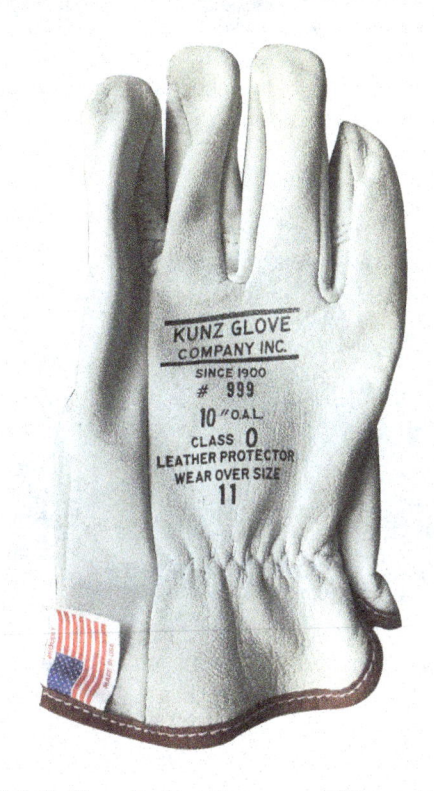

FIGURE 1-9 Clean leather gloves must be used to protect the HV rubber gloves.

gloves should be clean and free of any material that might puncture the lineman's glove or conduct electricity. ● SEE FIGURE 1-9.

SHOP UNIFORM Some manufacturers recommend arc flash clothing or long sleeve, 100% cotton clothing that is tucked into the gloves when working on HV components. Remove all jewelry, rings, watches, and bracelets before working on the vehicle.

INSULATED SHOES OR BOOTS Some manufactures recommend the use of insulated boots or shoes to protect against exposure to high voltage. These are particularly useful in areas where water, oil, and other substances cannot be wiped off the floor. ● SEE FIGURE 1-10.

INSULATED RUBBER MATS AND BLANKETS
Insulated rubber mats are placed on the floor when there is an exposure to high voltage. Insulated blankets are placed over

FIGURE 1-8 An electric glove inflator similar to this may be used for testing.

HYBRID AND ELECTRIC VEHICLE SAFETY **5**

FIGURE 1-10 The sole of this shoe is designed to prevent the transfer of electrical current.

FIGURE 1-11 Some work locations require the use of insulated rubber mats in the work area.

the battery or other HV components after removal and during disassembly. ● **SEE FIGURE 1-11.**

FIRE EXTINGUISHERS Use ONLY a Class C fire extinguisher rated for electrical fires. An ABC rated fire extinguisher may be used if a Class C is not available. ● **SEE FIGURE 1-12.**

OTHER PERSONAL PROTECTION EQUIPMENT Some manufactures recommend that a 10-foot insulated fiberglass pole be available outside the safety zone to be used to pull a technician away from the vehicle in the unlikely event of an accident where the technician is shocked or electrocuted. Other manufacturers require a second set of safety equipment be available.

FIGURE 1-12 Make sure a proper fire extinguisher is available in the work area.

? FREQUENTLY ASKED QUESTION

Is the Radiation from a Hybrid Dangerous?

No. While there is a changing magnetic field surrounding any wire carrying an electrical current, the amount of electromagnetic radiation is very low. ● **SEE FIGURE 1-13.**

FIGURE 1-13 The radiation emitted from a hybrid electric vehicle is very low and is being measured in units of milligauss.

HIGH-VOLTAGE TOOLS AND EQUIPMENT

CAT III RATED DIGITAL MULTIMETER Hybrid and electric vehicles are equipped with electrical systems whose voltages can exceed 600 volts DC. A **category three (CAT III)** certified **digital multimeter (DMM)** is required for making measurements on these high-voltage systems.

The **International Electrotechnical Commission (IEC)** has several categories of voltage standards for meter and meter leads. These categories are ratings for over voltage protection and are rated CAT I, CAT II, CAT III, and CAT IV. The higher the category (CAT) rating of the meter, the greater the level of protection to the technician when measuring high-energy voltage. Under each category, there are various voltage ratings.

- **CAT I**—Typically a CAT I meter is used for low-voltage (LV) measurements, such as voltage measurements at wall outlets in the home. Meters with a CAT I rating are usually rated at 300–800 volts. CAT I is for relatively low-energy levels. While the voltage level is high enough for use when working on a hybrid electric vehicle, the protective energy level is lower than what is needed.

- **CAT II**—A CAT II meter is a higher-rated meter that would be typically used for checking voltages at the circuit-breaker panel in the home. Meters with a CAT II rating are usually rated at 300–600 volts. CAT II-rated meters have similar voltage ratings as the other CAT ratings, but the energy level of protection is higher with a CAT II compared to a CAT I.

- **CAT III**—CAT III is the minimum-rated meter that should be used for hybrid and electric vehicles. Meters with a CAT III rating are usually rated at 600–1,000 volts and the highest energy level which is needed to protect the servie technician. ● **SEE FIGURES 1-14 and 1-15.**

- **CAT IV**—CAT IV meters are for clamp-on meters only. A clamp-on meter is used to measure current (amperes) in a circuit by placing the clamp around the wire carrying the current. If a clamp-on meter also has meter leads for voltage measurements, that part of the meter will be rated as CAT III.

FIGURE 1-14 Use only a meter that is CAT III rated when making electrical measurements on an electric or hybrid electric vehicle.

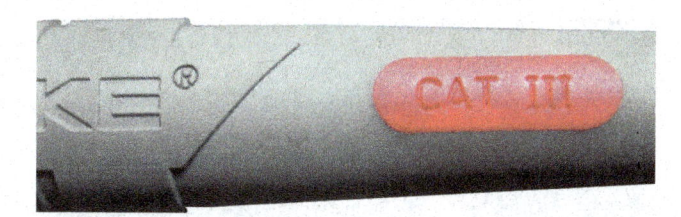

FIGURE 1-15 The meter leads should also be CAT III rated when checking voltages on an electric or hybrid electric vehicle.

MEGOHMMETER (INSULATION TESTER) A megohmmeteror insulation tester is used to check for continuity between the HV cables and the vehicle chassis. It contains an internal DC-DC converter that allows for the continuity test to occur at a much higher voltage than a conventional ohmmeter.
● **SEE FIGURE 1-16.**

INSULATED HAND TOOLS Although they are not required by all manufacturers, insulated tools such as a ratchets, extensions, sockets, pliers, and screwdrivers provide an additional margin of safety to the service technician when working around HV components and systems.
● **SEE FIGURE 1-17.**

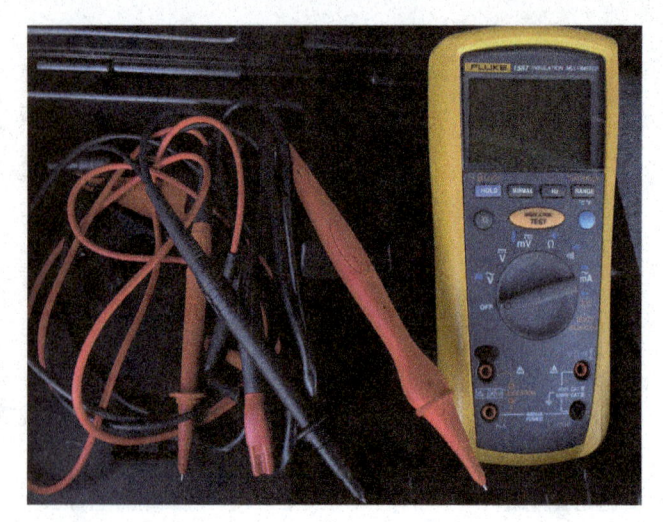

FIGURE 1-16 The Fluke 1587 is an example of an insulation tester that is able to test the HV circuit insulation to 1,000 volts. The resistance between the HV circuit and ground should be higher than one million ohms (1.0–22.2 MΩ).

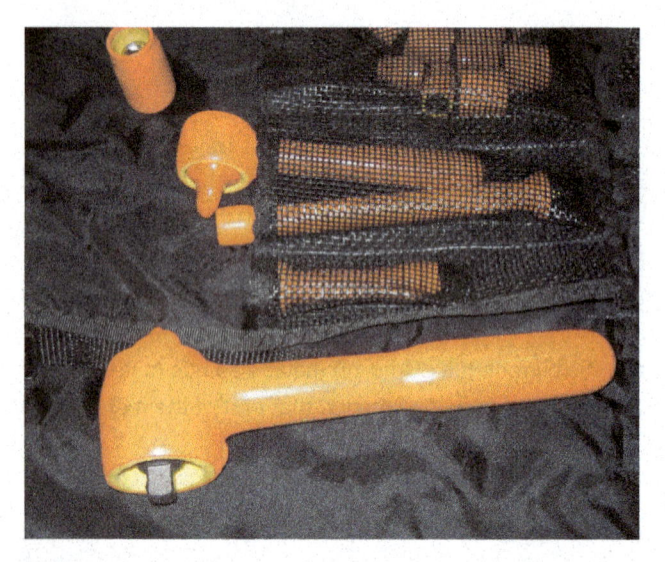

FIGURE 1-17 Insulated tools, such as this socket set, provide an additional margin of safety to the service technician when working around HV components and systems.

FIGURE 1-18 The manual disconnect on this Ford battery contains a fuse and safety interlock.

- On a hybrid vehicle, if the engine is running, it will detect a fault and set a diagnostic trouble code (DTC). It also opens the power relays, turning off the "ready" light.
- If the hybrid vehicle is moving, it will allow it to continue until a stop, and will disable the internal combustion engine (ICE).
- If the hybrid vehicle is not moving, it will disable the ICE immediately.
- The HV system will be depowered on an electric vehicle.

SAFETY INTERLOCK SYSTEM

PURPOSE AND FUNCTION The HV system uses contactors or heavy-duty relays to detect opens in the HV circuits.

This is a safety system that keeps the power circuits from closing with an open HV circuit. The manual safety disconnect switch protects the HV battery pack and it includes a safety interlock switch that uses two small terminals. With an open detected, the HV controller does the following to keep the vehicle safe. ● **SEE FIGURE 1-18.**

LOCAL INTERLOCK A local interlock is a LV circuit that uses separate switches and contacts to detect when there has been an open in LV circuits or components that are associated with the HV system. The local interlock can detect the removal of items such as covers, battery disconnects, air-conditioning compressors, or any other component that is associated with a HV circuit. ● **SEE FIGURE 1-19.** If an open has been detected, the controller (ECM) signals the hybrid controller to open the contactors or power relays and discharge the HV capacitors.

FIGURE 1-19 The small white connector is the local interlock on the HV connection to the battery.

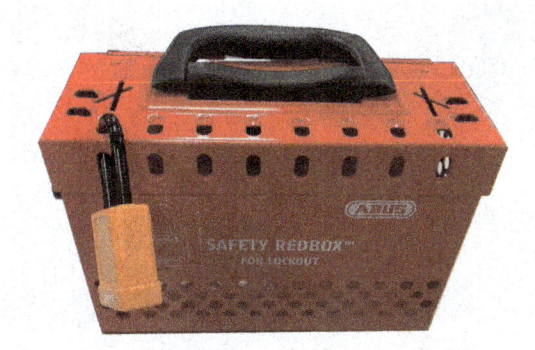

FIGURE 1-20 A lock box is a safe location to keep the ignition keys of a hybrid or electric vehicle while it is being worked on.

DEPOWERING THE HIGH-VOLTAGE SYSTEM

THE NEED TO DEPOWER THE HIGH-VOLTAGE SYSTEM

During routine vehicle service work, there is no need to go through any procedures needed to depower or shut off the HV circuits. However, if work is going to be performed on any of the following components, service information procedures must be followed to prevent possible electrical shock and personal injury.

- The HV battery pack
- Any of the electronic controllers that use orange cables, such as the inverter and converters
- The air-conditioning compressor, if electrically driven, and has orange cables attached

To safely depower the vehicle, always follow the instructions found in service information for the exact vehicle being serviced. The steps usually include the following:

STEP 1 Turn the ignition off and remove the key (if equipped) from the ignition and store it in a lock box to prevent accidental starting. ● **SEE FIGURE 1-20.**

CAUTION: If a push-button start is used, remove the key fob at least 15 feet (5 meters) from the vehicle to prevent the vehicle from being powered on. With the key fob out of the vehicle, attempt to start the vehicle to confirm no other key fobs are present in the vehicle.

STEP 2 Remove the 12-volt power source to the HV controller and wait 10 minutes for all capacitors to discharge. This step could involve:
- Removing a fuse or a relay
- Disconnecting the negative battery cable from the auxiliary 12-volt battery

STEP 3 Remove the HV fuse or service plug or switch.

STEP 4 Confirm there is no HV power present before beginning the repair.

HOISTING A HYBRID OR ELECTRIC VEHICLE

When hoisting or using a floor jack, refer to the manufacturer's service information for proper lift points. ● **SEE FIGURE 1-21.** Orange cables run under the vehicle just inside the frame rails on most hybrid and electric vehicles. The battery for many electric vehicles is underneath the vehicle and can be easily damaged by a hoist. In addition to the electrical circuits, many electric vehicles use coolant or refrigerant to maintain the temperature of the battery. Caution should be used to avoid damaging these lines. Some Honda hybrid vehicles use an aluminum pipe painted orange that includes three HV cables for the starter/generator and also three more cables for the HV air-conditioning compressor. If any damage occurs to any HV cables, the malfunction indicator; Lamp (MIL) will light up and a no-start will result if the powertrain control module (PCM) senses a fault. The cables are not repairable and are expensive. The cables can be identified by an orange outer casing, but in some cases, the orange casing is not exposed until a black plastic underbelly shield is removed first.

HYBRID AND ELECTRIC VEHICLE SAFETY

FIGURE 1-21 The HV wiring on this Honda hybrid is colored orange for easy identification.

MOVING A HYBRID OR ELECTRIC VEHICLE AROUND THE SHOP

After a hybrid or electric vehicle has been serviced, it may be necessary to push the vehicle to another part of the shop or outside as parts are ordered. Make sure to tape any orange HV cable ends that were disconnected during the repair procedure. Permanent magnets are used in all the drive motors and generators and it is possible that a HV arc could occur as the wheels turn and produce voltage. Another way to prevent this is to use wheel dollies. A sign that says "HIGH VOLTAGE—DO NOT TOUCH" could also be added to the roof of the vehicle or across the steering wheel. Remove the keys from the vehicle and keep in a safe location.

? FREQUENTLY ASKED QUESTION

What Is That Sound?

Electric vehicles and most hybrid electric vehicles emit a sound through a speaker in the front at low speeds to warn pedestrians that a moving vehicle is nearby. This system is called **acoustic vehicle alerting system (AVAS)**. It creates the sound whenever the vehicle is traveling at low speed. The U.S. National Highway Traffic Safety Administration (NHTSA) requires the device to emit warning sounds when travelling at speeds less than 19 MPH (30 km/h) with compliance by September, 2020. While easily heard from outside the vehicle, it is usually not heard inside the vehicle unless the windows are down. Some customers ask their service technician to disable this system, but it is a safety device and could help prevent personal injury if someone were to step in front or back of a moving vehicle that is almost silent.

SUMMARY

1. All high-voltage circuits are covered in orange plastic conduit.
2. For a safe working environment:
   - Be sure the work area is clean and dry.
   - Care should be taken that high-voltage warnings and safety cones are posted.
   - Additional precautions, such as a roof cone or warning tape, are also recommended.
3. Eye protection should include the following features:
   - Plastic frames (Avoid metal frames as these are conductive and could cause a shock hazard.)
   - Side shields
   - Meet the standard ANSI Z87.1
4. Before working on the high-voltage system of a hybrid electric vehicle, ensure that high-voltage lineman's gloves are available. Be sure that the gloves are rated at least 1,000 volts and class "0" by ANSI/ASTM.
5. Hybrid and electric vehicles are equipped with electrical systems whose voltages can exceed 600 volts DC. A category three (CAT III) certified digital multimeter (DMM) is required for making measurements on these high-voltage systems.
6. Local interlock is a low-voltage circuit that uses separate switches and contacts to detect when there has been an open in low-voltage circuits or components that are associated with the high-voltage system. The local interlock can detect the removal of items such as covers, battery disconnects, air-conditioning compressors, or any other component that is associated with a high-voltage circuit.
7. If work is going to be performed on any of the following components, service information procedures must be followed to prevent possible electrical shock and personal injury.
8. When hoisting or using a floor jack, refer to the manufacturer's service information for proper lift points.
9. Electric vehicles and most hybrid electric vehicles emit a sound through a speaker in the front at low speeds to warn pedestrians that a moving vehicle is nearby. This system is called acoustic vehicle alerting system (AVAS).

HIGH-VOLTAGE GLOVE PHOTO SEQUENCE

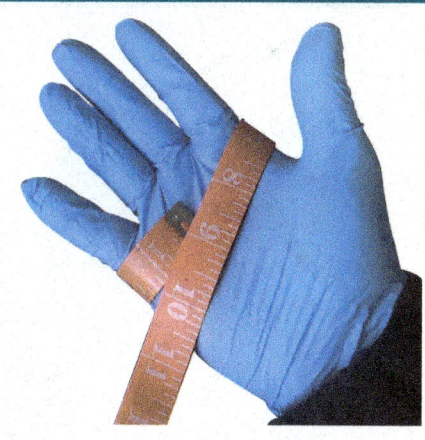

1 The cuff of the rubber glove should extend at least ½ inch beyond the cuff of the leather protector.

2 To determine the correct glove size, use a soft tape measure around the palm of the hand. A measurement of 9 inches would correspond with a glove size of 9.

3 The glove rating and the date of the last test should be stamped on the glove cuff.

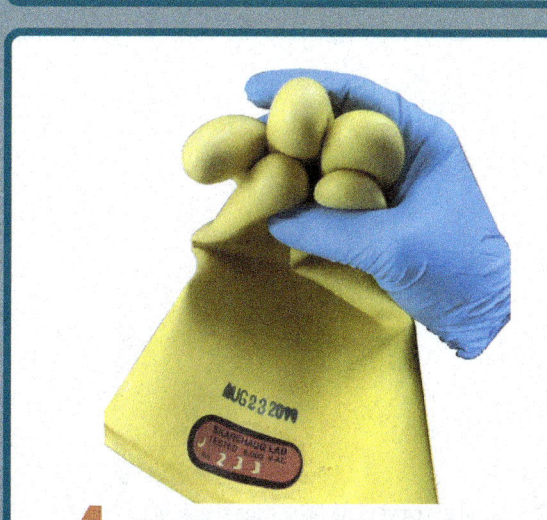

4 Start a visual inspection of the glove fingertips, making sure that no cuts or other damages are present.

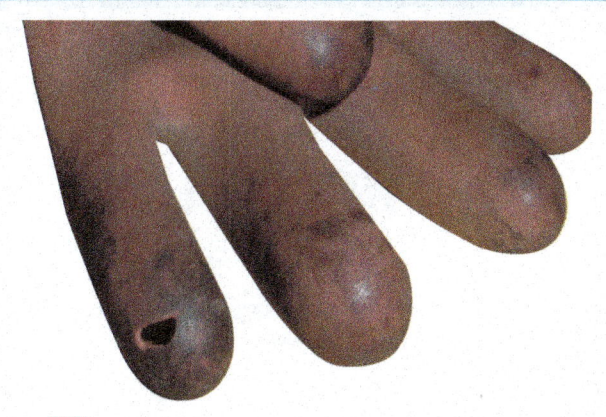

5 The damage on this glove was easily detected with a simple visual inspection. Note that the rubber glove material can be damaged by petroleum products, detergents, certain hand soaps, and talcum powder.

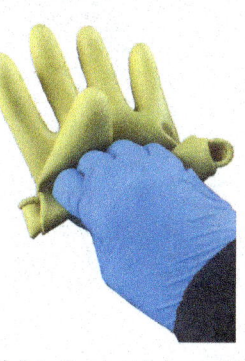

6 Manually inflate the glove to inspect for pinhole leaks. Starting at the cuff, roll up the glove and trap air in the finger end. Listen and carefully watch for deflation of the glove. If a leak is detected, the glove must be discarded.

CONTINUED ▶

STEP BY STEP

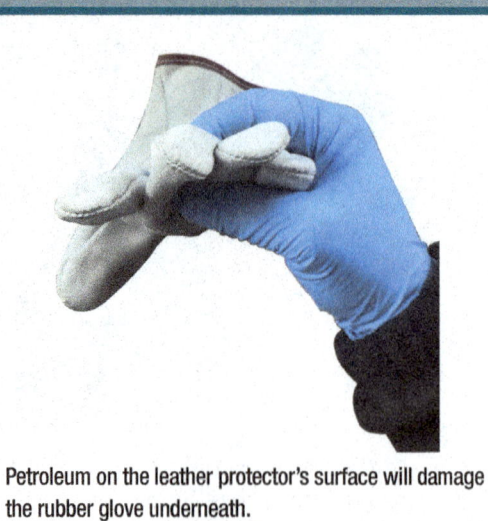

7 Petroleum on the leather protector's surface will damage the rubber glove underneath.

8 Glove powder (glove dust) should be used to absorb moisture and reduce friction.

9 Put on the gloves and tighten the straps on the back of the leather protectors (if equipped).

10 Technicians MUST wear HV gloves whenever working around the HV areas of a hybrid or electric vehicle.

11 HV gloves should be placed in a canvas storage bag when not in use. Note the ventilation hole at the bottom of this bag.

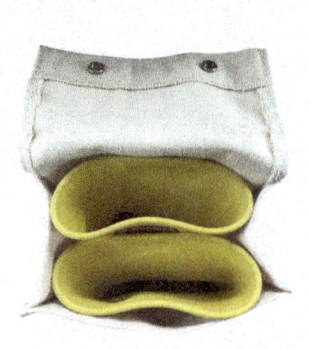

12 Make sure the rubber gloves are not folded when placed in the canvas bag. Folding increases mechanical stress on the rubber and can lead to premature failure of the glove material.

REVIEW QUESTIONS

1. What actions are needed to disable the high-voltage (HV) circuit?
2. What are the personal safety precautions that service technicians should adhere to when servicing hybrid or electric vehicles?
3. What are the recommended tools and equipment that should be used when working on the HV circuits of a hybrid or electric vehicle?
4. What precautions should be taken when hoisting a hybrid or electric vehicle?
5. When should the HV system be depowered?

CHAPTER QUIZ

1. Rubber gloves should be worn whenever working on or near the HV circuits or components of a hybrid electric vehicle. Technician A says that the rubber gloves should be rated at 1,000 volts or higher. Technician B says that leather gloves should be worn over the HV rubber gloves. Which technician is correct?
   a. Technician A only
   b. Technician B only
   c. Both Technician A and Technician B
   d. Neither Technician A nor Technician B

2. A CAT III certified DMM should be used whenever measuring HV circuits or components. The CAT III rating relates to _____.
   a. high voltage
   b. high energy
   c. high electrical resistance
   d. both high energy and high voltage

3. All of the following will shut off the high voltage to components and circuits, except _____.
   a. opening the driver's door
   b. turning off the ignition
   c. disconnecting the auxiliary 12-volt battery
   d. removing the main fuse, relay, or HV plug

4. What can occur if a hybrid electric vehicle is pushed in the shop?
   a. The HV battery pack can be damaged.
   b. The tires will be locked unless the ignition is on.
   c. Damage to the electric control will occur.
   d. High voltage will be generated by the motor/generator as the wheels turn.

5. When hoisting a hybrid or electric vehicle, what precautions must the technician follow to ensure personal safety and avoid damage to the vehicle?
   a. Make sure the lift points do not contact HV cables.
   b. Do not lift the vehicle by the battery case.
   c. Ensure the lift points are clear of battery cooling and refrigeration lines.
   d. All of the answers are correct.

6. When does the HV system NOT need to be depowered?
   a. Removing the HV battery pack
   b. Performing routine service
   c. Replacing the HV cables
   d. Replacing the HV air-conditioning compressor

7. What will occur if the safety interlock system detects an open circuit on a hybrid vehicle?
   a. If the engine is running, it will detect a fault and set a DTC. It also opens the power relays, turning off the "ready" light.
   b. If the vehicle is moving, it will allow it to continue until a stop, and will disable the ICE.
   c. If the vehicle is not moving, it will disable the ICE immediately.
   d. All of the answers are correct.

8. What precautions need to be taken to ensure the hybrid or electric vehicle work area is safe?
   a. The area should be clean and dry.
   b. The work area should be clearly marked.
   c. No special precautions are needed.
   d. The area should be clean and dry and clearly marked.

9. What is the purpose of a megohmmeter or insulation tester?
   a. Check for continuity between the HV cables and the vehicle chassis.
   b. Measure the resistance of connections in the LV system.
   c. Measure the current flow through the HV cables.
   d. None of the answers is correct.

10. What should be done if the HV rubber gloves inspection dates are found to be expired?
    a. Use them anyway if they look ok.
    b. Use them if they pass the air test.
    c. Send the gloves to a qualified inspection laboratory.
    d. Throw the gloves away.

Chapter 2
INTRODUCTION TO ELECTRIC AND HYBRID ELECTRIC VEHICLES

LEARNING OBJECTIVES

After studying this chapter, the reader should be able to:

- Explain the definition of a hybrid and electric vehicle.
- Describe the unique characteristics of owning or driving a hybrid or electric vehicle.
- Explain the differences in the levels of hybrid vehicles.
- Describe the different powertrain configurations in a hybrid vehicle.
- Explain the differences between one-, two-, and three-motor systems.

KEY TERMS

Battery electric vehicles (BEV) 15
Electric vehicle (EV) 15
Hybrid electric vehicle (HEV) 15
Internal combustion engine (ICE) 15
Medium hybrid 20
Micro hybrid 20
Mild hybrid 20
One-pedal driving 18
Phone as a Key (PAAK) 15
Plug-in hybrid electric vehicle (PHEV) 15
Range anxiety 18
Strong hybrid 20

HYBRID ELECTRIC VEHICLES

DEFINITION OF TERMS A hybrid vehicle is one that uses two different methods to propel the vehicle. A **hybrid electric vehicle (HEV)** uses both an internal combustion engine and an electric motor to propel the vehicle. Most hybrid vehicles use a high-voltage battery pack and a combination electric motor and generator to help or assist a gasoline engine. The **internal combustion engine (ICE)** used in a hybrid vehicle can be either gasoline or diesel, although only gasoline-powered engines are currently used in hybrid vehicles. An electric motor is used to help propel the vehicle, and in some designs, it is capable of propelling the vehicle alone without having to start the ICE.

A **plug-in hybrid electric vehicle (PHEV)** is an HEV with a larger capacity battery that can be recharged by the ICE or by plugging it in to an AC power source or charging station. A PHEV can drive in electric-only mode for up to 40 miles on some vehicles.

? FREQUENTLY ASKED QUESTION

What is meant by "Phone as a Key (PAAK)"?

Many hybrid electric and electric vehicles, as well as some regular (ICE) vehicles can be controlled using a smart phone application (app). This control of the vehicle, including remote start from the smart phone, is referred to as **Phone as a Key (PAAK).** There are apps for using a smart watch as a key which makes it very convenient to start and unlock a vehicle using just the smart watch.

ELECTRIC VEHICLE

DEFINITION OF TERMS An **electric vehicle (EV)**, also referred to as an electric drive vehicle, uses one or more electric motors to propel the vehicle. Electricity is used as the transportation fuel to power the EV. The electrical energy is typically stored in an energy storage device, such as a battery. The electrical energy is replenished by connecting to an electrical source, usually stationary. The Environmental Protection Agency (EPA) and the California Air Resources Board (CARB) define an EV as a zero-emission vehicle.
● SEE FIGURE 2-1.

FIGURE 2-1 The official emission sticker lists the vehicle as electric and producing zero emissions.

HISTORY

EARLY ELECTRIC VEHICLES Early EVs, also called **battery electric vehicles (BEVs)**, were first used in the late 1800s, and it was not until the early 1900s that EVs were practically possible using rechargeable lead–acid batteries.

- One of the first was the 1903 Baker Electric Car, produced by the Baker Motor Vehicle Company in Cleveland, Ohio.
- The Detroit Electric Car Company (1907–1939) produced very practical fully EVs.

The old EV mechanical controller was able to switch all six batteries in various combinations of series and parallel configurations to achieve lower voltage for slow speeds and higher voltages for higher speeds. EVs did not have a long range and needed to have the batteries charged regularly, which meant that EVs could only be used for short distances. In fact, EVs were almost more popular than steam-powered vehicles in 1900—while steam-powered vehicles had 40% of the sales, EVs had 38% of the sales. The gasoline-powered cars represented only 22% of the vehicles sold.

EARLY HYBRID VEHICLES In 1901, Ferdinand Porsche developed the Lohner-Porsche Mixte Hybrid, the first gasoline-electric hybrid automobile in the world. It was originally an electric-powered vehicle and then a gasoline engine was added to recharge the battery. One of the first hybrid electric cars was produced by the Owen Magnetic Motor Car Corporation, manufactured in New York City and then in Wilkes-Barre, PA, from 1915 until 1922. It failed because the fuel economy was about the same as a conventional gasoline-powered vehicle, yet cost more. Another vehicle that used both a gasoline engine and an electric motor to power the vehicle was built by Woods Motor Company of Chicago, Illinois, and was called the "Woods Dual Power" (1915–1918).

INTRODUCTION TO ELECTRIC AND HYBRID ELECTRIC VEHICLES   **15**

NOTE: Due to the oil embargo of 1973 and an increased demand for alternative energy sources, Congress enacted Public Law 94-413, the *Electric and Hybrid Vehicle Research, Development, and Demonstration Act of 1976*, which was designed to promote new technologies.

The hybrid electric vehicle did not become widely available until the release of the Toyota Prius in Japan in 1997, followed by the Honda Insight sold in the United States starting in 1999. In 2001, the first Toyota Prius was introduced in the United States.

EFFICIENCIES OF ELECTRIC MOTORS AND ICEs

Electric motors are more efficient compared to any ICE and have just one moving part compared to hundreds of moving parts in a typical gasoline-powered or diesel-powered ICE.

- An electric motor can have efficiency (including controller) of over 90%, while a gasoline engine has efficiency of only 35% or less.
- An ICE does not have the overload capability of an electric motor. That is why the rated power of an ICE is usually much higher than that required for highway cruising. Operating smoothly at idle speed produces a much lower efficiency than while operating at a higher speed.
- Maximum torque of an ICE is reached at intermediate speed and the torque declines as speed increases further.
- There is a maximum fuel efficiency point in the speed range for the ICE, and this speed is optimized by many hybrid vehicle manufacturers by using a transmission that keeps the engine speed within the most efficient range.
  ● **SEE FIGURE 2-2.**

Electric motors offer ideal characteristics for use in a vehicle because of the following factors:

- Constant power over all speed ranges
- Constant torque at low speeds needed for acceleration and hill-climbing capability
- Constant torque below base speed
- Constant power above base speed
- Only single gear or fixed gear is needed in the electric motor transmission

DRIVING A HYBRID OR ELECTRIC VEHICLE

DRIVING A HYBRID VEHICLE Driving a hybrid electric vehicle (HEV) is the same as driving any other conventional vehicle. In fact, many drivers and passengers are often not aware that they are driving or riding in a hybrid electric vehicle. Some unique characteristics that the driver may or may not notice include the following:

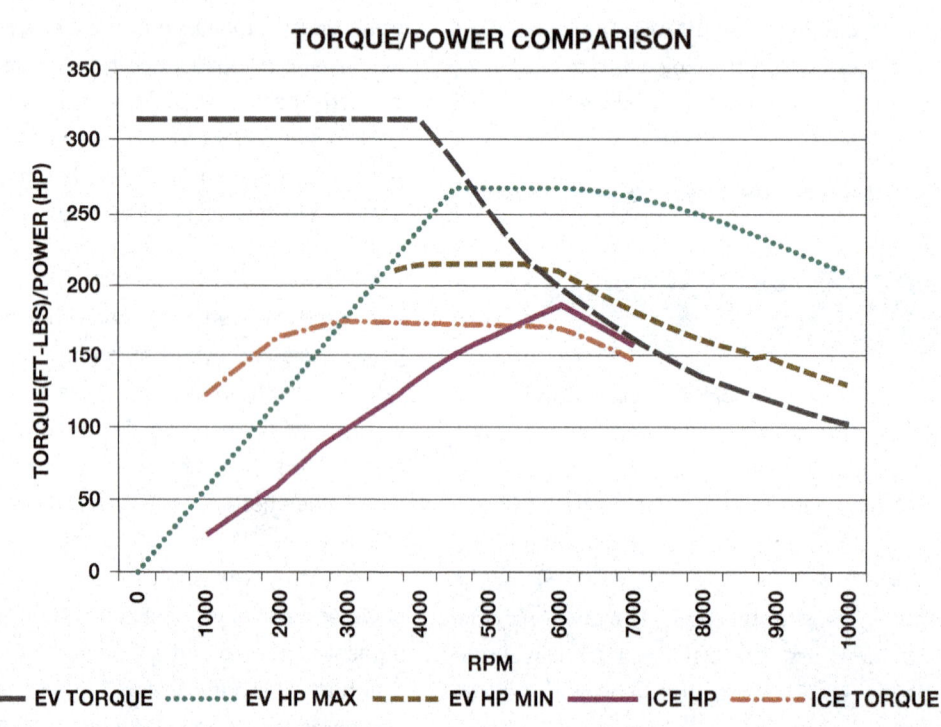

FIGURE 2-2 The graph shows a comparison of torque and power between an electric vehicle and a vehicle with an ICE.

- After the ICE has achieved normal operating temperature and other conditions are met, the engine will stop when the vehicle slows down and stops. This condition may cause a concern to some drivers who may think that the engine has stalled and may try to restart it.
- The brake pedal may feel different, especially at slow speeds of about 5 MPH and 15 MPH when slowing to a stop. It is at about these speeds that the brake system switches from regenerative braking to actually applying brake force to the mechanical brakes. A slight surge or pulsation may be felt at this time. This may or may not be felt and is often not a concern to drivers.
- The power steering works even when the engine stops because all HEV and PHEV use an electric power steering system.
- Some HEVs and all PHEVs are able to propel the vehicle using the electric motor alone, resulting in quiet, almost eerie operation.
- If an HEV is being driven aggressively and at a high rate of acceleration, there is often a feeling that the vehicle is not going to slow down when the accelerator pedal is first released. This is caused by two factors:
    1. The inertia of the rotor of the electric motor attached to the crankshaft of the ICE results in the engine continuing to rotate after the throttle has been closed.
    2. The slight delay that occurs when the system switches the electric motor from powering the vehicle to generating (regenerative braking). While this delay would rarely be experienced, it is not at all dangerous. For a fraction of a second, it gives a feeling that the accelerator pedal did not react to a closed throttle.

DRIVING AN ELECTRIC VEHICLE Driving an EV is a very different driving experience than a conventional vehicle. Some of the unique characteristics include the following:

- The startup and shutdown procedures are enough different than a conventional vehicle that many drivers need to be retrained on the processes.
- The lack of an ICE results in a much quieter ride. In many cases, the most predominate noise heard is the tires on the various road surfaces. Most electric vehicles come from the factory with tires that have acoustical foam inside of the tire to reduce the tire noise by up to 9 db. ● **SEE FIGURE 2-3.**

NOTE: The EV may be silent when in park or neutral. When put in drive or reverse, an artificial "running engine" sound is generated at the front of the vehicle

FIGURE 2-3 This Continental tire with acoustical foam on the inside is from a Tesla Model 3.

? FREQUENTLY ASKED QUESTION

How Fast Does the Motor-Generator Turn the Engine When Starting?

The typical starter motor used on a conventional gasoline or diesel engine rotates the engine from 100 to 300 revolutions per minute (RPM). Because the typical engine idles at about 600 to 700 RPM, the starter motor is rotating the engine at a speed slower than it operates. This makes it very noticeable when starting because the sound is different when cranking compared to when the engine actually starts and runs.

However, when the motor-generator of a HEV rotates the engine to start it, the engine is rotated about 1000 RPM, which is about the same speed as when it is running. As a result, engine cranking is just barely heard or felt. The engine is either running or not running, which is a truly unique sensation to those not familiar with the operation of hybrid electric vehicles.

through a speaker behind the front bodywork. Some vehicles have a second speaker mounted in the rear of the vehicle. Typically, the sound is present until the vehicle reaches approximately 20 MPH. ● SEE FIGURE 2-4.

- The electric motors that propel the vehicle provide exceptional torque and responsiveness.
- The regenerative braking systems tend to slow the vehicle more aggressively than a conventional vehicle. Often the system can be set so that the brake pedal is not used during normal driving except to keep the vehicle stationary when stopped. This feature is usually called **one-pedal driving**.
- Seasonal temperature changes, weather, and driving style will affect the battery range.
- Careful mapping of charging stations will be required when traveling a distance beyond the battery range capacity.
- **Range anxiety** is the fear that many potential owners of EV have that the vehicle will have insufficient range to reach their destination, and therefore could get stuck with a dead vehicle on the road. According to owners of EV, this fear tends to go away after about two weeks of ownership after seeing that the range, and the charging can be easily controlled.

Plug-in hybrid and electric vehicle owners will save money at the gasoline pump; however, they will experience a higher electric bill, depending on the amount of electricity these use. The increase in the cost of the electricity will vary based on the electrical providers' purchase plan. Some providers offer discounted rates when the electricity is consumed during off-peak hours.

ROUTINE MAINTENANCE Most hybrid and electric vehicles have a different maintenance schedule than a conventional vehicle. In the case of an EV, most of these costs are eliminated. A typical EV requires just the following as part of routine maintenance:

- Windshield washer fluid
- Windshield wiper blades
- Cabin filter
- Tire rotation

● SEE FIGURE 2-5.

In the case of a hybrid vehicle, certain costs may actually increase because of materials used because a hybrid vehicle typically uses full-synthetic motor oil which is more expensive

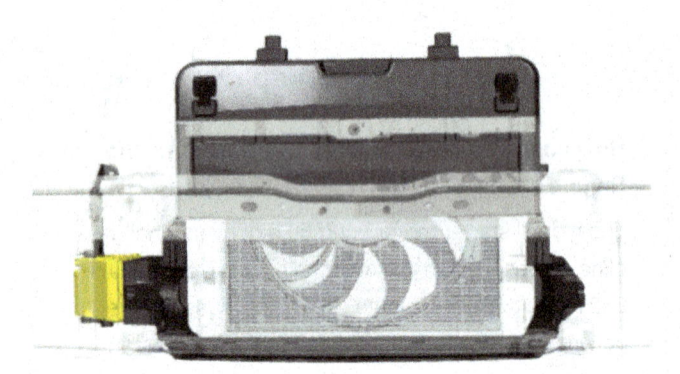

FIGURE 2-4 The sound generator on this 2021 VW ID.4 is located behind the front bumper assembly.

OWNING A HYBRID OR ELECTRIC VEHICLE A hybrid or electric vehicle will cost and weigh more than a conventional vehicle. The increased initial purchase price is due to the batteries, electric motor(s), and controllers used plus the additional components needed to allow operation of the heating and air-conditioning systems during idle stop periods. The cost is offset, in part, by improved fuel economy as well as state and national government energy credits awarded at the time of purchase for some new technology vehicles.

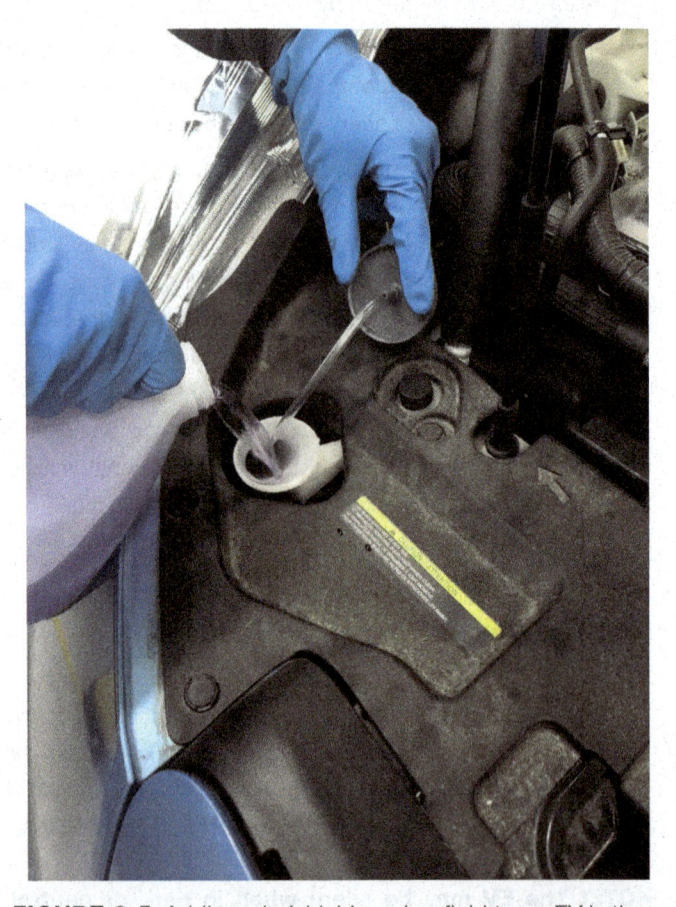

FIGURE 2-5 Adding windshield washer fluid to an EV is the item that requires most frequent maintenance depending on driving conditions.

than conventional motor oil. Additionally, the owner of a plug-in vehicle will need to make an investment in a recharging network for the home. See Chapter 12 for the details about charging an EV or PHEV.

> **? FREQUENTLY ASKED QUESTION**
>
> **Can the Nissan Leaf be Taken Through a Car Wash?**
>
> Yes, the Nissan Leaf, and all hybrid and electric vehicles can be taken through the car wash. All the high-voltage components, including the battery, that are outside of the passenger compartment, are sealed from outside water entry. If there has been no damage to protective coverings, the components will not be damaged and there is no chance of electrical shock.

> **🚗 Case Study**
>
> **The Case of the Vibrating Tesla**
>
> An owner of a Tesla Model Y visited a tire shop complaining of a vibration in the steering wheel at highway speeds. A local tire shop balanced both front tires. The right front only needed a quarter ounce whereas the left front required over four ounces to balance. After leaving the shop, the owner immediately noticed that the vibration was much worse. The owner returned to the shop and this time the tire was removed from the rim. It became apparent that the vibration issue was caused by the foam inside the tire. This foam that generally played the role of reducing noise had separated and was loose inside the tire. The shop removed the foam and did not try to reinstall it. The wheel was balanced which solved the vibration concern. The driver did not notice any increase in noise. ● **SEE FIGURE 2-6.**
>
> **Summary:**
> - **Complaint**—A Tesla owner complained of a vibration in the steering wheel at highway speeds.
> - **Cause**—The acoustical foam inside a tire that is supposed to reduce noise had separated from the inner liner of the left front tire.
> - **Correction**—The foam was removed from the tire and the tire/wheel assembly was balanced which corrected the vibration concern.

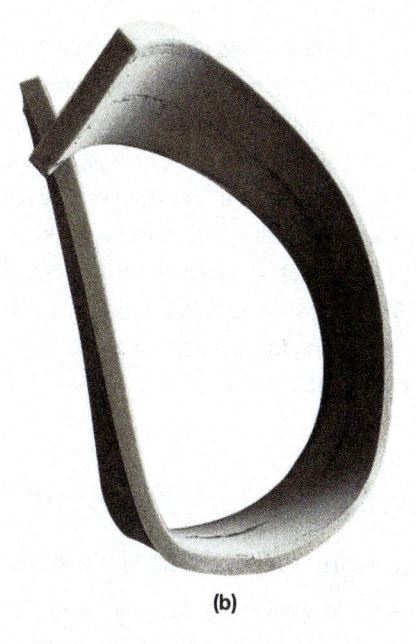

FIGURE 2-6 (a) The dismounted tire shows where the foam had become detached. (b) The foam removed in its entirety.

> **? FREQUENTLY ASKED QUESTION**
>
> **Why Are EVs and PHEVs Taxed in Some States?**
>
> Recently some states have added fees to the cost of the license plate on hybrid and electric vehicles to recover loss fuel taxes. Typically, these fees have been in the $100 to $200 range. Depending on the number of miles driven per year, these fees may have a negative impact on the cost of ownership.

All of these factors must be considered when making an informed decision to purchase a hybrid or electric vehicle. It may take many years of operation before the extra cost is offset by cost savings from the improved fuel economy. However, many owners purchase a hybrid or electric vehicle for other reasons besides fuel savings, including a feeling that they are helping the environment and the love of the high technology involved.

LEVELS OF HYBRID VEHICLES

MICRO HYBRID A **micro hybrid** will incorporate idle stop, but is not capable of propelling the vehicle without starting the ICE. A micro-hybrid system has the advantage of costing less, but saves less fuel compared to a full hybrid vehicle. The micro hybrid usually uses a second 12-volt battery and a heavy-duty starter motor and flywheel to restart the ICE when accelerating from a stop.

MILD HYBRID A **mild hybrid** will incorporate idle stop and regenerative braking, but is not capable of using the electric motor to propel the vehicle on its own without help from the ICE. A mild-hybrid system has the advantage of costing less, but saves less fuel compared to a full hybrid vehicle and usually uses a 42-volt electrical motor and battery package (36-volt batteries, 42-volt charging). An example of this type of hybrid is the 2004–2007 General Motors Silverado pickup truck and the 2007 Saturn VUE. The fuel savings for a mild type of hybrid design is about 8% to 15%.

> **? FREQUENTLY ASKED QUESTION**
>
> **Is a Diesel-Hybrid Electric Vehicle Possible?**
>
> Yes, using a diesel engine instead of a gasoline engine in a HEV is possible. While the increased efficiency of a diesel engine would increase fuel economy, the extra cost of the diesel engine is the major reason this combination is not currently in production.

> **? FREQUENTLY ASKED QUESTION**
>
> **What Is an Assist Hybrid?**
>
> An assist hybrid-electric vehicle is a term used to describe a vehicle where the electric motor is not able to start moving the vehicle on electric power alone. This type of hybrid would include micro hybrids (12 volt), all mild hybrids (36 to 42 volts), as well as the medium hybrids that use 144- to 158-volt systems.

MEDIUM HYBRID A **medium hybrid** uses 144- to 158-volt batteries that provide for engine stop/start, regenerative braking, and power assist. Like a mild hybrid, a typical medium hybrid is not capable of propelling the vehicle from a stop using battery power alone. Examples of a medium-hybrid vehicle include the Honda Insight, Civic, and Accord. The fuel economy savings are about 20% to 25% for medium-hybrid systems.

FULL HYBRID A **strong hybrid**, also called a *full hybrid*, uses idle stop, regenerative braking, and is able to propel the vehicle using the electric motor(s) alone. Each vehicle manufacturer has made its decision on which hybrid type to implement based on its assessment of the market niche for a particular model. Examples of a full or strong hybrid include the General Motors Silverado/Sierra (two-mode hybrid), Ford Escape SUV, Toyota Highlander, Lexus RX400h, Lexus GS450h, Toyota Prius, and Toyota Camry. The fuel economy savings are about 30% to 50% for full-hybrid systems.

CLASSIFICATIONS OF HYBRID VEHICLE POWERTRAIN

SERIES HYBRID POWERTRAIN In a series-hybrid design, sole propulsion is by a battery-powered electric motor, but the electric energy for the batteries comes from another onboard energy source, such as an ICE. In this design, the engine turns a generator and the generator can either charge the batteries or power an electric motor that drives the transmission. The ICE never powers the vehicle directly. ● **SEE FIGURES 2-7 AND 2-8.**

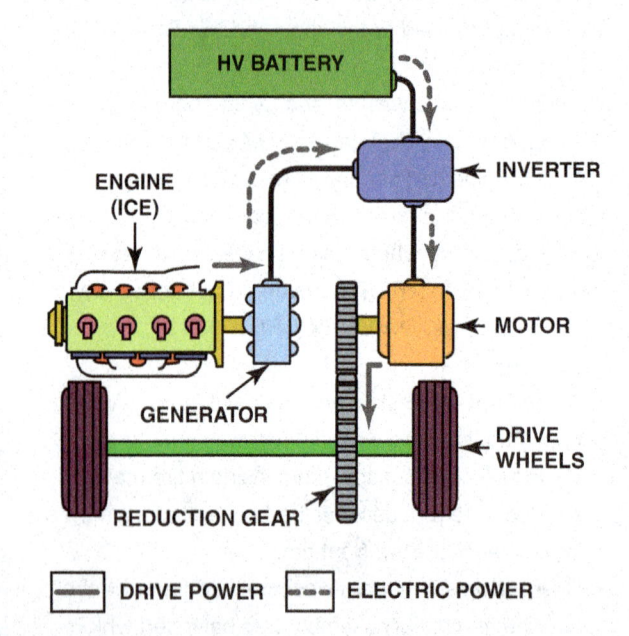

FIGURE 2-7 A drawing of the power flow in a typical series-hybrid vehicle.

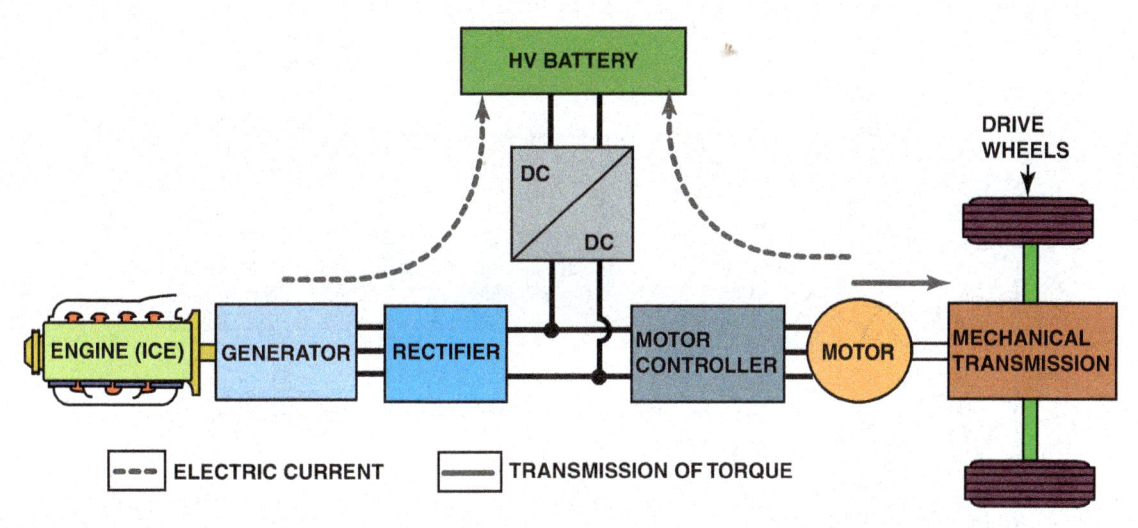

FIGURE 2-8 This diagram shows the components included in a typical series-hybrid design. The solid line arrow indicates the transmission of the torque to the drive wheels. The dotted line arrows indicate the flow of the electrical current.

The engine is operated only to keep the batteries charged. Therefore, the vehicle could be moving with or without the ICE running. Series-hybrid vehicles also use regeneration braking to help keep the batteries charged. The Chevrolet Volt is an example of a series-hybrid design. The engine is designed to just keep the batteries charged, and, therefore, is designed to operate at its most efficient speed and load.

An advantage of a series-hybrid design is that no transmission, clutch, or torque converter is needed.

A disadvantage of a series-hybrid design is the added weight of the ICE to what is basically an EV. The engine is actually a heavy on-board battery charger. Also, the electric motor and battery capacity have to be large enough to power the vehicle under all operating conditions, including climbing hills.

All power needed for heating and cooling must also come from the batteries, so using the air conditioning in hot weather and the heater in cold weather reduces the range that the vehicle can travel on battery power alone.

PARALLEL HYBRID POWERTRAIN
In a parallel-hybrid design, multiple propulsion sources can be combined, or one of the energy sources alone can drive the vehicle. In this design, the battery and engine are both connected to the transmission.

The vehicle using a parallel-hybrid design can be powered by the ICE alone, by the electric motor alone (full hybrids only), or by a combination of engine and electric motor propulsion. In most cases, the electric motor is used to assist the ICE. ● **SEE FIGURES 2-9 AND 2-10.**

One of the advantages of using a parallel-hybrid design is that by using an electric motor or motors to assist the ICE, the engine itself can be smaller than would normally be needed.

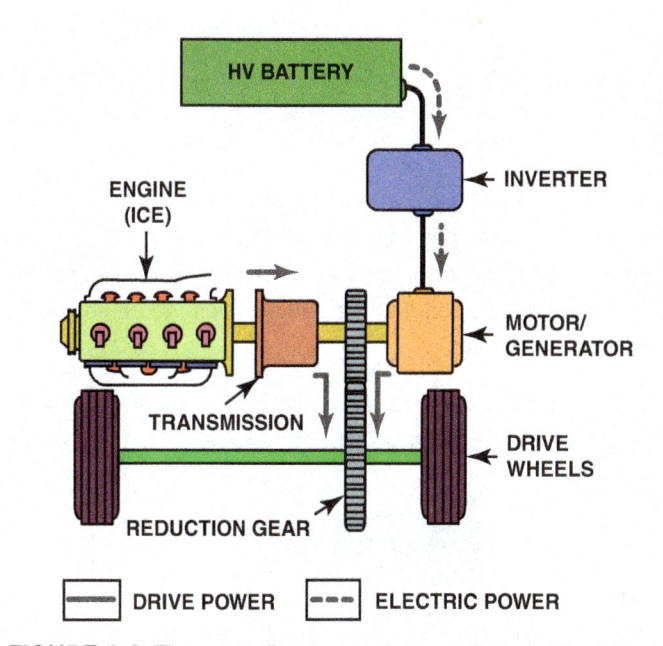

FIGURE 2-9 The power flow in a typical parallel-hybrid vehicle.

NOTE: A parallel-hybrid design could include additional batteries to allow for plug-in capability, which could extend the distance the vehicle can travel using battery power alone.

One disadvantage of a parallel-hybrid design is that complex software is needed to seamlessly blend electric and ICE power. Another concern about the parallel-hybrid design is that it has to be engineered to provide proper heating and air-conditioning system operation when the ICE stops at idle.

SERIES-PARALLEL HYBRID POWERTRAIN
The Toyota and Ford hybrids are classified as series-parallel hybrids because they can operate using electric motor power alone or

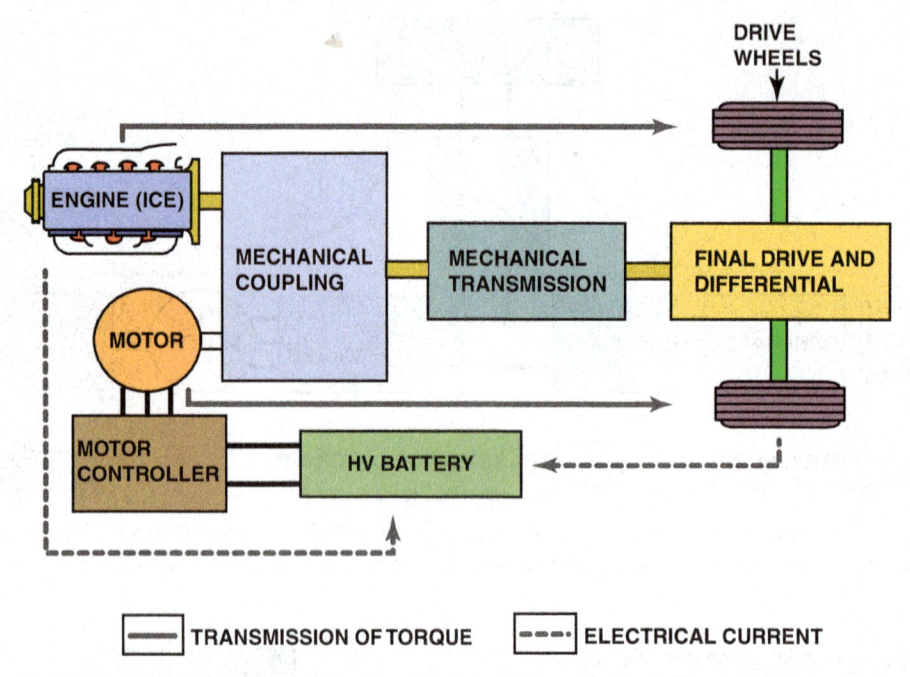

FIGURE 2-10 Diagram showing the components involved in a typical parallel-hybrid vehicle. The solid line arrows indicate the transmission of torque to the drive wheels, and the dotted line arrows indicate the flow of electrical current.

with the assist of the ICE. Series-parallel hybrids combine the functions of both a series and a parallel design. The ICE may be operating even though the vehicle is stopped if the electronic controller has detected that the batteries need to be charged.
● SEE FIGURE 2-11.

NOTE: The ICE may or may not start when the driver starts the vehicle, depending on the temperature of the engine and other conditions. This can be confusing to some who are driving a HEV for the first time and sense that the engine did not start when they tried to start the engine.

ONE-, TWO-, AND THREE-MOTOR HYBRID SYSTEM

ONE-MOTOR HYBRID SYSTEMS HEV that use one electric motor include VW, Nissan, Honda, and General Motors. In these units, an electric motor is attached to the ICE (engine) crankshaft which is used to perform two functions:

1. Start the ICE engine
2. Act as a generator to charge the high-voltage batteries

Hybrids that use one motor are often called mild hybrids, and usually are not able to power the vehicle using electric power alone. ● SEE FIGURE 2-12.

TWO-MOTOR HYBRID SYSTEMS HEVs that use two motors are the most commonly used hybrids by Toyota, Ford, and General Motors in their full-size two-mode trucks. Each electric motor serves two purposes:

- The motor/generator attached to the engine, usually labeled M/G1 or M/G A, is used to start the gasoline engine and to charge the high-voltage batteries.

FIGURE 2-11 A series-parallel hybrid design allows the vehicle to operate in electric motor mode only or in combination with the ICE.

FIGURE 2-12 The exploded view of this Honda IMA motor assembly is an example of a one-motor hybrid system.

- The motor/generator that is connected to the drive wheels, usually labeled M/G2 or M/G B, is used to propel the vehicle and to recharge the high-voltage battery during deceleration (regenerative braking).

Two-motor HEVs are full (strong) hybrids and are capable of propelling the vehicle using electric motor power alone for short distances. ● **SEE FIGURE 2-13.**

THREE-MOTOR HYBRID SYSTEMS Three-motor HEVs are usually two-motor hybrids that use an additional electric motor to propel the rear wheels for all-wheel-drive capability. HEVs that use three electric motors include the Toyota Highlander and Lexus RX400h/450h SUVs.

ADVANTAGES AND DISADVANTAGES OF AN ELECTRIC VEHICLE

ADVANTAGES There are many advantages of an EV compared to a vehicle powered by an ICE, which include the following:

- **Initial torque**—Electric vehicles have high torque at the starting from a stop and can provide a rapid acceleration experience to the driver. ● **SEE FIGURE 2-14.**

- **Better handling and stability**—The high-voltage battery in an EV, being the heaviest electric component, is placed very low, on the body floor resulting in a very low center of mass. This gives the vehicle more stability, resulting in better handling for the vehicle.

- **Maximum traction**—Electric motors are independently controlled, thereby providing precise control on each wheel for maximum traction in all wheel drive EVs.

- **More efficient than gasoline vehicles**—An EV is more efficient than a gasoline vehicle in converting stored energy into energy of motion. The efficiency of an electric motor is around 85% to 90%, whereas that of an ICE-powered vehicle is 35% to 40%.

- **Less cost of operation**—Cost of operation of an EV is less when compared to gasoline vehicle because the cost of electricity is less when compared to fossil fuels, as well as the high efficiency of the electric motor.

FIGURE 2-13 The cutaway of a second-generation Prius transmission (P112) shows two electric motors (MG1 and MG2). The vehicle can drive a short distance using just the electric motors.

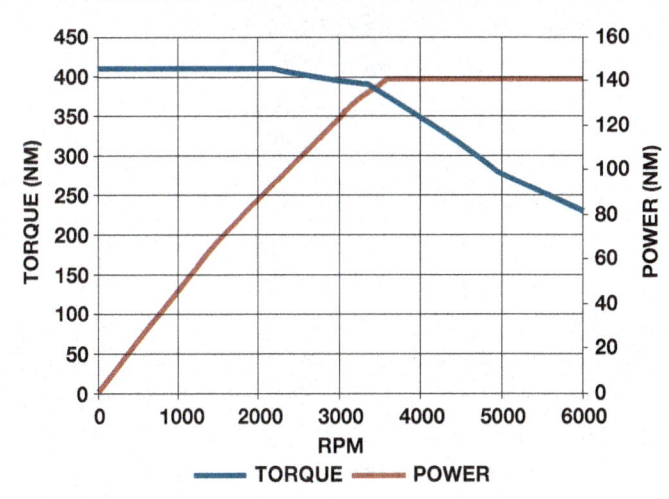

FIGURE 2-14 The graph shows how high the initial torque is in an electric motor and how quickly it generates power.

INTRODUCTION TO ELECTRIC AND HYBRID ELECTRIC VEHICLES

- **Less maintenance**—Fewer moving parts are included in EVs so the maintenance required is reduced. There is no need for oil changes and the brakes may last the life of the vehicle because of the regenerative braking technology. Only some items require periodical maintenance, which include tire rotation, changing the cabin filter, adding windshield washer fluid, and replacing the windshield wiper blades.
- **EVs are quiet and ecofriendly**—EVs are very quiet and do not make any sound while operating. So EVs will be more suitable for big cities where noise pollution is a concern. Also due to zero emission, it is considered ecofriendly.
- **Charge from your house**—Most of the EVs can be charged from the household itself.

DISADVANTAGES

There are several disadvantages of an EV compared to an ICE vehicle including:

- **Limited range**—While range is increasing due to improved battery designs, range is still a concern for many people. Early EVs had a range of up to 80 miles, but newer models are now reaching a range of 240 to 300 miles or more.
- **Electrical needs at home**—Most EVs are charged at home and this usually means that the electric service needs to be installed or upgraded to provide a 220–240-volt outlet near the vehicle to allow overnight charging.
- **High initial cost**—Because the cost of the high-voltage batteries is high, the cost of an EV is higher than an ICE vehicle of the same type and size.

TIPS FOR RANGE INCREASE

- Accelerate slowly.
- Avoid high-speed driving because as the speed increases, the aerodynamic drag is increased by the square of the speed.
- Avoid using the air-conditioning unless absolutely needed.
- Check tire pressure. The door placard pressure offers the best compromise in terms of tire rolling resistance, braking distance, comfort, lateral dynamics, and wear.
- Pre condition the vehicle. As long as the vehicle is attached to the charging station, it makes sense to pre condition the interior and to specify the departure time in winter, because the battery is only fully charged at the time of departure and is already at operating temperature.
- Reduce weight by removing unnecessary additional weight and roof structures, such as bike racks unless being used.

? FREQUENTLY ASKED QUESTION

Can an Electric Vehicle Be Towed?

Yes, with some precautions to prevent damage to the vehicle. Most vehicle manufacturers recommended towing any vehicle with all four wheels off the ground. ● SEE FIGURE 2-15. The manual for a Chevrolet Bolt includes the following steps:

- Place the front wheels on a dolly.
- Place the shift lever in P (Park).
- Secure the vehicle to the dolly.

However, under "Electric Parking Brake" the owner's manual says that the electric parking brake (EPB) may automatically apply in some situations when the vehicle is not moving to check the correct operation of the EPB system. Some Bolt owners have reported that the EPB has engaged while being towed with the rear wheels on the ground, which ruined the rear tires. If any front wheel drive vehicle is being towed with the rear wheels on the ground, many experts recommend the following precautions:

- Disconnect the 12-volt battery to prevent the possibility of the electric parking brake being applied.
- Listen carefully to ensure that the car does not automatically apply the EPB between the time that the car is turned off and the time that the battery is disconnected.
- Make sure to keep the driver's door open until after the battery is disconnected, otherwise the car may automatically lock the doors requiring the use of the physical key to unlock the door.
- Always make sure to test that the wheels are rolling freely before departure.

Obviously, all the aforementioned precautions are not necessary if the vehicle is towed with all four wheels off the ground.

Dinghy Towing 🚫

Dolly Towing

To tow the vehicle from the frond with the rear wheels on the ground.

🚫

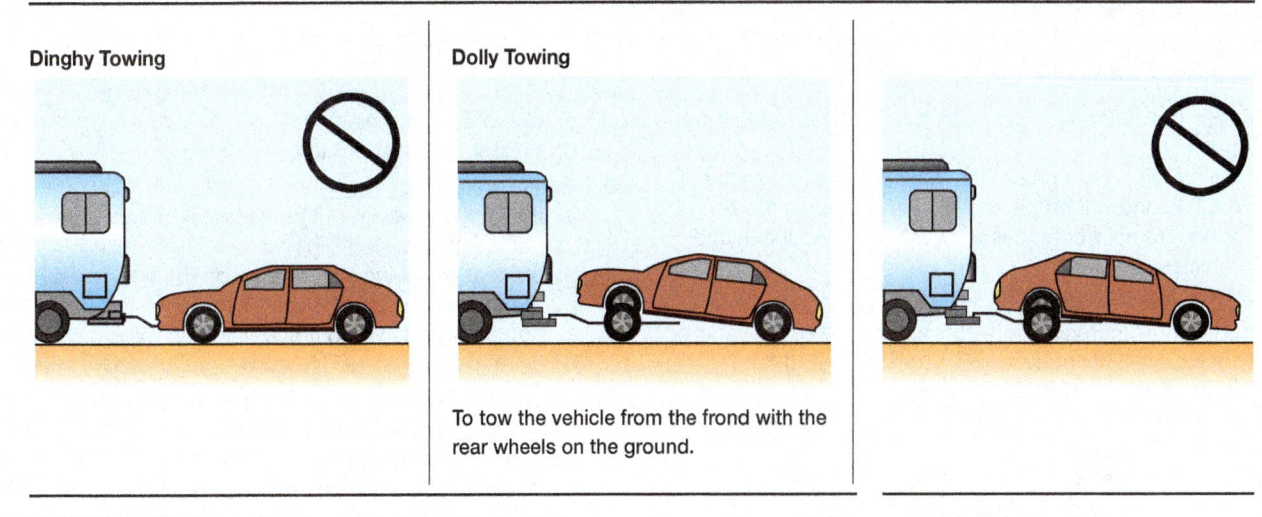

FIGURE 2-15 How a front-wheel-drive EV should be towed as per the vehicle manufacture's instructions.

SUMMARY

1. A hybrid electric vehicle (HEV) uses both an internal combustion engine (ICE) and an electric motor to propel the vehicle. Most hybrid vehicles use a high-voltage battery pack and a combination electric motor and generator to help or assist a gasoline engine.
2. An electric vehicle (EV), also referred to as an electric drive vehicle, uses one or more electric motors to propel the vehicle. Electricity is used as the transportation fuel to power the EV. The electrical energy is typically stored in an energy storage device, such as a battery.
3. The EV may be silent when in park or neutral. When put in drive or reverse, an artificial "running engine" sound is generated at the front of the vehicle through a speaker behind the front bodywork. Some vehicles have a second speaker mounted in the rear of the vehicle. Typically, the sound is present until the vehicle reaches approximately 20 MPH.
4. A hybrid or electric vehicle will cost and weigh more than a conventional vehicle. The increased initial purchase price is due to the batteries, electric motor(s), and controllers used plus the additional components needed to allow operation of the heating and air-conditioning systems during idle stop periods.
5. In a parallel-hybrid design, multiple propulsion sources can be combined, or one of the energy sources alone can drive the vehicle. In this design, the battery and engine are both connected to the transmission.
6. Each electric motor serves two purposes:
   - The motor/generator attached to the engine, usually labeled M/G1 or M/G A, is used to start the gasoline engine and to charge the high-voltage batteries.
   - The motor/generator that is connected to the drive wheels, usually labeled M/G2 or M/G B, is used to propel the vehicle and to recharge the high-voltage battery during deceleration (regenerative braking).
7. There are many advantages of an electric vehicle compared to a vehicle powered by an internal combustion engine.

REVIEW QUESTIONS

1. What are the advantages and disadvantages of a series-hybrid design?
2. What are the advantages and disadvantages of micro, mild, medium, and full hybrids?
3. What are some of the advantages and disadvantages of owning an electric vehicle (EV)?
4. What is the purpose of the third motor in a three-motor hybrid system?
5. What are the items that will affect the range of an electric vehicle?

CHAPTER QUIZ

1. What is the difference between a mild hybrid and a full hybrid?
   a. A mild hybrid will propel the vehicle in electric mode.
   b. A full hybrid will propel the vehicle in electric mode.
   c. There are no differences between mild and full hybrid vehicles.
   d. None of the answers are correct.

2. What is the difference between a hybrid electric vehicle (HEV) and plug-in hybrid electric vehicle (PHEV)?
   a. Both an HEV and PHEV have to be plugged in.
   b. Only the PHEV needs to be plugged in to achieve maximum range.
   c. A PHEV does not use an ICE.
   d. An HEV uses a high-voltage battery that has a higher capacity than a PHEV.

3. One-pedal driving means _____.
   a. the vehicle only has one pedal
   b. the vehicle has the ability to slow and often stop using just the accelerator pedal
   c. the vehicle does not use regenerative brakes but just friction brakes
   d. the vehicle uses the accelerator pedal to accelerate and the parking brake level to slow and stop

4. An electric vehicle (EV) is also called a _____.
   a. self-driving vehicle
   b. battery electric vehicle (BEV)
   c. hybrid electric vehicle (HEV)
   d. plug-in hybrid electric vehicle (PHEV)

5. Most hybrid and electric vehicles have a different maintenance schedule than a conventional vehicle. What is not commonly performed on an EV?
   a. Tire rotation
   b. Coolant flush
   c. Cabin filter replacement
   d. Windshield washer fluid

6. Range anxiety is_____.
   a. the fear of running out of electrical battery charge and being left stranded
   b. the fear of having to recharge on the way to work if the distance is greater than 5 miles
   c. normal anxiety when first owning an EV
   d. Both a and c

7. What is the typical battery configuration in a micro hybrid?
   a. A 12-volt battery and a 144-volt battery
   b. Two 12-volt batteries
   c. A 12-volt battery and a 42-volt battery
   d. A 12-volt battery and a 300-volt battery

8. A medium hybrid uses_____.
   a. a 12-volt battery and a 144-volt battery
   b. two 12-volt batteries
   c. a 12-volt battery and a 42-volt battery
   d. a 12-volt battery and a 300-volt battery

9. A full hybrid uses_____.
   a. a 12-volt battery and a 144-volt battery
   b. two 12-volt batteries
   c. a 12-volt battery and a 42-volt battery
   d. a 12-volt battery and a 300-volt battery

10. What is NOT an advantage of an EV?
    a. Higher cost
    b. Lack of required oil changes and other services that an ICE requires
    c. More economical to operate on a cost per mile basis
    d. All of the above.

Chapter 3
HEALTH AND ENVIRONMENTAL CONCERNS

LEARNING OBJECTIVES

After studying this chapter, the reader will be able to:

- Identify carbon-based fuels.
- Explain how ozone affects our environment.
- Describe how organic materials decompose into carbon-based fuels.
- Explain the difference between carbon-based and non-carbon-based energy sources.
- List alternatives to carbon-based fuels.
- List the factors that will be needed to reduce the carbon footprint.

KEY TERMS

Carbohydrates 28
Carbon (C) 28
Carbon footprint 33
Greenhouse gases (GHG) 29
Irradiance 31
Ozone 30
Ozone-depleting substances (ODS) 30
Sequestration 34
Smog 29
Stratosphere 31
Ultraviolet (UV) radiation 31
Volatile organic compounds (VOC) 30

NEED FOR ELECTRIC VEHICLES (EV) AND HYBRID ELECTRIC VEHICLES (HEV)

REDUCTION OF FOSSIL FUELS Electric vehicles do not consume fossil fuels directly, but instead are powered from the energy stored in on-board batteries. Hybrid electric vehicles are vehicles that have two sources of propulsion, either with an electric motor supplied energy from the high-voltage battery or an internal combustion engine. While an HEV still uses fossil fuels, they normally are able to achieve superior fuel economy compared to a similar vehicle that uses just fossil fuels for propulsion. The energy needed to create the electricity to charge the batteries can be from burning fossil fuels, such as coal or natural gas, or renewable solar and wind, as well as nuclear.

CARBON-BASED FUELS Throughout history, most of the energy used in the world has been generated by burning organic fuel that contains **carbon (C)**. An economy that uses only carbon-based fuels is often referred to as a *carbon-based society*. Carbon is formed from materials that were once alive on the earth, including:

- Plants that die and eventually are turned into coal, oil, and natural gas.
- Animal life of all types that also dies and decays to form carbon-fuels.

The source of carbon-based fuels is limited to the remains of dead plants and animals and is therefore not a limitless resource. ● SEE FIGURE 3–1.

CARBOHYDRATES All life-forms are able to collect, store, and use energy from their environment. In carbon-based biology, the basic energy storage compounds are in **carbohydrates**, where the carbon atoms are linked by single bonds into a chain. For example, carbon dioxide (CO_2) plus water (H_2O), when combined with chlorophyll in the plant and sunlight, produces glucose and oxygen (O_2). A carbohydrate is oxidized (combined with O_2) to release energy (and waste products of H_2O and CO_2). The carbon atoms are attached to hydrogen atoms to form hydrocarbons (abbreviated HC). There are literally thousands of hydrocarbons, and they differ not only by the number of carbon atoms, but also by the way they are attached to each other. The various bonds by which the molecule is constructed results in a change in the physical characteristics of the hydrocarbon. Molecules that have a high number of carbon atoms release more energy when burned, which translates into more power from the fuel and from the engine. Gasoline is composed of hundreds of different hydrocarbons that are blended together to create the specified volatility and other physical characteristic for use in an engine. SEE CHART 3–1.

CHEMISTRY OF CARBON-BASED EMISSIONS When carbon-based fuels are burned, the carbon and the hydrogen from the fuel combine with the 21% oxygen and the 88%

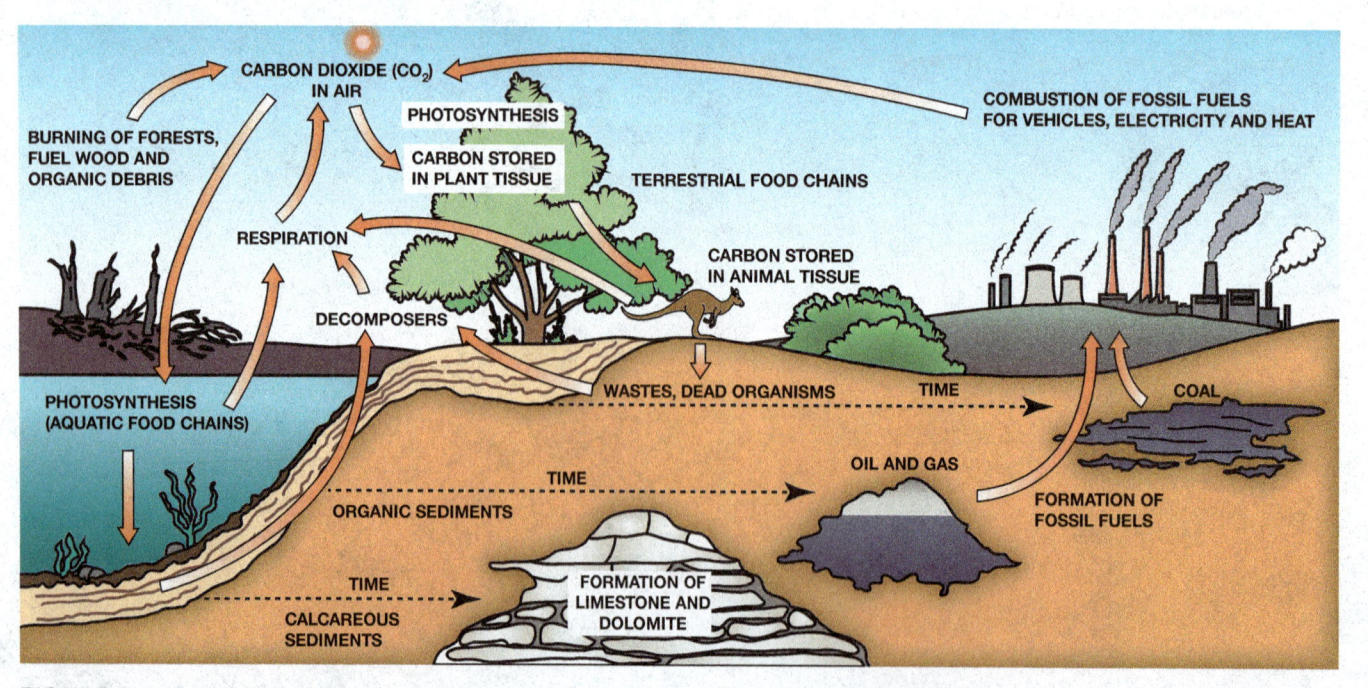

FIGURE 3-1 Carbon-based fuels are limited to the remains of dead plants and animals and their fossil remains create the carbon-based fuels used today.

FUEL	STATE	% OF CARBON	% OF HYDROGEN
Hydrogen	gas	0%	100%
Methane	gas	20%	80%
Gasoline	liquid	31%	69%
Oil	liquid	36%	64%
Coal	solid	62%	36%
Wood	solid	90%	10%

CHART 3-1 Carbon and hydrogen content of various fuels.

nitrogen in the air to create many new and often dangerous compounds, including:

- A colorless, odorless poisonous gas.
- Carbon dioxide (CO_2)—An inert greenhouse gas, which is thought to cause climate change.
- Hydrocarbons (HC)—This is simply unburned fuel and is one of the components of smog. **Smog** is a term used to describe a condition that looks like smoke and/or fog.

GREENHOUSE GASES Greenhouse gases (GHG) are those gases in our atmosphere that, if in too great a concentration, can prevent heat from escaping the surface, leading to an increase in the temperature on earth. In a nursery greenhouse, the glass panes are painted white to reflect the heat back into the greenhouse.

The ultraviolet light can penetrate through the paint and warms the interior so plants can be grown in colder periods of the year or in colder climates. Therefore, the gases in our atmosphere that act like the white paint on the glass panes of a greenhouse are called greenhouse gases. ● SEE FIGURE 3–2.

GHG tend to absorb this infrared radiation as it is reflected back toward space, trapping the heat in the atmosphere. Atmospheric concentrations of several important GHG (carbon dioxide, methane, nitrous oxide, and most man-made gases) have increased by about 25% since large-scale industrialization began some 150 years ago. The growth in the concentration of these gases is believed to be caused by human activity. Carbon dioxide that is generated as a result of human activity is known an anthropogenic greenhouse gas. In particular, anthropogenic carbon dioxide emissions have greatly increased since the beginning of the industrial age, due largely to the burning of fossil fuels and cutting down of forests for timber and other uses, such as paper and chemicals.

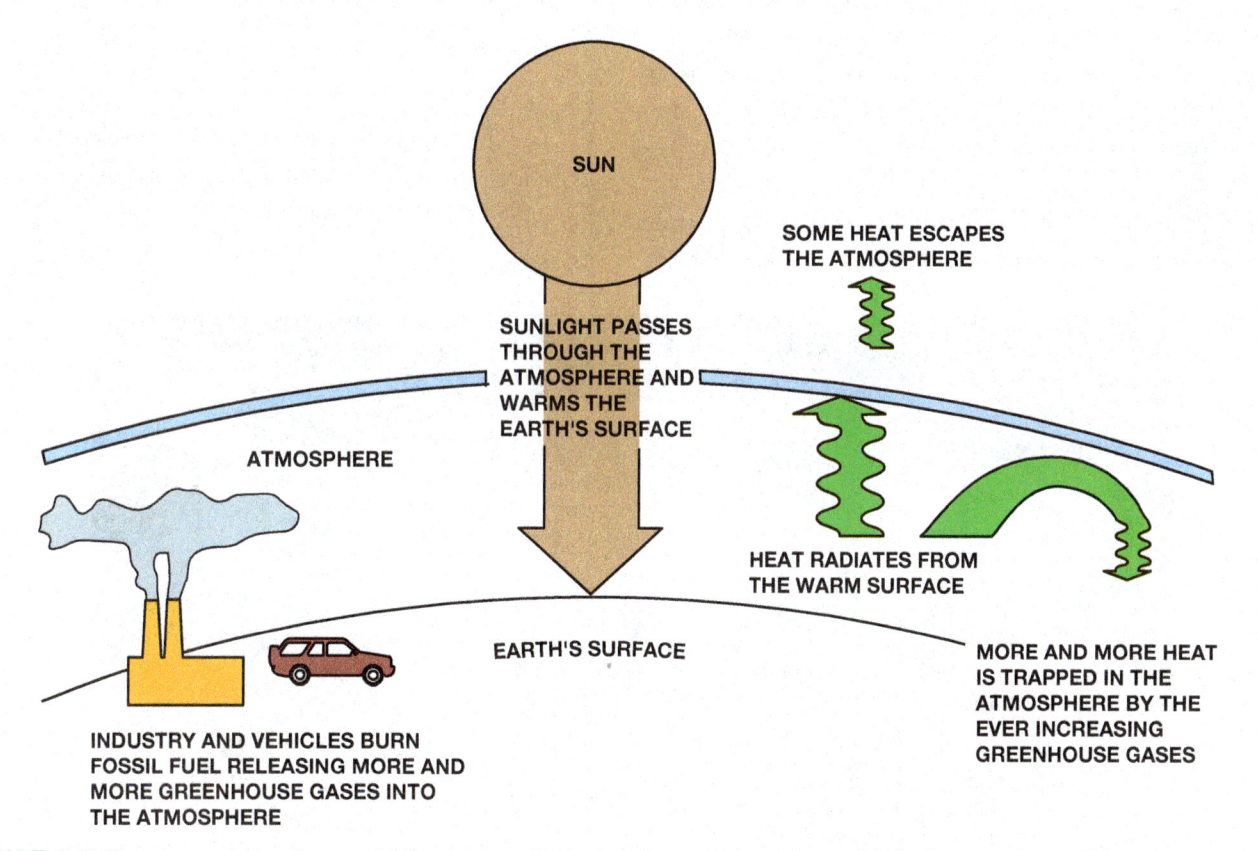

FIGURE 3-2 The atmosphere allows radiation to pass through to the earth's surface and blocks the release of heat back into space if there is too high a concentration of greenhouse gases.

HEALTH AND ENVIRONMENTAL CONCERNS

OZONE

DEFINITION Ozone is composed of three atoms of oxygen and is abbreviated O_3. Ozone occurs naturally in the atmosphere and can be detected by smell after a thunderstorm. Ozone has a strong clean smell, and in high concentrations, it can be a lung and respiratory irritant. Ozone can be created by lightning, which breaks the molecular structure of oxygen (O_2) into atoms (O), which then combine back into oxygen or combine to create ozone. ● **SEE FIGURE 3–3**.

GROUND-LEVEL OZONE Ozone that is located at ground level or in the atmosphere close to the earth is a health concern to humans because it causes health problems, including:

- Eye irritation
- Asthma
- Shortness of breath
- Chest tightness
- Wheezing

VEHICLES AND OZONE Exhaust from vehicles causes ground-level-ozone levels to increase because unburned hydrocarbons (HC) and oxides of nitrogen (NO_X), in the presence of sunlight, combine to create ozone, also called smog, which is a term used to describe the smoky or fog-like appearance of ground-level ozone.

UPPER-LEVEL OZONE Ozone located in the upper atmosphere (called the ozone layer) is helpful because it helps to block harmful ultraviolet rays from the sun from entering the lower atmosphere. Therefore, ozone is not a health concern when it is located in the upper regions of the atmosphere.

Depletion of the earth's upper ozone layer due to the release of man-made chemicals threatens human health and damages plant life. Certain man-made chemicals used in refrigeration, air conditioning, fire and explosion prevention, and as solvents can trigger reactions in the atmosphere that destroy the ozone layer. **Ozone-depleting substances (ODS)** include:

- Chlorofluorocarbons (CFCs)
- Hydrochlorofluorocarbons (HCFCs)
- Halons
- Methyl bromide

● **SEE FIGURE 3–4**.

? FREQUENTLY ASKED QUESTION

What Are Volatile Organic Compounds?

Volatile organic compounds (VOC) are gases emitted by paints, solvents, aerosol sprays, cleaners, glues, permanent markers, pesticides, and fuels. Health effects of VOC emissions into the atmosphere include:

- Eye, nose, and throat irritation
- Headaches
- Nausea

To reduce the levels of VOC released, always follow the manufacturer's directions for use of household and industrial products.

STRATOSPHERIC OZONE

GROUND - LEVEL OZONE
NO_x + VOC + SUN LIGHT = OZONE

INDUSTRIAL SOURCES | MOBILE SOURCES | AREA SOURCES | BIOGENIC SOURCES

AIR POLLUTION = GROUND-LEVEL OZONE + CO (CARBON MONOXIDE) + SO_x (SULPHUR OXIDES) + PM (PARTICULATE MATTER + NO_x (NITROGEN OXIDES) + VOC (VOLATILE ORGANIC COMPOUNDS)

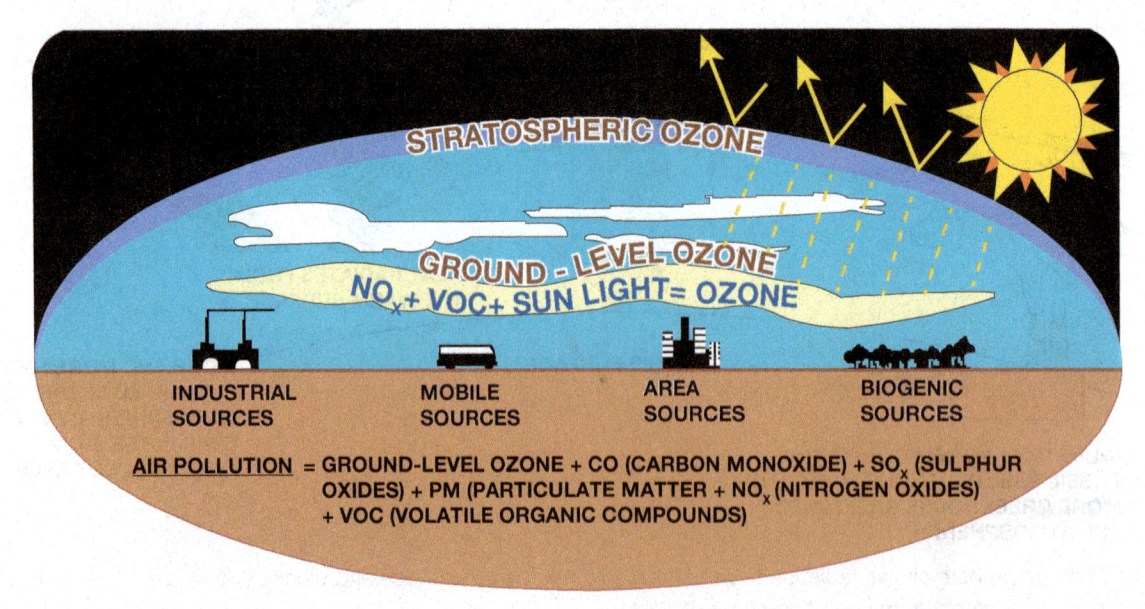

FIGURE 3-3 Ground-level ozone is created by pollutants, such as nitrogen oxides and volatile organic compounds reacting together by sunlight. Ozone in the upper atmosphere is good but ozone near the earth's surface is bad.

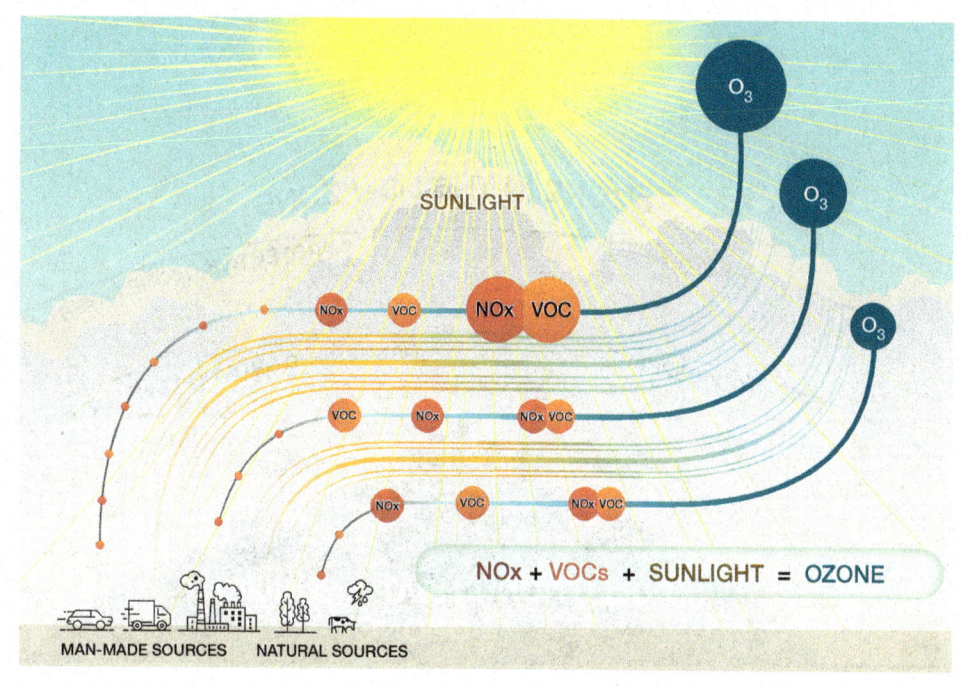

FIGURE 3-4 NO$_X$ plus VOCs interact with sunlight to create ozone.

ULTRAVIOLET RADIATION ABSORPTION

TYPES OF UV RADIATION **Ultraviolet (UV) radiation** is divided into three designations based on its impact on living organisms. The designations include:

- Designation "A," abbreviated UVA, is not absorbed by the ozone layer and generally is not damaging to biological organisms.
- Designation "B," abbreviated UVB, is only partially absorbed by the ozone layer and can cause damage to biological organisms.
- Designation "C," abbreviated UVC, is almost completely absorbed by the ozone layer and represents little, if any, health concerns.

INTENSITY OF RADIATION Another consideration in evaluating the effects of UV radiation is the intensity at the earth's surface—that is, how much radiation is reaching the earth's surface. For example, consider the difference in radiation between a 20-watt light bulb and a 100-watt bulb.

There is a large difference in intensity and thus in the amount of light or radiation. The term used to define the amount of solar radiation is **irradiance**. The solar irradiance at the earth's surface varies greatly depending on factors such as:

- Latitude
- Time of day
- Time of year
- Cloud cover
- Haze

In the case of the UV irradiance, additional factors are ozone density and elevation above sea level.

OZONE CONTROL OF UVB IRRADIANCE The protection of the earth's living systems from UVB and UVC radiation is a result of the absorption of this radiation by ozone. While there is some ozone in the lower atmosphere, called the troposphere, it is small compared to the amount in the upper atmosphere, called the **stratosphere**.

The most important factor is the total amount of ozone that solar radiation encounters before reaching the earth's surface. This is referred to as column ozone since it is the total amount of ozone in a column between the earth's surface and the top of the stratosphere. ● **SEE FIGURE 3–5**.

HEALTH AND ENVIRONMENTAL CONCERNS

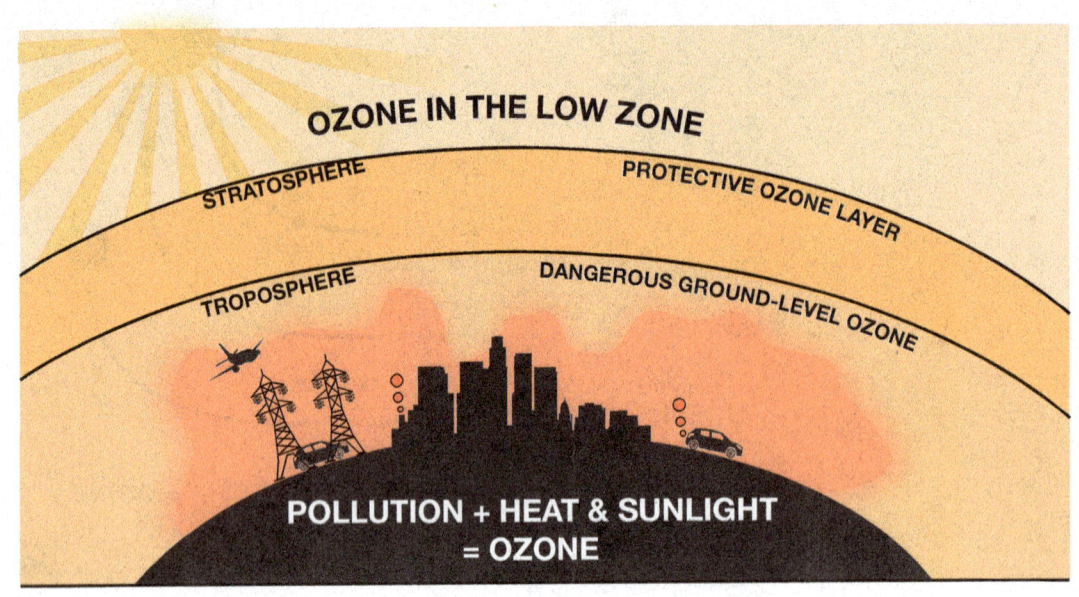

FIGURE 3-5 Column ozone is the total amount of ozone between the earth's surface and the top of the stratosphere.

> **TECH TIP**
>
> **Watch for Sunburn When at High Altitude**
>
> When at a location that is above 1,000 feet, and especially if above 5,000 feet, consider that there is much less atmosphere above to block the UV radiation. This means that sunburn and eye damage, such as cataracts, can more easily occur at high altitude compared to areas that are at or near sea level.

HEALTH EFFECTS OF AIR POLLUTION

TYPICAL HEALTH ISSUES According to medical experts, almost every disease has an environmental element, either minor or major. Skin cancer is largely thought to be caused by severe sunburn, often in childhood.

Unburned hydrocarbon (HC) emissions along with oxides of nitrogen (NO_X) combine in the atmosphere in the presence of sunlight to generate ground-level ozone (O_3). High levels of ozone, a respiratory irritant, can cause respiratory problems, including inflammation of the lungs.

Ozone exposure may lead to the following conditions:

- Premature death (due to long-term exposure to high levels of ozone)
- Shortness of breath
- Chest pain when inhaling deeply
- Wheezing and coughing

Another health concern involves particulate matter (PM), also called soot, which is found in the exhaust of diesel engines. PM has been linked to respiratory disease and cancer.

ACID RAIN

pH SCALE Acid rain refers to rain that has a pH lower than 7, indicating that it is acidic. Normal rain is pure water that is neither acidic (a pH of less than 7) nor alkaline (a pH greater than 7). Acid rain usually has a pH of 5.5 but can be as low as 4.3, according to the Environmental Protection Agency (EPA). The rain becomes acidic due to gases in the atmosphere, such as sulfur dioxide (SO_2) and oxides of nitrogen (NO_X). SO_2 combines with the rain water to form mild sulfuric acid. NO_X combine with rain water to form nitric acid. ● **SEE FIGURE 3–6**.

Both acids are harmful to the environment and can cause the following problems:

- Damage to forests and soils
- Damage to fish because the acid rain makes lakes and streams more acidic
- Damage to buildings and paint on vehicles
- Damage to roads and sidewalks. ● **SEE FIGURE 3–7**.

FIGURE 3-6 Acid rain is formed when sulfur dioxide (SO_2) and oxides of nitrogen (NO_X) combine with rain, forming acids.

FIGURE 3-7 The sidewalk section at the top is about 20 years old and shows the effects of acid rain, as compared to the lower section, which is about five years old. Notice that the acid rain has eroded the cement, leaving the aggregate (stones) exposed on the upper section.

Case Study

The Case of the Wrong pH

A museum was using a spray polish on an original paint blue 1937 Ford. After a few minutes, they noticed that the paint started to look purple. They immediately stopped using the spray polish and started to investigate the product they were using by checking with restoration experts. What they

...continued

...continued

discovered was that the polish they were using was slightly acidic and this was causing the original old paint to change color. While the product was okay to use on modern paints, it was not suitable for use on older original paint used before modern paint technology. To avoid causing damage or a color change on older paint, restoration experts recommend using a "pH balanced" product.

The pH is measured on a scale from 1 to 14 and is used to indicate the amount of chemical activity. The term pH is from the French word *pouvoir hydrogine*, meaning "hydrogen power."

Alkaline materials and acid materials neutralize each other, such as when baking soda (a caustic) is used to clean the outside of the battery (an acid surface). The caustic baking soda neutralizes any sulfuric acid that has been spilled or splashed on the outside of the battery. Most car shampoos are slightly alkaline with a pH of ranging from 7.1 to 8.5. Many car polishes are slightly acidic with a pH of 5 or 6. To check if the polish is acidic or is pH balanced, visit a parts store and ask that the safety data sheet (SDS) be printed out for the product being considered. The parts store counterperson will use the bar code to access the product information and from there, the SDS should be available and can be printed. Check the listed pH, and if the pH is 7, it is usable for all paints and finishes. However, if the pH is 4 to 6, most experts recommend that these not be used on old vehicles with their original paint.

Summary:
- **Complaint**—Using a spray wax, it was discovered to be the cause of turning the blue paint to purple on an old car.
- **Cause**—The spray wax was slightly acidic and this caused the blue paint to turn purple.
- **Correction**—The museum switched brands of spray wax to ones that were "pH balanced," meaning that the pH was 7 or about 7 (neutral).

CARBON FOOTPRINT

DEFINITION Total **carbon footprint** includes energy-related emissions from human activities, including heat, light, power, refrigeration, and all transport-related emissions from vehicles, freight, and distribution. The carbon footprint is a representation of the effect a person or organization has on the climate in terms of the total volume of GHG (mostly CO_2) produced.

Many actions generate carbon emissions, which contribute to accelerating climate change. For example, when gasoline is burned in a vehicle, it produces carbon in the form of carbon dioxide. Depending on the fuel efficiency of the vehicle and the miles traveled, a gasoline powered vehicle can easily generate its own weight in carbon dioxide each year. To prevent these conditions from occurring, GHG must be reduced by 60%, or a method must be used where CO_2 can be stored below the earth's surface. The process of storing carbon dioxide underground is called **sequestration**. ● SEE FIGURE 3–8.

REDUCING THE CARBON FOOTPRINT The following is a list of simple things that can be done immediately that will start to reduce the contribution to climate change. The items in this list will cost no money at all and will in fact save money.

1. Turn electrical devices off when not in use, such as lights, television, and computer.
2. Turn down the central heating slightly (try just 1 to 2 degrees).
3. Turn down the water heating setting (just 2 degrees will make a significant saving).
4. Check the central heating timer setting—there is no point in heating the house if everyone is at work during the day.
5. Fill the dishwasher and washing machine with a full load—this will save water and electricity, as well as detergent.
6. Unplug the cell phone as soon as it has finished charging.
7. Defrost the freezer regularly; if not done automatically, consider disabling the automatic function to save electricity.
8. Do shopping in a single trip.
9. Travel less and travel more using carbon-footprint-friendly vehicles.
10. Purchase a fuel-efficient vehicle, such an electric vehicle (EV) or hybrid electric vehicle (HEV).

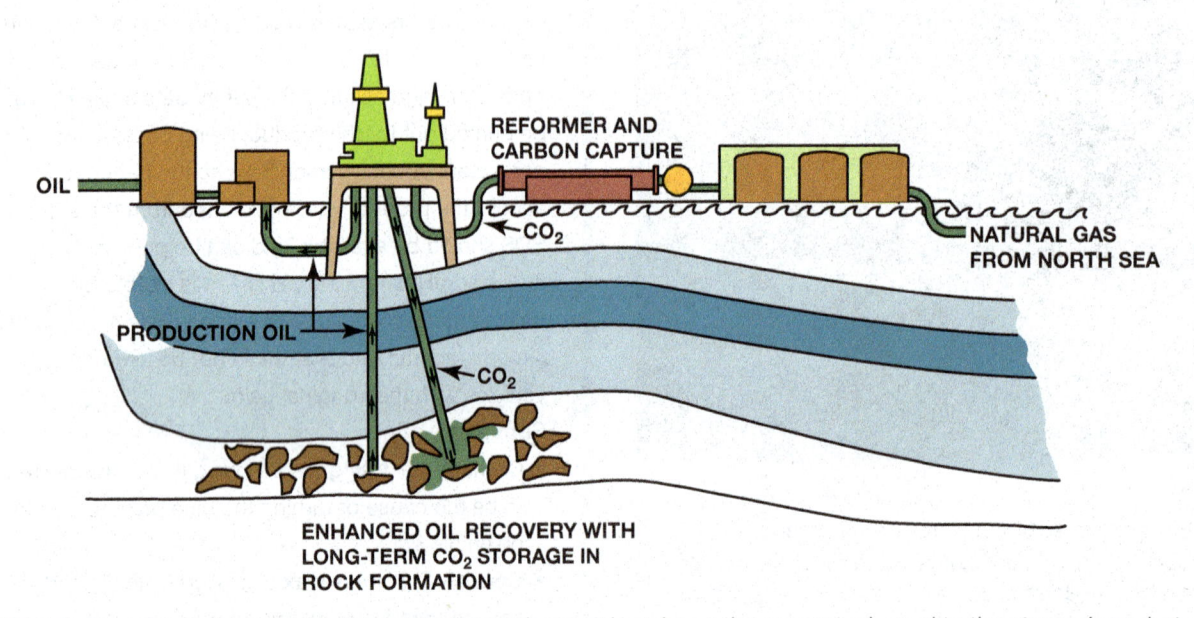

FIGURE 3-8 Pumping carbon dioxide back into the earth not only reduces the amount released to the atmosphere, but also helps force more crude oil to the surface, thereby increasing the efficiency of existing wells.

SUMMARY

1. Today's society is based on the use of carbon-based fuels, which are made from the remains of living plants and animals.
2. Carbon atoms are attached to hydrogen atoms to form hydrocarbons, abbreviated HC.
3. Ultraviolet (UV) radiation is divided into three designations based on its impact on living organisms.
4. Greenhouse gases (GHG) are those gases in our atmosphere that if in too great a concentration, can prevent heat from escaping the surface, leading to an increase in the temperature on earth.
5. The GHG in the atmosphere include:
   - Water vapor (H_2O)
   - Carbon dioxide (CO_2)
   - Methane (CH_4)
   - Nitrous oxide (N_2O)
   - Chlorofluorocarbons (CFCs)
6. Total carbon footprint includes energy-related emissions from human activities, including heat, light, power, refrigeration, and all transport-related emissions from vehicles, freight, and distribution.

REVIEW QUESTIONS

1. What is meant by the term "carbon-based society?"
2. What are hydrocarbons?
3. Which type of UV radiation is the most harmful to living organisms on earth?
4. What does carbon footprint mean?
5. What are six things people can do to reduce their individual carbon footprint?

CHAPTER QUIZ

1. Which fuel contains the least amount of carbon?
   a. Methane
   b. Hydrogen
   c. Coal
   d. Gasoline
2. What does the word organic mean?
   a. Any fuel
   b. Anything that was once alive
   c. Stone or rock
   d. Any part of the atmosphere above the ozone layer
3. The major greenhouse gas from gasoline-powered vehicles is _____.
   a. carbon monoxide (CO)
   b. carbon dioxide (CO_2)
   c. oxides of nitrogen (NO_X)
   d. unburned hydrocarbons (HCs)
4. The earth's upper ozone layer _____.
   a. is harmful to plants and animals, including humans
   b. helps reduce UV radiation from reaching the earth's surface
   c. Both a and b
   d. Neither a nor b
5. Which of the following result in smog when exposed to sunlight?
   a. Unburned hydrocarbon (HC)
   b. Oxides of nitrogen (NO_X)
   c. Carbon dioxide (CO_2)
   d. Both a and b
6. What is ozone?
   a. O_3
   b. CO_2
   c. NO_X
   d. H_2O
7. Which of the following UV radiation types is the most harmful to living organisms?
   a. UVA
   b. UVB
   c. UVC
   d. None of the above
8. Why is sunburn more likely to occur at high altitudes as compared to sea level?
   a. There is less ozone above to block the UV rays
   b. You are closer to the sun
   c. There is less oxygen
   d. It is colder at high altitudes and sunburn is therefore less likely
9. To reduce your carbon footprint, what action(s) can be performed?
   a. Drive a hybrid electric vehicle instead of a conventional gasoline-engine vehicle
   b. Drive fewer miles
   c. Insulate homes
   d. All of the above
10. Carbon dioxide is _____.
    a. manufactured gas
    b. occurs in our atmosphere normally
    c. is produced by plants and trees
    d. Both a and b

Chapter 4
HYBRID ENGINE SYSTEMS

LEARNING OBJECTIVES

After studying this chapter, the reader should be able to:

- Explain how a four-stroke cycle gasoline engine operates.
- Explain the Atkinson cycle and how it affects engine efficiency.
- Describe the importance of using the specified oil in the engine of a hybrid electric vehicle.
- Describe how the fuel injection and ignition systems work on hybrid gasoline engines.
- Explain how variable valve timing is able to improve engine power and reduce exhaust emissions.

KEY TERMS

Active grille shutters (AGS) 50
Atkinson cycle 38
Internal combustion engine (ICE) 37
Pumping losses 39
Variable valve timing (VVT) 42

HYBRID INTERNAL COMBUSTION ENGINES (ICE)

HYBRID ENGINE DIFFERENCES
The **internal combustion engine (ICE)** converts the energy contained in the fuel into heat energy in a process called combustion. A portion of this energy is lost due to the cooling and exhaust systems, but about a third is turned into useful power. This power is used to move the vehicle. The ICE used in hybrid electric vehicles (HEV) differs from those used in conventional vehicles. These differences can include:

- Smaller engine displacement than most similar vehicles of the same size and weight.
- Use of the Atkinson cycle to increase efficiency.
- Crankshaft offset to reduce internal friction.
- Often do not use a conventional starter motor.
- Some use spark plugs that are indexed so the open side of the spark is pointed toward the intake valve for maximum efficiency.
- Engine mounts are computer controlled to counteract and eliminate undesirable engine vibration.
- The use of low viscosity engine oil, such as SAE 0W-20 or SAE 0W-16.

The engines used in hybrid vehicles are also similar to those used in non-hybrid vehicles and share the following features:

1. Conventional fuel injection system
2. Conventional engine layout and number of cylinders (except for the Honda Insight, which uses a three-cylinder engine)
3. Uses the same engine parts as conventional
4. Same ignition system
5. Same or similar engine lubrication system, including the oil filter but with a lighter viscosity oil than that used in similar conventional vehicles

ENGINE FUNDAMENTALS

FOUR-STROKE CYCLE OPERATION
Engine cycles are identified by the number of piston strokes required to complete the cycle. A piston stroke is a one-way piston movement between the top and bottom of the cylinder (and vice versa). During one stroke, the crankshaft revolves 180° (1/2 revolution). A cycle is a complete series of events that continually repeat. Most automotive engines use the four-stroke cycle of events, begun by the starter motor, which rotates the engine. The four-stroke cycle is repeated for each cylinder of the engine. ● **SEE FIGURE 4–1.**

- **Intake stroke.** The intake valve is open and the piston inside the cylinder travels downward, drawing a mixture of air and fuel into the cylinder.
- **Compression stroke.** As the engine continues to rotate, the intake valve closes and the piston moves upward in the cylinder, compressing the air–fuel mixture.

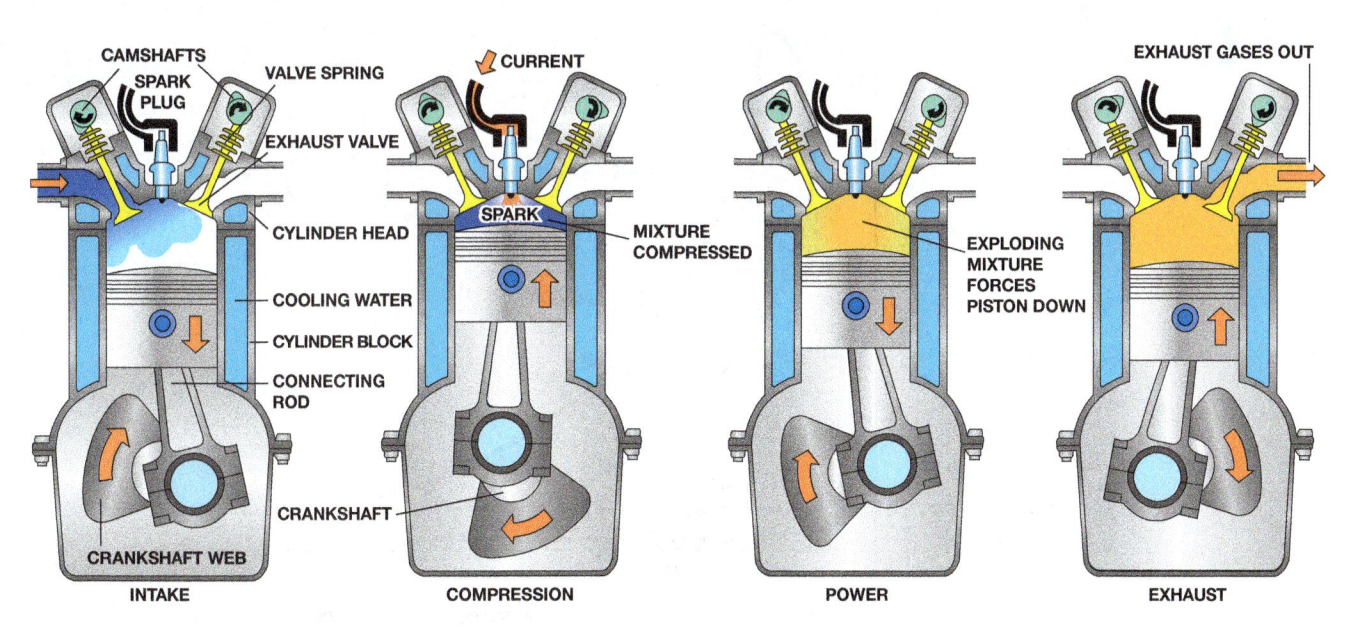

FIGURE 4–1 The downward movement of the piston draws the air–fuel mixture into the cylinder through the open intake valve on the intake stroke. On the compression stroke, the mixture is compressed by the upward movement of the piston with both valves closed. Ignition occurs at the beginning of the power stroke, and combustion drives the piston downward to produce power. On the exhaust stroke, the upward-moving piston forces the burned gases out the open exhaust valve.

- **Power stroke.** When the piston gets near the top of the cylinder, called top dead center (TDC), the spark at the spark plug ignites the air–fuel mixture, forcing the piston downward and the crankshaft to rotate.
- **Exhaust stroke.** The engine continues to rotate, and the piston again moves upward in the cylinder. The exhaust valve opens, and the piston forces the residual burned gases past the exhaust valve and into the exhaust manifold and exhaust system.

This sequence repeats as the engine rotates. To stop the engine, power to the ignition system and fuel system is shut off.

The piston is attached to a crankshaft with a connecting rod. This arrangement allows the piston to reciprocate (move up and down) in the cylinder as the crankshaft rotates. The combustion pressure developed in the combustion chamber at the correct time will push the piston downward to rotate the crankshaft.

ATKINSON CYCLE

BACKGROUND The **Atkinson cycle** engine is an engine that uses a late closing intake valve to reduce compression pressures and an extended power stroke event. In 1882, James Atkinson, a British engineer, invented an engine that achieved a higher efficiency than the Otto cycle, but produced lower power at low engine speeds. The Atkinson cycle engine was produced in limited numbers until 1890, when sales dropped, and the company that manufactured the engines finally went out of business in 1893.

OPERATION One key feature of the Atkinson cycle that remains in use today is that the intake valve is held open longer than normal to allow a reverse flow into the intake manifold. This reduces the effective compression ratio and engine displacement and allows the expansion to exceed the compression ratio while retaining a normal compression pressure. This is desirable for good fuel economy because the compression ratio in a spark ignition engine is limited by the octane rating of the fuel used, while a high expansion delivers a longer power stroke and reduces the heat wasted in the exhaust. This increases the efficiency of the engine because more work is being achieved. ● **SEE FIGURE 4–2.**

NOTE: Four-stroke engines of this type with forced induction, such as an engine-driven supercharger, are known as Miller cycle engines. At present, no hybrid engine uses a supercharger or the Miller cycle. Sometimes called a "five-stroke" cycle, the Atkinson cycle uses a normal intake stroke, but as the compression stroke is about to start, the intake valve is left open to reduce pumping losses. See Frequently Asked Question, "What Is Meant by 'Pumping Losses?'"

The open intake valve allows a "backflow stroke" of air from the cylinder into the intake manifold. As the piston moves up the cylinder, the intake valve closes and the compression stroke begins. A 12.3:1 compression ratio ensures there is sufficient cylinder pressure for good performance. The power stroke begins as the air–fuel mixture is ignited by the spark plug, and the cycle is completed as the piston forces the exhaust gases out the exhaust valve on the exhaust stroke.

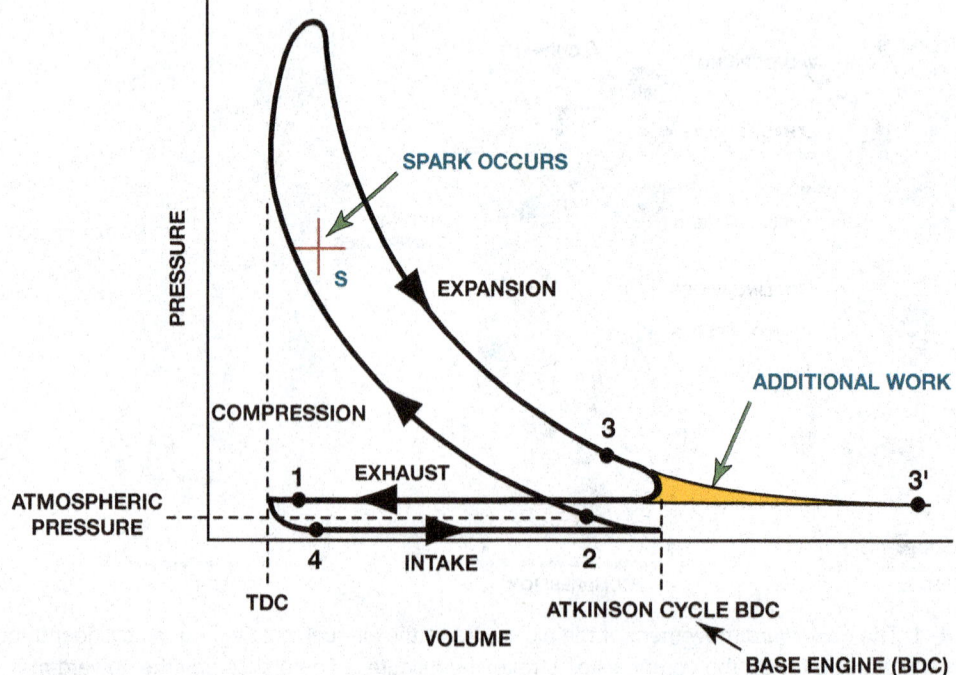

FIGURE 4–2 A pressure volume diagram showing where additional work is generated by the delayed closing of the intake valve. Point "S" is where the spark occurs.

> ### ❓ FREQUENTLY ASKED QUESTION
>
> **What Is Meant by "Pumping Losses?"**
>
> **Pumping losses** refer to the energy required to overcome the restriction in the intake system to fill the cylinders with air during the intake stroke. Pumping losses are created by the throttle valve that restricts the flow of air into the cylinders. Diesel engines do not have this concern because they are un-throttled, meaning that there is no restriction to airflow entering a diesel engine. To reduce pumping losses several methods are used:
>
> 1. Introduce a high percentage (over 30%) of exhaust gas recirculation (EGR) into the intake. Because the exhaust gases do not burn, but rather occupy space, the power of the engine is reduced. To achieve the original power from the engine, the throttle must be opened farther than normal, thereby reducing pumping losses due to the closed throttle.
> 2. The use of an electronic throttle allows the powertrain engineer to program the powertrain control module (PCM) to open the throttle at highway speeds to reduce pumping losses, and at the same time introduce additional EGR to maintain engine speed.
> 3. Reduce engine speed by using overdrive transmissions/transaxles. The slower the engine speed, the easier it is to increase its efficiency.
>
> The most efficient engines are huge ship diesel engines that operate at about 100 RPM and can achieve an efficiency of about 50%, or twice that of a conventional gasoline or diesel engine.

The Atkinson cycle is up to 10% more efficient than a conventional four-stroke gasoline engine, and produces more torque than a conventional engine at high engine speeds, but it does reduce low-end engine torque. A typical HEV can take advantage of this by using an electric motor to propel the vehicle at lower speeds. Electric motors excel at low RPM torque, so the hybrid transaxle makes up for the low-speed losses of the Atkinson cycle gasoline engine.

ATKINSON CYCLE ENGINES

The Atkinson cycle is used in many conventional, as well as HEV, including but not limited to the following:

- Chevrolet Volt
- Chrysler Pacifica plug-in hybrid model minivan
- Ford C-Max hybrid and plug-in hybrid models
- Ford Escape/Mercury Mariner hybrid electric
- Ford Fusion Hybrid/Mercury Milan Hybrid/Lincoln MKZ hybrid electric
- Honda Accord Plug-In Hybrid
- Honda Accord Hybrid
- Honda Clarity Plug-In Hybrid
- Honda Insight
- Honda Fit
- Hyundai Sonata Hybrid
- Hyundai Elantra Atkinson-cycle models
- Hyundai hybrid
- Hyundai Ioniq hybrid, plug-in hybrid
- Hyundai Palisade 3.8 L
- Infiniti M35h hybrid
- Kia Forte
- Kia Niro hybrid
- Kia Optima Hybrid Kia K5 hybrid 500h
- Kia Cadenza Hybrid Kia K7 hybrid
- Kia Telluride 3.8 L
- Kia Seltos 2.0L
- Lexus CT 200h
- Lexus ES 300h
- Lexus GS 450h hybrid electric
- Lexus RC F
- Lexus GS F
- Lexus HS 250h
- Lexus IS 200t
- Lexus NX hybrid
- Lexus RX 450h hybrid
- Lexus LC
- Mazda Mazda6
- Mercedes ML450 Hybrid
- Mercedes S400 Blue Hybrid
- Mitsubishi Outlander PHEV
- Toyota Camry Hybrid
- Toyota Avalon Hybrid
- Toyota Highlander Hybrid
- Toyota Prius hybrid
- Toyota Yaris Hybrid
- Toyota Tacoma V6
- Toyota RAV4 Hybrid
- Toyota Sienna
- Toyota C-HR Hybrid
- Subaru Crosstrek Hybrid

HYBRID ENGINE DESIGN FEATURES

PISTON PIN OFFSET The piston pin holes are usually not centered in the piston. They are located toward the major thrust surface, approximately 0.062 inch (1.57 millimeters) from the piston centerline. ● SEE FIGURE 4-3.

Pin offset is designed to reduce piston slap and noise that can result as the large end of the connecting rod crosses over TDC. The minor thrust side of the piston head has a greater area than does the major side. This is caused by the pin offset. The action includes the following steps:

- As the piston moves up in the cylinder on the compression stroke, it rides against the minor thrust surface.
- When compression pressure becomes high enough, the greater head area on the minor side causes the piston to cock slightly in the cylinder.
- This keeps the top of the minor thrust surface on the cylinder.
- It forces the bottom of the major thrust surface to contact the cylinder wall.
- As the piston approaches top center, both thrust surfaces are in contact with the cylinder wall.
- When the crankshaft crosses over top center, the force on the connecting rod moves the entire piston toward the major thrust surface.
- The lower portion of the major thrust surface has already been in contact with the cylinder wall. The rest of the piston skirt slips into full contact just after the crossover point, thereby controlling piston slap. ● SEE FIGURE 4-4.

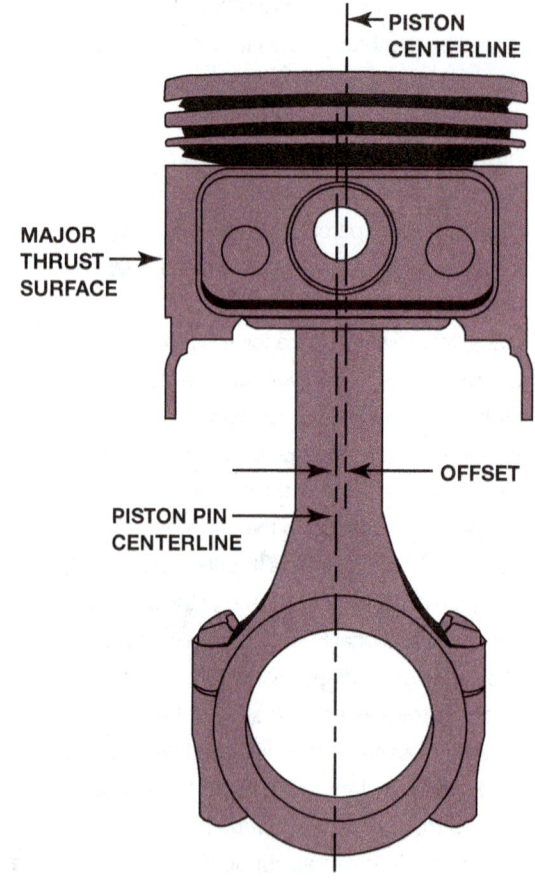

FIGURE 4-3 Piston pin offset toward the major thrust surface.

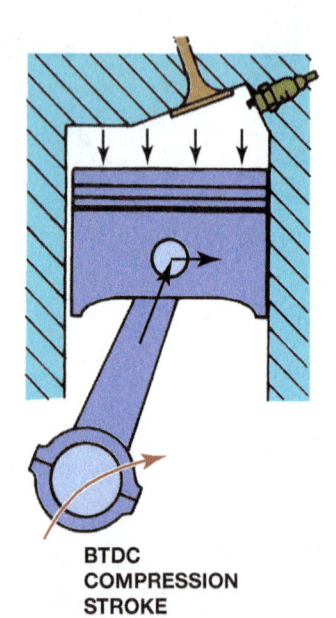

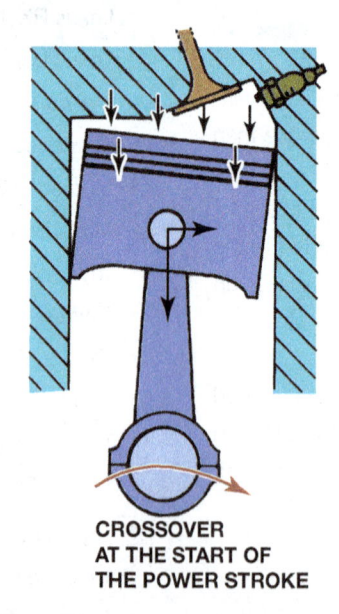

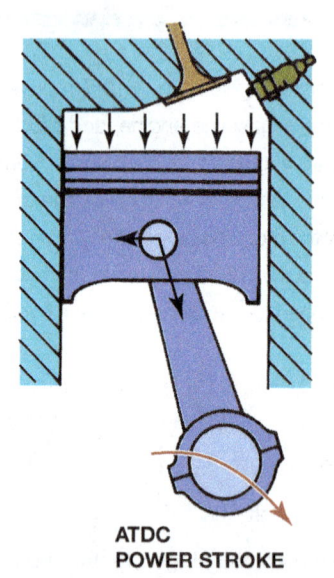

FIGURE 4-4 Engine rotation and rod angle during the power stroke cause the piston to press harder against one side of the cylinder, called the major thrust surface.

Offsetting the piston toward the minor thrust surface provides a better mechanical advantage. It also causes less piston-to-cylinder friction. For these reasons, the offset is often placed toward the minor thrust surface in racing engines. Noise and durability are not as important in racing engines as is maximum performance.

NOTE: All piston pins are offset. In fact, many engines operate without the offset to help reduce friction and improve power and fuel economy.

OFFSET CRANKSHAFT
The thrust side is the side of the cylinder that the connecting rod points to when the piston is on the power stroke. To reduce side loads, some vehicle manufacturers offset the crankshaft from center. This is called an *offset crankshaft*. For example, if an engine rotates clockwise as viewed from the front, the crankshaft may be offset to the left to reduce the angle of the connecting rod during the power stroke. The offset usually varies from 1/16 inch to 1/2 inch, depending on make and model. Some inline gasoline engines used in hybrid gasoline/electric vehicles use an offset crankshaft. ● **SEE FIGURE 4–5.**

? FREQUENTLY ASKED QUESTION

How Can the Motor/Generator Smooth Out ICE Power Pulses?

Most HEV use a motor/generator either attached to the ICE crankshaft either directly or through a drive belt. Every ICE creates the power by using combustion events inside the cylinder. Every time a cylinder fires, the crankshaft speed increases and starts to slow until the next cylinder in the firing order fires. The resulting speeding up and slowing down causes torsional harmonics to be transmitted to the crankshaft and eventually to the entire drivetrain. The motor/generator, commonly called an "electric machine," supplies a counter torque to the crankshaft to cancel out the torsional harmonics. This action results in smoother operation of the entire drivetrain.
● **SEE FIGURE 4–6.**

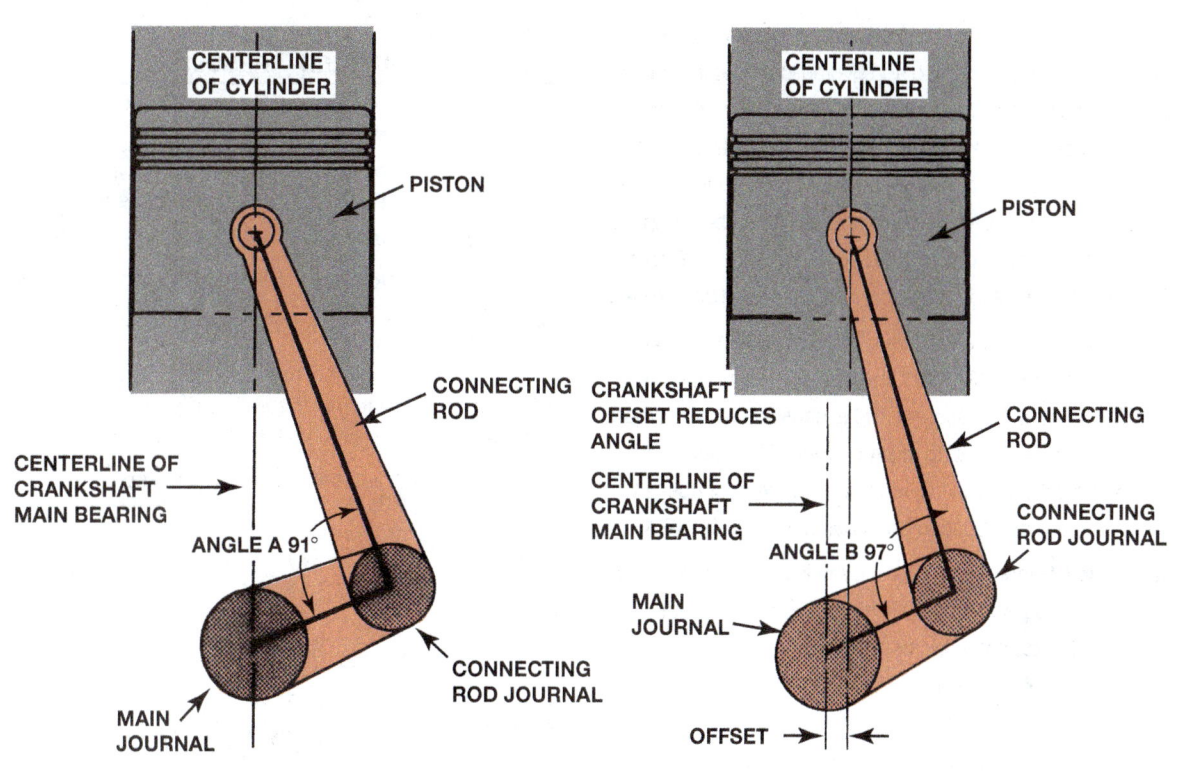

FIGURE 4–5 The crank throw is halfway down on the power stroke. The piston on the left without an offset crankshaft has a sharper angle than the engine on the right with an offset crankshaft.

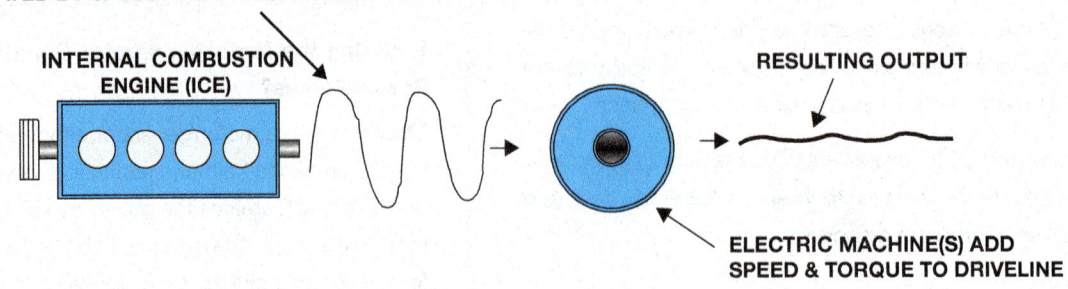

FIGURE 4–6 All ICE create crankshaft torsional harmonics when the cylinders fire. The attached motor/generator (electric machine) applies a counter torque to the crankshaft to smooth out these harmonics.

VARIABLE VALVE TIMING

PURPOSE OF VARIABLE VALVE TIMING Conventional camshafts are permanently synchronized to the crankshaft so that the valves operate at a specific point in each combustion cycle. In an engine, the intake valve opens slightly before the piston reaches the top of the cylinder and closes about 60 degrees after the piston reaches the bottom of the stroke on every cycle, regardless of the engine speed or load.

VARIABLE VALVE TIMING SYSTEMS Variable valve timing (VVT) involves the use of electric and hydraulic actuators that are used to change the timing of the camshaft(s) in relation to the crankshaft. VVT, also called *variable cam timing (VCT)*, allows the valves to be operated at different points in the combustion cycle to improve performance. As a result of being able to create overlap between the intake and exhaust valves, most engines equipped with VVT do not use an EGR valve. There are four basic types of VVT used on engines:

- **Exhaust only.** An engine that uses VVT on the exhaust only is used to create an EGR affect, thereby eliminating the need for an EGR valve. In this system, the exhaust valve is retarded when the engine is operating at part throttle. This delays the closing of the exhaust valves, which allows exhaust gases to be trapped in the combustion chamber. ● SEE FIGURE 4–7.

- **Intake only.** Changing the intake camshaft timing results in improved engine performance. This is due to commanding the intake valve to close earlier in the compression stroke, resulting in less of the air/fuel charge being pushed back into the intake port (reversions). The result is improved by low speed torque that the engine can produce.

- **Cam-in-block.** Some overhead valve (OHV) engines that use a single camshaft to control the valves are equipped with a phaser that allows the cam to be rotated in relation to the crankshaft to achieve VVT. The PCM retards the camshaft to achieve exhaust gases so an EGR valve is not needed to meet oxides of nitrogen (NOx) exhaust emissions. The camshaft can be changed to create a broad engine torque range and improved fuel economy.

- **Both Intake and Exhaust Cams.** Many double overhead camshaft (DOHC) engines use VVT on both the intake and the exhaust camshafts. By varying both camshafts, the engine torque is increased over a wide engine speed range. This allows the PCM to control the amount of exhaust gases trapped in the combustion chamber to control the formation of NOx emissions. This is achieved by allowing the intake valve(s) to open sooner or the exhaust valve(s) to stay open longer. ● SEE CHART 4–1.

CAMSHAFT PHASING CHANGED	RESULTS
Exhaust cam phasing	Reduces NOx exhaust emissions
Exhaust cam phasing	Increases fuel economy (reduced pumping losses)
Intake cam phasing	Increases low-speed torque
Intake cam phasing	Increases high-speed power

CHART 4–1
By varying the intake camshaft timing, engine performance is improved. By varying the exhaust camshaft timing, the exhaust emissions and fuel consumption are reduced.

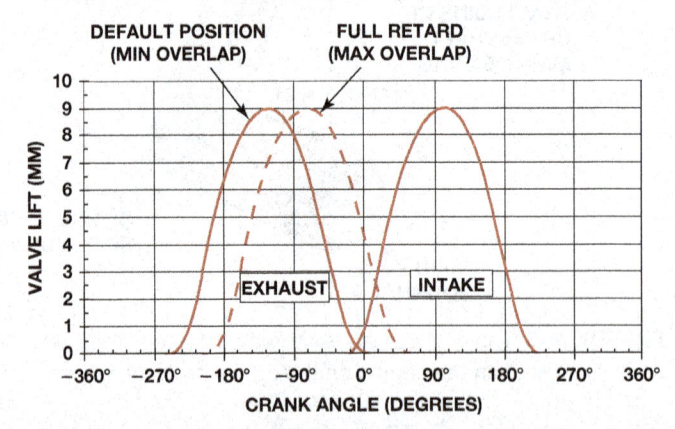

FIGURE 4–7 The exhaust on only VCT systems allows the overlap period where both valves are open to be changed. The at-rest position provides little valve overlap, whereas the maximum overlap allows for internal EGR needed to reduce NOx exhaust emissions.

TECH TIP

Always Use the Specified Oil in a HEV

Most HEV engines require a low viscosity engine oil such as SAE 0W-16, SAE 0W-20, or SAE 5W-20. There are three major reasons why this low viscosity oil is used:

1. Lower viscosity oil improves fuel economy by reducing drag inside the engine.
2. During starting after idle stop has occurred, the oil has to flow quickly to get oil to all of the moving parts especially in cold weather.
3. Most HEV engines use a type of VVT or displacement deactivation system that requires the rapid flow of oil to function as designed.

Therefore, for best overall performance and economy, always use the specified oil in all engines.

PARTS AND OPERATION The camshaft position actuator oil control valve (OCV) directs oil from the oil feed in the head to the appropriate camshaft position actuator oil passages. There is one OCV for each camshaft position actuator. The OCV is sealed and mounted to the front cover. The ported end of the OCV is inserted into the cylinder head with a sliding fit. A filter screen protects each OCV oil port from any contamination in the oil supply. The camshaft position actuator is mounted to the front end of the camshaft. The timing notch in the nose of the camshaft aligns with the dowel pin in the camshaft position actuator to ensure proper cam timing and camshaft position actuator oil hole alignment. ● **SEE FIGURE 4–8.**

CAMSHAFT PHASERS There are two types of cam phasing devices used:

1. Spline phaser is used on overhead camshaft (OHC) engines. ● **SEE FIGURE 4–9.**
2. Vane phaser is used on OHC and OHV cam-in-block engines.

SPLINE PHASER SYSTEM OPERATION On a typical OHC engine, the control valve is located on the front passenger side of the cylinder head. The OCV is controlled using a pulse-width modulation (PWM) signal from the PCM. Oil pressure is regulated by the control valve and directed to the ports in the cylinder head leading to the camshaft and cam phaser position. The cam phaser is located on the exhaust cams and is part of the exhaust cam sprocket. When the ECM commands an increase in oil pressure, the piston is moved inside the cam phaser and rides along the helical splines, which compresses the coil spring. This movement causes the cam phaser gear and the camshaft to move in an opposite direction, thereby retarding the cam timing. ● **SEE FIGURE 4–10.**

VANE PHASER SYSTEM ON AN OVERHEAD CAMSHAFT ENGINE The vane phaser system used on OHC engines uses a camshaft piston (CMP) sensor on each camshaft. Each camshaft has its own actuator and its own OCV. Instead of using a piston along a helical spline, the vane phaser uses a rotor with four vanes, which is connected to the end of the camshaft. The rotor is located inside the stator, which is bolted to the cam sprocket. The stator and rotor are not connected. Oil pressure is controlled on both sides of the vanes of the rotor, which creates a hydraulic link between the two parts. The OCV varies the balance of pressure on either side of the vanes and thereby controls the position of the camshaft. A return spring is used under the

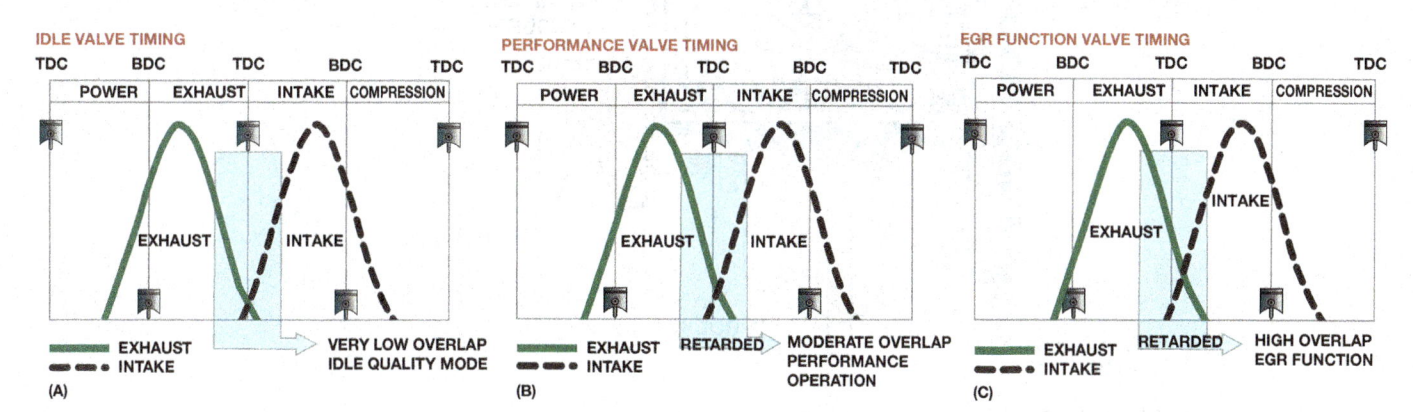

FIGURE 4–8 (a) At engine start, the camshaft timing has little valve overlap, which improves idle quality. (b) During acceleration, the valve overlap is increased to improve engine performance. (c) To reduce NOx emissions, the valve timing is changed to trap some of the exhaust gases in the combustion chamber, thereby eliminating the needs for an EGR valve.

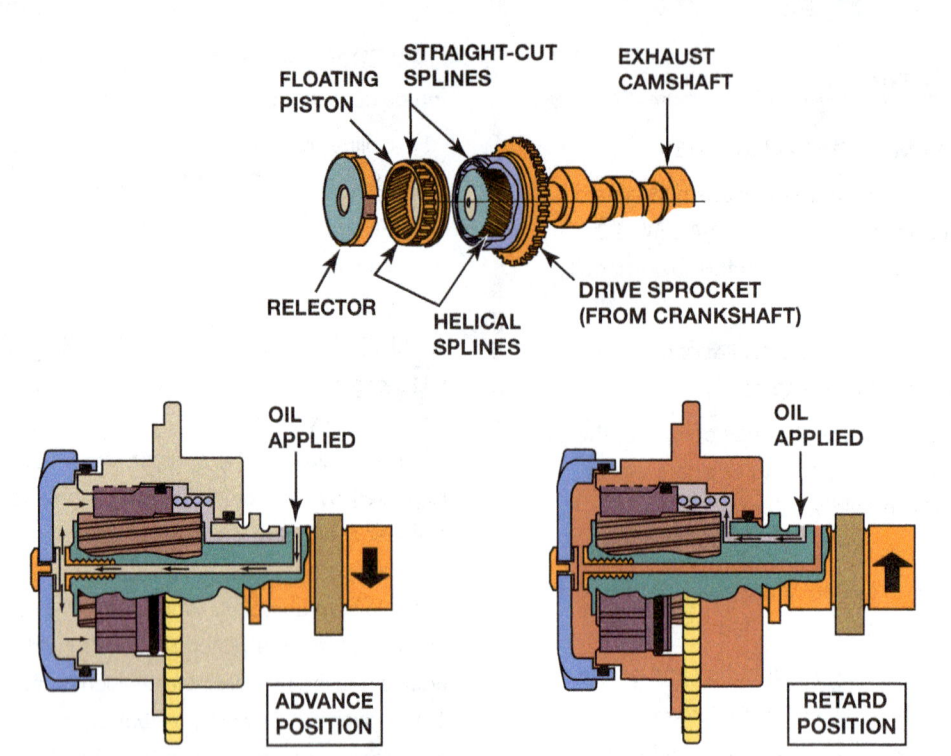

FIGURE 4–9 Spline cam phaser assembly.

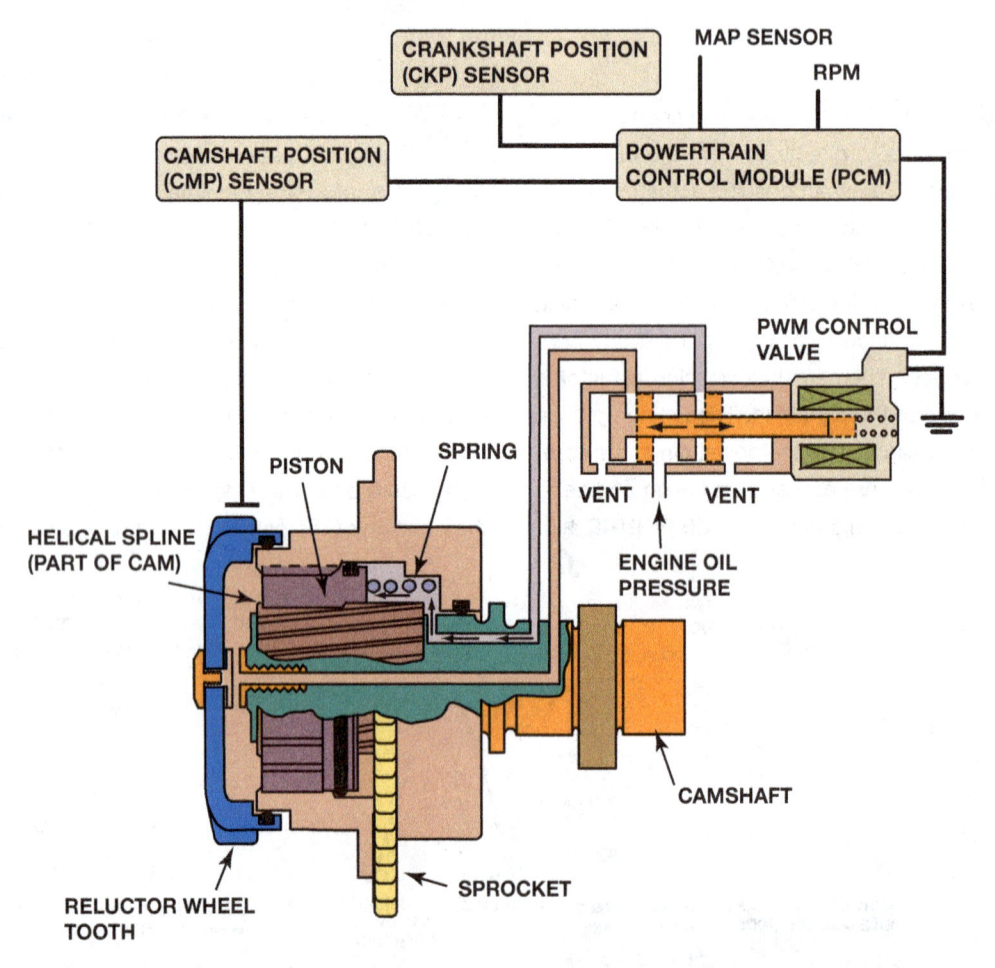

FIGURE 4–10 A spline phaser showing the control valve and how it works internally. The PCM uses the engine speed (RPM), crankshaft position (CKP) sensor, and the camshaft position (CMP) sensor to monitor and command the camshaft for maximum power and lowest possible exhaust emissions.

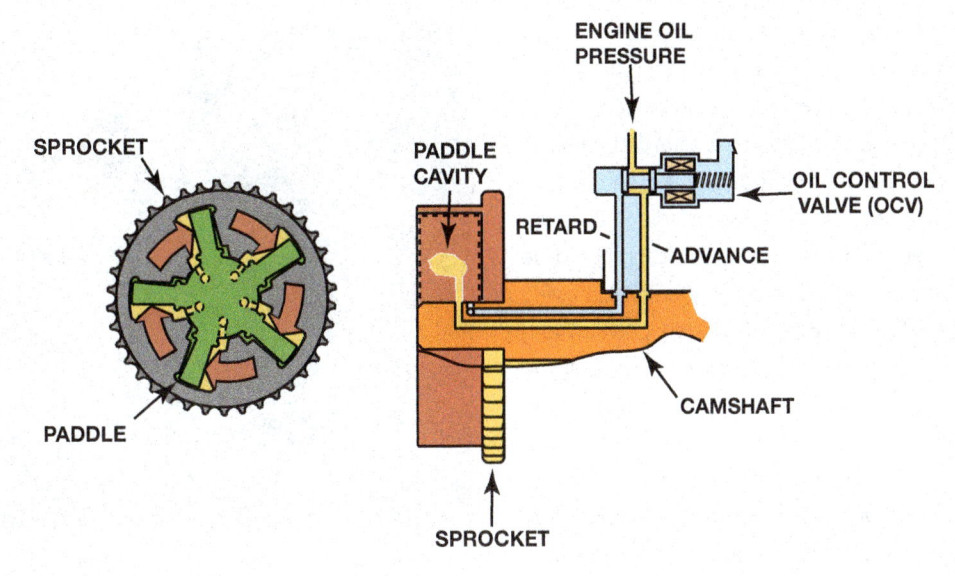

FIGURE 4–11 A vane phaser is used to move the camshaft using changes of oil pressure from the OCV.

reluctor of the phaser to help return it to the home or 0 position. ● SEE FIGURE 4–11.

The following occurs when the pulse width is changed:

- **0% pulse width.** The oil is directed to the advance chamber of the exhaust camshaft actuator and the retard chamber of the intake camshaft activator.

- **50% pulse width.** The PCM is holding the cam in the calculated position based on engine RPM and load. At 50% pulse width, the oil flow through the phaser drops to zero. ● SEE FIGURE 4–12.

- **100% pulse width.** The oil is directed to the retard chamber of the exhaust camshaft actuator and the advance chamber of the intake camshaft actuator.

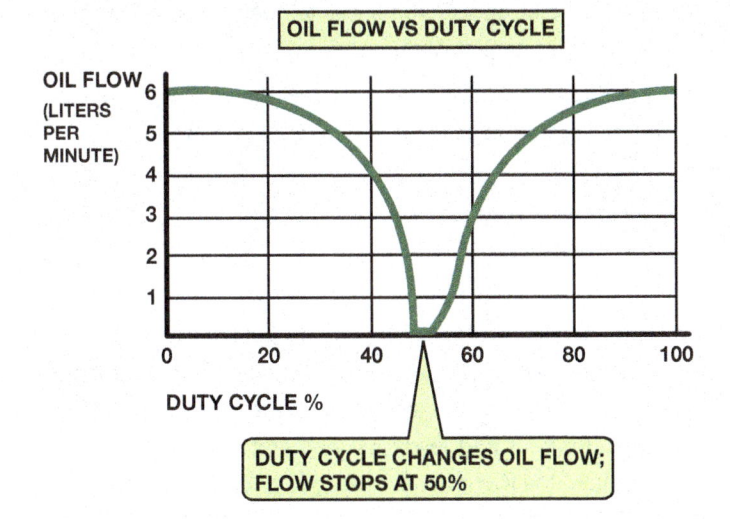

FIGURE 4–12 When the PCM commands 50% duty cycle, the oil flow through the phaser drops to zero.

The cam phasing is continuously variable with a range from 40 for the intake camshaft to 50 for the exhaust camshaft. The PCM uses the following sensors to determine the best position of the camshaft for maximum power and lowest possible exhaust emissions:

- Engine speed (RPM)
- MAP sensor
- Crankshaft position (CKP) sensor
- Camshaft position (CMP) sensor
- Barometric pressure (BARO) sensor

DIAGNOSIS OF VARIABLE VALVE TIMING SYSTEMS

DIAGNOSTIC STEPS The diagnostic procedure as specified by most vehicle manufacturers usually includes the following steps:

STEP 1 Verify the customer concern. This will usually be a "check engine light" (malfunction indicator light or MIL), as the engine performance effects would be minor under most operating conditions.

STEP 2 Perform a thorough visual inspection, including checking the oil for proper level and condition.

STEP 3 Check for stored diagnostic trouble codes (DTCs). Typical VVT–related DTCs include the following:

P0011—Intake cam position is over advanced bank 1
P0012—Intake cam position is over retarded bank 1

P0013—Exhaust camshaft position actuator
P0014—Exhaust camshaft too far advanced
P0021—Intake cam position is over advanced bank 2
P0022—Intake cam position is over retarded bank 2

STEP 4 Use a scan tool and check for duty cycle on the cam phase solenoid while operating the vehicle at a steady road speed. The commanded pulse width should be 50%. If the pulse width is not 50%, the PCM is trying to move the phaser to its commanded position and the phaser has not reacted properly. A PWM signal of higher or lower than 50% usually indicates a stuck phaser assembly.

STEP 5 Check the solenoid for proper resistance. If a scan tool with bidirectional control is available, connect an ammeter and measure the current as the solenoid is being commanded on by the scan tool.

STEP 6 Check for proper engine oil pressure. Low oil pressure or restricted flow to the cam phaser can be the cause of many DTC.

STEP 7 Determine the root cause of the problem and clear all DTCs.

STEP 8 Road test the vehicle to verify the fault has been corrected.

FIGURE 4–13 The screen(s) protects the solenoid valve from dirt and debris that can cause the valve to stick. This fault can set a P0017 DTC (crankshaft position–camshaft position correlation error).

> 🔧 **TECH TIP**
>
> **Change the Engine Oil If a DTC Is Set**
>
> A P000A DTC indicates that the intake camshaft timing changed too slowly. A P000B DTC is set when the exhaust camshaft timing changes too slowly. While these DTCs could be set due to a fault with the solenoids or the electrical circuits controlling the solenoids, the most likely cause is engine oil–related. Dirty oil, oil of the incorrect viscosity, or even a low oil level is often the most likely cause. If the electrical circuits are found to be within factory specification, changing the engine oil using the specified viscosity may well be the solution to either code fault. ● **SEE FIGURE 4–13.**

HEV ICE COOLING SYSTEM

ENGINE (ICE) COOLING The purpose of the engine cooling system is to bring the ICE up to the optimum temperature as quickly as possible and maintain that temperature under all operating conditions. ICE produce increased emissions during a cold start. This is because fuel has a tendency to condense on a cold air intake manifold and cylinder walls, requiring a richer air–fuel mixture to compensate. The cold surfaces in the combustion chamber also uses quench, where the flame along those surfaces is extinguished and the air–fuel mixture is only partially burned. These issues diminish significantly once the ICE is up to operating temperature. Coolant temperature is maintained at an optimum temperature for a number of reasons:

1. The ICE is able to run at the highest efficiency and lowest emissions when it is operating between 195°F and 215°F (90°C and 101°C).
2. Vehicle drivability (engine performance) is enhanced.
3. Engines that operate at normal temperatures tend to last longer than engines that run cold.
4. The optimum coolant temperature allows the passenger compartment heating system to operate properly.
5. Overheating of the ICE can lead to reduced efficiency and possible catastrophic failure of internal mechanical components.

All automotive ICEs are liquid-cooled. The cooling systems are sealed and liquid coolant is circulated through the water jacket (internal passages) by the water pump to absorb excess heat. The heated coolant is sent to the radiator to dissipate the heat and lower its temperature, and the coolant returns to the ICE internal passages to continue the cycle. ● **SEE FIGURE 4–14.**

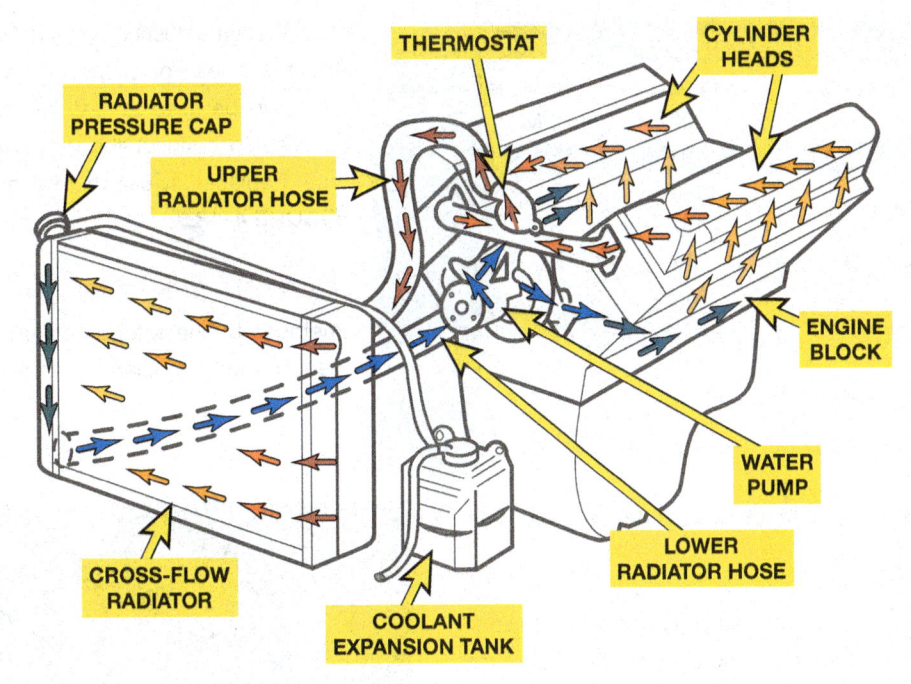

FIGURE 4–14 A series-type cooling system where the coolant first flows through the engine block and then to the heads before returning to the radiator after passing through the thermostat.

THERMOSTATS The thermostat is a temperature-controlled valve placed at the engine coolant outlet on most engines. An encapsulated wax-based plastic pellet heat sensor is located on the engine side of the thermostatic valve. As the engine warms, heat swells the heat sensor.

A mechanical link, connected to the heat sensor, opens the thermostat valve. As the thermostat begins to open, it allows some coolant to flow to the radiator, where it is cooled. The remaining part of the coolant continues to flow through the bypass, thereby bypassing the thermostat and flowing back through the engine. The bypass aids in uniform engine warm-up. Its operation eliminates hot spots and prevents the building of excessive coolant pressure in the engine when the thermostat is closed.

- The rated temperature of the thermostat indicates the temperature at which the thermostat starts to open.
- The thermostat is fully open at about 20°F higher than its opening temperature. If the radiator, water pump, and coolant passages are functioning correctly, the engine should always be operating within the opening and fully open temperature range of the thermostat.

An electronic thermostat allows the engine temperature to be more closely controlled during cruise, city driving, or heavy load conditions to optimize fuel economy, and reduce exhaust emissions. ● SEE FIGURE 4–15.

COOLING SYSTEM TESTING

SCAN TOOL A scan tool can be used on many vehicles to read the actual temperature of the coolant as detected by the engine coolant temperature (ECT) sensor. Although the sensor or the wiring to and from the sensor may be defective, at least the scan tool can indicate what the computer "thinks" is the coolant temperature. ● SEE FIGURE 4–16.

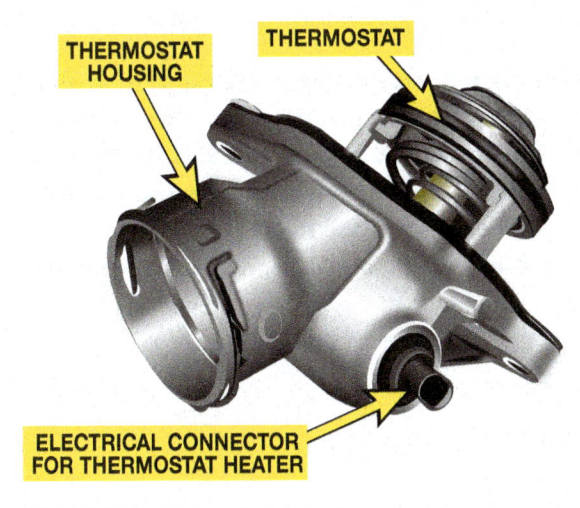

FIGURE 4–15 An electronic thermostat uses a wax pellet to open and a spring to close it, but it also uses an electric heater controlled by the PCM to accurately control ECT.

HYBRID ENGINE SYSTEMS

Engine Data		
Engine Speed	603	RPM
Desired Idle Speed	600	RPM
ECT Sensor	194	°F
IAT Sensor 1	143	°F
IAT Sensor 2	158	°F
Ambient Air Temperature	-36	°F
Cold Start-Up	No	
MAF Sensor	0.01	lb/s
Engine Load	14.5	%
Accelerator Pedal Position	0	%
Throttle Position	4	%

FIGURE 4–16 A scan tool can be used to monitor the ECT.

VISUAL INSPECTION
Many cooling system faults can be found by performing a thorough visual inspection. Items that can be inspected visually include the following:

- Water pump drive belt for tension or faults
- Cooling fan for faults
- Heater and radiator hoses for condition and leaks
- Coolant overflow or surge tank coolant level
- Evidence of coolant loss
- Radiator condition. ●SEE FIGURE 4–17.

PRESSURE TESTING
Pressure testing, using a hand operated pressure tester, is a quick and easy cooling system test. The radiator cap is removed (engine cold) and the tester is attached in the place of the radiator cap. By operating the plunger on the pump, the entire cooling system is pressurized.

CAUTION: Do not exceed the pressure beyond that specified by the vehicle manufacturer. Most systems should not be pressurized beyond 14 PSI (100 kPa). If a greater pressure is used, it may cause the water pump, radiator, heater core, or hoses to fail.

If the cooling system is free from leaks, the pressure should stay and not drop. If the pressure drops, look for evidence of leaks anywhere in the cooling system, including:

1. Heater hoses
2. Radiator hoses
3. Radiator
4. Heater core
5. Cylinder head
6. Core plugs in the side of the block or cylinder head

Pressure testing should be performed whenever there is a leak or suspected leak. The pressure tester can also be used to test the radiator cap. An adapter is used to connect the pressure tester to the radiator cap. Replace any cap that will not hold pressure. ●SEE FIGURE 4–18.

COOLANT DYE LEAK TESTING
One of the best methods to check for a coolant leak is to use a fluorescent dye in the coolant, one that is specifically designed

FIGURE 4–17 A heavily corroded radiator from a vehicle that was overheating. A visual inspection discovered that the corrosion had eaten away many of the cooling fins, yet did not leak. This radiator was replaced and it solved the overheating problem.

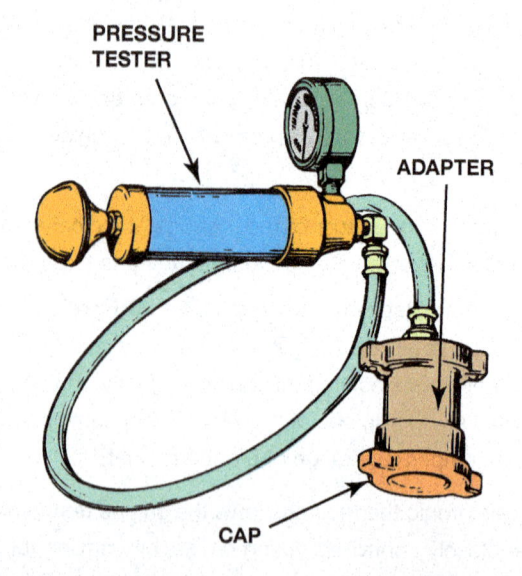

FIGURE 4–18 The pressure cap should be checked for proper operation using a pressure tester as part of the cooling system diagnosis.

for coolant. Operate the vehicle with the dye in the coolant until the engine reaches normal operating temperature. Use a black light to inspect all areas of the cooling system. When there is a leak, it will be easy to spot because the dye in the coolant will be seen as bright.

COOLANT HEAT STORAGE SYSTEM

PURPOSE Some hybrids, such as the third generation and newer Prius, use heat capture technology to help warm engines and catalytic converters more rapidly than conventional vehicles. They also store this heat so a few engine cycles on a short trip does not reduce the ability of the catalytic converter to work efficiently. This is one reason why the Prius earns the same perfect 10/10 EPA smog rating as the all-electric Chevrolet Bolt.

In the RAV4 Prime PHEV, Toyota uses what they call *Warm Up Control*. This system uses an electric water pump and electric thermostat that enables the RAV4 Prime to reduce emissions at an earlier stage than other vehicles.

NEED TO RETAIN HEAT One approach is to use a coolant heat storage system where heated coolant is stored during normal vehicle operation and is then used to warm the engine intake ports prior to a cold start. Toyota uses this system in the second-generation Prius.

The coolant heat storage system is part of the ICE cooling system, but adds the major components described below. ● **SEE FIGURE 4-19**.

The coolant heat storage tank is built very similar to a Thermos® bottle. The tank is built with an inner and outer casing, and a vacuum is formed between them. This is done to prevent heat transfer from the inner casing. Approximately 3 liters of coolant is stored inside the inner casing, and the coolant can be kept warm for up to three days. There is a standpipe that extends inside of the inner casing, so coolant must rise in order to exit the tank through the standpipe. ● **SEE FIGURE 4-20**.

The water valve is responsible for directing the coolant flow between the coolant storage tank, the ICE, and the vehicle heater core. The water valve is controlled by the ECM and consists of an electric motor, drive gears, a rotary valve, and a valve position sensor.

The storage tank pump is used to move coolant through the heat storage tank at times when the ICE is shut off. This pump is located on the side of the coolant heat storage tank and is plumbed in series with the tank inlet. ● **SEE FIGURE 4-21**.

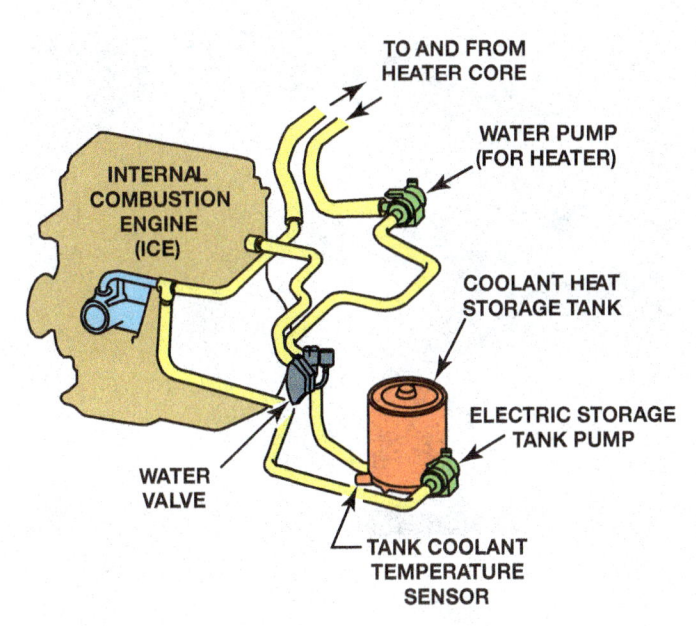

FIGURE 4-19 Toyota's coolant heat storage system. Note that the electric storage tank pump is located behind the coolant storage tank.

MODES OF OPERATION The coolant heat storage system has four modes of operation. These are:

1. Preheat
2. Engine warm-up
3. Storage during driving
4. Storage during ignition off

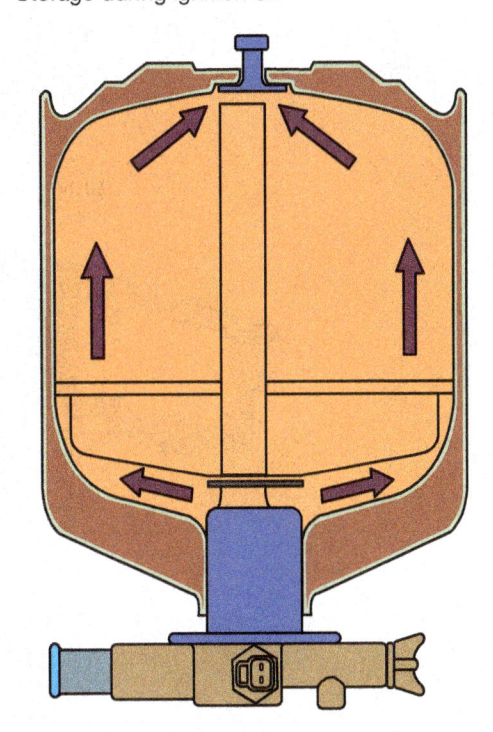

FIGURE 4-20 A vacuum exists between the inner and outer casing of the coolant heat storage tank. The outlet temperature sensor and the drain plug are located in the manifold at the bottom of the tank.

FIGURE 4–21 The storage tank and pump as seen from under the vehicle. This pump is energized when coolant must be moved through the tank, but the ICE is shut off.

> ## TECH TIP
>
> **Check the Active Grille Shutters**
>
> **Active grille shutters (AGS)** are designed to remain closed to decrease the aerodynamic drag by forcing the air to flow underneath the vehicle when closed. Only when there is a need for cooling, do the AGS open to allow air to flow through heat exchangers. They are used in all types of vehicle to help improve fuel economy. Even electric vehicle, such as the Mustang Mach E, uses AGS to open when additional cooling is needed to cool the high-voltage battery, electronics, and cabin. Because they are located at the front of the vehicle, AGS are prone to damage from road debris, as well as ice and snow during freezing weather conditions. If they are damaged, this can reduce fuel economy and/or cause an overheating condition to occur.
> - **SEE FIGURE 4–22.**

The preheat mode is enabled prior to the starting of the ICE. The ECM turns on the electric storage tank pump and directs the water valve to send hot coolant from the storage tank into the cylinder head. The heat from the coolant warms the cylinder head ports and minimizes fuel condensation on the port walls. This allows for easier starting and minimizes emissions during a cold start.

HYBRID ENGINE RUN MODE

PURPOSE There are times when the service technician or a vehicle inspector needs to bypass the idle-stop feature and to keep the engine running, such as:

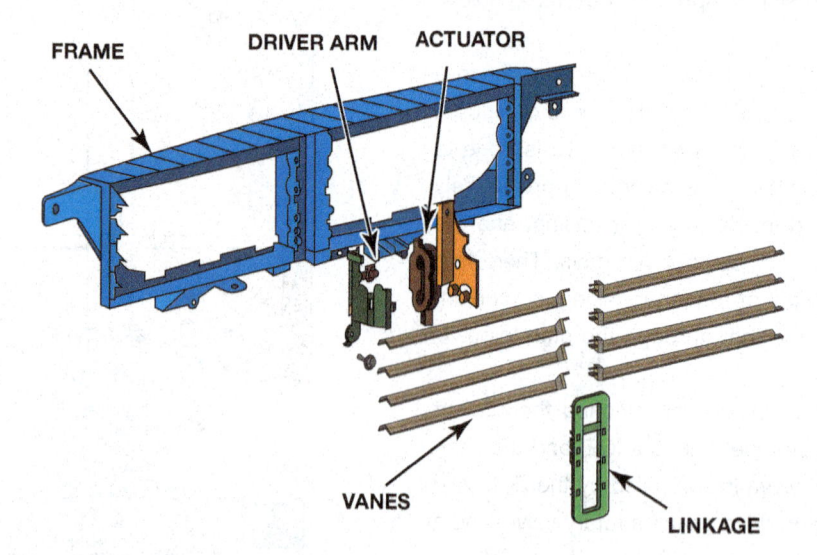

FIGURE 4–22 Active grille shutters(AGS) use a PCM-controlled actuator that operates movable vanes to either block off airflow when cooling is not needed, or open them to allow air to help cool the engine and electric components.

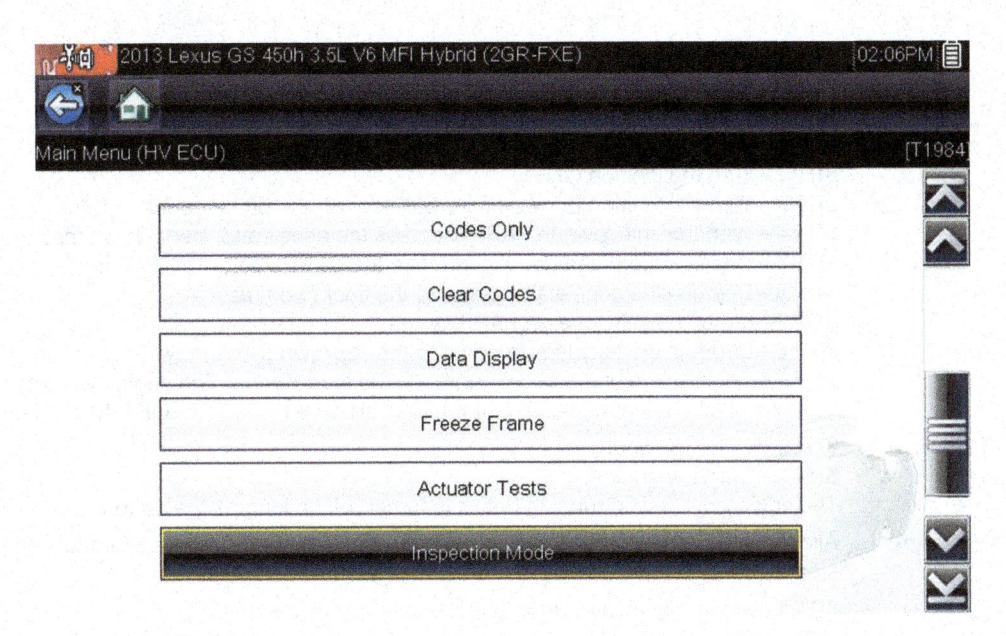

FIGURE 4–23 To enter the inspection mode, select this feature on a scan tool and follow the on-screen procedure.

- Checking the air-conditioning pressures on a unit that has an engine-driven air-conditioning compressor
- Attempting to get the engine (ICE) up to operating temperature in order to check for proper operation of the cooling system
- Safety inspection of the exhaust system

The mode to keep the ICE running can often be done using a scan tool, such as the Snap-on Solus Ultra, on a Lexus RX 450h hybrid. ● **SEE FIGURE 4–23.**

This mode is called any of the following:

- Service mode
- Maintenance mode
- Inspection mode

Most vehicle manufacturers warn not to drive the vehicle in this mode because many of the torque limiting factors are disabled in this mode, which could cause damage to the powertrain components if driven aggressively.

ENGINE OPERATING PROCEDURE ● **SEE CHART 4–2** for the method to use to keep the ICE operating and to prevent the idle-stop mode without using a scan tool.

VEHICLE MAKE	ENGINE START PROCEDURE
Toyota/Lexus	**STEP 1**—Turn the ignition to ON (NOT READY) **STEP 2**—While in PARK, press the accelerator two times. **STEP 3**—Press and hold the brake pedal, shift to NEUTRAL. **STEP 4**—While in NEUTRAL, press the accelerator pedal two times. **STEP 5**—Shift to PARK, while in PARK, depress the accelerator pedal two times **STEP 6**—Turn READY-ON
Ford/Lincoln/Mercury	**STEP 1**—Apply the parking brake and place the gear selector in PARK. **STEP 2**—Switch the ignition switch to ON. **STEP 3**—Within five seconds, fully depress the accelerator pedal and hold for 10 seconds. **STEP 4**—Within five seconds, release the accelerator pedal and shift into the DRIVE position and fully depress the accelerator pedal. **STEP 5**—Hold the accelerator pedal down for 10 seconds. **STEP 6**—Release the accelerator pedal and shift into the PARK position. **STEP 7**—The amber "wrench" lamp will flash if the procedure was successful. **STEP 8**—ICE can now be started. **STEP 9**—Exit by shifting into any other gear or by turning the ignition to OFF.

...continued

...continued

VEHICLE MAKE	ENGINE START PROCEDURE
Honda/Acura	STEP 1—Set the parking brake. STEP 2—Turn the ignition OFF. STEP 3—Turn the ignition on two times with foot off the brake pedal. STEP 4—With the shift lever in PARK, depress the accelerator pedal two times to the floor. STEP 5—Depress the brake pedal and move the gear selector to NEUTRAL. STEP 6—Depress the accelerator pedal to the floor two times. STEP 7—Move the shift lever to PARK. STEP 8—Depress the accelerator pedal to the floor two times. STEP 9—Depress the brake pedal and push the start button. The engine will start in the maintenance mode. To exit the maintenance mode, turn OFF the engine.
Chevrolet/GMC Truck (PHT or 2-Mode)	STEP 1—Open the hood. STEP 2—Start the engine. The engine will remain running until it is turned off as long as the hood is open.
Buick, Chevrolet, Saturn (BAS system)	Allow the ICE to idle when the engine is at normal operating temperature for two minutes. Idle stop is disabled.
Nissan Altima	STEP 1—Press the power button twice to turn on the ignition. STEP 2—Place Trans in "P" fully depressing the accelerator pedal twice. STEP 3—Place Trans in "N" fully depressing the accelerator pedal twice. STEP 4—Place Trans in "P" fully depressing the accelerator pedal twice. STEP 5—Start the engine. Idle stop is disabled.

CHART 4–2

Hybrid engine service mode chart.

TECH TIP

Look for Positive Torque

Some owners of hybrid vehicles have been fooled into thinking that their vehicle starts, runs for a while, and then stops running. What was happening was that the engine was being spun by the motor/generator and it sounded as if the engine was running. It stopped after a time when the PCM did not detect positive torque from the ICE. Using a scan tool, look for positive torque from the ICE or negative torque from the motor/generator.

HYBRID ENGINE TESTING

COMPRESSION TEST Unlike a conventional engine that uses a starter motor, most HEV do not use a starter, but rather use the electric motor attached to the crankshaft to rotate the ICE often at about 1000 RPM instead of the normal cranking speed or 250 RPM. The typical procedure to perform a compression test on a HEV so that it cranks at about 250 RPM includes the following steps:

- Remove all of the spark plugs from the engine. This ensures that the engine speed will be consistent.
- Install the compression gauge into the cylinder being checked. ● SEE FIGURE 4–24.
- Connect a factory or factory-level scan tool to the data link connector (DLC).
- Select engine and follow the onscreen messages to find and select compression test.
- Command the engine to crank at 250 RPM and read the compression gauge.
- Compare the reading to factory specifications. For example, a typical Toyota Prius has a specification of compression test pressure of 118 PSI with a minimum pressure of 90 PSI and a difference between cylinders no more than 14.5 PSI.

NOTE: That is lower than the 13.5:1 compression ratio specification than is anticipated. This results in an effective compression ratio of about 9:1. Therefore, the compression values are right for the effective compression ratio.

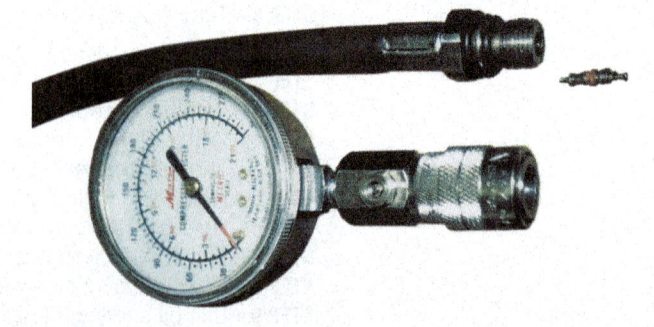

FIGURE 4-24 A two-piece compression gauge showing the Schrader valve removed from the end that is screwed into the spark plug hole.

TECH TIP

Use a Scan Tool to Determine Engine Vacuum

Using a scan tool and monitoring the MAP sensor value is a quick and easy way to help determine engine condition.

- If the MAP values are high and steady (high engine vacuum), the engine condition is sound.
- If the MAP sensor value fluctuates, this indicates a fault for which a further investigation is needed to determine the root cause.

CYLINDER LEAKAGE TEST One of the best tests that can be used to determine engine condition is the cylinder leakage test. This test involves injecting air under pressure into the cylinders one at a time. The amount and location of any escaping air helps the technician determine the condition of the engine. The air is injected into the cylinder through a cylinder leakage gauge into the spark plug hole. To perform the cylinder leakage test, take the following steps:

STEP 1—For best results, the engine should be at normal operating temperature (upper radiator hose hot and pressurized).

STEP 2—The cylinder being tested must be at TDC of the compression stroke. ● **SEE FIGURE 4–25**.

NOTE: The greatest amount of wear occurs at the top of the cylinder because of the heat generated near the top of the cylinders. The piston ring flex also adds to the wear at the top of the cylinder.

STEP 3—Calibrate the cylinder leakage unit as per manufacturer's instructions.

STEP 4—Inject air into the cylinders one at a time, rotating the engine as necessitated by the firing order to test each cylinder at TDC on the compression stroke.

STEP 5—Evaluate the results:
- Less than 10% leakage: good
- Less than 20% leakage: acceptable
- Less than 30% leakage: poor
- More than 30% leakage: definite problem

NOTE: If leakage seems unacceptably high, repeat the test, being certain that it is performed correctly and that the cylinder being tested is at TDC on the compression stroke.

STEP 6—Check the source of air leakage.
- If air is heard escaping from the oil filler cap, the piston rings are worn or broken.
- If air is observed bubbling out of the radiator, there is a possible blown head gasket or cracked cylinder head.

FIGURE 4–25 A whistle stop is used to find TDC. Remove the spark plug and install the whistle stop, then rotate the engine by hand. When the whistle stops making a sound, the piston is at the top.

- If air is heard coming from the throttle body or air inlet on fuel-injected engines, there is a defective intake valve(s).
- If air is heard coming from the tailpipe, there is a defective exhaust valve(s). ● **SEE FIGURE 4–26**.

Case Study

Toyota Prius Engine Oil Consumption

A customer of a Prius IV hatchback brought their vehicle into the dealership with the complaint of a yellow light appearing on the dashboard when the vehicle makes a sharp turn. The vehicle had 112,000 miles and had been serviced every 5,000 miles by Toyota dealerships.

The technician confirmed the concern and found an extremely low oil level. The sharp turns caused insufficient oil for the pickup tube, and created a low oil pressure concern. An oil consumption test was performed and the technician determined that the engine was burning a quart of oil every 1,200 miles. Further diagnosis by the service technician determined the excessive oil consumption was a result of weak or worn piston rings. A replacement engine was recommended.

Depending on the way the vehicle is driven, the low oil level between oil service intervals at high mileage is not uncommon on some hybrid vehicle engines. It is recommended that the engine be allowed to reach full operating temperature each time the vehicle is driven. This will help to minimize the possibility of this condition. The engine oil level should be checked at each fill-up when the vehicle reaches higher miles.

Summary:
- **Concern**—Yellow light appears on the dashboard on a sharp turn.
- **Cause**—Low oil level caused by an oil consumption problem.
- **Correction**—A replacement engine was recommended.

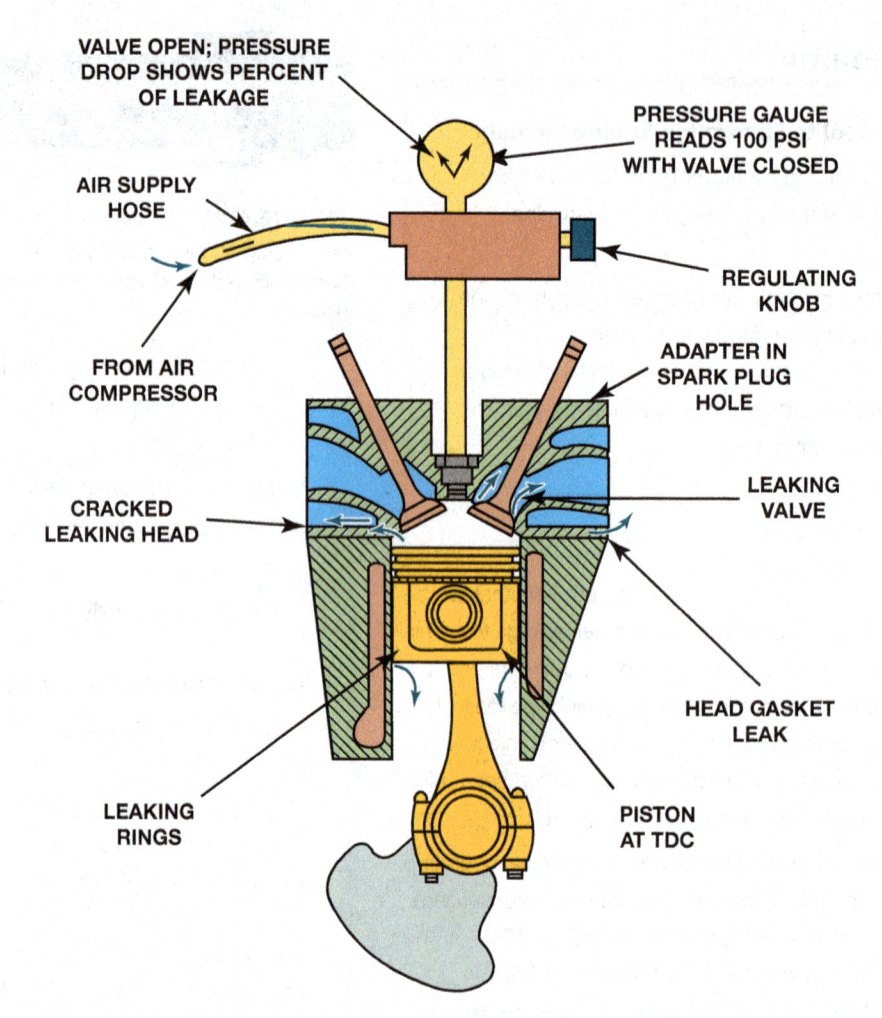

FIGURE 4–26 A cylinder leakage test is performed by inserting compressed air into the cylinder and checking for any leakage past the piston rings, head gasket or head, and valves.

SUMMARY

1. The internal combustion engine (ICE) used in hybrid electric vehicles (HEV) differs from those used in conventional vehicles because they usually use the Atkinson cycle to increase efficiency.
2. Offsetting the piston toward the minor thrust surface would provide a better mechanical advantage as well as results in less piston-to-cylinder friction.
3. Variable valve timing (VVT) involves the use of electric and hydraulic actuators that are used to change the timing of the camshaft(s) in relation to the crankshaft.
4. A factory or factory-level aftermarket scan tool is required to command the HEV ICE to rotate the engine at 250 RPM in order to perform a compression test.

REVIEW QUESTIONS

1. What is the difference between an Atkinson cycle and a conventional four-stroke cycle engine?
2. What features are different between an engine used in a hybrid vehicle and the engine used in a conventional vehicle?
3. What is an indexed spark plug?
4. How does the changing of the valve timing or opening affect the engine?
5. How is the ICE kept operating to prevent the idle-stop mode without using a scan tool?

CHAPTER QUIZ

1. Which of the following is a characteristic of many HEV gasoline engines?
   a. Smaller in displacement
   b. Offset crankshaft
   c. Variable valve timing and/or displacement
   d. All of the above

2. A HEV gasoline engine usually uses what viscosity of engine oil?
   a. SAE 0W-20 or SAE 5W-20
   b. SAE 5W-30
   c. SAE 10W-30
   d. SAE 20W-50

3. The Atkinson cycle engine design _____.
   a. requires special fuel and oil designed for this type of engine
   b. operates differently than the normal four-stoke cycle gasoline engine
   c. uses the same four-stroke cycle, but delays the closing of the intake valve
   d. Both a and b are correct

4. An offset crankshaft is used to _____.
   a. improve power output of the engine
   b. improve the fuel economy by reducing internal engine friction
   c. reduce engine noise
   d. All of the above

5. The oil flow through the phaser drops to zero when _____.
   a. 0% pulse width of the solenoid
   b. 10% pulse width of the solenoid
   c. 50% pulse width of the solenoid
   d. 100% pulse width of the solenoid

6. The screen(s) protects the VVT solenoid valve from dirt and debris that can cause the valve to stick. If this screen is clogged with debris, what is the most likely cause?
   a. P0300 DTC (random misfire)
   b. P0017 DTC (crankshaft position–camshaft position correlation error)
   c. Either a or b
   d. Both a and b

7. Most engines equipped with VVT do not use a(an) _____.
   a. PCV valve
   b. EGR valve
   c. MAP sensor
   d. MAF sensor

8. The VVT cam phasers are controlled by _____.
   a. oil pressure
   b. springs
   c. Both a and b
   d. Neither a nor b

9. Pumping losses are created by the throttle valve that _____ the flow of air into the cylinders.
   a. restricts
   b. enhances
   c. improves
   d. supercharges

10. When servicing an HEV, it is often needed to keep the ICE running. The mode that keeps the ICE operating is called _____.
    a. service mode
    b. maintenance mode
    c. inspection mode
    d. Any of the above Tech Tip

Chapter 5
HYBRID AND ELECTRIC VEHICLE PREVENTATIVE MAINTENANCE

LEARNING OBJECTIVES

After studying this chapter, the reader should be able to:

- Describe routine service procedures for both hybrid and electric vehicles.
- Explain how to place a hybrid vehicle in maintenance mode.
- Describe the service cautions when changing the oil and filter on a hybrid vehicle.
- Explain how to service the base brake system on a hybrid or electric vehicle.
- List the different voltages at which hybrid and electric steering systems operate, and explain the safety precautions when performing service.
- Explain the purpose of noise-reducing tires.

KEY TERM

Noise-reducing tire 61

ROUTINE SERVICE PROCEDURES

CUSTOMER PERCEPTION Many customers love their hybrid and electric vehicle; however, routine maintenance is frequently overlooked because it is different from a vehicle with just an internal combustion engine (ICE). Over time, the customer begins to notice a decrease in the fuel economy. The perception is that the decrease is a result of a failing high-voltage battery. In many cases the decrease in fuel economy or performance is a result of a lack of routine maintenance. ● SEE CHART 5-1.

INSTRUMENT CLUSTER WARNING MESSAGES As part of correctly diagnosing a hybrid or electric vehicle, the technician must understand what the indicators in the instrument cluster and message center mean. These indicators will help to confirm the customer's concern and provide a clue as to what may be wrong with the vehicle. The failure to understand these symbols may lead to unnecessary or incorrect initial diagnostic assumptions. ● SEE FIGURE 5-1.

NON-HIGH VOLTAGE COMPONENTS THAT IMPACT FUEL ECONOMY When performing a vehicle inspection, it is important to notice the absence or change in any of the following components as it may affect the vehicles' fuel economy:

- Low rolling resistance tires
- Low-mass wheels
- Spoilers
- Underbody trays
- Aerodynamic assist steps

HEV/PHEV MAINTENANCE ITEMS	EV MAINTENANCE ITEMS
Oil changes (once a year or when the OLM indicates)	NA
Engine air filter (every 2–3 years)	NA
Cabin filter (every 2–3 years)	Cabin filter (every 2–3 years)
Tire rotation (every 7,500 miles)	Tire rotation (every 7,500 miles)
Windshield washer fluid (as needed)	Windshield washer fluid (as needed)
Windshield wiper blades (as needed)	Windshield wiper blades (as needed)

CHART 5-1

Routine maintenance service.

PLACING THE HYBRID VEHICLE IN MAINTENANCE MODE There are times when the service technician needs to bypass the idle-stop feature and keep the engine running. These conditions can include the following:

- Checking air-conditioning pressures
- Bringing the engine to operating temperature
- Safety inspection of the exhaust system

Depending on the manufacturer, this mode is called any of the following:

- Service mode
- Maintenance mode
- Inspection mode

The vehicle can be placed in this mode either with a scan tool or through a specific sequence of steps inside

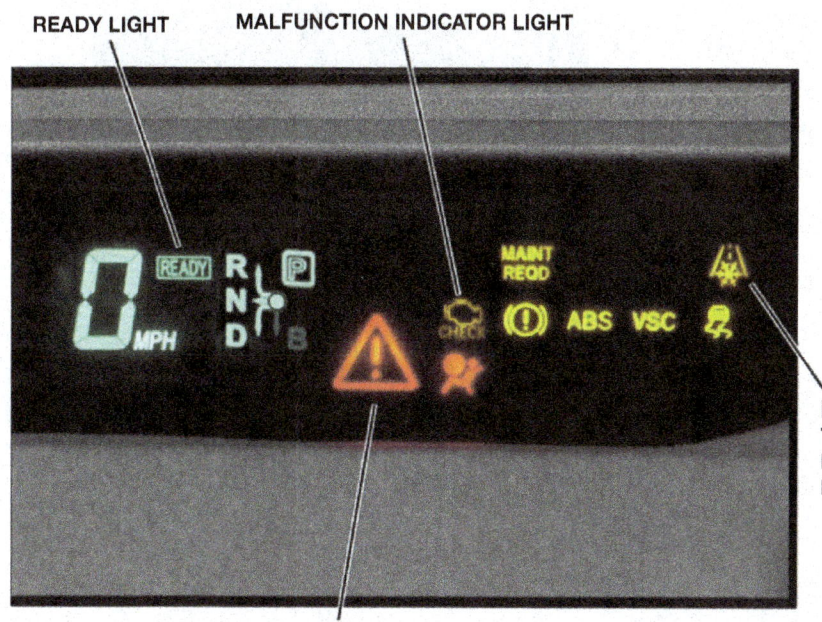

FIGURE 5-1 An example message screen from a Generation 2 Toyota Prius provides a wealth of information for the driver and the service technician.

HYBRID AND ELECTRIC VEHICLE PREVENTATIVE MAINTENANCE

the vehicle. Most vehicle manufacturers warn not to drive the vehicle while in this mode because torque limiting factors are disabled and damage to powertrain components could occur.

LIFTING AN ELECTRIC VEHICLE Most electric vehicle chassis are developed using a "skateboard design." In this configuration, the high-voltage battery and its covers fill a large portion of the underside of the vehicle. As a result, some vehicles require special adapters for lifting so that the battery and its covers are not damaged by the lift pads. Always follow the manufacturer's specific instructions to ensure the vehicle is safely lifted and damage does not occur. ● SEE FIGURE 5-2.

OIL AND FILTER SERVICE Performing an oil change in a hybrid vehicle is similar to changing oil in any vehicle equipped with an ICE. However, there are several items to know when changing oil in a hybrid electric vehicle (HEV).

Always use the specified oil viscosity. Most HEVs require either SAE 0W-20, SAE 0W-16, or SAE 5W-20.

Most hybrid vehicles use a full synthetic oil. Using the specified oil viscosity is important because the engine stops and starts many times and using the incorrect viscosity not

FIGURE 5-2 When positioning the lift, make sure the arms and contact points are clear of any high-voltage cables.

only can cause a decrease in fuel economy, but also could cause engine damage. ● SEE FIGURE 5-3.

When replacing the oil filter make sure it meets the manufacturer's original equipment specifications and it is correctly installed. A Honda Civic hybrid service procedure requires the oil filter to be prefilled upon installation to avoid a potential P1021 DTC.

Always follow the specified procedures. Be sure that the ICE is off and that the "READY" lamp is off. If there is a smart

> **? FREQUENTLY ASKED QUESTION**
>
> **When Do I Need to Depower the High-Voltage System?**
>
> During routine service work, there is no need for a technician to depower the high-voltage system. The only time when this process is needed is if service repairs or testing is being performed on any circuit that has an orange cable attached. These include:
>
> - AC compressor if electrically powered
> - High-voltage battery pack or electronic controllers
>
> The electric power steering system usually operates on 12 volts or 42 volts and neither is a shock hazard. However, an arc will be maintained if a 42-volt circuit is opened. Always refer to service information if servicing the electric power steering system, or any other system that may contain high voltage.

FIGURE 5-3 This Toyota Prius uses SAE 0W-20 as indicated by the oil filler cap.

key or the vehicle has a push-button start, be sure that the key fob is at least 15 feets (5 meters) away from the vehicle to help prevent the engine from starting accidentally.

ENGINE MAINTENANCE
Hybrid vehicles may have specific engine maintenance requirements. These may include the following:

- Honda Insight requires the indexing of spark plugs.
- Some Honda engines require mechanical valve lash adjustments.
- Atkinson cycle engines may require more frequent throttle body service.

COOLING SYSTEM SERVICE
Performing cooling system service is similar to performing this service in any vehicle equipped with an ICE. However, there are several items to know when servicing the cooling system on a hybrid and electric vehicle, including there may be two or three systems that require service. Always check service information for the exact procedure to follow. The procedure will include the following:

1. The specified coolant. Most vehicle manufacturers will recommend using premixed coolant because using tap water (half of the coolant) that has minerals could cause corrosion issues.
2. The specified coolant replacement interval. While this may be similar to the coolant replacement interval for a conventional vehicle, always check to be sure that this service is being performed at the specified time or mileage interval.
3. The specified precautions. Some Toyota Prius HEVs use a coolant storage bottle that keeps the coolant hot for up to three days. Opening a coolant hose could cause the release of this hot coolant and can cause serious burns to the technician.
4. Always read, understand, and follow all of the service information instructions when servicing the cooling system on a hybrid or electric vehicle. In many cases a vacuum lift or evacuation system will be needed in order to get all the air out of the system and the system completely full of the coolant mixture. A failure to get the system completely full may result in an overheat condition and possible component failure.
5. When replacing the coolant bottle caps, make sure the cap goes back onto the correct bottle. Some hybrid vehicles use a different pressure cap on the engine as compared to the electronics cooling systems. ● SEE FIGURES 5-4 AND 5-5.

BRAKING SYSTEM SERVICE
Performing braking system service is similar to performing this service in any vehicle equipped with an ICE. However, there are several items to

---

Case Study

A No-Start Prius After a Routine Oil Change

A technician went to start a Toyota Prius after completing a routine oil and filter service. He discovered the engine would crank over briefly and then fail to start. A visual inspection was performed and no components were found to be damaged or disconnected as a result of the oil service. Further diagnosis revealed the engine crankcase was significantly overfilled. When motor generator 1 (MG1) turned over the crankshaft on startup, it was unable to achieve the desired engine RPM as a result of the extra resistance created by the excess oil in the crank case. The fail-safe or limp-in operation was a no-start condition. After the engine oil level was lowered to the correct level the vehicle started and operated normally.

Summary:
The vehicle failed to start due to a crankcase overfill condition which caused MG1 to go into a fail-safe or limp-in condition.
- **Concern**—The vehicle would not start.
- **Cause**—An over-full engine crank case was observed.
- **Correction**—Lowered the engine oil to the correct level.

FIGURE 5-4 Chevrolet Volt engine cooling system with a 20 PSI rated reservoir cap.

FIGURE 5-5 Chevrolet Volt electronic cooling system with a 5 PSI rated reservoir cap.

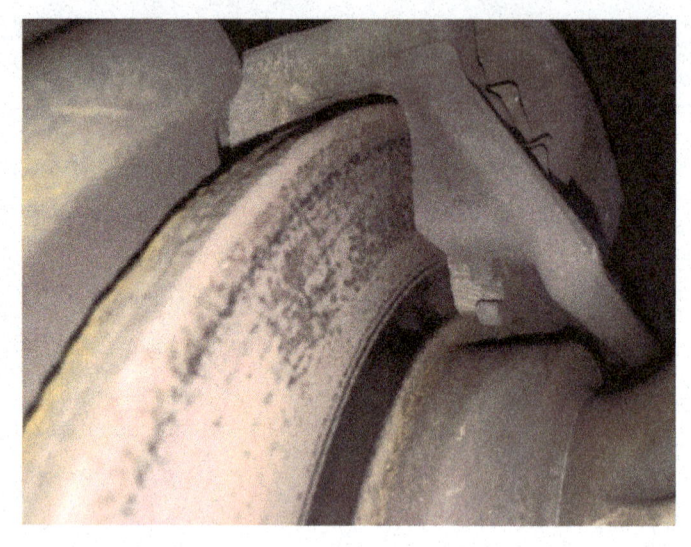

FIGURE 5-6 The brake rotor on this Audi Q5 hybrid is rusted and has very little pad contact due to a seized brake caliper pin.

know when servicing the braking system on a hybrid or electric vehicle. They are as follows:

1. Check service information for any precautions that are specified to be followed when servicing the braking system on a hybrid or electric vehicle.

2. Before beginning any base brake service on a hybrid or electric vehicle, make sure to have the needed scan tools, pressure bleeders, and other required tools to properly disable, bleed, and re-enable system.

3. All hybrid and electric vehicles use a regenerative braking system, which captures the kinetic energy of the moving vehicle and converts it to electrical energy and is sent to the high-voltage battery pack. The amount of current produced during hard braking can exceed 100 amperes. This current is stored in the high-voltage battery pack and is used as needed to help power the vehicle.

4. The base brakes used on HEVs are the same as any other conventional vehicle except for the master cylinder and related control systems. There are no high-voltage circuits associated with the braking system as the regeneration occurs inside the electric drive (traction) motors and is controlled by the motor controller.

5. The base brakes on many hybrid and electric vehicles are often found to be stuck or not functioning correctly because the brakes are not doing much work and can rust. The use of regenerative braking decreases the amount of heat generated at the brake assembly and reduces the amount of evaporation of moisture. This is a very common occurrence in the part of the country that the auto manufacturers refer to as the "salt belt." ● **SEE FIGURE 5-6.**

HIGH-VOLTAGE BATTERY AIR FILTER Many hybrid vehicles rely on the air that is heated and cooled for the passenger compartment to regulate the temperature of the high-voltage battery. To prevent the intrusion of passenger compartment debris from the entering the high-voltage battery cooling system, a filter is placed in the air-intake system. These filters must be replaced at specific service intervals to ensure proper cooling. ● **SEE FIGURE 5-7.**

FIGURE 5-7 This Toyota Prius has a high-voltage battery air filter that must be replaced at the documented time or mileage to prevent the battery from overheating.

AIR-CONDITIONING SERVICE

Performing air-conditioning system service is similar to performing this service in any vehicle equipped with an ICE. However, there are several items to know when servicing the air-conditioning system on a hybrid or electric vehicle. They are as follows:

- Many hybrid and electric vehicles use an air-conditioning compressor that uses high voltage from the high-voltage battery pack to operate the compressor.
- Make sure the high-voltage system has been properly depowered before removing the compressor for service.
- If the system is electrically driven, special refrigerant oil, POE oil, is used that is nonconductive and will not degrade the insulation on the electric motor windings. This means that a separate recovery machine should be used to avoid the possibility of mixing regular refrigerant oils with the oil used in hybrid and electric systems. ● **SEE FIGURE 5-8**.

TIRE SERVICE

Performing tire-related service is similar to performing this service in any vehicle equipped with an ICE. However, there are several items to know when servicing tires on a hybrid or electric vehicle. They are as follows:

1. Tire pressure is very important not only to the fuel economy but also to the life of the tire. Lower inflation pressure increases rolling resistance and reduces load-carrying capacity and tire life. Always inflate the tires to the pressure indicated on the door jamb sticker or found in service information or the owner's manual.
2. All tires create less rolling resistance as they wear. Even if the same identical tire is used as a replacement, the owner may experience a drop in fuel economy.
3. Tires can have a big effect on fuel economy. It is best to warn the owner that replacement of the tires can and often will cause a drop in fuel economy, even if low rolling resistance tires are selected.
4. Try to avoid using tires that are larger than used from the factory. The larger the tire, the heavier it is, and it takes more energy to rotate, resulting in a decrease in fuel economy.
5. Follow normal tire inspections and tire rotation intervals as specified by the vehicle manufacturer.

NOISE-REDUCING TIRES

The purpose of a **noise-reducing tire** is to eliminate noise in the 130–240 Hz range that would be normally covered up by normal engine noise in a vehicle with an ICE. The noise reduction is accomplished by adding acoustical foam to the inside of a tire. The sound is created within the structure of the tire itself and is not transmitted through the air, but rather through the chassis of the vehicle. The sound is similar to the sound heard when blowing across a partially filled glass Coke bottle. As result, this sound is often referred to a "Coke bottle resonance." This sound is most noticeable with electric vehicles (EVs) because there is no drivetrain noise to drown out the resonance. ● **SEE FIGURE 5-9**.

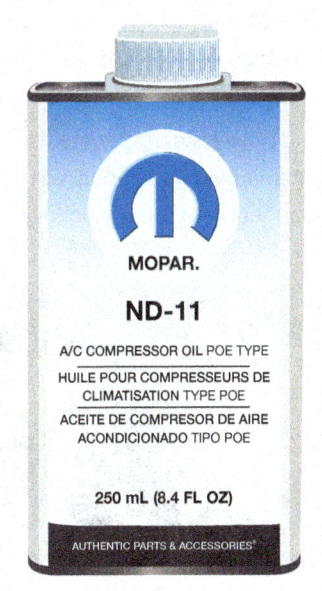

FIGURE 5-8 This POE refrigerant oil is specific to FCA brand products.

FIGURE 5-9 Blowing across the top of an empty "Coke" bottle creates a noise similar to a vehicle without noise-reducing tires.

The tire repair process is different on many noise-reducing tires because of the use of acoustical foam. In most instances, the acoustical foam must be carefully cut from the area of the wound and after the repair is complete it must be reattached. ● SEE FIGURE 5-10.

AUXILIARY BATTERY TESTING AND SERVICE

Performing auxiliary battery service is similar to performing this service in any vehicle equipped with an ICE. However, there are several items to know when servicing the auxiliary battery on a HEV. They are as follows:

1. Auxiliary 12-volt batteries used in hybrid or electric vehicles are located in one of two general locations.

   - Under the hood—If the 12-volt auxiliary battery is under the hood, it is generally a flooded-type lead–acid battery and should be serviced the same as any conventional battery.

   - In the passenger or trunk area—If the battery is located in the passenger or trunk area of the vehicle, it is usually of the absorbed glass mat (AGM) design. This type of battery requires that a special battery charger that limits the charging voltage be used.

2. The auxiliary 12-volt battery is usually smaller than a battery used in a conventional vehicle because it is not used to start the engine.

3. The 12-volt auxiliary battery can be tested and serviced the same as any battery used in a conventional vehicle.

4. Some micro hybrids with the stop-start feature will have two 12-volt batteries. The batteries must be isolated during testing to obtain accurate results.

5. Always read, understand, and follow all of the service information instructions when servicing the auxiliary battery on a hybrid or electric vehicle. ● SEE FIGURE 5-11.

STEERING SYSTEM SERVICE Performing steering system service is similar to performing this service in any vehicle equipped with an ICE. However, there are several items to know when servicing the steering system on a hybrid or electric vehicle which include the following:

1. Check service information for any precautions that are specified to be followed when servicing the steering system on a hybrid or electric vehicle.

2. Most hybrid or electric vehicles use an electric power steering system. These can be powered by one of two voltages:

   - 12 volts—These systems can be identified by the red or black wiring conduit and often use an inverter that increases the voltage to operate the actuator motor (usually to 42 volts). While this higher voltage is contained in the controller and should not create a shock hazard, always follow the specified safety precautions and wear protective high-voltage gloves as needed.

   - 42 volts—These systems use a yellow or blue plastic conduit over the wires to help identify the possible hazards from this voltage level. This voltage level is not a shock hazard, but can maintain an arc if a circuit carrying 42 volts is opened.

   - Many electric power steering systems contain capacitors that provide additional voltage to the system under heavy operating loads. When

FIGURE 5-10 A tire off a Tesla Model 3 with acoustical foam.

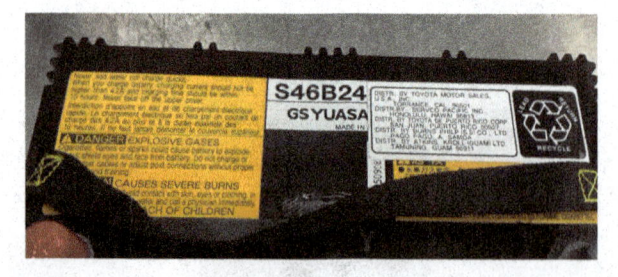

FIGURE 5-11 This Toyota battery is rated using the Japanese Industrial Standard (JIS) rather than cold-cranking amperes.

depowering the power steering system to make repairs, it is important to follow the specific wait times to ensure the capacitors are completely discharged. ● SEE FIGURE 5-12.

DIAGNOSIS PROCEDURES Hybrid and electric vehicles should be diagnosed the same as any other type of vehicle.

FIGURE 5-12 The capacitors in the power steering assist unit provide additional power when needed but must be allowed to discharge before service work begins.

This means following a diagnostic routine, which usually includes the following steps:

STEP 1   Verify the customer concern.
STEP 2   Check for diagnostic trouble codes (DTCs). An enhanced or factory level scan tool may be needed to get access to codes and sub codes.
STEP 3   Perform a thorough visual inspection. If a DTC is stored, carefully inspect those areas that might be the cause of the trouble code.
STEP 4   Check for technical service bulletins (TSBs) that may relate to the customer concern.
STEP 5   Follow service information specified steps and procedures. This could include checking scan tool data for sensors or values that are not within normal range.
STEP 6   Determine and repair the root cause of the problem.
STEP 7   Verify the repair and clear any stored DTCs unless in an emission testing area. If in an emission test area, drive the vehicle until the powertrain control module (PCM) passes the fault and turns off the malfunction indicator lamp, thereby allowing the vehicle to pass the inspection.
STEP 8   Complete the work order and record the "three Cs" (complaint, cause, and correction).

SUMMARY

1. Routine service for hybrid electric vehicles is similar to maintenance required for any internal combustion vehicle.
2. The maintenance required of electric vehicles consists of tire rotation, cabin filter, windshield washer fluid and wiper blade replacement as needed
3. Most HEVs require low viscosity engine oil such as SAE 0W-16, 0W-20 or 5W-20.
4. Hybrid and electric vehicles use separate cooling systems for the battery and electronics that require inspection and maintenance.
5. Hybrid and electric vehicles use regenerative brakes and as a result the base brakes do not suffer much wear. However, a routine inspection is needed to insure proper operation.
6. Tires used on electric vehicle usually have foam inside to reduce tire noise called "Coke bottle resonance."
7. The auxiliary battery used in hybrid and electric vehicle are either flooded lead acid type if they are located under the hood or AGM type if they are located in the trunk or in the passenger compartment area.
8. Hybrid and electric vehicles should be diagnosed the same as any other type of vehicle.

REVIEW QUESTIONS

1. What is the purpose of the hybrid vehicle maintenance mode?
2. Why do most manufactures of hybrid vehicles use full synthetic engine oil?
3. Why do most manufacturers recommend premixed coolant when servicing the hybrid or electric vehicle cooling systems?
4. Why does the base brake system require more frequent maintenance in the "salt belt" portion of the country?
5. What is the purpose of the acoustical foam in the noise-reducing tire?

CHAPTER QUIZ

1. The purpose of the hybrid vehicle maintenance mode is to _____.
   a. bypass the idle stop feature
   b. service the base brake system
   c. change the oil and filter
   d. service the cooling system

2. Why do most hybrid vehicles use a full synthetic engine oil?
   a. The engine stops and starts more frequently.
   b. It helps to reduce engine damage.
   c. It helps to improve fuel economy.
   d. All of the above are correct.

3. Why do most manufacturers recommend using a pre-mixed replacement coolant when servicing a hybrid or electric vehicle cooling system?
   a. The minerals in tap water can cause corrosion issues.
   b. It is difficult to get the mixture ratio correct.
   c. Both a and b are correct.
   d. Neither answer is correct.

4. Why do base brake systems require more frequent maintenance in the "salt belt" portion of the country?
   a. Salt causes the brake pads to separate from their backing.
   b. The use of regenerative brakes causes less heat at the brake rotor and leads to a decrease in the evaporation rate of moisture on the brake system.
   c. Corrosion causes the brake pins and sliders to stick.
   d. All of the answers are correct.

5. Why special procedures may need to be performed when repairing a leaking tire on an electric vehicle?
   a. The tire cannot be repaired, it must be replaced.
   b. The acoustical foam in the area of the leak will need to be removed prior to repairing the wound.
   c. The acoustical foam will need to be reattached after the repair is complete.
   d. Both b and c are correct.

6. What special procedure must be followed when testing the batteries in a micro-hybrid vehicle?
   a. The batteries must be electrically separated to obtain accurate test results.
   b. The batteries must be tested together.
   c. The batteries must be replaced together.
   d. There are no special test procedures.

7. Electric power steering systems operate at what voltage level?
   a. 12 volts
   b. 42 volts
   c. 60 volts
   d. Both a and b are correct.

8. What cautions should be observed when servicing an electric air-conditioning compressor?
   a. Make sure the high-voltage system has been properly depowered.
   b. Make sure the proper refrigerant oil is used in the repair.
   c. Use the appropriate refrigerant recovery machine.
   d. All of the answers are correct.

9. What is the purpose of the high-voltage battery cabin filter?
   a. To prevent the intrusion of passenger compartment debris.
   b. To help regulate the temperature of the battery.
   c. Both a and b are correct.
   d. Neither a nor b is correct.

10. Why is the eight-step diagnostic procedure used when diagnosing a hybrid or electric vehicle?
    a. To ensure a problem is not overlooked.
    b. To ensure the vehicle is repaired as efficiently as possible.
    c. To make sure the repair is properly documented.
    d. All of the answers are correct.

Chapter 6
DIGITAL STORAGE OSCILLOSCOPE TESTING

LEARNING OBJECTIVES

After studying this chapter, the reader should be able to:

- Explain the advantages of a digital storage oscilloscope.
- Describe the process for adjusting the oscilloscope time base and voltage scale.
- Explain the difference between AC and DC coupling.
- Describe the different pulse train measurement scales.
- Explain the purpose of a trigger.

KEY TERMS

AC coupling 68
BNC connector 71
Cathode ray tube (CRT) 66
Channel 70
Current clamp 71
DC coupling 68
Digital storage oscilloscope (DSO) 66
Duty cycle 68
External trigger 70
Frequency 68
Graticule 66
Hertz 68
Oscilloscope 66
Pressure transducer 71
Pulse train 68
Pulse width 68
pulse-width modulation (PWM) 68
Time base 67
Trigger level 70
Trigger slope 70

TYPES OF OSCILLOSCOPES

TERMINOLOGY An **oscilloscope** (usually called a scope) is a visual voltmeter with a timer that shows when a voltage changes. Following are two types of oscilloscopes.

- An *analog scope* uses a **cathode ray tube (CRT)** similar to a television screen to display voltage patterns. The scope screen displays the electrical signal constantly.

- A *digital scope* commonly uses a liquid crystal display (LCD), but a CRT may also be used on some digital scopes. A digital scope takes samples of the signals that can be stopped or stored and is therefore called a **digital storage oscilloscope (DSO)**.

A digital scope does not capture each change in voltage, but instead captures voltage levels over time and stores them as dots. Each dot is a voltage level. Then the scope displays the waveforms using the thousands of dots (each representing a voltage level) and electrically connects the dots to create a waveform.

A DSO can be connected to a sensor output signal wire and can record the voltage signals over a long period of time. It can be replayed, and a technician can see if any faults were detected. This feature makes a DSO the perfect tool to help diagnose intermittent problems.

A digital storage scope, however, can sometimes miss faults called *glitches* that may occur between samples captured by the scope. Therefore, a DSO with a high "sampling rate" is preferred. Sampling rate means that a scope is capable of capturing voltage changes that occur over a very short period of time. Some digital storage scopes have a capture rate of 25 million (25,000,000) samples per second. This scope can capture a glitch (fault) that lasts just 40 nano (0.00000040) seconds.

- A scope has been called "a voltmeter with a clock."
- The voltmeter part means that a scope can capture and display changing voltage levels.
- The clock part means that the scope can display these changes in voltage levels within a specific time period; with a DSO, it can be replayed so that any faults can be seen and studied.

CAUTION: When using a DSO on high-voltage or high-current circuits, follow the manufacturer's recommendations to protect the scope and other equipment from damage due to over current or over voltage conditions.

OSCILLOSCOPE DISPLAY GRID A typical scope face usually has 8 or 10 grids vertically (up and down) and 10 grids horizontally (left to right). The transparent scale (grid), used for reference measurements, is called a **graticule**. This arrangement is commonly 8 × 10 or 10 × 10 divisions. ● **SEE FIGURE 6–1**.

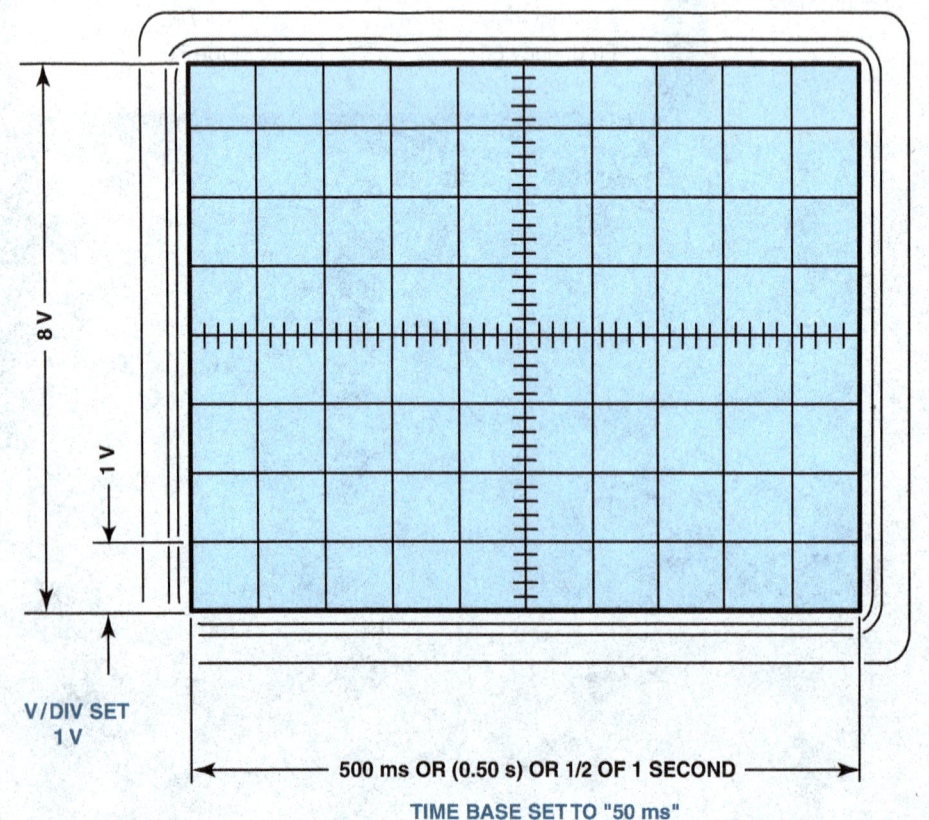

FIGURE 6–1 A scope display allows technicians to take measurements of voltage patterns. In this example, each vertical division is 1 volt, and each horizontal division is set to represent 50 milliseconds.

NOTE: These numbers originally referred to the metric dimensions of the graticule in centimeters. Therefore, an 8 × 10 display would be 8 centimeters (80 millimeters or 3.14 inches) high and 10 centimeters (100 millimeters or 3.90 inches) wide.

- Voltage is displayed on a scope starting with 0 volts at the bottom and higher voltage being displayed vertically.
- The scope illustrates time left to right. The pattern starts on the left and sweeps across the screen from left to right.

SCOPE SETUP AND ADJUSTMENT

SETTING THE TIME BASE Most scopes use 10 graticules from left to right on the display. Setting the **time base** means setting how much time will be displayed in each block called a division. For example, if the scope is set to read 2 seconds per division (referred to as *s/div*), the total time displayed would be 20 seconds (2 × 10 divisions = 20 seconds). The time base should be set to an amount of time that allows two to four events to be displayed. Milliseconds (0.001 second) are commonly used in scopes when adjusting the time base. Sample time is milliseconds per division (indicated as *ms/div*) and total time. ● **SEE CHART 6–1**.

The horizontal scale is divided into 10 divisions (sometimes called *grats*). If each division represents 1 second of time, the total time period displayed on the screen will be 10 seconds. The time per division is selected so that several events of

MILLISECONDS PER DIVISION (MS/DIV)	TOTAL TIME DISPLAYED
1 ms	10 ms (0.010 sec.)
10 ms	100 ms (0.100 sec.)
50 ms	500 ms (0.500 sec.)
100 ms	1 sec. (1.000 sec.)
500 ms	5 sec. (5.0 sec.)
1,000 ms	10 sec. (10.0 sec.)

CHART 6–1

The time base is milliseconds (ms) and total time of an event that can be displayed.
NOTE: Increasing the time base reduces the number of samples per second.

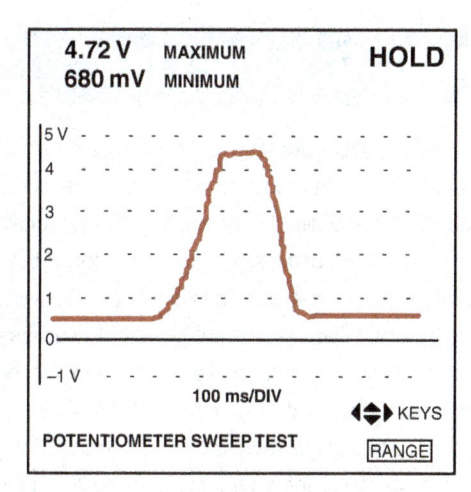

FIGURE 6–2 The DSO displays the entire waveform of a throttle position (TP) sensor. Note that the waveform starts on the left side at about 0.5 volts when the throttle is closed. When the throttle is opened and then closed, the voltage gores up to about 4.5 volts at wide open throttle and then returns to the closed position.

the waveform are displayed. Time per division settings can vary greatly in hybrid and electric use.

- Electric Motors: 2 ms/div (20 ms total)
- Network (CAN) communications network: 2 ms/div (20 ms total)
- Resolver (speed sensor): 2 ms/div (20 ms total)
- Sensor voltage measurements (hybrid engines): 5 ms/div (50 ms total)

The total time displayed on the screen allows comparisons to see if the waveform is consistent or is changing. Multiple waveforms shown on the display at the same time also allow for measurements to be seen more easily. ● **SEE FIGURE 6–2.**

VOLTS PER DIVISION The volts per division, abbreviated *V/div*, should be set so that the entire anticipated waveform can be viewed. Examples include the following:

- Electric Motor: 1 V/div (20 V total)
- 12-volt Battery and DC–DC Converter: 2 V/div (16 V total)
- Resolver: 500 mV/div (10 V total)

Notice from the examples that the total voltage to be displayed exceeds the voltage range of the component being tested. This ensures that all the waveforms will be displayed. It also allows for some unexpected voltage readings. For example, a resolver should read between 0 V and 2 V (2,000 mV). By setting the V/div to 500 mV, up to 10 V higher voltages will be displayed.

DC AND AC COUPLING

DC COUPLING DC coupling is the most used position on a scope because it allows the scope to display both alternating current (AC) voltage signals and direct current (DC) voltage signals present in the circuit. The AC part of the signal will ride on top of the DC component. For example, as the electric inverters and converters manage the energy flow between different powertrain subsystems and deliver the necessary torque and power requirements at the wheels. These power subsystems can generate undesired electrical harmonics on the DC bus of the powertrain. The normal DC volts will be displayed as a horizontal line on the screen. Any AC ripple voltage created as the electric machines will be displayed as an AC signal on top of the horizontal DC voltage line. Therefore, both components of the signal can be observed at the same time.

AC COUPLING When the **AC coupling** position is selected, a capacitor is placed into the meter lead circuit, which effectively blocks all DC voltage signals, but allows the AC portion of the signal to pass and be displayed. AC coupling can be used to show output signal waveforms from sensors such as:

- Magnetic engine speed sensors
- Magnetic position sensors
- The AC ripple from the inverters and converters.
  ● **SEE FIGURE 6–3**.
- Magnetic vehicle speed sensors

NOTE: Check the instructions from the scope manufacturer for the recommended settings to use. Sometimes it is necessary to switch from DC coupling to AC coupling, or from AC coupling to DC coupling to properly see some waveforms.

PULSE TRAINS

DEFINITION Scopes can show all voltage signals. Among the most commonly found in automotive applications is a DC voltage that varies up and down and does not go below zero like an AC voltage. A DC voltage that turns on and off in a series of pulses is called a **pulse train**. Pulse trains differ from an AC signal in that they do not go below zero. An alternating voltage goes above and below zero voltage. Pulse train signals can vary in several ways.
● **SEE FIGURE 6–4**.

FREQUENCY Frequency is the number of cycles per second measured in **hertz**. The engine revolutions per minute (RPM) is an example of a signal that can occur at various frequencies. At low engine speed, the ignition pulses occur fewer times per second (lower frequency) than when the engine is operated at higher engine speeds (RPM).

DUTY CYCLE Duty cycle refers to the percentage of on-time of the signal during one complete cycle. As on-time increases, the amount of time the signal is off decreases and is usually measured in percentage. Duty cycle is also called **pulse-width modulation (PWM)** and can be measured in degrees. ● **SEE FIGURE 6–5**.

PULSE WIDTH The **pulse width** is a measure of the actual on-time measured in milliseconds. Fuel injectors are usually controlled by varying the pulse width. ● **SEE FIGURE 6–6**.

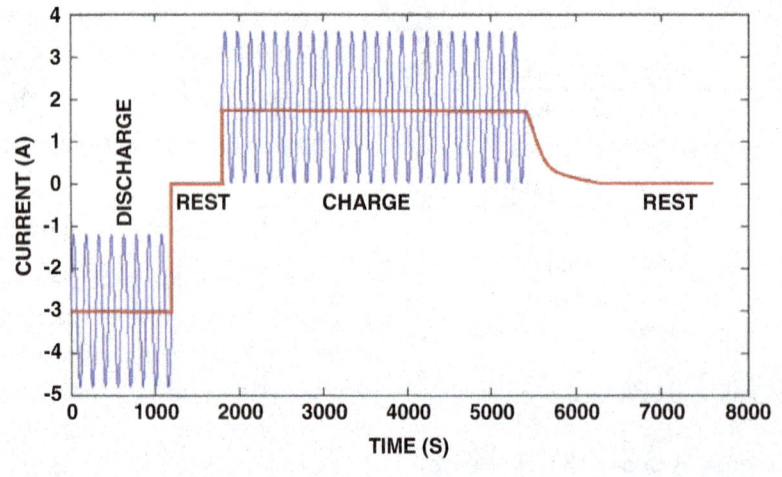

FIGURE 6–3 Ripple voltage created from the inverters and converters is shown on the DC voltage circuit for the high-voltage batteries.

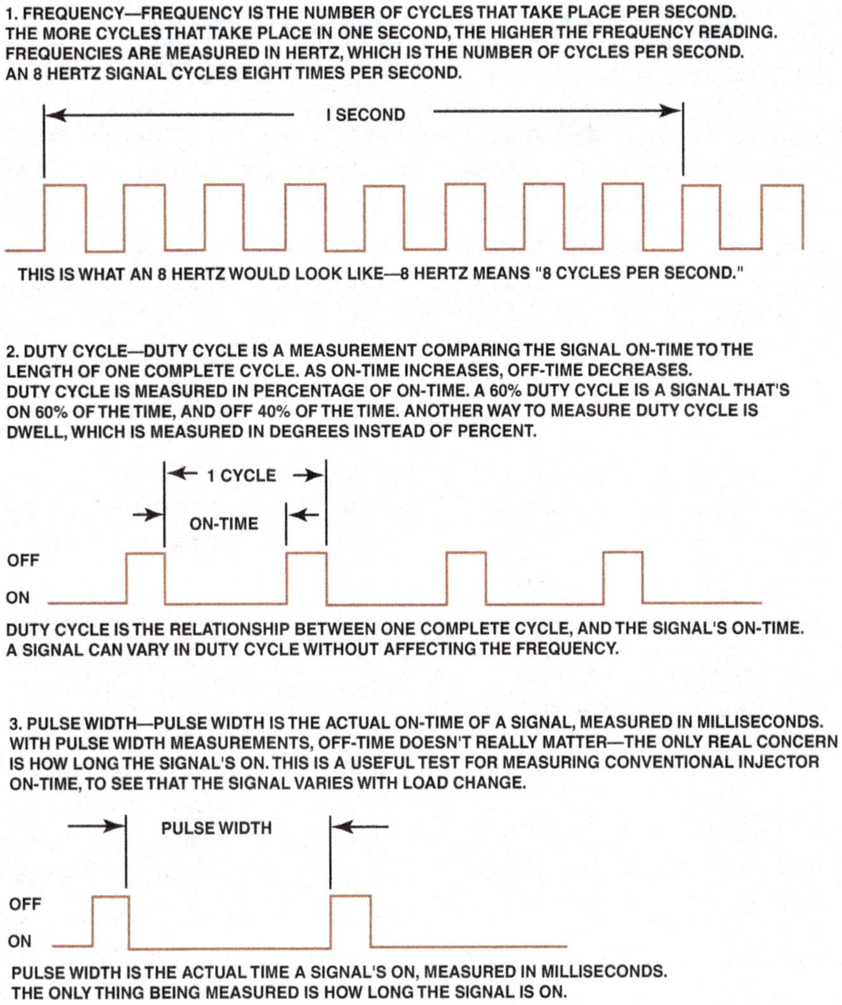

1. **FREQUENCY**—FREQUENCY IS THE NUMBER OF CYCLES THAT TAKE PLACE PER SECOND. THE MORE CYCLES THAT TAKE PLACE IN ONE SECOND, THE HIGHER THE FREQUENCY READING. FREQUENCIES ARE MEASURED IN HERTZ, WHICH IS THE NUMBER OF CYCLES PER SECOND. AN 8 HERTZ SIGNAL CYCLES EIGHT TIMES PER SECOND.

THIS IS WHAT AN 8 HERTZ WOULD LOOK LIKE—8 HERTZ MEANS "8 CYCLES PER SECOND."

2. **DUTY CYCLE**—DUTY CYCLE IS A MEASUREMENT COMPARING THE SIGNAL ON-TIME TO THE LENGTH OF ONE COMPLETE CYCLE. AS ON-TIME INCREASES, OFF-TIME DECREASES. DUTY CYCLE IS MEASURED IN PERCENTAGE OF ON-TIME. A 60% DUTY CYCLE IS A SIGNAL THAT'S ON 60% OF THE TIME, AND OFF 40% OF THE TIME. ANOTHER WAY TO MEASURE DUTY CYCLE IS DWELL, WHICH IS MEASURED IN DEGREES INSTEAD OF PERCENT.

DUTY CYCLE IS THE RELATIONSHIP BETWEEN ONE COMPLETE CYCLE, AND THE SIGNAL'S ON-TIME. A SIGNAL CAN VARY IN DUTY CYCLE WITHOUT AFFECTING THE FREQUENCY.

3. **PULSE WIDTH**—PULSE WIDTH IS THE ACTUAL ON-TIME OF A SIGNAL, MEASURED IN MILLISECONDS. WITH PULSE WIDTH MEASUREMENTS, OFF-TIME DOESN'T REALLY MATTER—THE ONLY REAL CONCERN IS HOW LONG THE SIGNAL'S ON. THIS IS A USEFUL TEST FOR MEASURING CONVENTIONAL INJECTOR ON-TIME, TO SEE THAT THE SIGNAL VARIES WITH LOAD CHANGE.

PULSE WIDTH IS THE ACTUAL TIME A SIGNAL'S ON, MEASURED IN MILLISECONDS. THE ONLY THING BEING MEASURED IS HOW LONG THE SIGNAL IS ON.

FIGURE 6–4 A pulse train is any electrical signal that turns on and off or goes high and low in a series of pulses. Ignition module and fuel injector pulses are examples of a pulse train signal.

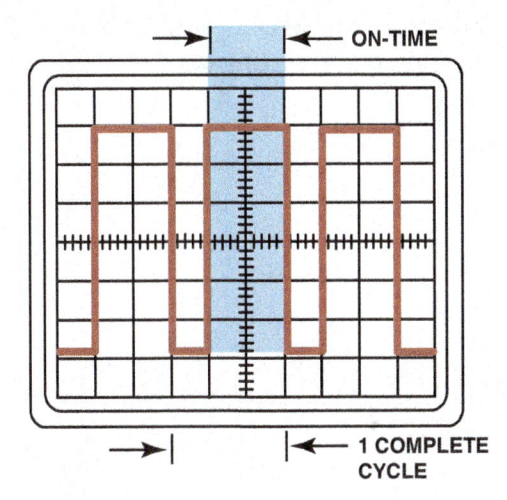

FIGURE 6–5 A scope representation of a complete cycle showing both on-time and off-time.

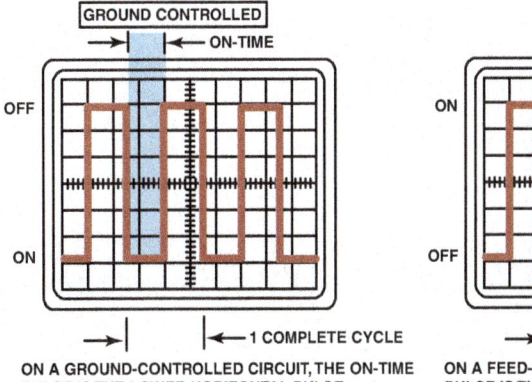

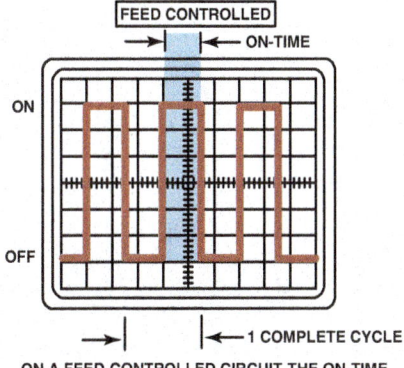

FIGURE 6–6 The computer can control the device by either turning on or off the ground or power side of the component.

ON A GROUND-CONTROLLED CIRCUIT, THE ON-TIME PULSE IS THE LOWER HORIZONTAL PULSE.

ON A FEED-CONTROLLED CIRCUIT, THE ON-TIME PULSE IS THE UPPER HORIZONTAL PULSE.

NUMBER OF CHANNELS

DEFINITION Scopes are available that allow the viewing of more than one sensor or event at the same time on the display. The number of events, which require leads for each, is called a **channel**. A channel is an input to a scope. Commonly available scopes include the following:

- **Single channel.** A single-channel scope is capable of displaying only one sensor signal waveform at a time.
- **Two channel.** A two-channel scope can display the waveform from two separate sensors or components at the same time. This feature is very helpful when testing the accelerator position sensor or brake switch inputs to ensure they change at the appropriate voltage levels.
  ● SEE FIGURE 6–7.
- **Four channel.** A four-channel scope allows the technician to view up to four different sensors or actuators on one display.
- **Eight channel.** An eight-channel scope is now available for technicians who need to view more data than can be graphed by a four-channel scope.

NOTE: Often the capture speed of the signals is slowed when using more than one channel.

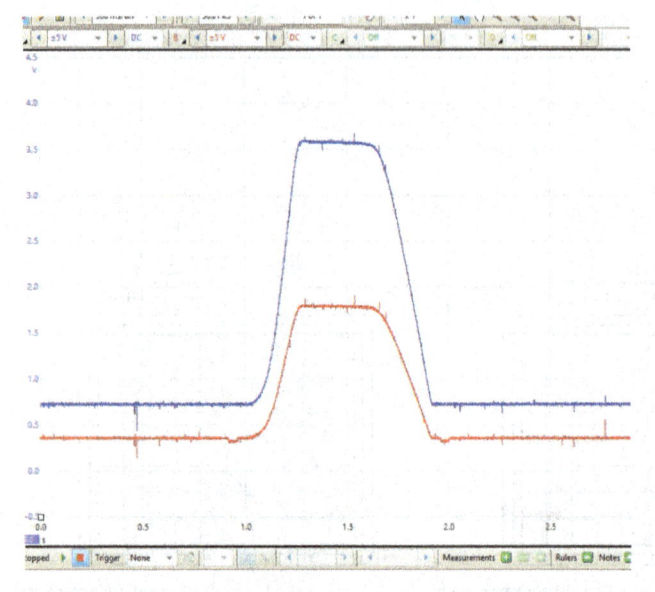

FIGURE 6–7 A two-channel scope being used to compare the two inputs from an accelerator position sensor.

TRIGGERS

EXTERNAL TRIGGERS An **external trigger** is when the waveform that starts as a signal is received from another external source, rather than from the signal pickup lead. A common example of an external trigger comes from the probe clamp around the cylinder #1 spark plug wire to trigger the start of an ignition pattern.

TRIGGER LEVEL **Trigger level** is the voltage that must be detected by the scope before the pattern will be displayed. A scope will start displaying a voltage signal only when it is triggered or is told to start. The trigger level must be set to start the display. If the pattern starts at 1 volt, the trace will begin displaying on the left side of the screen *after* the trace has reached 1 volt.

TRIGGER SLOPE The **trigger slope** is the voltage direction that a waveform must have in order to start the display. Most often, the trigger to start a waveform display is taken from the signal itself. Besides trigger voltage level, most scopes can be adjusted to trigger only when the voltage rises past the trigger level voltage. This is called a *positive slope*. When the voltage falling past the higher level activates the trigger, this is called a *negative slope*.

The scope display indicates both a positive and a negative slope symbol. For example, if a waveform, such as a magnetic sensor used for crankshaft position or wheel speed, starts moving upward, a positive slope should be selected. If a negative slope is selected, the waveform will not start showing until the voltage reaches the trigger level in a downward direction. A negative slope should be used when a fuel-injector circuit is being analyzed. In this circuit, the computer provides the ground and the voltage level drops when the computer commands the injector on. Sometimes the technician needs to change from negative to positive or positive to negative trigger if a waveform is not being shown correctly. ● SEE FIGURE 6–8.

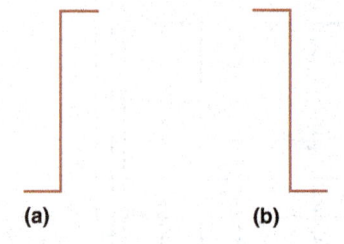

FIGURE 6–8 (a) A symbol for a positive trigger—a trigger occurs at a rising (positive) edge of the waveform. (b) A symbol for a negative trigger—a trigger occurs at the falling (negative) edge of the waveform.

USING A SCOPE

SCOPE LEADS Most scopes, both analog and digital, normally use the same test leads. These leads usually attach to the scope through a **BNC connector**, which is a miniature standard coaxial cable connector. BNC is an international standard that is used in the electronics industry. If using a BNC connector, be sure to connect one lead to a good clean, metal engine ground. The probe of the scope lead attaches to the circuit or component being tested. Many scopes use one ground lead and each channel has its own signal pickup lead.

MEASURING AUXILIARY BATTERY VOLTAGE WITH A SCOPE One of the easiest things to measure and observe on a scope is battery voltage. A lower voltage can be observed on the scope display as the hybrid engine is started, and a higher voltage should be displayed after the engine starts. ● **SEE FIGURE 6–9**.

An analog scope displays rapidly and cannot be set to show or freeze a display. Therefore, even though an analog scope shows all voltage signals, it is easy to miss a momentary glitch on an analog scope.

CAUTION: Check the instructions for the scope being used before attempting to scope household AC circuits. Some scopes are not designed to measure high-voltage AC circuits.

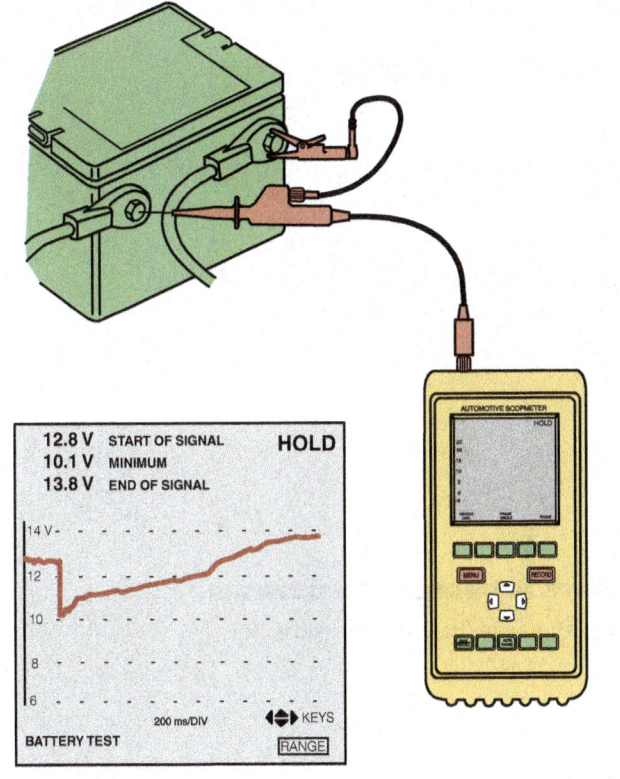

FIGURE 6–9 The battery voltage is represented by the single scope trace. The drop in voltage occurred when the vehicle was started.

USING DSO ACCESSORIES

CURRENT CLAMPS A **current clamp** (also called an *amp clamp*) is an electrical probe with jaws that open to allow the clamping around an electrical conductor. The probe measures the magnetic field created by the current flow and converts it into a waveform on the scope. It can be used with a scope to measure AC or DC current in a circuit without disconnecting any wires or components. Current clamps, depending on their design, can measure very small current or large current flow. A current clamp can be a useful tool when diagnosing components, such as an electrical motor. When measuring the current generated by an electrical motor in a hybrid or electric vehicle, a special high-current clamp or clamp adapter is used to protect the scope from unintended spikes in current. ● **SEE FIGURE 6–10**.

PRESSURE TRANSDUCERS A **pressure transducer** is an electrical device that converts pressure into an electrical signal. Pressure transducers are divided into two categories:

1. Actual: An actual transducer measures the actual pressure of the system being tested.
2. Relative: A relative transducer measures the change in system pressure.

A pressure transducer can be used with a scope to measure operating pressures of various hybrid powertrain systems, such as fuel pressure, engine vacuum, exhaust pressure, and cylinder compression. ● **SEE FIGURE 6–11**.

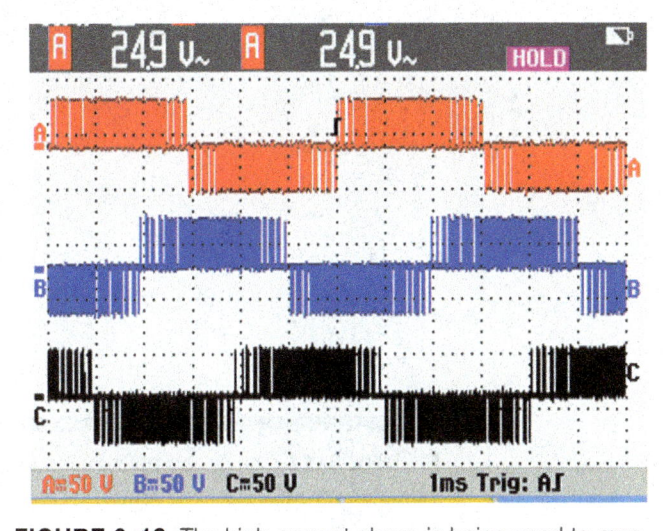

FIGURE 6–10 The high-current clamp is being used to measure the operating current of an electrical motor.

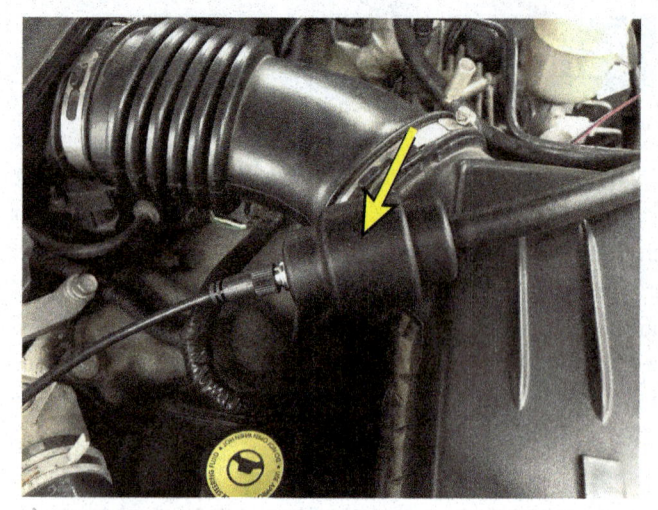

FIGURE 6–11 The relative vacuum transducer is attached to the intake manifold and is measuring the change in engine vacuum.

WAVEFORM ANALYSIS

DATA RECORDING Most oscilloscopes and DSOs have the ability to record and playback the data that is being monitored. In some cases, the recording can be saved for viewing at a later time. In a typical scenario, the technician will record the data until a malfunction is detected. The data would be saved and then reviewed in an effort to determine what failure had occurred. When looking at the data, it is important to first understand how the circuit or component is supposed to work and look for specific failures.

CAN THE CONDITION EXIST NORMALLY? When analyzing a waveform, first look to see if the condition can exist under normal operating conditions. In ● **FIGURE 6-12**, the coolant temperature drops from almost 200°F to below zero and back to almost 200°F in less than the span of 45 seconds. There is no possible way this could happen on a normal operating engine and should therefore be a clue that something is wrong electrically.

LINE CHARACTERISTICS The characteristics of the line of data being recorded can be an indicator of a failure. The nearly vertical change in the MAP sensor voltage in ● **FIGURE 6-13** is an indication of an electrical failure. In this case, the voltage had increased to source voltage, indicating an open circuit. If the voltage had dropped to near zero volts, this would have indicated a short circuit.

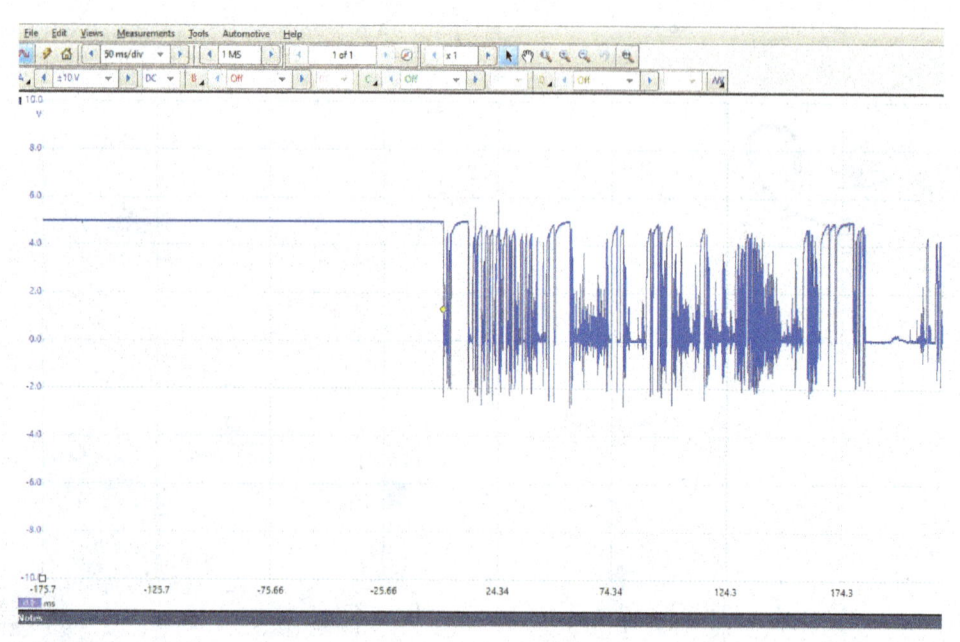

FIGURE 6–12 The scope pattern shows a temperature change that is not possible. This indicates an electrical problem.

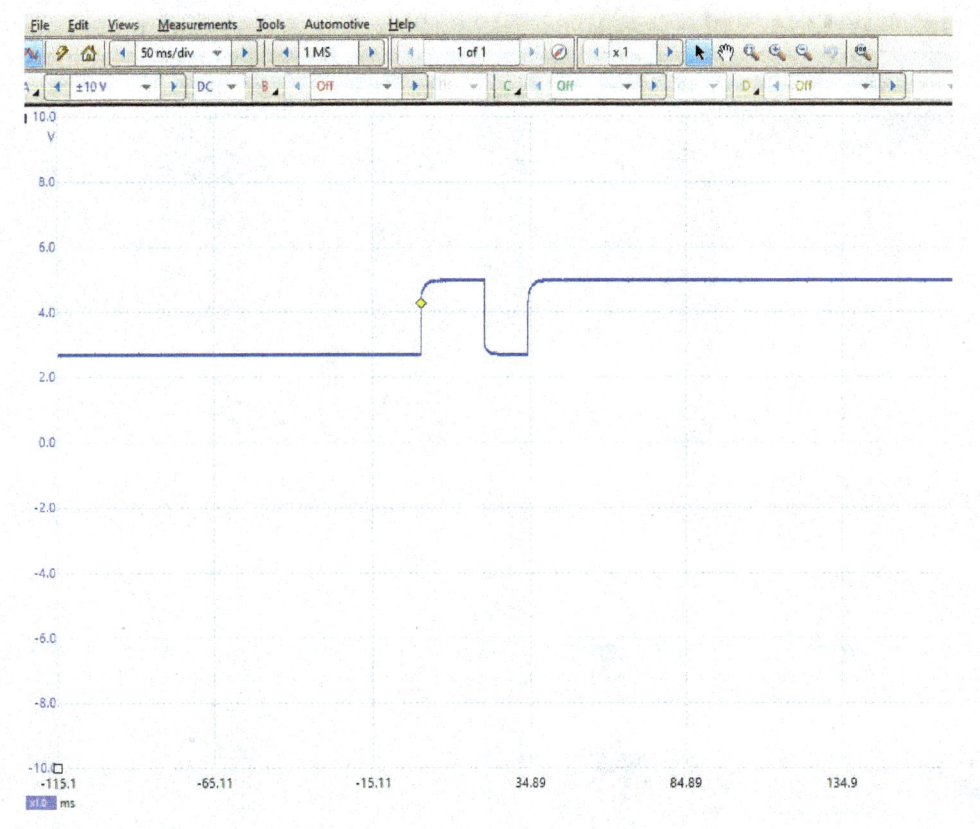

FIGURE 6–13 The scope pattern shows a nearly vertical change in voltage indicating an electrical open circuit.

SCOPE SETUP PHOTO SEQUENCE

1 Plug the scope interface into the USB port on the computer.

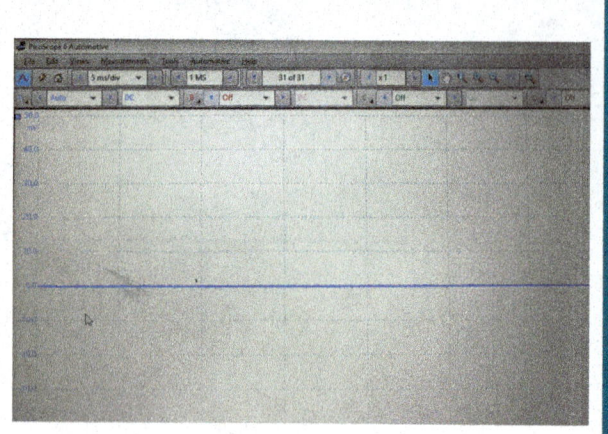

2 Start the program.

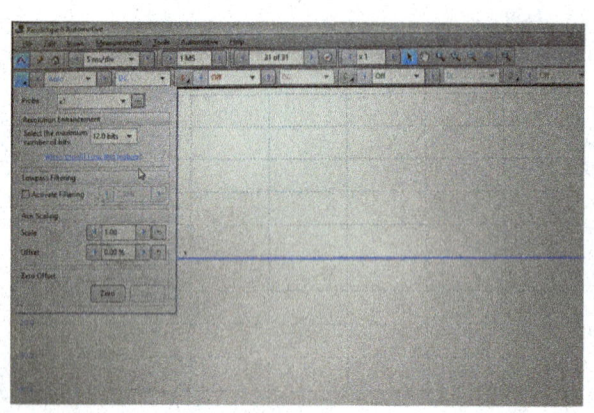

3 Select the probe for channel A.

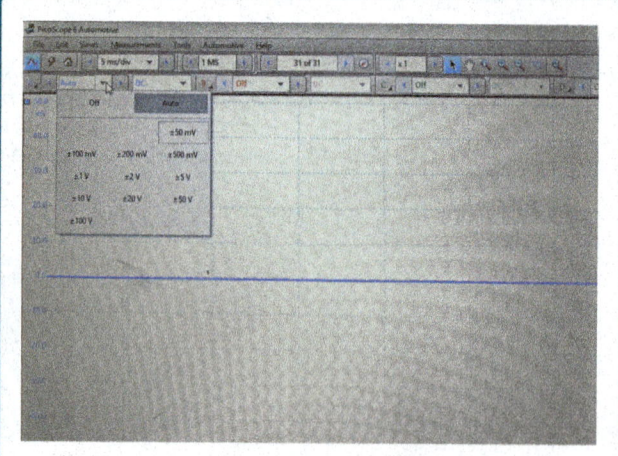

4 Select the voltage range for channel A.

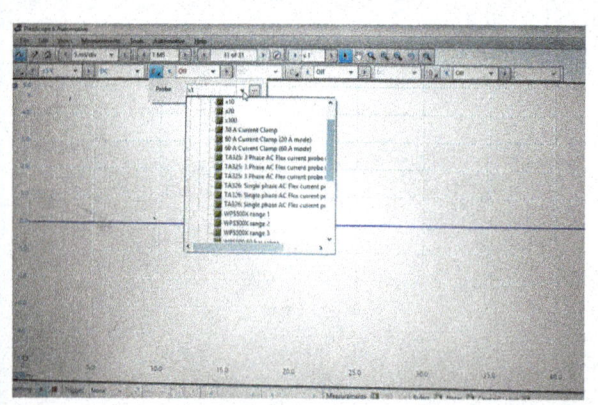

5 If more than one channel is being used, select the probe for these channels.

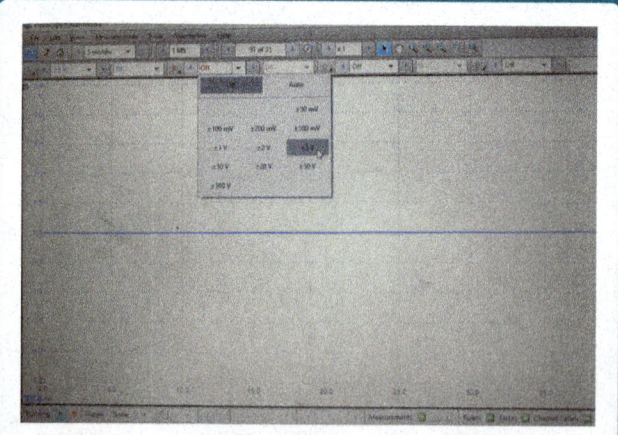

6 Select the voltage range for the additional channels.

CONTINUED >

STEP BY STEP

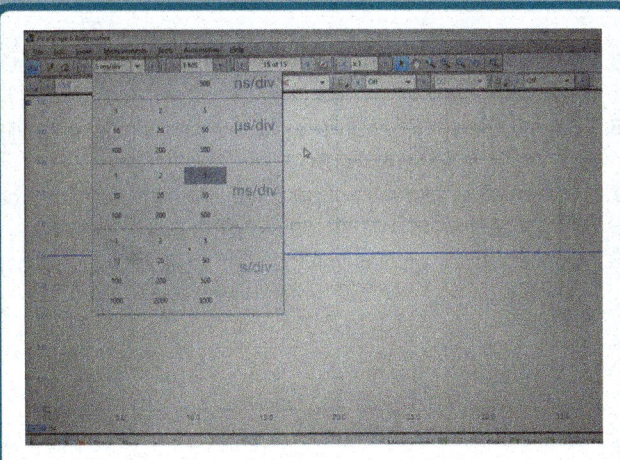

7 Select the sample rate.

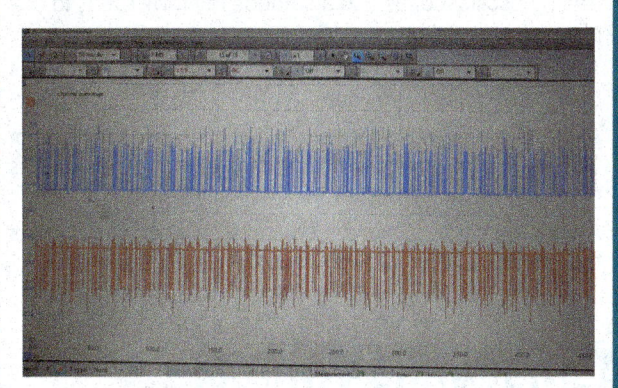

8 Capture the signal (for example, high-speed CAN bus).

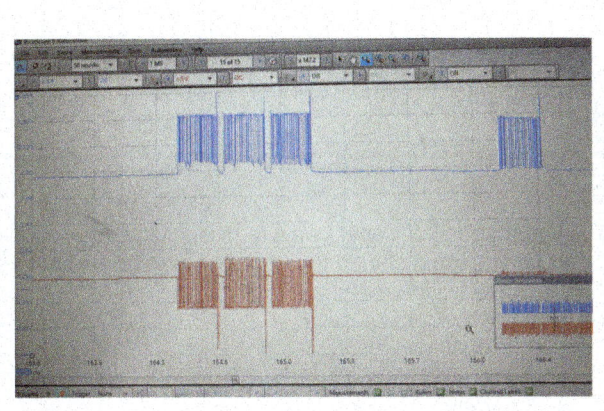

9 Zoom in on the sample to view the data.

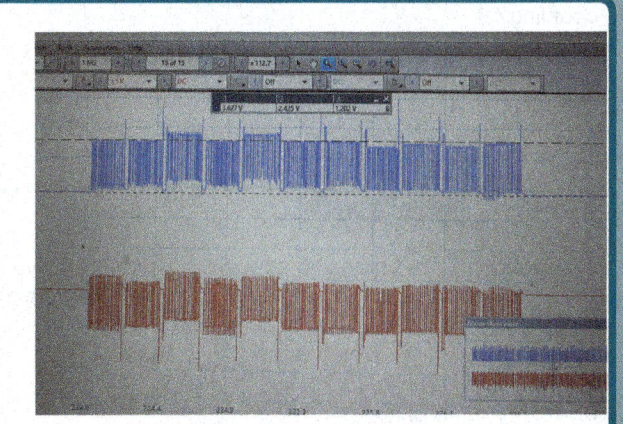

10 Use the rulers to measure the high and low voltage.

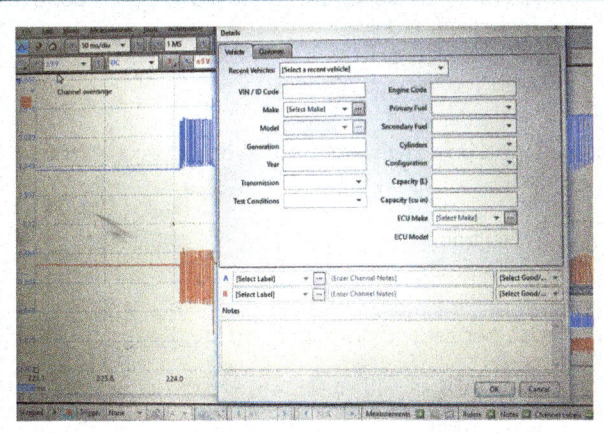

11 Save the data for future analysis.

DIGITAL STORAGE OSCILLOSCOPE TESTING

SUMMARY

1. Analog oscilloscopes use a cathode ray tube (CRT) to display voltage patterns.
2. The waveforms shown on an analog oscilloscope cannot be stored for later viewing.
3. A digital storage oscilloscope (DSO) creates an image or waveform on the display by connecting thousands of dots captured by the scope leads.
4. An oscilloscope display grid is called a graticule. Each of the 8 × 10 or 10 × 10 dividing boxes is called a division.
5. Setting the time base means establishing the amount of time each division represents.
6. Setting the volts per division allows the technician to view either the entire waveform or just part of it.
7. DC coupling and AC coupling are two selections that can be made to observe different types of waveforms.
8. Oscilloscopes display voltage over time. A DSO can capture and store a waveform for viewing later.

REVIEW QUESTIONS

1. What are the differences between an analog and a digital oscilloscope?
2. What is the difference between DC coupling and AC coupling?
3. Why is a DC signal that changes called pulse trains?
4. What is the benefit of recording oscilloscope and DSO waveforms?
5. What is the purpose of a trigger when capturing data on a DSO?

CHAPTER QUIZ

1. Technician A says an analog scope can store the waveform for viewing later. Technician B says that the trigger level has to be set on most scopes to be able to view a changing waveform. Which technician is correct?
   a. Technician A only
   b. Technician B only
   c. Both Technicians A and B
   d. Neither Technician A nor B

2. An oscilloscope display is called a _____.
   a. grid
   b. graticule
   c. division
   d. box

3. A signal showing the voltage of a battery displayed on a digital storage oscilloscope (DSO) is being discussed. Technician A says that the display will show one horizontal line above the zero line. Technician B says that the display will show a line sloping upward from zero to the battery voltage level. Which technician is correct?
   a. Technician A only
   b. Technician B only
   c. Both Technicians A and B
   d. Neither Technician A nor B

4. Setting the time base to 50 milliseconds per division will allow the technician to view a waveform how long in duration?
   a. 50 ms
   b. 200 ms
   c. 400 ms
   d. 500 ms

5. A motor position sensor waveform is going to be observed. At what setting should the volts per division be set to see the entire waveform from 0 to 5 volts?
   a. 0.5 V/div
   b. 1.0 V/div
   c. 2.0 V/div
   d. 5.0 V/div

6. Two technicians are discussing the DC coupling setting on a DSO. Technician A says that the position allows both the DC and AC signals of the waveform to be displayed. Technician B says this setting allows just the DC part of the waveform to be displayed. Which technician is correct?
   a. Technician A only
   b. Technician B only
   c. Both Technicians A and B
   d. Neither Technician A nor B

7. Voltage signals (waveforms) that do not go below zero are called _____.
   a. AC signals
   b. pulse trains
   c. pulse width
   d. DC coupled signals

8. Cycles per second are expressed in _____.
   a. hertz
   b. duty cycle
   c. pulse width
   d. slope

9. A MAP sensor signal voltage on a hybrid engine is being observed using a DSO. The pattern on the scope

occasionally, and instantaneously, rises to 5 volts (source voltage). What does this indicate?
   a. A drop in manifold vacuum
   b. A momentary short circuit
   c. Normal operation
   d. A momentary open circuit

10. Two technicians are discussing pulse train signals. Technician A says a fuel injector pulse on a hybrid engine is an example of a pulse train signal. Technician B says that an ignition module pulse on a hybrid engine is an example of a pulse train signal. Which technician is correct?
   a. Technician A only
   b. Technician B only
   c. Both Technicians A and B
   d. Neither Technician A nor Technician

Chapter 7
ENERGY AND POWER

LEARNING OBJECTIVES

After studying this chapter, the reader should be able to:

- Explain the difference between energy and power.
- Explain the units of energy and power.
- Describe DC current and its generation process.
- Describe AC current and its generation process.
- Describe the process to calculate the formulas for Watts and Power.

KEY TERMS

Energy 79
Energy efficiency ratio (EER) 87
Geothermal energy 85
Geothermal heat pump (GHP) 86
Hydroelectricity 85
Joule 79
Kilowatt (kW) 81
Kilowatt-hour (kWh) 81
Photovoltaics (PV) 82
Power 80
Solar cell 82
Torque 80
Watt 82
Watt's law 82
Watt-hour 81
Wind power 83
Wind farms 83
Work 80

ENERGY

DEFINITION Energy is defined as the ability to do work. The sun is the source of energy for life on Earth. It releases the following:

- Thermal energy
- Heat energy
- Radiant (light) energy

Physics defines energy as a property of objects which can be transferred to other objects or converted into different forms including:

- Thermal energy
- Electrical energy
- Magnetic energy
- Nuclear energy
- Chemical energy
- Potential and kinetic energy

● **SEE FIGURE 7–1.**

Some types of energy are a varying mix of both potential and kinetic energy. Thermal or heat energy is internal energy present in a system due to its temperature. This is a thermodynamic concept where heat is defined as a transfer of energy (just as work is another type of transfer of energy).

LAWS OF THERMODYNAMICS Internal combustion engines use the theory of thermodynamics to generate power.

- The first law of thermodynamics is a law of energy conservation: energy cannot be created or destroyed. The amount of internal energy in a system is a direct result of the heat transferred into that system and the work done. Heat and work are means by which natural systems exchange energy with each other. Basically, it is the relationship between heat and mechanical energy.

- The second law of termodynamic concerns the thermodynamic cycle. In a perfect heat engine, all of the heat produced would be completely converted to mechanical work. Nicolas Leonard Sadi Carnot, a 19th century French scientist, proved that this ideal cycle could not exist. The best engine loses heat and work because the burned gases must be exhausted. The exhaust removes a great deal of heat.

ENERGY UNITS

- In SI units (International System of Units), the modern form of the metric system, energy is measured in joules, and one **joule** is defined mechanically as being the energy transferred to an object by the mechanical work of moving it a distance of 1 meter with a force of 1 newton. 1 N-m (newton-meter) = 1 joule

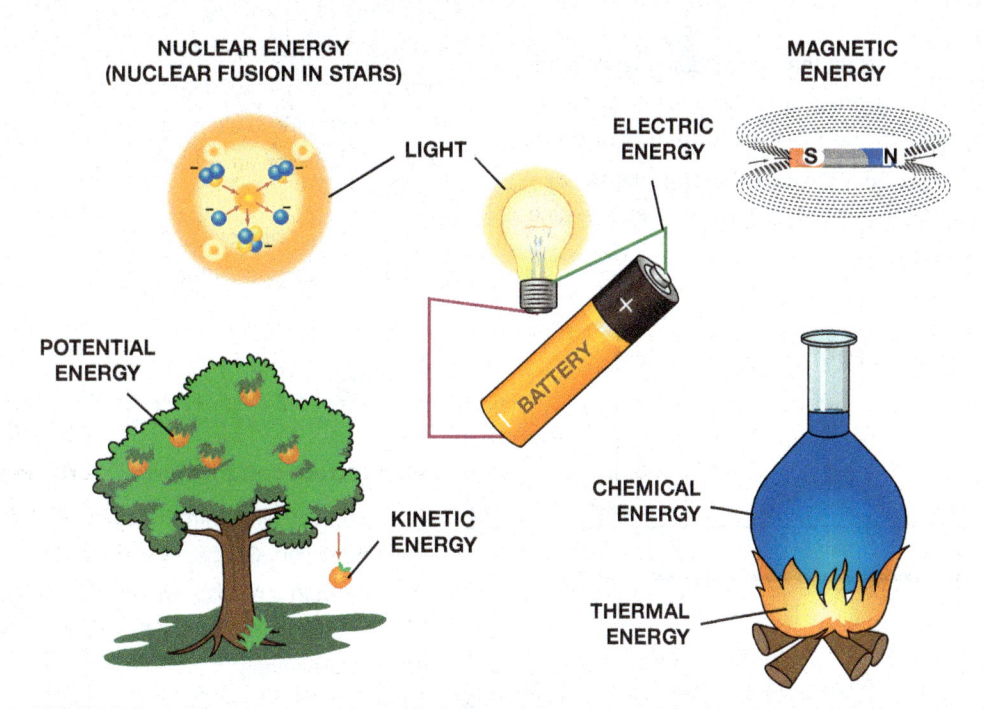

FIGURE 7–1 Energy is found in many forms and each has the potential to perform work.

- In the MKS (Meter Kilogram Second) measuring system, joule is equivalent to the *dyne centimeter*.
- In the CGS (Centimeter Gram Second) measuring system, joule is equivalent to the *erg*.

TORQUE, WORK, AND POWER

TORQUE Torque is the term used to describe a rotating force that may or may not result in motion. Torque is measured as the amount of force multiplied by the length of the lever through which it acts. If a one-foot-long wrench is used to apply 10 pounds of force to the end of the wrench to turn a bolt, then 10 pound-feet of torque is being applied. ● SEE FIGURE 7–2.

The metric unit for torque is newton-meters because newton is the metric unit for force and the distance is expressed in meters.

1 pound-foot = 1.3558 newton-meters
1 newton-meter = 0.7376 pound-foot

WORK Work is defined as actually accomplishing movement when force (torque) is applied to an object. A service technician can apply torque to a bolt in an attempt to loosen it, yet no work is done until the bolt actually moves. Work is calculated by multiplying the applied force (in pounds) by the distance the object moves (in feet). If you applied 100 pounds of force to move an object 10 feet, you accomplished 1,000 foot-pounds of work (100 pounds × 10 feet = 1,000 foot-pounds). ● SEE FIGURE 7–3.

POWER Power is defined as the rate of doing work or the rate at which work is being done. It is the amount of energy consumed per unit time. In the SI system, the unit of power is the joule per second, also known as the watt, named after James Watt, the 18th century developer of the steam engine.

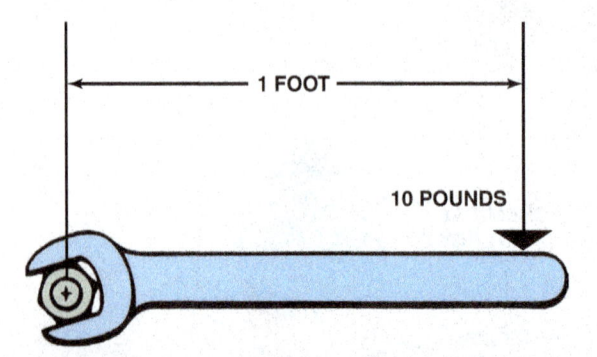

FIGURE 7–2 Torque is a twisting force equal to the distance from the pivot point times the force applied expressed in units called pound-feet (lb-ft) or newton-meters (N-m).

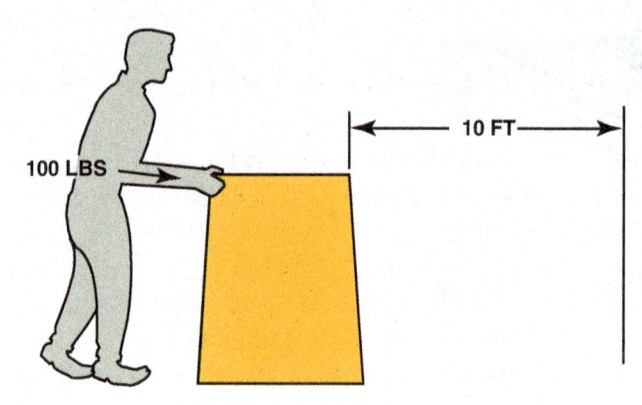

FIGURE 7–3 Work is calculated by multiplying force times distance. If you push 100 pounds 10 feet, you have done 1,000 foot-pounds of work.

Another common and traditional measure is horsepower (comparing to the power of a horse). As the rate of work over time, the equation for power is shown below:

$$\text{Power} = \frac{\text{Work}}{\text{Time}}$$

The faster a given amount of work is done, the greater is the power. In terms of the above formula, the smaller the time, the greater is the fraction or power result. The watt is a common unit of power used in electricity.

HORSEPOWER Horsepower is the unit of measurement that expresses the power output of an internal combustion engine. One horsepower is equivalent to 33,000 ft-lb (foot-pounds) of work done in one minute. For example, if it takes one minute to lift a weight of 550 pounds a distance of 60 feet, the work done is 550 × 60 = 33,000 lb-ft done in one minute. One horsepower is consumed, since 33,000 ft-lb per minute is equal to one horsepower. In the metric system, power of an engine is expressed in kilowatts (0.746 kilowatt = 1 horsepower, or 1.341 horsepower = 1 kilowatt).

The horsepower of an engine as measured by a dynamometer is expressed by the formula:

? FREQUENTLY ASKED QUESTION

Who Introduced the Term "Work" in Physics?

The term work was introduced in 1826 by the French mathematician, Gaspard-Gustave Coriolis, as "weight lifted through a height," which is based on the use of early steam engines to lift buckets of water out of flooded ore mines.

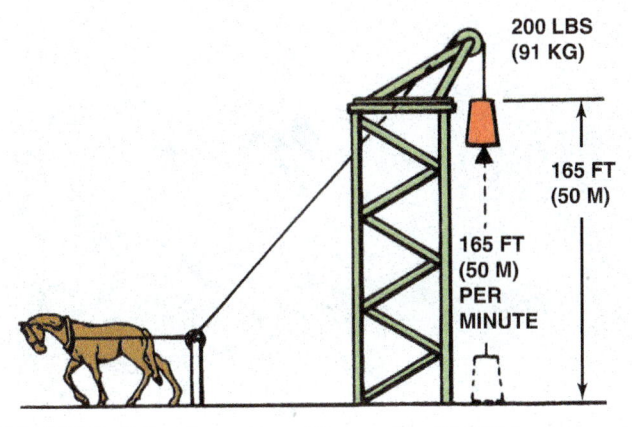

FIGURE 7–4 One horsepower is equal to 33,000 foot-pounds (200 lbs × 165 ft) of work per minute.

$$hp = \frac{2\pi FRN}{33,000}$$

- hp = Horsepower
- F = Dynamometer load, in pounds
- R = Radius arm of dynamometer, in feet
- 33,000 = Conversion factor, foot-pounds per minute, to produce one horsepower
- N = Engine speed, in revolutions per minute (RPM)
- π = 3.1416, a constant

● **SEE FIGURE 7–4.**

FREQUENTLY ASKED QUESTION

Where Did the Term Horsepower Come From?

The term horsepower came from the act of a horse pulling or lifting a weight of 200 pounds for a distance of 165 feet; that is, 200 times 165 equal to 30,000 foot-pounds accomplished in 1 minute. Brake or shaft horsepower is the power delivered at the shaft of the engine. The term brake horsepower comes from the method of testing early engines. This consisted of putting a mechanical brake on the engine and measuring the force required to hold the brake from turning. The energy produced was dissipated as heat. Water or air was used to cool the friction surfaces of the brake. Brakes, called Prony brakes, were an early type of the absorption dynamometer.

ELECTRICAL POWER

BACKGROUND The Greeks discovered electricity. They found that when they took amber (a translucent, yellowish resin that comes from fossilized trees) and rubbed it against other materials, it became charged with an unseen force that had the ability to attract lightweight objects, such as feathers, in the same way that a magnet picks up metal objects. In 1600, a scientist named William Gilbert discovered that other materials shared the ability to attract, such as sulfur and glass. He also used the Latin word *electricus*, which means "amber," and the word electrical for the effect. Sir Thomas Browne used the word electricity during the early 1600s.

ELECTRICAL POWER Energy is a measure of how much fuel is contained within something, or used by something over a specific time period.

- **Kilowatt-hour (kWh)** is a unit of energy.
- **Kilowatt (kW)** is a measure of power.

Electric power is the rate at which electrical energy is transferred by an electric circuit. The SI unit of power is the watt, one joule per second. It is usually produced by electric AC (alternating current) generators (invented by Nikola Tesla). Direct current (DC) can be supplied by other sources, such as batteries or solar cells. It is supplied to businesses and homes by the electric power industry through an electric power grid. Electric power is usually sold by the kilowatt-hour (3.6 MJ), which is the product of power in kilowatts multiplied by running time in hours. The **watt-hour** is a unit of energy equal to a power of one watt operating for one hour. One watt-hour equals 3,600 joules. The kilowatt-hour is a unit of energy equal to 1,000 watt-hours, or 3.6 megajoules. If the energy is being transmitted or used at a constant rate (power) over a period of time, the total energy in kilowatt-hours is the product of the power in kilowatts and the time in hours. Electric utilities measure power using an electricity meter, which keeps a running total of the electric energy delivered to a customer. ● **SEE FIGURE 7–5.**

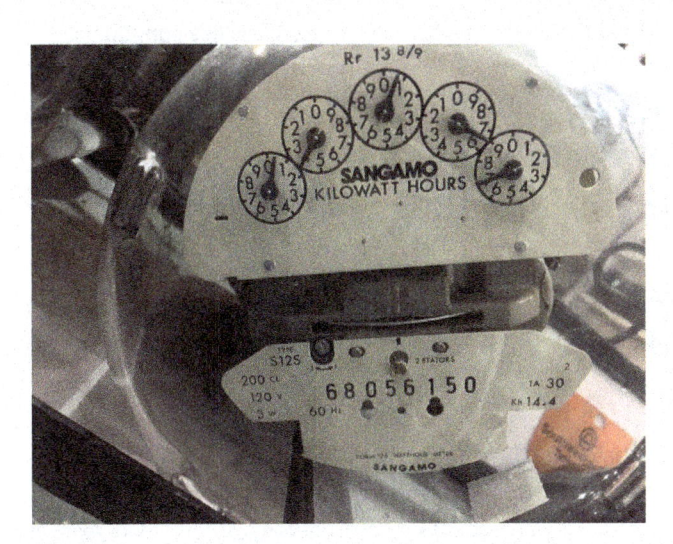

FIGURE 7–5 A typical power meter that measures the amount of electrical power supplied to a home.

ENERGY AND POWER 81

VALUE	SYMBOL	NAME
10^3	kWh	kilo watt-hour
10^5	MWh	mega watt-hour
10^9	GWh	giga watt-hour
10^{12}	TWh	tera watt-hour
10^{15}	PWh	peta watt-hour

CHART 7–1

Kilowatt-hours (kWh) are for household electrical service and electric vehicle power consumption. Megawatt-hours (MWh) are for city wide power generation. Terawatt-hours (TWh) and petawatt-hours (PWh) would be for larger producers of electrical power like wind farms, large solar arrays, laser systems, and concentrating solar power (CSP) systems.

One megawatt is equal to the electrical needs for 1,000 homes. ● SEE CHART 7–1.

A **watt** is a basic unit of power. Power is the rate at which electrical energy is delivered to a circuit. Watts and horsepower are both measures of power. The power formula, sometimes called **Watt's law**, describes the relationship between power (P), voltage (E), and current (I). The relationship among power voltage and current can be expressed by the formula $P = I \times E$ and its derivatives $P/E = I$ and $P/I = E$. For example, a 60-watt light bulb uses 0.5 amps of current at 120 volts (60/120 = 0.5).

Power is the product of current multiplied by voltage.

- In a circuit if voltage or current increases, power increases.
- When the voltage or current decreases, the power will decrease.

One watt is equal to one ampere times one volt. One of the most common applications of a rating in watts is the light bulb. The number of watts consumed classifies light bulbs.

SOLAR ELECTRIC GENERATION

THE SUN Solar energy used to generate electricity is a very promising form of renewable energy. Without the sun, the Earth would not exist.

PHOTOVOLTAICS Photovoltaics (PV) is the direct conversion of light into electricity at the atomic level. Certain materials exhibit a property known as the photoelectric effect that causes this material to absorb photons of light and release electrons. ● SEE FIGURE 7–6.

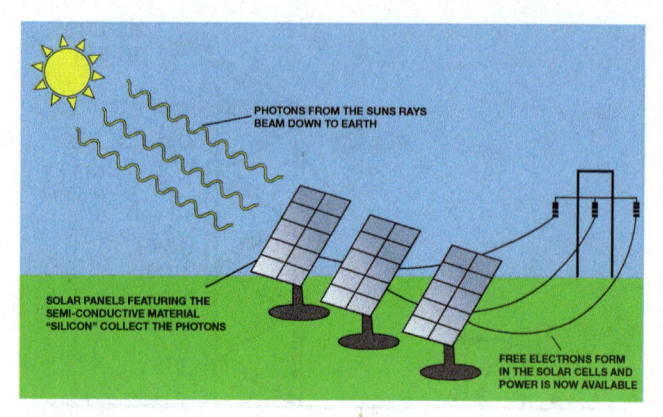

FIGURE 7–6 Solar panels are one of the most efficient sources of electrical energy.

FREQUENTLY ASKED QUESTION

Who Invented Photovoltaics?

The photoelectric effect was first listed by a French physicist, Edmond Becquerel, in 1839, who discovered that certain materials would produce small amounts of electric current when exposed to sunlight. *Albert Einstein* described the nature of light and the photoelectric effect on which photovoltaic technology is based, for which he won a Nobel Prize in physics in 1905. The first photovoltaic module was developed by Bell Laboratories in 1954. It was promoted as a solar battery and was too costly for common use. The space industry, notably NASA (National Aeronautics & Space Administration), began first serious use of the technology to provide power aboard spacecraft in the sixties. Through the efforts of NASA and advanced technology, the dependability of PV was established, and the costs began to go down. Photovoltaic technology has gained recognition as a source of power during the oil embargo of the seventies.

PHOTOVOLTAIC (PHOTOELECTRIC CELL) OPERATION

A basic photovoltaic cell, also called a **solar cell**, is made from semiconductor materials, such as silicon, that has been used in the electronics industry for decades. In a solar cell, a thin semiconductor wafer is used to form an electric field, positive on one side and negative on the other. When light strikes the solar cell, electrons are loosened from the atoms in the semiconductor material N-type and P-type silicon wafers. With electrical

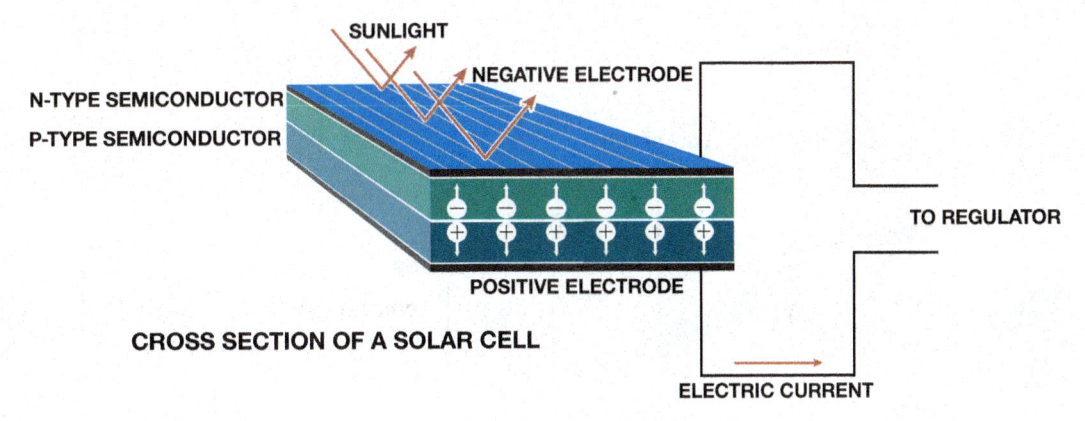

FIGURE 7–7 Sunlight striking a solar cell releases electrons causing an electric current to be generated.

conductors attached to the positive and negative sides, an electrical circuit is formed so the electrons can develop an electric current. This electricity can then be used to power anything that operates on electricity. ● **SEE FIGURE 7–7**.

The multi-junction PV cell (cascade/tandem cells) uses two or more different cells, with more than one bandgap and more than one junction to generate a voltage. These devices can achieve higher total conversion efficiency because they can convert more of the energy spectrum of light to electricity. The multi-junction device is a stack of individual single-junction cells in descending order of bandgap. ● **SEE FIGURE 7–8**.

WIND ENERGY GENERATION

WIND POWER Wind power is the generation of electricity using air flow through wind turbines, which are mechanically powered generators driven by a large turbine blade.

Wind energy, like solar energy, is used to generate electricity all around us. The two types of wind turbines used are as follows:

1. HAWT (horizontal axis wind turbines)
2. Gorlov-type wind turbines

Wind power is an alternative to burning fossil fuels and it is renewable. It is a variable renewable energy source because it does not generate greenhouse gas emissions during operation, does not use water, the energy can be varied, and only has a small footprint. Environment issues are far less with wind power than other nonrenewable power sources. ● **SEE FIGURE 7–9**.

WIND FARMS Wind farms are an array of many individual wind turbines that are connected to the electric power transmission network gird. Onshore and offshore wind farms are an inexpensive source of electricity, competitive with coal or gas plants. ● **SEE FIGURE 7–10**.

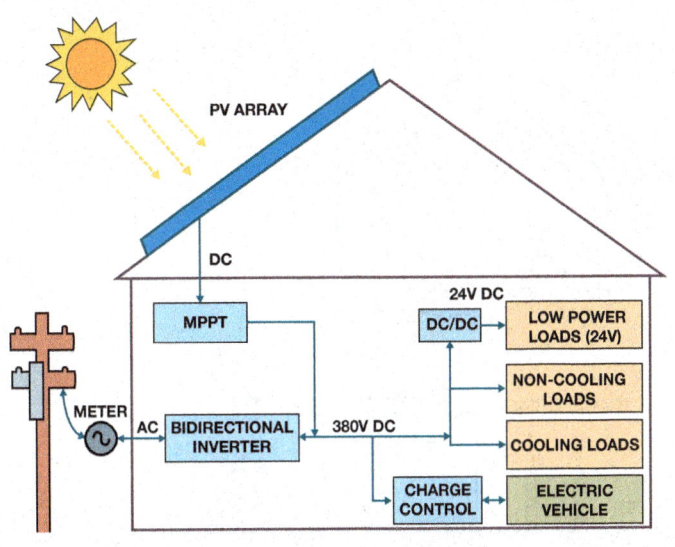

FIGURE 7–8 Solar panels are a cost-efficient way to use the energy from the sun for household uses including charging an electric vehicle.

ENERGY AND POWER

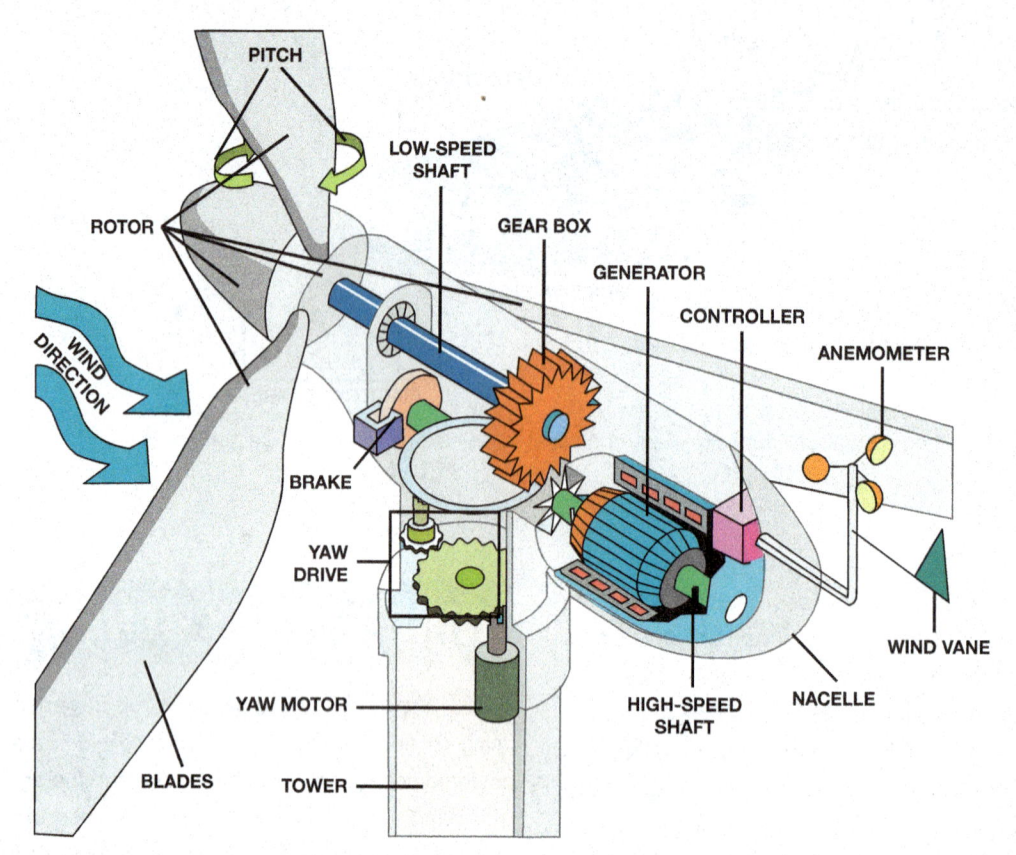

FIGURE 7–9 A typical wind generator is a complex set of mechanical and electric components.

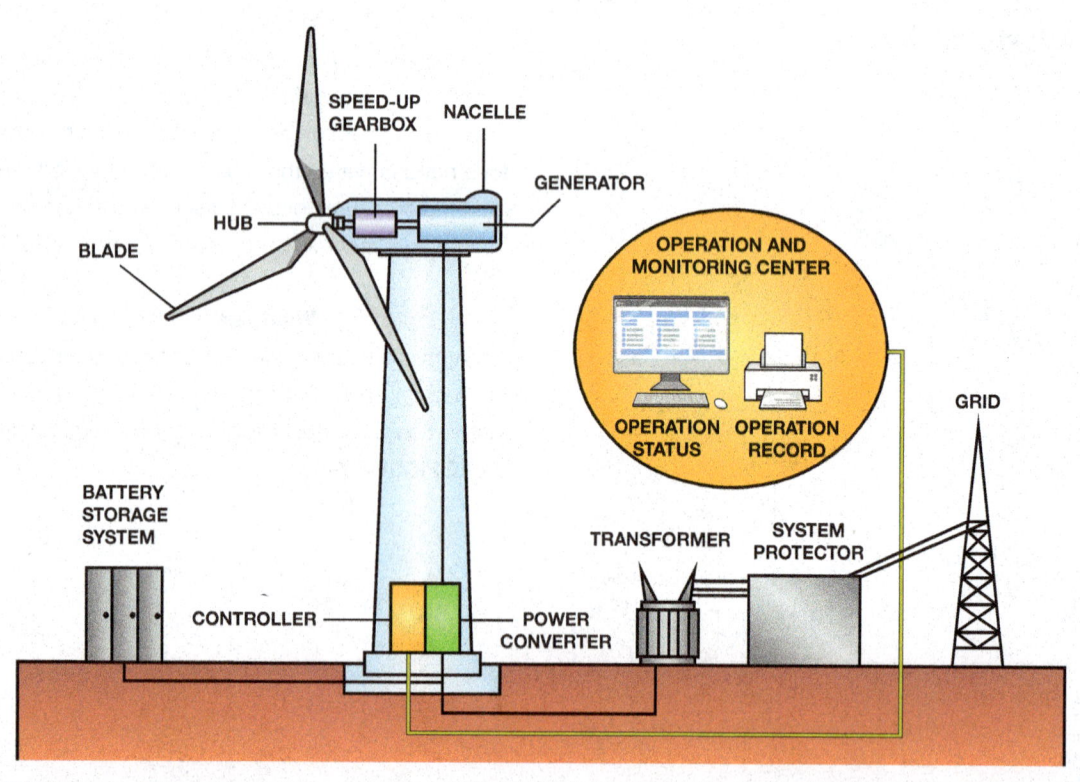

FIGURE 7–10 Groups of wind generators are commonly located where the wind blows above 8 MPH (13 km/h) and where it is close to the electric grid.

84 CHAPTER 7

HYDROELECTRIC GENERATION

DEFINITION **Hydroelectricity** is defined as converting the energy of flowing water into the mechanical energy of a turbine to turn a hydroelectric generator to generate electricity. In 2020, hydroelectricity generated 16.6% of the world's total electricity and 70% of all renewable electricity, and is expected to grow 3.1% each year for the next 25 years. It is produced in 150 countries. China is the largest producer of hydroelectricity, producing about 920 TWh a year, which represents 16.9% of its electricity use. ● SEE FIGURE 7–11.

ECONOMIC IMPACT Hydroelectricity is relatively cheap to produce, so it is a very competitive source of renewable electricity. The hydroelectric plant does not consume or use any fuel, unlike coal or gas plants that consume fossil fuels. The average cost of electricity from a hydro station larger than 10 MW is 3–5 cents per kilowatt-hour. Using a dam and reservoir is a very flexible source of electricity since what is produced can be increased or decreased quickly to adjust to changing demands. A dam is a barrier that impounds water or underground streams. Reservoirs created by dams not only suppress floods, but also provide a water supply for the following:

- Hydroelectricity
- Irrigation
- Human consumption (drinking and bathing water)
- Industrial use
- Aquaculture
- Recreation (boating, fishing, etc.)

Hydropower is used in conjunction with dams to generate electricity in a hydroelectricity plant. The hydroelectric plant produces no waste, and has a lower output level of greenhouse gases than fossil fuel powered electricity plants.

GEOTHERMAL ENERGY

DEFINITION **Geothermal energy** is energy derived from the heat of the earth. The earth's core is approximately 4,000 miles from the surface and is so hot that it is molten. Temperatures are believed to be at least 9,000°F (5,000°C). A well is drilled and the earth's core heats water into steam that drives a turbine to drive an AC generator to produce electricity. ● SEE FIGURE 7–12.

Geothermal power is cost-effective, reliable, sustainable, and environmentally friendly, but has historically been limited

> **? FREQUENTLY ASKED QUESTION**
>
> **Where Does Geothermal Energy Come From?**
>
> The geothermal energy of the earth's crust originates from the original formation of the planet and from radioactive decay of materials. The geothermal gradient, which is the difference in temperature between the core of the planet and its surface, drives a continuous conduction of thermal energy in the form of heat from the core to the surface.

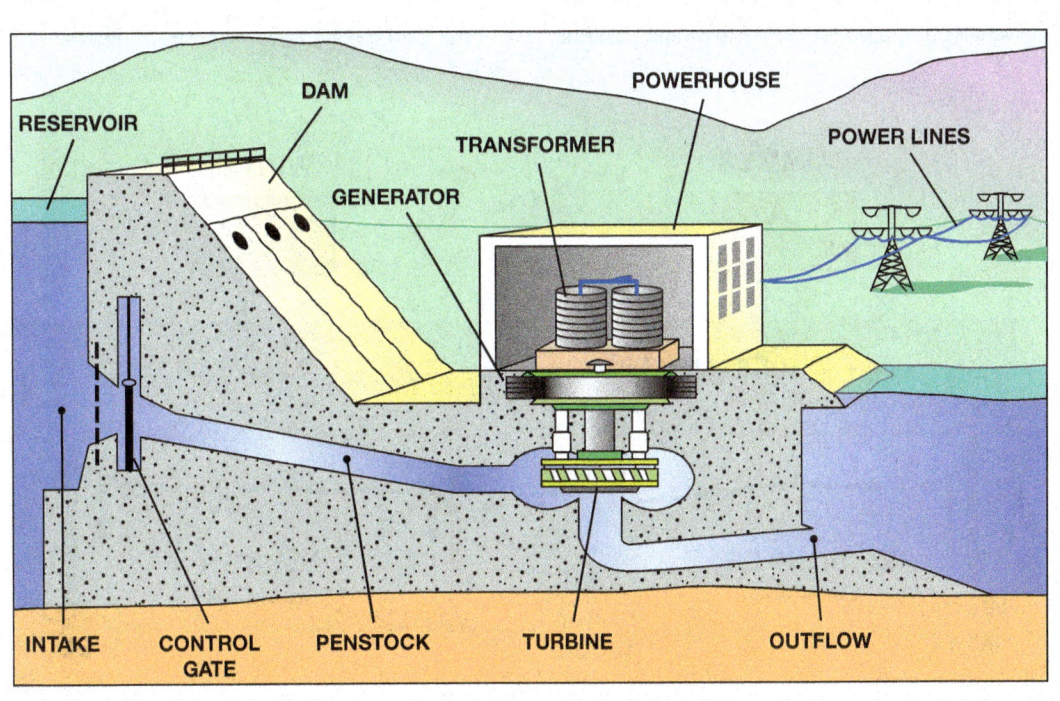

FIGURE 7–11 A conventional hydroelectric dam showing the cross section of the inner components involved with the generation of electrical power using the flow of water.

ENERGY AND POWER

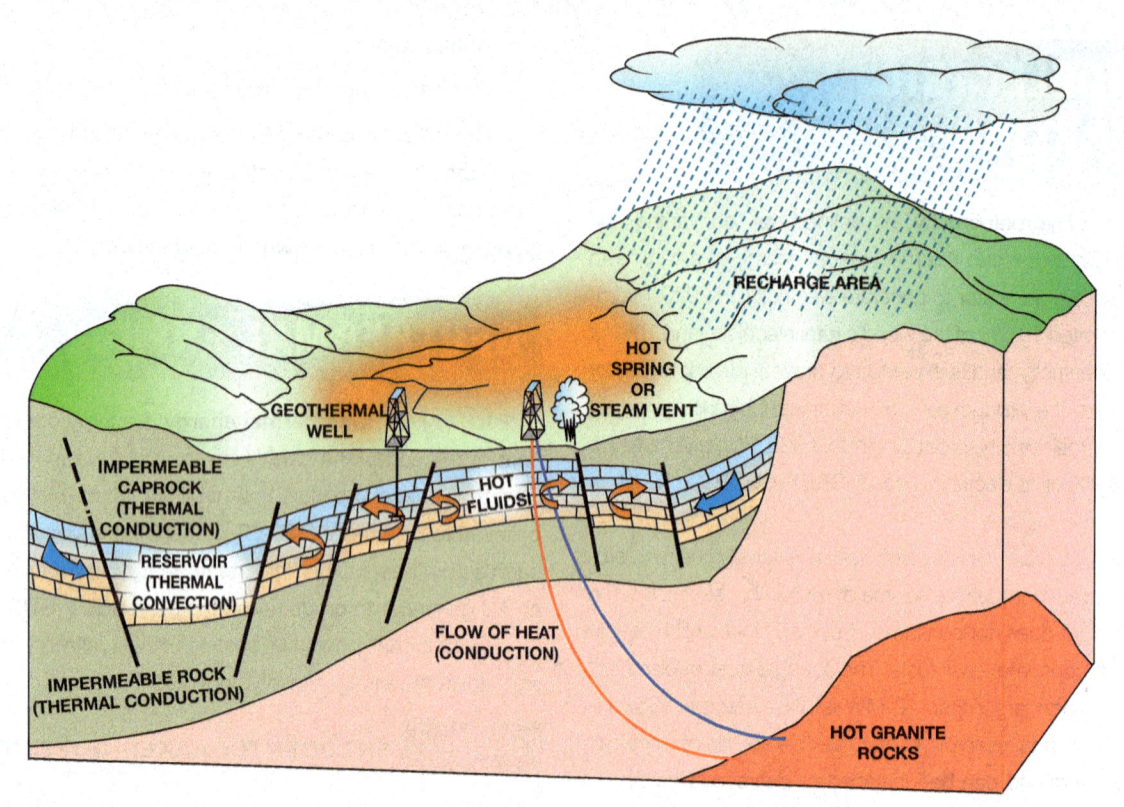

FIGURE 7–12 Geothermal energy is energy derived from the heat of the earth's core.

to areas near tectonic plate boundaries. Recent technological advances have dramatically expanded the range and size of viable resources, especially for applications, such as home heating, opening a potential for widespread exploitation. Geothermal energy costs between $0.02 and $0.10 cents per kilowatt-hour.

Geothermal power is renewable because any projected heat extraction is small compared to the earth's heat content. Geothermal use will not endanger the capability of future generations to use energy sources that are presently used.

GHP SYSTEM Geothermal can be used in cold weather to warm the interior of a building and can be used in warm weather to cool the inside of a building using a **geothermal heat pump (GHP)** system. ● SEE FIGURE 7–13.

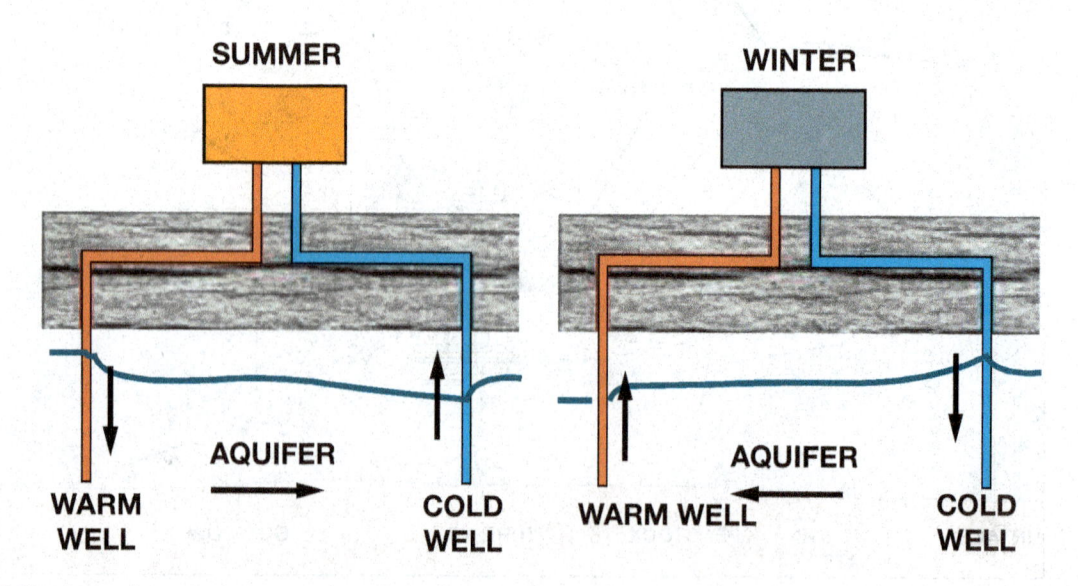

FIGURE 7–13 Geothermal energy is energy that can be used to heat or cool.

86 CHAPTER 7

During warm weather, a GHP is used to lower the indoor temperature by transferring heat from inside a building into the ground that is usually at a constant temperature ranging from 45°F (7°C) to 75°F (23°C). Like a cave, this ground temperature is warmer than the air above it during the winter and cooler than the air in the summer. The GHP takes advantage of this by exchanging heat with the earth through a ground heat exchanger. Piping may be arranged as coils buried horizontally, as a single well, or as a series of vertical wells. In the winter, a GHP draws heat from the ground and transfers it to inside the building.

EER **Energy efficiency ratio (EER)** is a value representing the relative electrical efficiency of cooling equipment in the cooling season. EER is calculated by dividing cooling capacity (in British thermal units per hour [Btu/h]) by the power input (in watts or W). The higher the EER, the less electricity the equipment uses to cool the same amount of air. A unit with an EER of 7 costs about twice as much to operate as one with an EER of 14.

SUMMARY

1. Energy is defined as the ability to do work. The sun is the source of energy for life on Earth. It releases the following: thermal energy, heat energy, and radiant (light) energy.
2. Physics defines energy as a property of objects which can be transferred to other objects or converted into different forms.
3. A watt is a unit of electrical power represented by a current of 1 ampere through a circuit with a potential difference of 1 volt.
4. Hydroelectricity is defined as converting the energy of flowing water into mechanical energy to turn an AC hydroelectric generator to generate electricity.
5. Geothermal energy is energy derived from the heat of the earth's core.
6. A well is drilled to the core and heat from the earth's core heats water into steam that drives a turbine to drive an AC generator to produce electricity.

REVIEW QUESTIONS

1. What is electrical power?
2. What is the difference between work and power?
3. What is a kWh?
4. What is the most common component used to generate a DC current?
5. How can geothermal energy be used to heat or cool?

CHAPTER QUIZ

1. What is defined as the ability to do work?
    a. Energy
    b. Power
    c. Horsepower
    d. Wattage
2. Thermal or heat energy is internal energy present in a system due to its _____.
    a. weight
    b. temperature
    c. mass
    d. density
3. In SI units (International System of Units) energy is measured in which of these units?
    a. Ohms
    b. Joules
    c. Volts
    d. Newtons
4. _____ is defined as the production of electric current at the interface of two semiconductor materials.
    a. Photovoltaics
    b. Ohm's law
    c. Watt's law
    d. Any of the above
5. Which of these energies is energy of motion?
    a. Potential
    b. Kinetic
    c. Static
    d. Work
6. Which of these is defined as the product of a force and the distance through which the force acts?
    a. Kinetic energy
    b. Potential energy
    c. Torque
    d. Work

7. Which of these is defined as the rate of doing work or the rate at which work is being done?
   a. Kinetic energy
   b. Power
   c. Torque
   d. Work

8. Which of these is defined as the product of a force and the perpendicular distance between the line of action of the force and the axis of rotation?
   a. Kinetic energy
   b. Potential energy
   c. Torque
   d. Work

9. A watt-hour is a unit of _____?
   a. energy
   b. power
   c. torque
   d. heat

10. Which of these is the SI unit of power?
    a. Joule
    b. Ampere
    c. Watt
    d. Volt

Chapter 8
ADVANCED AC AND DC ELECTRICITY

LEARNING OBJECTIVES

After studying this chapter, the reader should be able to:

- Describe DC current and its generation process.
- Describe AC current and its generation process.
- Describe the process to calculate the formulas for watts and power.
- Explain the purpose of a capacitor.
- Describe the differences between a milliohm, ohm, and megohm.
- Explain how to perform a loss of isolation test.
- Explain electromagnetism and the electric motor principle.
- Describe the operation of CAN bus communication.
- Explain the process of programming a module.

KEY TERMS

Alternating current (AC) 91
Controller Area Network (CAN) 97
Direct current (DC) 90
Electromagnetic induction 94
Insulated-gate bipolar transistor (IGBT) 95
Kilowatt 92
Locksmith ID 99
Loss of isolation 97
Megohm 96
Milliohm 96
National Automotive Service Task Force (NASTF) 99
SAE J2534 98
Watt 92

DC ELECTRICITY

DEFINITION In **direct current (DC)**, the electric charge (current) only flows in one direction. ● SEE FIGURE 8-1.

DC is used in batteries and the charging of all batteries including smartphones and electric vehicles. Hybrid electric and electric vehicles use an auxiliary 12-volt battery for most lighting and accessories. DC voltage can be viewed flowing in a single line from battery through an electrical load and back to the battery. ● SEE FIGURE 8-2.

DC GENERATION An alternator generates alternating current within itself, but the output is DC. The induced current in the stator windings is an alternating current because of the alternating magnetic field of the rotor. The current induced in the stator windings connects to diodes (one-way electrical check valves) that permit the alternator output current to flow in only one direction, thereby changing AC voltage to DC voltage. All alternators contain six diodes, one pair (a positive and a negative diode) for each of the three stator windings. Some alternators contain eight diodes with another pair connected to the center connection of a wye-type stator. ● SEE FIGURE 8-3.

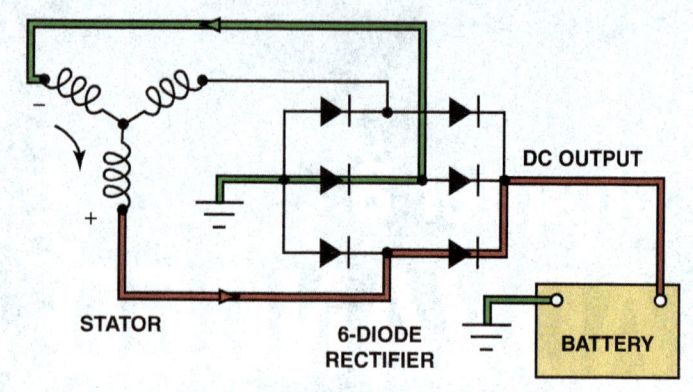

FIGURE 8-3 As the magnetic field, created in the rotor, cuts across the windings of the stator, a current is induced. Notice that the current path includes passing through one positive (+) diode on the way to the battery and one negative (−) diode as a complete circuit is completed through the rectifier and stator. It is the flow of current through the diodes that converts the AC voltage produced in the stator windings to DC voltage available at the output terminal of the alternator.

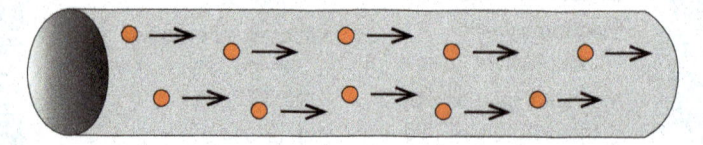

FIGURE 8-1 Electrons flow in only one direction in DC circuits.

DC WAVEFORM DC has only one waveform consisting of a straight horizontal line. This line represents the change (or the lack of change) of voltage over time. In practice, the intensity of the voltage and the current may change, but the direction of the flow stays the same. Over time, for example, batteries lose their power and the voltage will start dropping at some point, producing a horizontal line that drops down slightly over time. ● SEE FIGURE 8-4.

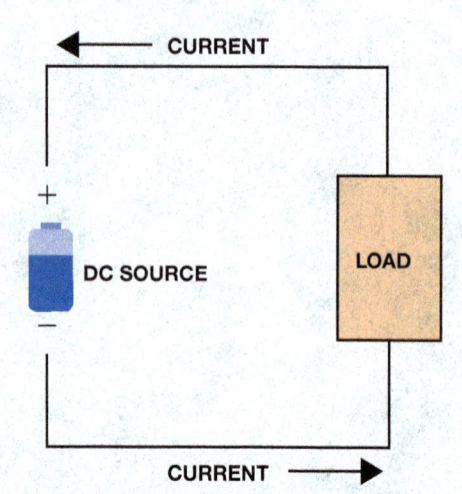

FIGURE 8-2 A DC source is often a battery and a simple circuit that allows current to flow in one direction through the circuit.

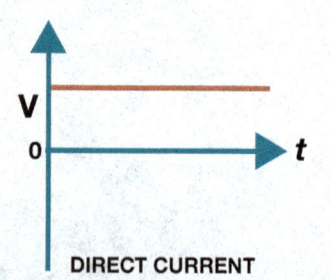

FIGURE 8-4 The waveform of a DC current flow is a flat line representing the voltage over time.

AC ELECTRICITY

DEFINITION Electric charge in **alternating current (AC)** changes direction periodically. The voltage in AC circuits also periodically reverses because the current changes direction. AC is supplied to households and office buildings and can be converted to DC if needed. ● **SEE FIGURE 8-5**.

AC GENERATION An AC is produced by an electric generator. An electric generator consists of a magnet and a loop of wire which rotates in the magnetic field of the magnet. The rotor generates a moving magnetic field around the stator, which induces a voltage difference between the windings of the stator. This produces the AC output of the generator. To produce AC current, this wire needs to have some kind of rotation, which can be produced by flowing water, steam turbine, or wind turbine. During the spinning process, the wire periodically changes its magnetic polarity which makes both current and the voltage alternate. ● **SEE FIGURE 8-6**.

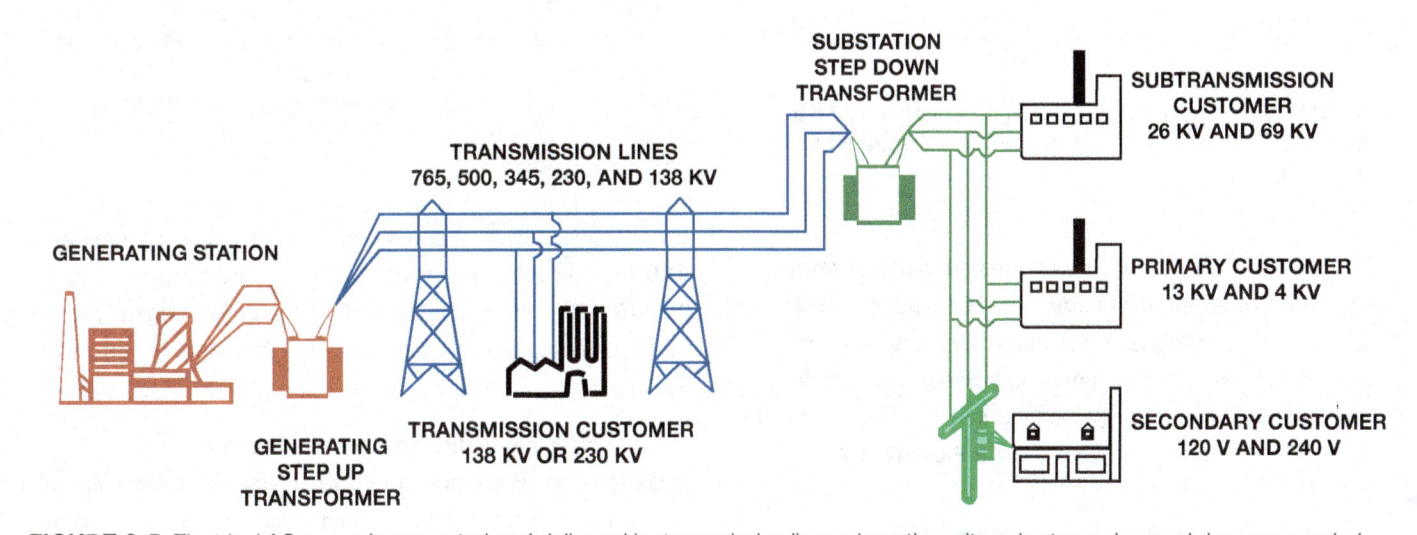

FIGURE 8-5 Electrical AC power is generated and delivered by transmission lines where the voltage is stepped up and down as needed.

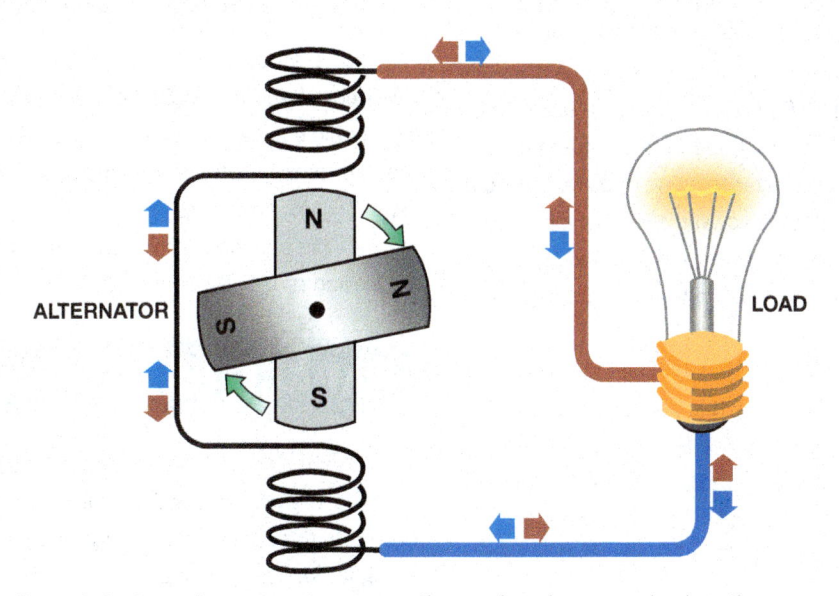

FIGURE 8-6 AC is the flow of electrons from one atom to another and performs work when the movement is applied to an electrical load.

ADVANCED AC AND DC ELECTRICITY

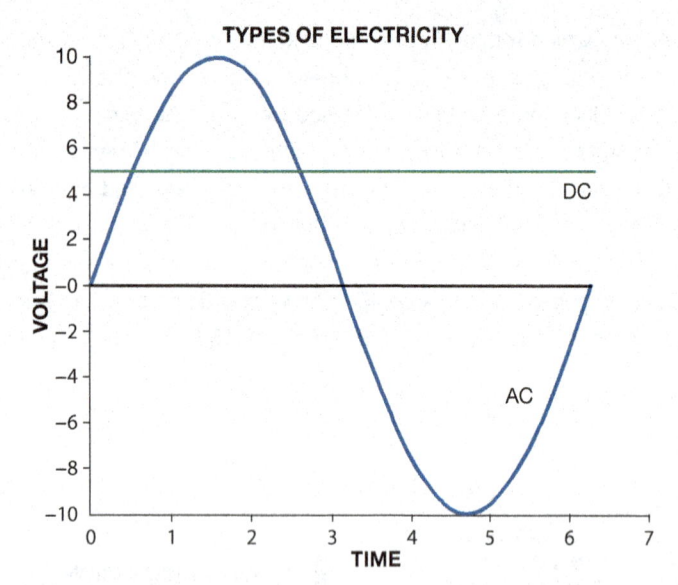

FIGURE 8-7 Compared to DC that is shown to be a flat horizontal line on a scope, the AC waveform is continuously changing.

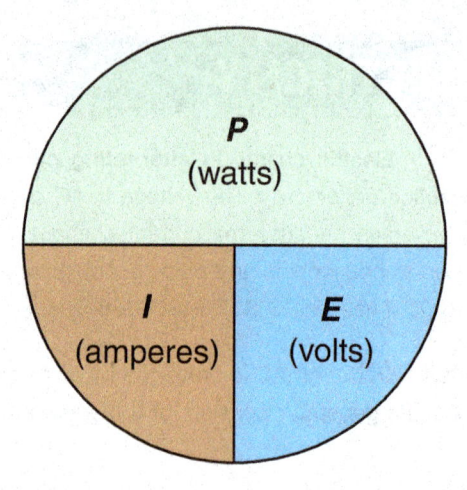

FIGURE 8-8 To calculate one unit when the other two are known, simply cover the unknown unit to see what unit needs to be divided or multiplied to arrive at the solution. The power of electric motors, such as starter motors and propulsion (traction) motors used in electric and hybrid electric vehicles, are rated in watts.

AC WAVEFORMS AC waveforms are different from a DC waveform. Most AC waveforms are a sine wave. This can be seen easily if an oscilloscope is connected to an AC circuit. For example, the AC used in homes and offices have a sine wave when viewed on a scope, indicating that the amplitude of the current flow changes over time. ● **SEE FIGURE 8-7**.

POWER OUTPUT (WATTS)

BACKGROUND James Watt (1736–1819), a Scottish inventor, first determined the power of a typical horse while measuring the amount of coal being lifted out of a mine. The power of one horse was determined to be 33,000 foot-pounds per minute. Electricity can also be expressed in a unit of power called a watt and the relationship is known as Watt's law, which states:

A **watt** is a unit of electrical power represented by a current of 1 ampere through a circuit with a potential difference of 1 volt.

FORMULAS The symbol for a watt is the capital letter W.
The formula for watts is: $W = I \times E$
Another way to express this formula is to use the letter P to represent the unit of power. The formula then becomes:
$$P = I \times E$$

NOTE: An easy way to remember this equation is that it spells "pie."

Engine power is commonly rated in watts or **kilowatts** (1,000 watts equal 1 kilowatt), because 1 horsepower is equal to 746 watts. For example, a 200-horsepower engine can be rated as having the power equal to 149,200 watts or 149.2 kilowatts (kW).

To calculate watts, both the current in amperes and the voltage in the circuit must be known. If any two of these factors are known, the other remaining factor can be determined by the following equations:

$P = I \times E$ (watts equal amperes times voltage)
$I = P / E$ (amperes equal watts divided by voltage)
$E = P / I$ (voltage equals watts divided by amperes)

For example, the amperage required to operate a 55-watt low-beam headlight bulb can be calculated using Watt's law. The vehicle's 12-volt battery supplies the voltage to operate the lamp. Using the formula, $I = P/E$, the calculation is $55/12 = 4.6$ amperes.

A Watt's circle can be drawn and used like the Ohm's law circle diagram. ● **SEE FIGURE 8-8**.

CAPACITORS

CONSTRUCTION A capacitor (also called a condenser) consists of two conductive plates with an insulating material between them. The insulating material is commonly called a *dielectric*. This substance is a poor conductor of electricity and can include air, mica, ceramic, glass, paper, plastic, or any similar nonconductive material. The dielectric constant is the relative strength of a material against the flow of electrical current. The higher the number is, the better are the insulating properties.

OPERATION When a capacitor is placed in a closed circuit, the voltage source (battery) forces electrons around the circuit. Because electrons cannot flow through the dielectric of the capacitor, excess electrons collect on what becomes the negatively charged plate. At the same time, the other plate loses electrons, and therefore becomes positively charged.
● **SEE FIGURE 8-9**.

Current continues until the voltage charge across the capacitor plates becomes the same as the source voltage. At that time, the negative plate of the capacitor and the negative terminal of the battery are at the same negative potential.
● **SEE FIGURE 8-10**.

The positive plate of the capacitor and the positive terminal of the battery are also at equal positive potentials. There is a voltage charge across the battery terminals and an equal voltage charge across the capacitor plates. The circuit is in balance, and there is no current. An electrostatic field now exists between the capacitor plates because of their opposite charges. It is this field that stores energy. In other words, a charged capacitor is similar to a charged battery.

If the circuit is opened, the capacitor holds its charge until it is connected into an external circuit through which it can discharge. When the charged capacitor is connected to an external circuit, it discharges. After discharging, both plates of the capacitor are neutral because all the energy from a circuit stored in a capacitor is returned when it is discharged. ● **SEE FIGURE 8-11**.

Theoretically, a capacitor holds its charge indefinitely. Actually, the charge slowly leaks off the capacitor through the dielectric. The better the dielectric, the longer the capacitor holds its charge. To avoid an electrical shock, any capacitor should be treated as if it were charged until it is proven to be

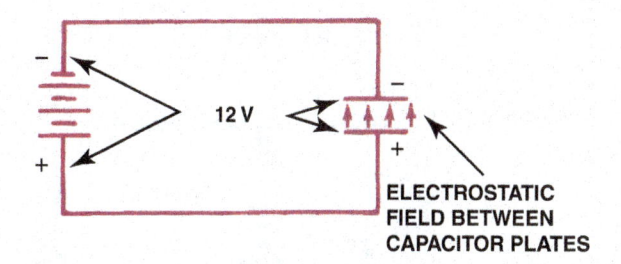

FIGURE 8-10 When the capacitor is charged, there is equal voltage across the capacitor and the battery. An electrostatic field exists between the capacitor plates. No current flows in the circuit.

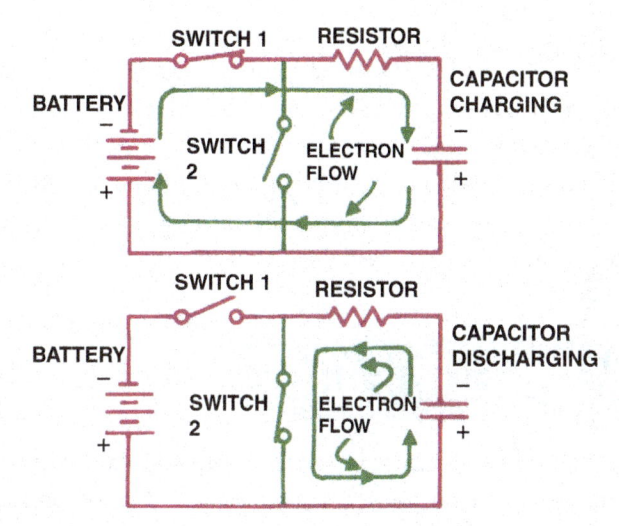

FIGURE 8-11 The capacitor is charged through one circuit (top) and discharged through another (bottom).

discharged. To safely discharge a capacitor, follow the manufacturer's procedure. In most cases the technician must wait a specific amount of time (typically 5–10 minutes) for the capacitors to self-discharge before continuing with the task. ● **SEE FIGURE 8-12** for the symbol for capacitors as used in electrical schematics.

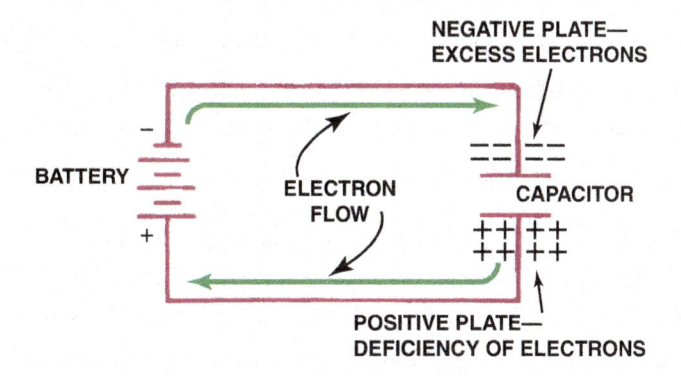

FIGURE 8-9 As the capacitor is charging, the battery forces electrons through the circuit.

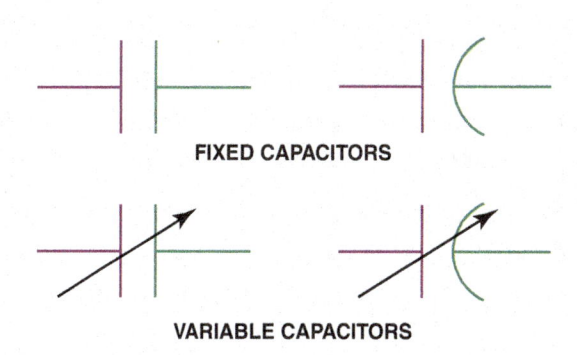

FIGURE 8-12 Capacitor symbols as shown in electrical diagrams. The negative plate is often shown curved.

ADVANCED AC AND DC ELECTRICITY **93**

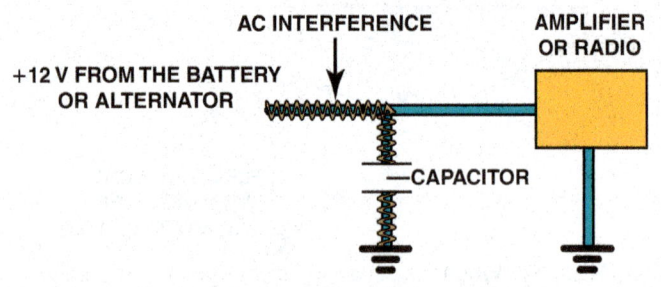

FIGURE 8-13 A capacitor blocks DC, but passes AC. A capacitor makes a very good noise suppressor because most of the interference is AC, and the capacitor conducts this AC to ground before it can reach the radio or amplifier.

SPIKE SUPPRESSION A capacitor can be used in parallel to a coil to reduce the resulting voltage spike that occurs when the circuit is opened. The energy stored to the magnetic field of the coil is rapidly released at this time. The capacitor acts to absorb the high voltage produced and stop it from interfering with other electronic devices, such as automotive radio and video equipment. ● **SEE FIGURE 8-13**.

MAGNETIC FORCE

MAGNETISM Magnetism is a form of energy that is caused by the motion of electrons in some materials. It is recognized by the attraction it exerts on other materials. Like electricity, magnetism cannot be seen. It can be explained in theory, however, because it is possible to see the results of magnetism and recognize the actions that it causes. Magnetite is the most naturally occurring magnet. Naturally magnetized pieces of magnetite, called *lodestone*, attract and hold small pieces of iron. Many other materials can be artificially magnetized to some degree, depending on their atomic structure. Soft iron is very easy to magnetize, whereas some materials, such as aluminum, glass, wood, and plastic, cannot be magnetized at all.

ELECTROMAGNETISM Scientists did not discover that current-carrying conductors also are surrounded by a magnetic field until 1820. These fields may be made many times stronger than those surrounding conventional magnets. Also, the magnetic field strength around a conductor may be controlled by changing the current.

- As current increases, more flux lines are created and the magnetic field expands.
- As current decreases, the magnetic field contracts. The magnetic field collapses when the current is shut off.
- The interaction and relationship between magnetism and electricity is known as electromagnetism.

FIGURE 8-14 Conductors with opposing magnetic fields move apart into weaker fields.

ELECTROMAGNETIC INDUCTION Electricity can be produced by using the relative movement of an electrical conductor and a magnetic field. The following three items are necessary to produce electricity (voltage) from magnetism.

1. An electrical conductor (usually a coil of wire)
2. A magnetic field
3. Movement of either the conductor or the magnetic field
   Therefore:
   - Electricity creates magnetism.
   - Magnetism can create electricity.

Magnetic flux lines create an electromotive force, or voltage, in a conductor if either the flux lines or the conductor is moving. This movement is called *relative motion*. This process is called induction, and the resulting electromotive force is called *induced voltage*. This creation of a voltage (electricity) in a conductor by a moving magnetic field is called **electromagnetic induction**. ● **SEE FIGURE 8-14**.

MOTOR CONTROL

PRINCIPLES Most hybrid electric vehicles use an AC synchronous motor that is controlled as follows:

1. To change the speed of the motor, the frequency of the applied current is changed. The speed is synchronized to the frequency so when the frequency is changed, the speed changes.
2. The pulse-width and voltage is adjusted to change the power output to match the demands of the vehicle for electric assist or propulsion.

EXAMPLES An example of traction motor control is the motor control module (MCM) used on hybrid electric vehicles. The MCM has three inputs from three rotor position sensors, A, B, and C. They send digital information to the MCM to indicate rotor angular position. The MCM is programmed to use this information to determine which driver circuits in the power drive unit (PDU) are turned on. The PDU controls all functions of the motor, whether it is producing torque to drive the vehicle or is being used as a generator to charge the batteries during regenerative braking.

The MCM has three outputs: U, V, and W. Each winding sends control information (digital high-low) to the PDU. These three inputs tell the PDU which of the power transistors to turn on to drive current through the stator windings and continue rotation of the rotor. ● SEE FIGURE 8-15.

MOTOR CONTROL IGBTs The arrangement of transistors and diodes results in three-phase control of the electric motor for both moving the vehicle (assist) and recharging the battery pack. The current flow through the PDU is controlled by six **insulated-gate bipolar transistors (IGBTs)**. Three of these transistors control the voltage side of the circuit and are called positive or high-side IGBTs. The other three transistors are negative or low-side IGBTs because they are on the negative (ground) side of the stators coils. The base of each IGBT connects to an input terminal in the connector to the PDU. The IGBTs are current drivers that send current from the battery pack through the stator windings to energize the stator coils and move the rotor to power the drive wheels. Most motor controllers include Hall-effect current sensors. ● SEE FIGURE 8-16.

Each IGBT has a diode connected in parallel between the collector and the emitter. These six diodes work together to rectify stator AC to pulsating DC to charge the high-voltage

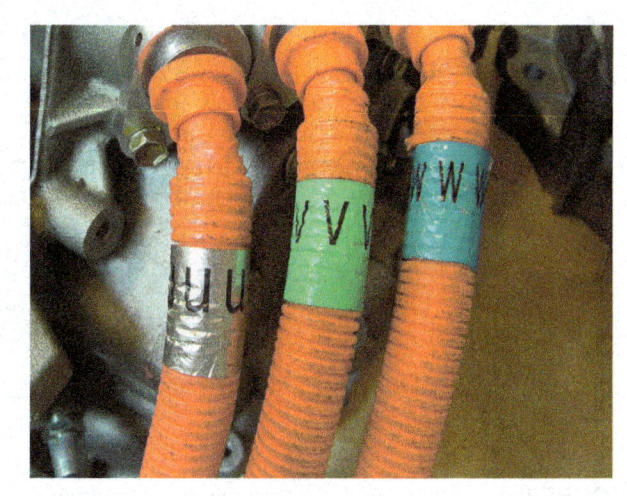

FIGURE 8-15 The power cables for a motor-generator in a Toyota hybrid transaxle.

batteries when the DC electric drive motor becomes a generator during regenerative braking. At that time, the IGBTs are instantly shut off by the MCM to stop powering the DC electric drive motor. Because the HEV is still moving forward, the crankshaft is rotating, which rotates the permanent magnet rotor (armature) in the DC electric drive motor. The rotation of the rotor causes the lines of flux from the powerful permanent magnets to induce an AC current in the stator coils. The six diodes are forward biased and turn on to rectify the AC current induced in the stator coils to pulsating DC to recharge the battery pack.

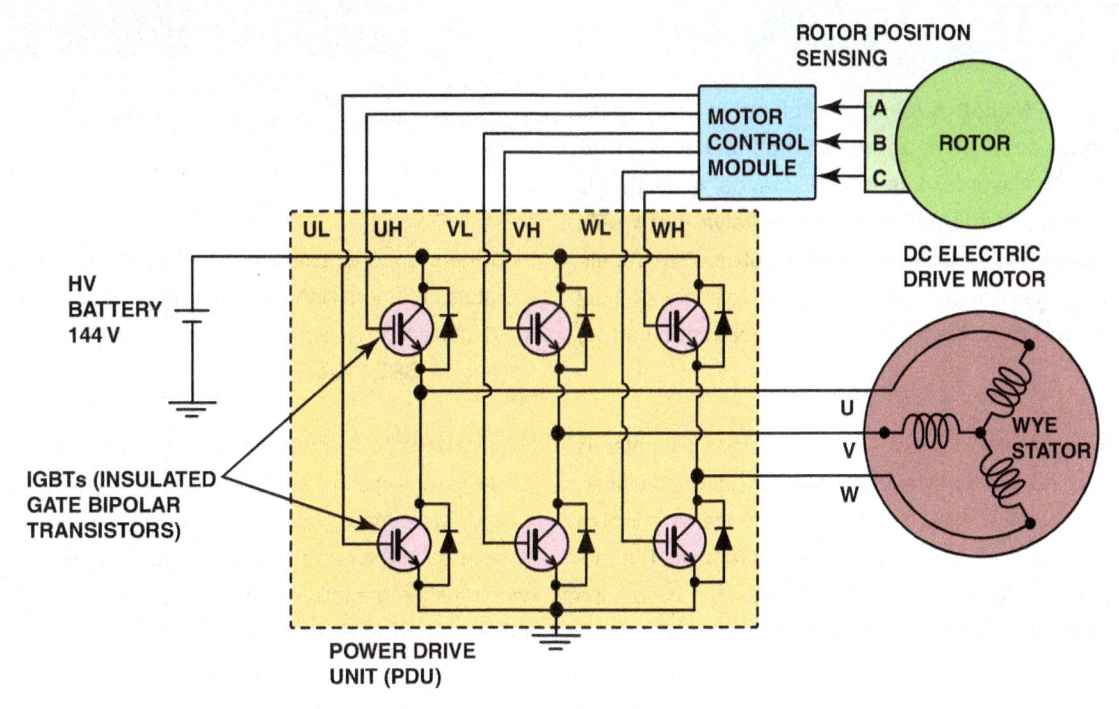

FIGURE 8-16 The drive control unit on a hybrid electric vehicle controls the current and voltage through the stator windings of the motor.

ADVANCED AC AND DC ELECTRICITY   **95**

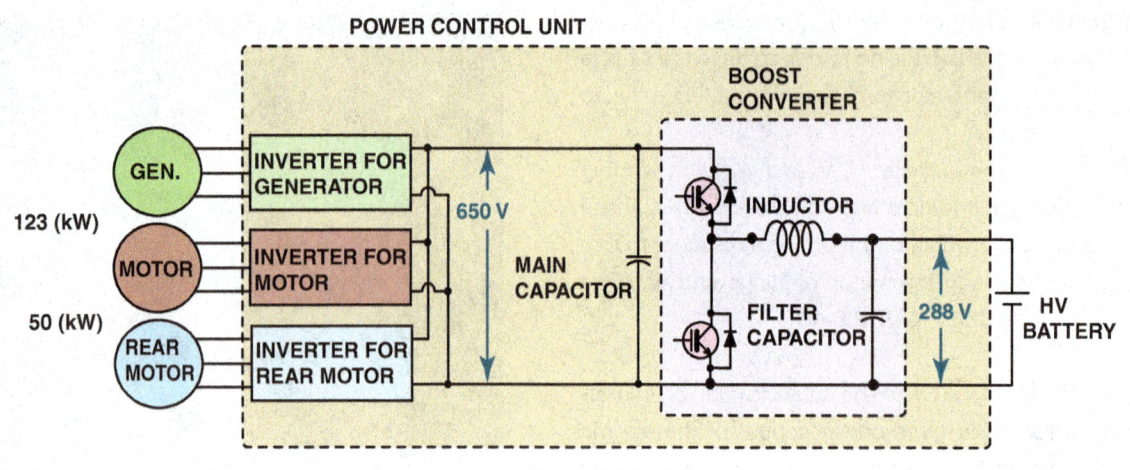

FIGURE 8-17 A schematic showing the motor controls for a Lexus RX 450h. Note the use of the rear motor to provide 4WD capability.

Rotor position information is sent to the MCM, which is programmed to turn on the correct IGBTs to keep the rotor turning. It is critical that the controller know the exact position of the rotor.

The IGBTs process drive current to the electric drive motor. The diodes form a rectifier bridge to change the AC generated in the electric drive motor to pulsating DC to charge the battery pack. ● **SEE FIGURE 8-17**.

EV AND HEV ELECTRICAL MEASUREMENTS

MILLIOHMS Milliohm (plural milliohms) is defined as one thousandth of an ohm, abbreviated as mΩ with a lowercase m. In other words, this is a resistance value that is less than 1 ohm. This is not a resistance valve that would be measured in the course of routine automotive repair. However, when testing the stator windings of an electrical motor in a hybrid or electric vehicle this level of accuracy is required.

MILLIOHMS MEASUREMENT A typical multimeter is not suitable for accurately measuring milliohms. Most multimeters are not accurate below 1 ohm of resistance. A milliohm meter must be used when making this measurement. The milliohm meter has unique test leads and a specific calibration procedure. Before making the measurement, both the meter

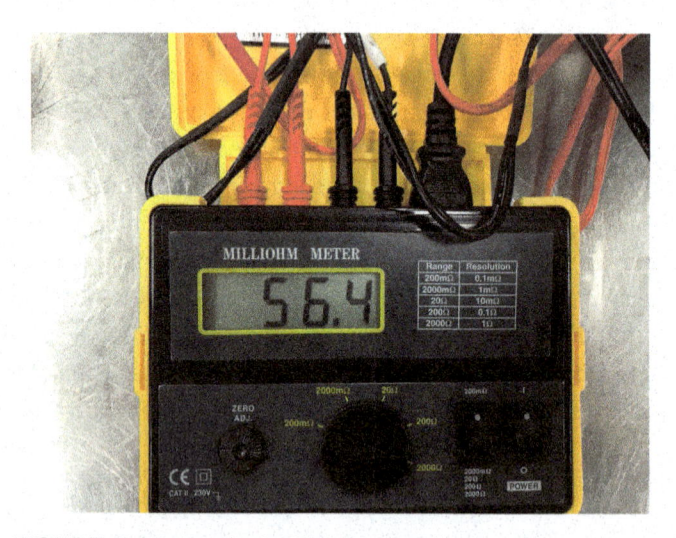

FIGURE 8-18 A typical milliohm meter that is able to measure resistance less than 1 ohm.

and the component being tested must be at a specified temperature. Many milliohm meters must be plugged into household current to ensure a minimum operating voltage during testing. ● **SEE FIGURE 8-18**.

MEGOHMS A **megohm** is defined as a unit of resistance, equal to one million ohms MΩ using an uppercase M and an abbreviation meg. This is not a resistance valve that would be measured in the course of routine automotive repair. However, when testing the integrity of the high-voltage system, this type of measurement is required.

FREQUENTLY ASKED QUESTION

What Is a Loss of Isolation Test?

The **loss of isolation** test is performed to detect unwanted continuity between the high-voltage system and the chassis ground. The test is performed to detect a high-voltage leakage problem and to verify that a defect has been repaired. The loss of isolation test is performed with a digital megohm meter that has an insulation resistance tester. For use on a hybrid or electric vehicle, the meter must be CAT III rated and capable of providing 1,000 volts. Follow the specific safety protocols and the manufacturer's procedure:

- The positive lead of the meter is connected to the high-voltage system.
- The negative lead of the meter is connected to chassis ground.
- The megohm meter is set to the appropriate voltage (typically 1,000 volts).
- The test button is depressed and the value is recorded.
- A reading of near 2.2 MΩ indicates a normal system without loss of isolation.
- A reading of less than 1 MΩ requires further diagnosis.
  - ● SEE FIGURE 8-19.

FIGURE 8-19 A loss of isolation test being performed on a Lexus NX 300h hybrid electric vehicle. The results indicate a resistance of 2.8 million ohms.

EV AND HEV MODULE COMMUNICATIONS

CAN BUS COMMUNICATION Robert Bosch Corporation developed the **Controller Area Network (CAN)** protocol, which was called CAN 1.2, in 1993. The CAN protocol was approved by the Environmental Protection Agency (EPA) for 2003 and newer vehicle diagnostics, and became a legal requirement for all vehicles by 2008. The CAN diagnostic systems use pins 6 and 14 in the standard 16 pin OBD-II (J-1962) connector. Before CAN, the scan tool protocol had been largely manufacturer specific.

CAN FEATURES The CAN protocol offers the following features.

- Faster than other bus communication protocols
- Cost-effective because it is an easier system than others to use
- Less affected by electromagnetic interference (Data is transferred on two wires that are twisted together, called twisted pair, to help reduce EMI interference.)
- Message-based rather than address-based, which makes it easier to expand
- No wake-up needed because it is a two-wire system
- Supports up to 15 modules plus a scan tool
- Uses a 120-ohm resistor at the ends of each pair to reduce electrical noise
- Applies 2.5 volts on both wires:
  H (high) goes to 3.5 volts when active
  L (low) goes to 1.5 volts when active

  ● SEE FIGURE 8-20.

CAN CLASS A, B, AND C There are three classes of CAN and they operate at different speeds. The CAN A, B, and C networks can all be linked using a gateway within the same vehicle. The gateway is usually one of the many modules in the vehicle.

CAN A. This class operates on only one wire at slow speeds and is therefore less expensive to build. CAN A operates a data transfer rate of 33.33 Kbs in normal mode and up to 83.33 Kbs during reprogramming mode. CAN A uses the vehicle ground as the signal return circuit.

CAN B. This class operates on a two-wire network and does not use the vehicle ground as the signal return circuit. CAN B uses a data transfer rate of 95.2 Kbs. CAN B (and CAN C) uses two network wires for differential signaling. This means that the two data signal voltages

ADVANCED AC AND DC ELECTRICITY **97**

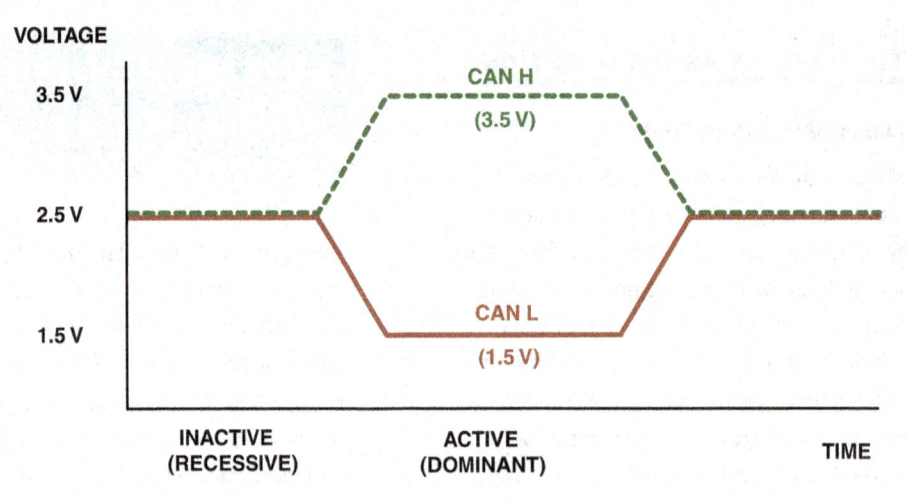

FIGURE 8-20 CAN uses a differential type of module communication where the voltage on one wire is the equal, but opposite voltage on the other wire. When no communication is occurring, both wires have 2.5 volts applied. When communication is occurring, CAN H goes up 1 to 3.5 volts and CAN L goes down 1 to 1.5 volts.

are opposite to each other and used for error detection by constantly being compared. In this case, when the signal voltage at one of the CAN data wires goes high (CAN H), the other one goes low (CAN L), hence the name *differential signaling*. Differential signaling is also used for redundancy, in case one of the signal wires shorts out.

CAN C. This class is the highest speed CAN protocol with speeds up to 500 Kbs. Beginning with 2008 models, all vehicles sold in the United States must use CAN bus for scan tool communications. Most vehicle manufacturers started using CAN in older models, and it is easy to determine if a vehicle is equipped with CAN. The CAN bus communicates to the scan tool through terminals 6 and 14 of the DLC indicating that the vehicle is equipped with CAN.

The total voltage remains constant at all times and the electromagnetic field effects of the two data bus lines cancel each other out. The data bus line is protected against received radiation and is virtually neutral in sending radiation.

MODULE REPROGRAMMING

PURPOSE Designing a program that allows a vehicle to meet strict air quality and fuel economy standards while providing excellent performance is no small feat. However, this is only part of the challenge faced by engineers assigned with the task of developing OBD-II software. The reason for this is the countless variables involved with running diagnostic monitors. Although programmers do their best to factor in any and all operating conditions when writing this complex code, periodic revisions are often required. Reprogramming consists of downloading new calibrations from the manufacturer into the PCM's electronically erasable programmable read only memory (EEPROM).

SAE J2534 STANDARD SAE J2534 is a standard for communications between a computer and a vehicle. The original standard was introduced in February 2002, and was identified as version 02.02. The EPA and CARB regulations require all automakers to provide a J2534 service to everyone in the United States for reflashing emission-related controllers. If the technician has a SAE J2534 pass-through device, they can reflash and, in some cases, diagnose vehicles with factory functionality.

The current standard is referred to as SAE J2534 version 5.00. The newest standard includes all the changes required in the previous updates and serves to improve the communication through the J1962 connector. It is important to have the most current equipment to ensure that the flash reprogramming process will be completed without any malfunctions.

PROGRAMMING HARDWARE Each manufacturer has developed their own J2534 pass-through device or application programming interface (API) that is specific to the brands the manufacturer sells. A pass-through device or API serves as a connection point that makes all the hardware look the same, and allows the computer with the reprogramming software to communicate with the vehicles control module through the data link connector (DLC). Generally, these tools are not designed with the functionality to support competitive brands. In many cases, these pass-through devices are designed to support the manufacturer scan tool in addition to providing reprogramming capabilities. The GM MDI and Ford VCI are both examples of this type of technology. **SEE FIGURE 8-21.**

The generic J2534 pass-through device is designed to support multiple manufacturers. These tools typically do not have the same level of scan tool diagnostics as a manufacturer-specific tool. These tools are more often found outside of the dealership environment in the independent repair facilities. The Drew

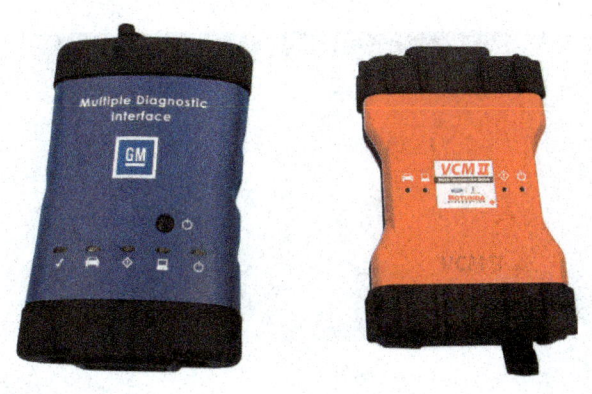

FIGURE 8-21 The GM MDI and Ford VCI are examples of manufacturer-specific pass-through devices.

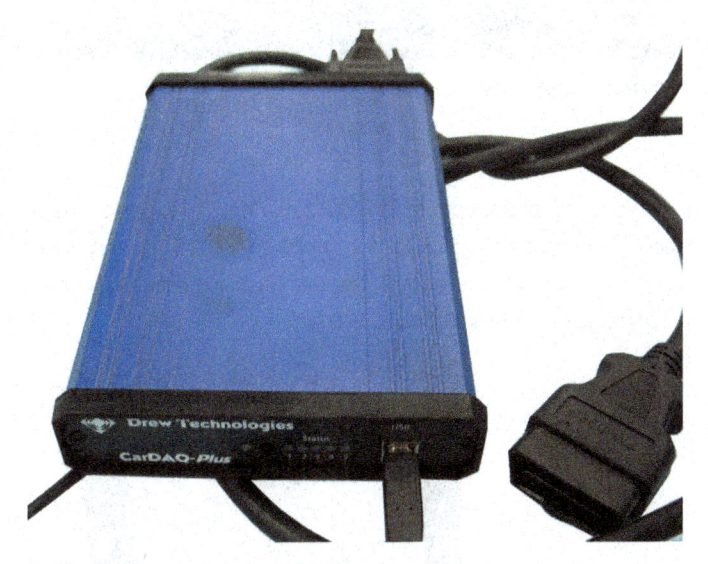

FIGURE 8-22 The CarDAQ Plus is a generic pass-through device.

Technologies CarDAQ-Plus series of J2534 pass-through devices is an example of a generic tool. ● **SEE FIGURE 8-22**.

PROGRAMMING SOFTWARE

The **National Automotive Service Task Force (NASTF)** is a cooperative effort of the automotive service industry, the tool industry, and the original equipment manufacturers to ensure that automotive professionals employed outside of the OEMs have all the information, training, and tools they need to diagnose and repair modern automobiles. The NASTF has created a portal for all automotive service professionals to access manufacturer-specific reprogramming information. This includes where to access the information, the tools needed, and in many cases a short video on how to complete the task. ● **SEE FIGURE 8-23**.

VEHICLE SECURITY PROFESSIONAL—LOCKSMITH ID

Many times, when a module must be reprogrammed or programmed upon replacement, the security codes or key specific information must be reentered during the process. In order to obtain this information, the shop or service technician must be a registered vehicle security professional and have a **locksmith ID** number. The NASTF, in conjunction with automotive manufacturers, insurance industry, independent repair, and law enforcement communities, has developed this system to allow the aftermarket repair industry to access to this sensitive data. The forms and instructions needed to apply for this identification number can be found on the NASTF website (www.nasft.org) under Locksmith/Vehicle Security. ● **SEE FIGURE 8-24**.

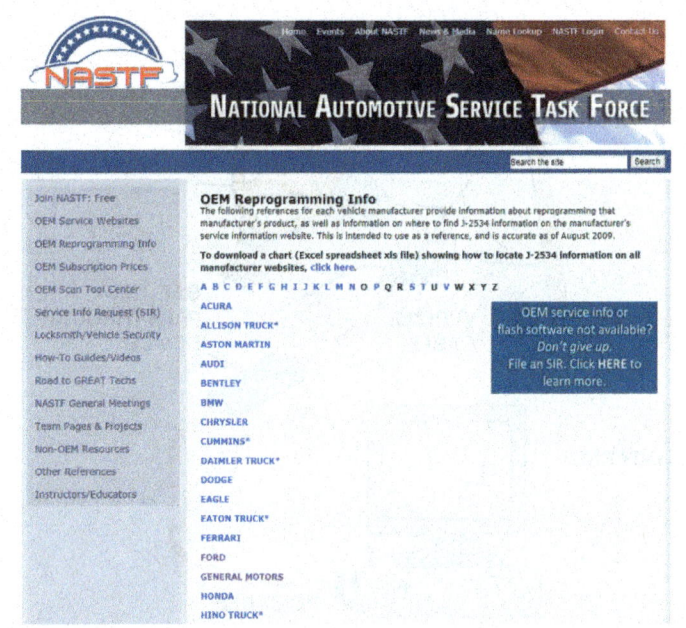

FIGURE 8-23 The screenshot of the NASTF website provides an access point for the aftermarket automotive professional to obtain the needed reprogramming information.

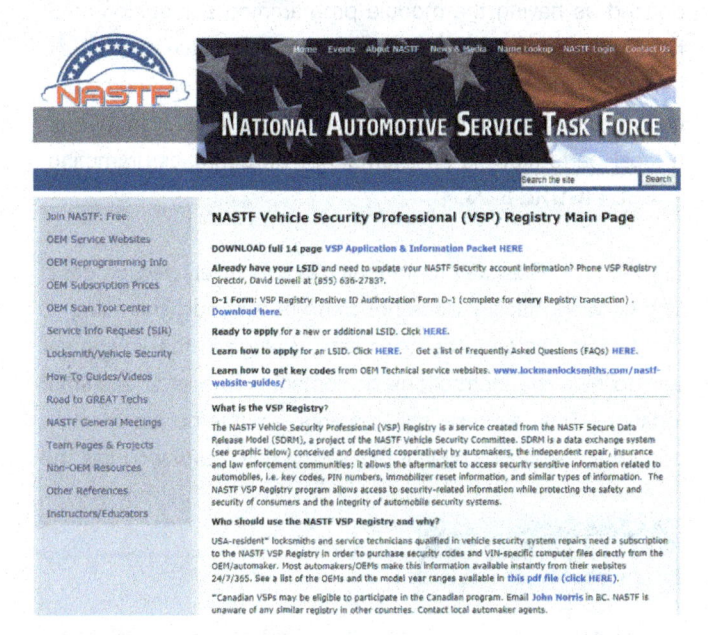

FIGURE 8-24 The screenshot from the NASTF website provides the resources for the technician to apply for a locksmith ID.

ADVANCED AC AND DC ELECTRICITY

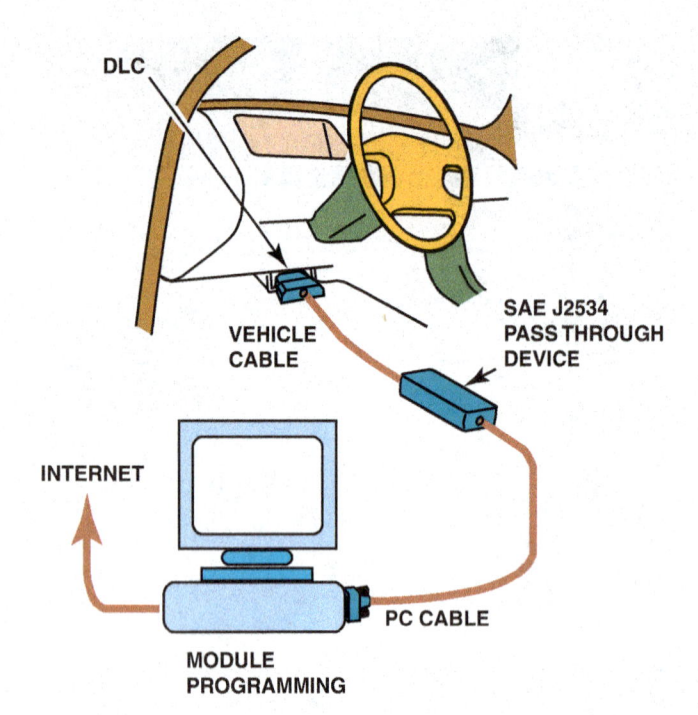

FIGURE 8-25 The J2534 device is being used to program the engine control module through the DLC.

FIGURE 8-26 The control module is being programmed at an off-board location.

ON-BOARD On-board reprogramming of the controller is defined as having the module connected to the vehicle during the process. The module uses its normal connection points to provide the power, ground, communication links, and any other needed support. This is the type of programming that occurs in a service facility. ● SEE FIGURE 8-25.

OFF-BOARD Off-board programming of the controller is defined as having the module programmed someplace other than in the vehicle. This could be done at an place where there is a computer and the needed power, ground, and communication links. The purchase and programming of a module at a local parts store is an example of off-board programming.
● SEE FIGURE 8-26.

REMOTE Remote programming is a relatively new process. The servicing facility does not perform the reprogramming of the vehicle. Instead, the shop simply plugs in the equipment and follows the instructions of someone who is at a distant location. This process still requires an Internet connection and equipment. However, it relies on a third party who has the manufacturer subscription for the software. This option has become increasingly popular for shops that perform very few reprogramming events or lack the technical expertise to complete the task. ● SEE FIGURE 8-27.

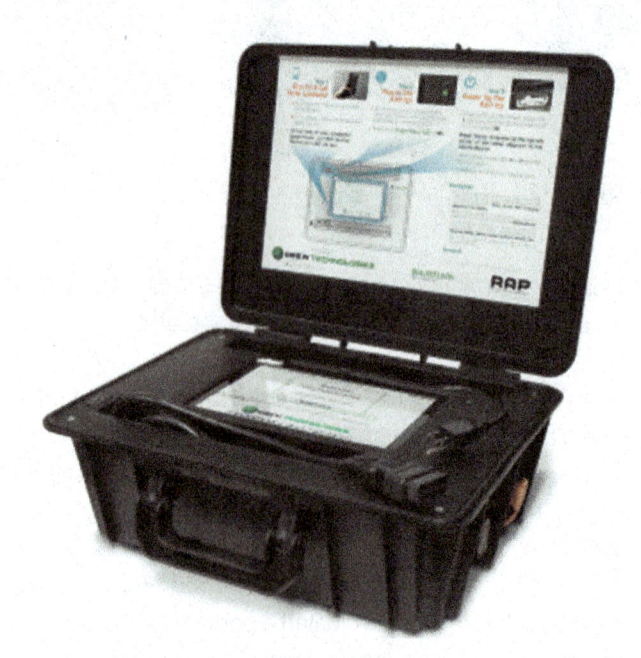

FIGURE 8-27 The Drew Technologies remote programming tool is an example of a tool that is connected to the vehicle and used remotely.

SUMMARY

1. Direct current (DC), the electric charge (current), only flows in one direction. The most common form of generation is through a rectifier.

2. A watt is a unit of electrical power represented by a current of 1 ampere through a circuit with a potential difference of 1 volt.

3. A capacitor (also called a condenser) consists of two conductive plates with an insulating material between them.
4. Milliohm (plural milliohms) is defined as one thousandth (10^{-3}) of an ohm, abbreviated as mΩ.
5. A megohm is defined as a unit of resistance, equal to one million ohms.
6. An insulated-gate bipolar transistor (IGBT) is a three-terminal power semiconductor device primarily used as an electronic switch.
7. The CAN diagnostic systems use pins 6 and 14 in the standard 16 pin OBD-II (J-1962) connector.
8. Reprogramming consists of downloading new calibrations from the manufacturer into the PCM's electronically erasable programmable read only memory (EEPROM).

REVIEW QUESTIONS

1. What is the most common component used to generate a DC current?
2. What is the purpose of a capacitor?
3. What is the purpose of the loss of isolation test?
4. What are the advantages of CAN bus compared to other communication protocols?
5. What are the three methods described to reprogram the EEPROM?

CHAPTER QUIZ

1. Direct current (DC) is being discussed. Technician A say that DC only flows in one direction. Technician B says that a common way to generate DC is with a rectifier bridge. Which technician is correct?
   a. Technician A only
   b. Technician B only
   c. Both Technicians A and B
   d. Neither Technician A nor Technician B

2. A capacitor is being discussed. Technician A says that a capacitor is used for electrical spike suppression. Technician B says that a capacitor is used as a supplemental power source. Which technician is correct?
   a. Technician A only
   b. Technician B only
   c. Both Technicians A and B
   d. Neither Technician A nor Technician B

3. The purpose of an insulated-gate bipolar transistor (IGBT) is to _____.
   a. provide an additional power source
   b. switch power or ground on and off very quickly
   c. suppress electrical spikes
   d. None of these answers are correct

4. The EEPROM in a module can be reprogrammed using which of the following methods?
   a. On-board
   b. Off-board
   c. Remote
   d. Any of these methods can be used

5. The loss of isolation test is used to determine _____.
   a. if the vehicle has a bad chassis ground
   b. if a high-voltage circuit has an unintended path to the vehicle chassis
   c. if the ignition-off draw on the battery is to high
   d. if the cable between the battery and the starter is defective

6. CAN bus features which of the following benefits?
   a. Faster than other communication protocols
   b. Less effected by electromagnetic interference
   c. Message-based rather than address-based, which makes it easier to expand
   d. All the answers are correct

7. An AC synchronous motor is controlled by changing the _____.
   a. voltage
   b. amperage
   c. frequency
   d. All of the above

8. Milliohm is defined as _____.
   a. one thousandth of an ohm
   b. one millionth of an ohm
   c. 100 ohms
   d. 1,000 ohms

9. A megohm is defined as a unit of resistance, equal to _____.
   a. one millionth of an ohm
   b. one million ohms
   c. 1,000 ohms
   d. 10,000 ohms

10. The security codes or key specific information must be reentered during the process. In order to obtain this information, the shop or service technician must be a registered vehicle security professional and have _____.
    a. a factory-level scan tool
    b. an aftermarket enhanced scan tool
    c. a J2534 device
    d. a locksmith ID number

Chapter 9
LOW-VOLTAGE BATTERIES AND STOP-START MICRO HYBRIDS

LEARNING OBJECTIVES

After studying this chapter, the reader should be able to:

- Describe the purpose of the 12-volt battery.
- Explain the 12-volt battery rating systems.
- Describe the 12-volt battery test procedures.
- Describe the function of the 36-48-volt battery.
- Explain the 36-48-volt battery test procedure.
- Describe the main advantages of a stop-start system.
- Explain the difference between a micro and mild hybrid.
- Explain how a disable condition prevents the operation of a stop-start system.

KEY TERMS

Belt alternator starter (BAS) 110
Body control module (BCM) 112
Engine control module (ECM) 112
Hybrid control module 116
Internal combustion engine (ICE) 110
Load test 107
SLI battery 103
Transmission control module (TCM) 112
Ultracapacitor 113

INTRODUCTION TO THE 12-VOLT BATTERY

PURPOSE AND FUNCTION Many may not realize that an electric or hybrid electric vehicle uses a 12-volt battery. Every vehicle, hybrid or electrical, has a 12-volt battery that is used to supply electrical current to the low-voltage components in the vehicle. The battery is one of the most important parts of a vehicle because it is the heart or foundation of the electrical system. The primary purpose of an automotive battery is to provide a source of electrical power for all of the vehicle electrical needs. In a hybrid or electric vehicle, the 12-volt auxiliary battery is used for the following purposes:

- Power all of the 12-volt accessories
- Power the electronic controller for the high-voltage system

WHY BATTERIES ARE IMPORTANT The battery also acts as a stabilizer to the voltage for the entire electrical system. The battery *must* be in good (serviceable) condition to assure correct hybrid or electric vehicle operation. The battery must be confirmed to be in serviceable condition before performing any electrical system testing.

THE HYBRID OR ELECTRIC VEHICLE WILL NOT START IF THE AUXILIARY BATTERY IS DISCHARGED If the 12-volt auxiliary battery is discharged or defective, it cannot power the electronic controller used to start the vehicle. The gasoline engine will not start and the vehicle will not move under high-voltage battery power. If "nothing happens" when the vehicle is attempted to be started, always start the diagnosis with the state of charge and condition of the auxiliary 12-volt battery.

HOW A BATTERY WORKS

PRINCIPLE INVOLVED How a battery works is based on a scientific principle discovered years ago that states:

- When two dissimilar metals are placed in an acid, electrons flow between the metals if a circuit is connected between them.
- This can be demonstrated by pushing a steel nail and a piece of solid copper wire into a lemon. Connect a voltmeter to the ends of the copper wire and nail, and voltage will be displayed.

? FREQUENTLY ASKED QUESTION

What Is a SLI Battery?

Sometimes the term *SLI* is used to describe a type of battery. An **SLI battery** means starting, lighting, and ignition, and describes the use of a typical automotive battery. The auxiliary battery used in hybrid and electric vehicles is an SLI-type battery compared to the high-voltage battery used to help propel the vehicle, which is sometimes called a *traction battery*.

A fully charged lead-acid battery has a positive plate of lead dioxide (peroxide) and a negative plate of lead surrounded by a sulfuric acid solution (electrolyte). The difference in potential (voltage) between lead peroxide and lead in acid is approximately 2.1 volts.

DURING DISCHARGING The positive plate lead dioxide (PbO_2) combines with the SO_4, forming $PbSO_4$ from the electrolyte and releases its O_2 into the electrolyte, forming H_2O. The negative plate also combines with the SO_4 from the electrolyte and becomes lead sulfate ($PbSO_4$). ● **SEE FIGURE 9–1**.

FULLY DISCHARGED STATE When the battery is fully discharged, both the positive and the negative plates are $PbSO_4$ (lead sulfate) and the electrolyte has become water (H_2O). As the battery is being discharged, the plates and electrolyte approach

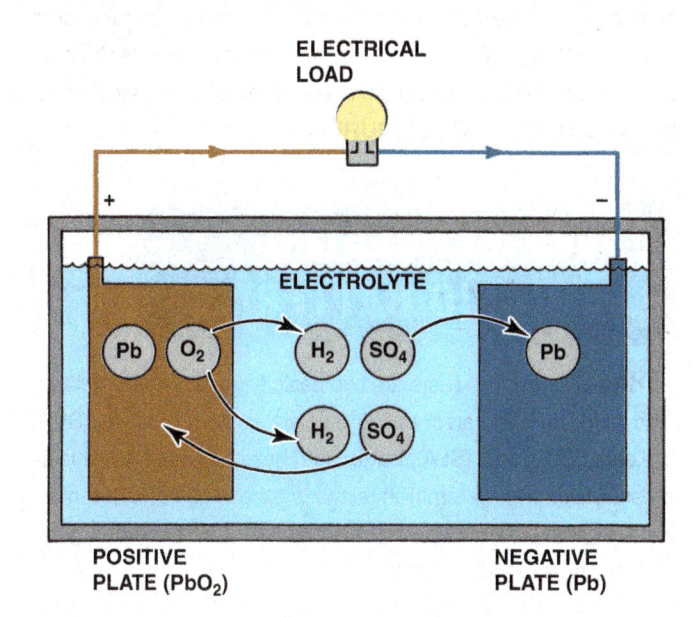

FIGURE 9–1 Chemical reaction for a lead-acid battery that is fully charged being discharged by the attached electrical load.

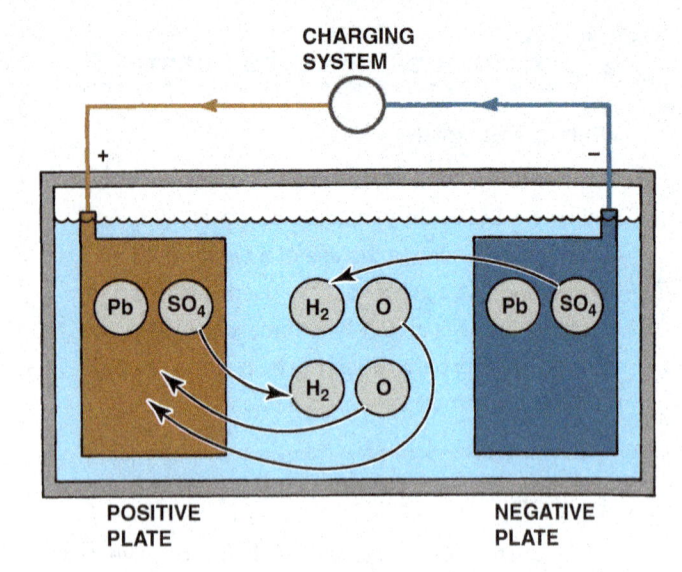

FIGURE 9–2 Chemical reaction for a lead-acid battery that is fully discharged being charged by the attached alternator.

the completely discharged state. When a battery is completely discharged, there are no longer dissimilar metals submerged in an acid. The plates have become the same material ($PbSO_4$) and the electrolyte becomes water (H_2O). This is a chemical reaction that can be reversed during charging.

CAUTION: Never charge or jump start a frozen battery because the hydrogen gas can get trapped in the ice and ignite if a spark is caused during the charging process. The result can be an explosion.

DURING CHARGING During charging, the sulfate that was deposited on the positive and negative plates returns to the electrolyte, where it becomes a normal-strength sulfuric acid solution. The positive plate returns to lead dioxide (PbO_2), the negative plate is again pure lead (Pb), and the electrolyte becomes H_2SO_4. ● **SEE FIGURE 9–2.**

VALVE-REGULATED LEAD-ACID BATTERIES

TERMINOLOGY There are two basic types of valve-regulated lead-acid (VRLA), also called sealed valve-regulated (SVR) or sealed lead-acid (SLA), batteries. These batteries use a low-pressure venting system that releases excess gas and automatically reseals if a buildup of gas is created due to overcharging. The two types include the following:

- Absorbed glass mat. The acid used in an absorbed glass mat (AGM) battery is totally absorbed into the separator, making the battery leak-proof and spill-proof. The battery is assembled by compressing the cell about 20%, then inserting it into the container. The compressed cell helps reduce damage caused by vibration and helps keep the acid tightly against the plates. The sealed maintenance-free design uses a pressure release valve in each cell. Unlike conventional batteries that use a liquid electrolyte, called flooded cell batteries, most of the hydrogen and oxygen given off during charging remains inside the battery. The separator or mat is only 90% to 95% saturated with electrolyte, thereby allowing a portion of the mat to be filled with gas. The gas spaces provide channels to allow the hydrogen and oxygen gases to recombine rapidly and safely. Because the acid is totally absorbed into the glass mat separator, an AGM battery can be mounted in any direction. AGM batteries also have a longer service life, often lasting 7–10 years. AGM batteries are used as standard equipment in vehicles where the battery is located inside the passenger compartment or trunk.
● **SEE FIGURE 9–3**.

- A recombinant-type battery means that the oxygen gas generated at the positive plate travels through the dense electrolyte to the negative plate. When the oxygen reaches the negative plate, it reacts with the lead, which consumes the oxygen gas and prevents the formation of hydrogen gas. It is because of this oxygen recombination that VRLA batteries do not use water.

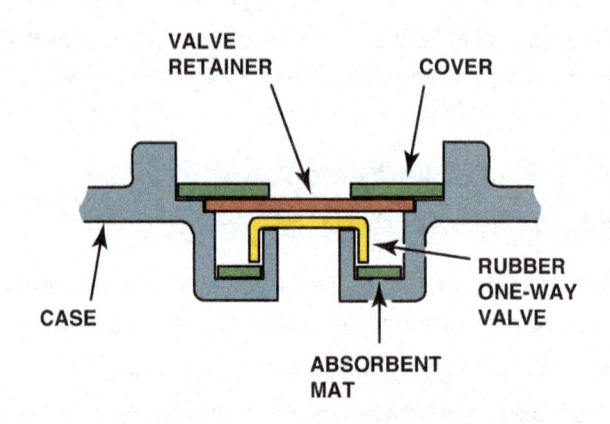

FIGURE 9–3 Pressure relief valve from a VRLA battery. This stays closed during normal operating conditions and prevents gases from entering or leaving the battery case.

12-VOLT BATTERY RATINGS

COLD-CRANKING AMPERES Every automotive battery must be able to supply electrical power to crank the engine in cold weather and still provide battery voltage high enough to operate the ignition system for starting. The cold-cranking ampere rating of a battery is the number of amperes that can be supplied by a battery at 0°F (–18°C) for 30 seconds while the battery still maintains a voltage of 1.2 volts per cell or higher. This means that the battery voltage would be 7.2 volts for a 12-volt battery and 3.6 volts for a 6-volt battery. The cold-cranking performance rating is called cold-cranking amperes (CCA). Try to purchase a battery with the highest CCA for the money. See the vehicle manufacturer's specifications for recommended battery capacity.

CRANKING AMPERES The designation CA refers to the number of amperes that can be supplied by a battery at 32°F (0°C). This rating results in a higher amperage rating than the more stringent CCA rating. ● **SEE FIGURE 9–4**.

RESERVE CAPACITY The reserve capacity rating for batteries is *the number of minutes* for which the battery can produce 25 amperes and still have a battery voltage of 1.75 volts per cell (10.5 volts for a 12-volt battery). This rating is actually a measurement of the time for which a vehicle can be driven in the event of a charging system failure.

AMPERE HOUR Ampere hour is an older battery rating system that measures how many amperes of current the battery can produce over a period of time. For example, a battery that has a 50 amp-hour (A-H) rating can deliver 50 amperes for 1 hour or 1 ampere for 50 hours or any combination that equals 50 amp-hours.

FIGURE 9–4 This battery has a rating of 1,000 cranking amperes (CA) and 900 amperes using the cold crank amperes (CCA) rating system.

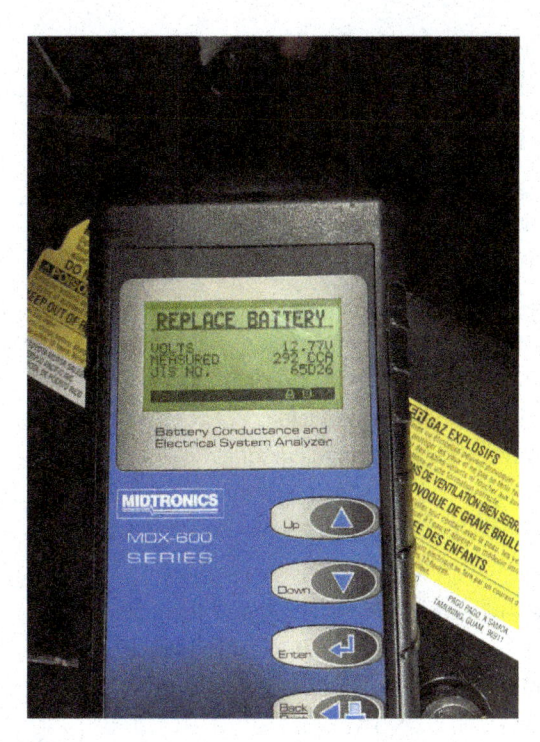

FIGURE 9–5 The JIS battery rating is stamped into the top of the battery.

JIS JIS stands for Japanese Industrial Standard. This rating standard can be found on AGM batteries found in Toyota and Nissan vehicles. It is important to use battery test equipment that includes this rating system when determining the functionality of the battery. ● **SEE FIGURE 9–5**.

BATTERY SERVICE SAFETY PRECAUTIONS

HAZARDS Batteries contain acid and release explosive gases (hydrogen and oxygen) during normal charging and discharging cycles.

SAFETY PROCEDURES To help prevent physical injury or damage to the vehicle, always adhere to the following safety procedures.

1. When working on any electrical component on a vehicle, disconnect the negative battery cable from the battery. When the negative cable is disconnected, all electrical circuits in the vehicle will be disabled, which will prevent accidental electrical contact between an electrical component and ground. Any electrical spark has the potential to cause explosion and personal injury.
2. Wear eye protection (goggles preferred) when working around any battery.

LOW-VOLTAGE BATTERIES AND STOP-START MICRO HYBRIDS

> **? FREQUENTLY ASKED QUESTION**
>
> **What Does "EN" and "DIN" Mean?**
>
> Many students trying to find the specifications for load testing a 12-volt battery on a European vehicle often run into two classifications:
>
> - **EN**—EN is short for European Norm. The European Norm is an agreement between the countries in Europe to consolidate the specification of standards to enhance the efficiency of commerce. In Europe, EN standards are gradually being adopted as a more uniform alternative to many different national standards. This EN standard has been applied to automotive batteries.
>
> - **DIN**—DIN stands for the Deutsches Institut für Normung. Recognized by the German Federal Government as Germany's national standards body, DIN has been a member of the International Organization for Standardization (ISO) since 1951. While these standards were developed for Germany, many of their automotive standards have been used to develop EN standards, but they are not always the same. It is important to remember that EN standards are for all of Europe and not just for one country. It is also important to note that there are some DIN battery part numbers, originally for German manufactured cars, that do not have a corresponding EN part number.

3. Wear protective clothing to avoid skin contact with battery acid.
4. Always adhere to all safety precautions as stated in the service procedures for the equipment used for battery service and testing.
5. Never smoke or use an open flame around any battery.
6. Never stand near a battery that is being jump started, especially in cold weather because the battery could explode.

12-VOLT BATTERY VOLTAGE TEST

STATE OF CHARGE Testing the battery voltage with a voltmeter is a simple method for determining the state of charge (SOC) of any battery. ● **SEE FIGURE 9–6**.

FIGURE 9–6 (a) A voltage reading of 12.28 volts indicates that the battery is not fully charged and should be charged before testing. (b) A battery that measures 12.6 volts or higher after the surface charge has been removed is 100% charged.

STATE OF CHARGE (SOC)	BATTERY VOLTAGE
Fully charged	12.6 volts or higher
75% charged	12.4 volts
50%	12.2 volts
25%	12.0 volts
Discharged	11.9 volts or lower

CHART 9–1

A comparison showing the relationship between battery voltage and SOC.

The voltage of a battery does not necessarily indicate whether the battery can perform satisfactorily, but it does indicate to the technician more about the battery's condition than a simple visual inspection. A battery that "looks good" may not be good. This test is commonly called a *terminal voltage test* or an *open circuit battery voltage test* because it is conducted with an open circuit, no current flowing, and no load applied to the battery.

1. If the battery has just been charged or the vehicle has recently been driven, it is necessary to remove the surface charge from the battery before testing. A surface charge is a charge of higher-than-normal voltage that is just on the surface of the battery plates. The surface charge is quickly removed when the battery is loaded, and therefore, does not accurately represent the true SOC of the battery.

2. To remove the surface charge, turn the headlights on high beam for 1 minute, then turn the headlights off and wait for 2 minutes. With the engine and all electrical accessories off, and the doors shut (to turn off the interior lights), connect a voltmeter to the battery posts. Connect the red positive lead to the positive post and the black negative lead to the negative post.

3. Read the voltmeter and compare the results with SOC shown in ● **CHART 9–1**. The voltages shown are for a battery at or near room temperature (70°F to 80°F, or 21°C to 27°C).

12-VOLT BATTERY LOAD TESTING

TERMINOLOGY One test to determine the condition of any 12-volt battery is the **load test**. Most automotive starting and charging testers use a carbon pile to create an electrical load on the battery. The amount of the load is determined by the original CCA rating of the battery, which should be at least 75% charged before performing a load test.

TEST PROCEDURE To perform a battery load test, take the following steps:

STEP 1 Determine the CCA rating of the battery. The proper electrical load used to test a battery is one-half of the CCA rating or three times the ampere-hour rating, with a minimum 150-ampere load.

STEP 2 Connect the load tester to the battery. Follow the instructions for the tester being used.

STEP 3 Apply the load for a full 15 seconds. Observe the voltmeter during the load testing and check the voltage at the end of the 15-second period while the battery is still under load. A good battery should indicate above 9.6 volts.

STEP 4 Repeat the test. Many battery manufacturers recommend performing the load tests twice, using the first load period to remove the surface charge on the battery and the second test to provide a truer indication of the condition of the battery. Wait 30 seconds between tests to allow time for the battery to recover.

RESULTS: If the battery fails the load test, recharge the battery and retest. If the load test is failed again, the battery needs to be replaced. ● **SEE FIGURE 9–7.**

FIGURE 9–7 The carbon pile tester can be used to test a flooded battery.

12-VOLT BATTERY CONDUCTANCE TESTING

TERMINOLOGY General Motors, Chrysler, Honda, and Ford specify that an electronic conductance tester be used to test batteries in vehicles still under factory warranty. Conductance is a measure of how well a battery can create current. This tester sends a small signal through the battery and measures a part of the AC response. As a battery ages, the plates can become sulfated and shed active materials from the grids, reducing the battery capacity. Conductance testers can be used to test flooded or AGM-type batteries. The unit can determine the following information about a battery:

- Tested CCA
- State of charge
- Voltage of the battery
- Defects such as shorts and opens
- Most conductance testers also display an internal resistance value

However, a conductance tester is not designed to accurately determine the SOC or CCA rating of a new battery. Unlike a battery load test, a conductance tester can be used on a battery that is discharged. This type of tester should only be used to test batteries that have been in service. ● **SEE FIGURE 9–8**.

TEST PROCEDURE To test a battery using an electronic conductance tester, perform the following steps.

STEP 1 Connect the unit to the positive and negative terminals of the battery. If testing a side post battery, always use the lead adapters and *never* use steel bolts as these can cause an incorrect reading.

NOTE: Test results can be incorrectly reported on the display if proper, clean connections to the battery are not made. Also be sure that all accessories and the ignition switch are in the off position.

STEP 2 Enter the CCA rating (if known).

STEP 3 The tester determines and displays the measured CCA of the battery as well as SOC and the voltage, plus one of the following:

- Good battery. The battery can return to service.
- Charge and retest. Fully recharge the battery and return it to service.
- Replace the battery. The battery is not serviceable and should be replaced.
- Bad cell—replace. The battery is not serviceable and should be replaced.

Some conductance testers can check the charging and cranking circuits, too.

12-VOLT BATTERY CHARGING

CHARGING PROCEDURE If the SOC of a battery is low, it must be recharged. It is best to slow charge any battery to prevent possible overheating damage to the battery. Perform the following steps.

STEP 1 Determine the charge rate. The charge rate is based on the current SOC and charging rate. ● **SEE CHART 9–2** for the recommended charging rate.

STEP 2 Connect a battery charger to the battery. Be sure the charger is not plugged in when connecting to a battery. Always follow the battery charger's instructions for proper use.

STEP 3 Set the charging rate. The initial charge rate should be about 35 amperes for 30 minutes to help start the charging process. Fast charging a battery increases the temperature of the battery and can cause warping of the plates inside the battery. Fast charging also increases the amount of gassing (release of hydrogen and oxygen), which can create a health and fire hazard. The battery temperature should not exceed 125°F (hot to the touch).

- Fast charge: 15 A maximum
- Slow charge: 5 A maximum

FIGURE 9–8 A conductance tester is very easy to use and has proved to accurately determine battery condition if the connections are properly made. Follow the instructions on the display for best results.

OPEN CIRCUIT VOLTAGE	STATE OF CHARGE (SOC) (%)	@60 A (MIN.)	@50 A (MIN.)	@40 A (MIN.)	@30 A (MIN)	@20 A (MIN.)	@20 A (MIN.)
12.6	100	N.A. (Fully charged)	N.A. (Fully charged)	N.A. (Fully charged)	N.A. (Fully charged)	N.A. (Fully charged)	N.A. (Fully charged)
12.4	75	15	20	27	35	48	90
12.2	50	35	45	55	75	95	180
12.0	25	50	65	85	115	145	260
11.8	0	65	85	110	150	195	370

CHART 9–2

Battery charging guidelines are based on the SOC of the battery and the charging rate.

CHARGING AGM BATTERIES

Charging an AGM battery requires a different charger than is used to recharge a flooded-type battery. ● **SEE FIGURE 9–9**. The differences include the following:

- The AGM can be charged with high current, up to 75% of the ampere-hour rating due to lower internal resistance.
- The charging voltage has to be kept at or below 14.4 volts to prevent damage.

Because most conventional battery chargers use a charging voltage of 16 volts or higher, a charger specifically designed to charge AGM batteries must be used. AGM batteries are often used as auxiliary batteries in hybrid electric vehicles when the battery is located inside the vehicle.

BATTERY CHARGE TIME

The time needed to charge a completely discharged battery can be estimated by using the reserve capacity rating of the battery in minutes divided by the charging rate.

Hours needed to charge the battery = Reserve capacity/Charge current

For example, if a 10-ampere charge rate is applied to a discharged battery that has a 90-minute reserve capacity, the time needed to charge the battery will be 9 hours.

90 minutes/10 amperes = 9 hours

THE 36-48-VOLT BATTERY

PURPOSE AND FUNCTION

The 36-48-volt battery is used to drive the integrated starter generator (ISG) unit. The ISG unit is used on vehicles where the starter and alternator are integrated into a single unit. The 36-48-volt battery system uses a DC-DC converter to charge the 12-volt battery.

CONSTRUCTION AND DESIGN

Typically 36-48-volt batteries are of lithium-ion design. In many cases the battery is integrated into a single module with other components. For example, the Chrysler/Ram eTorque 48-volt battery is incorporated into a power pack unit that contains the battery, contactors, the DC-DC converter, and the power pack control module. These modules are generally located within the passenger compartment. A few manufacturers, such as Mercedes, locate the 48-volt battery under the hood. ● **SEE FIGURE 9–10**.

FIGURE 9–9 This battery charger has settings for both a flooded battery and an AGM battery.

FIGURE 9–10 The 48-volt battery for the Ram eTorque system is incorporated into a power pack module that is located under the rear seat.

Early designs, such as the Chevrolet/GMC hybrid pickup truck used three VRLA connected in series to achieve a nominal voltage of 36 volts and a charging voltage of 42 volts.

DIAGNOSIS AND TESTING
The diagnosis of the 36-48-volt battery is dependent on the design. Early designs that use multiple 12-volt lead-acid batteries simply separate the batteries and test them individually like any other lead-acid battery. Vehicles that utilize 36-48-volt batteries that are lithium-ion rely on the hybrid or battery control module to continuously monitor the condition of the battery. When the control module detects a battery that is outside of normal operating range, a code is set and a warning indicator is illuminated. A scan tool and the manufacturers diagnostic procedure is used to determine the correct course of repair.

STOP-START DEFINED

PURPOSE AND FUNCTION
Stop-start systems can be categorized as either mild or micro hybrids based on their design and operating voltage. The main feature of either design is the idle-stop mode, in which the **internal combustion engine (ICE)** is stopped, rather than idling while stopped in traffic. The idle-stop mode improves the fuel economy slightly and reduces tailpipe emissions allowing manufacturers to meet emission standards. Other features, such as power assist and regenerative braking, can be part of the system based on the design.

TERM USED
Depending on the manufacturer, the term stop-start and start-stop are used to describe the technologies. A stop-start system may be called different names depending on the vehicle manufacturer. Those names are as follows:

- Stop-Start—GM and many others
- Idle-Stop—Honda
- Start-Stop—Audi/VW
- Smart Stop—Toyota
- Intelligent Stop & Go—Kia
- Auto Start/Stop—BMW
- Engine Stop-Start—FCA/Stellantis

STOP-START SYSTEMS

BAS SYSTEM
The **belt alternator starter (BAS)** system was the most common early stop-start system. The BAS system was the least expensive system that can be used and still claim that the vehicle is a hybrid. For many buyers, cost was a major concern and the BAS system allows certain hybrid features without the cost associated with an entire redesign of the engine and powertrain. Consumers were be able to upgrade from conventional models to BAS hybrids at a reasonable cost and will get slightly better fuel economy. The system was available on the Saturn VUE Hybrid, and the Chevrolet Malibu Hybrid.

The BAS concept is to replace the belt-driven alternator with an electric motor that serves as a generator and a motor. When the engine is running the motor, acting as a generator, it will charge a separate 36-volt battery (42-volt charging voltage). When the engine needs to be started again after the engine has been stopped at idle to save fuel (idle stop), the BAS motor is used to crank the engine by taking electrical power from the 36-volt battery pack and applies its torque via the accessory belt, and cranks the engine instead of using the starter motor.

NOTE: A BAS system uses a conventional starter motor for starting the ICE the first time, and only uses the high-voltage motor-generator to start the ICE when leaving idle-stop mode.

The motor-generator is larger than a standard starter motor so more torque can be generated in the cranking mode, also referred to as the motoring mode. The fast rotation of the BAS allows for quicker starts of the engine and makes the start/stop operation possible. Having the engine shut off when the vehicle is at a stop saves fuel. Of course, the stopping of the engine does create a sense that the engine has stalled, which is a common concern to drivers unfamiliar with the operation of hybrid vehicles.

A typical BAS system would achieve an 8% to 15% increase in fuel economy, mostly affecting the city mileage with little, if any, effect on the highway mileage. ● **SEE FIGURES 9-11 AND 9-12.**

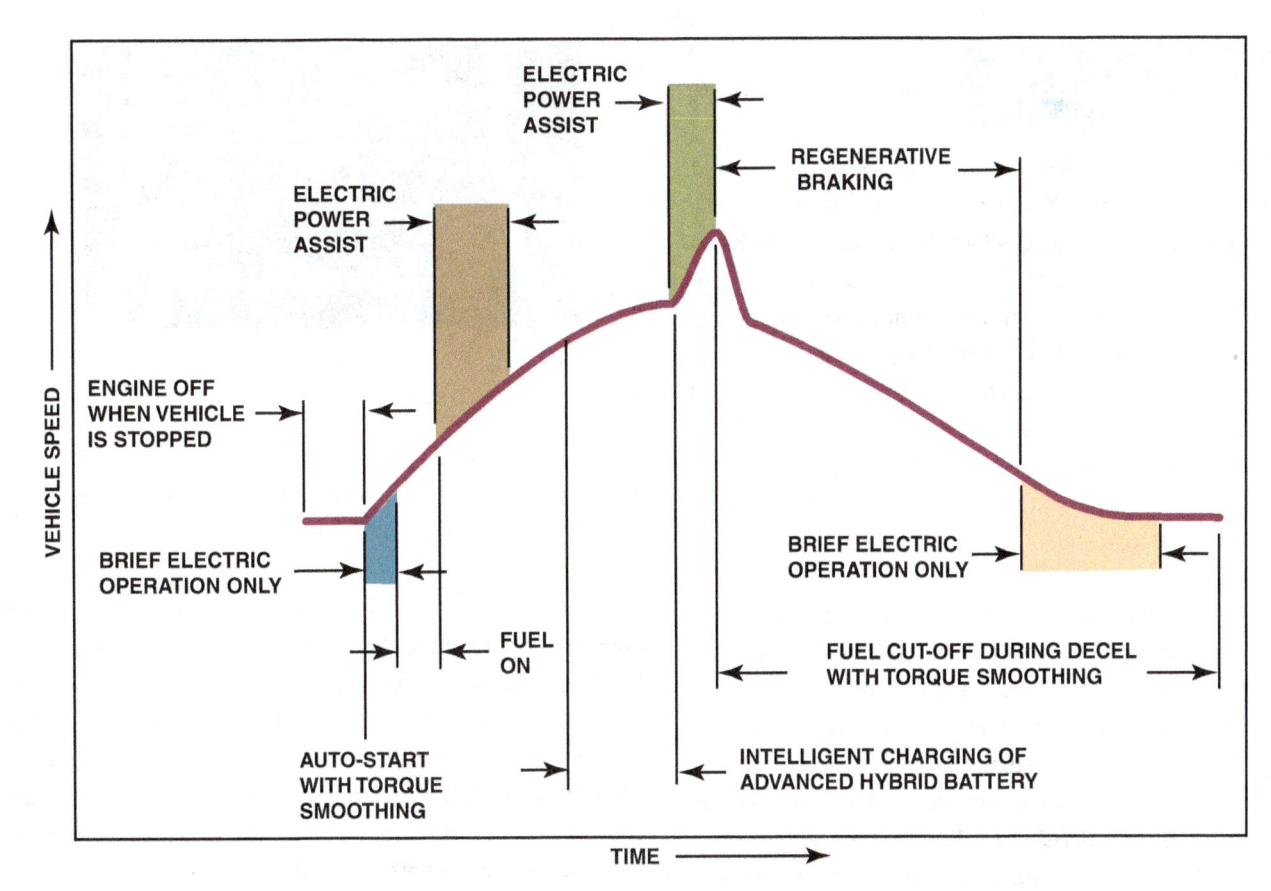

FIGURE 9–11 This figure shows what is occurring during various driving conditions in a BAS-type hybrid.

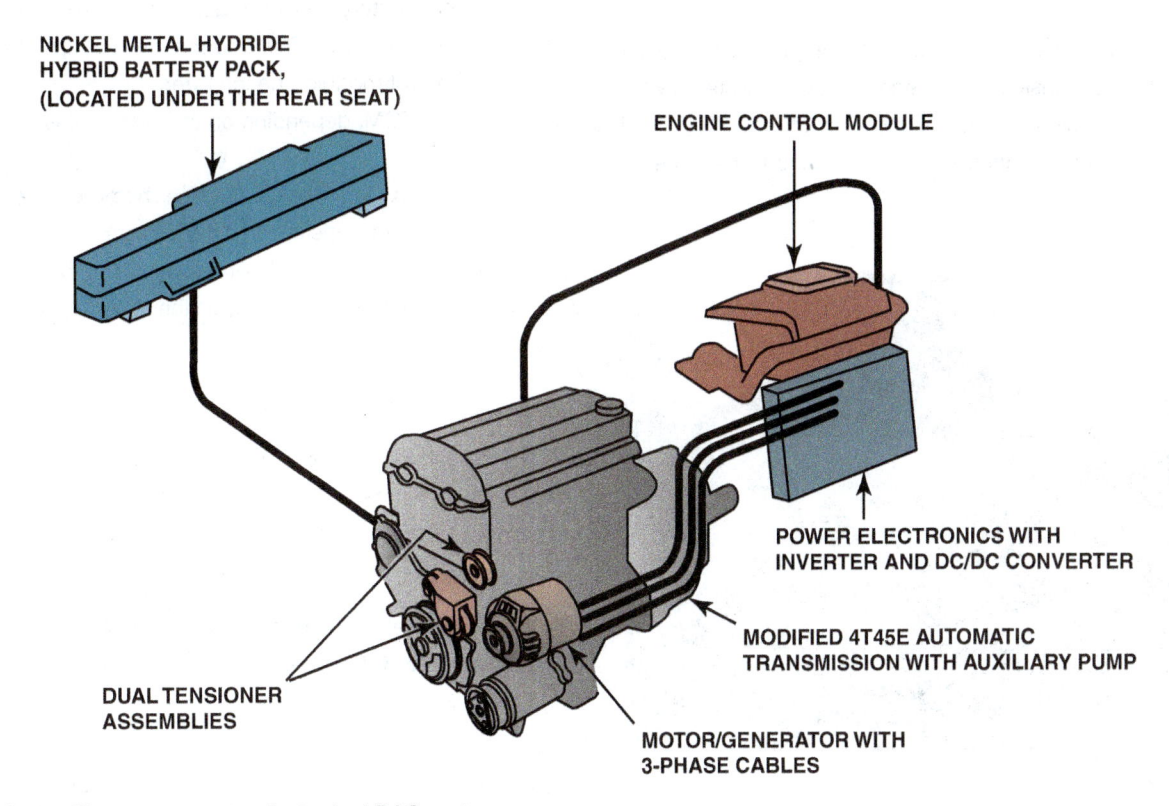

FIGURE 9–12 The components of a typical BAS system.

LOW-VOLTAGE BATTERIES AND STOP-START MICRO HYBRIDS **111**

MICRO HYBRIDS

PARTS INVOLVED A micro hybrid utilizes a stop-start system that operates on a 12-volt system and does not contain any high-voltage components. When the enabling conditions are met at a stop, the engine will shut off. During the engine off period, the 12-volt system will maintain vehicle operation including climate control, power steering, and brakes to keep the occupants comfortable and safe. The system will engage the starter motor to restart the engine when the driver releases the brake pedal. The system will automatically restart the engine if the system voltage or monitored conditions fall below minimum thresholds.

OPERATION A micro-hybrid system relies on a number of modules and enhanced components, depending on the make and model to operate. The heart of the system is an enhanced starter and heavy-duty flywheel as well as a second 12-volt battery. The micro-hybrid system also has a system disable button that allows the driver to turn off the feature when it is not desired. ● **SEE FIGURE 9–13.** The instrument cluster has an indicator that will illuminate when the system is disabled. ● **SEE FIGURE 9–14.** The default operation of the system is enabled on a restart.

ENGINE CONTROL MODULE The **engine control module (ECM)** is responsible for all engine control systems when the engine is running. When the engine is off, the ECM monitors the accelerator pedal position sensor, crankshaft position sensor, brake booster vacuum, brake pedal position, hood ajar switch, and engine coolant temperature.

FIGURE 9–13 The button on the left allows the driver to disable the stop-start feature for the drive cycle.

FIGURE 9–14 The indicator on the instrument cluster indicates the stop-start feature has been disabled.

TRANSMISSION CONTROL MODULE The **transmission control module (TCM)** monitors the range selector switch to determine what gear the driver has selected. This information is shared with the ECM. The TCM controls an additional electric transmission oil pump (if equipped) during the engine off mode of operation. The transmission also monitors the transmission output speed sensor if this input is used to determine vehicle speed.

INTELLIGENT BATTERY SENSOR MODULE If equipped, the intelligent battery sensor is used to measure battery voltage, current, and SOC. This information may be shared with the body control module, the intelligent power module or sent directly to the ECM, depending on the system design.

BODY CONTROL MODULE The **body control module (BCM)** monitors the operation of the climate control system as well as the driver's door switch and driver's seat belt. If the AC is on "MAX" or the driver's door is open the start-stop feature will be disabled.

MANUAL TRANSMISSION EQUIPPED VEHICLES When the vehicle comes to a complete stop and the transmission is placed in neutral with the clutch pedal released, and all other criteria are met, the engine will shut off. The engine will restart when the clutch pedal is depressed.

NOTE: If the vehicle comes to a stop and the driver keeps the clutch pedal depressed, the engine will not shut off.

HEAVY-DUTY STARTER A conventional starter is designed with a life cycle of less than 50,000 start cycles. A heavy-duty starter designed for a stop-start system is

FIGURE 9–15 The starter on this Jeep Compass is designed to last longer than a standard starter motor.

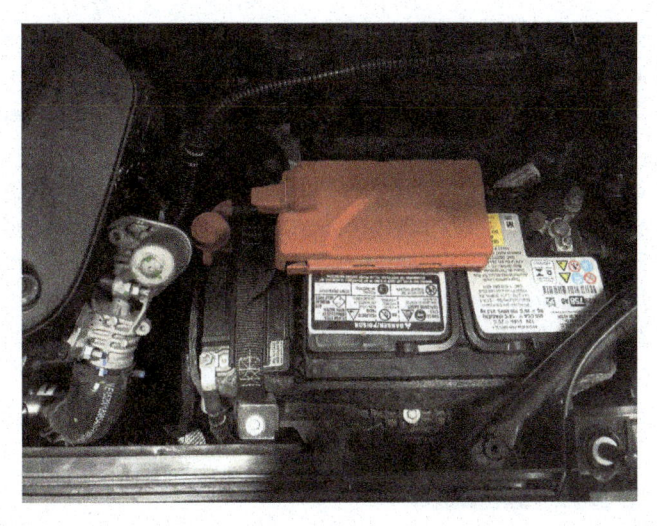

FIGURE 9–16 This Jeep Compass has two batteries under the hood. The smaller battery is used to maintain voltage during starting.

designed with a life cycle of over 300,000 start cycles. The design typically includes the following upgrades.

- Long life brushes
- Long life bearings
- Hardened gears
- Upgraded armatures and commutators

The starter system also includes a flywheel with stronger teeth and higher quality battery cables between the battery and the starter. ● **SEE FIGURE 9–15**.

BATTERIES Most 12-volt stop-start systems have two batteries. The main, or primary, battery supplies power to the starter during all cranking events. The secondary, or auxiliary, battery powers vehicle electrical loads except the starter during cranking. The secondary battery is smaller and may be an AGM battery based on the location. ● **SEE FIGURE 9–16**. Both batteries have more of a deep cycle capacity that can endure the frequent draws from the starter motor and the systems operating during the engine off periods. Ensure the batteries are electrically separated before testing to ensure that one battery does not affect the test results of the other.

ULTRACAPACITORS An **ultracapacitor** delivers a quick burst of energy during peak power demands. Some models use an ultracapacitor to help restart the engine. ● **SEE FIGURE 9–17**. Ultracapacitors store energy in an electrical field and can be rapidly charged and discharged many times. The ultracapacitors are switched on in series with the battery during the cranking event. This keeps the system voltage above 10 volts, which allows all systems to maintain normal operation and prevents modules from resetting.

AUXILIARY COMPONENTS Some models are equipped with auxiliary electric coolant pumps to help maintain engine

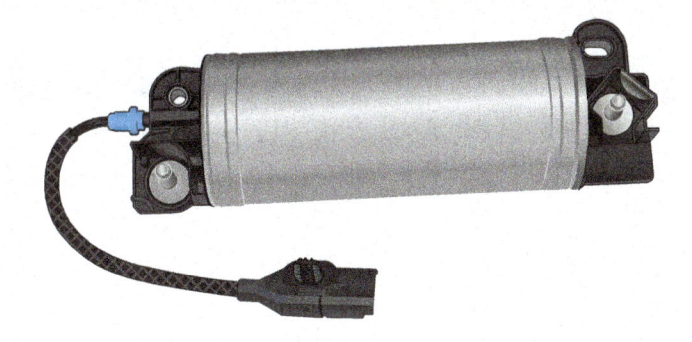

FIGURE 9–17 This ultracapacitor manufactured by Continental is an example of a system used in stop-start systems by General Motors.

cooling and aid in keeping the passenger compartment warm in colder temperatures. Some engines may be equipped with special engine mounts that help dampen the vibrations created during the cranking events. The alternator may have a higher amperage output than a vehicle without a stop-start system to ensure both the primary and secondary battery stay charged. The climate control system may have additional humidity and temperature sensors to monitor passenger compartment temperature during the shutdown period.

DIAGNOSIS

FIRST STEPS FIRST There are many key safety conditions that will cause the stop-start system to become disabled. Before beginning diagnosis ensure one or more of these conditions do not exist. On many vehicles, an open door, an unlatched hood, or unbuckled driver's seat belt latch will disable the system. When the climate control system is placed in MAX AC mode or the transmission is taken out of drive, the system is disabled. When a 4 × 4 truck is placed in low range or is placed in towing mode, the system is disabled. These are not system failures but rather driver education concerns. The technician may be able to view the start-stop disable reason on a scan tool to confirm the condition. ● SEE FIGURE 9–18.

DIAGNOSIS PROCEDURE To begin stop-start system diagnosis refer to the flowchart. Not all faults may illuminate a warning lamp on the instrument panel.

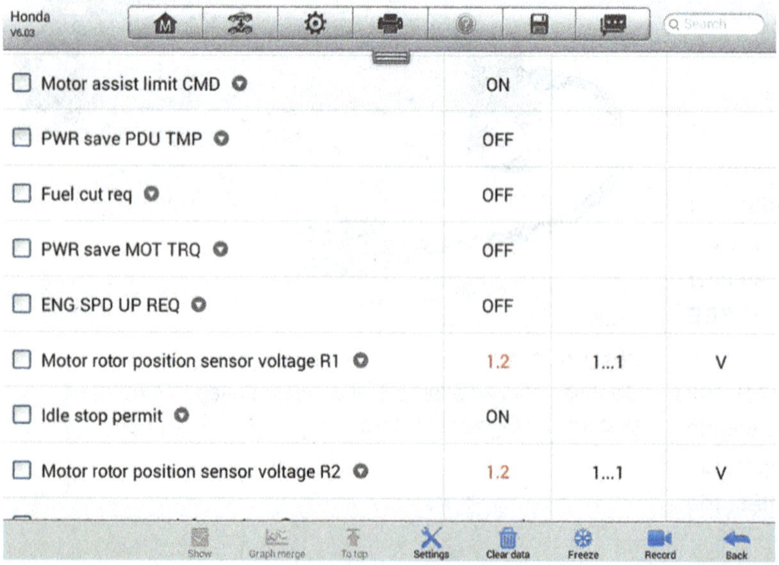

FIGURE 9–18 The PIDs displayed on the scan tool may indicate why the start-stop system is disabled.

Step 1	Ignition On	
	Test battery for greater than 12v	If 12v or less – test battery
Step 2	If greater than 12 volts	
	Verify no DTCs in modules	DTCs present – refer to DTC list
Step 3	If no DTCs	
	Verify proper operation of stop-start system. Drive vehicle under conditions for stop-start	
Step 4	If vehicle does not auto stop	
	Observe scan tool auto stop **Disable Reason**	Observe scan tool for auto stop **Inhibit Reason**

Diagnostic trouble codes that are associated with the 12-volt stop–start systems can refer to issues with the starter relay, the intelligent battery sensor module, network communications, and various switch inputs. Examples on these DTCs include:

- P0615: Starter Relay Control Circuit
- P058A: Battery Monitor Module Performance
- U135C: Lost Communication with the Stop-Start Control Module
- B3006: Hood Ajar Circuit Open
- P0556: Brake Booster Pressure Sensor Performance

The codes associated with the stop-start system are not all going to be found in a single module. It is important to perform a complete module scan when looking for DTCs to ensure that nothing is overlooked. Before beginning diagnostics for codes associated with the stop-start system, review the technical service bulletins for updated information. Many conditions may have been addressed with revised parts and updated programming. Scan tool data PIDs may help identify these conditions.

The replacement of some parts will require a reset or relearn process before the system will operate normally. A battery replacement is a common example of this condition. After the battery is replaced, a vehicle with a battery sensor module will need to be reset. Failure to reset the module may cause unwanted over charging results.

Stop-start systems may require special test procedures when performing other routine tests. For example: In order to perform a compression test or a relative compression test on some models, the vehicle must be placed in a special bi directional control mode with a scan tool. ● SEE FIGURE 9–19.

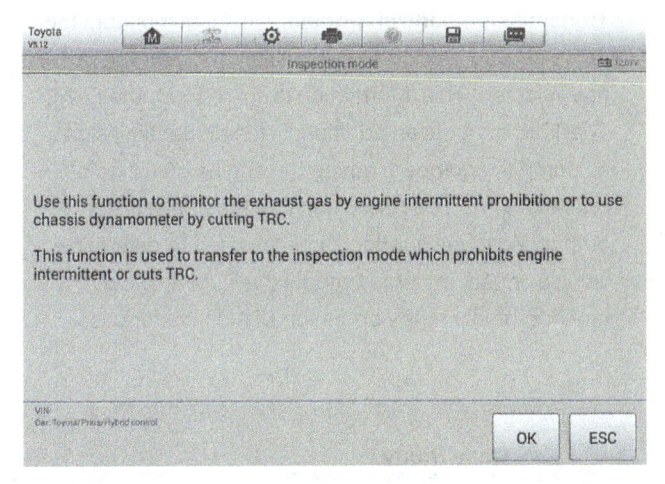

FIGURE 9–19 The scan tool is used to place the vehicle in the required mode to perform specific service procedures.

FIGURE 9–21 The electric motor on a Honda IMA system is mounted between the engine and transmission.

MILD HYBRIDS

TERMINOLOGY A mild hybrid utilizes a stop-start system that operates on a voltage that is greater than normal system voltage. The voltage can vary from 36 to 144 volts, depending on the model. When the enabling conditions are met, the engine will shut off. During the engine off period, the 12-volt system will maintain vehicle operation including climate control, power steering, and brakes to keep the occupants comfortable and safe. The system will engage an electric motor to restart the engine when the driver releases the brake pedal. The electric motor can be located between the engine and transmission or mounted on the engine and connected with a belt and tensioner. ● **SEE FIGURES 9–20 AND 9–21.** On some models the electric motor can provide supplemental torque to the engine on acceleration to improve performance. The system will automatically restart the engine if the system voltage or monitored conditions fall beyond minimum thresholds.

PARTS AND OPERATION

- **Battery.** The high-voltage battery will be either nickel metal hydride or lithium-ion construction. The location of the battery will vary based on vehicle design. In many cases, because of the relatively small size, the battery is mounted under or behind a seat in passenger compartment of the vehicle. ● **SEE FIGURE 9–22.**
- **Electric motor.** Typically this is a permanent magnet motor. On start or auto start, it is used in motor mode to start the ICE. In generator mode it is used to recharge

FIGURE 9–20 The eTorque system on the Ram truck is mounted on the engine.

FIGURE 9–22 The battery in this Honda is located behind the back seat.

the high-voltage battery. On some models it can be used to supplement the ICE to supply additional torque to the powertrain.

- **Inverter/converter.** The inverter is used to convert AC voltage generated by the motor to DC voltage so that it can be stored in the high-voltage battery. The converter is used to step the high voltage down to system voltage to power all the systems on the vehicle. The inverter and converter may be housed together or mounted separately in the vehicle. ● SEE FIGURE 9–23.

- **High-voltage cables.** Blue or yellow cables are used on vehicles when the system voltage is below 60 volts. Orange cables are used on vehicles where the system voltage is above 60 volts. These cables are isolated from the vehicle chassis. Follow the service safety precautions outlined by the vehicle manufacturer when servicing these cables.

- **Engine control module.** The ECM is responsible for all engine control systems when the engine is running. When the engine is off, the ECM monitors the accelerator pedal position sensor, crankshaft position sensor, brake booster vacuum, brake pedal position, hood ajar switch, and engine coolant temperature.

- **Hybrid control module.** The **hybrid control module** is responsible for controlling the electric portion of the powertrain. This includes functions related to the high-voltage battery, the inverter, and converter. It communicates with the powertrain control module to send and receive critical information needed for the high-voltage operation. Some system designs include a dedicated high-speed data BUS between these modules.

- **Transmission control module.** The TCM monitors the range selector switch to determine what gear the driver has selected. This information is shared with the ECM. The TCM controls an additional electric transmission oil pump (if equipped) during the engine off mode of operation. The TCM also monitors the transmission output speed sensor if this input is used to determine vehicle speed. In a 4 × 4 model the TCM also may monitor for low range operation of the transfer case.

Case Study

Not All High-Voltage Problems Are a High-Voltage System Failure

A 2010 Honda Insight with a 1.3L hybrid engine was towed into the shop. The customer complained that the vehicle battery would not stay charged, and that the IMA and check engine lights were both illuminated. The customer also stated that the 12-volt battery had recently been replaced. A visual inspection of the vehicle confirmed that the IMA and Check Engine lights were both illuminated. ● SEE FIGURE 9-24. A scan tool was plugged into the data link connector (DLC) to check for codes. The scan tool was not able to communicate with any vehicle module. Further diagnosis indicated that there was no battery (B+) at pin 16 in the DLC and the fuse that provided power to that circuit was good. A review of the wiring diagrams revealed that the same fuse also provided power to the dome lights, cargo lights, and the motor control module (MCM). An additional visual inspection revealed that the dome lights and cargo lights were inoperative. After carefully jumping fused battery voltage (B+) to the back side of pin 16 at the DLC, the scan tool was able to communicate, the dome and cargo lights illuminated, and the IMA light went out. Additional testing revealed that the charging system was now operating. It was determined that the problem was internal to the fuse block. After the fuse block was replaced and the keys were relearned, all systems were verified to be operating as designed.

Summary:
- **Complaint**–The battery would not stay charged.
- **Cause**–An internal open in the fuse block.
- **Correction**–The fuse block was replaced and the keys were relearned which restored proper operation.

FIGURE 9–23 The inverter/converter assembly is located above the transmission with the orange cables connecting it to the transmission.

FIGURE 9–24 The Check IMA and Check Engine lights are both illuminated in the instrument cluster.

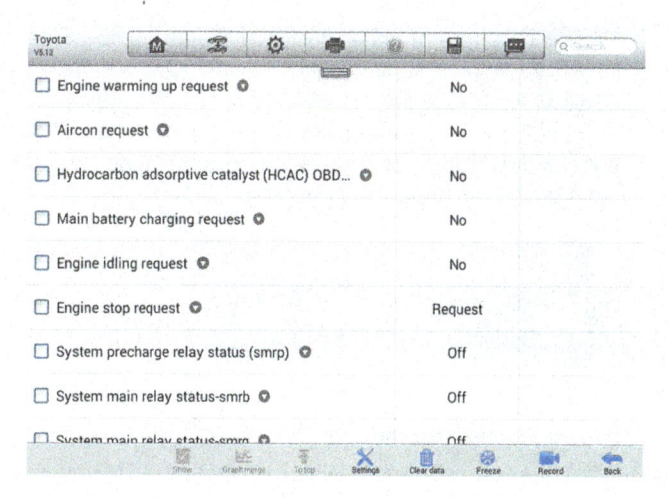

FIGURE 9–25 The PIDs displayed on the scan tool may help to identify the failed component or abnormal condition.

DIAGNOSIS AND TESTING Like a micro-hybrid stop-start system, there are many key safety conditions that will cause the mild-hybrid stop-start system to become disabled. Begin diagnosis by checking the battery and charging system for proper operation. A low-battery charge level is the number one reason for a stop-start system to become disabled.

The second step in the diagnostic process is to complete a module scan and check for codes in any of the modules associated with the stop-start system. If a code is present, the diagnostics should be followed. A review of the data PIDs in the modules associated with the stop-start system may also help identify an abnormal condition or failed component.
● **SEE FIGURE 9–25**. Review the service information for technical service bulletins, and recalls. Software updates are often associated with component replacements.

If the diagnosis reveals a failed high-voltage component, such as the battery, electric motor, inverter or converter, check the manufacturer recommended service procedures. These components are typically replaced and not repaired. High-voltage safety precautions must be followed when servicing these parts. This includes properly depowering the system, and the use of personal protective equipment, such as class "0" gloves and safety glasses.

> **TECH TIP**
>
> **Test Motor Before Replacing the Inverter**
>
> Before replacing a failed inverter, test the electric motor for any defects. It is relatively common for shorted electric motor windings to cause a failure of the inverter. The new inverter is likely to fail upon installation if the electric motor failure is not resolved first.

SUMMARY

1. The 12-volt battery may be either a flooded or absorbed glass mat (AGM) design based on location and manufacturer design.
2. The 12-volt battery capacity is rated in either cold-cranking amps, cranking amps, reserve capacity, or ampere hours.
3. Stop-start systems can be categorized as either mild or micro hybrids based on their design and operating voltage.
4. A micro hybrid stop-start system operates on 12 volts and a mild hybrid operates on 36–144 volts.

5. The main feature of either design is the idle-stop mode, in which the internal combustion engine (ICE) is stopped, rather than idling while in traffic.
6. The idle-stop mode improves the fuel economy slightly and reduces tailpipe emissions, allowing manufacturers to meet government regulatory targets.
7. A micro- or mild-hybrid powertrain will not move the vehicle in electric only mode.
8. Other features, such as power assist and regenerative braking, can be part of the system based on the manufacturer design.

REVIEW QUESTIONS

1. What are the differences between a flooded and an absorbed glass mat (AGM) style battery?
2. What are the differences when testing an AGM battery when compared to a flooded battery?
3. What are the main advantages of a micro- or mild-hybrid system?
4. Explain how a disable condition will prevent the stop-start system from operating.
5. What is the difference between a mild- and micro-hybrid vehicle?

CHAPTER QUIZ

1. A micro stop-start system operates on what voltage system?
   a. 12 volts
   b. 36 volts
   c. 144 volts
   d. 330 volts

2. A 12-volt battery can be rated for _____.
   a. cold-cranking amperes
   b. reserve capacity
   c. cranking amperes
   d. All the answers are correct

3. Load testing of an absorbed glass mat (AGM) battery is being discussed. Technician A says that a carbon pile tester can be used. Technician B says that a conductance tester must be used. Which technician is correct?
   a. Technician A only
   b. Technician B only
   c. Both Technicians A and B
   d. Neither Technician A nor Technician B

4. Which of the following conditions may disable a start-stop system?
   a. An open driver's door
   b. An air-conditioning system that is placed in the "Max Cold" position
   c. A transfer case that has been placed in the 4 × 4 low range
   d. All the answers are correct

5. Which module is responsible for the operation of a mild-hybrid operating system?
   a. Engine control module
   b. Transmission control module
   c. Hybrid control module
   d. All the answers are correct

6. Micro-hybrid vehicles are being discussed. Technician A says that micro-hybrid vehicles have two 12-volt batteries. Technician B says that some micro-hybrid vehicles have one 12-volt battery and an ultracapacitor. Which technician is correct?
   a. Technician A only
   b. Technician B only
   c. Both Technician A and B
   d. Neither Technicians A nor Technician B

7. What color are the covers on high-voltage cables when the voltage is above 12 volts and less than 60 volts?
   a. Yellow
   b. Blue
   c. Orange
   d. Yellow or Blue

8. The heavy-duty starter in a micro-hybrid vehicle is being discussed. Technician A says that the starter contains long-life bearings. Technician B says that the starter has hardened gears. Which technicians is correct?
   a. Technician A only
   b. Technician B only
   c. Both Technicians A and B
   d. Neither Technician A nor Technician B

9. What high-voltage components are typically found in a mild-hybrid vehicle?
   a. Electric motors
   b. Inverters and converters
   c. High-voltage battery
   d. All of the above

10. Diagnosis of a micro-hybrid stop-start system is being discussed. Technician A says that it is important to verify the concern because there are many conditions that will prevent the system from operating. Technician B states that the two batteries must be electrically separated before testing. Which technician is correct?
    a. Technician A only
    b. Technician B only
    c. Both Technicians A and B
    d. Neither Technician A nor Technician B

Chapter 10
HIGH-VOLTAGE BATTERIES

LEARNING OBJECTIVES

After studying this chapter, the reader should be able to:

- Prepare for ASE L3 certification test section "A" (Battery Systems).
- Discuss hybrid and electric vehicle high-voltage batteries.
- Describe nickel-metal hydride batteries and designs used in hybrid electric vehicles.
- Explain the operation of lithium-ion high-voltage batteries including the various types and designs.
- Discuss battery capacity versus vehicle range.
- Explain the need for high-voltage battery cooling and heating.
- Discuss battery capacity versus vehicle range.
- Discuss the high-voltage battery control components.
- Describe the purpose and function of the battery management system (BMS).
- Discuss the Electrical Distribution System (EDS).
- Explain the HEV high-voltage battery monitor.
- Discuss the factory authorized lithium-ion battery repair procedure.
- Describe battery degradation and balancing.

KEY TERMS

Active balancing 136
Battery density 126
Battery control module (BCM) 130
Battery management system (BMS) 131
Electrical Distribution System (EDS) 131
Guess-O-Meter (GOM) 129
Lithium iron phosphate (LiFePO$_4$) 125
Nickel, cobalt, and aluminum (NCA) 125
Nickel, manganese, and cobalt (NMC) 125
Nickel-metal hydride (NiMH) 120
MPGe 129
Passive balancing 136
Pouch cell 125
System Main Relays (SMRs) 130
Worldwide harmonized Light vehicles Test Procedure (WLTP) 129

HYBRID AND ELECTRIC VEHICLE HIGH-VOLTAGE BATTERIES

PURPOSE AND FUNCTION Hybrid electric vehicles (HEVs) use a dual-voltage electrical system.

- The high-voltage (HV) system is used to power the electric drive (traction) motor.
- A conventional 12-volt system is used to power all other aspects of vehicle operation.

One advantage to using this system is that the vehicle can use any conventional electrical accessories in its design.

NOTE: It is possible for an HEV to have three separate voltage systems. The Toyota Highlander HEV, for example, has a 12-volt auxiliary system, a 42-volt system for the electric power assist steering, and a 288-volt system for the hybrid drive.

ELECTRIC MOTOR REQUIREMENTS EVs and HEVs use high-output electric motors to drive and assist vehicle movement. These motors are rated anywhere from 10 to 50 kW for HEVs and as much as 450 kW for some EVs, so they consume large amounts of electrical power during operation. If a conventional 12-volt electrical system was used to power these motors, the amount of current flow required would be extremely large and the cables used to transmit this energy would also be so large as to be impractical. Also, the motors used in these systems would have large gauge windings and would be big and heavy relative to their power output. Automotive engineers overcome this problem by increasing the voltage provided to the motors, thus decreasing the amount of current that must flow to meet the motor's wattage requirements. (see Frequently Asked Question, "Why Do Higher Voltage Motors Draw Less Current?"). Smaller amounts of current flowing in the cables mean that the cables can be sized smaller, making it much more practical to place a battery in the rear of the vehicle and run cables from there to the drive motor in the engine compartment.
● **SEE FIGURE 10-1**.

The motors can also be made much smaller and more powerful when they are designed to operate on higher voltages.

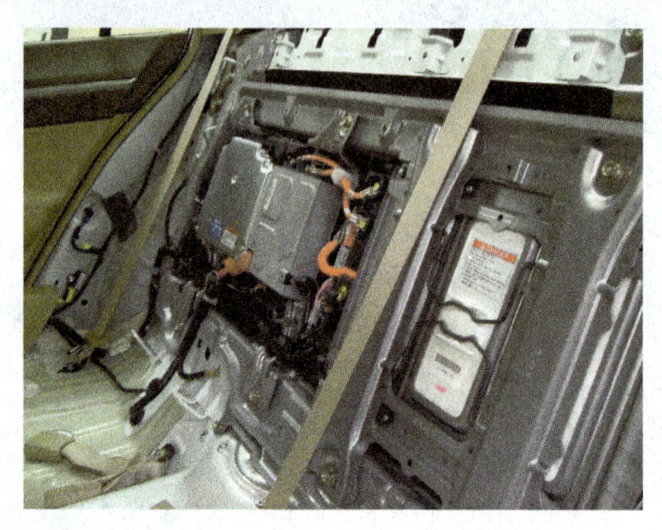

FIGURE 10-1 The high-voltage battery and motor controls are located behind the rear passenger's seat in a Honda.

NICKEL-METAL HYDRIDE BATTERIES

USES Most current production HEVs use **nickel-metal hydride (NiMH)** battery technology for the high-voltage battery. NiMH batteries are being used for these applications because of their performance characteristics, such as specific energy, cycle life, and safety. From a manufacturing perspective, the NiMH battery is attractive because the materials used in its construction are plentiful and recyclable.

DESCRIPTION AND OPERATION NiMH batteries have a positive electrode made of nickel hydroxide. The negative electrode is unique, in that it is a hydrogen-absorbing alloy, also known as a metal hydride. The electrolyte is an alkaline, usually potassium hydroxide. The nominal voltage of an NiMH battery cell is 1.2 volts.

ELECTROLYTE NiMH batteries are known as alkaline batteries due to the alkaline (pH greater than 7) nature of the electrolyte. The electrolyte is aqueous potassium hydroxide. Potassium hydroxide works well for this application because it does not corrode the other parts of the battery and can be housed in a sealed steel container. Also, potassium hydroxide does not take part in the chemical reaction of the battery, so the electrolyte concentration stays constant at any given state-of-charge. These factors help the NiMH battery achieve high-power performance and excellent cycle life. ● **SEE FIGURE 10-2**.

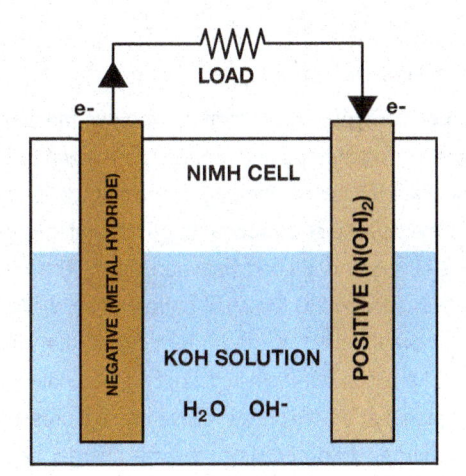

FIGURE 10-2 An NiMH cell. The unique element in a nickel metal hydride cell is the negative electrode which is a hydrogen-absorbing alloy. The positive electrode is nickel hydroxide. The electrolyte does not enter into the chemical reaction and is able to maintain a constant conductivity regardless of the state-of-charge of the cell.

OPERATION DURING CHARGING
During battery charging, hydrogen ions (protons) travel from the positive electrode to the negative electrode, where they are absorbed into the metal hydride material. The electrolyte does not participate in the reaction and acts only as a medium for the hydrogen ions to travel through.

OPERATION DURING DISCHARGING
When the battery is discharged, this process reverses, with the hydrogen ions (protons) traveling from the negative electrode back to the positive electrode. The density of the electrodes changes somewhat during the charge/discharge process, but this is kept to a minimum as only protons are exchanged during battery cycling. Electrode stability due to minimal density changes is one of the reasons why the NiMH battery has a very good cycle life.
● **SEE FIGURE 10-3**.

? FREQUENTLY ASKED QUESTION

Why Do Higher Voltage Motors Draw Less Current?

Keep in mind that an electric motor is powered by wattage. Every electric motor is rated according to the amount of power (in watts) it consumes. Power is calculated using the following formula:

$$P = I \times E$$

or

$$\text{Power (in watts)} = \text{Current (in amperes)} \times \text{Voltage (in volts)}$$

An electric motor rated at 144 watts will consume 12 amperes at 12 volts of applied voltage (12 volts × 12 amperes = 144 watts). If this same motor was powered with 6 volts, it would draw 24 amperes to achieve the same power output. This increase in current draw would require a much bigger cable to efficiently transmit the electric current and minimize voltage drop. The motor windings would also have to be much heavier to handle this increased current. Imagine that we power this same motor with a 144-volt battery. Now we require only 1 ampere of electrical current to operate the motor (144 volts × 1 ampere = 144 watts). The cable required to transmit this current could be sized much smaller and it will now be much easier to run the cables over the length of the car without significant power loss. Also, the electric motor can be made much smaller and more efficient when less current is needed to power it. Some hybrid systems have motors that operate at up to 650 volts in an effort to increase system efficiency.

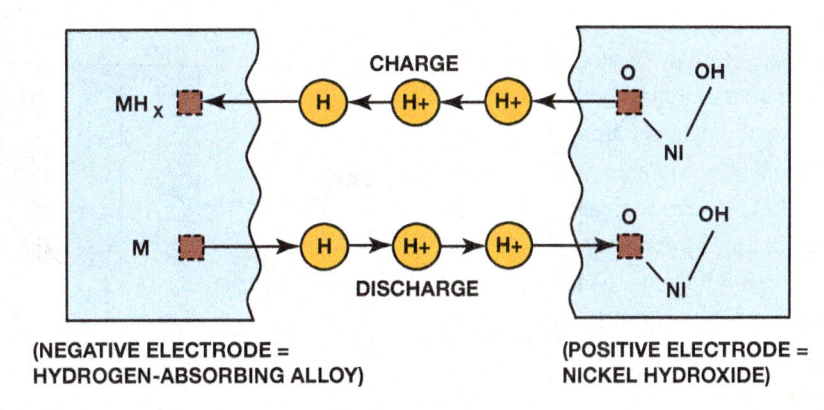

FIGURE 10-3 Chemical reactions inside an NiMH cell. Charging and discharging both involve an exchange of hydrogen ions (protons) between the two electrodes

ADVANTAGES Nickel-based alkaline batteries have a number of advantages over other battery designs. These include the following:

- High specific energy.
- The nickel electrode can be manufactured with large surface areas, which increase the overall battery capacity.
- The electrolyte does not react with steel, so NiMH batteries can be housed in sealed steel containers that transfer heat reasonably well.
- The materials used in NiMH batteries are environmentally friendly and can be recycled.
- Excellent cycle life.
- Durable and safe.

DISADVANTAGES Disadvantages of the NiMH battery include the following:

- High rate of self-discharge, especially at elevated temperatures.
- Moderate levels of memory effect, although this seems to be less prominent in newer designs.
- Moderate to high cost.

? FREQUENTLY ASKED QUESTION

How Is an Alkaline Battery Different from a Lead–Acid Battery?

Lead–acid batteries use sulfuric acid as the electrolyte, which acts as the medium between the battery's positive and negative electrodes. Acids have a pH that is below 7, and pure water has a pH of exactly 7. If electrolyte from a lead–acid battery is spilled, it can be neutralized using a solution of baking soda and water (an alkaline solution). Alkaline batteries use an electrolyte such as potassium hydroxide, which has a pH greater than 7. This means that the electrolyte solution is basic, which is the opposite of acidic. If an alkaline battery electrolyte is spilled, it can be neutralized using a solution of vinegar and water (vinegar is acidic). Both nickel-cadmium (Ni-Cd) and nickel-metal hydride (NiMH) batteries are alkaline battery designs.

NiMH BATTERY DESIGNS There are two primary designs for an NiMH battery cell. These are:

1. **Cylindrical type.** The cylindrical type has the active materials made in long ribbons and arranged in a spiral fashion inside a steel cylinder (case). The negative electrode is wound alongside the positive electrode, and the separator material holding the electrolyte is placed between them. The negative electrode is attached to the steel battery case, while the positive electrode attached to the (–) terminal at the top of the battery. There is a self-resealing safety vent located at the top of the battery case, which will relieve internal pressure in case of overcharge, short circuiting, reverse charge, or other abuse. Cylindrical cells are often constructed very similar to a conventional "D" cell. Cylindrical cells are most often incorporated into modules with a group of six cells connected in series. This creates a single battery module with a 7.2-volt output. Groups of these modules can then be connected in series to create higher voltage battery packs. ●**SEE FIGURE 10-4.**

2. **Prismatic type.** The prismatic type is a rectangular or boxlike design with the active materials formed into flat plates, much like a conventional lead–acid battery. The positive and negative plates are placed alternately in the battery case, with tabs used to connect the plate groups. Separator material is placed between the plates to prevent them from touching, but still allow electrolyte to circulate freely. ●**SEE FIGURE 10-5.**

BATTERY CELLS ARE CONNECTED IN SERIES Battery designers are limited by the nominal cell voltage of the battery technology. In the case of NiMH batteries, each cell is capable of producing only 1.2 volts. A high-voltage battery based on NiMH technology must be built using multiples of 1.2 volts. In order

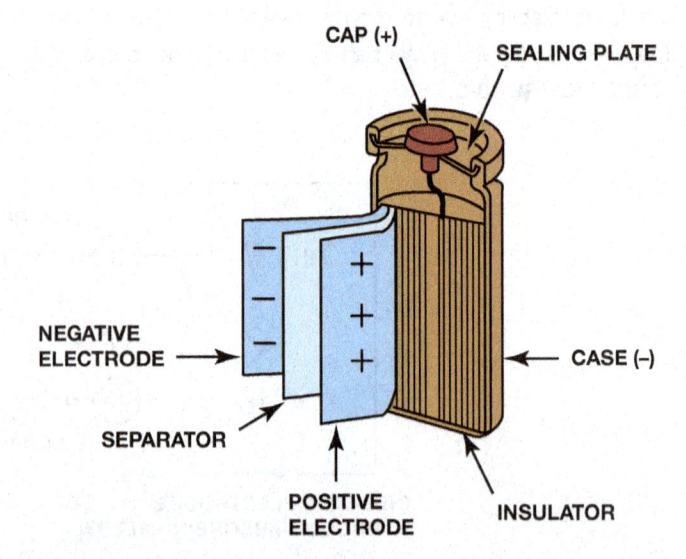

FIGURE 10-4 Cylindrical-type NiMH batteries are made with a stainless-steel housing.

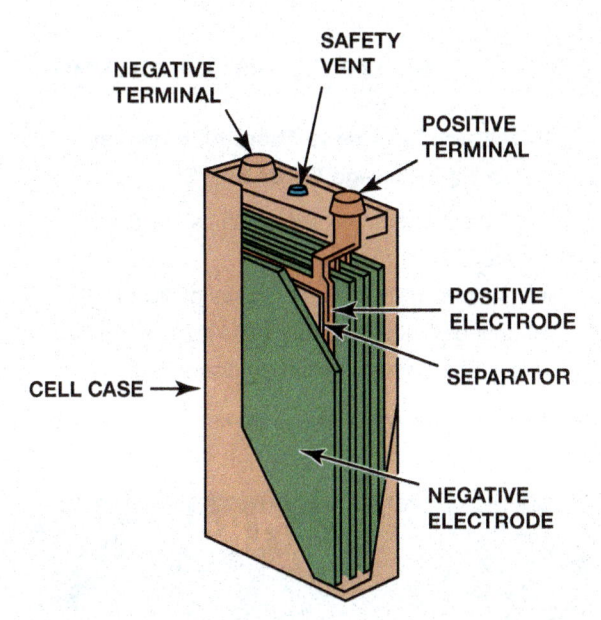

FIGURE 10-5 A prismatic NiMH cell. Prismatic cells are built with flat plates and separators similar to conventional lead–acid batteries.

to build a 144-volt battery, 114 individual NiMH cells must be connected together in series (144 × 1.2 volts). Obviously, the higher the voltage output of the battery, the greater the number of individual battery cells that must be used to achieve the necessary voltage. ● **SEE FIGURES 10-6, 10-7, AND 10-8**.

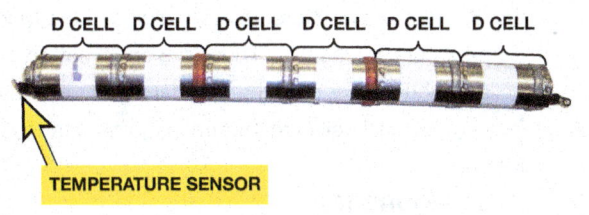

FIGURE 10-6 Each cell has 1.25 volts and a group of six as shown has 7.5 volts. These sections are connected to other sections to create the HV battery pack.

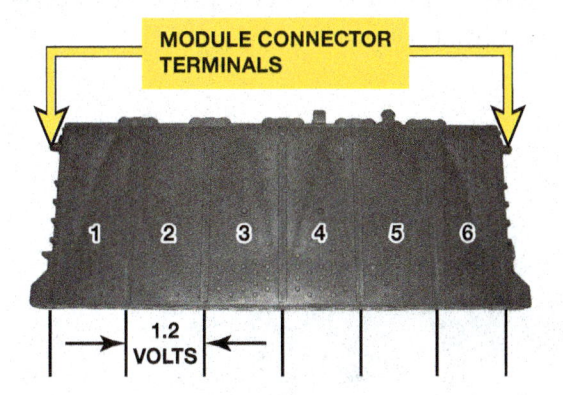

FIGURE 10-7 A prismatic NiMH module from a Toyota Prius HV battery pack. The battery posts are located on the left and right sides of the module. A self-resealing vent is located on the top right for venting hydrogen gas if the module overheats.

FIGURE 10-8 A Toyota Camry Hybrid HV battery pack.

LITHIUM-ION HIGH-VOLTAGE BATTERIES

USES A battery design that shows a great deal of promise for electric vehicles (EV) and hybrid electric vehicles (HEV) applications is lithium-ion (Li-ion) technology. Lithium-ion batteries have been used extensively in consumer electronics since the early 1990s and are currently used in most electric and plug-in hybrid electric vehicles (PHEVs).

DESCRIPTION A lithium-ion cell is named because during battery cycling, lithium ions move back and forth between the positive and negative electrodes. Lithium-ion has approximately twice the specific energy of nickel-metal hydride.

CONSTRUCTION The positive electrode in a conventional lithium-ion battery has lithium cobalt oxide as its main ingredient, with the negative electrode being made from a specialty carbon. The electrolyte is an organic solvent, and this is held in a separator layer between the two electrode plates. To prevent battery rupture and ensure safety, a pressure release valve is built into the battery housing that will release gas if the internal pressure rises above a preset point. ● **SEE FIGURE 10-9**.

OPERATION The lithium-ion cell is designed so that lithium ions can pass back and forth between the electrodes when the battery is in operation.

1. During battery discharge, lithium ions leave the anode (negative electrode) and enter the cathode (positive electrode) through the electrolyte and across the separator.

2. During charging, lithium ions leave the cathode and move through the electrolyte into the anode.

ADVANTAGES Lithium-ion batteries have the following advantages:

- High specific energy
- Good high temperature performance

HIGH-VOLTAGE BATTERIES 123

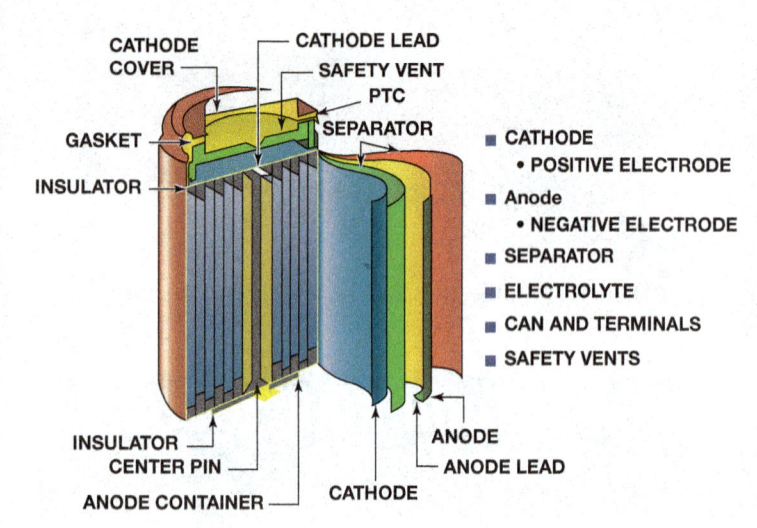

FIGURE 10-9 Construction of a cylindrical lithium-ion cell. Note the pressure relief valve and exhaust gas hole that will relieve internal battery pressure if it gets too hot.

- Low self-discharge
- Minimal memory effect
- High nominal cell voltage. The nominal voltage of a lithium-ion cell is 3.6 volts, which is three times that of nickel-based alkaline batteries. This allows for fewer battery cells being required to produce high voltage from an HV battery.

DISADVANTAGES Disadvantages of the lithium-ion battery include:

- High cost
- Issues related to battery overheating

NOTE: Early lithium-ion battery designs have experienced problems with thermal runaway, which has led to fire and even explosions. Lithium-ion battery packs in automotive applications are designed with cooling and safety systems that prevent overheating and isolate cell failures.

FREQUENTLY ASKED QUESTION

How Much Lithium Is There in a Typical Li-Ion High-Voltage EV Battery?

In a typical electric vehicle, such as the Tesla Model S, it is estimated that there is a total of about 15 pounds (7 kg) of lithium used in all of the cells. This is about the weight of a bowling ball.

DESIGNS OF LITHIUM-ION CELLS

CYLINDRICAL A cylindrical cell has high specific energy, good mechanical stability, and lends itself to automated manufacturing. Cylindrical cell design cycles well, offers a long life and is low cost, but it has less than ideal packaging density. The cylindrical cell design is used by many electric vehicle manufacturers such as Tesla.

Tesla, for example, uses several sizes of cylindrical cells including:

- 18650 cells manufactured by Panasonic in the Models S and X cars since 2012. These are small battery cells, slightly larger than the standard AA cells. The Tesla cylindrical cells are 18 mm in diameter and 65 mm tall.
  ● **SEE FIGURE 10-10**.
- Tesla Model 3 and Y use 2170 batteries, which are 21 mm in diameter and 70 mm tall.
- Tesla Cyber Truck uses 4680 cells which are 46 mm in diameter and 80 mm tall.

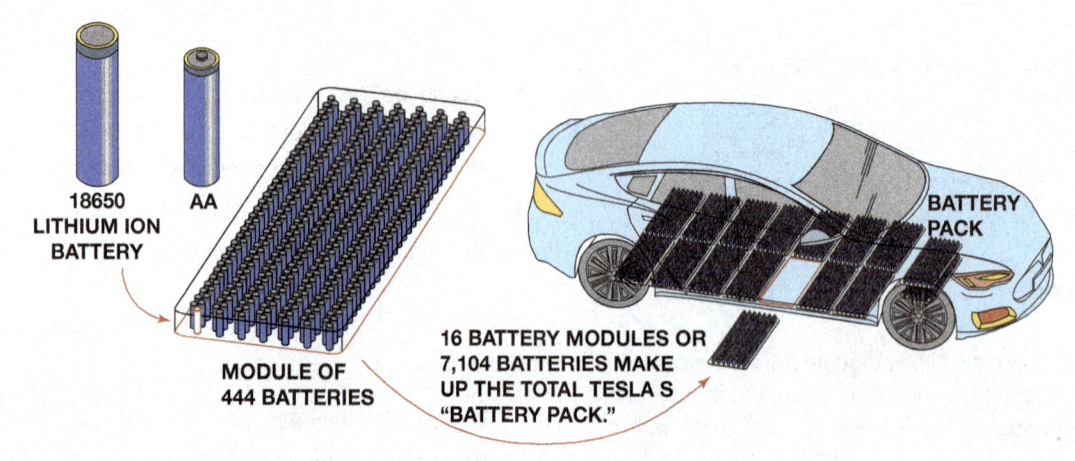

FIGURE 10-10 A Tesla Model S uses 7,104 18650 batteries located under the floor of the vehicle and weighs 1,200 pounds (544 kg).

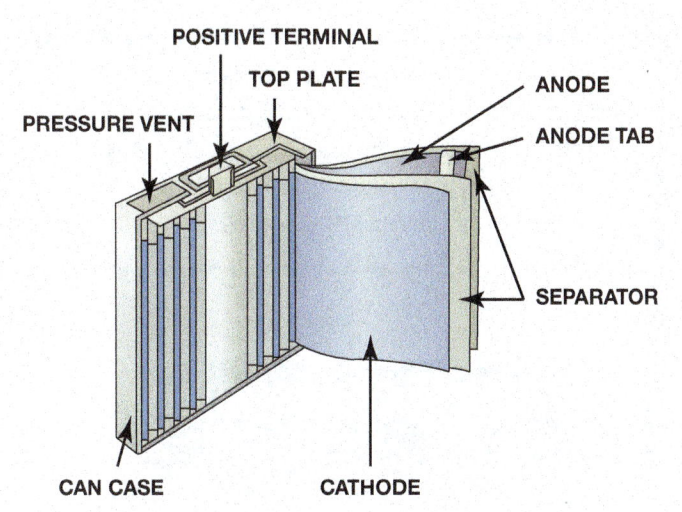

FIGURE 10-11 The prismatic type is a rectangular or boxlike design that allows them to be stacked close together to create a HV battery pack.

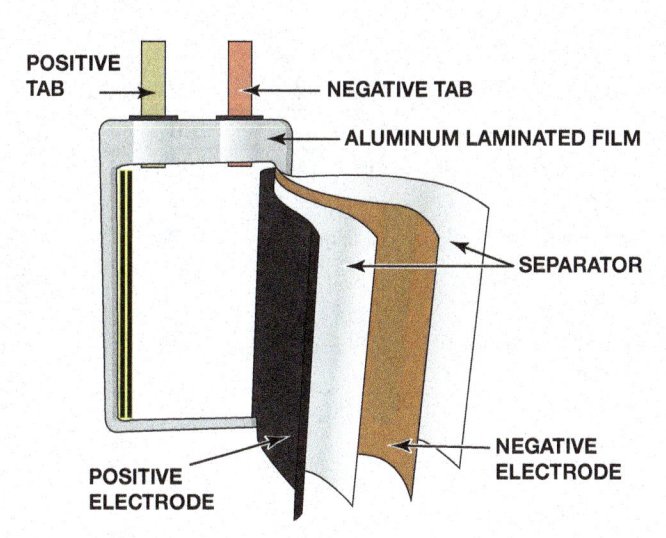

FIGURE 10-12 The pouch design uses a flexible outer container that is able to expand when being charged without damaging the battery.

PRISMATIC—HARD CASE
The prismatic type is a rectangular or boxlike design with the active materials formed into flat plates, much like a conventional lead–acid battery. The positive and negative plates are placed alternately in the battery case, with tabs used to connect the plate groups. Separator material is placed between the plates to prevent them from touching, but still allow electrolyte to circulate freely. ● **SEE FIGURE 10-11**.

PRISMATIC—POUCH TYPE
Pouch design HV battery uses laminated architecture in a bag referred to as **pouch cell**. It is light and cost-effective, but exposure to humidity and high temperature can shorten its life. The pouch cell offers a simple, flexible, and lightweight battery design. The pouch cell makes most efficient use of space and achieves 90–95% packaging efficiency, the highest among battery packs.

Eliminating the metal enclosure reduces weight, but the cell needs support and allowance to expand in the battery compartment. The pouch packs are used in consumer, military and automotive applications, and are used in the Jaguar I-Pace, Mustang Mach E, and the GMC Hummer EV electric vehicles. The General Motor's Ultium batteries are unique because of their large-format, pouch-style cells, which can be stacked vertically or horizontally inside the battery pack. No standardized pouch cells exist as each manufacturer designs its own. ● **SEE FIGURE 10-12**.

TYPES OF LITHIUM-ION BATTERIES

NUMEROUS MATERIALS
There are numerous types of lithium-ion batteries, and the list is growing. While every component of the battery is under development, the primary difference between the various designs is the materials used for the positive electrode or cathode. The original Li-ion cell design used lithium cobalt oxide for its cathode, which has good energy storage characteristics, but suffers chemical breakdown at relatively low temperatures. This failure results in the release of heat and oxygen, which often leads to a fire or explosion as the electrolyte ignites. In order to make lithium-ion batteries safer and more durable, a number of alternative cathode materials have been formulated.

CATHODE MATERIAL
Vehicle manufacturers use several different cathode materials:

- A combination of **nickel, manganese, and cobalt (NMC)** for the cathode material. This cathode material results in slightly lower energy, but is less volatile and can withstand variation in temperature.

  NOTE: This design of battery is used in the 48-volt mild-hybrid Ram truck.

- Tesla uses **nickel, cobalt, and aluminum (NCA)** cathode material, which results in a long battery life and faster charging capability.

- Another cathode design for automotive applications includes **lithium iron phosphate (LiFePO$_4$)**, which is stable at higher temperatures and does not contain cobalt, which is in limited supply worldwide.

The lithium iron phosphate battery is the most promising future battery and is constructed using lithium iron phosphate as the cathode, and a graphitic carbon electrode with a metallic backing as the anode. The lithium iron phosphate battery offers a longer life cycle, low cost, low toxicity, well-defined performance, and long-term stability making it a likely battery for use in future electric vehicles. ● **SEE CHART 10-1**.

CHART 10-1

CHEMICAL NAME	MATERIAL	ABBREVIATION
Lithium Cobalt Oxide	$LiCoO_2$	LCO
Lithium Nickel Cobalt Oxide	$LiNi_xCoyAl_zO_2$	LNCO
Lithium Nickel Manganese Cobalt Oxide	$LiNiMnCoO_2$	NMC
Lithium Manganese Oxide	$LiMn_2O_4$	LMO
Lithium Iron Phosphate	$LiFePO_4$	LFP
Lithium Nickel Cobalt Aluminum Oxide	$LiNiCoAlO_2$	NCA

Chart of the most commonly used Li-ion batteries.

? FREQUENTLY ASKED QUESTION

What Is "Battery Density?"

Battery density refers to the amount of energy in kilowatt-hours (kWh) that a battery can store per kilogram of mass (kWh per kilograms) or volume (kWh per liter) of volume. The higher the number, the higher the energy density of the battery. ● **SEE CHART 10-2**.

BATTERY TYPE	ENERGY DENSITY (KWH/KG)	ENERGY DENSITY (KWH/L)
Lead–Acid	0.11–0.14	0.22–0.27
Nickel-Metal Hydride	0.36	1.44
Lithium Cobalt Oxide	0.70	2.0

CHART 10-2

The higher the number, the higher the energy density of the battery. Notice that the lithium-ion battery has the highest energy density compared to lead–acid and nickel-metal hydride batteries.

? FREQUENTLY ASKED QUESTION

What Is a "Solid State" Battery?

Many manufacturers including Toyota are working on a solid-state battery that does not use a liquid or gel electrolyte. A prototype solid-state battery is said to use a lithium-nickel-manganese-cobalt cathode and a flexible ceramic separator. The lithium ions from the cathode create a metal film on the collector when charging. The advantages of a solid-state battery include a faster charging rate, lower weight, and higher capacity.

HEV/EV ELECTRONICS COOLING

NEED FOR COOLING Hybrid electric vehicles are unique in that they have electric motors and electronic controls that are not found in vehicles with conventional drivetrains. These components are designed to operate under heavy load with high current and voltage demands, so they tend to generate excessive heat during vehicle operation. Special auxiliary cooling systems are incorporated into hybrid electric vehicles to prevent overheating of these critical components and keep those components at efficient operating temperatures.

EFFECTS OF HEAT ON THE ELECTRICAL/ELECTRONIC SYSTEM Electronic components operate more efficiently as their temperature decreases, but can suffer permanent damage if they overheat. All hybrid electric vehicles have cooling systems for their motors and motor controls, and some use air-cooling to remove excess heat from these components. ● **SEE FIGURE 10-13**.

For example, a Chevrolet Bolt electric vehicle has two expansion valves in the A/C system. One is used to cool the

FIGURE 10-13 The underside of the Toyota Prius controller showing the coolant passages used to cool the electronic control unit.

> **FREQUENTLY ASKED QUESTION**
>
> **Why Isn't the ICE Cooling System Used to Cool HEV Motors and Motor Controls?**
>
> Most ICE cooling systems operate at over 200°F (93°C). For maximum efficiency, it is important that the ICE operate at close to this temperature at all times. Electric motors and the motor controls, however, tend to operate more efficiently at lower temperatures. The ICE cooling system runs too hot to allow these components to operate at peak efficiency, so a separate low-temperature system is often used.

passenger compartment and the other is used to cool the electronics and the high-voltage battery.

Many hybrid electric vehicles use a liquid cooling system for their motors and motor controls. These systems are often separate from the ICE's cooling system and typically operate at lower temperatures.

SYSTEM CONSTRUCTION The liquid cooling systems used for the motors and motor controls on hybrid electric vehicles have much in common with conventional ICE cooling systems. There is a separate expansion tank that acts as a coolant reservoir for the system, and the coolant is often the same type that is used for the ICE cooling system. A radiator is used to dissipate excess heat, and is located at the front of the vehicle. Some designs may have the radiator incorporated into the ICE radiator, or it may be separate. ● **SEE FIGURE 10-14**.

A low-voltage electric water pump is used to circulate the coolant, and it is often configured to run whenever the vehicle is in operation. The coolant is circulated through the various components in the system, which could include the following:

- Electric motor-generator(s)
- DC–DC converter
- Inverter
- Transmission oil cooler
- Other high-load control modules

NOTE: The first- and second-generation Ford Escape Hybrid also uses a cabin filter in the auxiliary climate control (battery zone) system to prevent particulate matter from collecting on the traction battery cooling passages. ● **SEE FIGURE 10-15.**

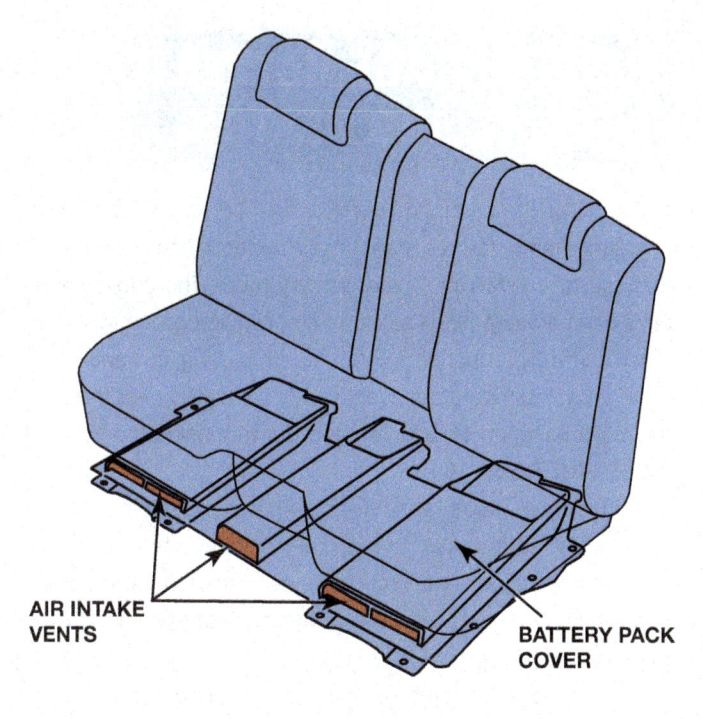

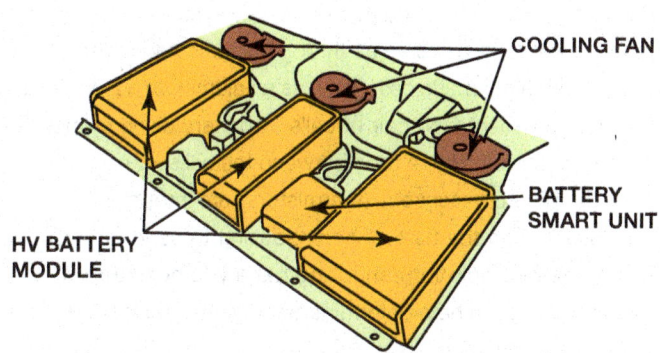

FIGURE 10-14 The motor and HV battery electronics on Toyota hybrid SUV.

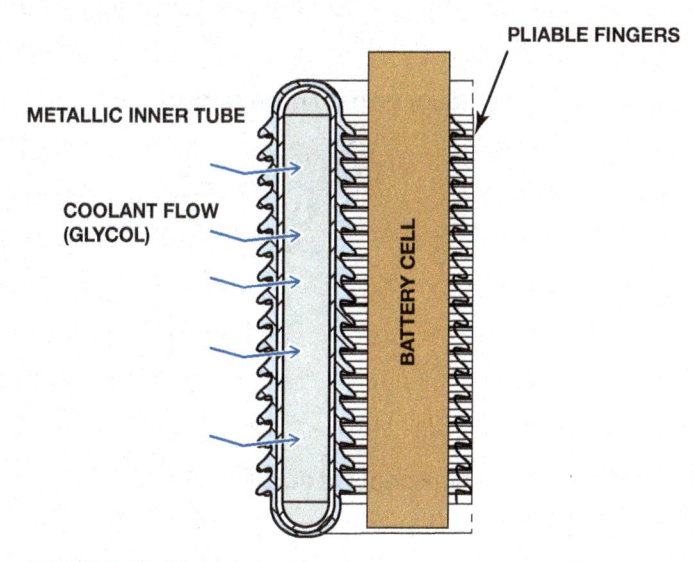

FIGURE 10-15 The electric motors and the motor controls are cooled using a separate cooling system. This Toyota Hybrid Synergy Drive (HSD) system uses a radiator that is integral with the ICE cooling system radiator.

HIGH-VOLTAGE BATTERY COOLING AND HEATING

THE NEED TO HEAT/COOL HV BATTERIES High operating temperatures can lower performance and cause damage to a NiMH or lithium battery pack. The cooling systems can be categorized as either air or liquid cooling systems. Most current production HEVs use air cooling to control HV battery pack temperature. Cabin air is circulated over the battery cells using an electric fan and ducting inside the vehicle.
● SEE FIGURE 10-16.

In some cases, the air-conditioning system has an extra zone that cools the air being circulated over the HV battery pack. The first- and second-generation Ford Escape Hybrid is an example of this type of system. ● SEE FIGURE 10-17.

Most current electric vehicles use a liquid cooling system. Coolant is circulated through a dedicated system that transfers battery heat to the outside air through a dedicated radiator. In a battery using prismatic cells, there is an aluminum cooling plate inserted between each pair of cells. A battery using cylindrical cells uses a ribbon-type tube between the cells.

Temperature sensors (thermistors) are mounted in various locations in the battery pack housing to send data to the module responsible for controlling battery temperature. These inputs are used to help determine battery charge rate and cooling system operation

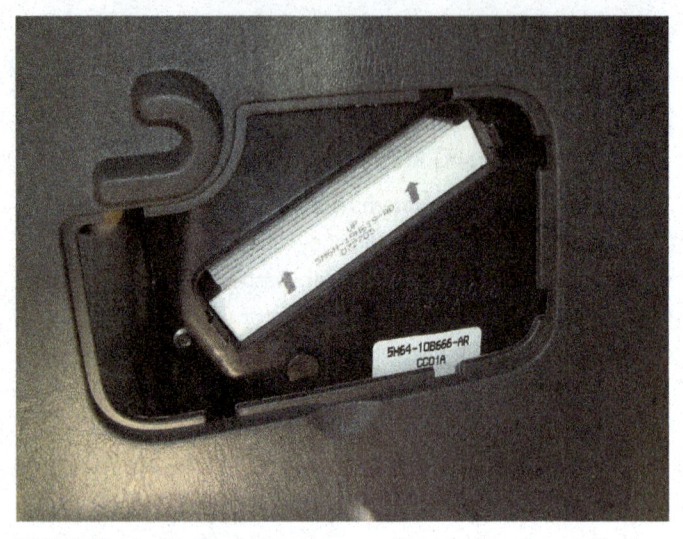

FIGURE 10-17 The HV battery cooling system from a Ford Escape Hybrid. Ford uses outside air to cool the battery pack, then increases cooling with a separate zone in the A/C system when necessary. The battery zone filter was only used on a first generation Ford Escape Hybrid.

HIGH-VOLTAGE BATTERY COOLING SYSTEM SERVICE The service of high-voltage battery cooling systems falls into two main categories:

1. Service of the air distribution system
2. Service of the liquid system

The service of the air distribution system is similar to HVAC systems. The blower motor must be operational and the fan must be free of debris. The air intake inlets must be inspected

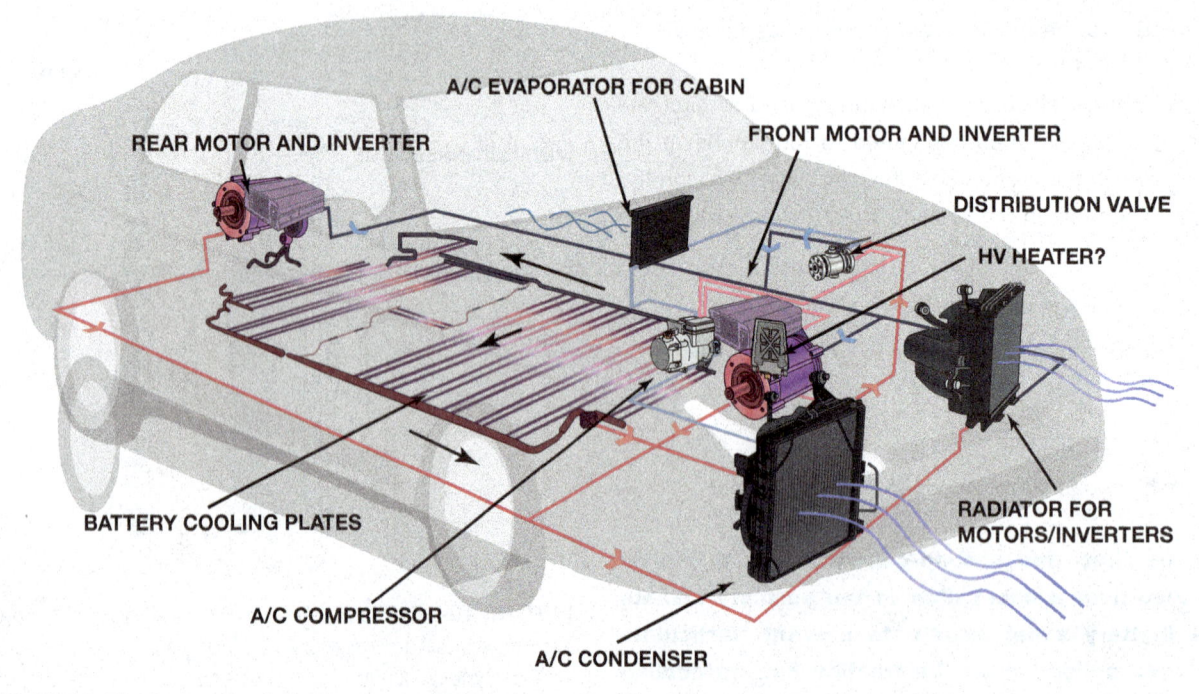

FIGURE 10-16 The battery and electronics are included as part of the temperature control system.

128 CHAPTER 10

and found to be free of anything that would restrict airflow. If the system has a dedicated cabin filter, it must be replaced at the specified interval.

The service of the liquid cooling system is similar to a conventional cooling system. On a regular basis the cooling system level must be checked to ensure there are no leaks and the freeze protection and pH level should be checked with a refractometer or test strip. The coolant should be replaced at the specified service interval using the recommended replacement coolant. The electric water pump must be inspected for proper operation. This is verified by actuating the pump with a factory-level scan tool. The dedicated radiator needs to be checked for airflow obstructions and for proper cooling fan operation.

EV BATTERY HEATER
The electric vehicle battery heating methods include heater pads that are typically 0.011 inch (0.28 mm) thick and can be applied between cells, wrapped around cells, or modules bonded to the surface of a cold plate directly under a module. The pads ensure quicker time to temperature while achieving better uniformity from cell to cell, and function as a dielectric barrier between cells/modules/plates with minimal impact on cooling performance.

NOTE: A water-cooling system for Hyundai and Kia's EV battery packs, rather than air cooling, have yielded further increases in range because water-cooling channels take up less space than air-cooling channels, increasing battery density by up to 35%.

BATTERY CAPACITY VS VEHICLE RANGE

ICE VEHICLE MILEAGE
In the United States, fuel economy for an internal combustion engine (ICE) vehicle is expressed in miles per gallon (MPG). Outside of the United States, fuel economy is measured in the number of liters of fuel needed to travel 100 kilometers (62 miles), abbreviated L/100 km. This means that as the number increases, the fuel economy decreases. In the metric system, the fuel is measured; in the United States, the miles are measured.

EPA VS WLTP
In the United States the Environmental Protection Agency (EPA) estimates electric vehicle range, while in Europe electric vehicle range uses the **Worldwide harmonized Light vehicles Test Procedure (WLTP)**. When the range is expressed using the WLTP standard, drivers can convert it to approximate EPA range estimates by dividing the WLTP value by 1.12. However, the EPA range is in fact just an estimate and real-world range can be different.

EV EQUIVALENT ECONOMY
A kilowatt (kW) is a rate of energy flow similar to the gallons per minute that a water hose or pump can deliver. A kilowatt-hour (kWh) is a quantity of electricity, similar to what a gallon is with water. A bigger battery pack with a higher number of kWh will hold more electricity, just as a bigger bucket will hold more gallons of water.

With an electric vehicle, how far it can travel is measured in *miles per kilowatt-hours*. A typical electric vehicle can travel about 3 to 4 miles per kilowatt-hour of battery capacity. The larger the battery in kwh, the greater the range, like an ICE vehicle that has a larger fuel tank capacity.

To help consumers compare the energy consumption of electric vehicles with those that run on fossil fuel, the EPA created a miles-per-gallon measurement, called **MPGe**. This is calculated based on a conversion factor of 33.705 kilowatt-hours of electricity equaling one gallon of gasoline. Therefore, a battery that has a capacity of 100 kWh is equal to the energy of about three gallons of gasoline.

? FREQUENTLY ASKED QUESTION

'What Is a "Guess-O-Meter?"

The dash display that shows the miles per kWh is often called a **Guess-O-Meter (GOM)** because it is often not accurate. Good numbers for miles per kWh are 4.3 to 4.9 miles of travel for each kWh consumed. It can be used to help plan a trip. For example, if the GOM indicates the battery capacity is 60 kWh in the battery, this usually means the vehicle can travel about 235 miles, so plan on charging at about 200 miles. ● **SEE FIGURE 10-18**.

TECH TIP

The Rule of Thumb Is 3

To help estimate the range of an electric vehicle (EV), multiply the battery capacity in kilowatt-hours (kWh) by three to get a good idea as to the range of the vehicle. For example, a Tesla Model 3 has a battery capacity of 75 kWh and when multiplied by 3 equals 225 miles ($75 \times 3 = 225$).

FIGURE 10-18 The dash display on a Chevrolet Bolt indicates the miles per kWh, which may or may not be accurate. Because the displayed estimated range varies, it is often referred to as "Guess-O-Meter".

HIGH-VOLTAGE BATTERY CONTROL COMPONENTS

BATTERY CONTROL MODULE The **battery control module (BCM)** is responsible for controlling the operation of the high-voltage battery based on the requests from the hybrid control module. The BCM monitors the voltage blocks, the current sensor, and temperature sensors to determine the need for charging. The BCM communicates with the other vehicle modules on the CAN BUS network and its data is accessible with a scan tool.

SYSTEM MAIN RELAYS (SMRs) System Main Relays (SMRs) are heavy duty relays that control the high-voltage circuit between the battery and the other components of the high-voltage system. SMRs are often referred to as contactors. Depending on the design of the battery control system, the battery will contain one to three SMRs. The battery control module controls the low-voltage side of the SMR. When the load side of the SMR closes, high-voltage current is allowed to flow from the battery. In a three SMR system design, one SMR controls the positive circuit and two SMRs control the negative circuit. On the negative side, one SMR is in-series with a high-wattage resistor that pre-charges the system capacitors. To allow current to flow:

- The BCM will first close the SMR for the positive cable.
- The BCM will close the SMR with the resistor on the negative cable. This will reduce the initial current flow to the system capacitors and also reduce the possibility of arcing across the high-current SMR contacts.
- The BCM will then close the second SMR on the ground cable and open the SMR in-series with the resistor. This will allow for full current flow.

CURRENT SENSORS The current sensor is used to measure the current flowing into the battery during charging and is used to measure current flowing out of the battery when it is discharging. The sensor may be mounted on the positive or the negative cable based on design. This data is combined with individual cell temperature and voltage to provide an overall state-of-charge (SOC) of the battery. The sensor will be either a Hall-effect design or a shunt, depending on the manufacturer and the design of the system. The BCM will set a fault code if the senor becomes open, shorted, or if the current running through the sensor becomes abnormally high or low. ● **SEE FIGURE 10-19.**

VOLTAGE BLOCK MONITORING CIRCUITS Each cell block, which consists of multiple battery cells, is monitored by the BCM for voltage level. These are low-voltage circuits that allow the BCM to flag a group of cells that are out of range when compared to the cell groups in the battery. A variance of .3 volts between cell groups is allowed. Any variance of measured voltage that is greater than .3 volts will set a fault code. This condition could be as a result of a bad cell or an imbalance condition.

TEMPERATURE SENSORS Temperature sensors are used to measure the temperature of the battery cells and temperature of the air entering the pack if a forced air system is used to cool the battery. The primary use of this data is to control the fan speed of the blower used to cool the battery. The data is also used in the

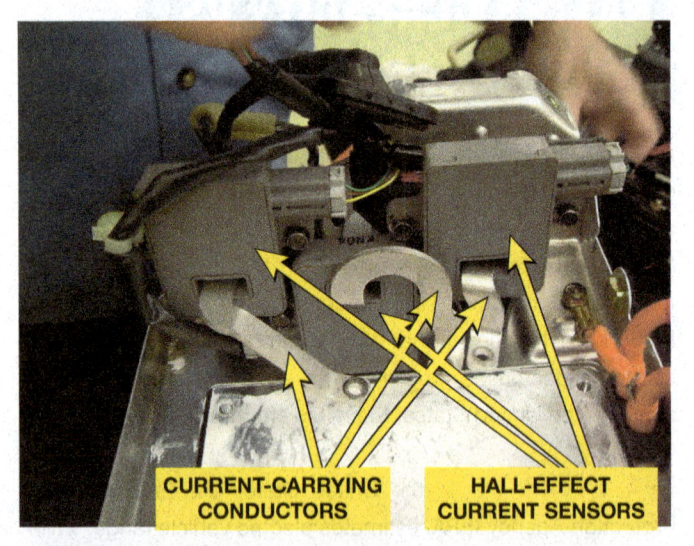

FIGURE 10-19 The three legs of the brushless motor run through three Hall-effect-type current sensors. The conductors used in the Honda unit are flat aluminum and attach to the motor controller terminals.

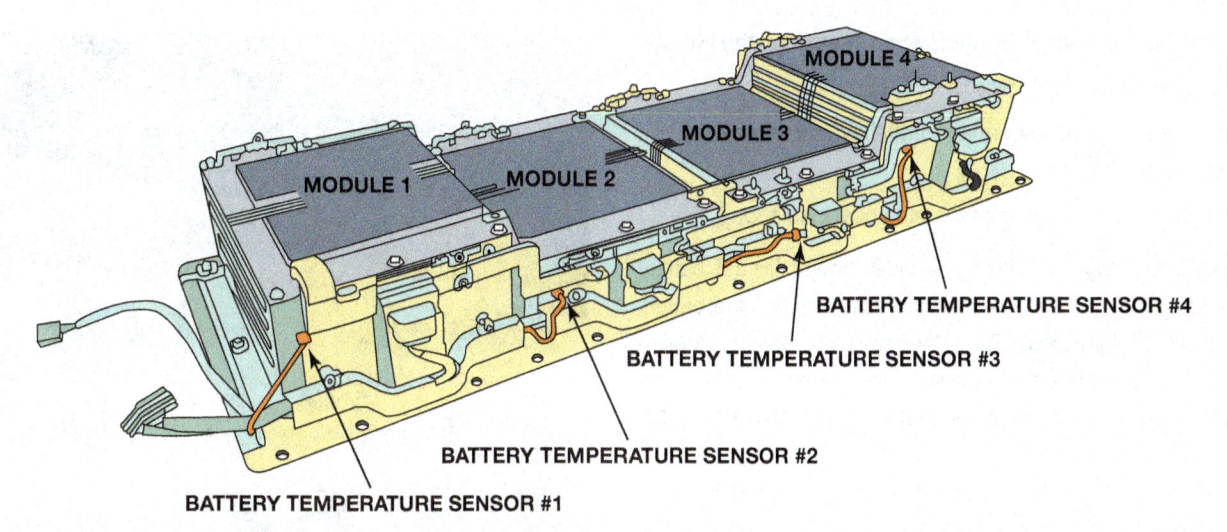

FIGURE 10-20 Temperature sensors are located throughout a HV battery pack.

calculation of the battery state-of-charge (SOC). The sensors are PTC thermistors so the higher the battery temperature, the lower the resistance of the sensor. ● **SEE FIGURE 10-20.**

NOTE: The General Motors electric vehicles using the Ultium batteries incorporate a wireless transmitter connected to the battery cells. Instead of running wires from each battery cell to the battery control module, the wireless system is able to reduce the number of wires and connections.

HV DISCONNECT The purpose of the HV battery disconnect switch is to remove power from the high-voltage system prior to repairs. When removing the HV disconnect switch, personal protective equipment (PPE) must be worn to protect against electrocution. Many HV disconnect switches contain a high-voltage fuse. Most HV disconnect switches also contain a low-voltage monitoring circuit. Failure to properly install and latch the HV disconnect switch will result in a no-start or failure to power-up condition. ● **SEE FIGURE 10-21.**

FIGURE 10-21 The battery disconnect on a Chevrolet Volt is located under the center console.

BATTERY MANAGEMENT SYSTEM (BMS)

PURPOSE The battery cells or modules need to be monitored and controlled for temperature and voltage. The **battery management system (BMS)** is an electronic system that manages cells in a battery pack. The BMS monitors and controls:

- State-of-charge (SOC)
- State of health (SOH)
- State of function (SOF)
- Safety and critical safeguards
- Temperature
- Load balancing/individual cell efficiency

The BMS receives inputs from voltage and temperature sensors in the modules. In some packs, the BMS may also provide outputs to drive other components, such as fans, pumps, or valves for the battery cooling system. External connectors enable robust and safe connection between the battery pack and other vehicle systems.

ELECTRICAL DISTRIBUTION SYSTEM (EDS)

PURPOSE The primary function of the **Electrical Distribution System (EDS)** is to provide the electrical conduction path through the battery pack and includes the following features:

- Isolates the conduction path
- Measures current and voltage in the high-voltage (HV) line

- Provides pre-charge function when energizing the HV line
- Fuses the HV line in case of over-current
- Provides manual disconnect of the HV line for vehicle servicing
- Monitors effectiveness of the electrical insulation

The low-voltage (LV) wiring provides power for the battery control functions and allows communication between the battery and vehicle (CAN protocol). The LV wiring is also used to confirm all external connectors are correctly in place, and to ensure that HV conductors cannot be contacted externally. ●SEE FIGURE 10-22.

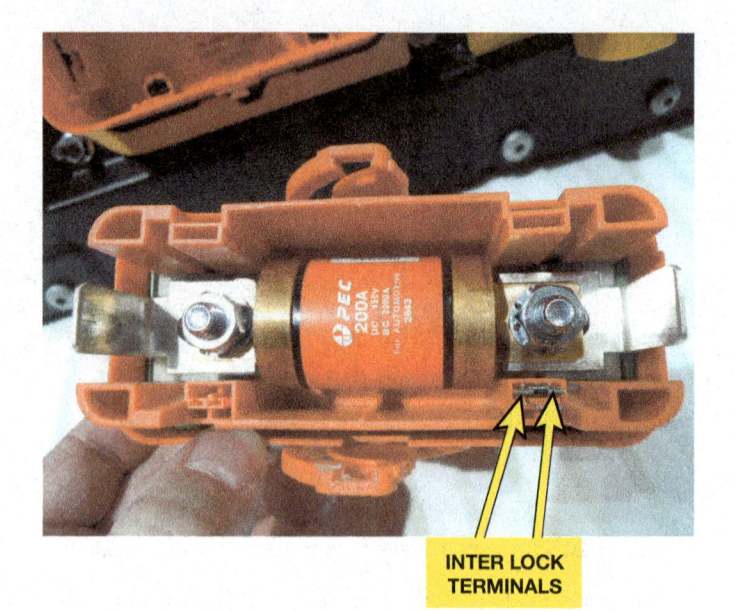

FIGURE 10-22 The HV disconnect plug has two small terminals used to signal the HV controller that the safety/service plug has been removed.

ISOLATION TESTING
The high-voltage system is completely isolated from the vehicle. A loss of isolation in the high-voltage system will result in a vehicle that will not power-up to the ready mode and set a series of diagnostic trouble codes. Some vehicles will set additional information codes that will help to identify the area where the loss of isolation has occurred.

To verify the loss of isolation has occurred, a meg ohm meter will be used to perform the isolation test. The use of class 0 high-voltage safety gloves is required when performing this test. With the high-voltage battery disconnected, the meg ohm meter is connected between the high-voltage system and chassis ground. During the test, the meter will charge its internal capacitor to up to 1,000 volts and measure the resistance between the high-voltage system and chassis ground. If continuity is detected, the loss of isolation needs to be identified and repaired. The system should be tested again after the repair is complete to verify the repair was successful.

STATE-OF-CHARGE MANAGEMENT
The HV battery in a hybrid electric vehicle (HEV) is subjected to constant charging and discharging during normal operation. The battery can overheat under the following conditions:

- The battery state-of-charge rises above 80%.
- The battery is placed under a load when its SOC is below 20%. In order to prevent overheating and maximize service life, the battery SOC must be carefully managed. In most hybrid-electric vehicle applications, a target SOC of 60% is used, and the battery is then cycled so its SOC varies no more than 20% higher or lower than the target. ●SEE FIGURE 10-23.

NOTE: The Chevrolet Volt is designed to allow the state-of-charge to drop to 25–35% before the gasoline engine is started to maintain that level of state-of-charge. The cooling system and software are designed to allow this reduced SOC so that the vehicle can be driven for an extended distance without having to start the engine.

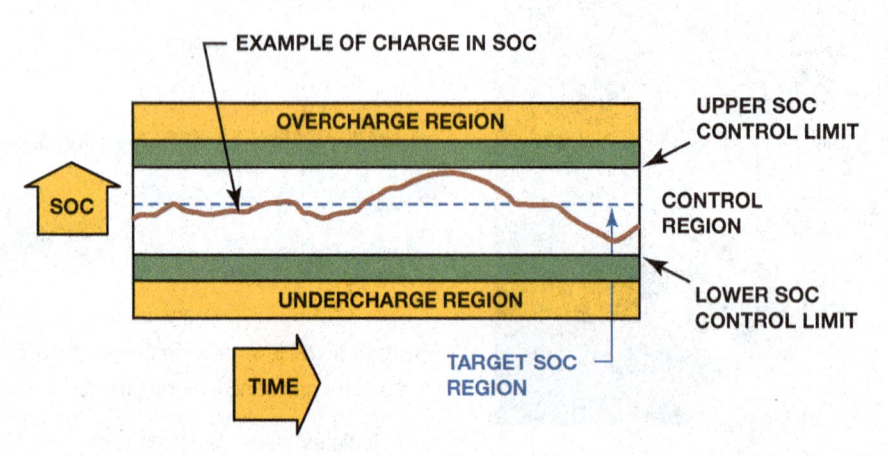

FIGURE 10-23 The HV battery pack SOC is maintained in a relatively narrow range to prevent overheating and maximize service life.

HEV HIGH-VOLTAGE BATTERY MONITOR

STATE-OF-CHARGE The HV battery pack controller monitors the state-of-charge.

- During acceleration, the battery pack state-of-charge (SOC) may drop slightly, and rise when the vehicle decelerates as a result of regenerative braking which charges the HV battery.
- Scan data displays charge and discharge levels. Normal operating HV battery SOC range for most hybrid electric vehicles is within 52–68%.
- When the SOC drops to 50%, the ICE starts to recharge the HV batteries. This means that the idle stop (start-stop) function is disabled if the SOC is at or below 50%, and will resume after it reaches 52% or higher in most cases.
  ● SEE FIGURE 10-24.
- If the SOC reaches 80% or higher, the regenerative braking stops. This means that during vehicle braking when the SOC is high, a harder than normal brake pedal effort is often noticed.
- Reduction of electric traction motor power occurs when the state-of-charge falls to 40%. If the ICE does start, there will be little or no electric assist from the electric traction motor. This will likely only occur if the vehicle runs out of fuel for the ICE and the vehicle operates on electric power alone. However, the main warning light will be on and the system will set and store multiple diagnostic trouble codes (DTCs) if this happens.

SCAN DATA TEST PROCEDURE Connect the scan tool and select the vehicle, and then select the following parameter identification (PID) items:

- State-of-charge
- Battery temperature
- Battery voltage
- Battery current draw
- Check the battery block internal resistance as displayed on a scan tool for Toyota/Lexus HEVs. Normal internal resistance is 15 to 40 milliohms (0.015 to 0.040 ohms).

● SEE FIGURE 10-25.

> **TECH TIP**
>
> **Check State-of-Charge First**
>
> If a hybrid vehicle owner complains of a lack of power on acceleration, check the state-of-charge (SOC) first. There may be nothing wrong with the traction motor or its controller. It may be simply that the HV battery pack is not within a normal state-of-charge, usually due to a fault with the battery pack or related electrical connections.

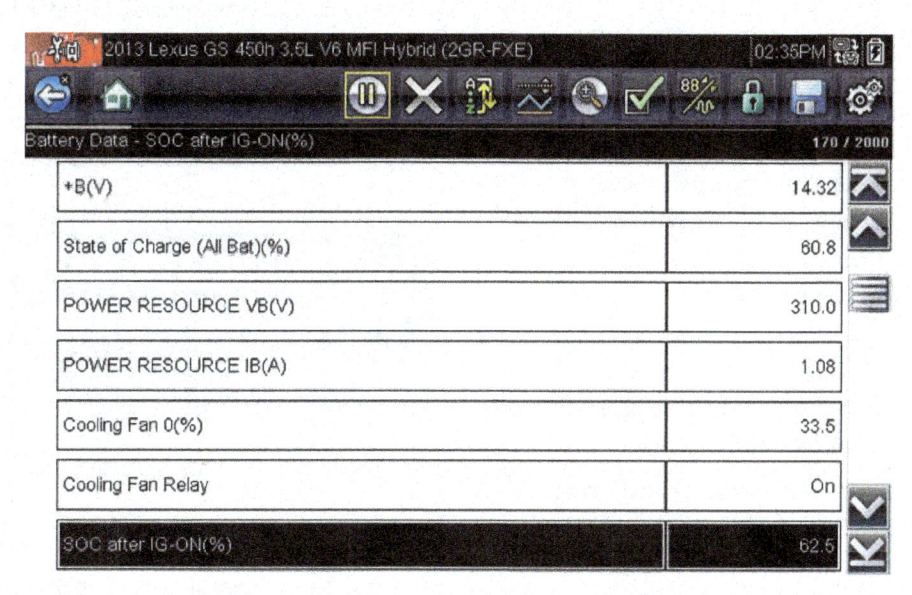

FIGURE 10-24 A Snap-on Solus scan tool displays the state-of-change of the high-voltage battery under the heading of "HV ECM".

HIGH-VOLTAGE BATTERIES **133**

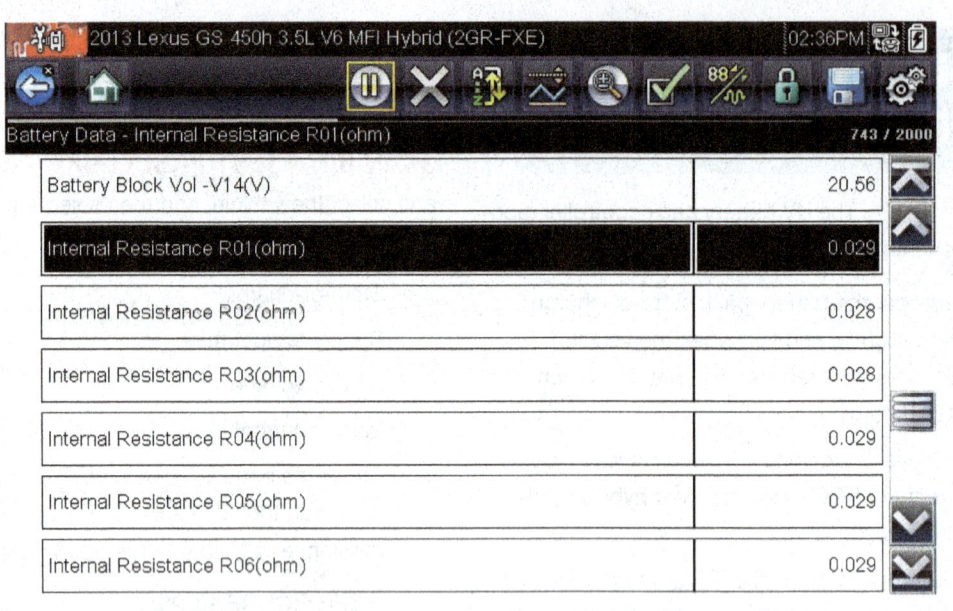

FIGURE 10-25 The internal resistances of the battery blocks are available on the data stream as shown using an aftermarket scan tool. The internal resistance should be between 15 and 40 milliohms (0.015 to 0.040 ohms).

LITHIUM-ION BATTERY REPAIR

PURPOSE Some original equipment manufacturers (OEMs) are replacing defective high-voltage battery components rather than replacing the entire battery. This reduces the amount of time the vehicle is in a non-drivable condition and it reduces the cost of the repair. Included in the list of replaceable components is the high-voltage battery module.

PROCEDURE A typical example of a factory-authorized procedure that addresses failed high-voltage battery modules used by Nissan/Infinity on specific hybrid and electric vehicles includes a battery cell replacement as determined by a diagnostic trouble code. A P3374 DTC indicates that a cell is more than 100 mV lower than other cells. The scan tool data indicates that cell #27 was more than 100 mV lower than the rest of the cells. ● **SEE FIGURE 10-26**.

Before the battery is removed, it is essential that all the required tools are available. The specified tools include the required PPE, insulated tools, and the module balance adjuster tool. The procedure includes the following steps:

STEP 1 Following the service procedures and observing all high-voltage cautions, the battery should be removed from the vehicle and made ready for repair.

STEP 2 Using the service information, identify the location of the defective module within the pack.

STEP 3 Remove the battery covers, the controller, and other components needed to access the battery modules as described in the service procedures. ● **SEE FIGURE 10-27**.

STEP 4 Prior to completing the final disassembly of the battery, all module voltages must be measured using a digital multimeter to determine the module charge balance of the battery. This data will be used to determine the adjustment voltage for the replacement module.

STEP 5 The new replacement battery module must be installed in the module charge balancer, and the adjustment voltage must be entered into the charger. This will allow the charge to be adjusted to match the rest of the battery.

STEP 6 The defective module can now be removed and the new module installed.

STEP 7 Reinstall all parts that have been removed during the disassembly process and make the battery ready for reinstallation.

ALTERNATIVE OUT-OF-VEHICLE HV BATTERY SERVICE

PROCEDURE Start HV battery pack service by performing the following steps:

STEP 1 Remove the safety disconnect switch. When the safety disconnect switch is removed, the high voltage is isolated within the battery pack itself.
● **SEE FIGURE 10-28**.

23	3.560 V
24	3.576 V
25	3.519 V
26	3.558 V
27	3.277 V
28	3.547 V
29	3.556 V
30	3.529 V

FIGURE 10-26 The scan tool data indicates that cell #27 was a lot lower than the rest of the cells, which indicates a problem and the reason for the diagnostic trouble code to be set.

FIGURE 10-27 Whenever working on any potential high-voltage components, always follow the recommended safety procedures including using insulated tools and rubber gloves.

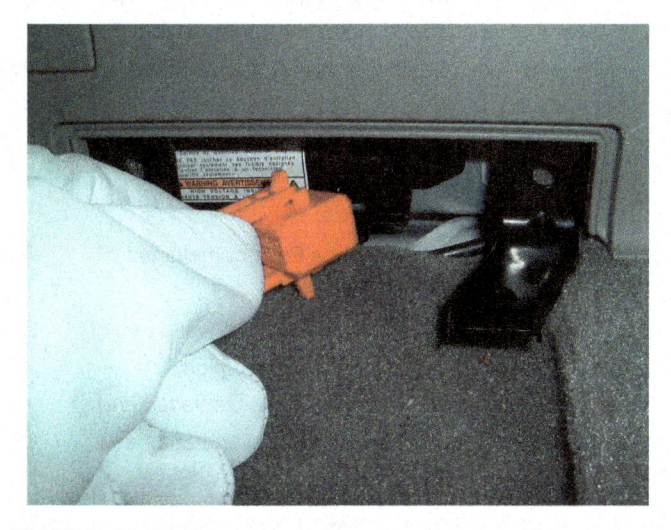

FIGURE 10-28 Removing the service plug on a Toyota Highlander Hybrid. This service plug is located behind a plastic panel on the left side of the rear passenger seat.

STEP 2 Wait 15 minutes for the capacitors to discharge.

STEP 3 Wear class zero gloves.

STEP 4 Place HV battery pack on wood or a rubber mat, and use insulated tools. After disassembling the HV battery pack, work will involve individual battery modules. As long as there is contact with just one block of batteries at a time, there is no danger as the voltage level is about the same as with a conventional 12-volt battery.

- Check the voltage of each module.
  Do not use battery modules that are below 5.4 volts (10.8 V for a block), which is the lower limit on cell voltage. Even if the modules can be recharged, they will have a short service life.
  If batteries are below 7.5 volts, charge at a maximum of 16 volts at 2- to 6-ampere rate.
  Monitor battery temperature and do not allow the battery to overheat and do not allow the temperature to exceed 120°F (50°C).
- Allow the voltage to stabilize after being charged and record the no load voltage to be used for the internal resistance calculation. In this example, assume a voltage of 15.21 volts.
- Use a high-wattage resistor to apply a load to the batteries. A 1.5-ohm resistor rated at 25 watts is often used to provide a load.
- Apply the load resistor and measure the new voltage and current values.

DETERMINE INTERNAL RESISTANCE To determine the internal resistance of a battery block (two modules), compare the unloaded voltage to the voltage of the block under the load that was applied by the resistor. This is called the delta (Δ) or the change in the voltage. This difference is then divided by the measured current (amperes) that was measured during the load test using the 1.5-ohm resistor. For example, if the current is 9.6 amperes with voltage at 15.50 volts, the internal resistance is. 0.29 Δ volts (15.50 − 15.21) ÷ 9.6 amperes = 0.0302 or 30 milliohms. A tested salvage battery can be used to replace a defective battery module in a vehicle that has battery block resistance of 25 to 35 milliohms. Always try to match the internal resistance as close as possible.

MATCH STATE-OF-CHARGE Connecting batteries in series requires the batteries to be close to the same voltage. Series connected batteries receive the same charge/discharge current, and an undercharged battery will never catch up with the rest of the battery pack. A diagnostic trouble code (DTC), if there is a 0.30-volt difference in battery, blocks voltages.

HIGH-VOLTAGE BATTERIES 135

BATTERY DEGRADATION AND BALANCING

RATE OF DEGRADATION Most HV batteries will outlast the usable life of the vehicle. However, some factors that affect battery life and the rate of degradation include the following:

- The average decline in energy storage is 2.3% per year.
- EV batteries decline in a non linear fashion, which means that at the beginning of the battery life, there is an early drop, but the rate of decline slows down in subsequent years.
- Liquid-cooled batteries decline slower than air-cooled packs. For example, a liquid-cooled EV has an average annual degradation rate of 2.3%, compared to an air-cooled EV rate of 4.2%.
- Higher vehicle use does not necessarily equal higher battery degradation.
- Vehicles driven in hot temperatures show a faster decline in battery health.
- The use of DC fast-chargers speeds up the process of degradation, but there is not much difference in battery health based on frequent use of Level 1 versus Level 2 charging. Losses that happen with frequent DC charging are made worse in hot climate conditions.

PASSIVE AND ACTIVE CELL BALANCING Long battery life requires that the electronics in the vehicle perform passive and active battery cell balancing.

- **Passive balancing** is achieved by having energy drawn from the most charged cell and dissipated as heat, usually through resistors. Passive balancing allows the stack to act as if every cell has the same capacity as the weakest cell. Using a relatively low current, it drains a small amount of energy from high SOC cells during the charging cycle so that all cells charge to their maximum state-of-charge (SOC).
- **Active balancing** is achieved when energy is drawn from the most charged cell and transferred to the least charged cells, usually through DC–DC converters.

NORMAL OPERATION During normal vehicle operation, the charge and discharge cycles of the high-voltage battery in an HEV are monitored and controlled by the battery management system (BMS). This module monitors battery temperature, current, and voltage to calculate SOC and determine at what rate the battery should be charged. While dealerships sometimes have a special high-voltage battery charger for recharging HEV battery packs, the best charger is the vehicle itself. If the HV battery in an HEV becomes discharged, the first step should be getting the vehicle started to recharge the battery pack. The procedure will vary depending on the model in question. Always follow the manufacturer's specified procedures when starting a disabled hybrid vehicle.

Case Study

The Case of the Broken Prius

The owner of a Prius complained that "the engine never shuts off" and fuel economy has dropped to as low as 25 MPG instead of the normal 40+ MPG. By "never shuts off," the customer means that the idle stop (auto start/stop function) is suspended. The master warning light was also on, indicating a serious problem has been detected. The technician used a scan tool and retrieved the following diagnostic trouble codes (DTCs).

- P0A80—The difference in voltage between two of the blocks in the battery pack is too high.
- P3006—Uneven state-of-charge.

Scan tool data showed battery block voltages reading ranging from 4.65 to 15.01 volts. Generally, if a battery block is under 7.5 volts, it cannot be restored to useful service. Even if it can be charged, the module will have a short service life. The shop recommended, and the customer approved, a replacement reconditioned battery pack supplied by a nationally known company. The battery pack was replaced and the vehicle was restored to normal operation and fuel economy.

Summary:

- **Complaint**—The owner of a Prius complained of reduced fuel economy.
- **Cause**—The difference in voltage between two of the blocks in the battery pack is too high.
- **Correction**—The battery pack was replaced and the vehicle was restored to normal operation and fuel economy.

PHOTO SEQUENCE HEV-HV BATTERY INSPECTION AND TESTING

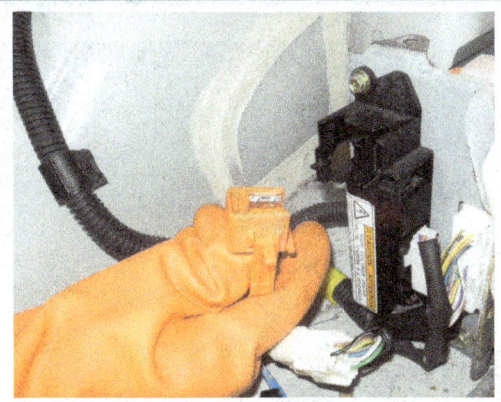

1 To depower the high-voltage system, the ignition was off and the negative battery cable was disconnected from the 12-volt auxiliary battery, then the HV battery safety plug was removed.

2 After checking that the voltage level is safe, the rear seat and HV battery cover were removed. Always follow the safety procedures specified by the manufacturer for the vehicle being serviced and adhere to all safety warning and precautions.

3 The high-voltage wires were removed from the battery pack while wearing HV gloves.

4 The HV battery pack is being removed through the rear of the vehicle.

5 The HV battery pack is placed on a workbench that is covered with a thick rubber (insulating) mat. A wood top bench can also be used.

6 A visual inspection shows that many electrical connections between battery modules are corroded.

HIGH-VOLTAGE BATTERIES

STEP BY STEP

7 The HV battery pack temperature sensors are removed.

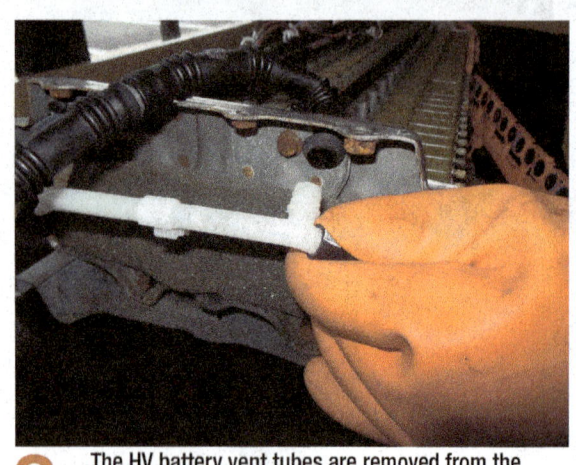

8 The HV battery vent tubes are removed from the battery pack.

9 The end caps are removed from the battery pack.

10 The fasteners that hold the battery modules to the base of the battery pack are removed.

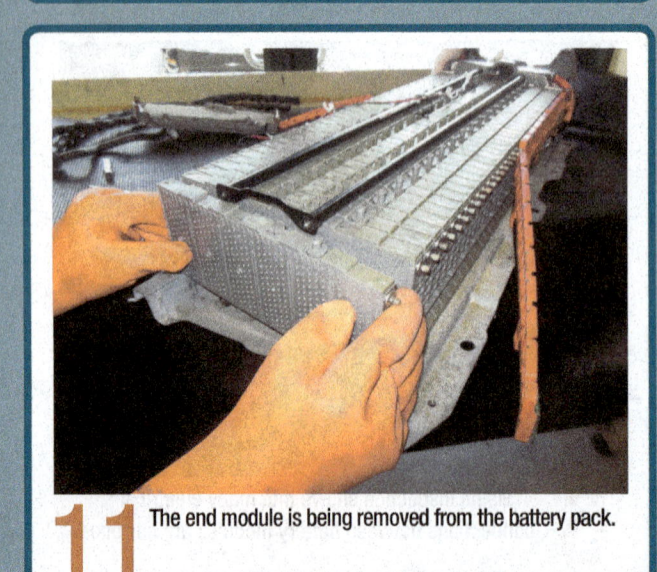

11 The end module is being removed from the battery pack.

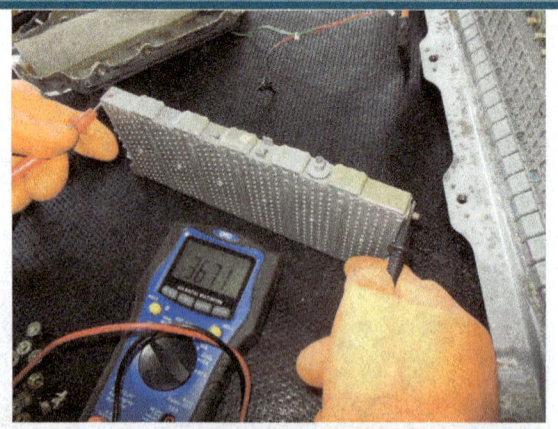

12 The individual modules were measured using a voltmeter and most modules were found to be about 3.6 volts which is far below the minimum of 5.4 volts that most experts think can be restored by charging.

SUMMARY

1. Most current production HEVs use nickel-metal hydride (NiMH) battery technology for the high-voltage battery.
2. The cylindrical type has the active materials made in long ribbons and arranged in a spiral fashion inside a steel cylinder (case).
3. The prismatic type is a rectangular or boxlike design with the active materials formed into flat plates, much like a conventional lead–acid battery.
4. All current production HEVs use air cooling to control HV battery pack temperature.
5. A lithium-ion cell is named because during battery cycling, lithium ions move back and forth between the positive and negative electrodes.
6. To help consumers compare the energy consumption of electric vehicles with those that run on fossil fuel, the EPA created a miles-per-gallon measurement, called MPGe.
7. System Main Relays (SMRs) are heavy-duty relays that control the high-voltage circuit between the battery and the other components of the high-voltage system.
8. The low-voltage (LV) wiring provides power for the battery control functions and allows communication between the battery and vehicle (CAN protocol).
9. Most HV batteries will outlast the usable life of the vehicle.
10. Long battery life requires that the electronics in the vehicle perform passive and active battery cell balancing.

REVIEW QUESTIONS

1. Why do high-voltage batteries need to be heated if cold or cooled if hot?
2. What advantages do lithium-ion batteries have comparted to NiMH batteries?
3. What is the primary function of the Electrical Distribution System (EDS)?
4. What are the steps involved to address failed high-voltage battery modules?
5. What occurs if the state-of-charge exceeds 80%?

CHAPTER QUIZ

1. A 12-volt system is used in both HEV and EV vehicles to _____.
   a. provide a source for the high voltage through a DC-to-DC converter
   b. power all accessories and other aspects of vehicle operation except propulsion
   c. Both a and b
   d. Neither a nor b
2. The nominal voltage of an NiMH battery cell is _____.
   a. 1.2 volts
   b. 3.2 volts
   c. 3.6 volts
   d. 4.8 volts
3. A lithium-ion cell produces _____ per cell.
   a. 1.2 volts
   b. 3.2 volts
   c. 3.6 volts
   d. 4.8 volts
4. Vehicle manufacturers use several different cathode materials including _____.
   a. nickel, manganese, and cobalt (NMC)
   b. nickel, cobalt, and aluminum (NCA)
   c. lithium iron phosphate (LiFePO$_4$)
   d. Any of the above
5. Lithium-ion cells can be _____.
   a. cylindrical cell
   b. prismatic—hard case
   c. prismatic—pouch type
   d. Any of the above
6. _____ is responsible for controlling the operation of the high-voltage battery based on the requests from the hybrid control module.
   a. Battery control module (BCM)
   b. System Main Relays (SMRs)
   c. Battery management system (BMS)
   d. Electrical Distribution System (EDS)
7. In most hybrid electric vehicle applications, a target SOC of _____ is used, and the battery is then cycled so its SOC varies no more than _____ higher or lower than the target.
   a. 100%; 50%
   b. 80%; 20%
   c. 70%; 50%
   d. 80%; 40%

8. In a three SMR system design, one SMR controls the positive circuit and two SMRs control the negative circuit. On the negative side an SMR is in-series with a _____.
   a. capacitor
   b. resistor
   c. diode
   d. inductor (coil)

9. During normal vehicle operation, the charge and discharge cycles of the high-voltage battery in an HEV are monitored and controlled by the _____.
   a. battery control module (BCM)
   b. System Main Relays (SMRs)
   c. battery management system (BMS)
   d. Electrical Distribution System (EDS)

10. The primary function of the _____ is to provide the electrical conduction path through the battery pack.
    a. battery control module (BCM)
    b. System Main Relays (SMRs)
    c. battery management system (BMS)
    d. Electrical Distribution System (EDS)

Chapter 11
EV AND HEV MOTORS, CONVERTERS, AND INVERTERS

LEARNING OBJECTIVES

After studying this chapter, the reader should be able to:

- Describe the operation of DC and AC electric motors.
- Explain how a brushless DC motor works.
- Discuss the advantages and disadvantages of using electric motors in hybrid electric vehicles.
- Describe how a DC-to-DC converter works.
- Discuss how a DC-to-AC inverter works.
- Prepare for the ASE L3 certification text area "D" (Power Electronics).

KEY TERMS

AC induction motor (ACIM) 146
Armature 145
Boost converters 155
Brushless motors 147
Commutator 146
DC-to-DC converters 153
Electromagnetic induction 143
Electromagnetism 142
Flux lines 142
Insulated-gate bipolar transistors (IGBTs) 149
Interior permanent magnets (IPMs) 147
Inverters 155
Lenz's law 144
Resolver 150
Right-hand rule 142
Rotor 145
Snubbers 153
Squirrel-cage rotor 146
Stator 145
Surface permanent magnets (SPMs) 147

ELECTROMAGNETISM

PRINCIPLES Scientists discovered around 1820 that current-carrying conductors are also surrounded by a magnetic field. The creation of a magnetic field by the use of an electrical current is called **electromagnetism**. These fields may be made many times stronger than those surrounding conventional magnets. Also, the magnetic field strength around a conductor may be controlled by changing the current. These magnetic lines of force are called **flux lines**. As current increases, more flux lines are created, and the magnetic field expands and becomes stronger. As current decreases, the magnetic field contracts, or collapses. These discoveries greatly broadened the practical uses of magnetism and opened an area of study known as *electromagnetics*.

CREATING AN ELECTROMAGNET A magnet can be created by magnetizing a piece of iron or steel or by using electricity to make an electromagnet. An easy way to create an electromagnet is to wrap a nail with 20 turns of insulated wire and connect the ends to the terminals of a 1.5-volt dry-cell battery. When energized, the nail will become a magnet and will be able to pick up tacks or other small steel objects.

STRAIGHT CONDUCTOR The magnetic field surrounding a straight, current-carrying conductor consists of several cylinders of flux lines that exist along the entire length of the wire. The strength of the current determines how many flux lines there will be and how far out they extend from the surface of the wire. ● **SEE FIGURE 11-1**.

RIGHT-HAND RULE Magnetic flux cylinders have direction, just as the flux lines surrounding a bar magnet have direction. Most automotive circuits use the conventional theory of current flow (+ to –), and therefore the **right-hand rule** is used to determine the direction of the magnetic flux lines. ● **SEE FIGURE 11-2**.

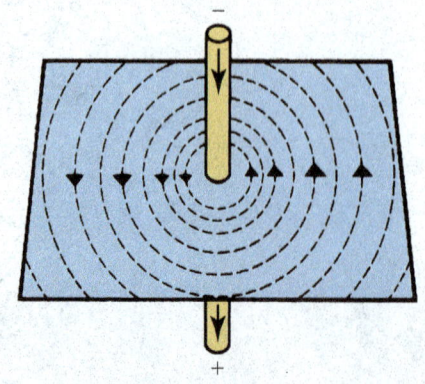

FIGURE 11-1 A magnetic field surrounds a current-carrying conductor.

FIGURE 11-2 The right-hand rule for magnetic field direction is used with the conventional theory of electron flow.

FIELD INTERACTION The area of flux surrounding current-carrying conductors interacts with other magnetic fields. In the following illustrations, the cross symbol (+) indicates current moving inward, or away from you. It represents the tail of an arrow. The dot symbol (•) represents an arrowhead and indicates current moving outward. If two conductors carry current in opposite directions, their magnetic fields also rotate in opposite directions. If they are placed side-by-side, the opposing flux lines between the conductors create a strong magnetic field. Current-carrying conductors tend to move out of a strong field into a weak field, so the conductors move away from each other. ● **SEE FIGURE 11-3**.

If the two conductors carry current in the same direction, their fields are in the same direction. The flux lines between the two conductors cancel each other out, leaving a very weak field between them. The conductors are drawn into this weak field, and they tend to move toward each other.

MOTOR PRINCIPLE Electric motors, such as automobile starter motors, use this field interaction to change electrical energy into mechanical energy. If two conductors carrying current in opposite directions are placed between strong north and south poles, the magnetic field of the conductor interacts with the magnetic fields of the poles. The clockwise field of the top conductor adds to the fields of the poles and creates a strong field beneath the conductor. The conductor tries to move up to get out of this strong field. The counterclockwise field of the lower conductor adds to the field of the poles and creates a strong field above the conductor. The conductor tries to move

FIGURE 11-3 Conductors with opposing magnetic fields will move apart into weaker fields.

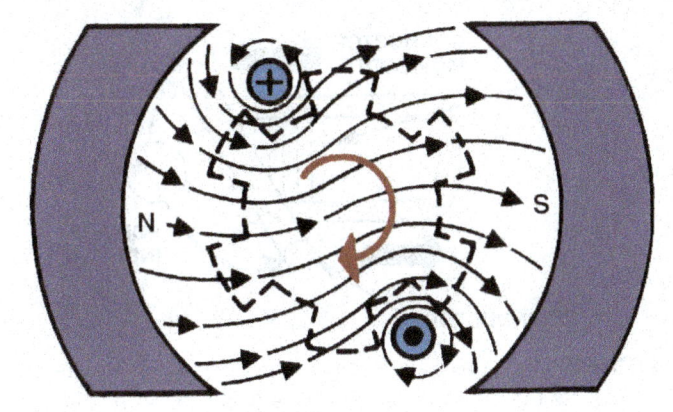

FIGURE 11-4 Electric motors use the interaction of magnetic fields to produce mechanical energy.

down to get out of this strong field. These forces cause the center of the motor, where the conductors are mounted, to turn clockwise. ● **SEE FIGURE 11-4**.

COIL CONDUCTOR If several loops of wire are made into a coil, the magnetic flux density is strengthened. Flux lines around a coil are the same as the flux lines around a bar magnet.

They exit from the north pole and enter at the south pole. The magnetic field of a coil can be strengthened by increasing the number of turns in the wire, by increasing the current through the coil, or both. ● **SEE FIGURE 11-5**.

ELECTROMAGNETS The magnetic field surrounding a current-carrying coil of wire can be strengthened by using a soft iron core. Because soft iron is very permeable, magnetic flux lines pass through it easily. If a piece of soft iron is placed inside a coiled conductor, the flux lines concentrate in the iron core, rather than pass through the air, which is less permeable. The concentration of force greatly increases the strength of the magnetic field inside the coil. Coils with an iron core are called electromagnets. ● **SEE FIGURE 11-6**.

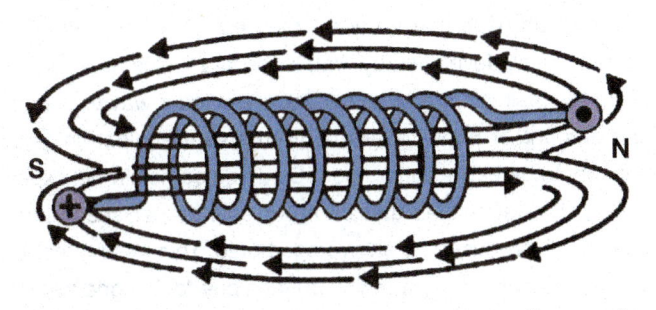

FIGURE 11-5 The magnetic lines of flux surrounding a coil look similar to those surrounding bar magnets.

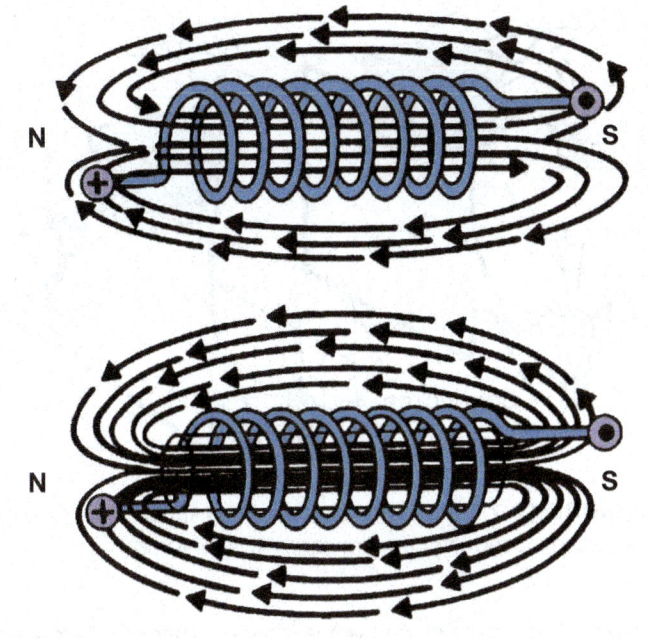

FIGURE 11-6 An iron core concentrates the magnetic lines of force surrounding a coil.

ELECTROMAGNETIC INDUCTION

PRINCIPLES INVOLVED Magnetic flux lines can create an electromotive force, or voltage, in a conductor if either the flux lines or the conductor is moving. This movement is called relative motion. In other words, there is relative motion between the flux lines and the conductor. This process is called induction, and the resulting electromotive force is called induced voltage. This creation of a voltage in a conductor by a moving magnetic field is called **electromagnetic induction**. If the conductor is in a complete circuit, current flows. Voltage is induced when magnetic flux lines are broken by a conductor. This relative motion can be a conductor moving across a magnetic field or a magnetic field moving across a stationary conductor (as in alternators and ignition coils). In both cases, the induced voltage is generated by relative motion between the conductor and the magnetic flux lines. The highest voltage is generated when the motion is at right angles. ● **SEE FIGURE 11-7**.

VOLTAGE STRENGTH Induced voltage depends upon magnetic flux lines being broken by a conductor. The strength of the voltage depends upon the rate at which the flux lines are broken. The more flux lines broken per unit of time, the greater the induced voltage. If a single conductor breaks one million

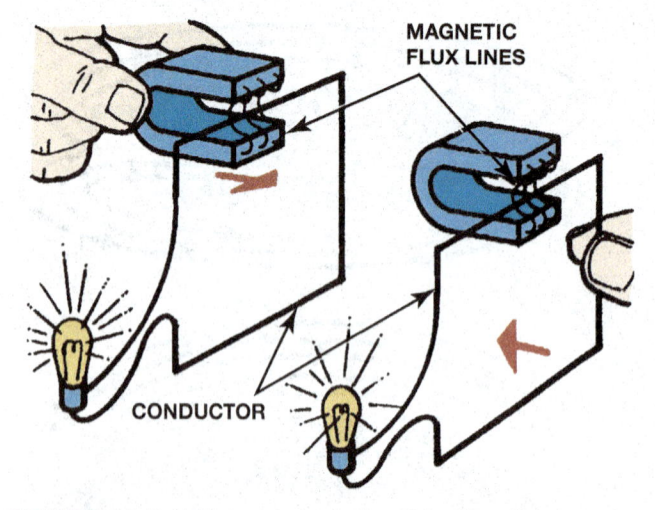

FIGURE 11-7 Voltage can be induced by the relative motion between a conductor and magnetic lines of force.

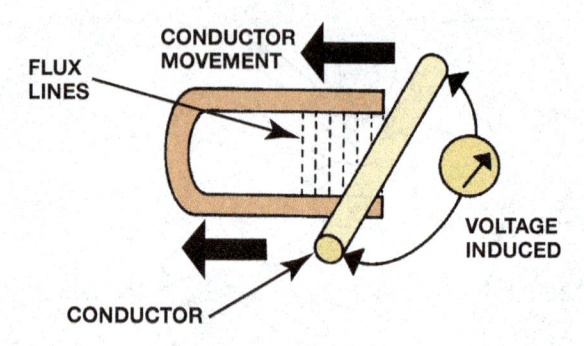

FIGURE 11-9 Maximum voltage is induced when conductors cut across the magnetic lines of force (flux lines) at a 90-degree angle.

flux lines per second, one volt is induced. There are four ways to increase induced voltage:

- Increase the strength of the magnetic field, so there are more flux lines.
- Increase the number of conductors that are breaking the flux lines.
- Increase the speed of the relative motion between the conductor and the flux lines so that more lines are broken per time unit.
- Increase the angle between the flux lines and the conductor to a maximum of 90 degrees. There is no voltage induced if the conductors move parallel to, and do not break any, flux lines. ● **SEE FIGURE 11-8.**

Maximum voltage is induced if the conductors break flux lines at 90 degrees and the voltage decreases when the flux lines are cut at angles between 0 and 90 degrees. ● **SEE FIGURE 11-9.**

Voltage can be electromagnetically induced and can be measured. Induced voltage creates current. The direction of induced voltage (and the direction in which current moves) is called polarity and depends upon the direction of the flux lines, as well as the direction of relative motion. An induced current moves so that its magnetic field opposes the motion that induced the current. This principle is called **Lenz's law**. The relative motion between a conductor and a magnetic field is opposed by the magnetic field of the current it has induced.

ELECTRIC MOTORS

ELECTRIC MOTOR POWER Electric motor power is expressed in kilowatts (kW). This is the preferred international standard for rating mechanical and electrical power. A 100% efficient motor would produce one kilowatt of mechanical power with an input of one kilowatt of electrical power. A kilowatt is equal to 1,000 watts. A watt is the amount of power that would lift an object weighing 3.6 ounces (102 grams) a distance of 39 inches (one meter) in one second. The watt scale of power measurement is named after the Scottish engineer, James Watt. One horsepower (hp) is equal to 746 watts. The hp rating was developed by Watt in the late 1700s when horses were the main source of power. Watt wanted a way to express the amount of power available from steam engines in terms that could be easily understood. By doing some simple experiments, he determined that 550 foot-pounds per second was the power produced by an average horse. This means that the horse could lift a weight of 550 pounds one foot in one second. ●**SEE CHART 11-1** for a conversion between horsepower and kilowatts.

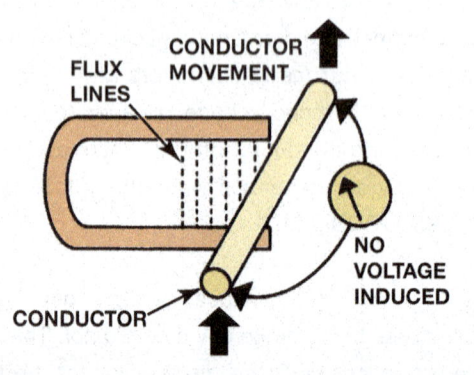

FIGURE 11-8 No voltage is induced if the conductor is moved in the same direction as the magnetic lines of force (flux lines).

HORSEPOWER (HP)	KILOWATT (KW)
25	19
50	37
75	56
100	75
125	93
150	112
175	131
200	149

CHART 11-1 Horsepower to kilowatt conversion chart.

FREQUENTLY ASKED QUESTION

Why Don't the Horsepower Ratings Add Up?

When looking at the specifications for an all-wheel-drive electric vehicle, a potential buyer noticed the rear motor had a 250-horsepower rating and the front motor had a 200-horsepower rating. However, the customer noticed that the "combined" horsepower was just 380 horsepower whereas both combined should be 450 hp.

The reason the horsepower does not add up is not due to the rating of the motors, but rather is due to the total energy the high-voltage battery can supply. The battery management system is only capable of supplying 380 horsepower worth of energy even though the electric motors themselves are capable of producing more power individually.

ELECTRIC MOTOR OPERATION Most electric motors work by electromagnetism and the fundamental principle that there is a mechanical force on any wire when it is conducting electricity while contained within a magnetic field. The force is described by the Lorentz force law and is perpendicular to both the wire and the magnetic field. In an electric motor, the rotating part (usually on the inside) is called the **rotor**, and the stationary part is called the **stator**. The motor contains electromagnets that are wound on a frame. One basic principle of electromagnetism is that a magnetic field surrounds every conductor carrying a current. The strength of the magnetic field is increased as the current flow (in amperes) is increased. Inside the starter housing is a strong magnetic field created by the field coil magnets. The **armature**, made up of many conductors, is installed inside this strong magnetic field, with very little clearance between the armature and the field coils.

The two magnetic fields act together, and their lines of force "bunch up" or are strong on one side of the armature loop wire and become weak on the other side of the conductor. This causes the conductor (armature) to move from the area of strong magnetic field strength toward the area of weak magnetic field strength.

This causes the armature to rotate. This rotation force (torque) is increased as the current flowing through the starter motor increases. The torque of a starter is determined by the strength of the magnetic fields. Magnetic field strength is measured in ampere-turns. If the current or the number of turns of wire is increased, the magnetic field strength is increased.
● SEE FIGURE 11-10.

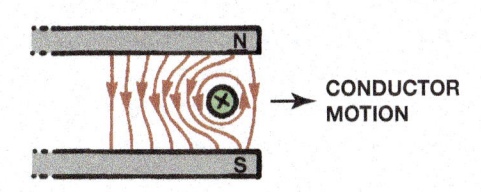

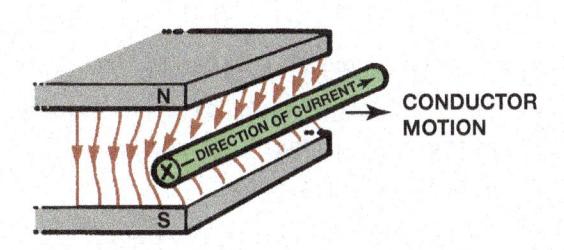

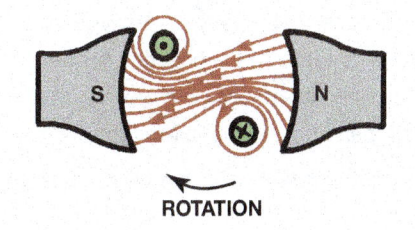

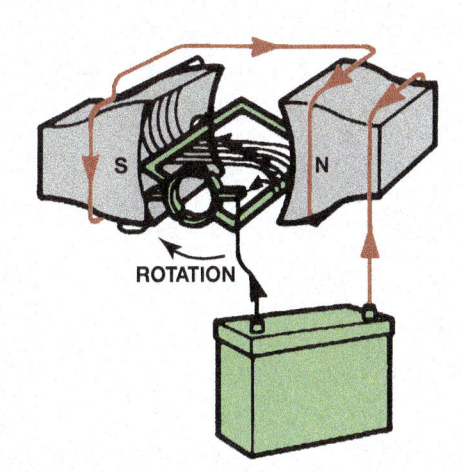

FIGURE 11-10 The armature loops rotate due to the difference in the strength of the magnetic field. The loops move from a strong magnetic field strength toward a weaker magnetic field strength.

One of the first electromagnetic rotary motors was invented by Michael Faraday in 1821. The classic DC motor uses a rotating armature in the form of an electromagnet with two poles. A rotary switch called a **commutator** reverses the direction of the electric current, twice every cycle, to flow through the armature so that the poles of the electromagnet push and pull against the permanent magnets on the outside of the motor. As the poles of the armature electromagnet pass the poles of the permanent magnets, the commutator reverses the polarity of the armature electromagnet. During that instant of switching polarity, inertia keeps the motor going in the proper direction. A typical DC motor today uses four poles.

DC motor speed generally depends on a combination of the voltage and current flowing in the motor coils and the motor load or braking torque. The following are the basic principles of a typical DC motor:

- The speed of the motor is proportional to the applied voltage.
- The torque is proportional to the applied current.
- The speed is typically controlled by altering the voltage or current flow by using taps in the motor windings or by using a variable voltage supply.

The speed can also be controlled by using an electronic circuit that switches the supply voltage on and off very rapidly. As the "on" to "off" time is varied to alter the average applied voltage, the speed of the motor varies. This type of DC motor uses carbon brushes to make the connection with the commutator. The use of brushes in an electric motor has many disadvantages. Some of them include the following:

1. Any arcing of the brushes also causes electrical noise, which can cause serious problems with the electronics in the vehicle.
2. The brushes eventually wear out and require replacement.

This adds to the maintenance cost of the vehicle and could result in customer dissatisfaction due to motor failure and/or the cost involved in brush replacement.

BRUSHLESS MOTORS

TYPES There are two types of electric **brushless motors**:

1. AC induction motor
2. AC synchronous motor.

AC INDUCTION MOTOR An **AC induction motor (ACIM)** uses electromagnetic induction from the stator to induce a current, and therefore creates a magnetic field in the rotor without the need for brushes. An AC induction motor is also known as an *AC asynchronous motor*, or **AC induction motor (ACIM)**, because it allows a certain amount of slip between the rotor and the changing magnetic field in the stator. The term *asynchronous* means that the speed of the motor is not necessarily related to the frequency of the current flowing through the stator windings. ACIMs include squirrel-cage and wound-rotor induction designs.

- A **squirrel-cage rotor** is composed of parallel thick copper or aluminum conductors connected to a ring of the same material at the ends. As the stator magnetic field rotates, the field interacts with the magnetic field established by the magnetic poles of the rotor, causing the rotor to turn at nearly the speed of the rotating stator magnetic field. ● SEE FIGURE 11-11.

- An alternate design is called the *wound rotor*. In this case, the rotor has the same number of poles as the stator, and the windings are made of wire. When the stator magnetic field rotates and the rotor windings are shorted, the stator magnetic field motion induces a field into the wound rotor, causing the rotor to turn at nearly the speed of the rotating stator magnetic field. ● SEE FIGURE 11-12.

AC SYNCHRONOUS MOTOR The AC synchronous motor rotates exactly at the supply frequency or a submultiple of the supply frequency. The speed is controlled by varying the frequency of the AC supply and the number of poles in the stator winding according to the following relation:

$$RPM = 120F \div p$$

where

RPM = Synchronous speed

F = AC power frequency

p = Number of poles, usually an even number, but always a multiple of the number of phases

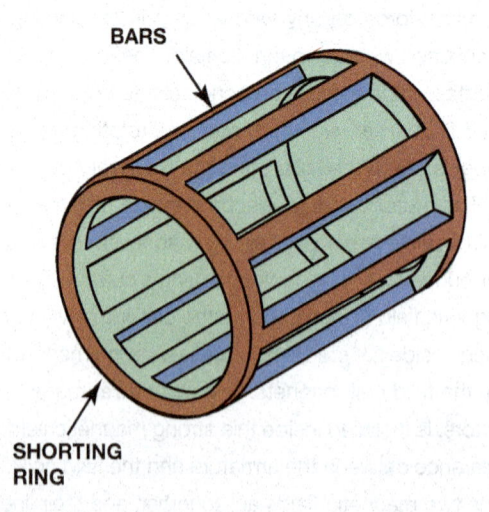

FIGURE 11-11 A squirrel-cage-type rotor used in an AC induction motor.

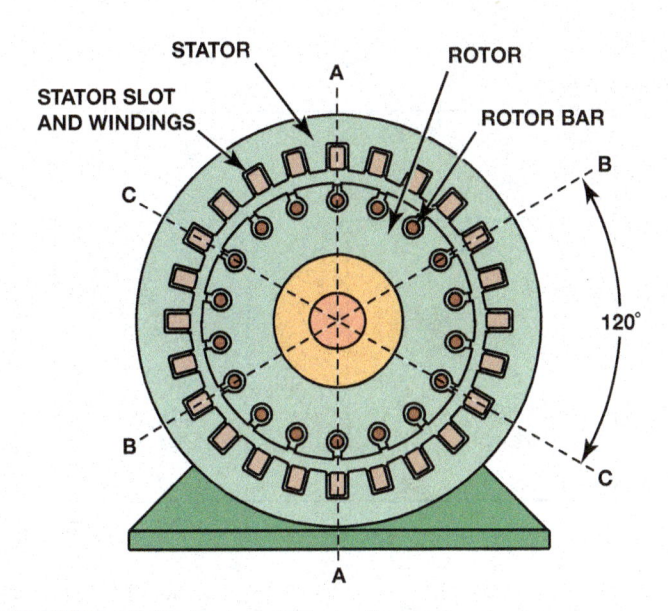

FIGURE 11-12 Typical AC induction motor design.

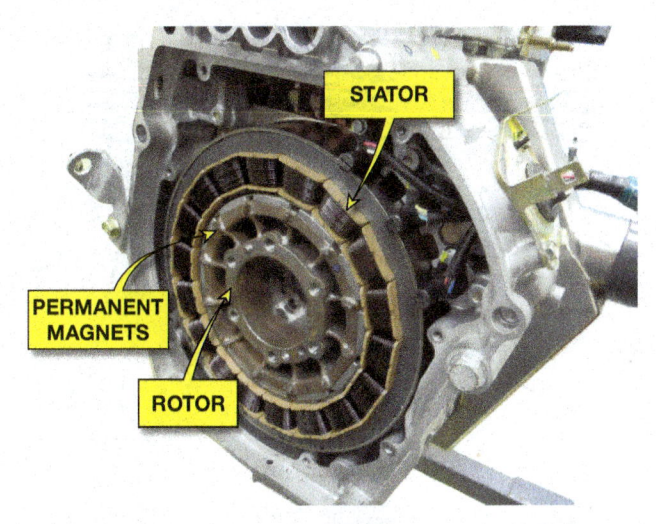

FIGURE 11-13 The rotor for the integrated motor assist (IMA) used on the Honda Civic is a surface permanent magnet (SPM) design. The magnets are made from neodymium.

An electronic switching circuit produces commutating currents in the stator windings based on the position of the magnetic poles on the rotor. The rotor of the motor rotates at the same speed as the stator commutation. The speed of the motor is controlled by the frequency of the AC current being used.

PERMANENT MAGNET MOTORS
Brushless motors, which use permanent magnet rotors, produce high starting torque and are typically over 90% efficient. Brushless permanent magnet motors use two designs of rotors:

1. In one type, the permanent magnets are mounted on the outside surface of the rotor. These are called **surface permanent magnets (SPMs)**. ● SEE FIGURE 11-13.

2. In the other type, the permanent magnets are housed inside the outer shell of the rotor and are called **interior permanent magnets (IPMs)**. The Honda Accord, Ford hybrids, and Toyota hybrids use an IPM-type rotor assembly.

OPERATION
In both types of motors, the stator coils are stationary and the permanent magnet assembly rotates. Alternating current (AC) is fed to the various phases in the stator in order to get the permanent magnets in the rotor to "chase" the changing magnetic field. ● SEE FIGURES 11-14 AND 11-15.

The current is fed into one of the three stator phases and flows out of a second phase. This current flows through the phases, acts as a position sensor, and helps the controller to determine when to energize which phase of the stator. This is sometimes called a *senseless DC motor* design.

Induction motors at rest draw a very high current, known as the *locked rotor current*. They also produce torque, which is known as the *locked rotor torque* (LRT). As the motor accelerates, both the torque and the current will tend to change with rotor speed if the voltage is maintained at a constant level. The starting current of a motor, with a fixed voltage, will drop very slowly as the motor accelerates and will only begin to fall when the motor has reached at least 80% full speed. Typically, the

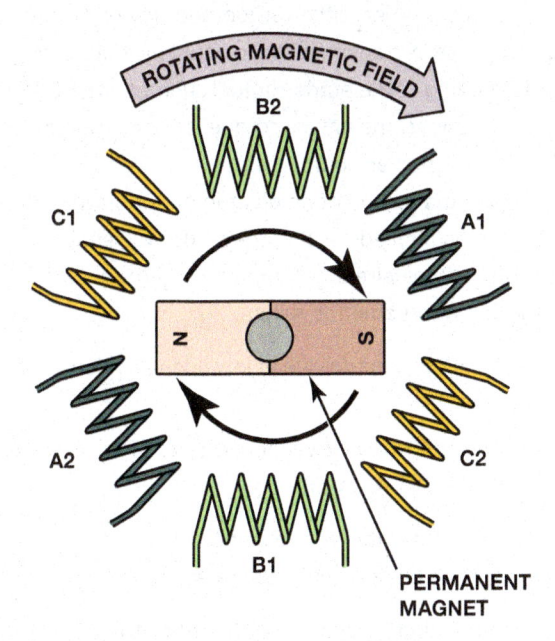

FIGURE 11-14 The rotor in most electric motors used to propel hybrid electric vehicles uses a permanent magnet design. The coils surrounding the rotor in the stator are pulsed on and off to control the speed and torque of the motor.

EV AND HEV MOTORS, CONVERTERS, AND INVERTERS

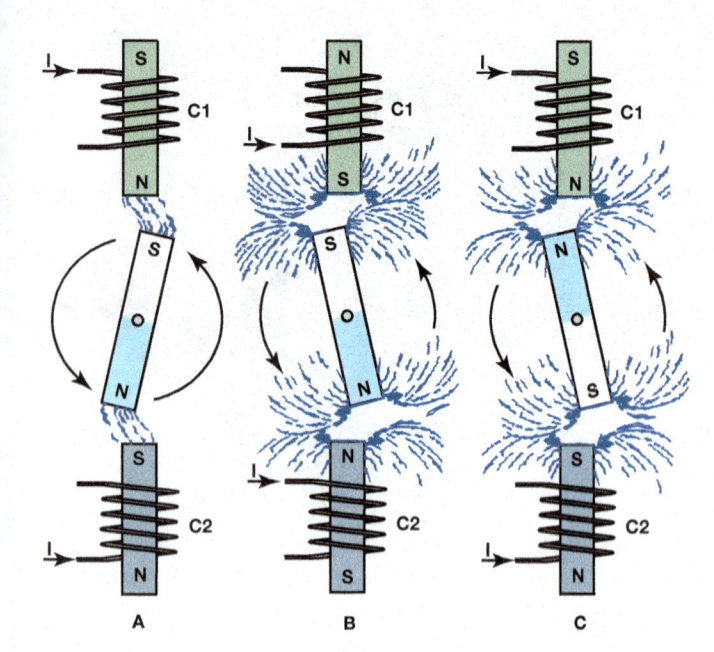

FIGURE 11-15 The rotor is forced to rotate by changing the polarity and the frequency of the coils surrounding the rotor.

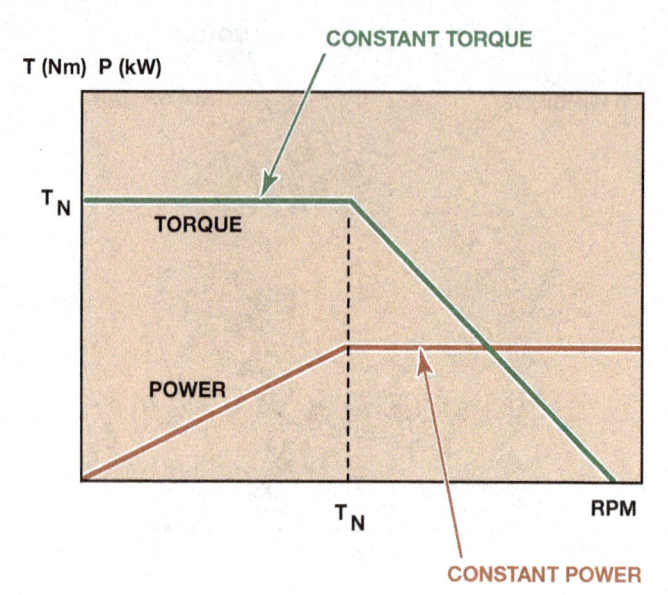

FIGURE 11-16 Notice on the graph that at lower motor speeds the torque produced by the motor is constant and at higher motor speeds the power is constant. Power is equal to torque times RPM; therefore, as the torque decreases the speed increases, keeping the power constant.

efficiency of an induction motor is greater than 92% for high-speed motors.

Most electric vehicles use permanent magnet traction motors except for Tesla. A PM motor has to be continuously driven, whereas an induction motor can freewheel making it more efficient.

ELECTRIC MOTOR TORQUE A gasoline or diesel engine produces very little torque and power at low speeds and must use a transmission to multiply torque to get the vehicle moving. An electric motor, such as an AC induction motor, produces maximum torque at low speeds, making it the perfect power source to get a vehicle moving from a stop. When the torque of an electric motor starts to drop off, the torque multiplied by the speed (RPM) results in power. Therefore, a typical electric motor used on a hybrid vehicle has the following characteristics:

- Delivers constant torque at low speed, typically from 0 to 1500 RPM.
- Delivers constant power above 1500 RPM.
  - **SEE FIGURE 11-16**.

For example, the rear electric motor used in a Toyota Highlander has the following specifications:

- Power output: 123 kW at 4500 RPM (167 hp)
- Maximum torque: 247 lb ft at 0 to 1500 RPM

ELECTRIC MOTOR CONTROL

PRINCIPLES Most hybrid and electric vehicles use one or more AC synchronous motors. They are controlled as follows:

1. To change the speed of the motor, the frequency of the applied current is changed. The speed is synchronized to the frequency so when the frequency is changed, the speed changes.
2. The pulse-width and voltage is adjusted to change the power output to match the demands of the vehicle for electric assist or propulsion.

EXAMPLES An example of traction motor control is the motor-generator (MG) ECU used on Toyota hybrid electric vehicles, which is typical of the controller used in most hybrid electric vehicles.

Motor Mode:

- **Low-Speed–Low-Load Condition:** MG ECU applies low current at low frequency for low output.
- **Low-Speed–High-Load Condition:** MG ECU applies high current at low frequency to produce high motor torque and power output at low speeds.
- **High-Speed–Low-Load Condition:** MG ECU applies low current at a high frequency when low motor torque and power at a high speed is required.

- **High-Speed–High-Load Condition:** MG ECU applies high current at a high frequency to produce high motor power output.

Generator Mode:

- **Low-Speed Voltage Output:** Voltage output is low at low speeds. The diodes in the inverter rectify the AC voltage into DC voltage.
- **High-Speed Voltage Output:** Voltage output is higher at high speeds because the magnetic fields created by the rotor magnets move through the stator windings at high speed.

The MG ECU relies on feedback from the resolver to maintain the highest possible efficiency during the electrochemical conversion of energy. The MG ECU controls all functions of the motor, whether it is producing torque to drive the vehicle or is being used as a generator to charge the batteries during regenerative braking. ● **SEE FIGURE 11-17.**

MOTOR CONTROL IGBTs The arrangement of transistors and diodes results in three-phase control of the electric motor for both moving the vehicle (assist) and recharging the battery pack. The current flow through the MG ECU is controlled by six **insulated-gate bipolar transistors (IGBTs)**.

- Three of these transistors control the voltage side of the circuit and are called positive or high-side IGBTs.

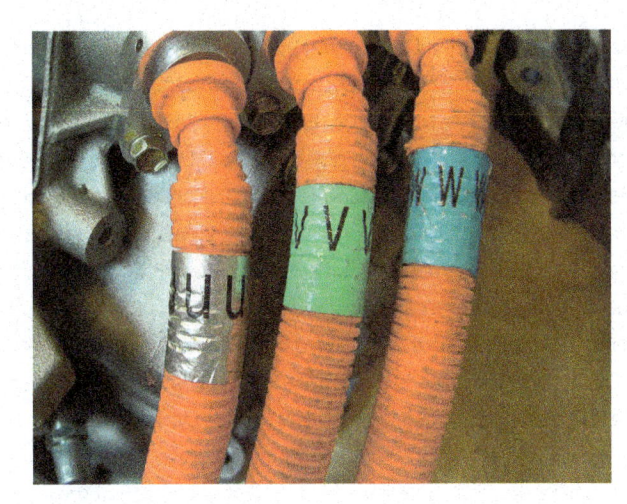

FIGURE 11-17 The power cables for a motor-generator in a Toyota hybrid transaxle.

- The other three transistors are negative or low-side IGBTs because they are on the negative (ground) side of the stator's coils.

The base of each IGBT connects to an input terminal in the connector to the MG ECU. The IGBTs are current drivers that send current from the battery pack through the stator windings to energize the stator coils and move the rotor to power the drive wheels. Most motor controllers include Hall-effect current sensors. ● **SEE FIGURE 11-18.**

Each IGBT has a diode connected in parallel between the collector and the emitter. These six diodes work together to rectify

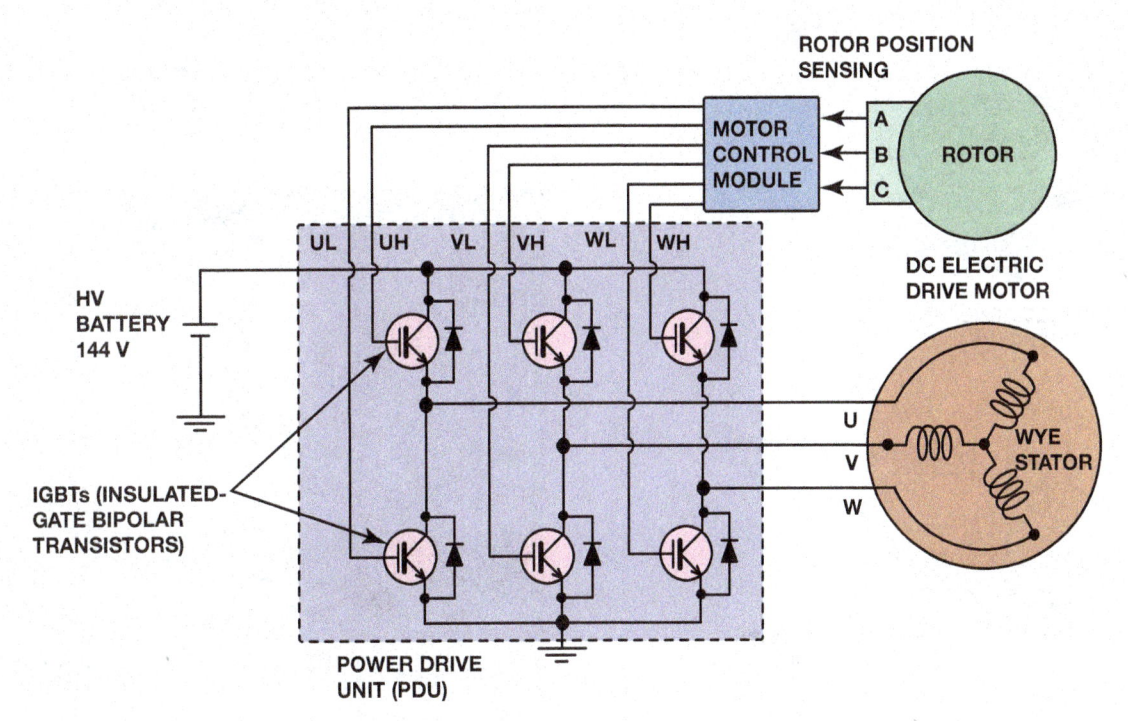

FIGURE 11-18 The drive control unit on a Honda hybrid electric vehicle controls the current and voltage through the stator windings of the motor.

EV AND HEV MOTORS, CONVERTERS, AND INVERTERS

stator AC to pulsating DC to charge the high-voltage batteries when the DC electric drive motor becomes a generator during regenerative braking. At that time, the IGBTs are instantly shut off by the motor control module to stop powering the DC electric drive motor. Because the HEV is still moving forward, the crankshaft is rotating, which rotates the permanent magnet rotor (armature) in the DC electric drive motor. The rotation of the rotor causes the lines of flux from the powerful permanent magnets to induce an AC current in the stator coils. The six diodes are forward biased and turn on to rectify the AC current induced in the stator coils to pulsating DC to recharge the battery pack. Rotor position information is sent to the MCM, which is programmed to turn on the correct IGBTs to keep the rotor turning. It is critical that the controller knows the exact position of the rotor.

The IGBTs process drives current to the electric drive motor. The diodes form a rectifier bridge to change the AC generated in the electric drive motor to pulsating DC to charge the battery pack. ● **SEE FIGURE 11-19**.

RESOLVER Most electric motors use an internal sensor to detect rotor position, speed, and direction that is called a **resolver** or encoder. The resolver consists of an AC generator or excitation coil and two AC pickup coils or detection coils. The resolver is triggered by a rotating iron egg-shaped wheel that is attached to the rotor.

The controller or ECU responsible for motor operation sends a fixed frequency signal to the excitation coil. This signal generates a magnetic field around the excitation coil which expands and contracts with the signal frequency. As the rotor turns the signal strength varies at the two detection coils. Based on the fixed frequency signal and the signal strength of the detection coils, the controller or ECU is able to determine rotor position, rotational direction, and speed. The position can be determined without turning the rotor. The ECU compares the height of the waveforms generated by the detection coils and the frequency of signal change to make the determination. ● **SEE FIGURES 11-20 AND 11-21**.

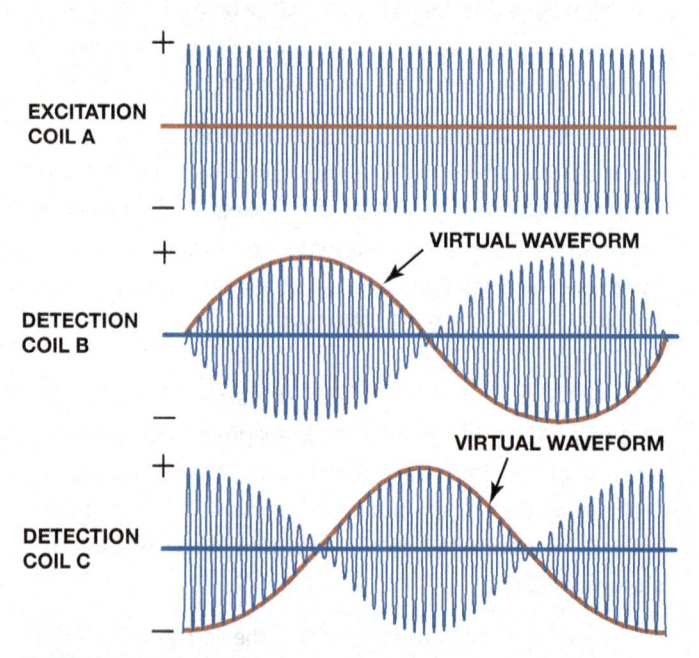

FIGURE 11-20 Each coil in the speed sensor (resolver) generates a unique waveform, allowing the motor controller to determine the position of the rotor in the motor. The top waveform is coil A, the middle waveform is coil B, and the bottom waveform is coil C. The controller uses the three waveforms to determine the position of the rotor.

FIGURE 11-19 A Toyota motor speed sensor called a resolver.

FIGURE 11-21 The underside of the Toyota Prius controller showing the coolant passages used to cool the electronic control unit.

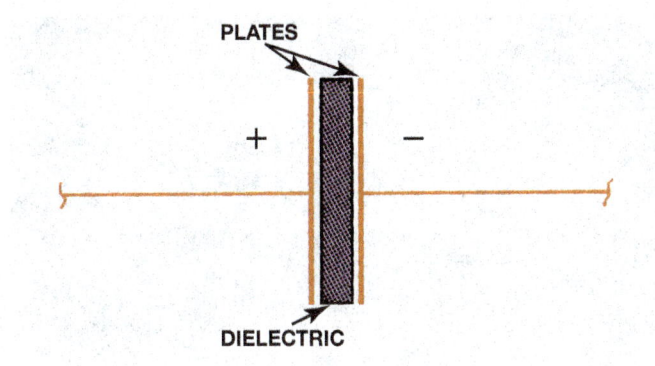

FIGURE 11-22 A capacitor is made using two plates separated by an insulating material called a dielectric.

Historically, resolvers or encoders were not serviceable because of the inability to properly install and calibrate the replacement sensor. As a result, a failed resolver would require motor replacement. However, more recently resolvers have become a serviceable component within the motor. The resolver in the motor of the Chevrolet Bolt is an example of a serviceable sensor. When servicing a resolver, it is important to remember that it is a low-voltage and low-current component and that the connections need to be properly torqued for proper operation.

TEMPERATURE SENSORS Temperature sensors are needed to help protect the motors from overheating. The controller responsible for motor operation reads the thermistor resistance much like an engine coolant sensor operates and they convert this reading to a temperature. An overheating electric motor will result in fail-safe or limp-in operation.

COOLING THE ELECTRONICS The current flow and the electronic devices in hybrid electric control units generate a lot of heat. Many hybrid and electric vehicles use a dedicated liquid cooling system to control the temperature of the electronics, including the motors. Others use a wet cooling method to cool the motors that utilizes the transmission fluid to remove the heat. ● **SEE FIGURE 11-22**.

CAPACITORS IN CONVERTERS

PRINCIPLES
Capacitance is the ability of an object or surface to store an electrical charge. In 1745, Ewald Christian von Kleist and Pieter van Musschenbroek independently discovered capacitance in an electric circuit. While engaged in separate studies of electrostatics, they discovered that an electric charge could be stored for a period of time.

A capacitor consists of two conductive plates with an insulating material between them. The insulating material is commonly called a dielectric. It may be air, mica, ceramic, glass, paper, plastic, or any similar nonconductive material. The higher the dielectric constant number of a material, the better it is as an insulator. Capacitors are also called *condensers*. This term developed because electric charges collect, or condense, on the plates of a capacitor much like water vapor collects and condenses on a cold bottle or glass. ● **SEE FIGURE 11-23 AND CHART 11-2.**

OPERATION When a capacitor is placed in a closed circuit, the voltage source, such as a battery, forces electrons around the circuit. Because electrons cannot flow through the dielectric of the capacitor, excess electrons collect on what becomes the negatively charged plate. At the same time the other plate loses electrons, and therefore becomes positively charged.

Current continues until the voltage charge across the capacitor plates becomes the same as the source voltage. At that time, the negative plate of the capacitor and the negative terminal of the battery are at the same negative potential. ● **SEE FIGURE 11-24.**

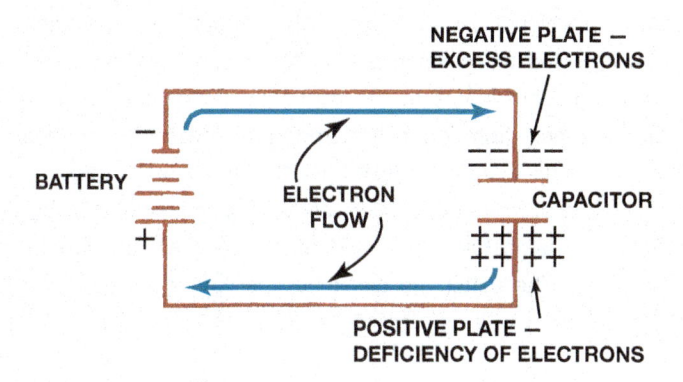

FIGURE 11-23 As the capacitor is charging, the battery forces electrons through the circuit.

MATERIAL	DIELECTRIC CONSTANT
Vacuum	1.0
Air	1.00059
Polystyrene	2.5
Paper	3.5
Mica	5.4
Flint Glass	9.9
Methyl Alcohol (Methanol)	35
Glycerin	56
Pure Water	81

CHART 11-2

The dielectric constant for selected materials.

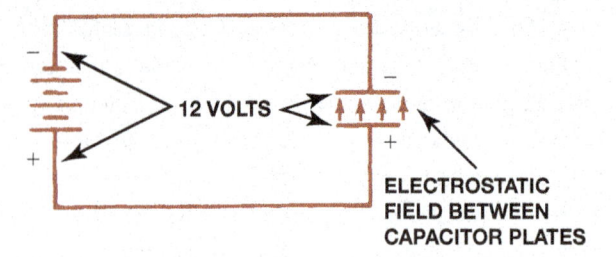

FIGURE 11–24 When the capacitor is charged, there is equal voltage across the capacitor and the battery. An electrostatic field exists between the capacitor plates. No current flows in the circuit.

The positive plate of the capacitor and the positive terminal of the battery are also at equal positive potentials. There is then a voltage charge across the battery terminals and an equal voltage charge across the capacitor plates. The circuit is in balance, and there is no current. An electrostatic field now exists between the capacitor plates because of their opposite charges. It is this field that stores energy. ● SEE FIGURE 11–25.

PRECAUTIONS If the circuit is opened, the capacitor will hold its charge until it is connected into an external circuit through which it can discharge. When the charged capacitor is connected to an external circuit, it discharges. After discharging, both plates of the capacitor are neutral because all the energy from a circuit stored in a capacitor is returned when it is discharged. ● SEE FIGURES 11–26 AND 11–27.

Theoretically, a capacitor can hold its charge indefinitely. Actually, the charge slowly leaks off the capacitor through the dielectric. The better the dielectric, the longer the capacitor

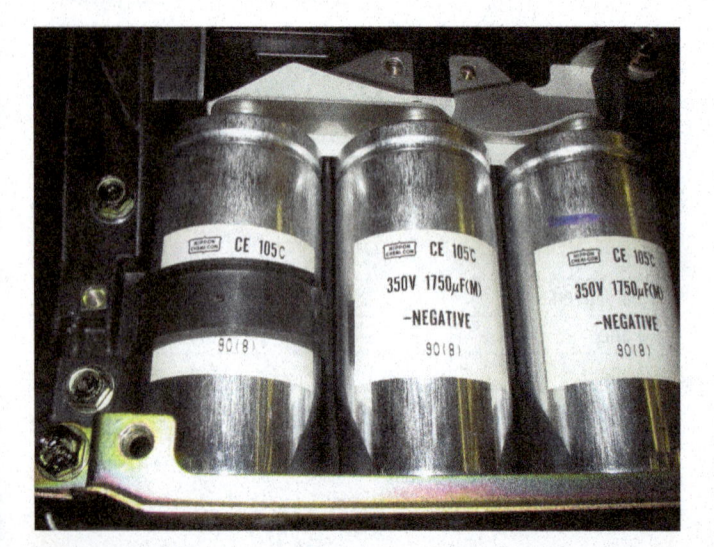

FIGURE 11–25 The three large capacitors absorb voltage spikes that occur when the voltage level is changed in the DC-DC converters.

FIGURE 11–26 The dark cylinders are capacitors that are part of the electronic control unit of this Toyota hybrid.

FIGURE 11–27 Using a CAT III-rated digital meter and wearing rubber lineman's gloves, this technician is checking for voltage at the inverter to verify that the capacitors have discharged.

holds its charge. When the ignition of an HEV is turned off, vehicle manufacturers warn that you must wait 5 to 10 minutes for the capacitors to discharge before servicing the high-voltage system. While these capacitors often discharge in less than five minutes, it is wise to wait the amount of time specified by the vehicle manufacturer. ● SEE FIGURE 11–28.

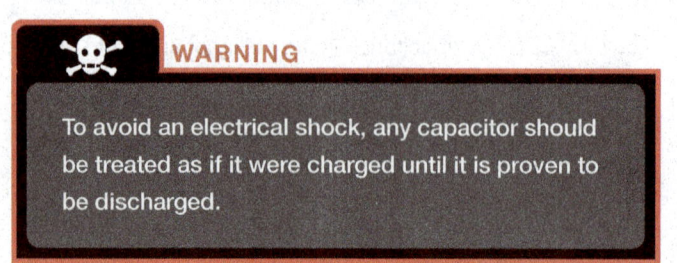

> **☠ WARNING**
>
> To avoid an electrical shock, any capacitor should be treated as if it were charged until it is proven to be discharged.

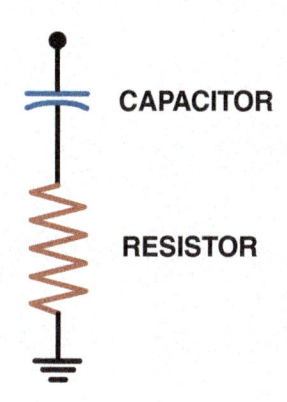

FIGURE 11-28 A typical snubber circuit showing a capacitor and a resistor in series and connected to ground.

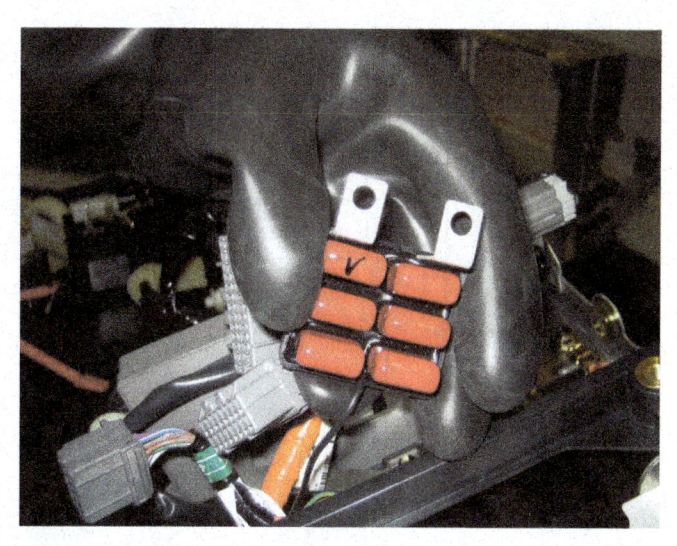

FIGURE 11-29 The snubber circuit from a hybrid showing the six capacitors used to control voltage spikes in the switching circuits.

FARAD RATING Capacitance is measured in farads, which is named after Michael Faraday (1791–1867). The symbol for farads is F. If a charge of 1 coulomb is placed on the plates of a capacitor and the potential difference between them is 1 volt, the capacitance is defined to be 1 farad. One coulomb is equal to the charge of 6.25×10^{18} electrons. One farad is an extremely large quantity of capacitance. Microfarads (0.000001 farad), abbreviated µF, are more commonly used.

The capacitance of a capacitor is proportional to the quantity of charge that can be stored in it for each volt difference in potential between its plates:

$$C = Q \div V$$

Where C is capacitance in farads, Q is the quantity of stored electrical charge in coulombs, and V is the difference in potential in volts. Therefore, stored electric charge can be calculated using the formula:

$$Q = CV$$

SNUBBERS Snubbers are capacitors and resistors arranged in a circuit to control the high-voltage surges that can occur when circuits containing coils are switched on and off. Snubbers are also called *flyback, freewheeling, suppressor,* or *catch diodes*.

Because the switch is being protected, this results in higher reliability, higher efficiency, higher switching frequency, smaller size, lower weight, and lower electromagnetic interference (EMI). ● **SEE FIGURE 11-29**.

CONVERTERS AND INVERTERS

CONVERTERS DC-to-DC converters (usually written DC–DC converter) are electronic devices used to transform DC voltage from one level of DC voltage to another higher or lower-level voltage. They are used to distribute various levels of DC voltage throughout a vehicle from a single power bus (or voltage source).

A more familiar example of a DC–DC converter circuit is the circuit the PCM uses to convert 14 to 5 volts. The 5 volts is called the reference voltage, abbreviated V-ref, and is used to power many sensors in a computer-controlled engine management system.

The PCM uses a DC–DC converter that is a small semiconductor device called a voltage regulator and is designed to convert battery voltage to a constant 5 volts regardless of changes in the charging voltage.

Hybrid and electric vehicles use DC–DC converters to provide system operating voltage (approximately 14.4 volts) that would normally be provided by an alternator. ● **SEE FIGURE 11-30**. This provides power for items such as lights, radios, and any other components that operate on the 12-volt system. The power transistor within the control module pulses the high-voltage coil of the center-tap transformer; the resulting changing magnetic field induces a voltage in the coil windings of the lower-voltage side of the transformer. The diodes and capacitors help control and limit the voltage and frequency of the circuit. Most DC–DC converters used on hybrid and electric vehicles are capable of maintaining 14 volts and 100 amperes of current flow under maximum load. The DC–DC converter may be air cooled or liquid cooled and integrated into the same housing as the inverter or it may be in a separate location depending on the vehicle design. ● **SEE FIGURE 11-31**.

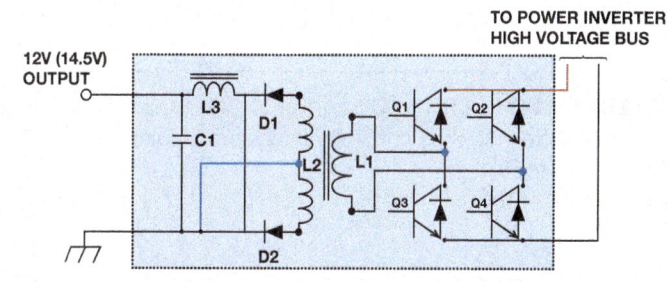

FIGURE 11-30 A DC to DC converter that changes the high voltage from the high-voltage battery (right) to 12 volts on the left.

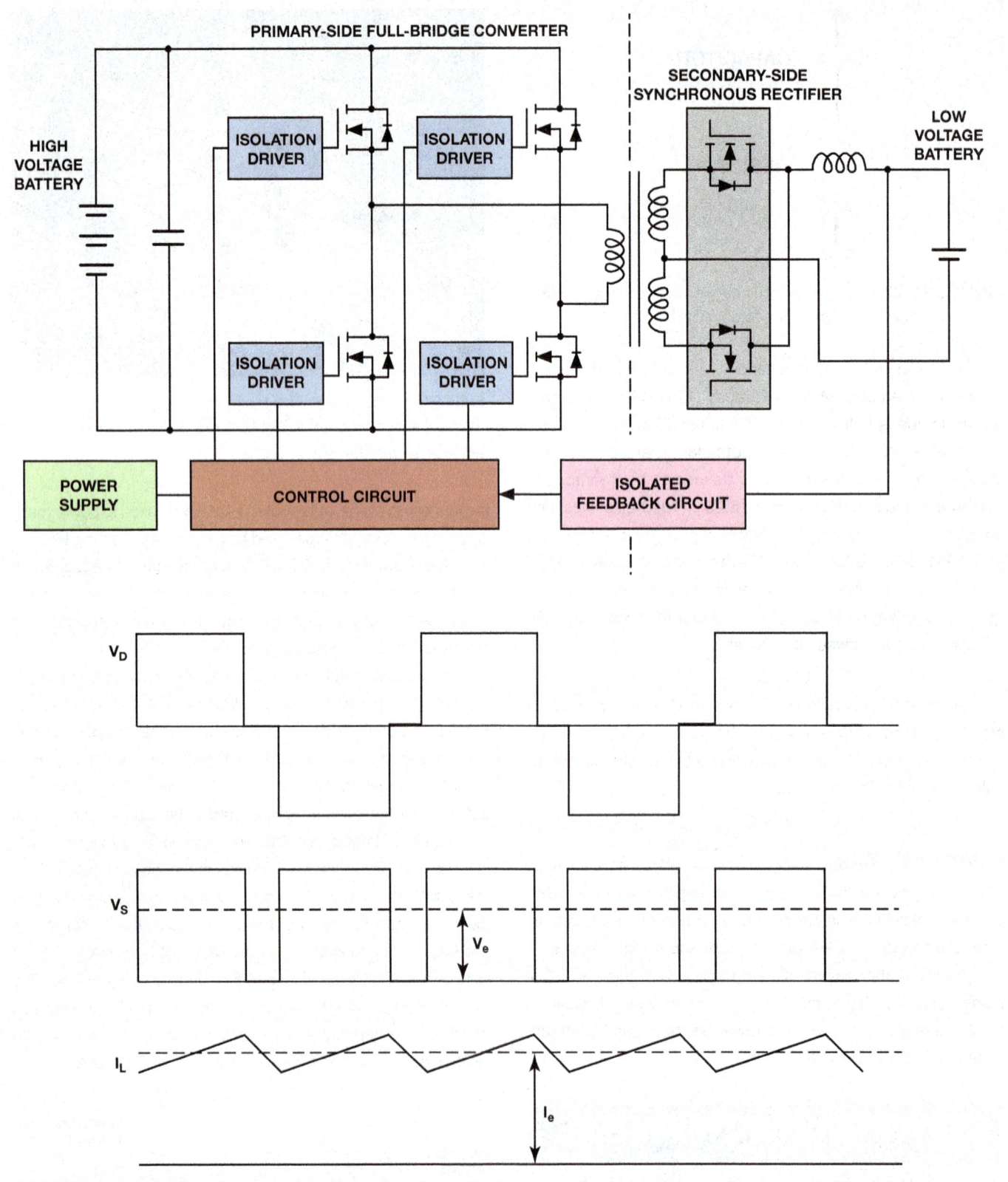

FIGURE 11-31 A DC-to-DC converter. The schematic at the top shows the high voltage battery on the left and the low voltage battery on the right. The circuits are able to change the pulsing DC into a pulse train and finally into an almost flat direct current.

INVERTERS Inverters are electronic devices that can turn DC (direct current) to AC (alternating current). It is also responsible for controlling speed and torque for electric motors. The inverter can provide a pulsed signal to the motor to move the vehicle or it can process the AC signal generated by the motors during a regeneration event. The inverter uses insulated-gate bipolar transistor (IGBTs) to control the motor. They are turned on alternately for short pulses. By changing the power and ground, as well as the polarity, the inverter is able to use DC current to drive an AC motor.

As a result, the transformer produces a modified sine wave output, rather than a true sine wave. The waveform produced by an inverter is not the perfect sine wave of household AC current, but is rather more like a pulsing DC current that reacts similar to sine wave AC in transformers and in induction motors.
● **SEE FIGURE 11-32**.

The inverter contains up to three smoothing capacitors. The purpose of these capacitors is to smooth the DC ripple. A resistor is wired in parallel to the capacitors that allows for them to be discharged after the vehicle is shut off.

IGBTs allow current to flow in two directions. As a result, the ECU is able to pulse the IGBTs as the vehicle decelerates. This controls the strength of the magnetic field in the motors as they are driven by the wheels. The strength of the magnetic field affects how rapidly the vehicle slows and how much energy is generated to recharge the battery.

PRE-CHARGE RELAY A pre-charge resistor is used to slowly charge the capacitors inside an electronic speed controller before it is powered up. Without this resistor, closing the contactor would generate a large amount of inrush current causing the contacts to arc.

Normal operation of a pre-charge circuit is to terminate pre-charge mode when the circuit voltage is 90% or 95% of the operating voltage. After pre-charging, the pre-charge resistor is switched out of the power supply circuit and returns to a normal mode.

BOOST CONVERTERS Integrated into some inverters is a boost converter. **Boost converters** are used to enhance high-voltage systems that operate on a lower high-voltage battery. The boost converter boosts the nominal voltage output by the battery to as much as 500 volts to meet increased electrical demand based on the load. The boost converter consists of the boost integrated power module (IPM) with a built-in insulated-gate bipolar transistor (IGBT), which performs the switching controls and a reactor which stores the energy. By using these components, the converter boosts the voltage. ● **SEE FIGURE 11-33**.

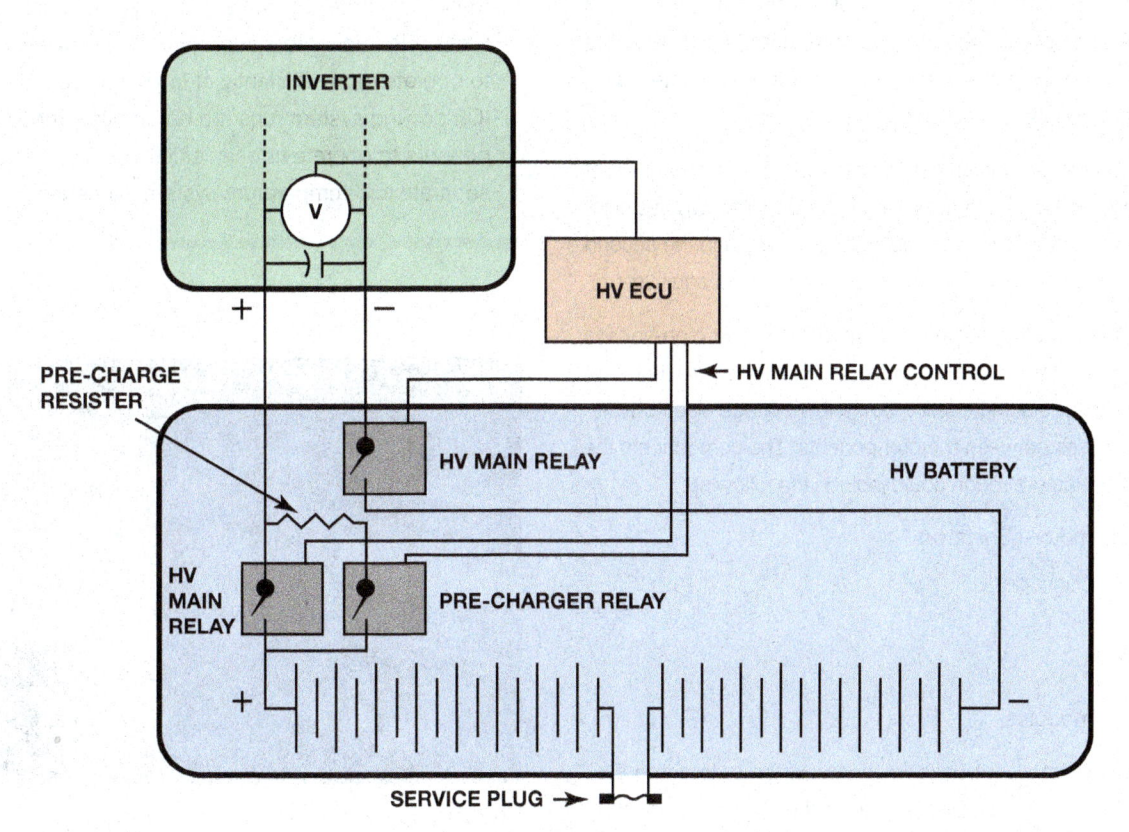

FIGURE 11-32 A typical HV battery and HV main relay schematic showing the pre-charge resistor and relay as well as the HV main relay.

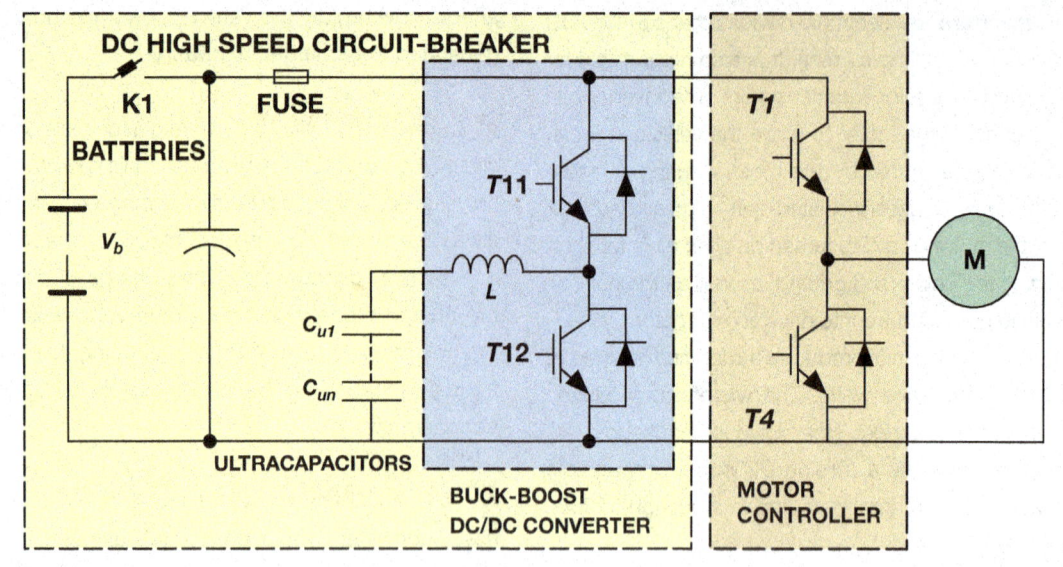

FIGURE 11-33 A boost converter is used to increase the voltage supplied to the drive motor to improve power output.

ELECTRONIC SYSTEM COOLING SYSTEM

NEED FOR COOLING The high-voltage electrical system on a HEV will have its own dedicated cooling system. The purpose of this system is to absorb the heat generated by the operation of the high-voltage components and dissipate it through a dedicated radiator. The coolant is circulated by a dedicated low-voltage electric pump.

Example: On some vehicles, like the second-generation Chevrolet Volt, the high-voltage cooling system is divided into two systems. One system is responsible for cooling the battery and the second system is responsible for the balance of the high-voltage system.

The liquid cooling system for the motors and high-voltage components consists of an expansion tank with a pressure cap, a radiator with an electric cooling fan, a low-voltage electric water pump, and hoses between the components. The components the coolant is circulated through could include the following:

- Electric motor-generators
- DC–DC converter
- Inverter
- Battery
- Control modules

A thermostat is not used in these systems. In some systems the electric pump runs any time the key is on. In other systems the pump speed and time vary with the temperature of the coolant. ● **SEE FIGURE 11-34**.

? FREQUENTLY ASKED QUESTION

Why Isn't the ICE Cooling System Used to Cool HEV Motors and Electronic Components?

Most ICE cooling systems operate at over 200°F (93°C). For maximum efficiency, it is important that the ICE operates as close to this temperature at all times. Electric motors and controllers, however, tend to operate more efficiently at lower temperatures. The ICE cooling system runs too hot to allow these components to operate at peak efficiency. Therefore, a separate low-temperature system is needed.

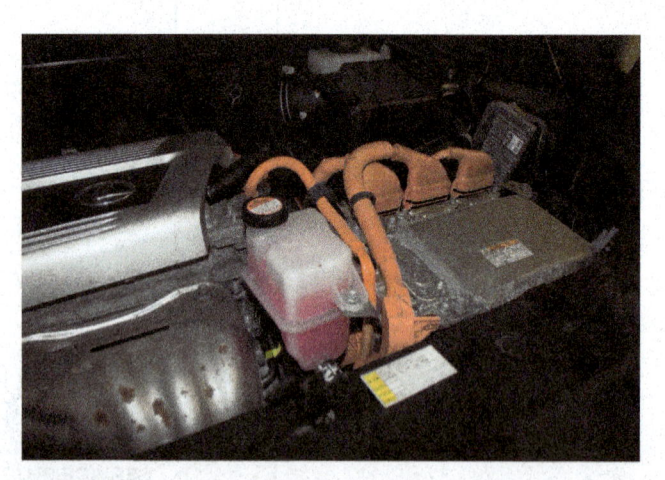

FIGURE 11-34 The reservoir and cap of the inverter/converter (orange cable) on a Toyota Highlander hybrid electric hybrid vehicle.

NOTE: The system will run when charging the batteries on EVs and PHEVs. This is to warm the batteries in cold weather or to cool the batteries/charging system during hot weather.

DIAGNOSTIC STEPS The coolant in these systems is the same as the internal combustion engine (ICE). Servicing the electronic cooling system includes the following steps:

STEP 1 The coolant should be tested, serviced, and replaced according to the specific manufacturer's recommendations. In many cases, a vacuum lift system will be required to remove and replace the coolant in the electronic cooling system.

STEP 2 A scan tool with the capability of actuating the electric water pump will be needed to ensure all air pockets are removed from the cooling system during service.

MOTOR–CONVERTER–INVERTER DIAGNOSTICS

GLOBAL (GENERIC) DIAGNOSTIC TROUBLE CODES

Whenever diagnosing a motor or control fault, use a scan tool and check for any stored diagnostic trouble codes and follow the vehicle manufacturer's recommended pinpoint tests to determine the root cause. ● **SEE CHART 11-3**.

TESTING THE ELECTRIC MOTOR STATOR

A stator can be tested for shorts to ground and for shorts to copper within the windings. A failed stator is likely to cause an imbalance between the windings. This is the equivalent of having uneven compression in the cylinders of an internal combustion engine. The MG ECU will typically set a DTC P3120 if the energy balance becomes too great. The stator can be tested by measuring the current flow through each leg or by measuring the resistance of each leg. The resistance through each leg of the windings is too small to be measured with a conventional multimeter. The resistance should be checked with a milliohm meter. The resistance of each leg should be approximately the same. Any significant variance indicates a failed stator.

The current flow through the stator can be measured on the bench using a stator tester or when the vehicle is operating using a scope. Using either method, all three legs of the windings must be balanced.

DC–DC CONVERTER TESTING

If a vehicle is being driven with a DC–DC converter malfunction, the voltage to the auxiliary battery will drop and the vehicle will no longer be operational. If the voltage drops below a specific threshold, a diagnostic trouble code (DTC) P3125 will be set indicating a malfunction. To test the DC–DC converter three CAT III multimeters and two amp clamps will be needed.

- Test the 12-volt (auxiliary) battery to ensure it is good. If not, charge and retest.
- Connect the first multimeter across the 12-volt battery to measure the DC voltage.
- Connect the first amp clamp around the cable between the DC–DC converter and the 12-volt battery. This will measure the amount of current the DC–DC converter is providing.
- Connect the second amp clamp around the battery negative cable. This will measure how much current the vehicle systems are drawing from the battery.

With the vehicle in the ready mode the DC–DC converter should be able to maintain a system voltage of 14.0 volts and provide up to approximately 100 amperes of current flow as needed to maintain the electrical load.

DIAGNOSTIC TROUBLE CODE (DTC)	MEANING
P0A00	Motor electronics coolant temperature sensor circuit
P0A01	Motor electronics coolant temperature sensor circuit range/performance
P0A02	Motor electronics coolant temperature sensor circuit low
P0A03	Motor electronics coolant temperature sensor circuit high
P0A04	Motor electronics coolant temperature sensor circuit intermittent
P0A05	Motor electronics coolant pump control circuit /open
P0A06	Motor electronics coolant pump control circuit low
P0A07	Motor electronics coolant pump control circuit high
P0A08	DC–DC converter status circuit/open
P0A09	DC–DC converter status circuit low
P0A10	DC–DC converter enable circuit/high
P0A11	DC–DC converter enable circuit/open
P0A12	DC–DC converter enable circuit low
P0A13	DC–DC converter enable circuit high

CHART 11-3

Sample global (generic) motor/controller-related diagnostic trouble codes (DTCs).

INVERTER TESTING In most cases, when the inverter fails, the vehicle will not move. Begin inverter testing by checking for trouble codes. Typically the presence of a P0A08 or P0A09 trouble code is an indicator of a failed inverter. The two most common causes of these codes are an inverter that is overheating due to a failed coolant pump or a customer has hooked up the battery cables backwards trying to jump start a second vehicle. Before replacing a failed inverter, check the electric motors. A failed stator winding in a motor may cause the inverter to fail. Failure to first replace the failed motor may result in failure of the replacement inverter.

LOSS OF ISOLATION TESTING One of the tests that can be performed using an isolation tester is to check for the resistance between the inverter and the engine block (chassis ground). ● **SEE FIGURE 11-35**.

FIGURE 11-35 Testing at the inverter for a loss of isolation. The reading of 1.4 million ohms indicates that there is not continuity between the inverter and chassis ground.

PHOTO SEQUENCE—INVERTER/CONVERTER REPLACEMENT

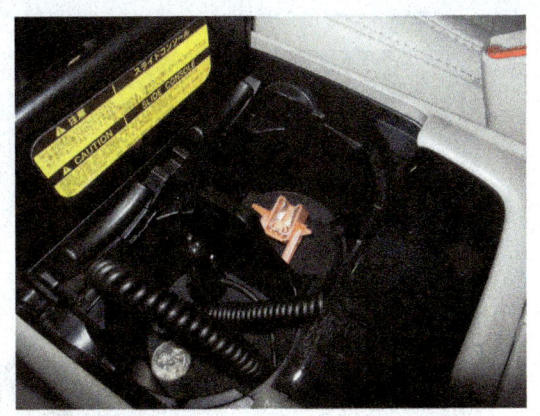

1 The first step when dealing with the high-voltage system on any hybrid electric vehicle is to remove the HV service plug while wearing high-voltage gloves for protection. The technician placed the orange plug in the cup holder in the center console to make sure it is out of the way.

2 Before gaining access to the inverter/converter assembly, the windshield wiper module and many other parts were removed.

3 The coolant reservoir bottle for the HV electronics was moved out of the way and secured using a rubber stretch cable.

4 After removing the protective cover plate, the terminals were checked to make sure that voltage was not present.

5 The meter was set to read DC volts and the meter displayed zero volts meaning that the system had been successfully depowered and was safe to work on the system.

6 A plastic cover was included with the replacement inverter/converter and was to be used to protect the upper part of the circuit board during the removal process.

EV AND HEV MOTORS, CONVERTERS, AND INVERTERS

STEP BY STEP

7 The retaining fasteners being removed that were used to attach the main relays to the base of the inverter/converter housing.

8 The technician was careful to keep the fasteners separated and yet together by using several magnetic trays.

9 To help retrieve fasteners so they did not get lost or drop down into the electronic circuit board, this technician used a magnetic finger glove.

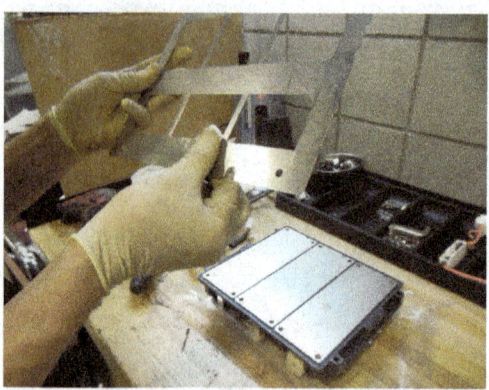

10 The replacement inverter is shipped to the dealer with a steel plate that is to be used as a template when applying heat-conductive grease to the base of the unit.

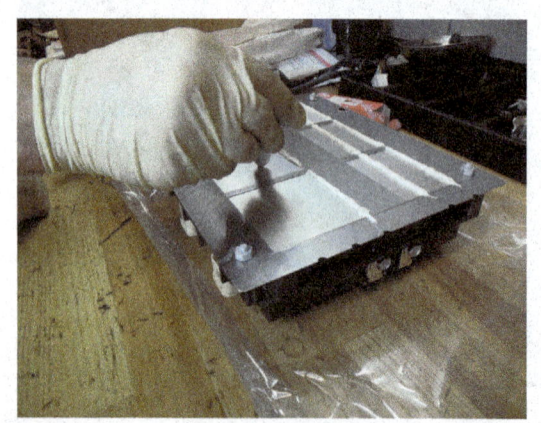

11 The instructions specified that rows of the conductive grease be applied across the surface.

12 Then the grease is spread over the surface using the supplied metal straight edge.

CONTINUED ▶

PHOTO SEQUENCE-INVERTER/CONVERTER REPLACEMENT

CONTINUED ➤

13 After the grease has been spread out, the steel template is removed which shows a perfectly flat layer of grease applied to the specified thickness to allow the heat from the inverter/converter to be transferred to the aluminum housing and then to the HV cooling system.

14 All of the original grease is being carefully removed in preparation for the installation of the replacement inverter/converter.

15 The instructions are checked at each step to make sure that all fasteners are tightened in the correct order and in the proper sequence.

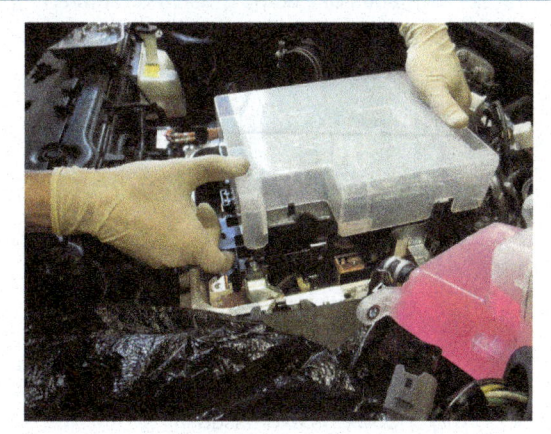

16 The upper electronic board with its protective cover is reinstalled and the fasteners tightened to factory specifications.

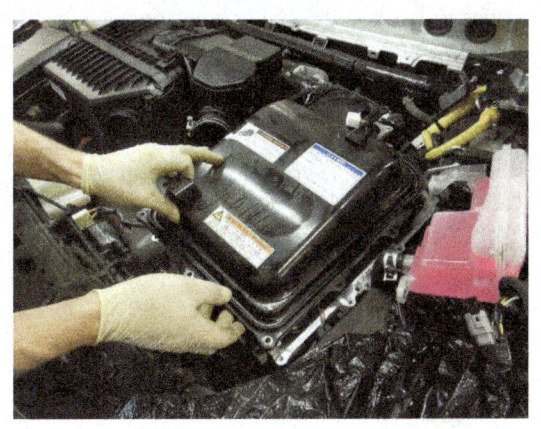

17 The outside cover is then installed.

18 The windshield wiper module and all other items removed are then reinstalled, completing the replacement.

SUMMARY

1. The creation of a magnetic field by the use of an electrical current is called electromagnetism.
2. Electric motor power is expressed in kilowatts (kW).
3. DC motor speed generally depends on a combination of the voltage and current flowing in the motor coils and the motor load or braking torque.
4. There are two types of electric brushless motors.
5. The AC synchronous motor rotates exactly at the supply frequency or a submultiple of the supply frequency.
6. A PM motor has to be continuously driven, whereas an induction motor can freewheel making it more efficient.
7. To change the speed of the motor, the frequency of the applied current is changed. The speed is synchronized to the frequency so when the frequency is changed, the speed changes.
8. The current flow through the MG ECU is controlled by six insulated gate bipolar transistors (IGBTs).
9. DC-to-DC converters (usually written DC–DC converter) are electronic devices used to transform DC voltage from one level of DC voltage to another higher or lower level voltage.
10. The purpose of the inverter is to control the electric motors in the transmission.

REVIEW QUESTIONS

1. How is magnetism created using electricity?
2. What are two types of electric brushless motors?
3. What do insulated gate bipolar transistors (IGBTs) do?
4. How does a DC-to-DC converter work?
5. What is the purpose of the inverter?

CHAPTER QUIZ

1. The creation of a magnetic field by the use of an electrical current is called _____.
   a. electromagnetism
   b. electricity
   c. permanent magnet
   d. electrostatic field
2. Electric motor power is expressed in _____.
   a. horsepower
   b. kilowatts
   c. kilowatt-hours
   d. amperes
3. The two types of electric brushless motors include _____.
   a. Faraday and Tesla
   b. Ohms and Faraday
   c. AC induction and AC synchronous
   d. pulse-width and voltage
4. The speed of the motor is proportional to the _____ and the torque is proportional to the _____.
   a. voltage and current
   b. current and voltage
   c. resistance and amperage
   d. current and frequency
5. An AC induction motor is also known as a/an _____.
   a. DC motor
   b. magnetic motor
   c. AC asynchronous motor
   d. AC synchronous motor
6. Most electric motors use an internal sensor to detect rotor position, speed, and direction that is called a/an _____.
   a. resolver
   b. encoder
   c. position sensor
   d. Either a or b
7. Snubbers are also called _____ diodes.
   a. flyback
   b. freewheeling
   c. suppressor, or catch
   d. Any of the above
8. What supplies the 12 volts needed to operate the accessories in a hybrid electric or an electric vehicle?
   a. An alternator driven by an electric motor
   b. A DC–DC converter
   c. An inverter
   d. Either a or c depending on the vehicle
9. With the vehicle in the ready mode, the _____ should be able to maintain a system voltage of 14.0 volts to the 12-volt auxiliary battery.
   a. inverter
   b. alternator
   c. DC-to-DC converter
   d. Any of the above
10. A P0A04 DTC is what type of trouble code?
    a. Global (generic)
    b. Vehicle manufacturer specific
    c. Enhanced scan tool
    d. Any of the above

Chapter 12
EV AND PHEV CHARGING

LEARNING OBJECTIVES

After studying this chapter, the reader should be able to:

- Identify a plug-in hybrid electric vehicle (PHEV).
- Explain how the high-voltage batteries are recharged in a PHEV and EV vehicle.
- Discuss range anxiety, battery capacity, and range correlation of an EV.
- Explain the safety precautions using Level 1, Level 2, and Level 3 charging.

KEY TERMS

Always Be Charging (ABC) 169
Battery electric vehicle (BEV) 166
DCFC (DC Fast Charge) 169
Destination charging 173
Electric vehicle (EV) 166
EV Range 164
Guobiao standard (GB or GB/T) 170
kilowatt-hour (kWh) 164
kWh/100 mi 167
Miles per hour (MPH) 169
Plug-in hybrid electric vehicle (PHEV) 164
Public Charging Stations (PCS) 173
Range 166
Range anxiety 167
Range per hour (RPH) 169
SAE Combo Charging System (CCS) 169
State-of-charge (SOC) 164
Time-of-use (TOU) 172
Work place charging (WPC) 173
Zero-emission vehicles (ZEVs) 166

PLUG-IN HYBRID ELECTRIC VEHICLES

TERMINOLOGY A **plug-in hybrid electric vehicle (PHEV)** is a vehicle that is designed to be plugged into an electrical outlet at home, at work, or when traveling to charge the batteries. By charging the batteries in the vehicle, it can operate using electric power alone (stealth mode) for a longer time, thereby reducing the use of the internal combustion engine (ICE). The less the ICE is operating, the less fuel is consumed, which lowers the emissions of the vehicle. Some PHEVs offer the driver an option to use the ICE first and switch to EV mode (electric only) later in the trip. This option is commonly used where the driver is first traveling on the highway and uses the ICE to propel the vehicle, saving the energy in the battery to be used when arriving in the city.

IDENTIFYING A PHEV Many PHEV are built using a conventional or a hybrid-electric vehicle (HEV) configuration with just added battery capacity. As a result, some PHEVs may be difficult to pick out, such as the plug-in version of the Toyota Prius. Features that identify a plug-in version of a HEV include the following:

- Different badges (usually stating that it is a PHEV, sometimes including PHEV on the badge).
- An access door for the charging cable in addition to the normal ICE fueling door.
- A different instrument panel cluster.
  - ● **SEE FIGURE 12-1**.

The operation of the plug-in version is the same as the HEV version of the same vehicle, so from a service or maintenance point of view, it does not really matter whether it is a PHEV or a HEV.

PHEV BATTERY CAPACITY The size or capacity of the battery pack used determines how far that the vehicle can travel without using the ICE, commonly called the **EV range**. Battery capacity is measured in **kilowatt-hour (kWh)**. A kilowatt is 1,000 watts and a watt is a volt times an ampere, which is a measurement of electrical power. The higher the kWh rating of the battery, the more electrical energy it can store.

- A lower kilowatt-hour (kWh) rated battery weighs less and is less expensive, but the range that the vehicle can travel on battery power alone is limited.

FIGURE 12-1 (a) About the only way to tell a plug-in Prius from a regular Prius is from the badge on the sides or (b) by the charge port door on the passenger side at the rear.

- A higher kWh rating battery means that the battery is capable of propelling the vehicle for a greater distance before the ICE is used. This reduces the fuel used, but the larger battery weighs and costs more.
- The high-voltage battery is continuously checked for state-of-charge. The **state-of-charge (SOC)** is the percentage of the available capacity that can be stored in a battery. A battery that has a state-of-charge of 100% is fully charged.

Therefore, a plug-in vehicle is a compromise between cost and weight of the battery.

PHEV EXAMPLES A standard Toyota Prius has a 1.3 kWh battery pack, whereas the plug-in version has a larger 4.4 kWh battery, allowing electric-only travel of about 10 miles before the ICE is used. When the battery pack state-of-charge has been depleted, the vehicle operates as a standard HEV with the ICE and electric motor both used to propel the vehicle.

A Chevrolet Volt has a larger 16 kWh battery pack and, as a result, can travel about 40 miles on electric power alone, without using the ICE until the battery has been discharged to about 25% to 35%. At this stage, the ICE is operated to keep the battery pack at a level high enough to keep propelling the vehicle. ● **SEE FIGURE 12-2**.

● **SEE CHART 12-1** A comparison of many of the current PHEVs.

FIGURE 12-2 Chevrolet Volt extended range electric vehicle (EREV), also called a plug-in hybrid electric vehicle (PHEV), being charged at a row of charging stations at the Corvette assembly plant in Blowing Green, KY.

VEHICLE MAKE AND MODEL	BATTERY CAPACITY
BMW i8	11 kWh
Chevrolet Volt	16 kWh
Ford C-Max Energi	7.6 kWh
Ford Fusion Energi	7.6 kWh
Honda Accord PHEV	6.7 kWh
Porsche Cayenne PHEV	9.4 kWh
Porsche Panamera S PHEV	9.4 kWh
Toyota Prius PHEV	4.4 kWh
Toyota RAV4	8.1 kWh
Volvo XC60/XC90	11.6 kWh
VW Golf PHEV	8.8 kWh

CHART 12-1

The higher the capacity of the HV battery, the further the vehicle can travel using electric power only; it takes longer to be fully charged when plugged into a charger.

FIGURE 12-3 Charging stations that are equipped with SAE standard J1772 chargers are often found at large companies, colleges, universities, and shopping malls in many parts of the country.

CHARGING A PHEV After the battery pack has been discharged propelling the vehicle, the ICE is used to keep the battery charged enough to propel the vehicle, but it does not fully recharge the battery pack. To fully charge the high-voltage battery pack in a plug-in hybrid electric vehicle, it should be plugged into either a 110/120-volt or a 220/240-volt outlet.
● **SEE FIGURE 12-3**.

TECH TIP

Turn on Heat or A/C While Still Connected

If charging a plug-in hybrid or an electric vehicle, use a smartphone app to access the vehicle to turn on the air conditioning (A/C) or heat 15 minutes before leaving from work. For example, an owner of a Nissan Leaf, who works in Phoenix, AZ, uses the phone app to start the A/C while it is still connected to the charging station at work. The interior is nice and cool when the owner is ready to leave work, even though the vehicle has been sitting in the hot sun on a 100-degree day. Because the operation of the A/C is occurring while still plugged into the charging station, the range of the Leaf is not affected, and the ride home is done in comfort. The same can be done to heat the interior in cold weather, too.

EV AND PHEV CHARGING 165

ELECTRIC VEHICLES

EV BATTERY CAPACITY An **electric vehicle (EV)**, also called a **battery electric vehicle (BEV)**, uses a high-voltage battery pack to supply electrical energy to an electric motor(s) to propel the vehicle under all driving conditions. Electric vehicles that use battery power alone to propel the vehicle are called **zero-emission vehicles (ZEVs)**. The capacity of the battery pack, in kilowatt-hours, determines the range of the vehicle. It has to be plugged in to recharge the battery before it can be driven further. The time it takes to charge an electric vehicle can be as little as 30 minutes or more than 12 hours, depending on the size of the battery and the speed of the charging station.

COLD-WEATHER CONCERNS Past models of electric vehicles, such as the General Motors electric vehicle (EV1), were restricted to locations, such as Arizona and southern California that had a warm climate. Cold weather is a major disadvantage to the use of electric vehicles for the following reasons:

- Cold temperatures reduce battery efficiency.
- Additional electrical power from the batteries is needed to heat the batteries themselves to be able to achieve reasonable performance.
- Passenger compartment heating is a concern for an electric vehicle because it requires the use of resistance units or other technology that reduces the range of the vehicle.

HOT-WEATHER CONCERNS Batteries do not function well at high temperatures, and therefore, some type of battery cooling must be added to the vehicle to allow for maximum battery performance. This results in a reduction of vehicle range due to the use of battery power needed just to keep the batteries working properly. Besides battery concerns, the batteries also have to supply the power needed to keep the interior cool, as well as all of the other accessories. These combined electrical loads represent additional battery drain and reduce the range of the vehicle.

RANGE How far an electric vehicle can travel on a full battery charge is called **range**. The range of an electric vehicle depends on many factors, including:

- Battery energy storage capacity
- Vehicle weight
- Outside temperature
- Terrain (driving in hilly or mountainous areas requires more energy from the battery)
- Use of heating or air-conditioning systems and other electrical devices
- Driving style or habits

EVs have a shorter driving range than most conventional vehicles although EV driving ranges are improving. Many early EVs could travel less than 100 miles on a charge, but now typical range for an electric vehicle is in excess of 200 miles, depending on the make and model. A typical electric vehicle will consume about 30 kW per 100 miles (62 km). ● **SEE FIGURE 12-4**.

> **TECH TIP**
>
> **Batteries Like the Same Temperature Range as Humans**
>
> Batteries work best when they are kept within a temperature range that is also the most comfortable for humans. Most people are comfortable when the temperature is between 68°F and 78°F (20°C and 26°C).
> - Below 68°F (20°C), most people want heat.
> - Above 78°F (26°C), most people want cooling.
>
> Batteries perform best when they are exposed to the same temperature range. Therefore, a proper heating and cooling system must be used to keep the batteries within this fairly narrow temperature range for best performance.

FIGURE 12-4 The "gas gauge" on an electric vehicle is the miles remaining and the state-of-charge. According to those who have owned an electric vehicle, range anxiety lasts only about 10 days after they see that their travel distance can be easily achieved after being charged.

TECH TIP

Use Phone App to Turn on Seat and Steering Wheel Heaters

If not plugged into a charging station on a cold day, most experts recommend that just the steering wheel and seat warmers be turned on to help conserve electrical power. Heating the seats and steering wheel will give the driver a sense of warmth without draining the HV batteries in an effort to heat the air in the entire passenger compartment.

COST OF CHARGING The national average for electricity is about $0.11 per kilowatt-hour. Charging an all-electric vehicle with a 250-mile range (assuming a fully depleted 96 kWh battery) will cost about $10.56 to reach a full charge. This cost is about the same as operating an average central air conditioner for about 6 hours. General Motors estimates the annual energy use of the Chevy Volt is about 2,520 kilowatt-hours, which is less energy than is required to power a typical water heater or central air conditioning.

KILOWATTS PER 100 MILES The EPA also expresses an EV's energy consumption in terms of the number of kilowatts per hour needed to run the vehicle for 100 miles shortened to **kWh/100 mi**. For example, a Tesla Model 3 uses about 28 kW per 100 miles.

FREQUENTLY ASKED QUESTION

What Is Range Anxiety?

Range anxiety is a feeling that many drivers experience when driving an electric vehicle because they fear running out of electric battery energy before they reach their destination. This condition is very common, but according to studies, this feeling lasts about two weeks after first getting an electric vehicle. Within those first two weeks, the driver develops experience regarding how far the vehicle can travel on a full charge and knows that their regular trip can be completed without any issues.

LEVEL 1 CHARGING

20-AMPERE CIRCUIT Level 1 charging uses 110/120-volt standard electric outlet (20-ampere circuit). The maximum power with a Level 1 charging is 1.9 kW. This low rate of charging means that it is best to charge the vehicle overnight, so it is ready to go the next morning. The advantage is that there is little, if any, installation cost because many houses are equipped with 110/120-volt outlets and can supply up to 16 amperes protected by a 20-ampere circuit breaker.
● **SEE FIGURE 12-5**.

FIGURE 12-5 (a) A Chevrolet Volt being charged using the supplied 120-volt charger. (b) Always lay out the entire length of the charging cord before plugging the vehicle into the outlet. If the cord is not kept straight, the current flow can not only create a coil, but the flow of current can overheat the wires and, in some cases, can actually cause the insulation to melt.

Level 1 charging results in 2 to 5 miles of range for each hour of charging. Before plugging an EV into any outlet, be sure that the circuit does not supply other appliances, such as refrigerators or lights. For the connector, nearly all EVs come with a portable Level 1 cord set, which has a standard three-prong household plug on one end for the outlet and a standard J1772 connector for the vehicle. For Level 1 charging when plugged into regular 120-VAC outlet, a lot of vehicles will limit the rate 12 A which is 1.4 kW, while the peak allowed by the standard (and typical household wiring) is 16 A (1.9 kW). **SEE FIGURE 12-6**.

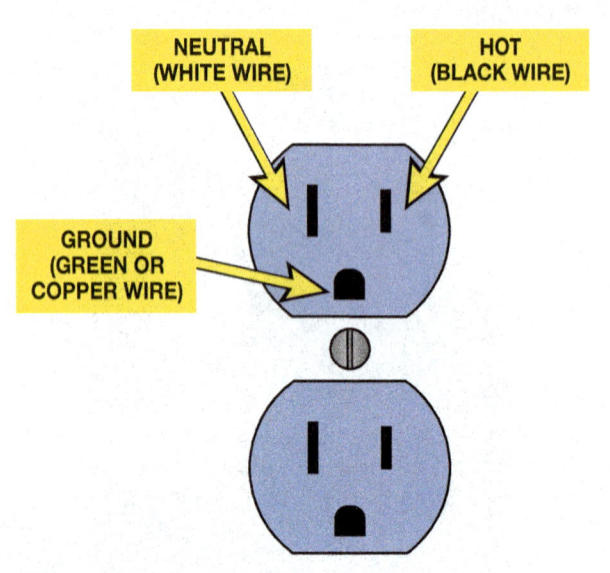

FIGURE 12-6 The electrical outlet must be wired correctly to the house wiring to avoid the possibility of an electrical shock and for proper charging of the vehicle.

TECH TIP

Tip on Using Some Generators

If trying to use a gasoline-powered generator to charge an electric vehicle, the neutral and ground have to be tied together or the charger errors out. For example, an owner of a Honda EU 2000i generator got a plug with the two lead (neutral and ground) tied together that it can be plugged into the other socket if needed to charge the vehicle. The electric vehicle needs to see 120 volts on the hot lead and 0 volt on neutral when referenced to ground. Some generators will show 60 volts and 60 volts, and then the vehicle may display a ground fault error.
NOTE—The neutral and ground *must* be electrically isolated. This is also true for any remote panel and all receptacles. The only place they can be connected together is in the main panel where the service ground (ground rod) is located. Some early generators combined them, which led to a whole host of problems, especially with household electronic equipment.

Case Study

The Case of the Older House

The owner of a Chevrolet Bolt was visiting a relative who lives in an older home. When visiting, the owner thought that they might as well charge their car even though it was at Level 1 (110/120-volt outlet). At least this could add some range added during the visit. Unfortunately, the house was so old that the electrical outlets did not have a separate ground wire and instead used just a neutral and power (hot) wire. The car knew that the connection did not have a proper ground and the connection was not completed. In this case, the car was smarter than the house.
Summary:
- **Complaint**—A Chevrolet Bolt would not charge when connected to a 110-volt outlet.
- **Cause**—The outlet did not have a ground terminal.
- **Correction**—The vehicle did not allow charging because of the missing ground terminal. This is normal operation and a safety feature of electric vehicles and no correction was needed.

PRECAUTIONS USING A LEVEL 1 CHARGING When using the 110/120-volt plug of the charging cord that comes with the vehicle, the following safety precautions should be adhered to preventing personal injury or property damage:

- Uncoil the cord before connecting the plug to an electrical outlet. If the cord is kept on the charger reel, heat can build up during charging that can cause the insulation to melt. Always unroll the entire length of the charge cord before charging.
- Plug the charging cord directly into a dedicated 110/120-volt, 20-ampere outlet. Do not use an extension cord.

LEVEL 2 CHARGING

HIGHER VOLTAGE EQUALS FASTER CHARGING

Level 2 chargers uses 208/240 volts to charge the same vehicle in about 4 hours. Level 2 chargers can be added to most houses, making recharging faster (up to 80 amperes) when at home, and are the most commonly used charging stations available at stores and colleges. A 208/240-volt Level 2 charger rated at 30 amperes will deliver 7.2 kW (240 × 30/1000). In one hour, that will send 7.2 kWh of electricity to a plug-in vehicle, so it will be fine to service vehicles with on-board chargers rated at 7.2 kW or less. Adding a Level 2 charging outlet to the garage or parking location can cost from $500 to $2,000 or more, depending on the location and the wiring of the house or condo. Level 2 charging adds about 25 miles of **range per hour (RPH)**, labeled as **miles per hour (MPH)** on the dash display of a Nissan Leaf. For Level 2 (220/240VAC) charging, vehicles have between a 3 kW and 10 kW on-board chargers, which is usually the limiting factors as to how many kWh of charging is actually achieved. ● SEE FIGURE 12-7.

FIGURE 12-7 Nissan Leaf plugged into a Level 2 charging station at a college.

ON-BOARD CHARGERS The Level 1 and 2 AC charging is done by the on-board charger. The charging station tells the vehicle the voltage and the maximum current available, and the vehicle will limit itself to no more than that current. Following that handshake (communications between the charging station and the vehicle), the charging station just switches on the power.

NOTE: For Level 3, the vehicle tells the charger how much voltage it can handle, and the external charger will limit the voltage and then the vehicle will take as much current as it can, up to the max the charger can provide.

FREQUENTLY ASKED QUESTION

What Is That Sound?
Many electric vehicle owners say that they hear their vehicle making humming sounds while parked in the garage like the climate control fans running. Checking the smartphone app indicated that the climate control was off. While this can cause some concerns to first time owner of electric vehicle, the noise is usually caused by one of the following:

- The fan, which keeps the battery cool, will run especially if charging or having just finished driving.
- A Chevrolet Volt, for example, often makes gurgling noises due to the A/C running to help cool the battery down in the garage on a hot sunny day.

Because these systems are working when the vehicle is stopped and not operating, many experts recommend that the vehicle is plugged in all the time when it is at home. This is what is often referred to as **Always Be Charging (ABC)**.

LEVEL 3 CHARGING

DC FAST CHARGING Level 3 charging stations use 440/480 volts AC input and outputs DC to charge most electric vehicles to 80% charge in less than 30 minutes. This high-charge rate may be harmful to battery life. Always follow the charging instructions and recommendations as stated in the owner's manual of the vehicle being charged. Level 3 chargers charge the vehicle using direct current (DC) at a rate up to 125 amperes. Level 3 chargers are often called a **DCFC (DC Fast Charge)** or *DC Quick Charge (DCQC)*. ● SEE FIGURE 12-8.

A Level 3 charger station can cost $50,000 or more, making this type of charger most suitable where facilities will be selling the service of rapidly charging the vehicle. For example, DCFC can provide 60 to 80 miles of range in as little as 20 minutes of charging time. ● SEE FIGURE 12-9.

LEVEL 3 ELECTRICAL CONNECTORS There are four different DCFC connectors currently being used by electric vehicle manufacturers all over the world.

- **CHAdeMO**—Nissan and other Japanese companies such as Mitsubishi. ● SEE FIGURE 12-10.
- **SAE Combo Charging System (CCS)**—(BMW, Ford, GM, VW, and other vehicle makers). ● SEE FIGURE 12-11.

AC VERSUS DC CHARGING

ALTERNATING CURRENT (AC) | **DIRECT CURRENT (DC)**

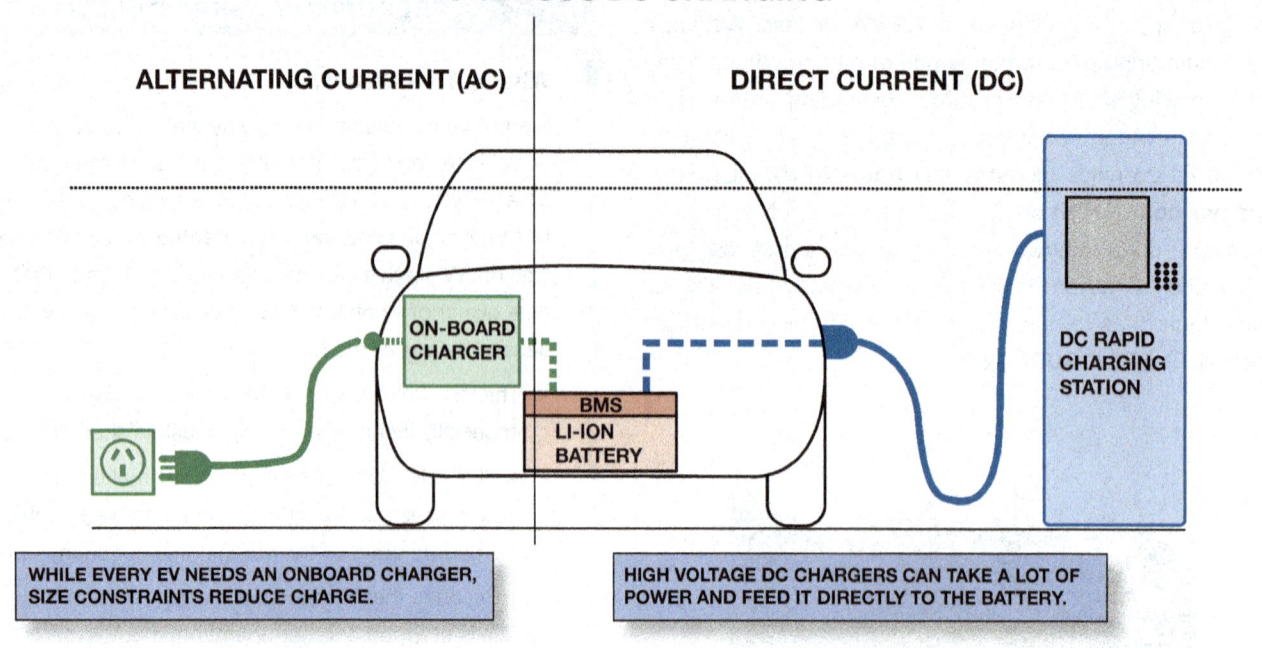

WHILE EVERY EV NEEDS AN ONBOARD CHARGER, SIZE CONSTRAINTS REDUCE CHARGE.

HIGH VOLTAGE DC CHARGERS CAN TAKE A LOT OF POWER AND FEED IT DIRECTLY TO THE BATTERY.

FIGURE 12-8 The difference between Levels 1, 2, and 3 charging is that by using AC (Levels 1 and 2) the onboard charger has to convert the alternating current (AC) to direct current (DC) in order to charge the high-voltage battery; using direct current (Level 3) this conversion is not needed so that the DC can be used directly to charge the battery.

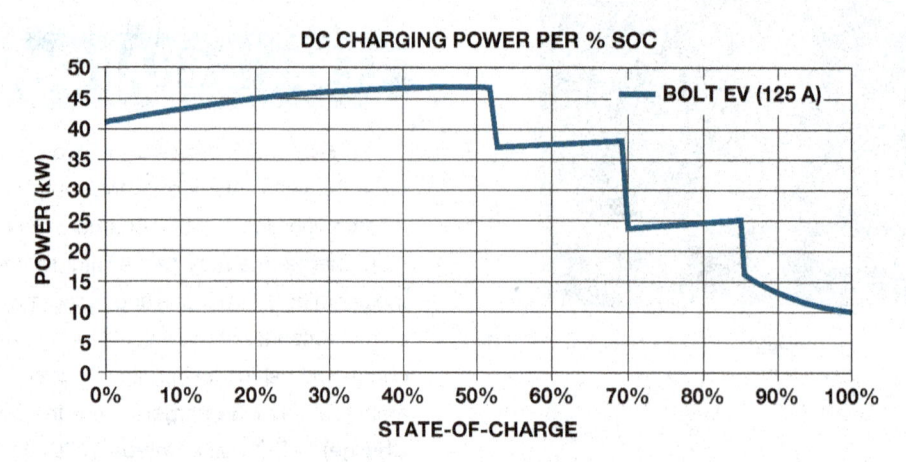

FIGURE 12-9 A chart showing a typical charging rate which is decreased once the state-of-charge reaches about 70%.

- **Tesla Supercharger**—Tesla standard connector. The Tesla "superchargers" are Level 3 chargers and are free to use by some Tesla owners. Tesla electric vehicles use their own unique plug and supply adaptors if the vehicle is going to be connected to a standard SAE J1772 charging station plug or a 110/120-volt electrical outlet. ● **SEE FIGURE 12-12**.

- **Guobiao standard (GB or GB/T)**—The Chinese national standard. BYD and other Chinese companies use this standard connector, as well as Mahindra and Tata electric vehicles. ● **SEE FIGURE 12-13**.
  ● **SEE CHART 12-2**.

FIGURE 12-10 A close-up view of CHAdeMO Level 3 charging plug.

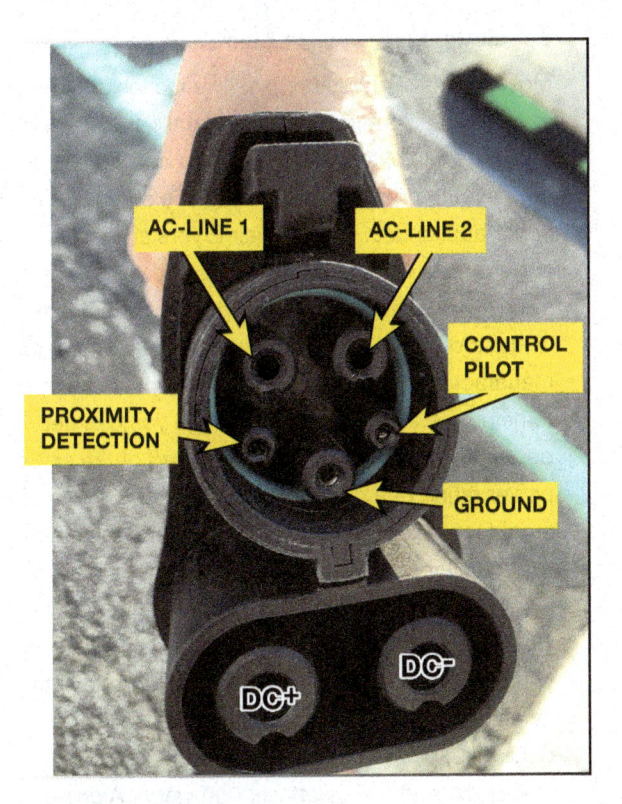

FIGURE 12-11 The SAE Combo Charging System (CCS) is a DCFC connector standard used by BMW, Ford, GM, VW, and other vehicle makers.

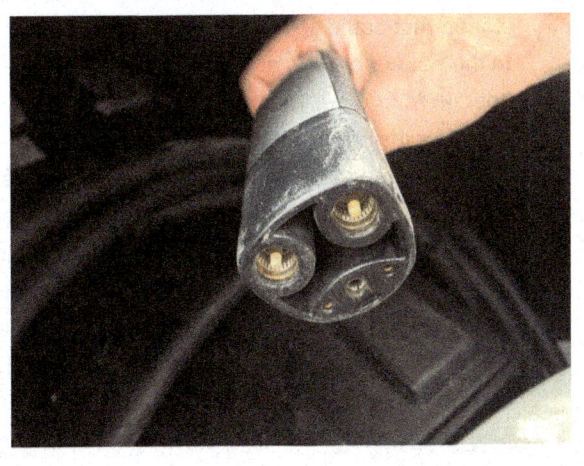

FIGURE 12-12 Tesla vehicles use a unique changing connector that is only used by Tesla.

EV AND PHEV CHARGING 171

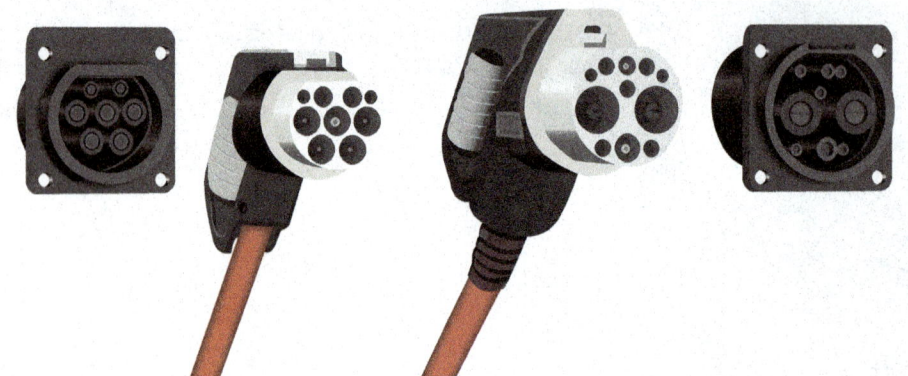

FIGURE 12-13 Connectors used for AC (left) and DC fast charging (right) using the GB/T standard.

SUMMARY CHARGING CHART

Level (voltage)	Rate	Time to Fully Charge	Miles per Hour (MPH) Range per Hour (RPH)
Level 1 (110/120 volts)	16 amperes (1.4 to 1.7 kW)	16 hours for 32 kWh battery 40 hours for 80 kWh battery	5 miles per hour
Level 2 (208/210/220 volts)	32-48 amperes (7 to 13 kW)	3.5 hours for 32 kWh battery 8 hours for 80 kWh battery	12 miles per hour with 3.7 kW on-board charger. 25 miles per hour with 6.6 kW on-board charger
Level 3 440/480 volts DC)	24 kW to 250 kW	Depends, but generally 80% charge in 30 minutes	Up to 200 miles per hour

CHART 12-2

The charge time and range per mile depend upon the voltage and current available during charging.

OWNING AND CHARGING AN EV

TIME-OF-USE For almost all EV owners, choosing a **time-of-use (TOU)** electric rate plan is needed to achieve the largest savings for charging. A TOU plan offers lower electric rates during off-peak periods (usually 11 PM until 5 AM), with higher rates for using electricity during high-demand times. Because most EVs are parked at home overnight, TOU rates are a wise choice for most EV owners.

TECH TIP

Speak the Language of Electricity

Most people understand units like inches and feet, meters and kilometers, cups and gallons, milliliters and liters, kilobytes and megabytes and gigabytes, but never learned the basic units of electricity. Many home appliances, such as hair dryers and microwave ovens, have the wattage printed right on the front. There are some people who think electricity is just too complicated. So, when it comes to EVs, manufacturers and charging station operators try to help by stating the miles of range you can get per minute or hour of charging instead of the actual power rating of a charging station. Also, vehicle manufacturers tend to mention just the range that the vehicle can achieve instead of the kWh capacity of the battery. The first battery electric vehicles were equipped with chargers rated at 3.3 kW. They could only accept a maximum of 3.3 kW of electricity each hour they were connected to a 240-volt, or Level 2, power supply. A watt is the basic unit of electricity, and a kilowatt is 1,000 watts. A charging station that could send only 1 kilowatt of electricity to the battery pack in an hour would be a 1 kilowatt-hour (kWh) device. The basic charging capacity of a Tesla, for instance, is 10 kWh, and buyers can order a second on-board charger that doubles the charging speed to 20 kWh. To compute how much electrical current will be delivered to a plugged-in vehicle through any properly installed EVSE, multiply the amperes by the volts and divide by 1,000. Typically, most EVs on a Level 2 charging station can achieve about 25 miles per charging hour.

PUBLIC CHARGING STATIONS (PCS)

Public Charging Stations (PCS) are available at many locations and most commercial Level 2 charging stations come with added features, which include the following:

- Authentication
- Integrated payment gateways
- Software for remote monitoring

The electric power consumed needs to be billed and payment needs to be collected. The power utilities may also want to manage power drawn by these chargers over time.

> **? FREQUENTLY ASKED QUESTION**
>
> **What Is Plug & Charge?**
>
> "Plug & Charge" uses the ISO 15118 international standard, which specifies the secured communication protocol that an EV and the charging stations should use. Plug & charge improves the public charging experience for electric vehicle owners. Until now, networked public EV charging stations required the use of:
>
> - an RFID card,
> - a smartphone app, and
> - a credit card.
>
> Some owners of EV find using a public charging station a frustrating experience. This is because the station often fails to communicate properly and the session either takes a couple of attempts to initiate. Using the plug & charge will simplify public charging and is available for use by many EV makes and models, except Tesla that have their own network.

NOTE: Some commercial charging stations will stop charging at 80%, whereas others may stop after 30, 45, or 1 hour while others have no limits. Use the website for the charging system being used to check for locations and the charging limits.

WORK PLACE AND DESTINATION CHARGING

Work place charging (WPC) is very popular because the vehicle owner can charge their vehicle while at work and usually for free. Hotels and motels often provide charging stations known as **destination charging**. Hotels are adding chargers to their properties to help attract EV drivers traveling on long trips.

Other charging locations include the following:

- Large factories
- Small businesses
- Museums
- Colleges and universities
- Shopping centers

The usual charging station at these locations is a Level 2 (220/240 volt).

> **🔧 TECH TIP**
>
> **Charge to 80% Unless Traveling**
>
> Batteries do not have a long service life if the **state-of-charge (SOC)** is above 80% or below 20%. To help protect the high-voltage battery and extend its life, use the menu in the vehicle display main screen to charge to 80% and input the charging stations at work or a free charger used frequently. Usually at 80% SOC, the charging rate drops and then holds steady until 95% where it tapers again. Even when charged to 80%, the display may say fully charged and needs to be manually changed to indicate charge capacity closer to 100%. The only difference will be the number of miles to zero. The two ways that batteries can degrade are as follows:
>
> 1. Over discharging starts eating copper once no more lithium is left to move and this action will destroy the battery.
> 2. Heat created by a high-charge level can cause acid to eat the battery more rapidly.
> 3. Once the charging station has been inputted, the vehicle will start to precondition the battery in preparation to being charged. Try to charge to 100% only for trips and charge to 80% for daily runs to help protect the battery life.

LOCATING A CHARGING STATION

Most electric vehicles will display where to charge if a trip is entered into the navigation system. Plus, there are numerous smartphone apps that can be used to locate charging stations. Some of them are as follows:

- Charge Point
- Charge Way
- Electrify America

- Drive the Arc
- EV Match
- Plug Share
- Pod Point

? FREQUENTLY ASKED QUESTION

Why Doesn't My EV Charge at the Rated Output of the Charging Station?

The Bolt owner's manual states to use at least 80 kW to get a full charge in 30 minutes. However, trying to locate a DCFC unit that does in fact supply 80 kW may be a challenge. For example, one Chevrolet Bolt owner was able to locate a DCFC rated at 50 kW, but when using it, the charger was only supplying 35 kW. Other EV owners report the same situation where the rated charger output is not what is actually being supplied to the vehicle. The reasons for this apparent reduced charger include that the vehicle battery may be limiting the amount of current that is be used to charge the battery. This could be the result of the state-of-charge, the battery temperature, or other parameters. As a result of the many factors involved, it is difficult to know what the charging rate will be. Best to use the smartphone app for the vehicle which will provide the information on the charging statues.

COST TO CHARGE Some businesses provide chargers at no cost to their customers as a way to add value to the service they provide and to help alleviate range anxiety, while others charge a fee. This can either be on a pay-as-you-go basis using a credit card, or via an account with a charging network like ChargePoint or Blink. Blink charges between $0.04 and $0.06 per minute or from $0.39 to $0.79 per kWh, in states where permitted. ● **SEE FIGURE 12-14**.

FIGURE 12-14 Commercial charging stations are often located in shopping areas and while most charge a fee, either by the minute of the kWh, some, such as some businesses and schools, are free to use.

? FREQUENTLY ASKED QUESTION

Can a Solar Panel on the Roof Charge My EV?

While this sounds like a neat idea, it is not practical. If a vehicle's surface was covered with solar panels, they might be able to produce 50-watt hours of electricity. A standard 110/120-volt electrical outlet that takes 8 hours to charge a Chevrolet Volt by supplying about 1,400 watts per hour. A full solar charge would roughly take 350 hours. To answer the question…, probably not.

PHOTO SEQUENCE

1 A Mustang Mach E electric SUV is showing 66 miles (27%) of charge remaining.

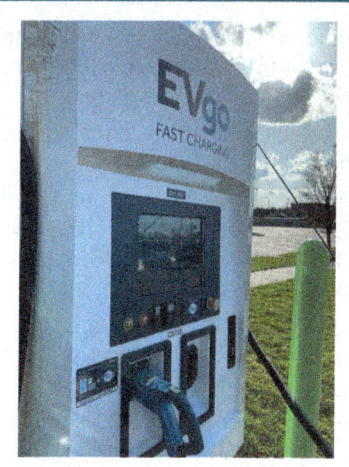

2 Using a smartphone app, Plug Share in this case, the driver located a Level 3 charging station.

3 After using a credit card to gain access, the driver removed the SAE CCS charge plug from the charging station.

4 The charge post on the Mustang Mach E is located on the left front fender.

5 During charging, the Mach E lights a series of lights around the charge receptible to let the driver know the level of charge. When all lights are on, the vehicle has been fully charged.

6 The charging station also shows the state-of-change on the display. Most experts recommend only charging to 80% unless traveling when the extra range is required to help protect the HV battery.

SUMMARY

1. A plug-in hybrid electric vehicle (PHEV) is a vehicle that is designed to be plugged into an electrical outlet at home, at work, or when traveling to charge the batteries.
2. How far an electric vehicle can travel on a full battery charge is called range.
3. The national average for electricity is about $0.11 per kilowatt-hour. Charging an all-electric vehicle with a 250-mile range (assuming a fully depleted 96 kWh battery) will cost about $10.56 to reach a full charge.
4. Level 1 charging uses 110/120-volt standard electric outlet (20-ampere circuit). The maximum power with a Level 1 charging is 1.9 kW.
5. A 208/240-volt Level 2 charger rated at 30 amperes will deliver 7.2 kW.
6. Level 3 charging stations use 440/480 volts AC input and outputs DC to charge most electric vehicles to 80% charge in less than 30 minutes.
7. Work place charging (WPC) is very popular because the vehicle owner can charge their vehicle while at work and usually for free. Hotels and motels often provide charging stations known as destination charging.
8. The standards established by the National Electrical Manufacturers Association (NEMA) define a product, process, or procedure with terminology, construction, dimensions, and performance ratings.
9. According to the National Highway Safety Administration (NHTSA), the average American travels about 13,500 vehicle miles per year. At that level of driving, most EVs will require around 4,000 kWh of electricity per year to operate.
10. Wireless power transfer (WPT) uses electromagnetic induction between the transmitting pad on the ground and a receiving pad attached for the underside of the vehicle.

REVIEW QUESTIONS

1. What is the difference between a hybrid electric vehicle (HEV) and a plug-in hybrid vehicle (PHEV)?
2. What precautions are needed when charging a vehicle using a Level 1 charging cable that comes with the vehicle?
3. What are the types of electrical outlets that can be used to power a Level 2 charger at home?
4. What are the typical charging rates for Level 3 (DCFC) chargers?
5. What are some of the smartphone apps that can be used to locate charging stations?

CHAPTER QUIZ

1. What identifies a plug-in version of a hybrid electric vehicle?
   a. Different badges
   b. An access door for the charging cable in addition to the normal ICE fueling door
   c. Different instrument panel cluster
   d. Any of the above
2. What is true about Level 1 charging?
   a. Uses 110/120 volts
   b. Can supply 2–5 miles per hour of range per hour of charging
   c. Can supply 1.4 to 1.9 kW
   d. All of the above
3. Level 2 charging _____.
   a. uses J1772 connector
   b. uses 110/120-volt outlet
   c. can supply 1.4 to 1.9 kW
   d. does not need EVSE
4. Level 3 charging _____.
   a. charges the high-voltage battery using DC
   b. uses 110/120-volt outlet
   c. uses the SAE J1772 connector
   d. Both a and c
5. A typical electric vehicle will consume about _____ per 100 miles (62 km).
   a. 10 kWh
   b. 20 kWh
   c. 30 kWh
   d. 50 kWh
6. Level 3 chargers use what type of connector?
   a. SAE J1772
   b. SAE Combo Charging System (CCS)
   c. NEMA 14-50
   d. NEMA 6-50

7. Destination charging means _____.
   a. charging at home
   b. charging at the workplace
   c. charging at a hotel/motel
   d. Any of the above

8. Using a J1772 plug can charge _____.
   a. Most PHEV and EVs
   b. Can use 110/120 volts
   c. Can used 220/240 volts
   d. All of the above

9. Public Charging Stations (PCS) often charge _____.
   a. by the hour of usage
   b. by the kWh
   c. by the level of voltage required
   d. Either a or b

10. Charging at 7.2 kW rate is achieved using _____.
    a. Level 1 charger
    b. Level 2 charger
    c. Level 3 charger
    d. None of the above

Chapter 13
ELECTRIC VEHICLE CHARGING EQUIPMENT

LEARNING OBJECTIVES

After studying this chapter, the reader should be able to:

- Discuss National Electric Code (NEC), National Electrical Manufacturers Association (NEMA), and Nationally Recognized Testing Laboratory (NRTL) rules and regulations.
- Discuss the use of solar to charge an electric vehicle.
- Discuss electric vehicle supply equipment.

KEY TERMS

Electric vehicle supply equipment (EVSE) 179
National Electric Code (NEC) 180
National Electrical Manufacturers Association (NEMA) 179
Nationally Recognized Testing Laboratory (NRTL) 180
Wireless power transfer (WPT) 184

ELECTRIC VEHICLE SUPPLY EQUIPMENT

PURPOSE AND FUNCTION Electric vehicle supply equipment (EVSE) supplies electricity to charge an electric vehicle (EV). The primary function of a plug-in vehicle charging station is to provide electrical safety for the operator and to address the risks of fire and electric shock. While the vehicle has a charger built-in that is used to convert AC from the electrical outlet to DC to charge the high-voltage battery, the vehicle manufacturers require that an EVSE be used between the electrical outlet and the vehicle. ● SEE FIGURE 13-1.

The purpose and function of the EVSE includes the following:

- To reduce the risk of electrical shock because there is no voltage potential at the terminals of the electrical connector until it has been plugged into the vehicle.
- The vehicle communicates with the EVSE and once all of the connections have been verified to be correctly made, the charging process can start.

An EVSE is a wall-mounted box or a part of the Level 2 charging cable that supplies electric energy to the vehicle onboard charger. It has safety components and software that works with the vehicle software to control charging. An EVSE supplies AC current to the vehicle's onboard charger, which in turn converts the AC power to DC, allowing the battery to be charged.

NEMA The standards established by the **National Electrical Manufacturers Association (NEMA)** define a product, process, or procedure with terminology, construction, dimensions, and performance ratings. The NEMA 14 devices are four-wire grounding devices (2 hot terminals, a neutral and a ground) from 15 to 60 amperes with a voltage rating of 250 volts. Both the NEMA 14-30 and 14-50 are in common residential use and either may also be used for home charging of electric vehicles.

- NEMA 14-30 is used for electric clothes dryers.
- NEMA 14-50 is used for electric cooking ranges.
- NEMA 6-50 is a three-wire connector with two hot terminals and a ground (no neutral). This type of outlet is often found in RV parks and campgrounds. It requires a dedicated 50 A circuit and is commonly used for welders or plasma cutters.

The EVSE equipment can be plugged into any of these outlets. ● SEE FIGURE 13-2.

> **TECH TIP**
>
> **Think of a Gas Pump and Hose**
>
> Think of the EVSE and its charging cord as a hose and the charger on the vehicle as the opening in the neck of a bottle. While a wider bottle neck can take in more water, it is limited by the volume of water being delivered through the hose. The hose is limited by the pressure of the water. In plug-in vehicle charging, the "pressure" that pushes the electrical current through the EVSE "hose" is measured in volts. While the charger on the vehicle is rated by the speed at which it can push electricity from the home connector through to the battery pack, the EVSE itself is rated for the maximum flow of current it can deliver. That volume is measured in amperage, or amps.

FIGURE 13-1 A typical SAE J1772 electric vehicle charging plug attached to an electric vehicle. Notice that the door lid shows that the plug can be used with 110 volts (Level 1) or 240 volts (Level 2).

FIGURE 13-2 The three most commonly used outlets that are suitable for use with an electric vehicle charging station. Most experts recommend the use of the 14-50 because it has a separate ground and neutral terminals.

> **WARNING**
>
> Electric vehicle charging station manufactures do not recommend the use a NEMA 10-30 plug. This type plug is commonly used for a clothes dryer or cooking range and is typically wired with a neutral wire instead of an earth ground. All electric vehicle charger manufacturers recommend the plug be connected to earth ground. When charging an electric vehicle, the ground is passed through to the vehicle from the station for safety. If a neutral is used instead of a ground, the neutral could generate a charge on the vehicle chassis, creating a potential safety hazard upon contact with the vehicle during or after charging. Do not use any EVSEs with a NEMA 10-30 adapter. Instead, it is recommended to have an electrician re-purpose the NEMA 10-30 receptacle into a NEMA 14-30 receptacle.

HARD WIRED Many home and company Level 2 220/240-volt charging stations are hard wired to the circuit breaker control panel in order to handle up to 60 amperes. Hard wiring the charger to the house wiring allows the charger to be able to supply the maximum possible charging current and saves the minor cost of an outlet. A possible disadvantage of connecting the charger directly to the wiring is that it would require a replacement charging unit to also be hard wired or installing a plug if the unit is to be replaced anytime in the future. It is a NEC requirement that any plugged device be able to be disconnected or if not, a switchable disconnect must be provided within sight of the component.

LOCATION Most house charging systems are installed in the garage, but can also be mounted in a car port or outside if a weather proof unit and receptacle are used.

NRTL AND UL Most charging station manufacturers send samples to a **Nationally Recognized Testing Laboratory (NRTL)**, such as Intertek (ETL mark) or Underwriter's Laboratory (UL mark) for testing of their device for safety. Safety engineers at these labs perform extensive safety testing that the products must pass before they can be safety certified and made available to the public for sale. Only products with these marks appearing on the manufactured product rating plate are safety certified. The UL Recognized Component Mark means that the product has been tested as a component. The UL Listed is the more stringent of the two and is recommended for any device installed in a garage or vehicle port to charge an electric vehicle. UL listing number such as the UL listing number in compliance with UL2202: "Standard for Electric Vehicle Charging System Equipment" should be on the EVSE. ● **SEE FIGURE 13-3**.

NEC The **National Electric Code (NEC)** is derived from the National Fire Protection Agency. The NEC codes are the standards to which buildings and equipment must meet minimum regulatory safety requirements in order to be safe enough for the general public to install and use. The NEC requires any charging station to be NRTL certified in order to be installed anywhere in the United States. In most places, installing an EVSE requires a building permit. One reason for a permit is to provide the opportunity for a building inspector to verify that the charging station is NRTL listed and that the electrical installation meets all other applicable aspects of the NEC, and therefore the equipment is safe to use.

PERMITS All EVSE installations must comply with local, state, and national codes and regulations, and the work should be done by a licensed electrical contractor. In addition to the National Fire Code, local building, fire, environmental, and electrical inspecting and permitting authorities may also require permits. In many areas, installers must submit a site installation plan to the permitting authority for approval before installation. The contractor should know the relevant codes and standards and should check with the local planning department before installing EVSE. There is a variety of equipment for Level 2 EVSE available, ranging from simple models with standard safety features and status lights to more advanced products

FIGURE 13-3 All electric vehicle charging equipment should be certified by Nationally Recognized Testing Laboratory (NRTL), such as Intertek (ETL mark) or Underwriter's Laboratory (UL mark) for testing of their device for safety.

FREQUENTLY ASKED QUESTION

What Does a "Fishy Smell" Mean While Charging?

A fishy smell indicates an overheated electrical component, such as a circuit breaker, outlet, or wiring. Electrical hazards that can cause overheating include the following:

- Incorrectly sized breakers/fuses
- Overloaded circuits
- Loose wires
- Frayed cords
- Wire insulation breakdowns
- Older homes with electrical systems that are not up to code

If a fishy smell is noticed, unplug the charging station and/or shut off the circuit breaker as soon as possible and call an electrician to test and repair the circuits.

that have features with enhanced displays, charging timers, smartphone connections, and keypads.

EVSE LOCATION According to the instructions for a typical charging station, the NEMA outlet should be located 20 to 26 inches (50 to 70 cm) from the ground and within 12 inches (30 cm) of a stud where the charging station will be mounted.

The EVSE wall unit also should be positioned to minimize the hazard of tripping over the power cord. This means keeping the cord out of walking areas and positioning the wall unit as close as possible to the electrical inlet. Another option is to install an overhead support that keeps the cord off the floor. ● **SEE FIGURE 13-4**.

HOME LEVEL 2 CHARGING The professional installing a 30-amp charging station system will wire the circuit from the home power service to handle 40 amps and will install the proper circuit breaker.

- A 40-amp EVSE will need a 50-amp breaker.
- A 48-amp EVSE will require a 60-amp breaker.

SEE CHART 13-1.

CIRCUIT BREAKER (AMPS)	MAX OUTPUT (AMPS)	POWER OUTPUT AT 240 VOLTS (KW)	ESTIMATED RANGE PER HOUR	PLUG-IN	HARD-WIRED
60	48	11.5	36 miles (58 km)	No	Yes
50	40	9.6	30 miles (48 km)	Yes	Yes
40	32	7.8	25 miles (40 km)	Yes	Yes
30	24	5.7	18 miles (29 km)	No	Yes
20	16	3.8	12 miles (19 km)	No	Yes

CHART 13-1

Circuit breaker rating and maximum output and estimated range per hour. Because the charger is a continuous load device, the circuit must be rated at 125% of the maximum load. The recommendation to be either a plug-in or hard-wired is based on a typical installation guide from a major charger suppler. Always follow the instructions for the charger being installed, as well as local electrical code requirements.

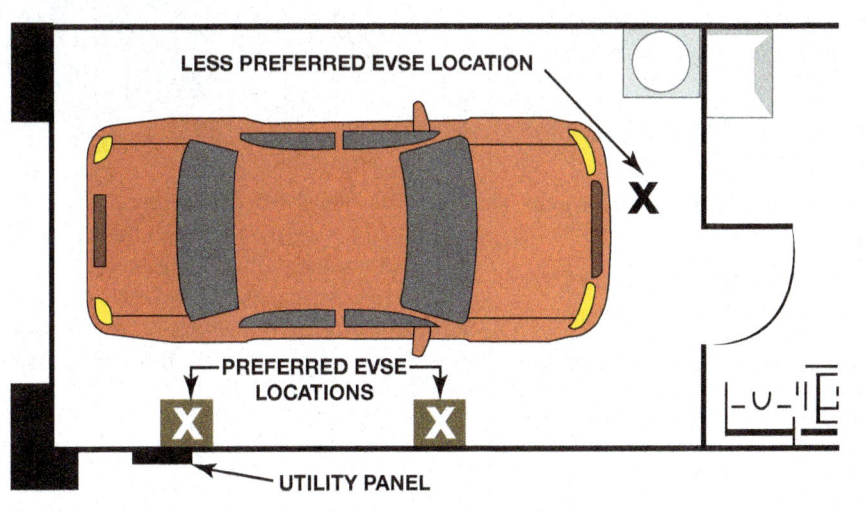

FIGURE 13-4 If the charger is mounted inside a garage, it should be located so that the charging cord will not create a trip hazard. Most house chargers are installed in the garage, but can also be mounted in a car port or outside, if a weather proof charger and plug are used.

- Some houses with very small or heavily used electric service capacity might need to have the service upgraded to handle an EVSE.
- Some home chargers are equipped with Wi-Fi access so that the charger can be controlled using a smartphone.

WATTAGE Electric vehicles can be charged at power draws comparable to various household appliances. Most electric vehicles charging at home on a 220/240-volt Level 2 charger will draw about 7,200 watts or less. For comparison, a typical electric furnace draws about 10,000 watts and a water heater uses 4,500 watts. The price of Level 2 residential EVSE varies, but ranges from $500 to $2,000 before installation and state or utility incentives.

Case Study

The Case of the No-Charge Chevrolet Volt

The owner of a Chevrolet Volt stated that sometimes the car would charge using a J1772 charging station, but most of the time it would not charge. The service technician was able to verify that the vehicle would not charge from a charging station. In an attempt to determine if it was the charging station or the vehicle, the service technician tried charging another Volt using the same charging station. The other Volt was successfully charged indicating that the issue was due to the vehicle and not due to a fault with the charging station. Following GM's procedure to conduct a visual inspection, the problem was found to be a small crack that allowed moisture into the charge connection. The moisture in the receptacle affected the resistance of the monitored circuit and shut down the charge process. Replacing the receptacle solved the issue.

Summary:
- **Complaint**—A Chevrolet Volt had intermittent issues charging from the charging station.
- **Cause**—A small crack that allowed moisture into the charge receptacle.
- **Correction**—Replacing the receptacle solved the issue.

CAUTION: When using the 220/240-volt plug of the charging cord, uncoil the wiring before connecting the plug to the vehicle. The normal cable ratings assume that the wire can adequately disperse heat generated in the cable due to the current flowing. If the cable is wrapped into a coil, it stands a good chance of melting the plastic insulation and causing a short and a fire.

SAE J1772 STANDARD CHARGER PLUG Most electric vehicles and plug-in hybrid electric vehicles use a standard charger plug. The standard charger plug meets the specification as designated by SAE standard J1772 (updated in 2009). ● **SEE FIGURE 13-5**.

Because electric vehicles have a relatively short range, charging stations must be made available in areas where these vehicles are driven. For example, when the state of California mandated the sale of zero-emission vehicles, charging stations were set up in many areas, usually in parking lots of businesses and schools. The parking spaces near the charging stations are designated for electric vehicles only and can be used for free to recharge electric vehicles. Vehicles sold in North America have the SAE J1772 plugs and support Level 1 (110/120VAC) and Level 2 (220/240VAC). ● **SEE FIGURE 13-6**.

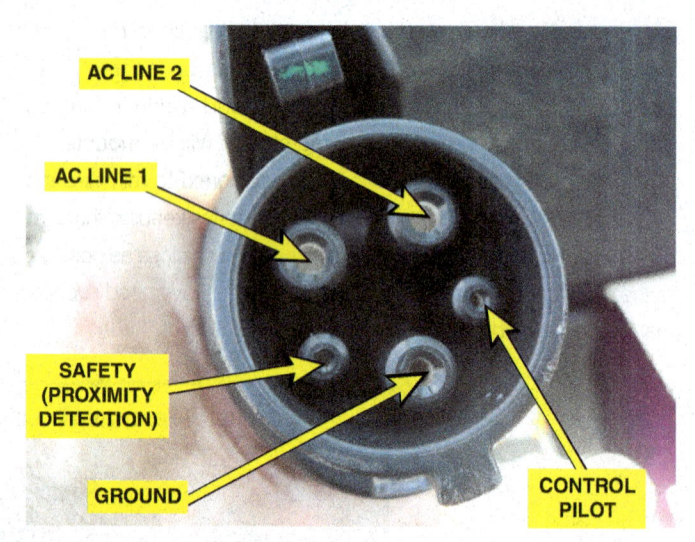

FIGURE 13-5 The terminals of a J1772 plug are not "hot" until the connection has been made to the vehicle and communications between the vehicle and the charger has been established. Then, and only then, is voltage applied to the terminals of the plug. Therefore, there is no danger of electrical shock to the person using the charger plug.

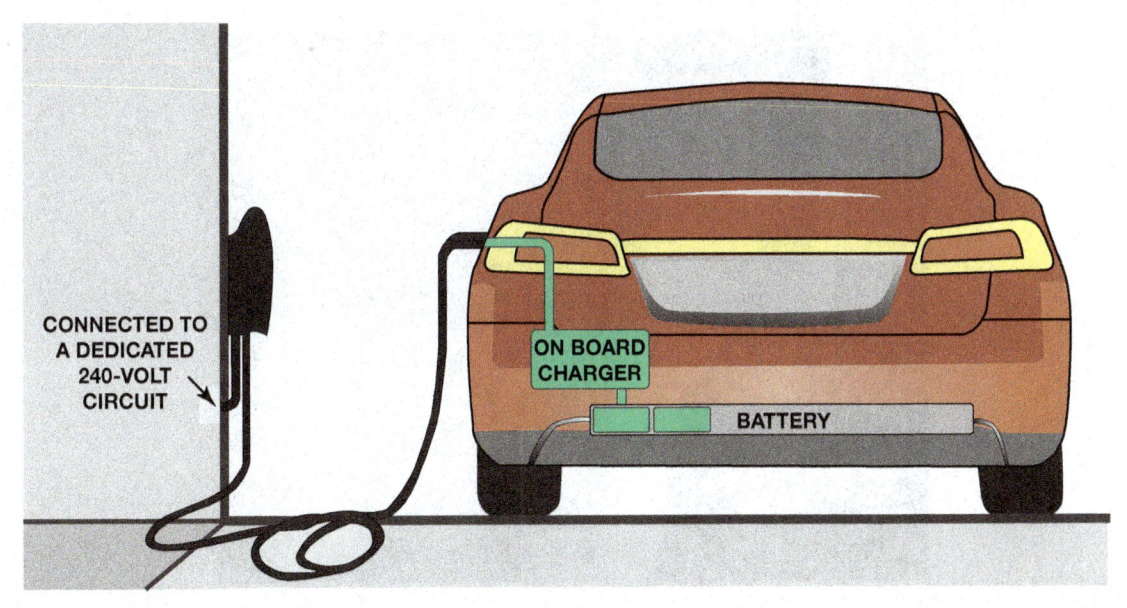

FIGURE 13-6 An electric vehicle charging station supplies alternating current, either 110/120 volts or 220/240 volts to the vehicle. The vehicle has an on-board charger that converts the AC to DC to charge the HV battery.

? FREQUENTLY ASKED QUESTION

What Is the Cost per Mile an Electric Vehicle Versus a Gasoline Powered Vehicle?

If electricity costs $0.11 per kWh and the vehicle consumes 34 kWh to travel 100 miles, the cost per mile is about $0.04. If electricity costs $0.11 per kWh, charging an EV with a 210-mile range (assuming a fully depleted 72 kWh battery) will cost about $7.92 to reach a full charge. This cost is about the same as operating an average central air conditioner for about 6 hours.

In comparison, a gasoline powered vehicle that achieves 25 miles per gallon (at $2.50 per gallon) would cost the owner (who drives 200 miles to use 8 gallons of gasoline) about $20 or $0.10 per mile.

In other words, the cost per mile driving an electric vehicle is about half the cost of driving a gasoline vehicle. In addition to the cost of the "fuel" (electricity for the EV and gasoline for the gasoline-powered vehicle), there is the added cost of oil changes and air filter expenses that an electric vehicle does not need or require.

Your electric bill will vary, depending on the type of vehicle, the size of the battery, how often you charge the battery, the efficiency of the charger, and the distance you drive. Driving 12,000 miles per year, 280 watt-hours per mile, 11.5¢ per kWh, and only drive on electric, your monthly electric bill will increase $32.24, much less than the average monthly cost for gasoline-powered cars.

TECH TIP

Charging Cable Tip

The charger cables that come with the vehicle are being stolen when the vehicle is charging. Some vehicles will sound an alarm if the vehicle is locked and the charge plug is disconnected. For example, on a Chevrolet Bolt, if it is plugged into charge and the remote lock button is pushed twice until it honks, it sets the alarm if the charger is removed without disarming the alarm by unlocking with the key fob. However, if the remote is depressed to lock it once, it will not set the charge cord removal alarm. There are several things that may help to avoid theft if the vehicle is being charged away from home and in a public area:

- Place the unit inside the vehicle and close the window to keep the unit safe inside.
- Drill a hole in the charge release arm and install a lock. ● **SEE FIGURE 13-7**.

On some electric vehicles such as Audi, the cable will not detach from the car if the car is locked.

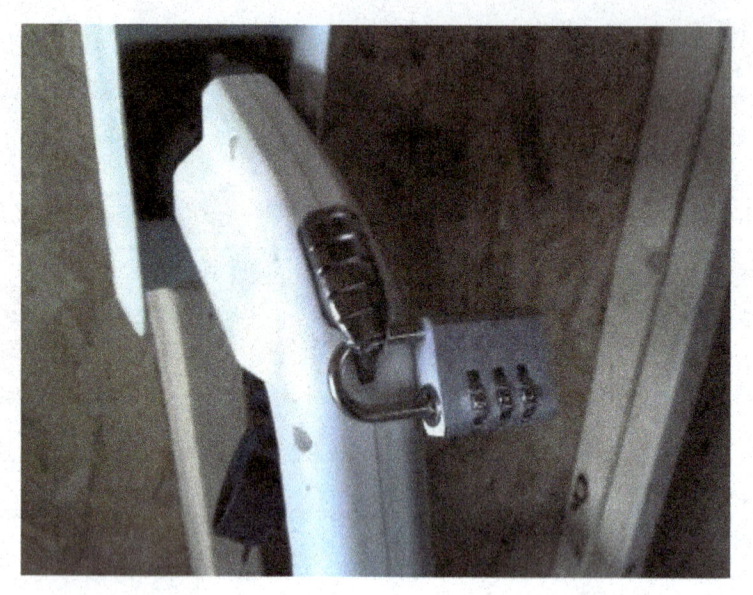

FIGURE 13-7 One way to prevent theft of the charging cord that comes with most electric vehicles is to drill a hole in the release handle and place a lock to prevent the handle from being released.

WIRELESS CHARGING

HOW IT WORKS Wireless power transfer (WPT) uses electromagnetic induction (magnetic resonance) between a transmitting pad on the ground and a receiving pad attached to the underside of the vehicle. Wireless charging allows the vehicle to be simply driven over the transmission pad and after a communication "handshake," electrical energy is transmitted from the transmission pad to the receiving pad and converted from AC to DC to charge the high-voltage battery.

WIRELESS CHARGING STANDARDS SAE international has established a world-wide standard for wireless charging under SAE J2954 which includes three levels of charging:

- WPT 1—3.7 kW
- WPT 2—7 kW
- WPT 3—11 kW

WPT will make it easier to charge an electric vehicle and also make an autonomous vehicle able to be charged by itself without the need to be plugged into a charging station. ● **SEE FIGURE 13-8**.

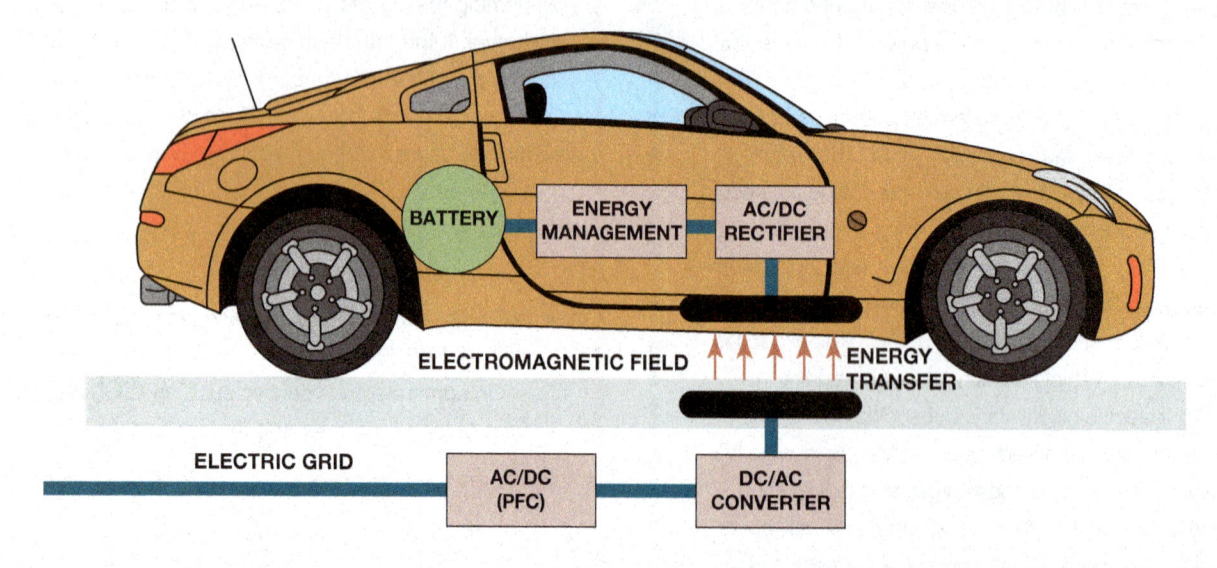

FIGURE 13-8 Wireless power transfer (WPT) uses electromagnetic induction between the transmitting pad on the ground and a receiving pad attached to the underside of the vehicle. For safety, an AC/DC power supply needs to incorporate isolation and power factor correction (PFC).

TWO MEASUREMENTS There are two different ways to determine the electricity that an EV requires.

1. The charge required per miles driven, typically expressed in kilowatt-hours per 100 miles driven (kWh/100 mi).
2. The electricity required to fully charge the vehicle.

The electricity required to "fill the tank" for an EV depends on the size of the battery. Most electric vehicle batteries can store between 40 and 100 kWh which determines the range on a single charge. How much electricity an EV consumes per day, month, or year depends primarily upon how far the vehicle is driven each day. According to the Federal Highway Administration, the average American travels nearly 13,500 vehicle miles per year. At that level of driving, most EVs will require around 4,000 kWh of electricity per year to operate.

> **? FREQUENTLY ASKED QUESTION**
>
> **How Many Solar Panels Are Needed to Charge an Electric Vehicle?**
>
> To calculate the number of solar panels required to power an electric vehicle, there are three variables that have to be considered:
>
> 1. How much electricity the vehicle will use annually
> 2. The wattage of the solar panels being used
> 3. The local area which determines how much electricity the solar panels produce
>
> Most solar panels are in the 320- to 330-watt range. The production from solar panels will vary from region to region, with each panel producing more electricity in sunnier climates—such as the Southwest—than they will in the Northeast part of the United States. Depending on the location, charging an electric vehicle typically requires 7 or 9 solar panels..

INSTALLING A HOME CHARGING STATION PHOTO SEQUENCE

1 A hole was cut in the wall of the garage to accept an NEMA 14-50 receptacle.

2 A four-conductor, six-gauge cable was routed from the garage to the fuse panel in the house.

3 The cable was run from the garage through the attic and then down to the fuse panel.

4 The wires were connected to a 60-amp circuit breaker in the fuse panel.

5 The NEMA 14-50 outlet box was installed in the garage opening.

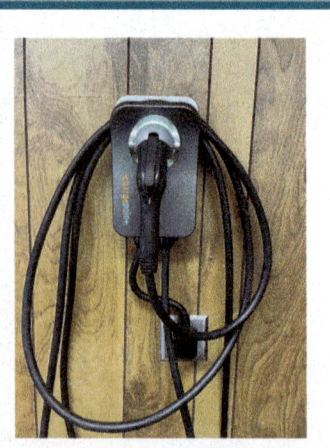

6 The Charge Point charging station was mounted to the wall, plugged into the outlet, and connected to Wi-Fi.

SUMMARY

1. The standards established by the National Electrical Manufacturers Association (NEMA) define a product, process, or procedure with terminology, construction, dimensions, and performance ratings.
2. According to the National Highway Safety Administration (NHTSA), the average American travels about 13,500 vehicle miles per year. At that level of driving, most EVs will require around 4,000 kWh of electricity per year to operate.
3. Wireless power transfer (WPT) uses electromagnetic induction between the transmitting pad on the ground and a receiving pad attached to the underside of the vehicle.

REVIEW QUESTIONS

1. When installing electric vehicle supply equipment (EVSE), what certifications should be checked?
2. What is defined by National Electrical Manufacturers Association (NEMA) regarding electrical outlets?
3. What does it mean if a "fishy smell" is noticed while charging?
4. What does wireless power transfer (WPT) use to transfer energy between the transmitting pad on the ground and a receiving pad attached for the underside of the vehicle?
5. When using a vehicle charging cord, why is it necessary to uncoil the wiring before connecting the plug to the vehicle?

CHAPTER QUIZ

1. What is used to convert AC from the electrical outlet to DC to charge the high-voltage battery?
   a. The electrical vehicle service equipment (EVSE)
   b. The on-board charger in the vehicle
   c. The inverter in the vehicle
   d. The converter in the vehicle
2. Both the NEMA _____ and _____ are four-wire grounding devices that are used in residential use and either may also be used for home charging of electric vehicles.
   a. 10-30; 10-50
   b. 14-30; 14-50
   c. 6-50; 10-50
   d. Any of the above
3. _____ codes are the standards to which buildings and equipment must meet minimum regulatory safety requirements.
   a. UL
   b. NEC
   c. NRTL
   d. NEMA
4. A "fishy smell" while charging indicates _____.
   a. overloaded circuits
   b. loose wires
   c. frayed cords
   d. Any of the above
5. A 48-amp EVSE will require a _____ breaker.
   a. 50-amp
   b. 60-amp
   c. 70-amp
   d. 80-amp
6. The terminals of a J1772 plug are _____.
   a. not "hot" until the connection has been made to the vehicle and communication between the vehicle and the charger has been established
   b. "hot" at all times and could result in a shock hazard if the terminals are touched
   c. power, one ground plus a control pilot and a safety terminal
   d. Both a and c
7. SAE J1772 plugs are used for _____.
   a. Level 1 charging
   b. Level 2 charging
   c. Level 3 charging
   d. Both a and b
8. Most house chargers are installed in the garage, but can also be mounted in a carport or outside if a _____ charger and plug are used.
   a. Level 1
   b. Level 2
   c. weather proof
   d. Either a or b
9. If electricity costs $0.11 per kWh and the vehicle consumes 34 kWh to travel 100 miles, the cost per mile is about _____.
   a. $4.00
   b. $8.00
   c. $0.04
   d. $0.80
10. Wireless power transfer (WPT) uses _____ between the transmitting pad on the ground and a receiving pad attached to the underside of the vehicle.
    a. Bluetooth
    b. CAN Buss
    c. internet
    d. electromagnetic induction

Chapter 14
REGENERATIVE BRAKES

LEARNING OBJECTIVE

After studying this chapter, the reader should be able to:

- Describe how regenerative braking works.
- Explain the principals involved in regenerative braking.
- Discuss the parts and components involved in regenerative braking systems.
- Describe the servicing precautions involved with regenerative brakes.

KEY TERMS

Inertia 189
Kinetic energy 189
One-pedal driving 194
Regeneration 190

REGENERATIVE BRAKING IN VEHICLES

INERTIA, FORCE, AND MASS If a moving object has a mass, it has inertia. **Inertia** is the resistance of an object to change its state of motion. In other words, as Newton's first law of motion states: "An object in motion tends to stay in motion, and an object at rest tends to stay at rest unless acted on by an outside force." An electric vehicle (EV) or hybrid electric vehicle (HEV) can reclaim energy by converting the energy of a moving object, called **kinetic energy**, into electric energy. According to basic physics:

A force applied to move an object results in the equation:

$$F = ma$$

where F = force
   m = mass
   a = acceleration

The faster an object is accelerated, the more force that has to be applied. Energy from the battery (watts) is applied to the coil windings in the motor. These windings produce a magnetic force on the rotor of the motor, which produces torque on the output shaft. This torque is applied to the wheels of the vehicle by use of a coupling of gears and shafts. When the wheel turns, it applies a force to the ground, which due to friction between the wheel and the ground, causes the vehicle to move along the surface. ● **SEE FIGURE 14-1**.

All vehicles generate torque to move the wheels to drive the vehicle down the road. During this time, it is generating friction and losses. When standard brakes are applied, it is just another friction device that has specially designed material to handle the heat from friction. This friction is applied to the drums and rotors that stop the wheel from turning. The friction between the wheel and the ground actually stops the vehicle. However, the energy absorbed by the braking system is lost in the form of heat and cannot be recovered or stored for use later to help propel the vehicle. The kinetic energy increases with the square of the speed. In other words, if the speed of a vehicle doubles, the kinetic energy is four times higher (speed is doubled (times 2) and the kinetic energy is squared (2 times 2 equals 4)). ● **SEE FIGURE 14-2**.

LAW OF INERTIA
THE TENDENCY OF OBJECTS TO RESIST CHANGES IN MOTION

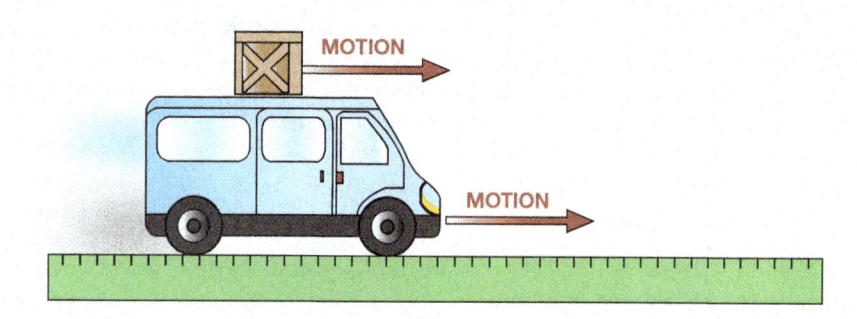

FIGURE 14-1 Any object tends to stay in motion unless acted on by an outside force.

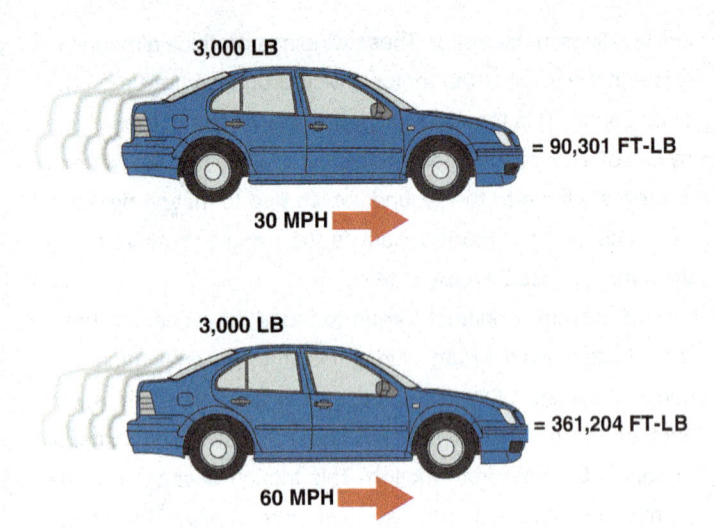

FIGURE 14-2 Kinetic energy increases as the square of any increase in vehicle speed.

FREQUENTLY ASKED QUESTION

Are the Friction Brakes Used During Regenerative Braking?

Yes. Most hybrid vehicles make use of the base (friction) brakes during stopping. The amount of regenerative braking compared to the amount of friction braking is determined by the electronic brake controller. It is important that the base brakes be used regularly to keep the rotors free from rust and ready to be used to stop the vehicle. A typical curve showing the relative proportion of brake usage is shown in **FIGURE 14-3**.

FREQUENTLY ASKED QUESTION

What Is the Difference Between Mass and Weight?

Mass is the amount of matter in an object. One of the properties of mass is inertia. Inertia is the resistance of an object to being put in motion, and the tendency to remain in motion once it is set in motion. The weight of an object is the force of gravity on the object and may be defined as the mass times the acceleration of gravity. Therefore, mass means the property of an object and weight is a force.

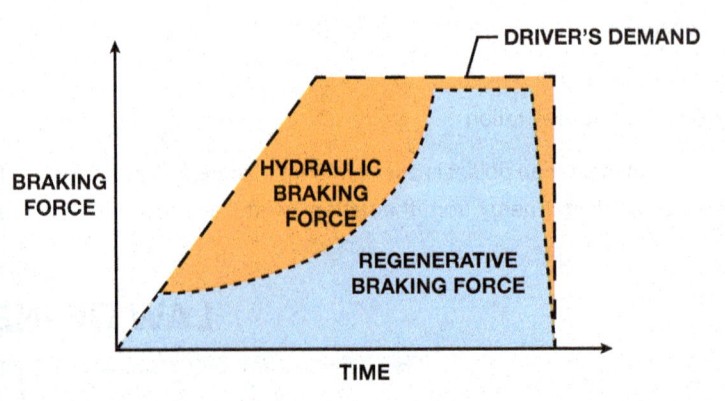

FIGURE 14-3 The regenerative braking system works with the mechanical and hydraulic brake system to provide the necessary braking force to slow and stop the vehicle. Regenerative brakes seldom work at speeds below 10 MPH (16 km/h).

TRANSFERRING ENERGY BACK TO THE MOTOR

Inertia is the fundamental property of physics that is used to reclaim energy from the vehicle. Instead of using 100% friction brakes (base brakes), the braking torque is transferred from the wheels back into the motor shaft. One of the unique things about most electric motors is that electrical energy can be converted into mechanical energy, and mechanical energy can be converted back into electrical energy. In both cases, this can be done very efficiently. Through the use of the motor and motor controller, the force at the wheels transfers torque to the electric motor shaft. The magnets on the shaft of the motor (called the rotor—the moving part of the motor) move past the electric coils on the stator (the stationary part of the motor), passing the magnetic fields of the magnets through the coils, producing electricity. This electricity is electrical energy, which is directed to and recharges the high-voltage battery. This process is called **regeneration**, *regen*, or simply "reclaiming energy."

LIMITATIONS OF REGENERATIVE BRAKES

There are some limitations that will always affect even the best regenerative braking systems, which include the following:

- It only acts on the driven wheels.
- The system has to be designed to allow for proper use of the antilock braking system (ABS).
- The batteries are commanded to be kept at a maximum of about 60%, plus or minus 20%, which is best for long battery life and to allow for energy to be stored in the batteries during regenerative braking. If the batteries were allowed to be fully charged, there would be no place for the electrical current to be stored and the conventional friction brakes alone have to be used to slow and stop the vehicle. Charging the batteries over 80% would also overheat the batteries.

BENEFITS OF REGENERATIVE BRAKING SYSTEMS

Depending on the type of vehicle, this would reduce fuel consumption by 10% to 25%.

Regenerative braking can be extremely powerful and can recover about 20% of the energy normally wasted as brake heat. Regenerative braking has the following advantages:

- Reduces the drawdown of the battery charge.
- Extends the overall life of the battery pack.
- Reduces fuel consumption.

All production EVs and HEVs use regenerative braking as a method to improve vehicle efficiency, and this feature alone provides the most fuel economy savings. How much energy is reclaimed depends on many factors, including the weight of the vehicle, speed, and the rate of deceleration. ● **SEE FIGURE 14-4**.

> **? FREQUENTLY ASKED QUESTION**
>
> **When Does Regenerative Braking Not Work?**
>
> There is one unusual situation where regenerative braking will not occur. What happens if, for example, the vehicle is at the top of a long hill and the battery charge level is high? In this situation, the controller can only overcharge the batteries. Overcharging is not good for the batteries, so the controller will disable regenerative braking and use the base brakes only. This is one reason why the SOC of the batteries is kept below 80% so regenerative braking can occur.

TYPES OF REGENERATIVE BRAKE SYSTEMS

SERIES REGENERATION In series regenerative braking systems, the amount of regeneration is proportional to the brake pedal position. As the brake pedal is depressed further, the controller that regulates the regenerative braking system computes the torque needed to slow the vehicle, as would occur in normal braking. As the brake pedal is depressed even further, the service brakes are blended into the regenerative braking to achieve the desired braking performance based on brake pedal force and travel. Series regenerative braking requires active brake management to achieve total braking to all four wheels. This braking is more difficult to achieve if the hybrid electric vehicle uses just the front or rear wheels to power the vehicle. This means that the other axle must use the base brakes alone, whereas the drive wheels can be slowed and stopped using a combination of regenerative braking and base brake action. All series regenerative braking systems use an electrohydraulic brake (eHb) system, which includes the hydraulic control unit (ABS modulator) that manages the brake system pressures, as well as the front-rear axle brake balance. Most hybrid vehicles use this type of regenerative braking system. The regenerative braking system mainly uses the regenerative capability, especially at higher vehicle speeds, and gradually increases the amount of the base braking force at low vehicle speeds. ● **SEE FIGURE 14-5**.

PARALLEL REGENERATION A parallel regenerative braking system is less complex because the base (friction)

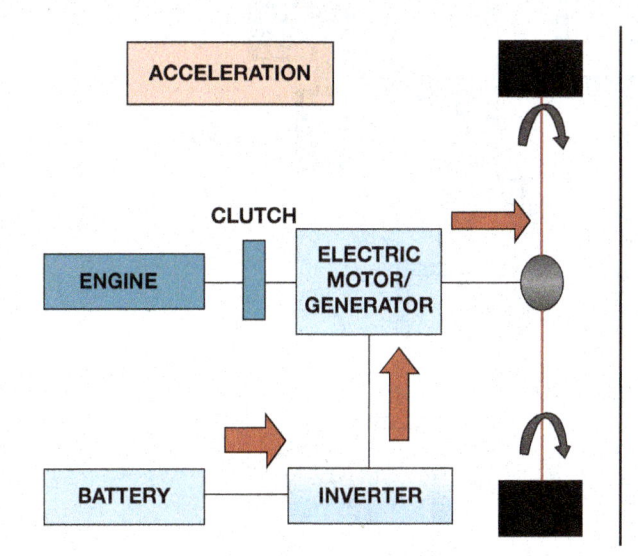

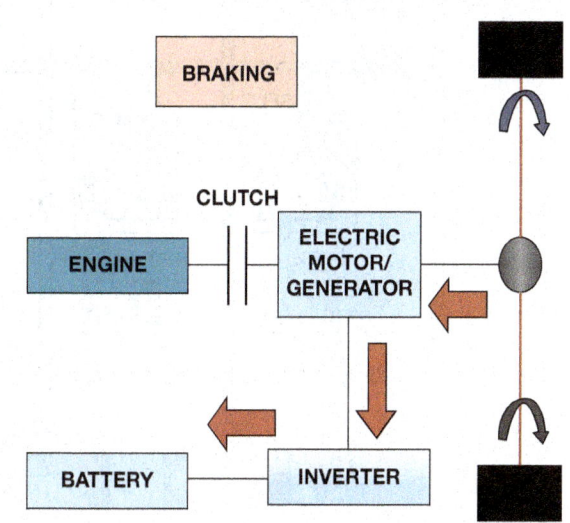

FIGURE 14-4 During acceleration, the ICE and motor/generator are used to propel the vehicle. During deceleration, the energy is returned to the HV battery through the inverter that changes the AC crated in the motor/generator to DC to charge the battery.

REGENERATIVE BRAKES 191

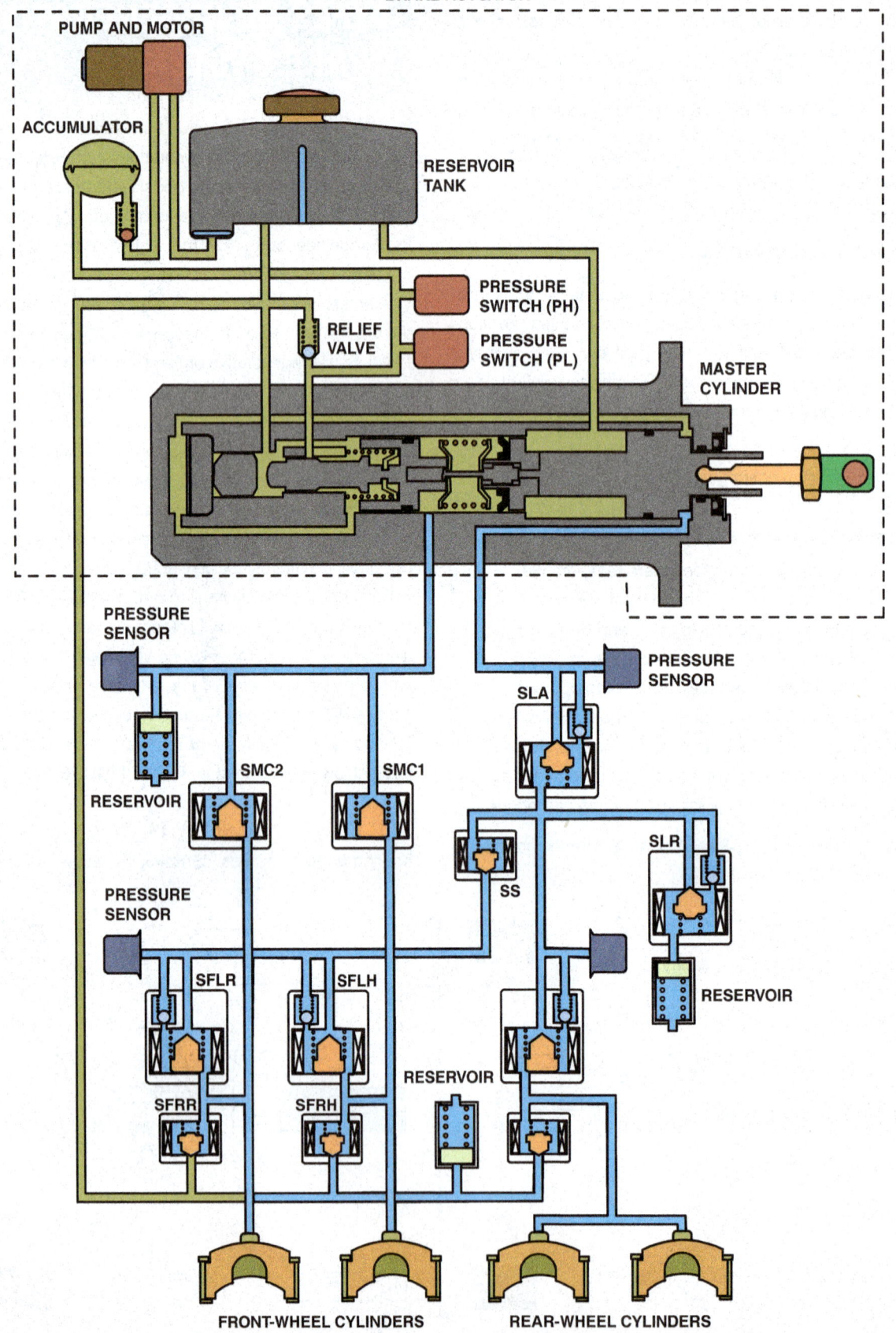

FIGURE 14-5 The Toyota Prius regenerative braking system component showing the master cylinder and pressure switches.

192 CHAPTER 14

brakes are used along with energy recovery by the motors, becoming generators. The controller for the regenerative braking system determines the amount of regeneration that can be achieved based on the vehicle speed. Front and rear brake balance is retained because the base brakes are in use during the entire braking event. The amount of energy captured by a parallel regenerative braking system is less than from a series system. As a result, the fuel economy gains are less.

REGENERATIVE BRAKE COMPONENTS
It is the ABS ECU that handles regenerative braking, as well as ABS functions, sending a signal to the hybrid ECU how much regeneration to impose. But how does the ABS ECU know what to do?

Rather than measuring brake pedal travel, which could vary with pad wear, the system uses pressure measuring sensors to detect master cylinder pressure. Some systems use a brake pedal position (BPP) sensor as an input signal to the brake ECU. A typical BBP sensor has two Hall-effect sensor elements on the vacuum booster body and a slide connected to the brake pedal with four Hall magnets. ● **SEE FIGURE 14-6**. The operation includes the following:

- The magnets are connected to the input push rod.
- When the driver presses the brake pedal, the Hall magnets move over the Hall sensors.

This movement (speed and position) is interpreted as a braking request by the brake control system.

The higher the master cylinder pressure, the harder the driver is pushing on the brake pedal. If the driver is pushing only gently, the master cylinder piston displacement will be small and the hydraulic brakes will be only gently applied. In this situation, the ECU knows that the driver wants only gentle deceleration and instructs the hybrid ECU to apply only a small amount of regeneration. However, as master cylinder pressure increases, so does the amount of regeneration that can automatically be applied.

If the electromechanical brake servo and ESC fail at the same time, purely mechanical braking is still possible.

There are four pressure sensors in the braking system and two pressure switches. However, it is the master cylinder pressure sensor that is most important. ● **SEE FIGURE 14-7**.

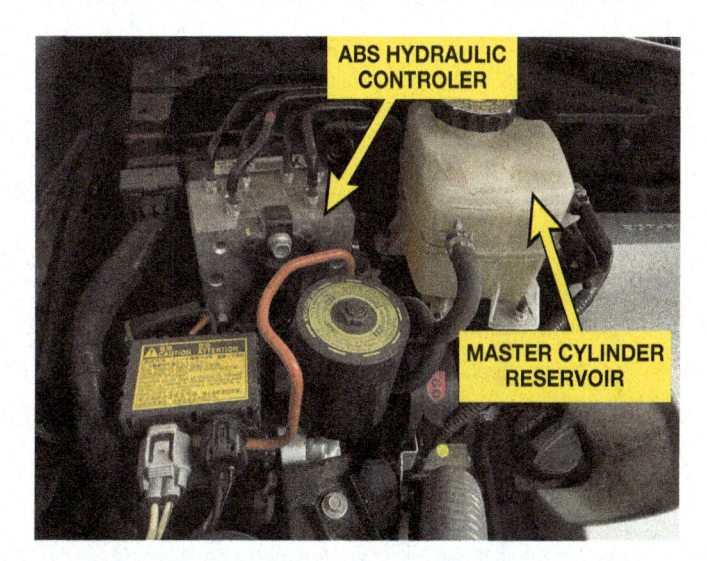

FIGURE 14-7 The components under the hood of a Toyota Highlander hybrid electric vehicle showing the master cylinder reservoir and the ABS controller.

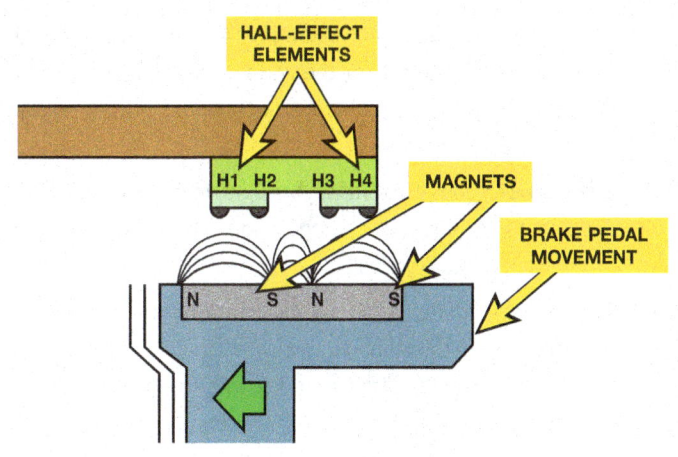

FIGURE 14-6 A contactless BPP sensor uses two Hall-effect elements and magnets to determine not only the position of the brake pedal, but also the speed that the driver is depressing the brake pedal.

? FREQUENTLY ASKED QUESTION

What Do Regenerative Brakes Look Like?

Regenerative brakes use the rotation of the wheels applied to the electric traction (drive) motor to create electricity. Therefore, the brakes themselves look the same as conventional brakes because the hydraulic brakes are still in place and work the same as conventional brakes. The major difference is that the standard wheel brakes work mostly at low vehicle speeds, whereas conventional brakes work at all speeds. As a result, the brakes on a hybrid electric vehicle should last many times longer than the brakes on a conventional vehicle. ● **SEE FIGURE 14-8**.

FIGURE 14-8 The front disc brakes on a Mustang Mach E electric vehicle look like most multi-piston front disc brakes used on conventional vehicles.

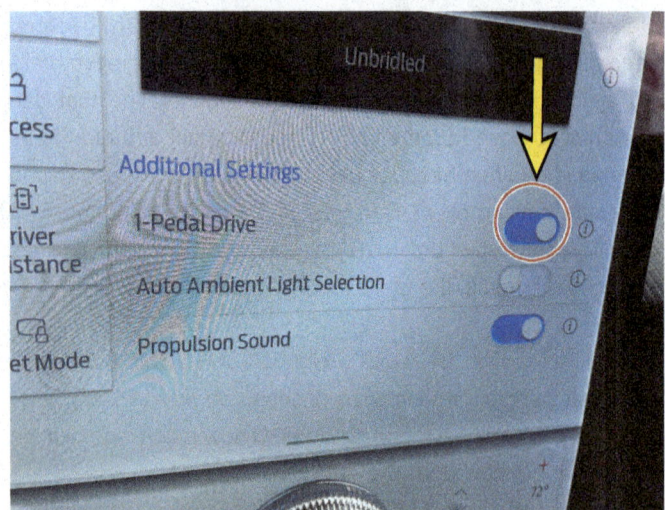

FIGURE 14-9 The display on the dash display of an electric vehicle shows where the one pedal feature can be turned on or off.

> **? FREQUENTLY ASKED QUESTION**
>
> **Can an On-Vehicle Brake Lathe Be Used on a Hybrid Electric Vehicle?**
>
> Yes. When a brake rotor needs to be machined on a hybrid electric vehicle, the rotor is being rotated. On most hybrids, the front wheels are also connected to the traction motor that can propel the vehicle and generate electricity during deceleration and braking. When the drive wheels are being rotated, the motor/generator is producing electricity. However, unless the high-voltage circuit wiring has been disconnected, no harm will occur.

more regenerative braking is achieved and the faster the vehicle slows down. If the deceleration rate is greater than 0.2 Gs, the brake lights come on to warn the driver behind that the vehicle is braking, just as if the driver depressed the brake pedal.

Drivers still have to use the brake pedal to come to a complete stop below 5 to 7 MPH (8 to 11 km/h). In a Nissan Leaf, the car can come to a complete stop in its "e-Pedal" mode. When the car stops totally, it engages the hydraulic brakes to hold it in place. This is not the case with most other vehicles that require the driver to depress the brake pedal to hold the vehicle from moving. ● **SEE FIGURE 14-9**.

ONE-PEDAL DRIVING

DEFINITION **One-pedal driving** means that for normal driving, the driver only needs to use the accelerator pedal to accelerate and decelerate. Tesla started using one-pedal driving in 2012 with the Tesla Model S. The brakes on a Tesla are stand alone and are not tied in and blended with the regenerative braking system. One-pedal driving involves the following:

- To accelerate, the driver depresses the accelerator pedal. To accelerate faster, the accelerator pedal is depressed further.
- To decelerate (slow down), the driver releases the accelerator pedal and the vehicle speed slows. The faster the driver lets up on the accelerator pedal, the

EXAMPLES

- The Nissan Leaf has a "L" setting for its drive selector that increases the strength of the regeneration. But it is not strong enough to permit proper one-pedal driving under many circumstances.
- The Volkswagen eGolf and the Chevrolet Bolt EV offer options for one-pedal driving or not depending on the driver needs and desires.
- The Bolt's default "D" position operates like an automatic-transmission car, while the "L" position provides strong regen, eliminating the idle creep, and allows one-pedal driving right down to 0 MPH.
- Audi, while it offers one-pedal driving, the feature has to be selected by the driver. The normal operation of an Audi EV is to allow the vehicle to coast, thereby maintaining the kinetic energy of the moving vehicle without converting

that energy back into electrical energy to be stored in the HV battery.

- One-pedal driving seems strange at first, but getting used to it occurs quickly and becomes easy to control the vehicle. The only time that the brake pedal is depressed is for emergency situations or to hold the vehicle from moving, and at very low speeds where regenerative braking is not active.

NOTE: When driving in one-pedal mode, the brake light will come on when the accelerator pedal is released and the vehicle starts to slow.

? FREQUENTLY ASKED QUESTION

Is One-Pedal Driving an Advantage?

Some dealers are recommending that their customers do not use one-pedal driving to maximized range. Some electric vehicle manufactures also limit regenerative braking and allow the vehicle to coast, thereby maintaining inertia. Regenerative braking is not 100% efficient. If you are coasting at 60 MPH, regen slows you down to 50, and then accelerates to 60 again, you will lose more energy than if the speed was kept at a steady 60 MPH. Regenerative braking is only useful if used for braking. The most efficient driving mode is the one that is smoothest. That means no hard acceleration or deceleration.

DECELERATION RATES

TERMINOLOGY Deceleration rates are measured in units of "feet per second, per second." What this means is that the vehicle will change in velocity during a certain time interval divided by the time interval.

Deceleration is abbreviated "ft/sec^2" (pronounced "feet per second, per second" or "feet per second squared") or meters per sec^2 (m/s^2) in the metric system.

EXAMPLES Typical deceleration rates include the following.

- Comfortable deceleration is about 8.5 ft/sec^2 (3 m/s^2).
- Loose items in the vehicle will "fly" above 11 ft/sec^2 (3.5 m/s^2).
- Maximum deceleration rates for most vehicles and light trucks range from 16 to 32 ft/sec^2 (5 to 10 m/s^2).

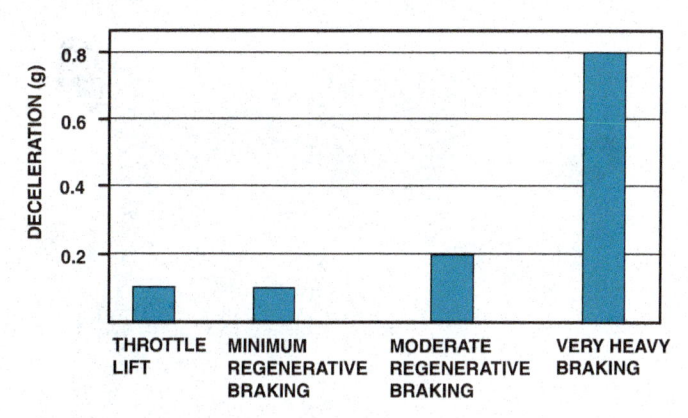

FIGURE 14-10 The graph compares the figures: at the far left, a throttle lift typically giving about 0.1 g deceleration; second from the left, a minimum regenerative braking of about 0.1 g; second from the right, a moderate regenerative braking is about 0.2 g; and on the far right, a hard emergency stop resulting in braking of (at least) 0.8 g, which uses both the regenerative braking system and the base hydraulic brake system.

An average deceleration rate of 15 ft/sec^2 (FPSPS) (3 m/s^2) can stop a vehicle traveling at 55 mph (88 km/h) in about 200 ft (61 m) and in less than 4 seconds. Deceleration is also expressed in units called a g. One g is the acceleration of gravity, which is 32 feet per second, per second. With a conventional hydraulic braking system, the driver can brake extremely gently, thereby only imperceptibly slowing the vehicle. A typical hybrid using regenerative braking will normally indicate a 0.1 g (about 3 ft/sec^2) deceleration rate when the throttle is released and the brake pedal has not been applied. This rate is what a driver would normally expect to occur when the accelerator pedal is released. This slight deceleration feels comfortable to the driver, as well as the passengers, because this is what occurs in a non-hybrid vehicle that does not incorporate regenerative braking. When the brake pedal is pressed, the deceleration increases to a greater value than 0.1 g, which gives the driver the same feeling of deceleration that would occur in a conventional vehicle. Maximum deceleration rates are usually greater than 0.8 g and could exceed 1 g in most vehicles. ● **SEE FIGURE 14-10.**

SERVICING REGENERATIVE BRAKES

UNIQUE MASTER CYLINDERS Most hybrid electric vehicles use unique master cylinders that do not look like conventional master cylinders. Some use more than one brake fluid reservoir and others contain sensors and other components, which are often not serviced separately. ● **SEE FIGURE 14-11.**

Late model GM EVs and PHEVs use an electromechanical brake booster combined with the ABS unit that allows the use of a more conventional master cylinder.

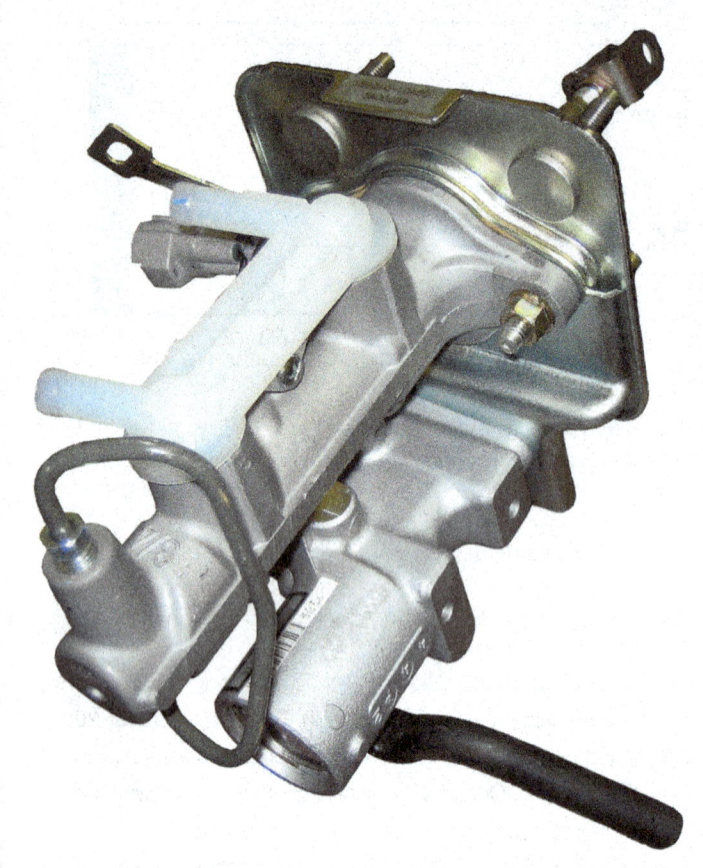

FIGURE 14-11 A master cylinder from a Toyota Highlander hybrid electric vehicle.

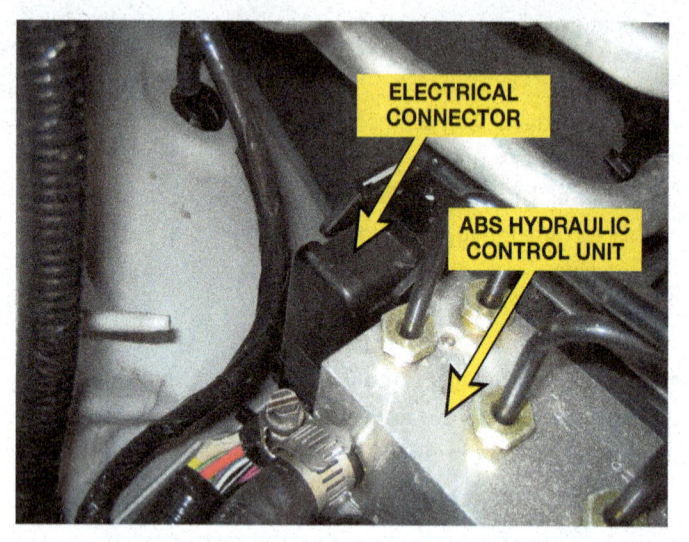

FIGURE 14-12 When working on the brakes on a Ford Escape or Mercury Mariner hybrid vehicle, disconnect the black electrical connector on the ABS hydraulic control unit located on the passenger side under the hood.

FORD ESCAPE PRECAUTIONS

On the Ford Escape hybrid system, the regenerative braking system checks the integrity of the brake system as a self-test. After a certain amount of time, the brake controller will energize the hydraulic control unit and check that pressure can be developed in the system.

- This is performed when a door is opened as part of the wake-up feature of the system.
- The ignition key does not have to be in the ignition for this self-test to be performed.
- This is done by developing brake pressure for short periods of time.

To prevent physical harm or causing damage to the vehicle when servicing the braking system, the technician should do the following:

1. In order to change the brake pads, it is necessary to enter the "Pad Service Mode" on a scan tool and disable the self-test. This will prevent brake pressure from being applied.
2. Disconnect the wiring harness at the hydraulic control unit. ● SEE FIGURE 14-12.
3. Check service information regarding how to cycle the ignition switch to enter the Pad Service Mode.

Case Study

Regenerative Brake Warning Message

The owner of an electric vehicle complained to the service department about a message on the dash that stated that the regenerative braking system is degraded. This can be considered normal in cold weather because lithium-ion batteries have no trouble discharging when cold, but do not accept a charge easily when cold. Regenerative braking relies on using the motors as generators, and the battery as the place to store that power. Cold batteries mean limited or no regenerative braking. Once the vehicle was driven and the high-voltage batteries increased in temperature, the regenerative braking system worked normally and the message was no longer displayed on the dash. ● SEE FIGURE 14-13.

Summary:
- **Complaint**—Vehicle owner saw a message on the dash warning that the braking system was degraded.
- **Cause**—The high-voltage batteries were cold and could not accept a charge from the regenerative brake system.
- **Correction**—Once the high-voltage batteries increased in temperature, the message was not displayed and is considered to be normal operation at very cold temperatures.

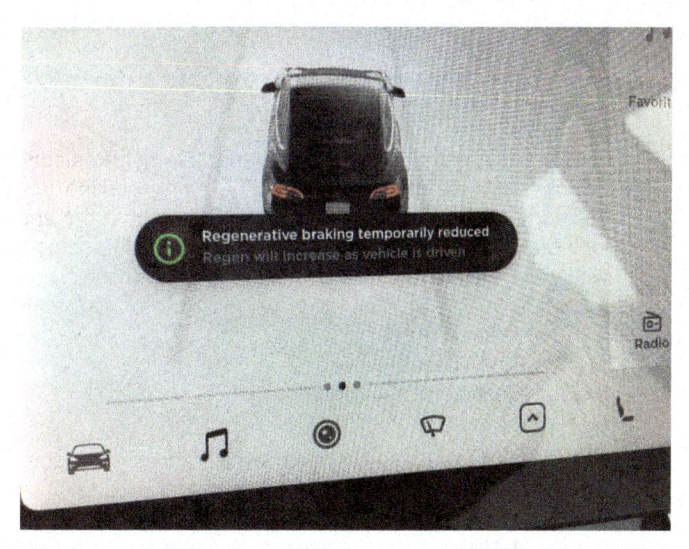

FIGURE 14-13 A notice displayed on the dash informing the driver that the regenerative brakes are degraded or temporarily reduced. When this occurs, the brake pedal feel will change because the system will use more of the base brakes, which may require a higher pedal effort.

SUMMARY

1. All moving objects that have mass (weight) have kinetic energy.
2. The regenerative braking system captures most of the kinetic energy from the moving vehicle and returns this energy to high-voltage batteries to be used later to help propel the vehicle.
3. The two types of regenerative braking include parallel and series.
4. Brushless DC and AC induction motors are used in hybrid electric vehicles to help propel it and to generate electrical energy back to the batteries during braking.
5. The controller is used to control the motors and turn them into a generator as needed to provide regenerative braking.

REVIEW QUESTIONS

1. What is inertia?
2. What is the difference between series and parallel regenerative braking systems?
3. What happens in the regenerative braking system when the high-voltage batteries are fully charged?
4. What is meant by "one-pedal driving"?
5. What occurs when the driver first releases the accelerator pedal and starts to brake on a hybrid electric vehicle equipped with regenerative braking?

CHAPTER QUIZ

1. Which type of regenerative braking system uses an electrohydraulic system?
   a. Series
   b. Parallel
   c. Both series and parallel
   d. Neither series nor parallel

2. Kinetic energy is _____.
   a. the energy that the driver exerts on the brake pedal
   b. the energy needed from the batteries to propel a vehicle
   c. the energy in any moving object
   d. the energy that the motor produces to propel the vehicle

3. Inertia is _____.
   a. the energy of any moving object that has mass (weight)
   b. the force that the driver exerts on the brake pedal during a stop
   c. the electric motor force that is applied to the drive wheels
   d. the force that the internal combustion engine and the electric motor together apply to the drive wheels during rapid acceleration

4. What are the benefits of regenerative brakes?
   a. Reduces the draw down of the battery charge.
   b. Extends the overall life of the battery pack.
   c. Reduces fuel consumption.
   d. All of the above

5. During braking on a hybrid electric vehicle equipped with regenerative braking system, what occurs when the driver depresses the brake pedal?
   a. The friction brakes are only used as a backup and not used during normal braking.
   b. The motors become generators.
   c. The driver needs to apply a braking lever instead of depressing the brake pedal to energize the regenerative braking system.
   d. The batteries are charged to 100% SOC.

6. Technician A says that a front-wheel-drive hybrid electric vehicle can only generate electricity during braking from the front wheel motor(s). Technician B says that the antilock braking (ABS) is not possible with a vehicle equipped with a regenerative braking system. Which technician is correct?
   a. Technician A only
   b. Technician B only
   c. Both Technicians A and B
   d. Neither Technician A nor B

7. In a regenerative braking system, which part of the electric motor is being controlled by the computer?
   a. The rotor
   b. The stator
   c. Both the rotor and the stator
   d. Neither the rotor nor the stator

8. Two technicians are discussing deceleration rates. Technician A says that a one "g" stop is a gentle slowing of the vehicle. Technician B says that a stopping rate of 8 ft/ sec^2 is a severe stop. Which technician is correct?
   a. Technician A only
   b. Technician B only
   c. Both Technicians A and B
   d. Neither Technician A nor B

9. One pedal system means _____.
   a. the vehicle is not equipped with a separate brake pedal
   b. the accelerator pedal is used to accelerate and decelerate the vehicle
   c. the vehicle uses regenerative braking only and not friction brakes
   d. the vehicle does not use regenerative braking

10. Which of these two is the more efficient type of regenerative braking?
    a. Series regeneration
    b. Parallel regeneration
    c. Both types are equally efficient
    d. A third type, not mentioned, is the most efficient

Chapter 15
ELECTRIC POWER STEERING

LEARNING OBJECTIVES

After studying this chapter, the reader should be able to:

- Describe the purpose, function, and types of electric power steering systems.
- Explain how electric power steering systems operate.
- Discuss how to diagnose electric power steering system faults.

This chapter will help prepare for the Steering and Suspension (A4) ASE certification test content area "A" (Steering Systems Diagnosis and Repair).

KEY TERMS

Column-mounted electric power steering (C-EPS) 200
Electric power-assisted steering (EPAS) 200
Electric power steering (EPS) 200
Power steering control module (PSCM) 203
Steering position sensor (SPS) 203
Steering shaft torque sensor 201

ELECTRIC POWER STEERING

TERMINOLOGY All HEV and EV vehicles use **electric power steering (EPS)** systems, also called **electric power-assisted steering (EPAS)**. Electric power steering takes the place of hydraulic components that were previously used by using an electric motor to provide power assist effort.

ADVANTAGES The advantages are as follows:

- Allows the vehicle manufacturer to save vehicle weight and complexity because there is no need for all of the hydraulic lines and engine-driven pump.
- Improved cold weather starting because of reduced engine load without the drag of a power steering pump.
- Simple two-wire connection in many cases, making vehicle assembly and vehicle service easier.

TYPES OR DESIGNS There are two basic types of EPS systems:

1. **Rack mounted.** The rack-mounted system has the assist motor attached to the rack and is often called a *rack-and-pinion electric power steering (R-EPS) system*. Another design has the assist motor surrounding the rack and this style is called a *direct-drive electric power steering (D-EPS) system*. ● **SEE FIGURES 15-1 AND 15-2**.

FIGURE 15-1 A Toyota Highlander hybrid EPS assembly.

2. **Column mounted.** Column-mounted electric power steering (C-EPS) has sensors and the assist motor located inside the vehicle so they are not exposed to the heat and outside elements as is the rack-mounted system.
 ● **SEE FIGURE 15-3**.

This is the most commonly used type and involves using a manual rack-and-pinion steering gear assembly with a motor assist in the steering column. While not directly mounted on the column itself, another type of electric power steering is the *pinion-mounted electric power steering system (P-EPS) system*. This system has the assist motor connected to the pinion shaft of the rack-and-pinion steering gear. ● **SEE FIGURE 15-4**.

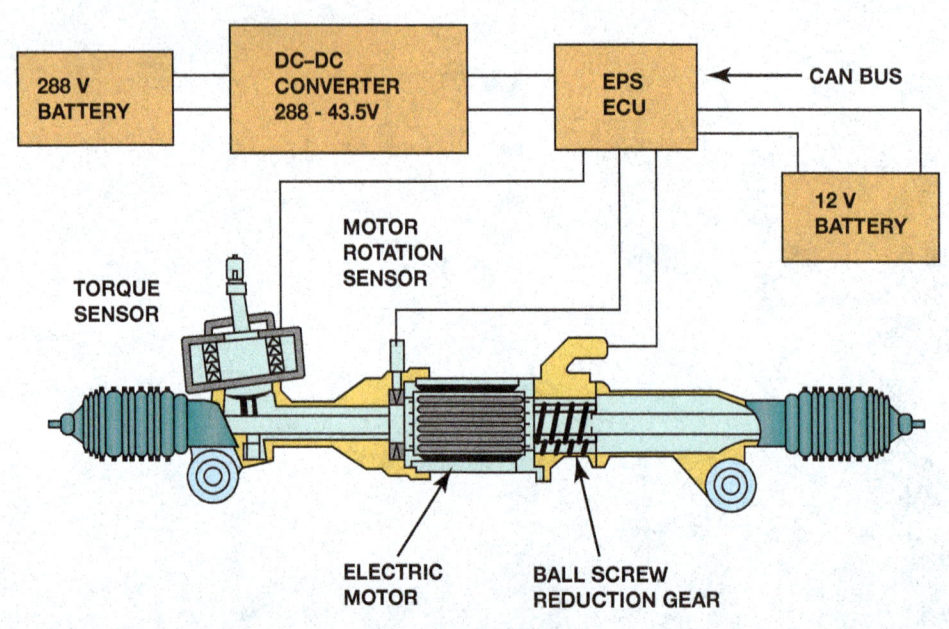

FIGURE 15-2 The electric power steering used in the Toyota/Lexus SUVs uses a brushless DC (labeled BLDC) motor around the rack of the unit and operates on 42 volts.

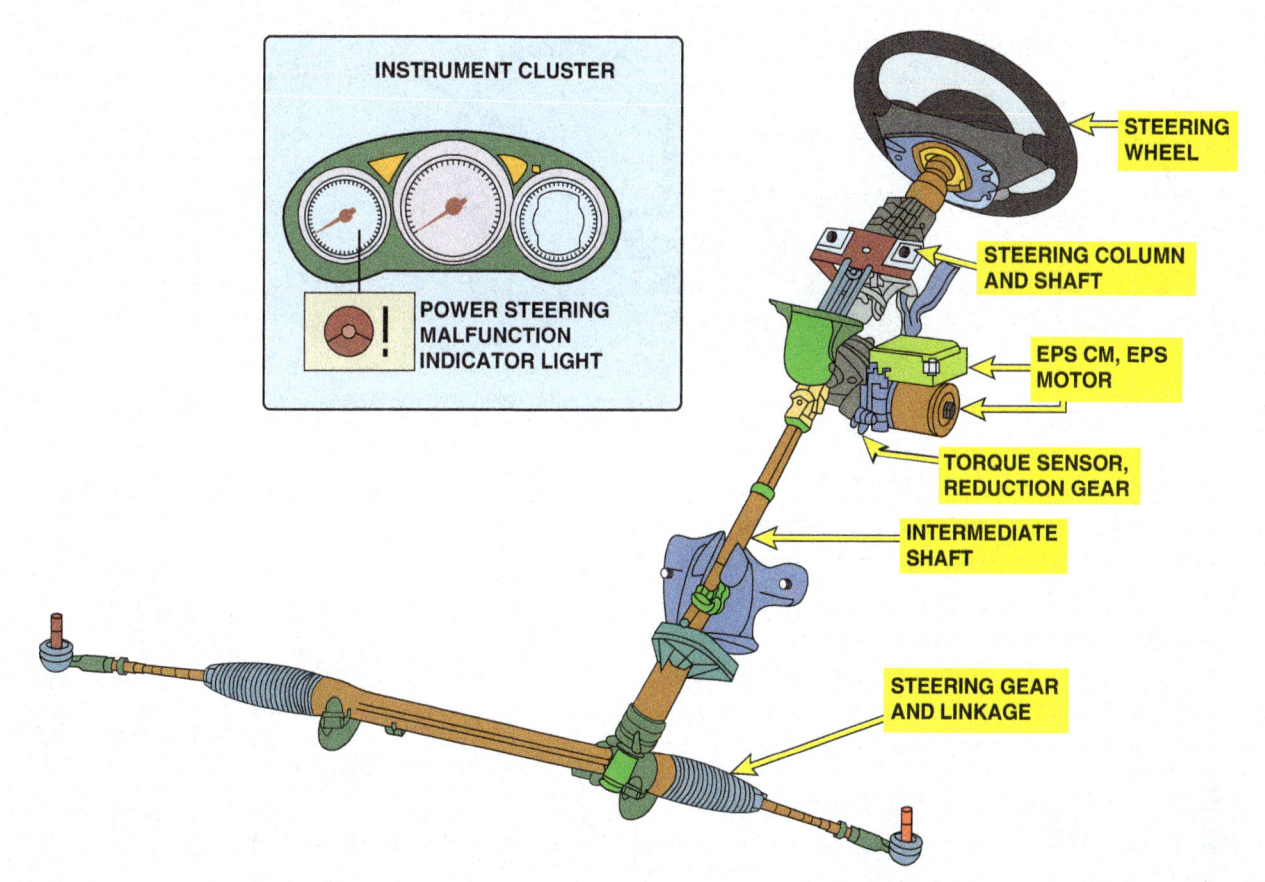

FIGURE 15-3 A column-mounted EPS system showing the location of the major components involved including the dash warning light symbol.

FIGURE 15-4 A pinion-mounted electric power steering system.

PARTS AND OPERATION

TYPES OF MOTOR USED Some EPS motors operate on 12 volts whereas others operate from 42 volts and use an electronic controller and a brushless DC motor as an actuator.

The power steering motor is a 12-volt brushless DC reversible motor with a 65-ampere rating. The motor assists steering through a worm gear and reduction gear located in the steering column housing. The motor draws about 750 to 1,000 watts or about 1 horsepower at full assist. The motor itself is usually replaced as an assembly or can be included with the control unit. ● **SEE FIGURE 15-5.**

EPS CONTROL UNIT The electric power steering is controlled by the EPS ECU, which calculates the amount of needed assist based on the input from the steering torque sensor. The steering torque sensor is a noncontact sensor that detects the movement and torque applied to the torsion bar. The torsion bar twists when the driver exerts torque to the steering wheel, and the more torque applied causes the bar to twist further. This generates a higher-voltage signal to the EPS ECU. ● **SEE FIGURE 15-6**.

The **steering shaft torque sensor** and the steering wheel position sensor are not serviced separately from each other or from the steering column assembly. The steering column assembly does not include the power steering motor and module assembly. The detection ring 1 and detection ring 2 are

ELECTRIC POWER STEERING 201

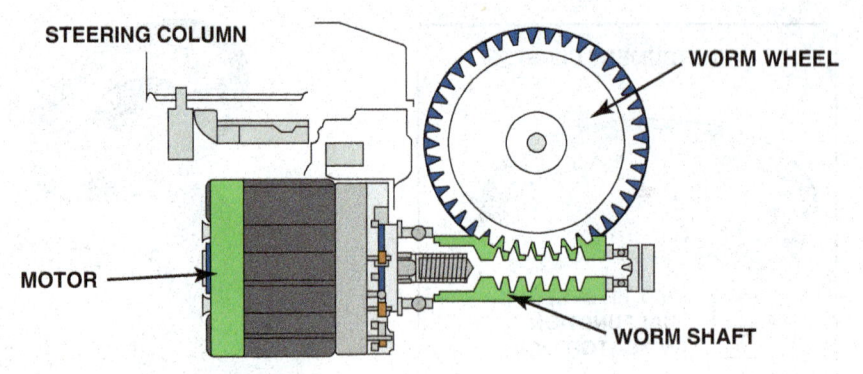

FIGURE 15-5 The EPS electric motor drives the rack through a worm gear in many electric power steering systems.

mounted on the input shaft, and detection ring 3 is mounted on the output shaft. The input shaft and the output shaft are connected by a torsion bar. When the steering wheel is turned, the difference in relative motion between detection rings 2 and 3 is sensed by the detection coil and sends two signals to the EPS ECU. These two signals are called Torque Sensor Signal 1 and Torque Signal 2. The EPS ECU uses these signals to control the amount of assist and also uses the signals for diagnosis.

NOTE: If the steering wheel, steering column, or the steering gear is removed or replaced, the zero point of the torque sensors must be reset using a scan tool. The Toyota Highlander and Lexus RX 400h use a different electric power steering unit due to the larger size of the vehicles. This unit uses a concentric brushless DC motor on the steering rack. ● **SEE FIGURE 15-7.**

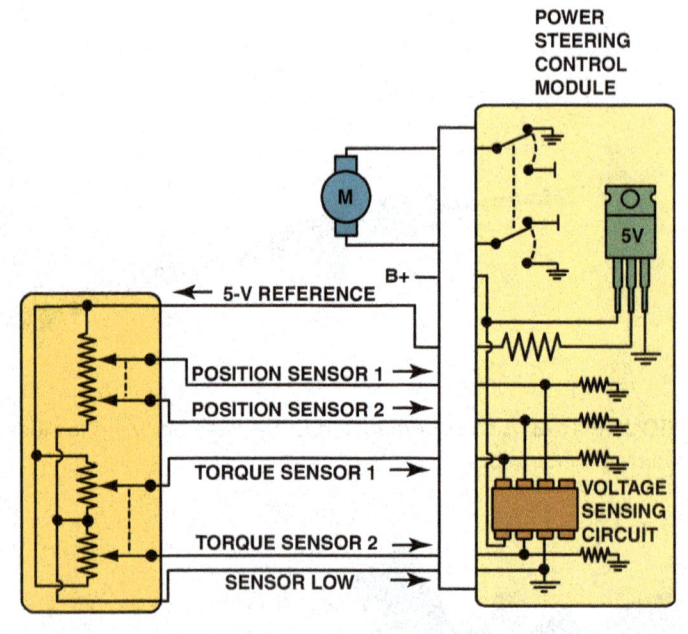

FIGURE 15-7 Schematic showing the EPS and the torque and position sensors.

INPUTS AND OUTPUTS The EPS system includes the following components and input signals from sensors and output signals to actuator components:

- Powertrain control module (PCM)
- Body control module (BCM)
- Power steering control module (PSCM)
- Battery voltage
- Steering shaft torque sensor
- Steering wheel position sensor
- Power steering motor
- Driver information center (DIC)
- Serial data communications circuits to perform the system functions

● **SEE FIGURE 15-8.**

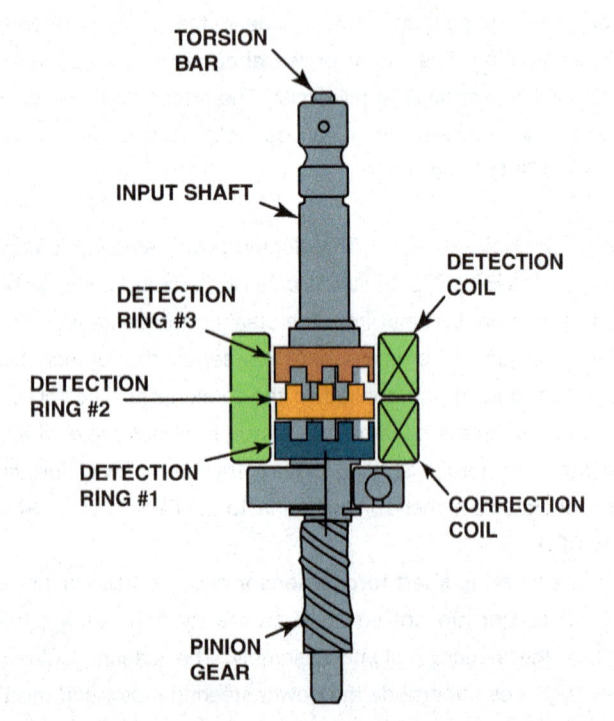

FIGURE 15-6 The torque sensor converts the torque the driver is applying to the steering wheel into a voltage signal.

202 CHAPTER 15

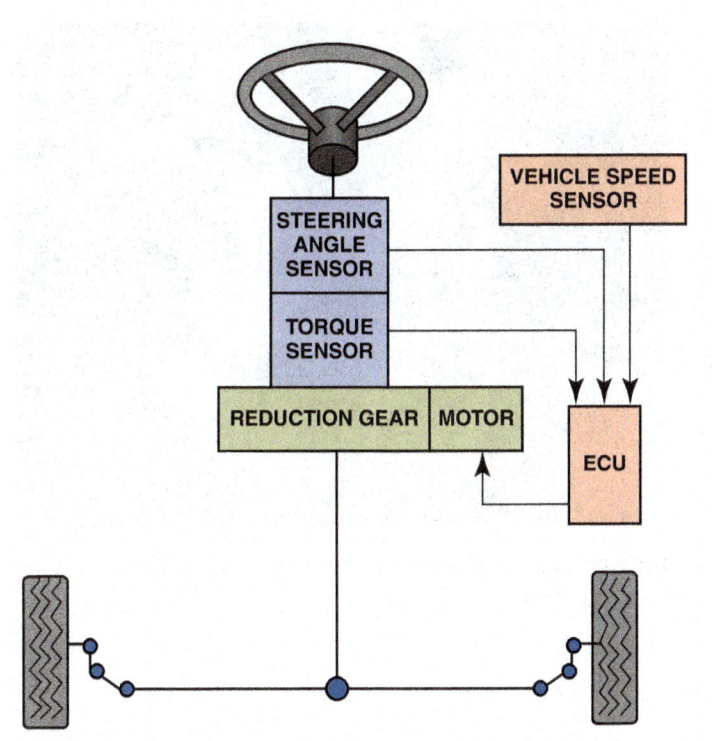

FIGURE 15-8 A graphical representation of the relationship of the various electric power steering components.

POWER STEERING CONTROL MODULE The **power steering control module (PSCM)** and the power steering motor are serviced as an assembly and are serviced separately from the steering column assembly. ● **SEE FIGURE 15-9**.

When the steering wheel is turned, the PSCM uses signal voltage from the steering shaft torque sensor to detect the amount of torque and steering direction being applied to the steering column shaft and then commands the proper amount of current to the power steering motor. The PSCM receives a vehicle speed message from the PCM by way of the serial data communications circuit. At low speeds, more assist is provided for easy turning during parking maneuvers, and at higher speeds, less assist is provided for improved road feel and directional stability. The steering shaft torque sensor and the steering wheel position sensor are not serviced separately from each other or from the steering column assembly. The steering column assembly does not include the power steering motor and module assembly.

STEERING SHAFT TORQUE SENSOR The PSCM uses the steering shaft torque sensor as a main input for determining steering direction and the amount of assist needed. The steering column has an input shaft, from the steering wheel to the torque sensor, and an output shaft, from the torque sensor to the steering shaft coupler. The input and output shafts are separated by a section of torsion bar, where the torque sensor is located. The torque sensor includes two different sensors in one housing. The sensors are used to detect the direction the steering wheel is being rotated.

- When torque is applied to the steering column shaft during a right turn, the sensor signal 1 voltage increases, while the signal 2 voltage decreases.
- When torque is applied to the steering column shaft during a left turn, the sensor signal 1 voltage decreases, while the signal 2 voltage increases.

The PSCM recognizes this change in signal voltage as steering direction and steering column shaft torque.

STEERING WHEEL POSITION SENSOR The PSCM uses the **steering position sensor (SPS)** to determine the steering system on-center position. Because the power steering motor provides a slight amount of return-to-center assist, the PSCM will command the power steering motor to the steering system center position and not beyond. The sensor is a 5-volt dual-analog signal device with a signal voltage range of 0 to 5 volts. The sensor's signal 1 and signal 2 voltage values will increase and decrease within 2.5 to 2.8 volts of each other as the steering wheel is turned.

FAULT DETECTION If a major fault were to occur, the control module will first try to maintain power-assisted steering even if some sensors have failed. If the problem is serious, the vehicle can be driven and steered manually. The EPS control unit will turn on the EPS dash warning light if a fault has been detected. A fault in the system will not cause the malfunction indicator light to come on because that light is reserved for emission-related faults only. Fault codes can be retrieved by using a scan tool, and the codes will be displayed by the flashing of the EPS warning lamp.

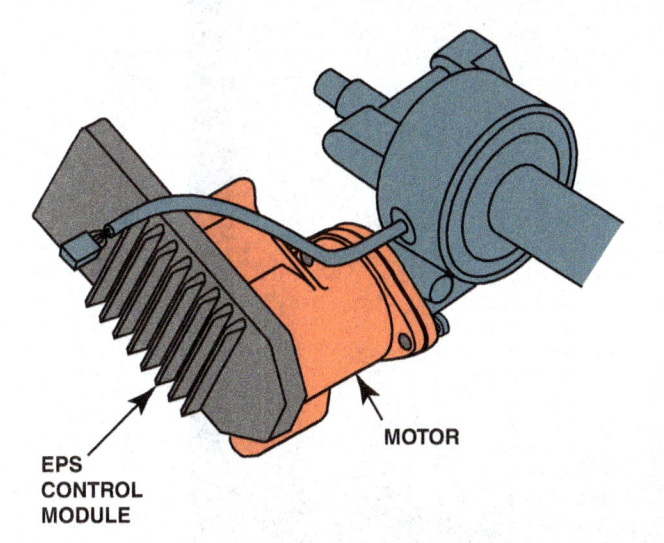

FIGURE 15-9 The PSCM is attached to the motor of the electric power steering assembly on some vehicles.

? FREQUENTLY ASKED QUESTION

What Is an Electrohydraulic Power Steering System?

Electrohydraulic power steering (EHPS) is used on the Chevrolet/GMC parallel hybrid truck (PHT) and on the Mini Cooper. This system uses an electric motor to drive a hydraulic pump. The EHPS module controls the power steering motor, which has the function of providing hydraulic power to the brake booster and the steering gear. A secondary function includes the ability to improve fuel economy by operating on a demand basis and the ability to provide speed-dependent variable-effort steering. ● SEE FIGURE 15-10.

FIGURE 15-10 An electrohydraulic power steering assembly on a Chevrolet hybrid pickup truck.

ELECTRIC POWER STEERING DIAGNOSIS

DIAGNOSTIC PROCEDURE The PSCM has the ability to detect malfunctions within the power steering system. Any malfunction detected will cause the driver information center to display the power steering warning message and/or the service vehicle soon indicator. The PSCM must also be set up with the correct steering calibrations, which are different in relation to the vehicle's powertrain configuration, model type, and tire and wheel size. A factory or aftermarket factory-level scan tool is needed to retrieve data and to perform relearn procedures if the unit is replaced. Always check service information for the exact procedures to follow when diagnosing and serving the electric power steering system. ● SEE FIGURE 15-11.

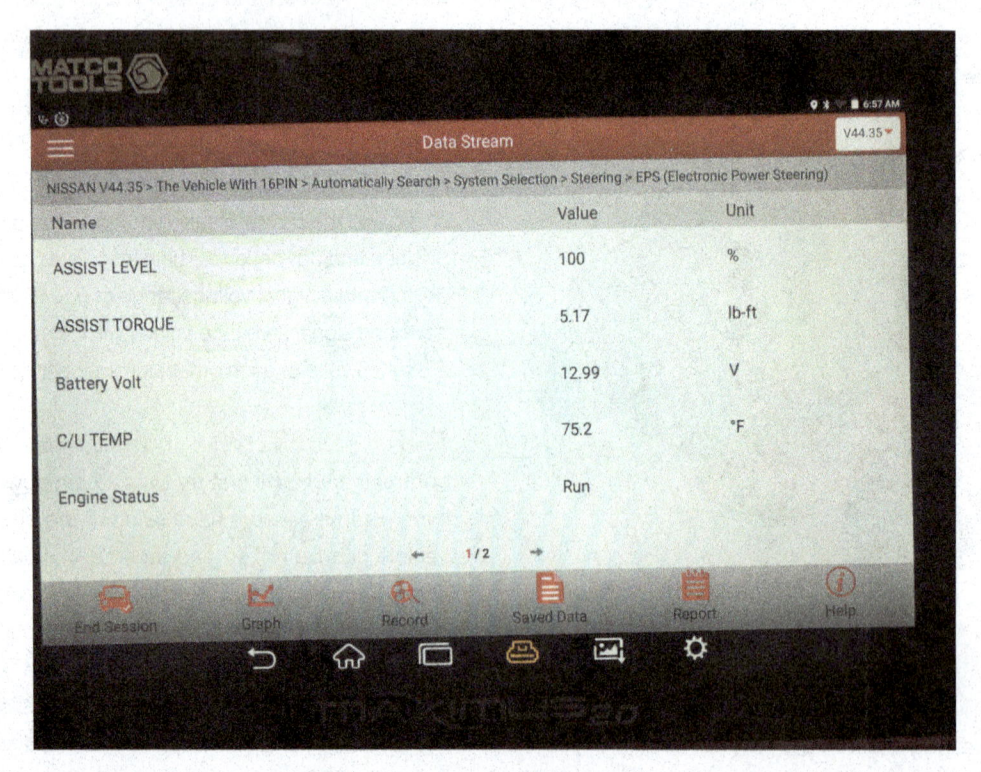

FIGURE 15-11 A screen shot showing some of the data that is available in a factory or factory-level scan tool when checking the electric power steering system.

CHAPTER 15

Case Study

Nissan Leaf Power Steering Fault

The owner of a Nissan Leaf SV drove home, parked the car in the driveway, left the car for 1/2 hour, then got into the car to drive it into the garage. After pushing brake and power, the car came on normally, but the PS warning light stayed on, the car wouldn't go into drive, and the steering wheel was very hard to turn. I could shift into neutral, but not drive. I kept my foot on the brake and hit power again, and it then powered on normally and allowed me to drive.

The owner repeated the sequence of events: Car off. Foot hard on brake. Push power. PS light stays on. Steering won't turn easily. Car won't go into drive. Held his foot on the brake and pushed power again, and the car powers up normally.

The local shop was able to verify the fault and suspected that the 12-volt battery was the cause. Testing of the 12-volt battery verified that it was not able to hold a charge and was replaced. This corrected the customer complaint.

Summary:

- **Complaint**—The power steering warning light was on and the steering was hard to turn.
- **Cause**—A defective 12-volt battery.
- **Correction**—The replacement of the 12-volt battery solved the hard steering and the warning light concern.

EPS DTCS Most electric power steering diagnostic trouble codes (DTCs) will be "C" codes for chassis-related faults or "U" codes for data communication faults. ● **SEE CHART 15-1** for same sample DTCs.

DIAGNOSTIC TROUBLE CODE (DTC)	DESCRIPTION OF FAULT
C1511; C1512; C1513; C1514	Torque sensor fault detected
C1521	Short in motor circuit
U0073	EPS control module lost communications

CHART 15-1

Sample DTCs for the electric power steering system.

SUMMARY

1. The use of electric power steering compared to conventional power steering results in more available engine power and improved fuel economy.
2. The two basic types of EPS include the rack-mounted and the column-mounted system.
3. The most commonly used system uses a manual rack and pinion gear with a column-mounted motor assist.
4. The sensors needed include the steering wheel position sensor and the steering shaft torque sensor.
5. Some vehicles that use electric power steering are capable of performing self-parking.
6. A few vehicles use an electric motor to power a hydraulic pump for steering assist.

REVIEW QUESTIONS

1. What are the types of electric power steering systems?
2. What sensors are needed for EPS systems?
3. What are the advantages of using an electric power steering system?
4. What type of motor is used in electric power steering systems?
5. How does an electrohydraulic power steering work?

CHAPTER QUIZ

1. The two basic types of electric power steering (EPS) include _____.
   a. engine mounted and column mounted
   b. column mounted and rack mounted
   c. electrohydraulic and rack mounted
   d. engine driven and battery powered

2. The advantages of EPS compared to hydraulic power steering include _____.
   a. less weight
   b. improved fuel economy
   c. increase usable engine power
   d. All of the above

3. What type of motor is used in most EPS systems?
   a. AC brush type
   b. DC brushless
   c. Stepper
   d. None of the above

4. Two technicians are discussing EPS systems. Technician A says that some systems operate on 12 volts. Technician B says that some systems operate on 42 volts, such as some hybrid electric vehicles. Which technician is correct?
   a. Technician A only
   b. Technician B only
   c. Both Technicians A and B
   d. Neither Technician A nor B

5. A typical electric motor used in EPS systems produces about how much power?
   a. ¼ horsepower
   b. ½ horsepower
   c. ¾ horsepower
   d. 1 horsepower

6. What is the relationship between the power steering control module (PSCM) and the powertrain control module (PCM)?
   a. Usually wired between the two
   b. No connection between the two
   c. Uses serial data lines between the two modules
   d. Mounted together on the EPS motor

7. If a fault is detected in the EPS system, what dash light is turned on?
   a. The "check engine" light
   b. The "service vehicle soon" light
   c. The power steering warning light
   d. Either b or c

8. What diagnostic equipment is usually needed to diagnose faults or relearn the EPS system?
   a. Special electronic diagnostic equipment designed to test each specific system
   b. Factory or factory-level scan tool
   c. A breakout box
   d. A 12-volt test light

9. What sensor is used to detect torque is applied to the steering column shaft?
   a. Torque sensor
   b. Steering shaft position sensor
   c. Steering shaft position sensor
   d. Power steering control module

10. Electrohydraulic power steering systems use _____.
    a. an electric motor to power a hydraulic pump
    b. a conventional hydraulic power steering gear
    c. an engine-driven hydraulic power steering pump and an electric motor steering gear
    d. Both a and b

Chapter 16
EV AND HEV HVAC SYSTEM

LEARNING OBJECTIVES

After studying this chapter, the reader should be able to:

- Describe the function of a hybrid electric vehicle's heating and cooling system.
- Explain the operation of the motor/electronics cooling system in an electric and hybrid electric vehicle.
- Describe the function of an electric vehicle's heating and air-conditioning (A/C) system.
- Discuss the operation and unique service procedures for electric-drive A/C compressors.
- Explain how an electric vehicle's battery is heated and cooled.

KEY TERMS

Cabin filter 214
Dog mode 225
Liquid-cooled condenser (LCC) 223
Positive temperature coefficient (PTC) 213
PTC heaters 213
Scroll compressor 216
Thermal storage material (TSM) 220

HEV ICE COOLING SYSTEM

ENGINE COOLING The purpose of the ICE (internal combustion engine) cooling system is to bring the ICE up to an optimum temperature as quickly as possible and then to maintain that temperature under all operating conditions. Coolant temperature for the ICE cooling system is maintained in a narrow range for a number of reasons including the following:

- The ICE is able to run at its highest efficiency and lowest emissions when it is at an operating temperature of 195°F to 215°F (90°C to 101°C). ICEs that run cold require richer air–fuel mixtures and suffer from reduced fuel economy and increased exhaust emissions.
- The engine will have better throttle response and produce greater output when it is at normal operating temperature.
- Engines that run cold tend to wear out much faster. A cold ICE will condense crankcase fumes and thus its engine oil will become contaminated more quickly.
- The ICE cooling system is also responsible for providing heat to the passenger compartment. The coolant temperature must be maintained at an optimum level to allow the heating system to work properly and to maximize passenger comfort.
- Overheating the ICE can lead to reduced efficiency and possible catastrophic failure of internal mechanical components.

Temperatures in the ICE combustion chamber can exceed 6000°F (3300°C). A portion of this heat energy (approximately one-third) is converted into mechanical energy to move the vehicle, but the vast majority is released as waste heat. Half of this waste heat is sent out the exhaust system, and the other half is absorbed by the ICE cooling system. The heat that is absorbed by the cooling system is then dissipated into the outside air by the vehicle's radiator. ● **SEE FIGURE 16-1**.

BASIC OPERATION All automotive ICEs are liquid-cooled. This means that the cooling system is sealed and liquid coolant is circulated through the water jacket (internal passages) by a water pump to absorb excess heat. The heated coolant is sent through a radiator to dissipate the heat and lower its temperature. The coolant then returns to the ICE internal passages to continue the cycle.

WATER PUMP The water pump is the "heart" of the ICE cooling system. It is most often driven by the ICE accessory drive belt, so it will circulate coolant whenever the ICE is running. When the ICE is first started, the cooling system is designed to reach operating temperature as quickly as possible. Therefore, the coolant is not circulated through the radiator until the correct temperature has been reached. A thermostat is used to allow coolant flow to the ICE water jacket and heater core until the coolant reaches approximately 195°F (91°C). At this point, the thermostat begins to open and allow coolant to flow to the radiator.

THERMOSTAT When the thermostat first starts to open, some coolant will flow to the radiator and some will continue to circulate in the ICE water jacket. Coolant that does not flow through the thermostat enters an internal bypass tube and returns

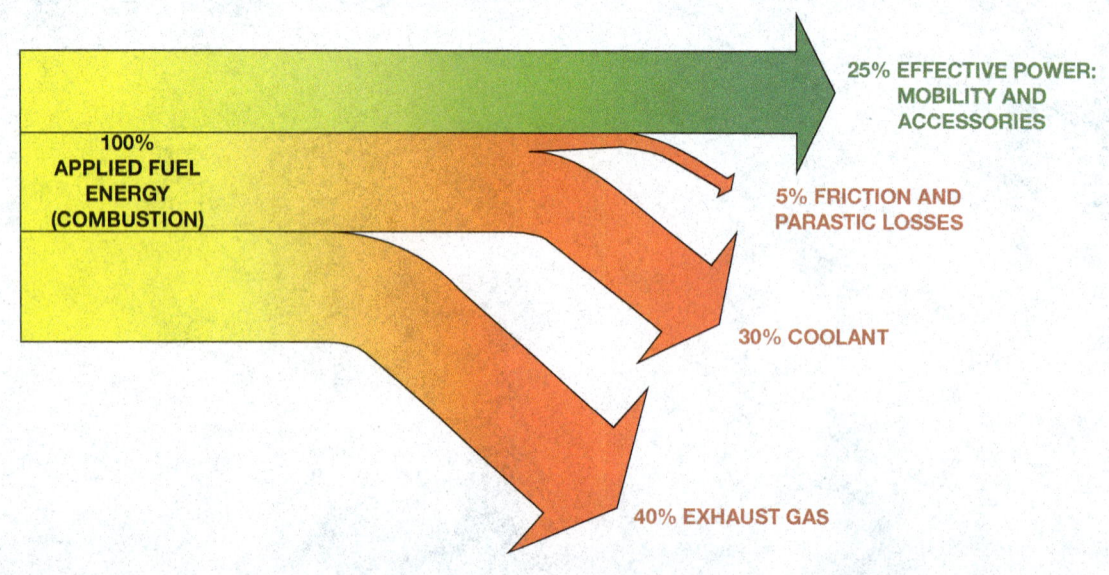

FIGURE 16-1 Only about a quarter of the total energy of the fuel in an internal combustion is used for useful work the rest is lost to the atmosphere through the exhaust and coolant.

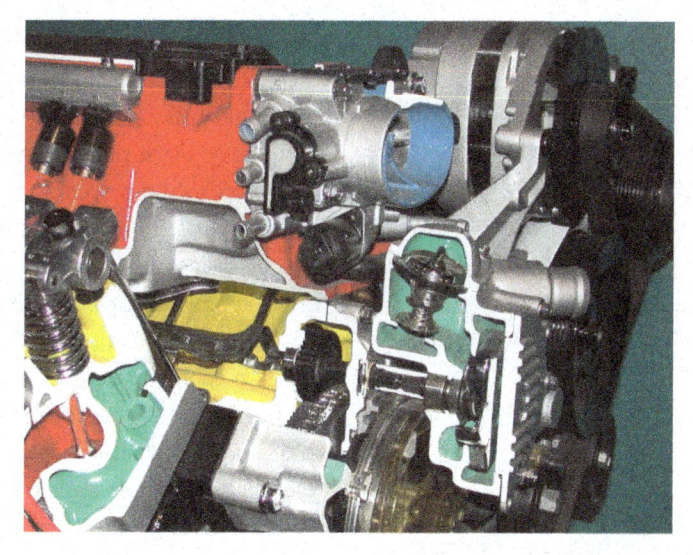

FIGURE 16-2 A cutaway of the front of an engine showing the coolant passages in green and the thermostat.

to the water pump inlet. As the coolant temperature continues to rise, the thermostat will open wider until it is fully open at about 215°F (20° above the opening temperature). Most of the coolant now flows through the radiator and the cooling system is removing heat from the ICE. If the coolant temperature continues to rise past this point, the electric fan will turn on and circulate air over the radiator to increase the amount of heat that can be dissipated.

- **SEE FIGURE 16-2**.

When engine temperature decreases, the electric fan will turn off and the thermostat will start to close. This causes more coolant to be recirculated through the water jacket and less to enter the radiator. The electric fan and thermostat work together to stabilize coolant temperature, and enable the ICE to operate at maximum efficiency and performance without overheating.

HEV CABIN HEATING SYSTEMS

PRINCIPLES Some of the waste heat absorbed by the ICE cooling system can also be dissipated by the heater core in the passenger compartment heating system. Hot coolant flows through the heater core and air is circulated through it to raise the temperature of the vehicle interior.

PARTS AND OPERATION Heater cores are similar to radiators, but are much smaller and usually have the inlet and outlet pipes located at the same end of the assembly. The heater core is located in the passenger compartment, inside the plenum chamber (HVAC air distribution box). ● **SEE FIGURE 16-3**.

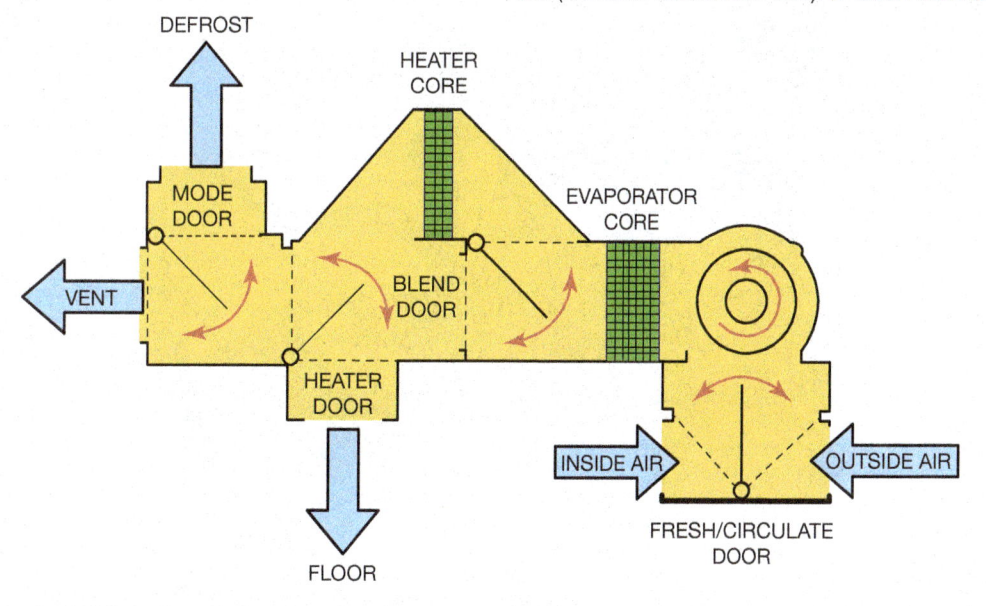

FIGURE 16-3 A typical HVAC plenum chamber showing the location of the various components.

EV AND HEV HVAC SYSTEM

In many systems, coolant is continually circulated through the heater core so it remains hot at all times. Air entering the plenum chamber must first pass through the air-conditioning (A/C) evaporator core, and is directed either through or around the heater core by the blend door (*air mix valve*). The temperature of the air can be adjusted by changing the position of the blend door and the percentage of air that is sent through the heater core.

Once the air leaves the heater core, it is blended with any air that has bypassed it and then is directed to specific areas of the vehicle, depending on the mode that is selected:

- In the defrost mode, the air can be directed toward the windshield outlets.
- In the heat mode, the air can be sent to the instrument panel outlets and/or the floor vents depending on the driver's preference.

HEATING SYSTEMS The amount of heat generated by the heating system is dependent on the temperature of the coolant that is circulated through the heater core. When the ICE is first started, it takes some time for the coolant to reach sufficient temperature for heat to be sent to the passenger compartment. This is further complicated with hybrid electric vehicles as the ICE coolant temperature is more difficult to maintain when the ICE enters into idle stop or the vehicle is operating in electric-only mode.

ELECTRIC ENGINE WATER PUMP An electric water pump uses a DC motor to power the impeller and is used on most hybrid electric vehicles and some internal combustion engines. The electric water pump usually is attached to the engine and is controlled by the powertrain control module (PCM). Being controlled by the PCM means that it can be operated only when needed to move coolant through the engine and radiator instead of being powered by the engine at all times. Also, not circulating coolant until needed allows the engine to reach operating temperature sooner than when using an engine-driven water pump. This results in increased efficiency for improved fuel economy and reduced exhaust emissions. Check service information for information about an electric water pump and where it is located because most are often hard to see. ● **SEE FIGURE 16-4**.

HEAT MODE When in the *heat mode,* the A/C compressor is turned off and the evaporator operates at ambient temperature. This means that any temperature change of the incoming air is now controlled only by the air temperature valve as it directs the air across the heater core.

NOTE: An auxiliary water (coolant) pump is a DC motor-operated water pump that is used to circulate coolant to the heater core to help keep the cabin warm. Hybrid electric vehicles have an electric water pump to cool the battery packs and inverters.

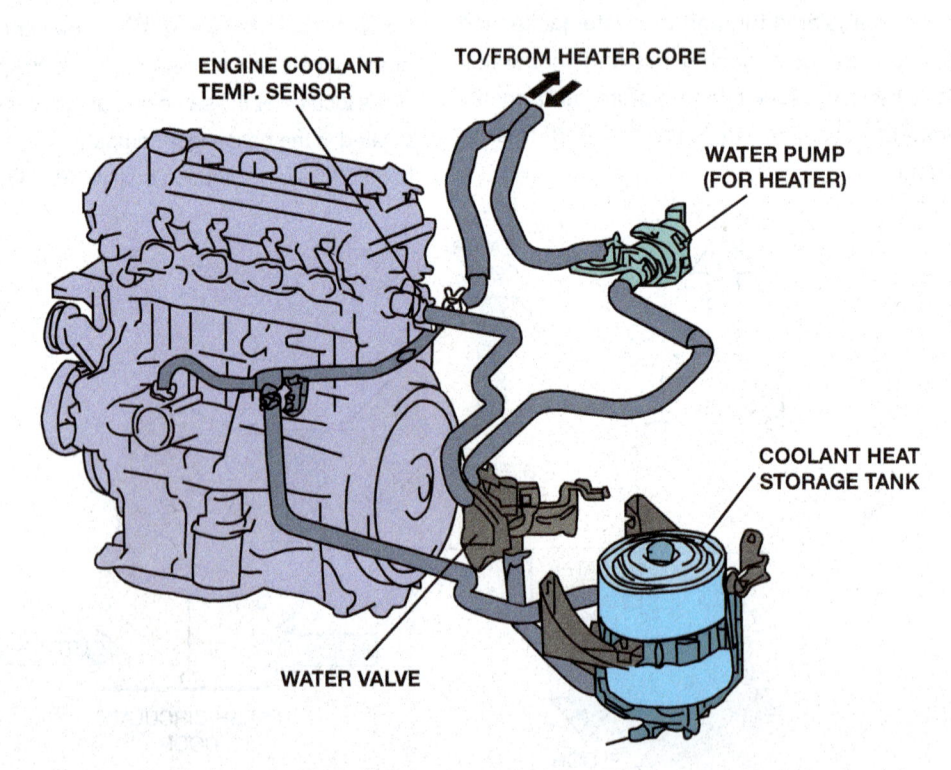

FIGURE 16-4 Toyota and many other hybrid electric vehicles use an electric water pump not only to circulate coolant though the engine, but also to circulate coolant through the heater core when operating at idle-stop mode.

MODES OF OPERATION The auxiliary water pump does not operate all the time. The BCM or controlling module will control and regulate the pump based on the following:

- Battery voltage
- Exterior temperature
- Interior temperature
- Vehicle speed
- Engine RPM
- Coolant temperature
- Temperature selected by the driver
- Blend door position
- Fan speed

FAILURE MODE A failed auxiliary water pump will usually not cause the engine to overheat. If the auxiliary coolant pump is inoperative, the customer might notice reduced heater performance at low speeds and at idle. While this fault is often caused by a defective thermostat, the wise service technician should check to SEE if the vehicle is equipped with an auxiliary water pump before replacing the thermostat. If the auxiliary water pump fails on some hybrids, the system will disable the hybrid drive system or put the vehicle into a limp mode.

AUXILIARY WATER PUMP DIAGNOSIS The diagnostic process includes the following steps:

STEP 1 Verify the customer concern. Operate the vehicle under the same conditions as the customer to verify a lack of cabin heating.

STEP 2 Perform a thorough visual inspection of the engine cooling system looking for leaks, coolant level, condition, and other possible reasons for a lack of cabin heat.

STEP 3 Check for codes with a scan tool. For example, a P2600 on a Mercedes indicates a fault with the auxiliary water pump or water pump circuit. Some codes may appear to be unrelated such as door module operation and loss of communications, but they can cause the auxiliary pump to stop operating. A scan tool can be used to command the pump on and off so its operation can be tested.

STEP 4 Check service information for the exact diagnostic procedure to follow for the vehicle being diagnosed. The electric auxiliary water pump may be called an auxiliary cooling circuit in the service information.

Case Study

The Case of the Hot Chevrolet Volt

Customer complained that their Chevrolet Volt had a coolant leak and lack of heat when the engine was running. The Volt heater system uses an electrical element for heat in electric mode and a pump and valve assembly to circulate engine coolant when the engine is running. Initial inspection found a coolant leak in the radiator. The radiator was replaced and the cooling system was refilled using a vacuum lift system. The cooling system has many places air can be trapped if any other method to refill the system is used. Following the repair, the leak was corrected but the lack of heat concern continued. Further inspection, draining, flushing, and refilling of the system revealed someone had put stop-leak into the system. The stop-leak had plugged the mesh filter in the upper heater hose. ● SEE FIGURE 16-5. The coolant heater hose and pipe assembly were replaced and the system was refilled. The lack of heat condition was corrected.

Summary:
- **Concern**—Coolant leak and lack of heat.
- **Cause**—Leaking radiator and the addition of stop-leak to the engine cooling system.
- **Correction**—Replacement of the radiator, the heater hose and pipe assembly, and the proper refilling of the cooling system restored the cooling system.

FIGURE 16-5 A mesh filter used in the cooling system of a Chevrolet Volt.

COOLANT HEAT STORAGE SYSTEM

PURPOSE In order to meet ever-increasing emissions standards, engineers strive to limit the impact that cold starts have on emissions and drivability. One approach is to use a coolant heat storage system where heated coolant is stored during normal vehicle operation and is then used to warm the engine intake ports prior to a cold start. Toyota uses this system in the second-generation Prius (2004–2009).

PARTS AND OPERATION The coolant heat storage tank is built very similar to a Thermos® bottle. The tank is built with an inner and outer casing, and a vacuum is formed between them. This is done to prevent heat transfer from the inner casing. Approximately 3 quarts (liters) of coolant are stored inside the inner casing, and the coolant can be kept warm for upto three days. There is a standpipe that extends inside of the inner casing, so coolant must rise in order to exit the tank through the standpipe. ● SEE FIGURE 16-6.

A water valve is used to direct the coolant flow between the coolant storage tank, the ICE, and the vehicle's heater core. The water valve is controlled by the ECM and consists of an electric motor, drive gears, a rotary valve, and a valve position sensor. ● SEE FIGURE 16-7.

The storage tank pump is used to move coolant through the heat storage tank at times when the ICE is shut off. This pump is located on the side of the heated coolant storage tank and is plumbed in series with the tank inlet. ● SEE FIGURE 16-8.

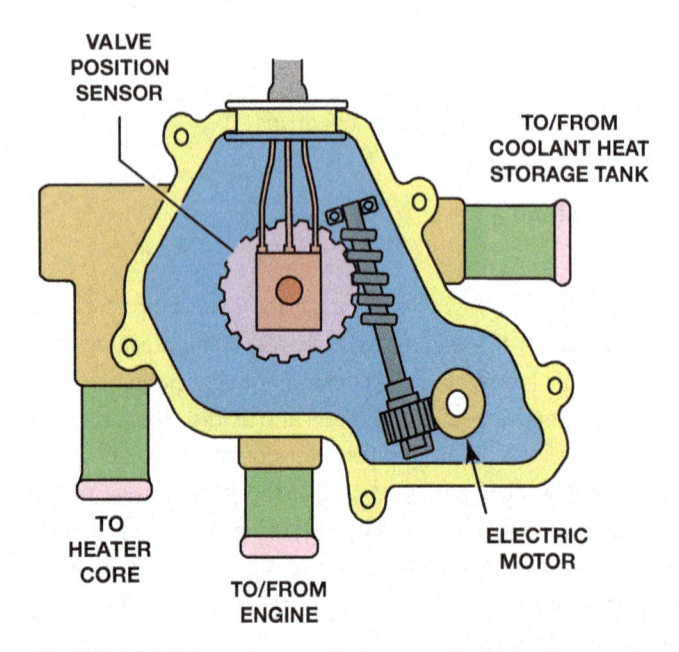

FIGURE 16-7 The valve position sensor in the water valve provides feedback to the ECM concerning the position of the water valve.

FIGURE 16-6 A vacuum exists between the inner and outer casing of the coolant heat storage tank. The outlet temperature sensor and the drain plug are located in the manifold at the bottom of the tank.

FIGURE 16-8 The storage tank and pump as seen from under the vehicle. This pump is energized when coolant must be moved through the tank but the ICE is shut off.

212 CHAPTER 16

PTC HEATERS

OPERATION Some vehicles are using the electrical system to boost the heat to the passenger compartment when the ICE coolant temperature is low. One approach is to use **PTC heaters** built into the heater core itself. **Positive temperature coefficient (PTC)** refers to the tendency of a conductor to increase its electrical resistance as its temperature increases. PTC heaters convert electrical energy into heat, and this is used to boost heat to the passenger compartment.

PTC heaters can also be located in the air ducts in the form of a honeycomb-shaped grid. Air that is leaving the plenum chamber passes through these heaters before it enters the passenger compartment. ● **SEE FIGURE 16-9**.

The Toyota Prius uses PTC heaters located in the heater core, as well as the footwell air ducts. The A/C electronic control unit turns on the PTC heaters when the coolant temperature is low and MAX HOT is requested. PTC heaters are sometimes referred to as "glow plugs" in service information. ● **SEE FIGURE 16-10**.

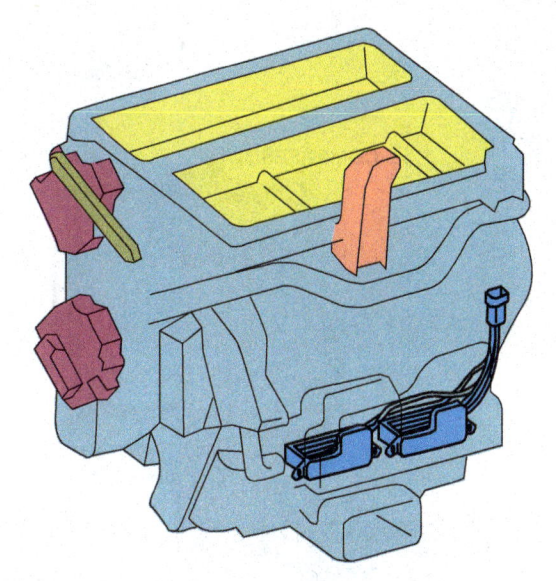

FIGURE 16-10 Two PTC heaters are located in the footwell air ducts in the Toyota Prius. These are energized when the coolant temperature is low and MAX HOT is requested in the FOOT or FOOT/DEF modes.

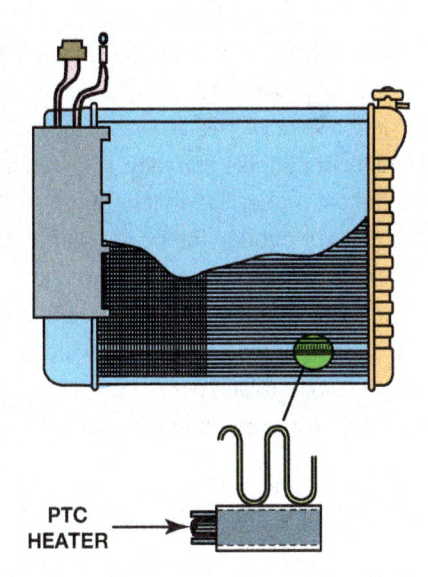

FIGURE 16-9 PTC heaters can be located on the heater core itself to help boost heat to the passenger compartment when coolant temperature is low.

HEV CABIN COOLING

BASIC OPERATION The fundamental purpose of any air-conditioning system is to absorb heat in one location and then release (dissipate) that heat in another location. Heat energy must be absorbed by a refrigerant (such as R-134a or R-1234yf) in order for it to change from a liquid to a gas. This is achieved by using an evaporator to absorb heat from inside the passenger compartment. The heat causes the refrigerant to change state form a liquid to a gas. The gaseous refrigerant is then compressed and sent to the condenser, located ahead of the radiator, where the absorbed heat is released to the outside air.

Changing the refrigerant from a gas to a liquid requires that it be compressed by the compressor to concentrate the heat and cooled by the condenser to remove the excess heat energy. The liquid refrigerant is then directed through a restriction (thermostatic expansion valve or orifice tube) in the line, where a pressure drop takes place. Moving from a high-pressure area to a low-pressure area allows the refrigerant to expand in the evaporator and absorb heat energy as it

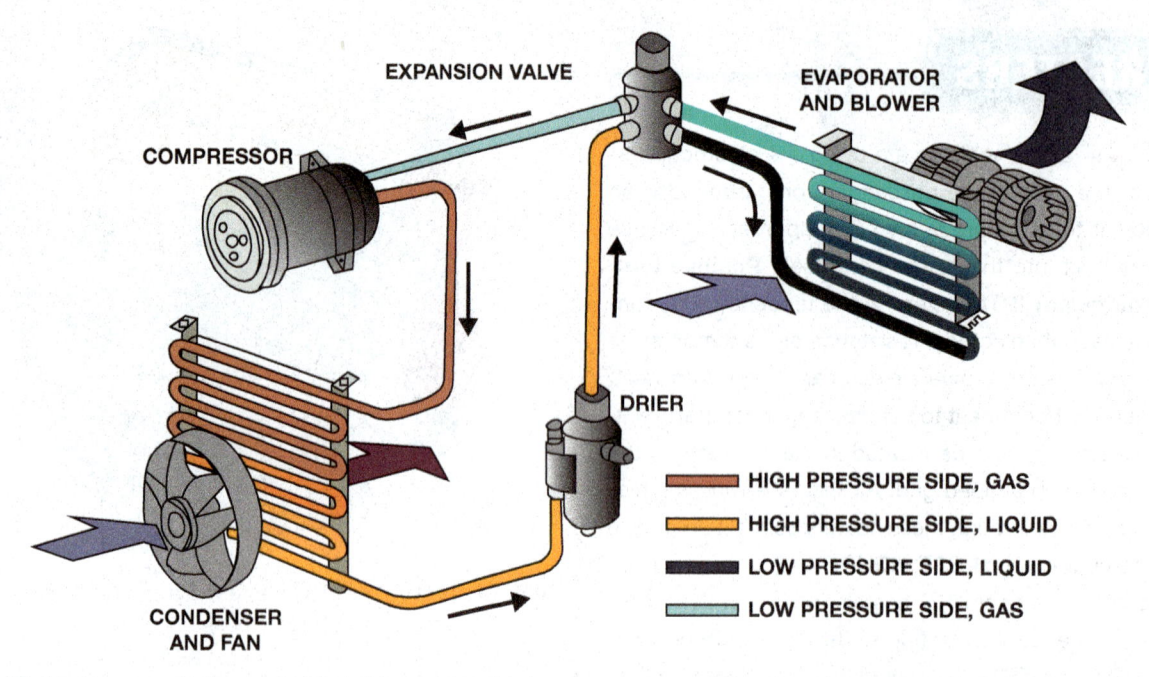

FIGURE 16-11 Newer vehicles and all hybrid electric vehicles use an expansion valve-type system because it requires less refrigerant.

changes into a gas. The cycle then starts over again as the refrigerant moves out of the evaporator and into the compressor inlet. ● **SEE FIGURE 16-11.**

Control of this type of air-conditioning system is accomplished through engagement of the compressor drive, as well as the airflow across the evaporator and condenser. The compressor is most often belt-driven by the ICE accessory drive. The belt drive often uses an electrically operated clutch, which allows the compressor pulley to disconnect from the compressor and stop refrigerant flow in the system while the ICE continues to run.

AIRFLOW Airflow into the passenger compartment is controlled by a blower motor, which sends the air through the evaporator and then into a series of passages and doors. In most situations, fresh air is brought in from outside the vehicle and then is heated or cooled before being sent to the appropriate vents. It is also possible to bring the air in from the passenger compartment itself, when the system is placed in the recirculation mode. The fresh air coming into the vehicle is sent through a **cabin filter**. A cabin filter is used for two purposes:

1. to remove particulate matter
2. prevent dirt and debris from clogging the evaporator.

Note that all the incoming air must pass through the A/C evaporator core after leaving the blower motor to remove moisture/water from the entering air and move it into the passenger area. ● **SEE FIGURE 16-12.**

DEFROST In defrost mode, the A/C compressor is activated and the evaporator core is cooled to the point where any humidity in the air will condense on the evaporator and then be drained outside the vehicle. This allows for rapid clearing of the windshield and a comfortable humidity level inside the vehicle.

While in defrost mode, the air leaving the A/C evaporator core can then be sent through the heater core to raise its temperature. This warm air is now sent to the defrost outlets and is passed over the driver and passenger side of the vehicle's windshield. The temperature of the air is controlled by the position of the air temp valve (blend door), as it either directs varying amounts of air over the heater core or bypasses it completely.

A/C MODE When the system is placed in the *A/C mode*, the A/C compressor is engaged and the blower motor circulates air over the evaporator. The cool, dehumidified air is then sent to the air temp valve, where it can bypass the heater core completely if maximum cooling effect is required. However, if warmer air is desirable, its temperature can be increased by changing the position of the air temperature/blend door valve so that some of the air passes through the heater core on its way to the distribution ducts. The final air temperature is achieved by blending the heated air from the heater core with the unheated air.

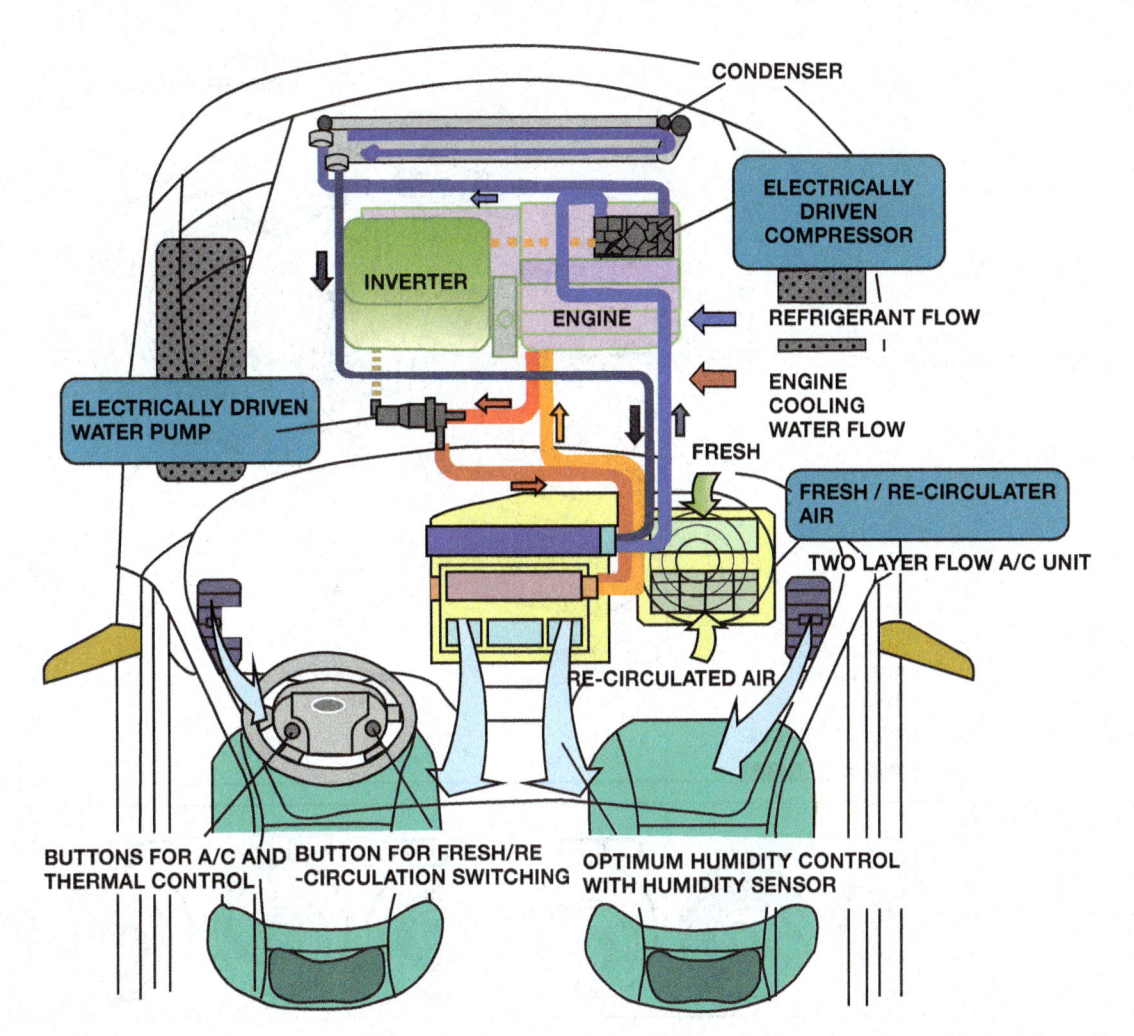

FIGURE 16-12 Typical airflow though an HVAC system. Outside air is drawn for the outside or from the cabin and flows through a cabin filter before flowing to the evaporator and heater core.

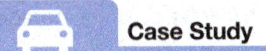

> **Case Study**
>
> **The Case of the Intermittent Blower Motor**
>
> The owner of a Ford Explorer hybrid electric vehicle complained that the blower motor would work for a while when the air conditioning was on but then stop. The blower motor would start working again at times. The service technician was able to duplicate the fault. A diagnostic trouble code B10b9 was retrieved (blower control circuit short to ground or open). During an inspection of the blower motor circuit components, the blower relay was hot to the touch. Using a clamp-on ammeter, the technician measured 30 amperes of current being drawn by the blower motor which exceeded the maximum specifications of 20 amperes. The blower motor and the relay were both replaced and the circuit current draw tested again. This time the blower motor drew 14 amperes and the operated normally.
>
> ...continued
>
> ...continued
> **Summary:**
> - **Complaint**—Customer stated that the blower would work intermittently.
> - **Cause**—The blower motor was found to be drawing an excessive amount of current causing the relay to open the circuit.
> - **Correction**—The blower motor and the relay were both replaced which restored proper blower motor operation.

HEV A/C COMPONENTS

COMPRESSORS There are many different compressor designs, with most utilizing either a rotary vane or a piston and cylinder arrangement. However, the most commonly used compressor design in hybrid electric vehicles is the scroll compressor. ● **SEE FIGURE 16-13**.

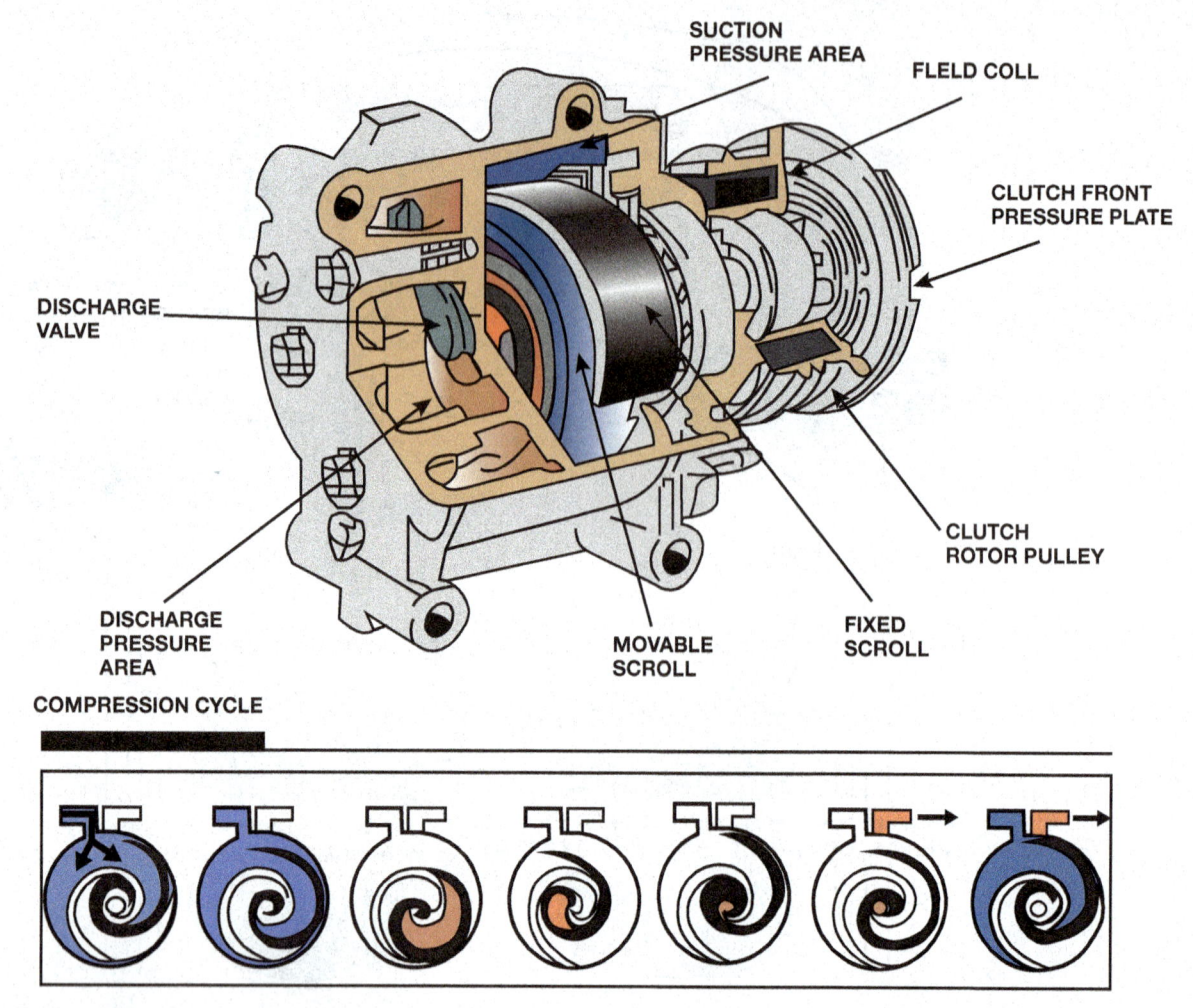

FIGURE 16–13 Basic components of a scroll compressor. Note the "pockets" of refrigerant that occupy the spaces labeled with arrows.

The **scroll compressor** is a highly efficient and durable design, with very good noise, vibration, and harshness (NVH) characteristics. This is because it is a balanced unit that uses an orbiting motion rather than sliding to compress the gases. It also has very low power consumption relative to other compressor designs, making it especially attractive for hybrid applications.

A scroll compressor has two primary components:

1. stationary scroll
2. movable scroll

In a scroll compressor the movable scroll *does not rotate* but instead it *orbits* inside the stationary scroll.

A low-pressure area is created at the inlet (outer) port of the scroll mechanism, and refrigerant enters this area and moves in a spiral pattern toward the delivery port in the center. There are several "pockets" of refrigerant being compressed at any one time as the movable scroll orbits inside the stationary scroll.

The compressor is on the dividing line between the high- and low-pressure sections of the air-conditioning system. Low-pressure gas enters the suction (inlet) port of the compressor, and high-pressure gas leaves the discharge (outlet) port. The temperature of the refrigerant rises as it is compressed and it is sent on for cooling in the condenser.

> **? FREQUENTLY ASKED QUESTION**
>
> **Why Are Electrically Driven A/C Compressors Mounted to the Engine?**
>
> If an A/C compressor is electrically driven, it seems as if it could be mounted anywhere there is room in the vehicle. The main reason why the compressor is mounted on the engine is because the engine acts as a large damper which helps reduce noise, vibration, and harshness (NVH) from being created and transmitted to the passenger compartment.

COMPRESSOR DRIVES There are two types of compressor drives used in hybrid electric vehicles:

1. **Belt-driven.** This type is used in many micro-hybrid electric vehicles and uses a standard A/C system. Another type or engine-driven compressors uses a portion that is ICE powered and the smaller section of a compressor to provide cooling when at idle-stop is driven by high voltage from the hybrid battery pack. The electric motor can be "piggybacked" with the conventional belt drive. ● **SEE FIGURE 16-14**.

2. **Electrically powered.** An electrically powered A/C compressor is used in all electric vehicle and many hybrid electric vehicles. There are two basic configurations of electric A/C compressors:

   - **Two High-Voltage Wires**—The two wires carry high-voltage DC current and the compressor itself includes an inverter to change the DC to AC for the operation of the AC motor used to drive the compressor.

   - **Three High-Voltage Wires**—The three wires carry high-voltage AC from an external inverter to power the motor used to power the A/C compressor.

   ● **SEE FIGURE 16-15 AND CHART 16-1.**

COMPRESSOR OIL Hybrid vehicle A/C systems that use electric-driven compressors must use POE (polyol ester) oil, unlike all other compressors. PAG (polyalkylene glycol) oil, which is used in non-hybrid vehicles, is slightly conductive and can cause deterioration of the insulation on the windings of the compressor motor. This can cause the compressor to become electrically conductive, which can result in electrical leakage. This leakage can potentially be hazardous during future service. ● **SEE FIGURE 16-16**.

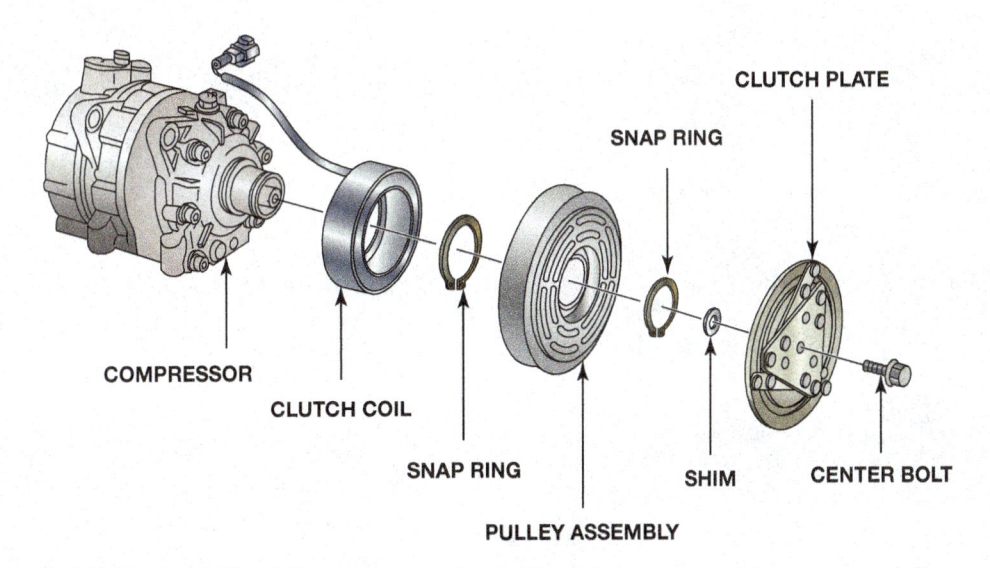

FIGURE 16-14 The A/C compressor clutch allows the compressor to engage and disengage as necessary while the ICE continues to run.

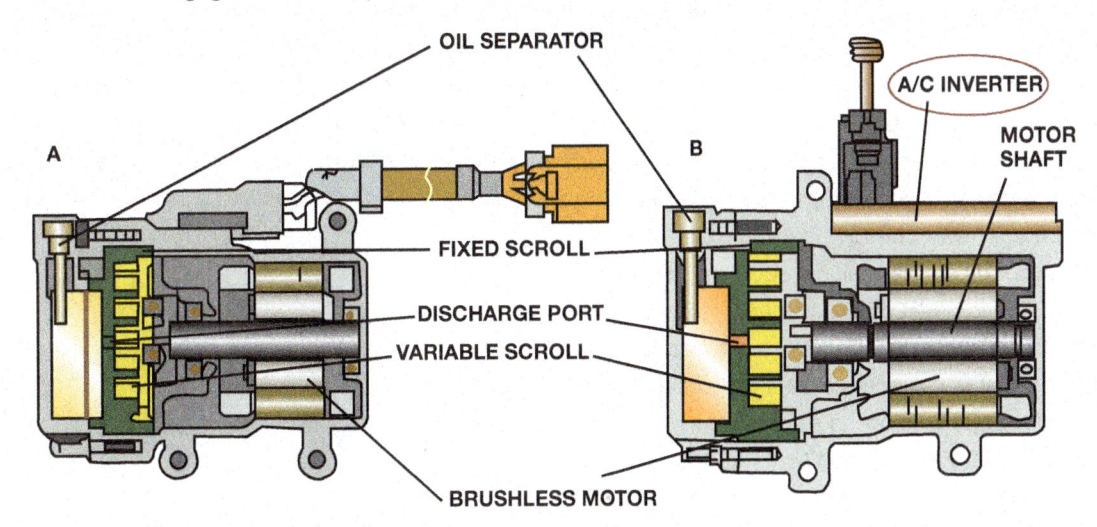

FIGURE 16-15 Two basic designs of compressors are used in HEV vehicles and both include an oil separator that is used to trap and hold refrigerant oil in the compressor. (a) This compressor uses a three-phase input from the vehicle inverter and operates on AC. (b) This compressor has two high-voltage wires from the battery pack and then uses a built-in inverter to convert DC to AC.

BELT-DRIVEN A/C COMPRESSOR	ELECTRICALLY POWERED A/C COMPRESSOR
Operation requires that the internal combustion engine (ICE) be running	No compressor clutch used or needed
Capable of removing more heat	Electrically powered—no drive belt needed
Optimal A/C performance similar to a non-hybrid vehicle	Uses a variable speed compressor
Does not operate during idle-stop	Operates during idle-stop

CHART 16-1 Performance comparison between a belt-driven A/C compressor and an electrically powered A/C compressor.

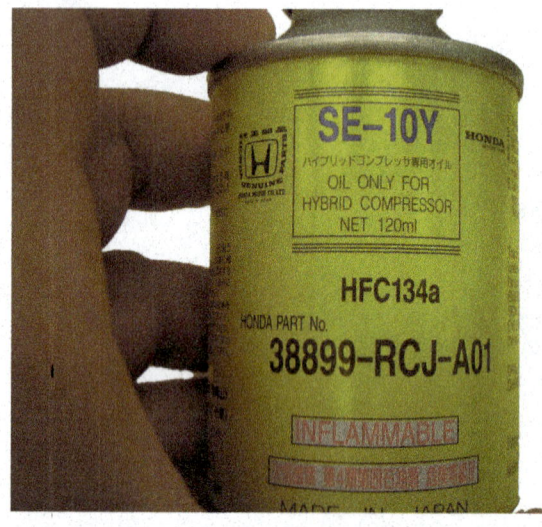

FIGURE 16-16 Specific A/C compressor oil designed for use in Honda hybrid vehicle air-conditioning systems.

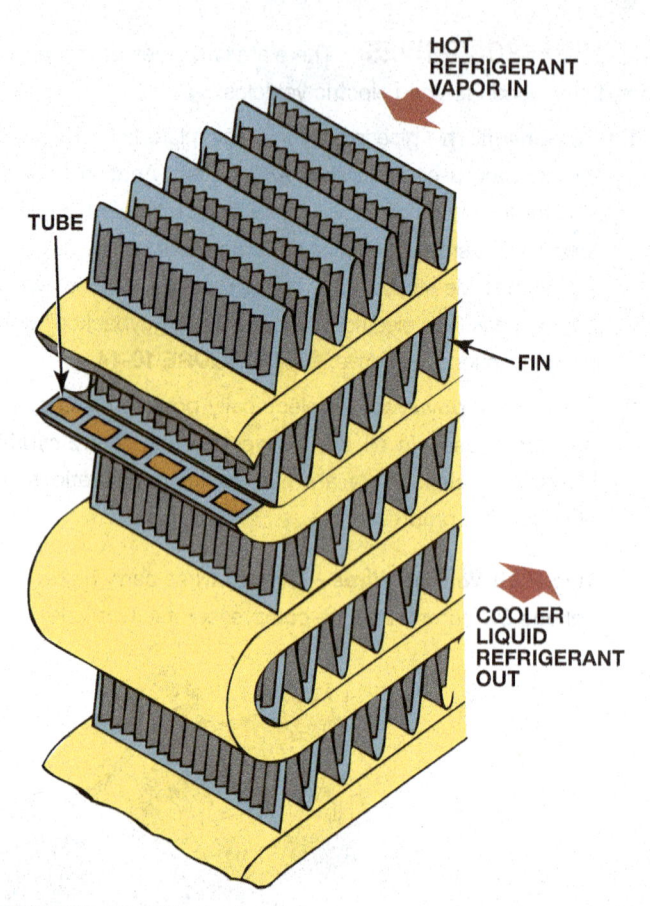

FIGURE 16-17 Condenser construction. Surface area is maximized with cooling fins and partitioned tubes to increase cooling capacity.

CONDENSERS

The condenser is part of the high-pressure section of the air-conditioning system and is another type of heat exchanger. It receives high-temperature, high-pressure refrigerant gas from the compressor and dissipates the heat from the refrigerant to the outside air. The refrigerant leaves the outlet of the condenser as a warm, high-pressure liquid. The condenser can be built with one long cooling tube following a serpentine path but most use multiple cooling tubes forming parallel paths. Surface area of the condenser is increased by the addition of thin fin material between the tubes, as well as partitioning in the tubes themselves. This ensures that sufficient air is in contact with the cooling surfaces and maximum heat is dissipated. ● **SEE FIGURE 16-17**.

The condenser is typically installed ahead of the vehicle's radiator and has airflow sent through it either through vehicle movement or by the cooling fan.

SUBCOOLING CONDENSERS Condenser subcooling is used on most recent condensers so that there is a liquid seal at the condenser's bottom so the liquid line or receiver will not be fed with vapors. On a subcooling condenser, the receiver/drier is integrated into one of the header tanks. The header tank is ported into the drier at several points from top to bottom. By integrating the receiver/drier, liquid/vapor separation within the condenser is improved, thus improving heat exchange efficiency. Most designs include an integrated drier. Some subcooling systems connect back to one or two tube rows at the bottom of the condenser.

NOTE: Many applications have the receiver drier attached to the condenser but not all of these are subcooling designs.

EXPANSION DEVICES

There are two primary types of expansion devices used in automotive air-conditioning systems:

1. Thermostatic expansion valve (TXV)
2. Orifice tube (OT)

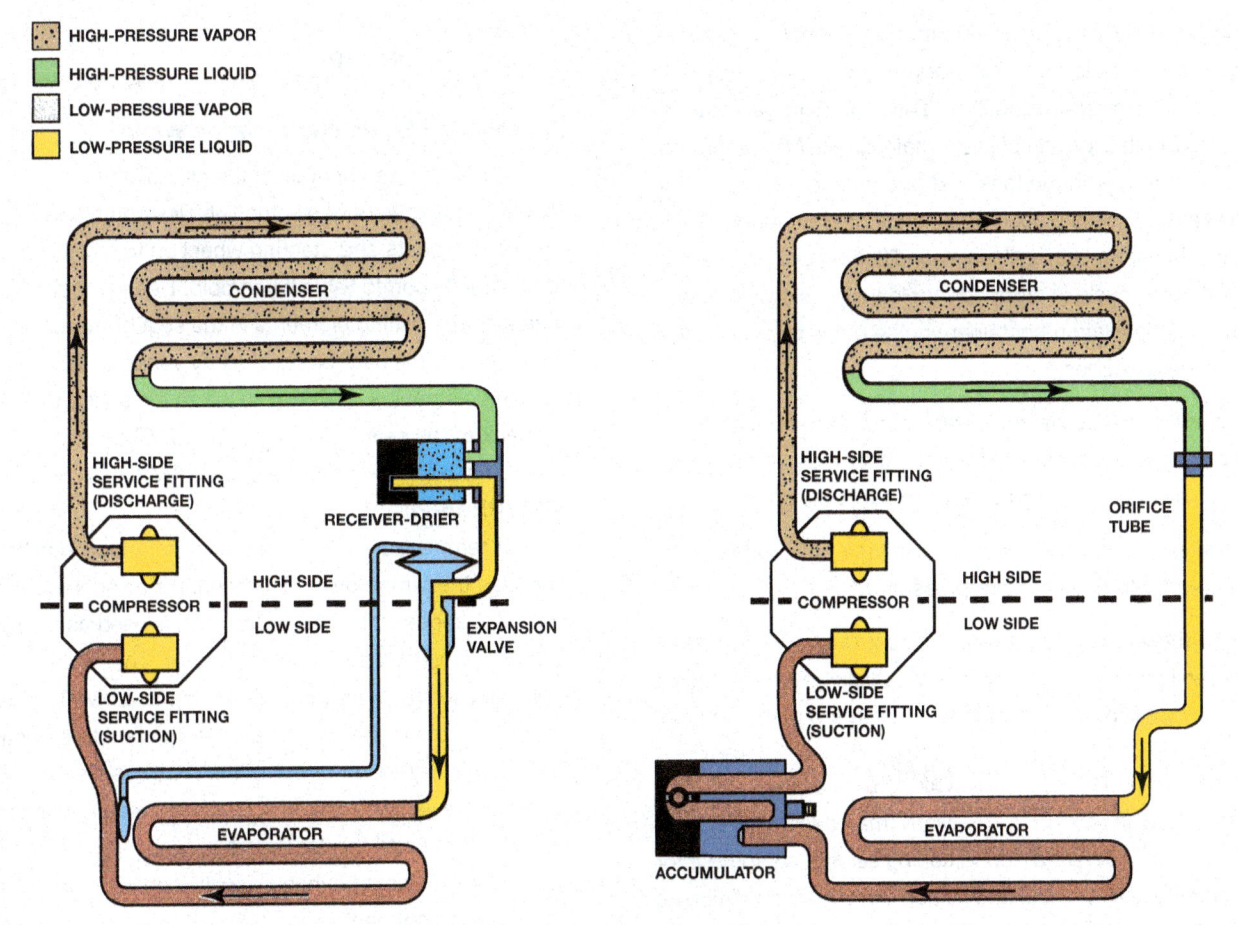

FIGURE 16-18 Basic components and refrigerant flow in an expansion-valve system and an orifice-tube system.

The type of expansion device used determines the configuration of the system, as there are differences between a system that uses a TXV and one that uses an orifice tube. ● SEE FIGURE 16-18.

- An expansion valve (TXV) system uses a receiver-drier in the high-pressure side.
- An orifice tube system has an accumulator on the low-pressure side between the evaporator and the compressor suction port.

EVAPORATORS The evaporator is located after the expansion device on the low-pressure side of the A/C refrigerant system. Its primary responsibility is to remove heat from the passenger compartment, but it is also tasked with reducing humidity as incoming air passes over its cool surfaces. Moisture in the air condenses on the evaporator surface, then exits the passenger compartment through a drain located beneath the evaporator housing. An added benefit is that pollen and other particulate matter will collect on the moist surface and be washed out through the evaporator drain with the water. Air entering the vehicle is thus conditioned for maximum passenger comfort. An evaporator is a heat exchanger, and therefore is constructed similar to a condenser. ● SEE FIGURE 16-19.

THERMAL STORAGE DURING IDLE STOP HEV and PHEV vehicles have engine stop-start systems but during A/C operation the air from the ducts start to warm in 5 to 15 seconds.

FIGURE 16-19 A typical thermal expansion valve (TXV) system used in most hybrid electric vehicles.

EV AND HEV HVAC SYSTEM

Reducing cooling on a warm summer day is not acceptable. One way that vehicle manufacturers use to prevent this is to use a thermal storage evaporator. **Thermal storage material (TSM)**, also called *phase change material (PCM)*, evaporator has a wax chamber in the tank end or between the tubes. The cold insulation case is placed between refrigerant tubes, which extracts cold energy during the air-conditioning cycle. When the air-conditioning cycle is stopped, cooled air is slowly released from the cold insulation container via the outer fins connected to the refrigerant tubes.

- When the A/C stops, refrigerant vapor rises through the tubing and condenses against the chamber, starting the thermosiphon loop and extending the cooling time.
- If the evaporator temperature rises too much, the engine will restart to drive the compressor.

With these functions, storing cold energy can be completed even in a relatively short time of vehicle travel and cooled air can be supplied to the cabin for an extended period of time.

UNIQUE HYBRID AND ELECTRIC VEHICLE AIR-CONDITIONING SERVICE Many manufacturers specify the separate or different air-conditioning service equipment for hybrid and electric vehicles that use an electric air-conditioning compressor. When the refrigerant is recovered from the system, typically small amounts of refrigerant oil are also removed from the system. To avoid cross contamination between PAG and POE oil, which might lead to an electric motor winding failure or a loss of isolation, separate air-conditioning recovery stations are specified.

When using dye to leak check the refrigerant system on a hybrid or electric vehicle, use a dye that is compatible with POE refrigerant oil and will not lead to an electric motor winding failure or loss of isolation.

EV HEATING

EMPHASIS IS ON RANGE Vehicles without an ICE do not have waste heat from coolant so they must create heat. Potential vehicle buyers of an electric vehicle (EV) want as much range as possible even though they can recharge every night at home. Range is often less than the manufacturer indicates. In order to counteract this disadvantage, manufacturers make efficient use of the available energy. Depending on ambient temperature, the heating, ventilation, and air-conditioning (HVAC) system can be the largest auxiliary load. The range of an EV is significantly reduced when the HVAC system is activated during extreme temperature conditions.

TECH TIP

Use Heated Seats and Steering Wheel

Instead of trying to heat all of the air inside the cabin, many drivers of electric vehicles command the heated seats and steering wheel on to make the cold vehicle comfortable when cold. Heated seats use electric heating elements in the seat bottom, as well as in the seat back, in many vehicles. The heating element is designed to warm the seat and/or back of the seat to about 100°F (38°C) or close to normal body temperature (98.6°F [37°C]). ● **SEE FIGURE 16-20**.

A temperature sensor in the seat cushion is used to regulate the temperature. The sensor is a variable resistor, which changes with temperature and is used as an input signal to a heated seat control module. The heated seat module uses the seat temperature input, as well as the input from the high–low (or variable) temperature control, to turn the current on or off to the heating element in the seat. Some vehicles are equipped with heated seats in both the front and the rear seats.

Heated steering wheels usually consist of the following components.

- Steering wheel with a built-in heater in the rim
- Heated steering wheel control switch
- Heated steering wheel control module

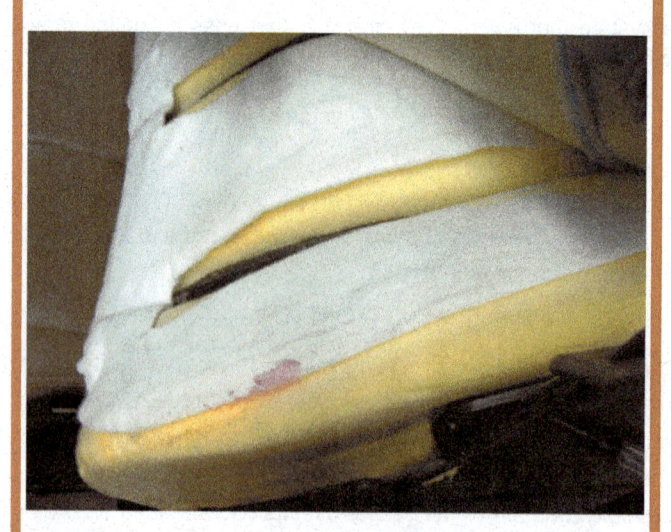

FIGURE 16-20 The heating element of a heated seat is a replaceable part, but service requires that the upholstery be removed. The yellow part is the seat foam material and the entire white cover is the replaceable heating element. This is then covered by the seat material.

...continued

...continued

When the steering wheel heater control switch is turned on, a signal is sent to the control module and electrical current flows through the heating element in the rim of the steering wheel. ● SEE FIGURE 16-21.

The system remains on until the ignition switch is turned off or the driver turns off the control switch. The temperature of the steering wheel is usually calibrated to stay at about 90°F (32°C), and it requires 3 to 4 minutes to reach that temperature, depending on the outside temperature. Many heated steering wheels only heat a part and often not all the steering wheel.

FIGURE 16-21 The heated steering wheel is controlled by a switch on the steering wheel in this vehicle.

ELECTRICAL RESISTANCE HEATING Some EVs use resistance heating for cabin temperature control. The heating effect of an electric current depends on three factors:

1. The resistance, R, of the conductor. A higher resistance produces more heat.
2. The higher the current flow, the greater amount of heat is generated. Heating a metal conductor makes it more difficult for electricity to flow through it. As electrons move through a metal conductor, some collide with atoms, other electrons or impurities. These collisions cause resistance and generate heat.

A good element will have a resistance between 5 and 25 ohms. To generate a significant amount of heat requires a significant amount of electricity. For example, a Tesla Model 3 draws about 4,800 W (20 A at 240 V) to heat the cabin using the resistance heating. ● SEE FIGURE 16-22.

PTC HEATERS One approach is to use PTC heaters built into the heater core itself. PTC refers to the tendency of a conductor to increase its electrical resistance as its temperature increases. PTC heaters convert electrical energy into heat, and this is used to boost heat to the passenger compartment.

PTC heaters are located in the air ducts in the form of a honeycomb-shaped grid. Air that is leaving the plenum chamber passes through these heaters before it enters the passenger compartment.

- **PTC Fluid Heaters.** These are self-regulating up to 460°F (240°C) and can be an immersion heater put into a fluid reservoir, or self-contained flow-through heater.

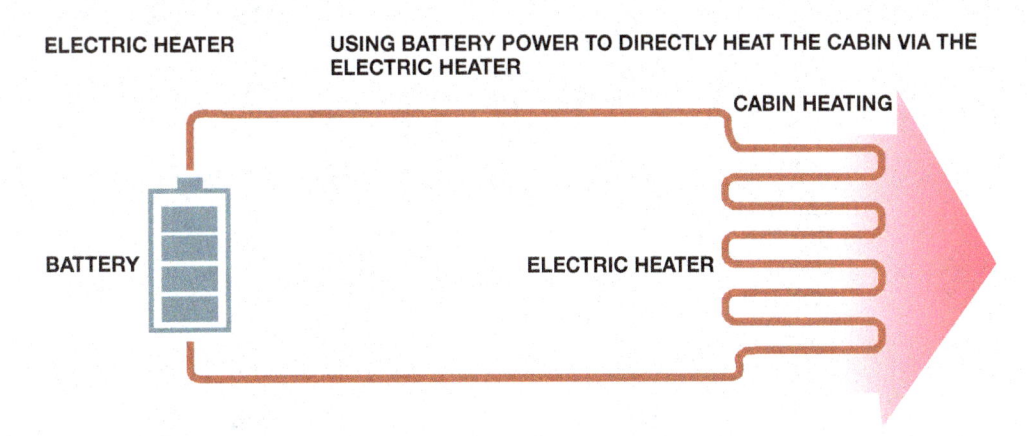

FIGURE 16-22 Electrical resistance heating is used in many electric vehicles including many Tesla models and the Mustang Mach E SUV.

> **FREQUENTLY ASKED QUESTION**
>
> **Why Doesn't the Heater Actually Turn Off?**
>
> The owners of Chevrolet Bolts often state that if they are running the heater and then turn it off, the fan continues to run so they think the heater doesn't actually turn off. The cause is due to the resistance heating; that is, heating the coolant and the heat dissipation of coolant retains heat longer than a metal resistor heater. It turns off, but it will just blow warm for a bit until the radiator cools off.

In this type of system, the coolant is heated electrically and then uses an electric water (coolant) pump to circulate the coolant though a heater core similar to the what is done when the coolant is heated by the ICE in a hybrid or conventional gasoline or diesel-powered vehicle.

- **PTC Air Heaters.** Self-regulating up to 460°F (240°C), primarily used for cabin heating, but can be used for heating the battery pack.

HEAT PUMP

PURPOSE AND FUNCTION Many automakers use a heat pump to maximize the range of an electric vehicle by scavenging waste heat to warm the cabin. A heat pump is more efficient than PTC/electric resistance heating. The original heat pump technology was introduced in 2014 on the first-generation Kia Soul EV. The 2013 Nissan Leaf was the first mass-produced vehicle in the world to offer a heat pump-based cabin heater which helped extend driving range during the winter months. Vehicles that use a heat pump include but not limited to the following:

- BMW i3 EV
- Jaguar I-Pace
- Audi E-tron
- Toyota Prius Prime
- Volkswagen e-Golf.
- Kia Niro EV does.
- Tesla Model Y

NOTE: Most Tesla models don't use a heat pump as part of the climate control system but do use waste heat from the motor and power electronics to help warm the battery.

Heat pumps can capture energy by recycling waste heat not only from power electrics (PE) modules, such as drive motors, on-board chargers, and inverters, but also from the battery pack. ● **SEE FIGURE 16-23.**

PARTS AND OPERATION A heat pump system is similar to an air-conditioning system where the operation can be reversed to provide both cabin heating and cabin cooling. A heat pump uses one refrigerant circuit that is used for both cooling and heating. ● **SEE FIGURE 16-24.**

- **Heating.** A heat pump system heats the cabin using the temperature difference between a refrigerant and the outside air making it possible to heat the vehicle cabin with less power than heating the air. When the heater is in use, the external condenser absorbs heat from the atmosphere and the compressor is used to compress it into a high-temperature gas. The cabin is heated as the hot air flows into the cabin out of the heating ducts. Heat

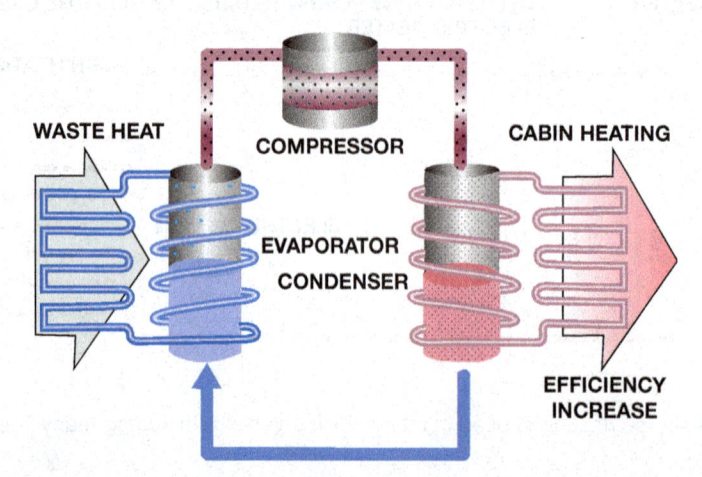

FIGURE 16-23 A heat pump is basically a reversible air-conditioning system that can provide both cabin heating and cabin cooling.

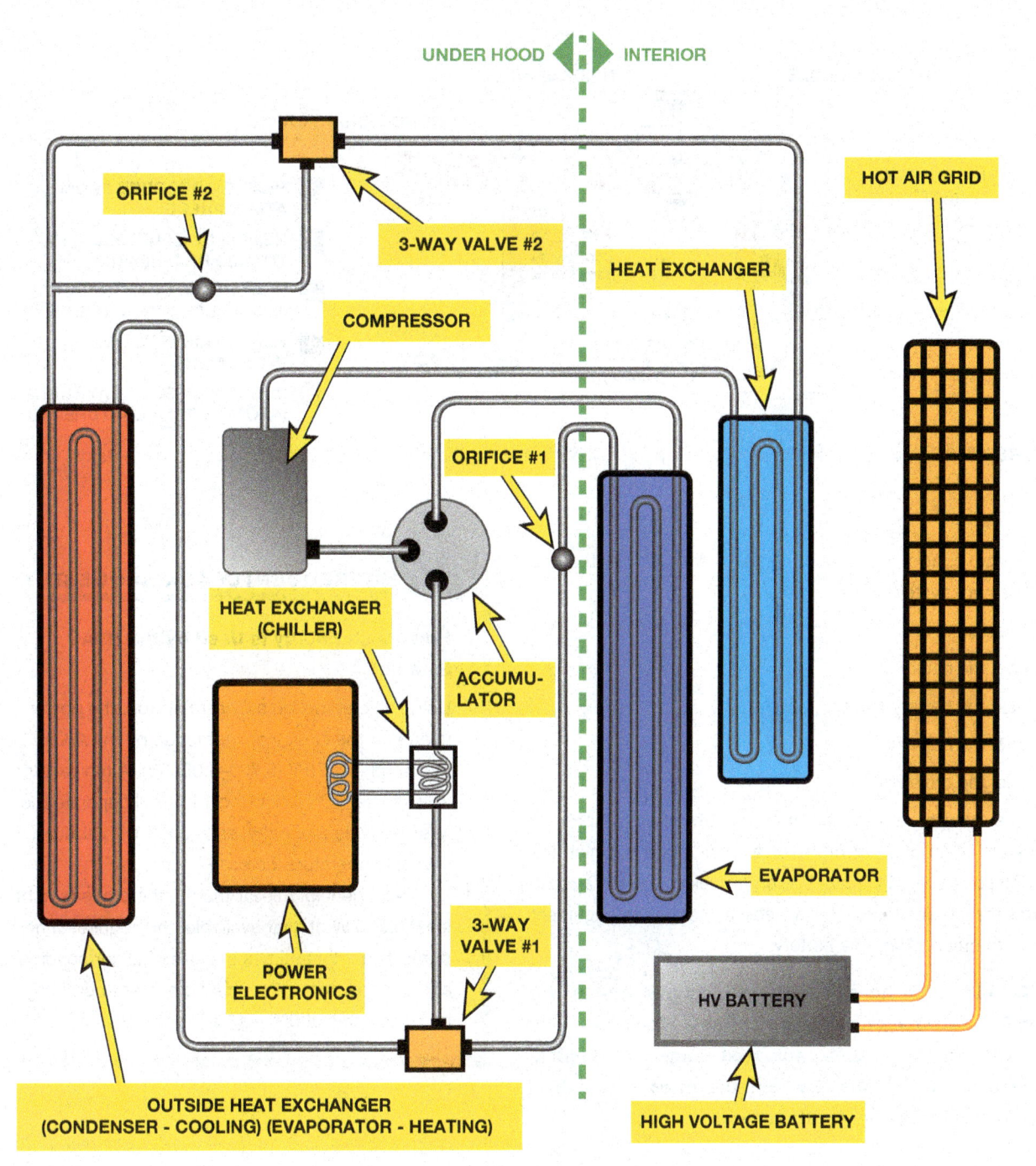

FIGURE 16-24 A heat pump is basically a reversible air-conditioning system that can provide both cabin heating and cabin cooling. It is used to the waste heat from the electronic components to heat the cabin.

pumps do not create heat, but instead they move heat. Heat can be moved using less electricity than it takes to heat the air in the cabin using resistive elements.

- **Cooling.** In the summer, heat is absorbed from inside the cabin and released outside by the external condenser, similar to that conventional air-conditioning works.
  - **SEE FIGURE 16-25**.

LIQUID-COOLED CONDENSER (LCC) Most vehicles use an air-to-refrigerant condenser ahead of the radiator. The job of the condenser is to cool refrigerant so that it can remove heat from the cabin. **Liquid-cooled condensers (LCC)** exchange heat by removing heat from one fluid and transferring it to another fluid. A liquid-cooled condenser is a heat exchanger that removes heat from refrigerant vapor and transfers it to the liquid running through it. In the case of the Tesla Model Y, it uses an air-to-glycol-based-coolant low-temperature radiator. That radiator sends cold coolant to the condenser which removes heat from the gaseous refrigerant to cause it to condense into a liquid. The control

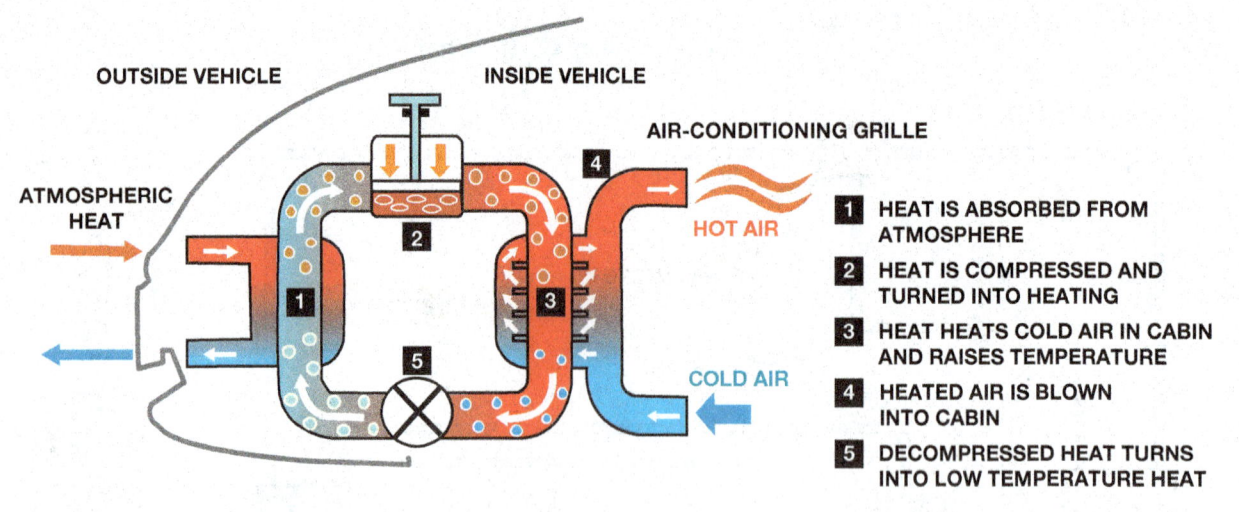

FIGURE 16-25 A typical electric vehicle heat pump system showing the components inside the cabin and outside, under the hood.

1. HEAT IS ABSORBED FROM ATMOSPHERE
2. HEAT IS COMPRESSED AND TURNED INTO HEATING
3. HEAT HEATS COLD AIR IN CABIN AND RAISES TEMPERATURE
4. HEATED AIR IS BLOWN INTO CABIN
5. DECOMPRESSED HEAT TURNS INTO LOW TEMPERATURE HEAT

electronics control the components of the vehicle thermal management system to:

1. heat the cabin
2. cool the cabin
3. heat the battery system
4. cool the battery system
5. cool the drivetrain

The control electronics may control the compressor to operate in an efficient mode or a lossy mode in which the compressor generates heat. The control electronics may also control the components of the vehicle thermal management system to precondition the battery.

NOTE: Although heat pumps are advantageous for extending cold-weather range, they don't actually increase the stated EPA-estimated range of a vehicle because the EPA does not test the effects of cabin-heating during its cold weather test.

> **? FREQUENTLY ASKED QUESTION**
>
> **How Much Energy Is Used by the HVAC System?**
>
> Using a scan tool on a Chevrolet Bolt, the power usage for the energy consumption by the A/C is 22 A maximum at 370 V (6,600–8,000 W). A typical automotive heat pump drawing 1 kW will generate the heat equivalent of between 2–3 kW with about a 60°F (16°C) temperature increase (delta).
>
> As a general rule-of-thumb, there needs to be at least 3,500 W of heat available, this requires a heat pump about three times the size of an air conditioner, and still may require a resistive heater to properly heat the cabin at 0°F (–18°C).

FREQUENTLY ASKED QUESTION

What Is "Dog Mode"?

Dog mode (also called *pet mode*) is a climate control feature in Tesla and some other electric vehicles that leaves the air conditioning or heater on when owners leave their pets in their vehicle. It is accessed through the climate-control settings by selecting "Dog" under the "Keep Climate On" settings. Then, a message is displayed that reads: "My owner will be back soon. Don't worry! The heater or A/C is on and it's 72 degrees." If the owner is gone for long periods of time and the battery goes below 20%, a push notification goes to the owner's phone to prompt them to get back to their pet. ● SEE FIGURE 16-26.

NOTE: Tesla has a feature referred to as "camp mode" where the climate control system can be kept on with the doors locked. Basically, this mode would be used if sleeping in the vehicle.

FIGURE 16-26 A message appears on the large center displace when the vehicle is placed in dog mode to notify anyone near that the pets are safe being locked in the vehicle.

SUMMARY

1. The heater core is located in the passenger compartment, inside the plenum chamber (HVAC air distribution box) for the vehicle's heater and air-conditioning components.
2. The amount of heat generated by the heating system is dependent on the temperature of the coolant that is circulated through the heater core.
3. An auxiliary water pump is a DC motor–operated water pump that is used to circulate coolant to the heater core.
4. The fundamental purpose of any air-conditioning system is to absorb heat in one location and then reject (dissipate) that heat in another location.
5. The fresh air coming into the vehicle is sent through a cabin filter.
6. There are two types of compressor drives used in hybrid electric vehicles—belt-driven and electrically driven.
7. PTC heaters convert electrical energy into heat, and this is used to boost heat to the passenger compartment.
8. A heat pump is more efficient than PTC/electric resistance heating.
9. A liquid-cooled condenser is a heat exchanger that removes heat from refrigerant vapor and transfers it to the liquid running through it.

REVIEW QUESTIONS

1. What is the purpose and function of the auxiliary water (coolant) pump?
2. How can it be determined if the inverter is located inside or outside an A/C compressor?
3. What type of refrigerant oil is used in an electrically powered A/C compressor?
4. What is the difference in the parts between a TXV and an orifice tube A/C system?
5. What are the advantages of a heat pump HVAC system?

CHAPTER QUIZ

1. A typical HEV uses waste heat from the _____ to heat the cabin.
   a. motor/generator
   b. ICE
   c. brakes
   d. exhaust

2. An electric water pump uses a _____ to power the impeller and is used on most hybrid electric vehicles and some internal combustion engines.
   a. stepper motor
   b. AC synchronize motor
   c. DC motor
   d. Any of the above

3. The fresh air coming into the vehicle is sent through a _____.
   a. cabin filter
   b. squirrel cage blower
   c. evaporator
   d. condenser

4. The type of A/C compressor most likely to be used is a _____ design.
   a. piston
   b. scroll
   c. variable displacement
   d. Both a and c

5. An electrically operated A/C compressor has two orange cables. This means the compressor _____.
   a. is powered by the 12-volt auxiliary battery
   b. has a built-in inverter
   c. is using an external inverter
   d. None of the above

6. _____ converts electrical energy into heat, and this is used to boost heat to the passenger compartment.
   a. Heater core
   b. Antifreeze/coolant
   c. PTC heater
   d. The 12-volt auxiliary battery

7. Many automakers use a _____ to maximize the range of an electric vehicle that can travel by scavenging waste heat to warm the cabin.
   a. heat pump
   b. scroll compressor
   c. variable compressor
   d. PTC

8. A _____ is a heat exchanger that removes heat from refrigerant vapor and transfers it to the liquid running through it.
   a. scroll compressor
   b. air-to-air heat exchanger
   c. liquid-cooled condenser
   d. Any of the above

9. The electric vehicle battery heating methods include _____.
   a. PTC fluid heaters
   b. PTC air heaters
   c. heater pads
   d. Any of the above

10. Dog mode, also called pet mode, is used to _____.
    a. heat the rear seats to keep dogs or pets warm
    b. cool the seats to keep dogs or pets cool
    c. keep the interior temperature comfortable for pets when they are left in a locked vehicle while the driver is gone
    d. All of the above

Chapter 17
EV AND HEV TRANSMISSIONS

LEARNING OBJECTIVES

After studying this chapter, the reader should be able to:

- Describe the function of a hybrid electric vehicle (HEV) transmission.
- Understand the relationship required between the ICE and electric motor(s).
- Explain the purpose of an auxiliary electric pump or hydraulic impulse storage generator.
- Describe the difference between a power-split system and an eCVT in a hybrid vehicle.
- Discuss the operation of a transmission in a fully electric vehicle.
- Explain the operation of a two-speed gearing in an electric vehicle

KEY TERMS

Electric auxiliary pump 230
Hydraulic impulse storage accumulator 231
Torque 230

TRANSMISSIONS AND TRANSAXLES

PURPOSE AND FUNCTION All vehicles, regardless of the power source, require the use of a transmission to achieve reasonable acceleration and efficiency. A transmission in a vehicle with an internal combustion engine (ICE) is designed to keep the torque and horsepower in the ideal range relative to the engine and road speed. The design of the transmission is different when it is coupled to a hybrid powertrain, or part of a fully electric powertrain as compared to a legacy ICE. The internal electric motors are responsible for much of the power. The transmission is responsible for providing the following:

- Torque applied to the drive wheel to accelerate the vehicle from a stop
- Power at higher speeds that allows the powertrain to operate efficiently

POWERTRAIN CONFIGURATION In rear-wheel-drive (RWD) applications, it is most common to use a transmission along with a driveshaft and differential at the rear axle to transmit torque to the drive wheels. The Lexus GS450h and LS600h are both examples of rear-wheel-drive hybrid electric vehicles. The Ford Mustang Mach-E standard configuration is an example of a rear-wheel-drive electric vehicle. In a front-wheel-drive (FWD) vehicle, a transaxle assembly is used with half-shafts to transmit torque to the drive wheels. A transaxle is the combination of a transmission, differential, and final drive gears built together as one assembly. A Toyota Prius and Hyundai Sonata hybrid are examples of FWD hybrid vehicles. The Chevrolet Bolt is an example of a FWD electric vehicle. ● **SEE FIGURE 17-1**.

In a four-wheel-drive (4WD) or all-wheel-drive (AWD) vehicle, a transfer case or rear electric motor is used to distribute power to all four wheels. The Toyota Highlander/Lexus RX450h uses a transaxle on the front of the vehicle and an electric motor to drive the rear wheels in the 4WD model. The 4WD version of the Ford Escape hybrid uses a separate power takeoff (PTO) from the transaxle to mechanically drive the rear axle.

Example Vehicle Transmission Configurations

Vehicle	FWD/RWD/AWD	Configuration
Toyota Prius 2001–2009	FWD	ECVT 2 Motors/1 Planetary
Chevrolet Volt 2011–2015	FWD	ECVT 2 Motors/1 Planetary/Clutches
Toyota Prius 2010–2015	FWD	ECVT 2 motors/2 Planetary
Toyota Prius 2016–2021	FWD/ AWD	ECVT 2 Motors/2 Planetary/One-way clutch
General Motors 2 Mode 2009	RWD/AWD	ECVT 2 Motors/ 3 Planetary/Clutches
Honda Accord Hybrid 2015	FWD	ECVT 2 Motors/ 2 Clutches
Nissan Leaf 2011	FWD	Electric Motor with gear reduction unit
Chevrolet Bolt 2017–2019	FWD	Electric Motor with gear reduction unit

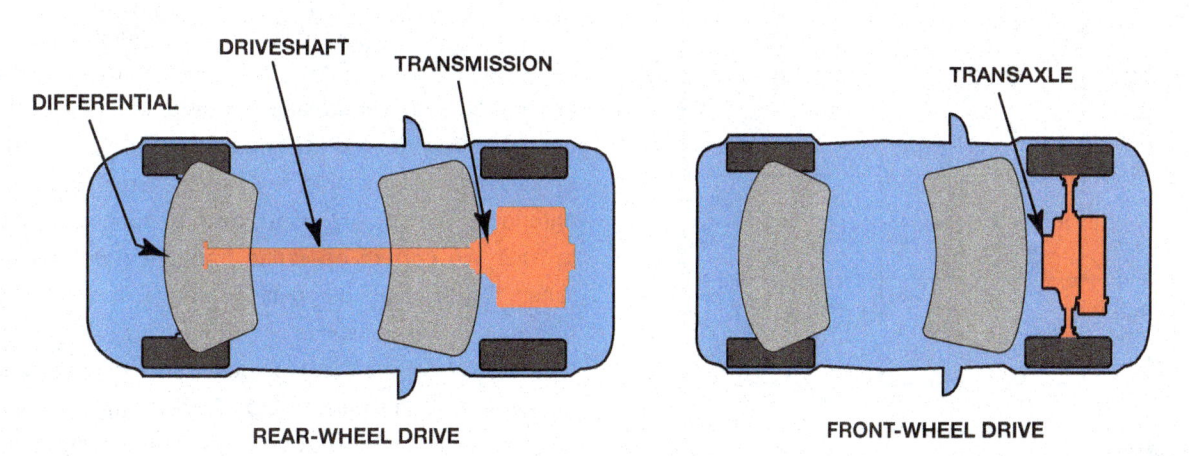

FIGURE 17-1 Rear-wheel-drive (RWD) vehicles use transmissions to send torque to the rear differential and final drive. Front-wheel-drive (FWD) vehicles use a transaxle, which incorporates the differential and final drive into the transaxle case.

PRINCIPLES INVOLVED

TORQUE DELIVERY To move a vehicle, torque must be applied to the drive wheels. **Torque** is *twisting force*.

Torque is applied to the drive wheels to make the vehicle accelerate. The vehicle transmission is responsible for increasing engine torque in the lower speed ranges when acceleration is required, and then reducing engine speed for the best fuel economy when the vehicle is cruising. ICE are very different from electric motors in that they only produce torque in a relatively narrow RPM range. ● SEE FIGURE 17-2.

An ICE is most efficient when it is operating near its torque peak. This is the RPM when the engine is breathing most efficiently, and is typically where the engine can deliver the best fuel economy. However, it is difficult to keep the engine in this range during all phases of vehicle operation. Automotive engineers overcome this difficulty in two ways.

1. By increasing the RPM range where the engine produces torque ("flattening" the torque curve).
2. By increasing the number of gear ratios in the transmission.

With more transmission ratios, it is easier to match the vehicle road speed with the most efficient engine RPM. Therefore, any torque increase is generated at the expense of speed. In other words, when torque is increased in a transmission, output speed is decreased. ● SEE FIGURE 17-3.

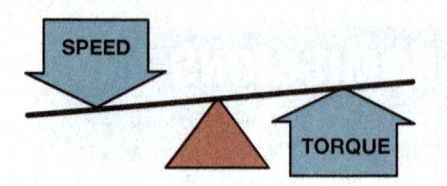

FIGURE 17-3 When output speed decreases in a transmission, output torque will increase.

MULTIPLE SPEED TRANSMISSIONS/TRANSAXLES

Years ago, it was common for vehicles with automatic transmissions to have only 2, 3, or 4 gear ratios. Currently, 5-, 6-, 7-, 8- and 10-speed automatic transmissions are becoming common. With more emphasis being placed on fuel economy and lower emissions, the continuously variable transmission (CVT) is becoming more popular as it provides infinite gear ratios and the best opportunity to maximize engine efficiency.

HEV TRANSMISSIONS

CLASSIFICATIONS HEV transmissions are different based on the level of the hybrid vehicle in which they are installed. A mild hybrid with stop-start system typically contains a transmission with a single electric motor. A full hybrid generally contains a transmission with two electric motors.

ELECTRIC AUXILIARY PUMP In order to adapt a conventional automatic transmission to a hybrid powertrain, an **electric auxiliary pump** is used to maintain fluid pressure in the transmission during ICE idle-stop. This pump is powered by a DC brushless (AC synchronous) motor, which requires a special controller to provide the correct operating frequency and pulse width. When the auxiliary pump is operating, it sends hydraulic pressure to the transmission regulator valve, and on to the manual valve where it is directed to the appropriate clutches. This prevents the transmission from shifting into "neutral" when the ICE is in idle-stop. Once the ICE restarts, the auxiliary pump is turned off and hydraulic pressure is again supplied by the mechanically driven transmission fluid pump.
● SEE FIGURE 17-4.

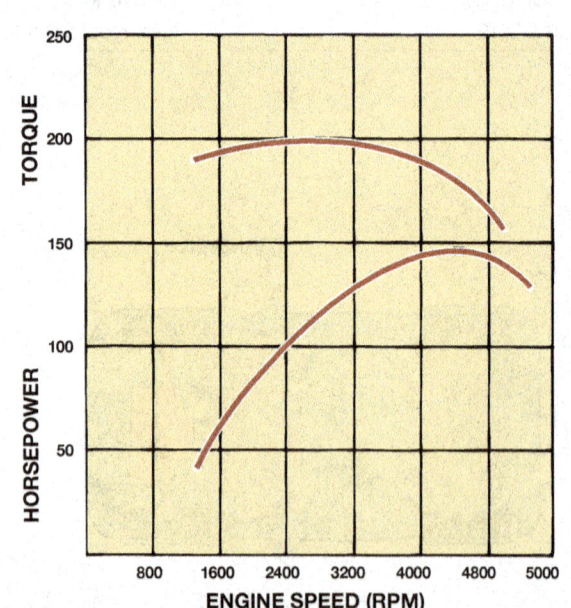

FIGURE 17-2 Graph showing engine torque vs horsepower output for a typical internal combustion engine. ICEs produce maximum torque at a high RPM, whereas electric motors produce maximum torque at low RPM.

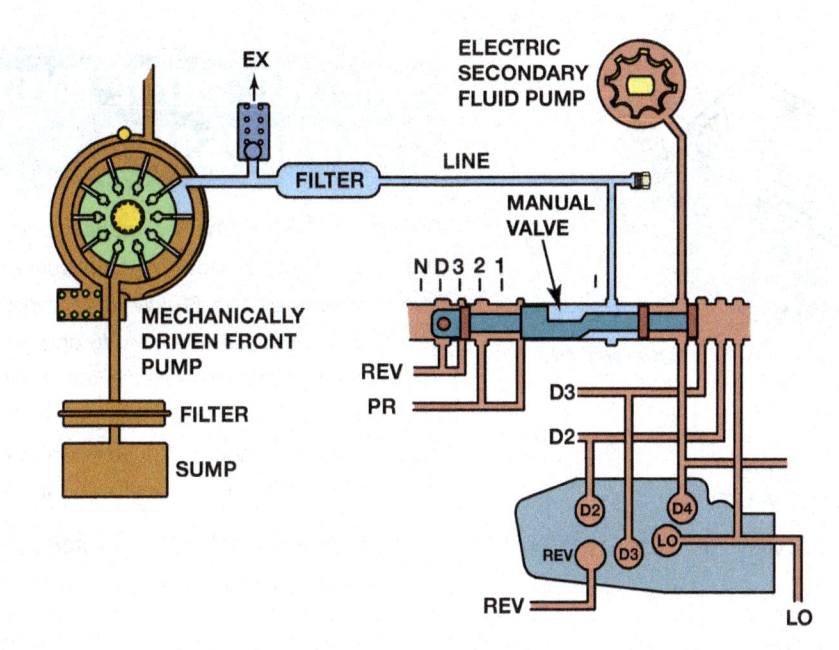

FIGURE 17-4 The hydraulic circuit diagram for this GM transmission includes a mechanical pump and an electric secondary fluid pump.

HYDRAULIC IMPULSE STORAGE ACCUMULATOR

A **hydraulic impulse storage accumulator** is used to provide fluid pressure as the ICE restarts after the idle-stop mode. During normal engine operation the mechanical transmission pump provides the hydraulic pressure and charges the accumulator. When the engine restarts, the accumulator provides the initial hydraulic pressure and the mechanical pump provides the continuation of the pressure. The pressure release from the accumulator ensures there is no delay in acceleration, and it eliminates the need for an electric auxiliary pump. ● **SEE FIGURE 17-5**.

GM PARALLEL HYBRID TRUCK (PHT)

DESCRIPTION The transmission in the 2004–2008 Chevrolet Silverado/GMC Sierra parallel hybrid truck (PHT) is based on the 4L60E electronically controlled automatic transmission design with minor modification to adjust for its new role in a hybrid powertrain. It has four forward speeds and one reverse, with the fourth speed being an overdrive. It is designed primarily for medium- and large-displacement engines and is used extensively in GM pickups and SUVs. The specific model used in the hybrid pickup is known as the M33.

OPERATION In idle-stop mode the engine stops, which will in turn stop the transmission oil pump and cause the transmission to go to "neutral." To prevent this, an electric secondary fluid pump is installed on the valve body inside the transmission oil pan. Whenever the engine goes into idle-stop, the electric fluid pump is turned on to maintain oil pressure on the transmission forward clutch, and keep the drivetrain connected to the engine. This results in a smoother transition between idle-stop and engine restarting as the vehicle resumes operation. ● **SEE FIGURE 17-6**.

The conventional 4L60E transmission is made to allow the vehicle to coast or brake without any interference from

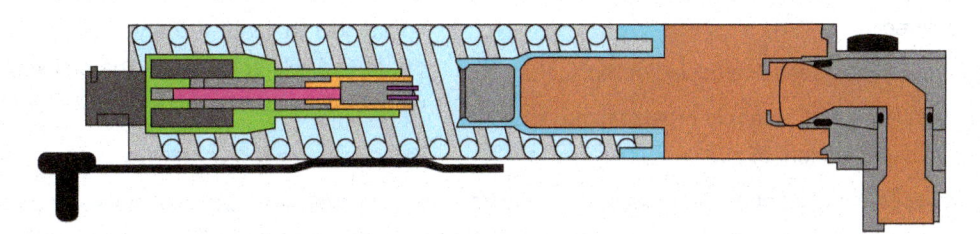

FIGURE 17-5 When the solenoid is energized, the accumulator releases the fluid creating the initial pressure needed at restart.

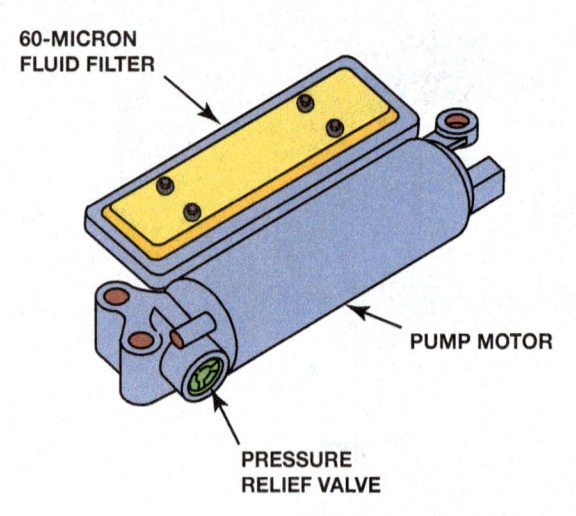

FIGURE 17-6 Electric secondary fluid pump from a transmission in a GM hybrid pickup.

the engine. To enable regenerative braking, the hybrid version of the 4L60E transmission is made to apply the overrun clutch during coast or braking in the D4 range and either third or second gear. This allows power to be transmitted back through the torque converter, which can then be used to generate electric current for recharging the 42-volt battery pack.

SERVICE Transmission service for the 4L60E model M33 is limited to fluid and filter changes. This transmission requires Dexron VI fluid. The filter on the electric secondary fluid pump is replaceable, but is not a regular maintenance item. Transmission pressure testing can be performed using the line pressure tap located on the transmission case. These tests are most often done by attaching a pressure gauge to the fitting on the side of the transmission and operating the transmission under various load conditions and road speeds. The test results are recorded and compared to charts to help determine what area(s) of the transmission might be malfunctioning.

A scan tool can be used to access DTCs (diagnostic trouble codes) and also to perform bidirectional testing of the transmission solenoids. A scan tool can also be used for clearing the *transmission adaptive pressure* (*TAP*) values if any of the following has occurred:

1. If the transmission has been overhauled or replaced.
2. Repair or replacement of an apply or release component (band, clutch, servo, piston, etc.).
3. Repair or replacement of a component that directly affects line pressure.

GM TWO-MODE HYBRID TRANSMISSION

DESCRIPTION The two-mode hybrid transmission used in 2009–2013 General Motors hybrid trucks is labeled a 2ML70. This unit features two 60-kW motors in the hybrid drivetrain, a 300-volt battery pack, and a V8 engine. A two-mode hybrid electric vehicle can increase the fuel economy by about 25%, depending on the type of driving conditions. Like all hybrids, the two-mode combines the power of a gasoline engine with that of electric motors and includes the following:

- Regenerative braking that captures kinetic energy that would otherwise be lost
- Idle-stop

Some full-hybrid systems have a single mode of operation, using a single planetary gear set to split engine power to drive the wheels or charge the battery. These systems are effective at low speeds because they can move the vehicle without running the gasoline engine (ICE). But at higher speeds, when the engine is needed, using the electric motors has much less benefit. As a result, sending power through electric motors and a variable transmission is roughly 20% less efficient than driving the vehicle through a purely mechanical power path, using gears.

COMPONENTS The two-mode unit is effectively an electronically variable transmission (EVT). It includes three simple planetary gear sets with four multiplate clutches. It has four fixed gear ratios with two EV ratios for smooth, more efficient operation. The components of the two-mode transmission include the following:

- Two 60-kW electric motor/generators assemblies.
- Three planetary gear sets (one is located in front of motor/generator A, called M/G A; another is located between the two motor/generators; and the last planetary gear set is located behind motor/generator B, called M/G B).
- Four wet plate clutches (two friction [rotating] and two [reaction/stationary] clutch assemblies). ● **SEE FIGURE 17-7**.

The vehicle starts moving in EV 1 with a variable ratio from infinite low to 1.7:1. If the vehicle is launched with the engine off, M/G A will spin the engine crankshaft so it can start running. EV 2 has a ratio between 1.7:1 and 0.5:1.

FIRST MODE OF OPERATION The first mode is for accelerating from standstill to second gear. At low speed and light load, the vehicle can be propelled by:

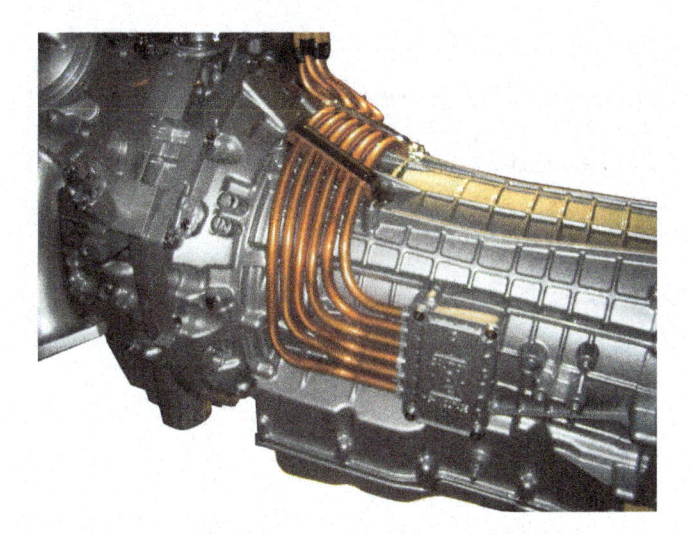

FIGURE 17-7 The two-mode transmission has orange high-voltage cables entering the unit to carry electric energy from the high-voltage battery pack to propel the vehicle and also charge the battery during deceleration.

- Either electric motor alone
- The ICE alone
- Or a combination of the two (electric motor and/or ICE)

In this mode, the engine (if running) can be shut off under certain conditions and everything will continue to operate on electric power alone. The hybrid system can restart the ICE at any time as needed. One of the motor/generators operates as a generator to charge the high-voltage battery, and the other works as a motor to assist in propelling the vehicle.

SECOND MODE OF OPERATION The second mode takes the vehicle from second gear through to overdrive. At higher loads and speeds, the ICE always runs. In the second mode, the motor/generators and planetary gear sets are used to keep torque and horsepower at a maximum. As the vehicle speed increases, various combinations of the four fixed ratio planetary gears engage and/or disengage to multiply engine torque, and allowing one or the other of the motor/generators to perform as a generator to charge the high-voltage battery. ● **SEE FIGURE 17-8**.

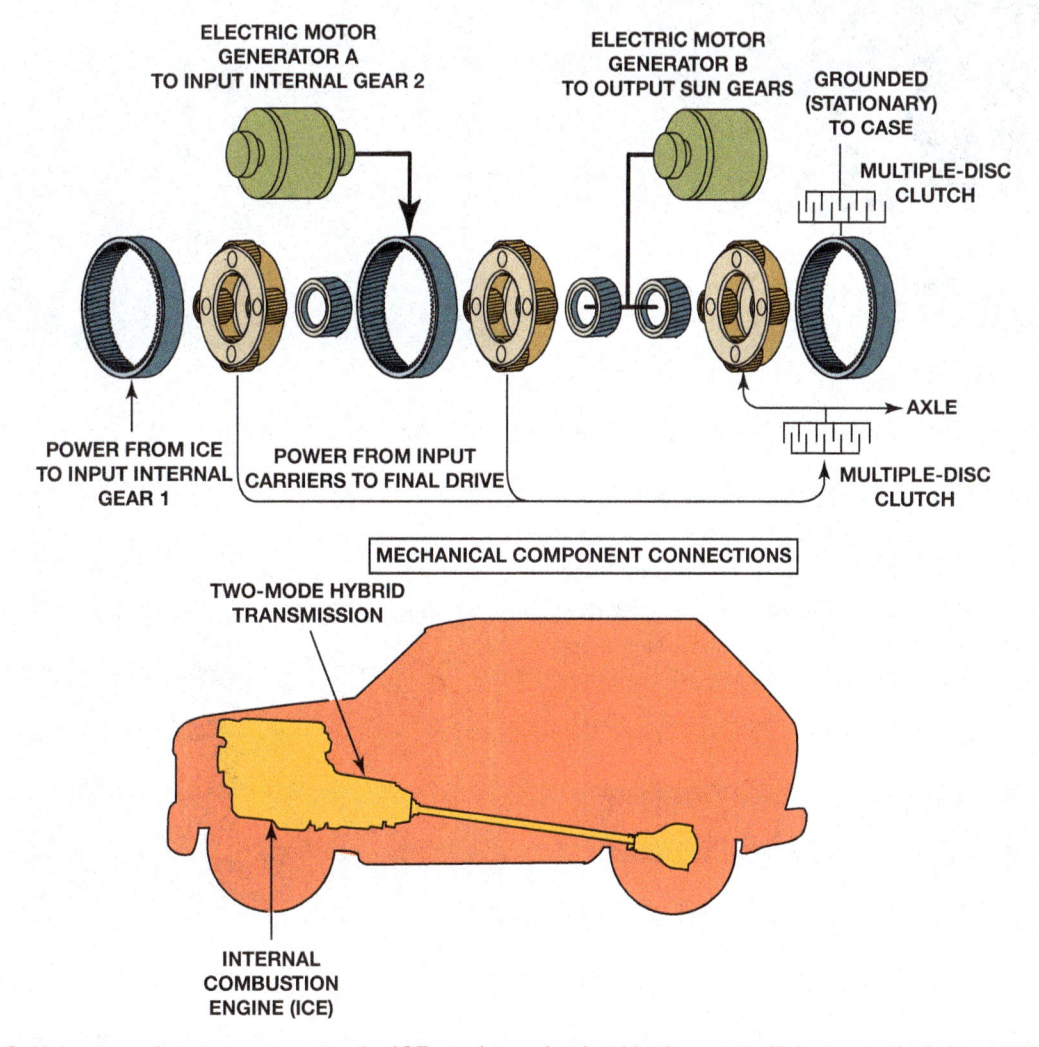

FIGURE 17-8 Using two planetary gear sets, the ICE can be maintained in the most efficient speed of about 2000 RPM under most operating conditions.

EV AND HEV TRANSMISSIONS

FIGURE 17-9 (a) Disassembly of the 2ML70 transmission requires the use of a special tool and a lift or engine hoist to remove the motor assembly. (b) The motor assembly after being removed from the transmission.

TWO-MODE SERVICE Routine service is all that is needed or required of the two-mode transmission. Fluid-level check and visual inspection should be all that is required until the first scheduled fluid change. Always use Dexron VI. Faults in the system will often set a diagnostic trouble code. Unit repair of the unit requires an engine hoist or the lift arm of a vehicle lift to remove the motor assembly. ● **SEE FIGURE 17-9 A AND B.**

FORD/LINCOLN 10R80 MHT

DESCRIPTION The 10R80 MHT is a modular ten-speed hybrid transmission that was introduced in the 2020 Explorer and the 2020 Lincoln Aviator plug-in hybrid. The transmission is unique because unlike most hybrid transmissions, it still uses a torque converter. The continued use of the torque converter improves towing and hauling capabilities. An electric motor and disconnect clutch are placed between the engine and the torque converter. In addition to providing stop-start capabilities, the electric motor provides low-speed torque and additional power. The MTH transmission is six inches longer than the non-hybrid model (10R80) and shares 90% of the same components. ● **SEE FIGURE 17-10 A AND B.**

COMPONENTS The components of the hybrid drive unit of the transmission are as follows:

- Electric motor
- Resolver (speed sensor)
- High-voltage connection
- Low-voltage connection

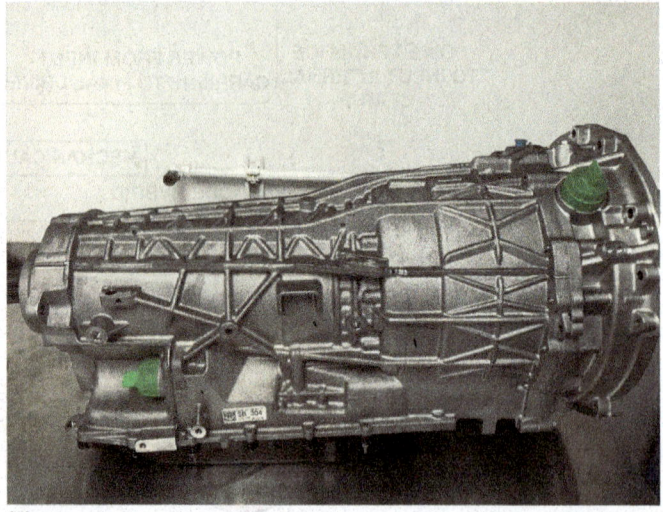

FIGURE 17-10 (a) The driver side of the transmission contains the high-voltage connections and the shift level assembly. The hybrid portion of the transmission is forward of the gasket. (b) The passenger side of the transmission contains the low-voltage connections.

The hybrid drive unit is removed from the transmission as a unit. An engine hoist and special adapter are recommended when completing this task because of the weight of the unit.
- SEE FIGURE 17-11 A AND B.

The electric motor is a permanent magnet three-phase motor that generates 33 kW of power. ● SEE FIGURE 17-12 A AND B.

The resolver (speed sensor) provides the powertrain control module (PCM) with the speed, location, and direction of rotation of the electric motor. ● SEE FIGURE 17-13.

The high-voltage connector at the transmission allows the electric motor in the hybrid section of the transmission to be connected to the Inverter System Controller (ISC) via the orange-colored high-voltage insulated wiring. ● SEE FIGURE 17-14.

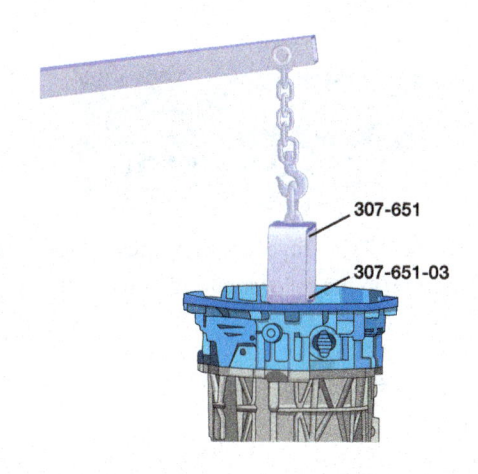

FIGURE 17-11 (a) An engine hoist and adapter are used to remove the hybrid portion of the transmission. (b) The hybrid portion of the transmission resting on two wooden blocks after being removed from the transmission.

FIGURE 17-12 (a) The motor windings attached to the housing after the rotor has been removed. (b) The rotor and torque converter assembly after being separated from the winding.

The low-voltage connectors at the transmission provide for traditional transmission control and monitoring by the powertrain control module. ● SEE FIGURE 17-15.

SERVICE Service procedures performed at specific service intervals include the transmission fluid and filter. If the non-hybrid section of the transmission experiences a failure, a detailed overhaul procedure is provided. If the hybrid section of the transmission experiences a failure, it is replaced as a unit. Most electrical components, such as solenoids and sensors,

FIGURE 17-13 The resolver is the black and gray electrical sensor bolted to the housing at the bottom of the motor housing.

FIGURE 17-15 The low-voltage connector is for transmission control and monitoring.

TOYOTA/LEXUS POWER-SPLIT SYSTEM

APPLICATIONS The Toyota/Lexus power-split device drive system is used in the following models:

- Toyota Prius
- Toyota Corolla Hybrid
- Toyota Sienna
- Toyota Venza
- Toyota Camry Hybrid
- Lexus CT200h
- Toyota Highlander
- Toyota RAVA Hybrid
- Lexus RX400h and RX450h

DESCRIPTION The power-split transaxle is a series-parallel hybrid technology. During most phases of vehicle operation, the system is operating as both series and parallel at the same time. While the control system is complex, the basic transaxle is very simple in design as it is built around a single planetary gear set (power-split device) and two electric motor/generators, called MG1 and MG2. ● **SEE FIGURE 17-16**.

A planetary gear set is composed of three main components:

1. Ring gear
2. Planet carrier
3. Sun gear

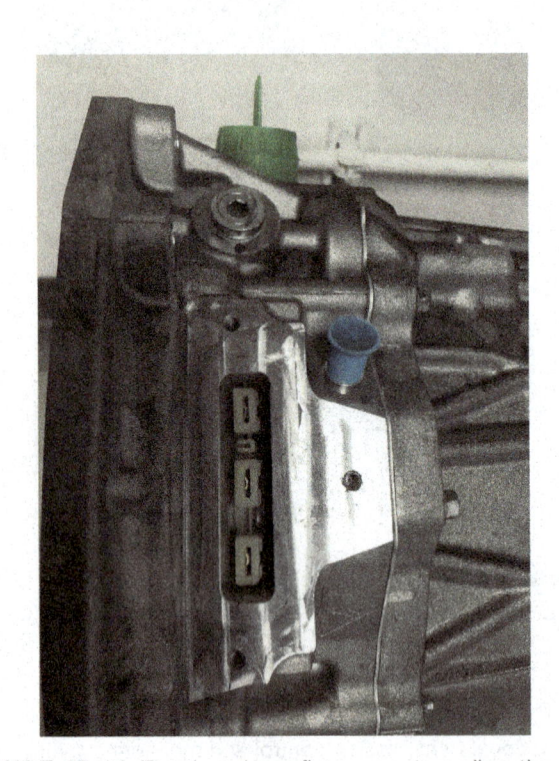

FIGURE 17-14 The three large flat connectors allow the electric motor to be connected to the ISC via the high-voltage cables.

are monitored by the powertrain control module (PCM) and supported with specific diagnostics related to a diagnostic trouble code (DTC). The external electrical components are serviceable.

236 CHAPTER 17

FIGURE 17-16 The Toyota Hybrid System uses two electric motor/generators (MG1 and MG2) and an ICE connected together by a power-split device which is a simple planetary gear set.

In the power-split transaxle, a large electric motor/generator (MG2) is directly attached to the transaxle final drive and to the planetary ring gear. The ICE is connected to the planet carrier, and the small electric motor/generator (MG1) is connected to the sun gear. ● SEE FIGURE 17-17.

The planetary ring gear always turns in the same direction as the drive wheels and its speed is directly proportional to vehicle speed. In other words, if the ring gear is not moving, the vehicle is not moving. The power-split device is so named because the ICE (attached to the planet carrier) splits its torque output between the sun gear (MG1) and the ring gear (MG2 and drive wheels).

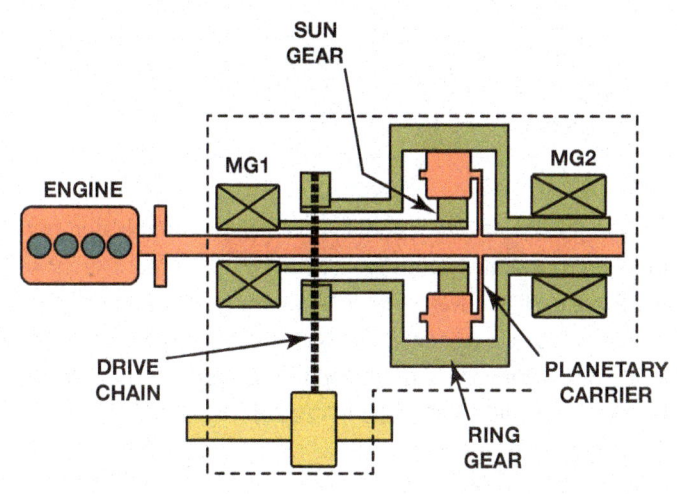

FIGURE 17-17 The power-split device from the Toyota Hybrid System. Note the vehicle will only move when MG2 (and the ring gear) is turning.

The gear ratio of the planetary gear set causes the ICE to send 72% of its torque to the ring gear and the remaining 28% to the sun gear. The torque split percentages remain the same regardless of what mode the transaxle is operating in because they are determined by the number of teeth on the planetary ring gear and the sun gear. ● SEE FIGURE 17-18.

While torque split percentages are always the same, power split percentages will vary depending on the RPM of the various components. Horsepower is the rate at which work is performed and is a function of torque and RPM. If a shaft has torque applied to it, but remains at zero RPM, no work is being performed and no horsepower is transmitted through the shaft. The same principle applies to the torque split planetary gear set. If the sun gear is stationary, it will still receive 28% of the torque of the ICE, but all of the engine horsepower will be directed through the ring gear and on to the drive wheels.

OPERATION

- **Vehicle Stopped.** When the vehicle is stopped, nothing is happening within the vehicle drive system. The ICE is

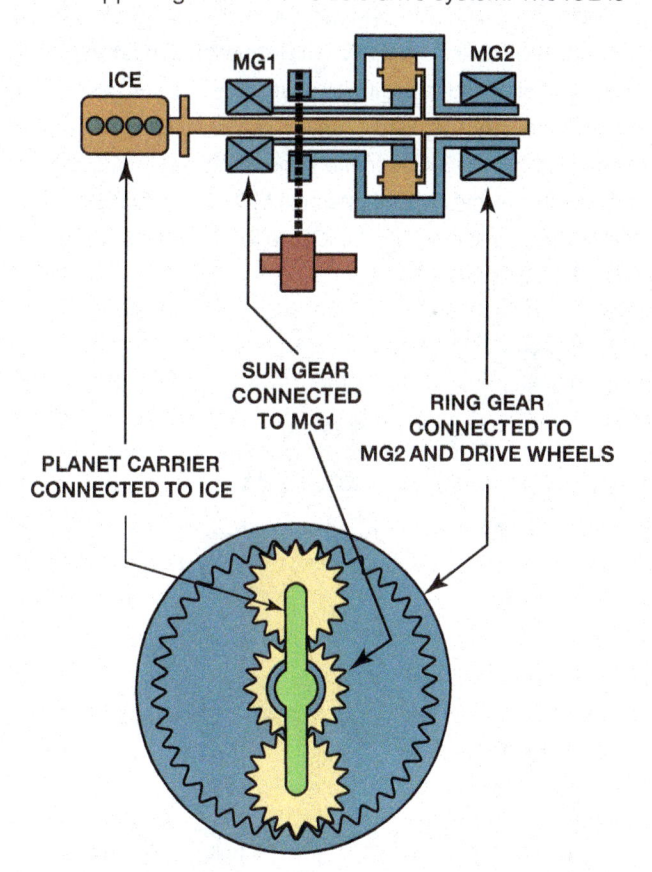

FIGURE 17-18 The planetary gearset used in the Toyota Hybrid System has 2.6 times the number of teeth in its ring gear as it has in its sun gear. This means that the ICE (attached to the planet carrier) will send 72% of its torque to the ring gear (drive wheels) and 28% of its torque to the sun gear (MG1).

EV AND HEV TRANSMISSIONS

shut off, and both electric motor/generators are shut off as well. There are circuits within the vehicle that will use electrical energy from the auxiliary battery, but the drive system itself is effectively inert. The Toyota hybrid system does not use an auxiliary starter, but instead uses the MG1 for starting under all conditions.
- **SEE FIGURE 17-19**.

- **Light Acceleration.** When the vehicle is driven at low speeds and light acceleration, it is driven by MG2 alone.
  - **SEE FIGURE 17-20**. This is because the electric motor is more efficient than the ICE at low vehicle speeds. Current from the high-voltage (HV) battery is sent through the inverter and on to MG2 to move the vehicle. A special graph, known as a monograph, shows the speed relationship between the various elements. When the engine is stopped (0 RPM), MG2 is turning forward (+), and this causes MG1 to turn backward (−). **SEE FIGURE 17-21**.

- **Normal Driving.** When higher vehicle speeds are required, the ICE must be started so that its output can be combined with that of MG2. The ring gear is already turning clockwise as the vehicle travels in a forward direction. Since the planet carrier (attached to the ICE) is stationary, the sun gear (driven by MG1) is used to drive the planet carrier clockwise and start the ICE. Current from the HV battery is directed through the inverter and operates MG1 as a motor, turning clockwise and spinning the ICE up to 1000 RPM for starting.
  - **SEE FIGURE 17-22**.

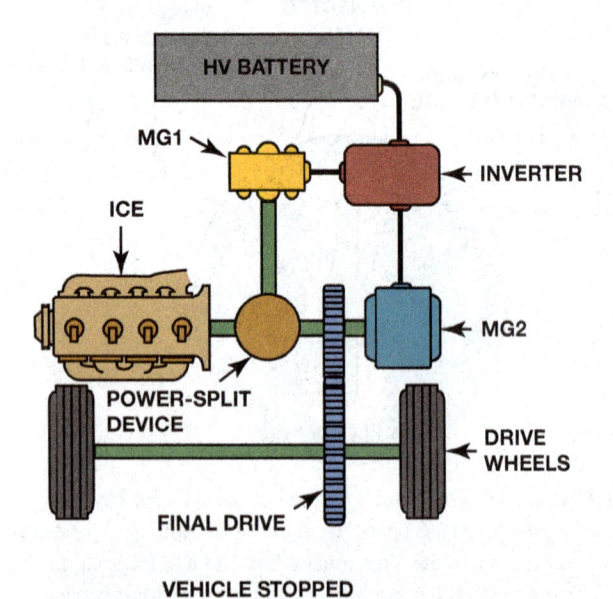

FIGURE 17-19 When the vehicle is stopped, the ICE is shut off along with both motor/generators.

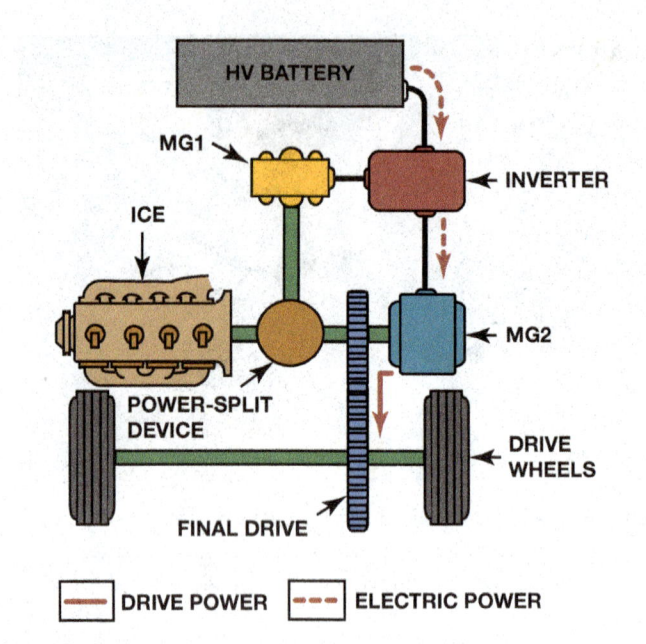

FIGURE 17-20 Under light acceleration, power is sent to MG2 to move the vehicle.

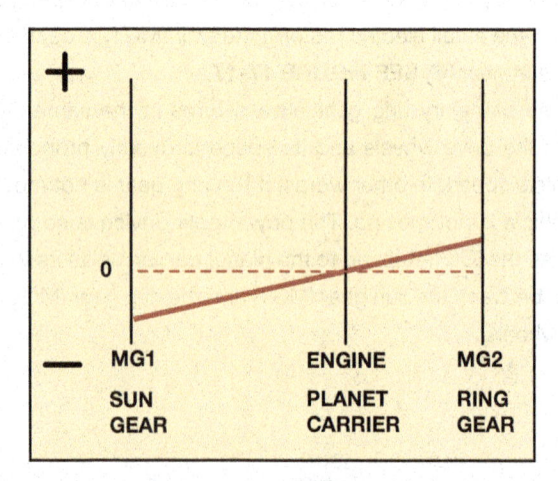

FIGURE 17-21 Under light acceleration, the engine is stopped (0 RPM), MG2 is turning forward (+), and MG1 is turning backward (−).

Once the ICE is started, MG1 operates as a generator, but turns in the counterclockwise direction. ICE output is now divided or "split" between the drive wheels (ring gear) and MG1 (sun gear). Power generated by MG1 is either directed to MG2 to help move the vehicle or is used to recharge the HV battery, if necessary. ● **SEE FIGURES 17-23 AND 17-24**.

- **Full-Throttle Acceleration and High-Speed Cruise.** When greater acceleration is required, both MG2 and the ICE continue sending torque to the vehicle drive wheels, but MG2 can also receive power from the HV battery to increase its output. As demand increases further, the

FIGURE 17-22 To start the ICE, MG1 (sun) acts as a motor and turns clockwise (CW), causing the planet carrier (attached to the ICE) to also turn CW.

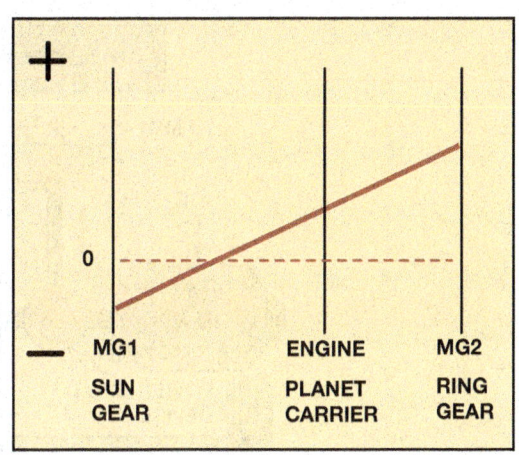

FIGURE 17-24 Normal driving—the engine is running, MG2 is turning forward (+), and MG1 is turning backward (–).

ICE speed is increased for more output. To enable an increase in ICE speed, the sun gear (MG1) must rotate in a clockwise direction. It is during these times that MG1 can be configured as a motor and will draw power from MG2 during a phase known as *energy recirculation*.

● **SEE FIGURES 17-25 AND 17-26.**

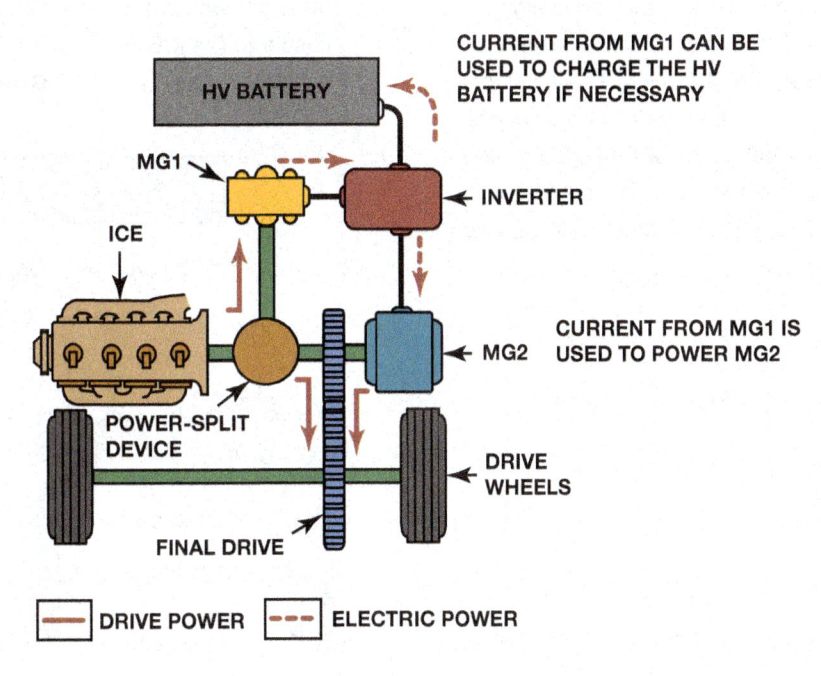

FIGURE 17-23 Normal driving—the ICE is now running and some of its torque is used to drive MG1. Electricity generated by MG1 is used to power MG2 or recharge the HV battery.

EV AND HEV TRANSMISSIONS 239

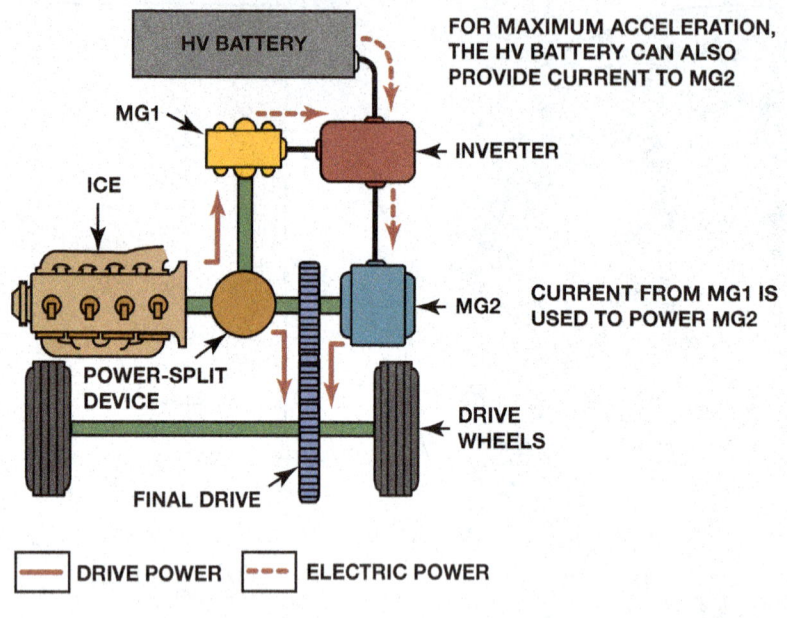

FIGURE 17-25 Full-throttle acceleration and high-speed cruise—with greater demand for acceleration, power from MG1 is combined with power from the HV battery to generate higher output from MG2. It is also possible to configure MG2 as a generator and send its power to MG1 (which then acts as a motor).

- **Deceleration and Braking.** As the vehicle is decelerating, MG2 is configured as a generator. The kinetic energy (energy of movement) of the vehicle is converted into electrical energy by MG2. The ICE and MG1 are shut off, and current from MG2 is sent through the inverter and is used to recharge the HV battery. ● **SEE FIGURE 17-27**.
- **Reverse.** If reverse is selected, power is sent from the HV battery to the inverter and on to MG2. MG2 operates in the reverse direction to back up the vehicle, but the other components in the drive system are turned off at this time. The ICE does not run when the vehicle is being driven in reverse. ● **SEE FIGURE 17-28**.

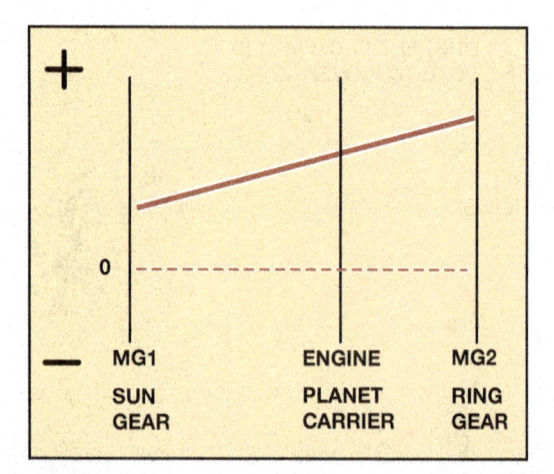

FIGURE 17-26 Full-throttle acceleration and high-speed cruise—this graph shows MG1 acting as a motor using power from MG2. This increases the speed of the ICE, allowing it to produce higher output.

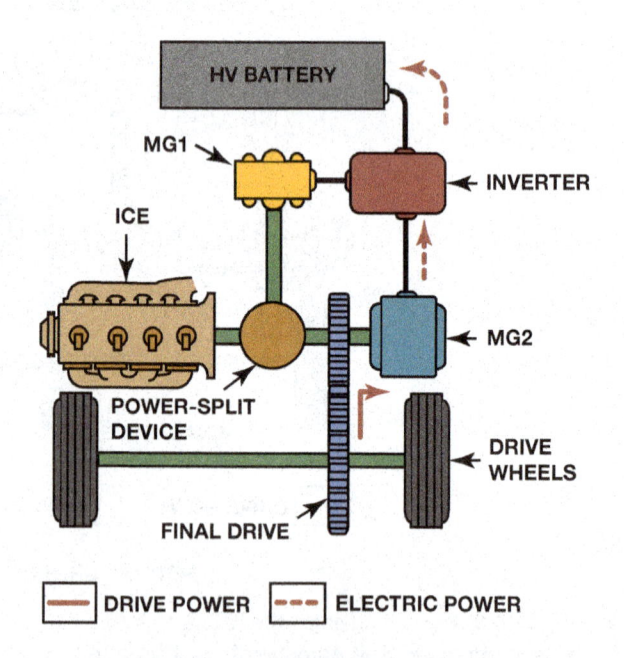

FIGURE 17-27 Deceleration and braking—MG2 is configured as a generator and recharges the HV battery.

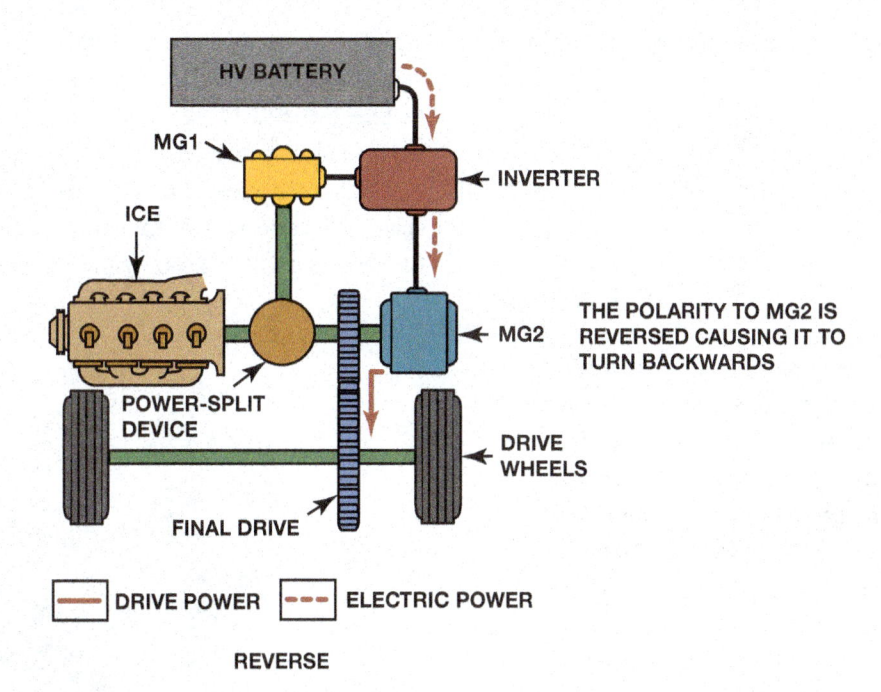

FIGURE 17-28 Reverse—MG2 alone is used to move the car in reverse. This is accomplished by reversing the direction of MG2.

CONSTRUCTION The Toyota power-split transaxle is built with an aluminum case composed of two major assemblies. These are known as the MG1 assembly and the MG2 assembly, and each houses its respective motor/generator.

Each of the motors/generators performs two functions:

- MG1—Used to crank the ICE and generate electrical current to charge the high-voltage battery.

- MG2—Used to propel the vehicle and to charge the high-voltage battery during deceleration.

Each of these major assemblies has its own water jacket for cooling the motor/generator windings in the housing. There are two water jacket unions installed in each major assembly, and these send coolant to the motors from the separate inverter cooling system. ● **SEE FIGURE 17-29 A AND B**.

FIGURE 17-29 (a) Coolant is circulated under the ring in the bellhousing area to remove heat generated by MG1. (b) Coolant is circulated in the passages near the rear of the transmission to remove heat generated by MG2.

EV AND HEV TRANSMISSIONS 241

The following components are assembled on a common axis:

- Internal combustion engine (ICE)
- MG1
- Power-split device
- MG2
- Oil pump

The final drive is housed between the two major assemblies and utilizes a conventional open differential for sending torque to the front-drive wheels. A chain drive attaches the ring gear of the power-split device to the counter drive gear, which drives the counter driven gear that is meshed with the ring gear of the differential assembly. ● **SEE FIGURE 17-30**.

This system does not use a conventional clutch or torque converter. With this design, there is no need to disconnect the engine from the input shaft. This is because the engine can turn at any speed while the vehicle is stopped (ring gear is stopped) by using MG1 (sun gear) as a generator. The ICE is connected directly to the transaxle input shaft using a damper disc mechanism. ● **SEE FIGURE 17-31**.

The transaxle oil pump is housed in the rear of the MG2 assembly and is attached to the input shaft from the ICE. ● **SEE FIGURE 17-32**. The oil is circulated by the pump only when the ICE is running.

When the vehicle is driven by MG2 only, the transaxle is splash-lubricated by the movement of the final drive gears. The transaxle for the 2001–2003 Prius has a cable-operated parking lock

FIGURE 17-31 The flywheel and clutch assembly serve as the dampener between the engine and transmission.

FIGURE 17-30 The view of the configuration of the final drive assembly after the front cover has been removed.

FIGURE 17-32 With the cover removed, the transmission oil pump is visible on the rear of the transmission.

FIGURE 17-33 The electronic actuated park lock mechanism is mounted externally beginning with the 2004 model year.

mechanism. This was replaced with an electrically actuated mechanism starting with the 2004 model year. ● **SEE FIGURE 17-33**.

SERVICE Service procedures to be performed at specified intervals include changing the transaxle oil and the coolant for the inverter (high-voltage) system. There are drain plugs for both at the bottom of the transaxle assembly. The transaxle oil is refilled through a hole in the front of the case, with the level being brought up to a specified distance from the bottom of the hole. The coolant is refilled at the reservoir that is located on the inverter assembly and must be bled properly before placing the vehicle back into service. Always use the recommended fluids and procedures when servicing any vehicle.

NOTE: The fastest and most reliable way to refill the inverter cooling system is to use an airlift fluid exchange machine. This pulls the cooling system into a vacuum and then injects the coolant into the evacuated system. This method fills the system quickly and eliminates air bubbles.

TOYOTA HYBRID eCVT TRANSMISSION

PURPOSE AND FUNCTION The Toyota electronically controlled continuously variable transmission (eCVT) is similar to the Toyota power-split transmission. It is built differently, however, to allow MG1 to control the gear ratio between the engine and the final drive of the transaxle. This maintains optimum engine RPM to achieve ideal tailpipe emissions and fuel economy when the ICE is operating. Toyota refers to this transmission as a P610 and a P710 depending on the application.

DESCRIPTION AND OPERATION The eCVt transmission uses a planetary gear set between the engine and MG1 to control the gear ratio to the final drive. This arrangement allows the ICE to provide power to the drive wheels. The planetary carrier of the gear set is connected to the engine crankshaft and turns at the same speed as the engine. The transmission oil pump is also connected to the planetary carrier to provide lubrication pressure when the ICE is operating. The sun gear of the planetary is connected to MG1. The ring gear of the gear set is connected to the counter gear that turns the pinion of the final drive assembly to move the vehicle. The speed and direction of MG1 will determine if the transmission is operating in and under-drive (UD), direct-drive, or over-drive (OD) mode of operation. The operation of MG1 provides for infinitely variable ratios within the transmission and eliminates the need for the older belt and pulley systems. MG1 is used to start the ICE, generate power for the high-voltage battery, and provide power to MG2, if needed. ● **SEE FIGURE 17-34**.

MG2 is connected to the final drive assembly through the counter gear to move the vehicle in electric mode. MG2 operates as a generator on deceleration providing regenerative braking.

FIGURE 17-34 A gear set is used to transfer power to the final drive assembly.

HYBRID ELECTRIC REAR AXLE

PURPOSE AND FUNCTION The electric rear drive axle is used for an AWD system without the use of a rear driveshaft. For example, the Toyota Q211, used in the RAV4 and the Highlander, and almost all systems used today regardless of the manufacturer, are of a similar design. The only items that vary are the size of the components depending on the kilowatt rating on the electric motor. The rear electric axle uses a single motor that Toyota refers to as MGR (motor generator rear). ● SEE FIGURE 17-35.

The electric rear axle has three modes of operation.

- Startup mode: The rear axle provides a small amount of torque up to approximately 3 MPH.
- Mode 2: During normal driving no torque is delivered unless front wheel slip is detected.
- Mode 3: Provides additional regenerative braking on deceleration.

DESCRIPTION AND OPERATION Vehicles with an electric rear axle use a special inverter that controls three electric motors. The unit is contained in a three-piece case. The unit is filled with automatic transmission fluid and relies on splash lubrication and cooling. As the ring gear on the final drive is turned, transmission fluid is splashed throughout the unit, including the electric motor, absorbing any heat generated. The heat is dissipated through the cooling fins that are molded into the exterior of the case. The electric motor in the Q211 is rated at 67 horsepower (55 Kw). Its position, speed, and location are determined by a resolver that

FIGURE 17-35 The cutaway of the rear axle assembly shows the arrangement of the electric motor and the transfer gears.

FIGURE 17-36 A rear motor unit in a Toyota RAV4 Hybrid, an all-wheel-drive HEV.

🔧 TECH TIP

Select the All-Wheel Drive Hybrid for Better Fuel Economy

The all-wheel drive versions of the Toyota/Lexus hybrid usually get better fuel economy compared to the front-wheel drive version. The reason is that the rear motor is used to generate electrical energy back to the high-voltage battery during deceleration. This rear electric motor is used for regeneration along with MG2.

is not serviceable due to the technician's inability to calibrate the replacement unit. The electric motor stator contains a temperature sensor that provides feedback to the hybrid control module. The rotor of MGR turns the MGR drive gear as it rotates. The MGR drive gear turns the counter gear which turns the ring gear on the final drive assembly. Each of the rear half-shafts is splined to the final drive assembly. The unit contains a fluid fill plug, drain plug, and level check plug should the fluid need to be serviced.
● SEE FIGURE 17-36.

HYBRID TRANSMISSION DIAGNOSIS

STEPS INVOLVED When diagnosing a hybrid electric vehicle (HEV) transmission concerns, perform the following steps:

STEP 1 The first step is to verify the customer complaint.
STEP 2 Check the fluid level and condition.

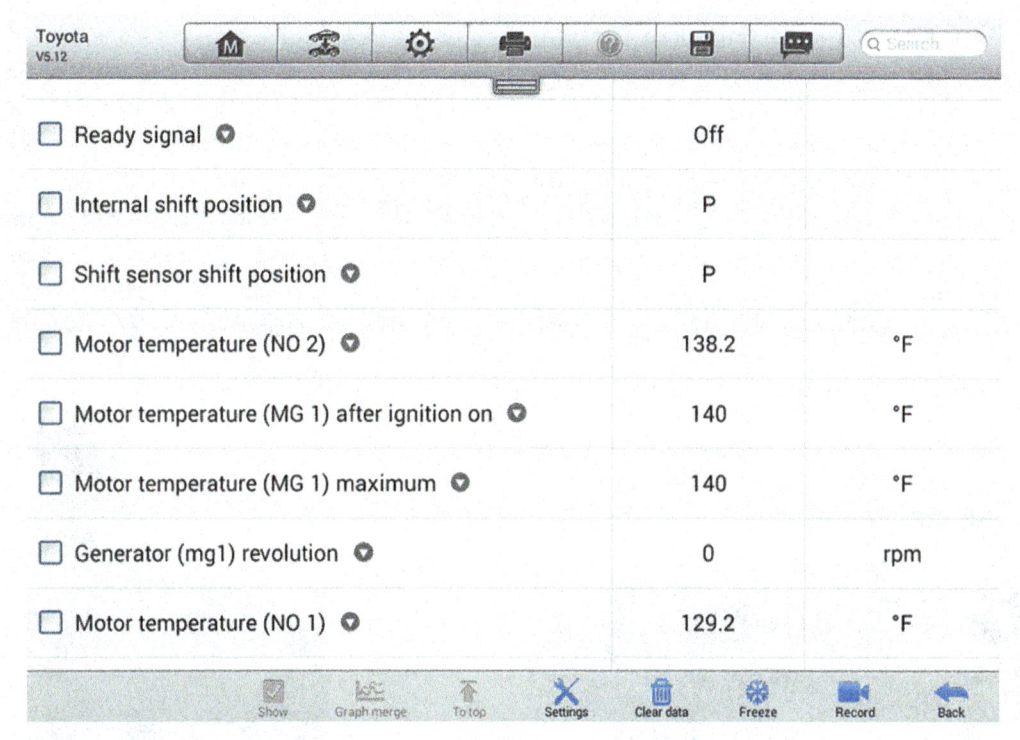

☐ Ready signal	Off
☐ Internal shift position	P
☐ Shift sensor shift position	P
☐ Motor temperature (NO 2)	138.2 °F
☐ Motor temperature (MG 1) after ignition on	140 °F
☐ Motor temperature (MG 1) maximum	140 °F
☐ Generator (mg1) revolution	0 rpm
☐ Motor temperature (NO 1)	129.2 °F

FIGURE 17-37 The data display of the transmission control module shows live values of various sensors and switches.

STEP 3 Check for stored diagnostic trouble codes (DTCs).
STEP 4 Check for any related technical service bulletins (TSBs).
STEP 5 Check scan tool data including checking the adaptive values. ● **SEE FIGURE 17-37**.
STEP 6 Perform visual inspections, including checking for recent accident damage, previous repairs, or other issues.
STEP 7 Perform bidirectional control of the transmission using a factory or an enhanced aftermarket scan tool to check operation. This helps to establish if the issue is inside or outside of the transmission/transaxle.
STEP 8 Locate and correct the root cause of the problem.

Always follow the specified diagnostic and repair procedures for the vehicle being serviced.

ELECTRIC VEHICLE TRANSMISSIONS

ACCELERATION VS TOP SPEED Most production electric vehicles use a single-speed transmission. ICE need many gears because they have a narrow RPM window within which they can operate efficiently. For electric motors, that window is much wider, so a single-speed works for both low-end acceleration and highway driving. It does require some compromise, and so EV manufactures usually design their system for optimum low-end acceleration instead of top speeds. Most electric vehicles have a top speed of 110–125 MPH (180–200 km/h). At top speed the electric motor RPM is 10000 and 18000 RPM, depending on the make and model.

SINGLE SPEED GEARING The objective of the motor and drivetrain is improving the conversion rate of battery power to actual wheel power. Every one percentage point in energy conversion efficiency translates into 2% more range. Most all-electric vehicles are equipped with just a single speed transmission/transaxle, yet are capable of delivering outstanding performance and acceptable range with motor torque of up to 230 lb-ft (315 Nm) and peak power of 188 HP (140 kW).

FORD MUSTANG MACH-E BorgWarner is producing an Integrated Drive Module (iDM) being used in the Ford Mustang Mach-E. The iDM consists within one compact assembly including the following components:

- Electric traction motor
- Single-speed gearbox
- Thermal-management system (liquid cooling)
- Motor and power electronics

The iDM uses parallel axis gearing, instead featuring a concentric design with outputs on the same axis as the electric motor, resulting in a more compact package.

CHEVROLET BOLT The Chevrolet Bolt drive unit consists of an electric motor and final drive assembly. ● SEE FIGURE 17-38.

The electric motor is a permanent-magnet synchronous AC motor. It is rated at 150 kW and has a maximum rotation speed of 8810 RPM (2017 model year specifications). The final drive section of the drive unit consists of the drive gear on the output end of the electric motor, the main shaft, and the ring gear which is mounted on the differential assembly. ● SEE FIGURE 17-39.

The final drive assembly provides a gear reduction of 7.05:1 between the electric motor and the drive wheels. The drive unit is internally lubricated and cooled using Dexron HP transmission fluid. ● SEE FIGURE 17-40.

The heat is transferred out of the transmission to an external radiator using coolant. ● SEE FIGURE 17-41.

The drive unit is completely serviceable following the specified procedures and General Motors supplied special tools.

NISSAN LEAF At the heart of LEAF's powertrain is its three-phase AC electric motor. It produces 80 kilowatts of power and can produce maximum torque within 0.1 seconds. This motor has a permanent magnet rotor core with high-density stator

FIGURE 17-38 The electric motor and final drive assembly installed in a Chevrolet Bolt.

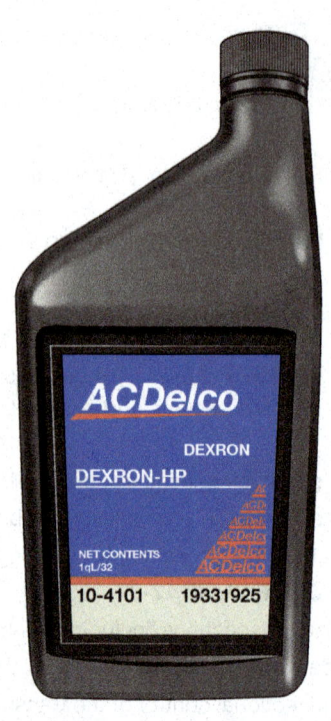

FIGURE 17-40 Dexron HP synthetic transmission fluid is specified for the Bolt final drive assembly.

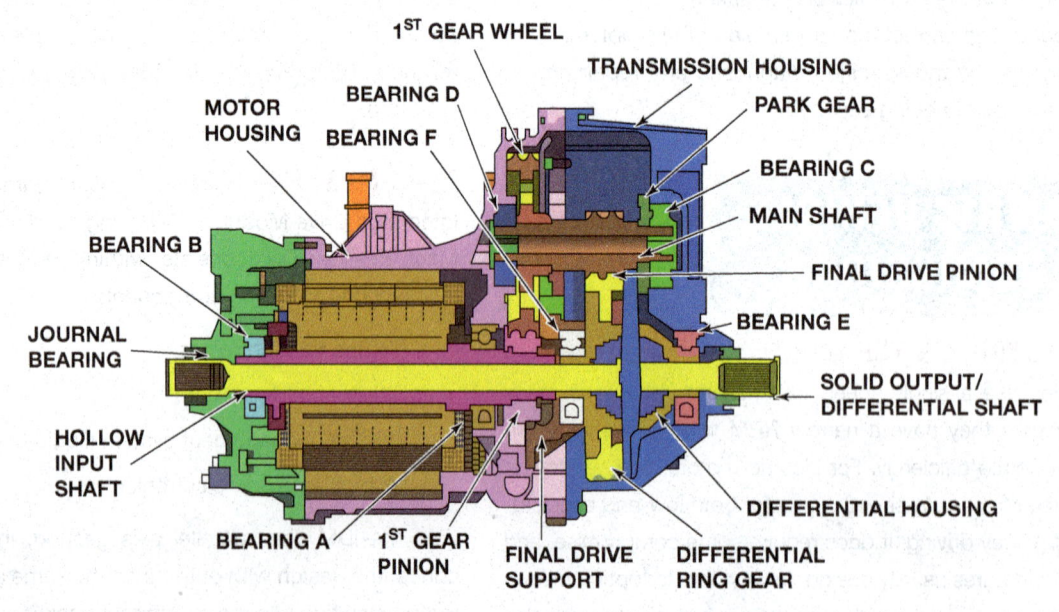

FIGURE 17-39 A CATIA drafting of a Chevrolet Bolt electric motor and final drive assembly.

FIGURE 17-41 Coolant enters through the hose on the left, travels through the passageway absorbing heat, and exits to the radiator through the hose on the right.

FIGURE 17-42 The electric motor assembly and reducer installed in a 2011 Nissan Leaf.

FIGURE 17-43 The external connection for the resolver.

winding. It produces 206.5 pound-feet of torque and weighs 129 pounds. ● **SEE FIGURE 17-42**.

A resolver is incorporated to input rotor position and speed to the Vehicle Control Module (VCM). Resolver calibration data to correct for variations in manufacturing is encoded on the traction motor housing. ● **SEE FIGURE 17-43**.

Instead of a conventional transmission, the LEAF incorporates a reducer that transfers the torque from the traction motor to the drive wheels. The reducer directs the motor's output to provide ideal torque at both low- and high-motor speeds. Compact and lightweight, the reducer minimizes energy loss due to friction. The LEAF's reducer is connected to the electric drive motor. Its components include the input gear, main gear, main shaft, final gear, differential, and parking unit. ● **SEE FIGURE 17-44**.

Nissan is not currently servicing any of the internal parts for the electric motor assembly; however, there is a procedure for repairing the reducer. According to the periodic maintenance schedule, the oil level in the reducer must be inspected. If the fluid level is found to be low, it should be filled to the desired level with Nissan genuine Matic Fluid S. The reducer holds approximately 1.1 liter of lubricant.

> **? FREQUENTLY ASKED QUESTION**
>
> **What Happens When You Shift to Neutral?**
>
> When neutral is selected, does it just disconnect the power connections? Or is the motor free to spin? In neutral, there is no power being supplied to the electric traction motor. The motor is never disconnected.

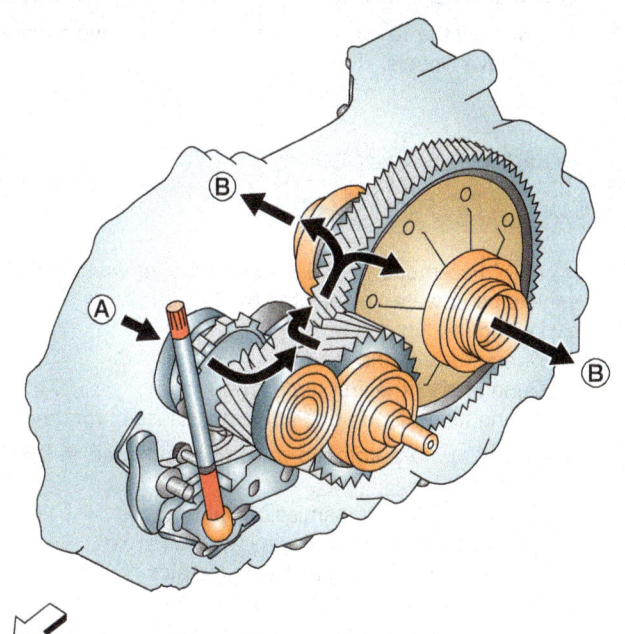

FIGURE 17-44 Power flow through the reducer.

EV AND HEV TRANSMISSIONS 247

TWO-SPEED GEARING The original Tesla Roadster featured a two-speed transmission and currently a two-speed unit is used in the Porsche Taycan. Using a multispeed transmission in an electric vehicle provides the same benefits that it does in a gasoline-powered vehicle with improved low-speed acceleration and increased efficiency by lowering the rotating speed of the electric motor at high speeds. The Porsche Taycan's rear gearbox uses a single planetary gearset and two clutches to create the ratio change. One clutch is used to decouple the rear motor altogether, allowing for efficient running using only the front (single-speed) axle. In most driving, the Taycan operates the rear axle in top gear. First-gear starts happen in Sport or Sport Plus mode.

SUMMARY

1. The transmission is responsible for providing torque applied to the drive wheel to accelerate the vehicle from a stop, and power at higher speeds that allow the engine to operate efficiently.
2. In order to move a vehicle, torque must be applied to the drive wheels.
3. In order to adapt a conventional automatic transmission to a hybrid powertrain, an electric auxiliary pump is used to maintain fluid pressure in the transmission during internal combustion engine (ICE) idle-stop.
4. The power-split transaxle is a series-parallel hybrid technology. During most phases of vehicle operation, the system is operating as both series and parallel at the same time.
5. Each of the motor/generators perform two functions: MG1—used to crank the ICE and generate electrical current to charge the high-voltage battery. MG2—used to propel the vehicle and to charge the high-voltage battery during deceleration.
6. An eCVT designed transmission does not use a belt or chain and instead uses a parallel gear design.
7. Most all-electric vehicles are equipped with just a single speed transmission/transaxle.
8. Using a multispeed transmission in an electric vehicle provides the same benefits that it does in a gasoline-powered vehicle with improved low-speed acceleration and increased efficiency by lowering the rotating speed of the electric motor at high speeds.

REVIEW QUESTIONS

1. What are the differences in FWD, RWD, and AWD powertrain configurations?
2. Explain how the transmission delivers torque and optimizes fuel economy.
3. Explain how the Toyota power-split system delivers power to the drive wheels.
4. What are the differences in single-speed and two-speed gearing in an electric vehicle?
5. Describe the operation of a single-speed transmission in a typical electric vehicle.

CHAPTER QUIZ

1. In a GM two-mode hybrid electric vehicle, when can the vehicle be powered by electric mode alone?
    a. During the first mode
    b. During the second mode
    c. During either the first or second mode
    d. During heavy load conditions regardless of mode
2. Modifications to automatic transmissions used in hybrid vehicles include _____.
    a. electric auxiliary transmission fluid pumps
    b. modified torque converter lockup schedule
    c. hydraulic impulse storage accumulator
    d. All of the answers are correct
3. In a Toyota/Lexus hybrid electric vehicle, how is reverse achieved?
    a. The ICE reverses direction and powers the drive wheels
    b. MG2 is used to power the vehicle in reverse
    c. MG1 is used to power the vehicle in reverse
    d. Either b or c depending on model and year
4. A FWD hybrid electric vehicle with an electric rear axle _____.
    a. has all-wheel drive capabilities
    b. uses a special inverter
    c. has a separate resolver and temperature sensor for the rear axle unit
    d. All of the answers are correct

5. The final drive assembly in an electric vehicle transmission assembly _____.
   a. transfers torque from the electric motor to the drive wheels
   b. reduces motor speed to produce ideal torque at low and high speeds
   c. provides for a parking mechanism for the assembly
   d. All of the answers are correct

6. What is the first step when diagnosing a hybrid vehicle transmission?
   a. Check the fluid level
   b. Verify the customer concern
   c. Check for trouble codes
   d. Check for Technical Service Bulletins (TSBs)

7. In a Toyota/Lexus hybrid electric vehicle, what is the purpose of MG1?
   a. Start the ICE
   b. Charge the HV battery
   c. Provide additional power to MG2
   d. All of the answers are correct

8. The oil pump in the Toyota/Lexus power-split hybrid system _____.
   a. only turns when the ICE is operating
   b. is located in the rear cover of the transmission behind MG2
   c. only turns when MG2 is operating
   d. Both answers a and b are correct

9. The electric motor in the Ford/Lincoln 10R80 MHT transmission provides _____.
   a. stop-start capabilities
   b. extra power
   c. extra low-speed torque
   d. All of the answers are correct

10. The GM parallel hybrid truck features _____.
    a. stop-start capabilities
    b. regenerative braking
    c. full electric mode
    d. Both answers a and b are correct

Chapter 18
EV AND HEV DRIVER ASSIST SYSTEMS

LEARNING OBJECTIVES

After studying this chapter, the reader should be able to:

- Describe the purpose and function of advanced driver assist systems.
- Discuss blind spot monitors and parking assist, as well as self-parking systems.
- Explain lane departure warning and lane keep assist systems.
- Describe how adaptive cruise control systems work.
- Discuss rear cross-traffic warning system operation.
- Explain automatic emergency braking and pre-collision systems.
- Describe the diagnostic and calibrations procedures for advanced driver assist systems.

KEY TERMS

Adaptive cruise control (ACC) 255
Advanced driver assist systems (ADASs) 251
Artificial intelligence (AI) 265
Automatic emergency braking (AEB) 258
Blind spot monitor (BSM) 252
Electromagnetic parking sensors (EPS) 253
Haptic actuator 252
Human–machine interface (HMI) 251
Intelligent Speed Advice (ISA) 257
Lane departure warning system (LDWS) 254
Lane keep assist (LKA) 255
Light Detection and Ranging 260
Parking-assist system 253
Rear cross-traffic warning (RCTW) 257
Self-parking 254
Ultrasonic object sensors 253

ADVANCED DRIVER ASSIST SYSTEMS

FOUNDATION OF DRIVER ASSIST Many of the existing systems on an electric or hybrid electric vehicle are also the foundation of driver assist systems including the following:

- Electronic power steering (EPS) allows the driver to steer the vehicle with ease without need of an engine-driven hydraulic pump. It also allows the driver assist system to steer the vehicle back into the lane if it drifts out of the lane.
- The antilock brake system (ABS) allows the driver to safely navigate slippery roads. It is the part of the emergency brake assist system that stops a vehicle when an obstacle is detected.
- The electronic throttle control (ETC) system allows the driver to accelerate smoothly. It also allows the adaptive cruise control system to maintain the proper following distance when engaged.

PURPOSE The purpose of **advanced driver assist systems (ADASs)** is to provide the driver with systems that help the driver by doing the following:

- Alert the driver of a potential issue, such as getting too close to the center line or too far to the right of the roadway.
- Help the driver maintain proper driving habits, such as maintaining an ensured clear distance from the vehicle in front while at the same time handling the accelerator pedal to maintain a set speed.
- Help the driver avoid a collision if a vehicle in front of the driver stops quickly.
- Make the parking safer through parking assist systems that use ultrasonic sensors to detect when the front or rear bumper is getting close to an object.

CAUTION: The advanced driver assist systems are designed as a driver aid and are not intended to replace the driver. It is the responsibility of the driver to be aware of the surroundings and be able to take control of the vehicle at all times.

HUMAN–MACHINE INTERFACE (HMI)

DEFINITION The **human–machine interface (HMI)** was very basic in the past because the vehicles were equipped with most of the following to let the driver know what the vehicle (the machine) was doing:

- Speedometer
- Fuel level gauge (HV battery charge level)
- Outside air temperature
- Tire pressures
- Instrument panel/dashboard warning icons

METHODS OF COMMUNICATION Vehicles with advanced technology need to communicate to the driver or occupants using the following:

1. Visual displays (eyes)
2. Sounds
3. Tactile (called "haptic" feedback vibrations of the seat or the steering wheel, which are created using a DC motor turning an offset weight to create the vibrations)

The hardware involved includes the following:

1. A display
2. Speakers

? FREQUENTLY ASKED QUESTION

How Do You Reboot the Digital Display?

For most electric vehicles, pull the first responder loop under the hood, then disconnect the negative battery terminal by the fuse box. Wait 5 minutes, reconnect the battery terminal and then the first responder loop.

On the Tesla Model 3, hold down both scroll wheels on the steering wheel until the display reboots. Press and hold both scroll wheels on either side of the steering wheel for up to 10 seconds and the main/central screen will reboot. A soft reboot is performed by holding in both scroll wheels until the touchscreen turns off. A hard reboot is allegedly doing the same thing, but pressing and holding the brake pedal until the Tesla logo appears on the touchscreen. Another variation of a "reboot" is to power off the car from the touchscreen and leave it off for a few minutes (you have to stay in the car).

On a Mustang Mach E, to reboot the SYNC 4 system, push Volume Down button and Forward seek button. Hold them both down at the same time until the screen reboots.

3. Input devices, such as a mouse, joystick, or touch screen
4. Microphone for voice commands

Behind the scenes, software is used to sort out the vast amount of information and reduce it to the levels where the driver can understand and react to situations as needed.

BLIND SPOT MONITOR

FUNCTION AND TERMINOLOGY The **blind spot monitor (BSM)** is a vehicle-based sensor device that detects other vehicles located to the side and rear of the vehicle. Warnings can be any of the following:

Visual—Usually a warning light in one or both of the outside rearview mirrors. ● SEE FIGURE 18-1.

- Audible—Usually a beep or buzzer sound.
- Vibrating (tactile)—A vibration is often created in the steering wheel or the driver's seat called a **haptic actuator**. ● SEE FIGURE 18-2.

The term used varies with vehicle manufacturers and includes the following:

- Acura—Blind Spot Information (BSI)
- Audi—Side Assist
- BMW—Active Blind Spot Detection
- Buick—Side Blind Zone Alert
- Cadillac—Side Blind Zone Alert
- Chevrolet—Side Blind Zone Alert

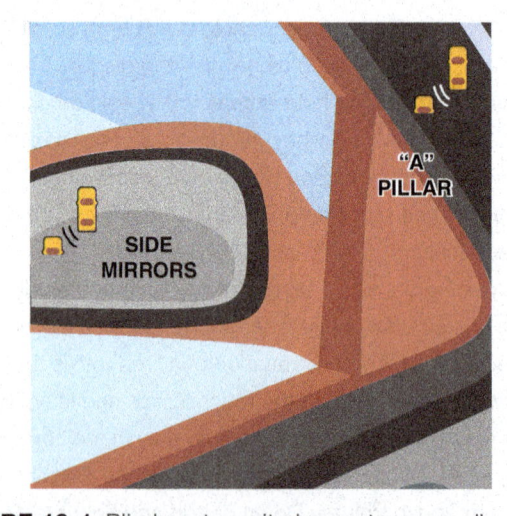

FIGURE 18-1 Blind spot monitoring systems usually use a warning system in the side-view mirror or in the "A" pillar near the side-view mirror to warn the driver that there is a vehicle in the potential blind spot.

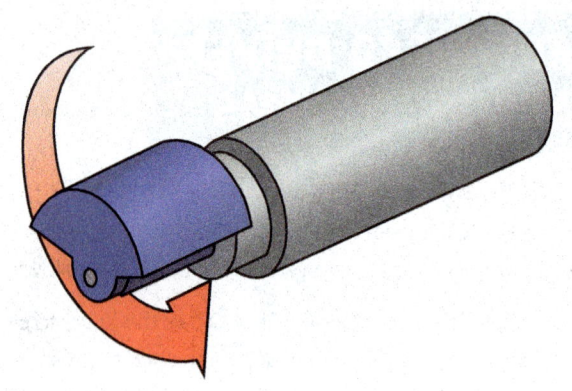

FIGURE 18-2 An actuator that causes the seat or the steering wheel to shake is a called a haptic actuator. The vibration is created by using a DC motor with a weight that is out of balance. When the motor rotates, a vibration is created.

- Dodge—Blind Spot Monitoring
- Fiat—Blind Spot Monitoring
- Ford—Blind Spot Information System (BLIS)
- GMC—Side Blind Zone Alert
- Honda—Lane Watch System
- Hyundai—Blind Spot Detection
- Infiniti—Blind Spot Intervention System
- Jeep—Blind Spot Monitoring
- Land Rover—Blind Spot Monitor
- Lexus—Blind Spot Monitor
- Mazda—Blind Spot Monitoring (BSM)
- Mercedes-Benz—Active Blind Spot Assist
- Mitsubishi—Blind Spot Warning (BSW)
- Nissan—Blind Spot Warning
- Porsche—Lane Change Assist
- Subaru—Blind Spot Detection
- Toyota—Blind Spot Monitor
- Volvo—Blind Spot Information System (BSIS)

PARTS AND OPERATION When the vehicle is first started, the outside mirrors display will come on briefly, indicating that the system is turned on and operating. The typical detection zone includes the following:

- Most systems are designed to detect objects that are as small as a motorcycle with rider.
- The detection zone extends out from the sides and behind the vehicle about 10 feet (3 m).

- It is capable of detecting objects that are about 2 to 6 feet (0.6 to 1.8 m) tall (above the ground).

NOTE: The blind spot monitoring system does not detect objects that are not moving, such as walls, curbs, bridges, or parked vehicles.

If the blind spot monitoring system fails to work as designed, check service information for the specified troubleshooting and repair procedure to follow.

PARKING-ASSIST SYSTEMS

FUNCTION AND COMPONENTS The **parking-assist system** is used to help drivers avoid contact with another object while moving slowly. When backing up at speed of less than 5 MPH (8 km/h), the system constantly monitors for objects located around the vehicle. The parking-assist system can usually detect objects that are greater than 3 inches (8 cm) wide and 10 inches (25 cm) tall, but the system cannot detect objects below the bumper or underneath the vehicle. As the vehicle gets closer to an object, there is an audible beep out of the speakers, and the time between the beeps becomes shorter, the closer to the object. The parking-assist system usually includes the following components:

- **Ultrasonic object sensors** are used to measure the distances to nearby objects and are built into the fender, and front and rear bumper assembly. The sensors send out acoustic pulses, and a control unit measures the return interval of each reflected signal, calculating object distances. ● **SEE FIGURE 18-3**.

- **Electromagnetic parking sensors (EPS)** detect when a vehicle is moving slowly and toward an object. Once detected, the sensor continues to give a signal of presence of the obstacle. If the vehicle continues to move toward the object, the alarm signal becomes more and more impressive as the obstacle approaches. Electromagnetic parking sensors do not require any holes in the bumper and cannot be seen from the outside of the vehicle. A BSM is an option that may include more than monitoring the front, rear, and sides of the vehicle. It can include cross-traffic alert, which can sound an alarm when backing out of a parking space and traffic is approaching from either side.

The system alerts the driver with warning tones with the frequency indicating object distance. The faster the tone sounds, the closer is the vehicle to the object. A continuous tone indicates a minimal predefined distance. Systems may also include visual aids, such as LED or LCD readouts, to indicate object distance. A vehicle may include a vehicle pictogram on the infotainment screen. ● **SEE FIGURE 18-4**.

OPERATION The system is activated automatically when the vehicle is started. The indicator light on the dash or driver information center indicates the system is on. The parking-assist system is active from the time the engine is started until the vehicle exceeds a speed of approximately 6 MPH (10 km/h). It is also active when the vehicle is backing up. The parking-assist system is automatically reactivated the next time the engine is started, even if the system was turned off by the driver the last time the vehicle was driven.

DIAGNOSIS The parking-assist control module can detect faults and store diagnostic trouble codes. If a fault has been detected

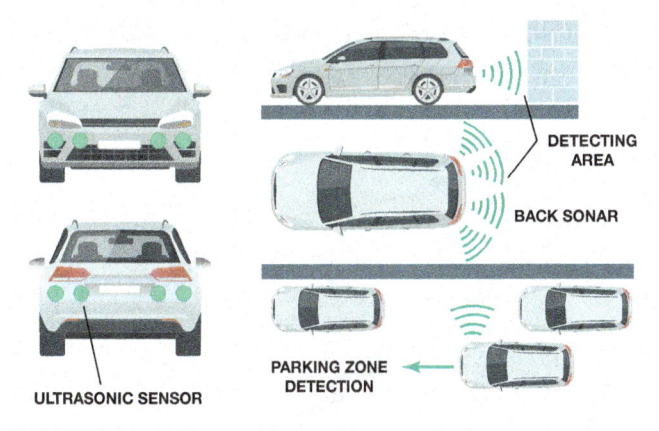

FIGURE 18-3 The small round buttons in the rear bumper are ultrasonic sensors used to sense distance to an object.

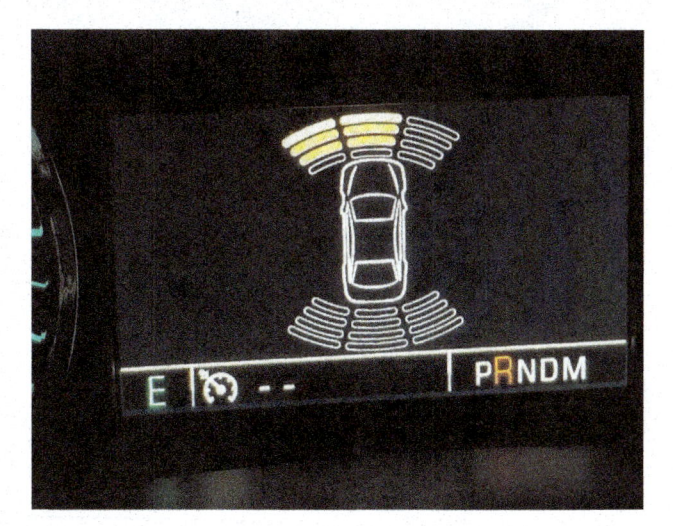

FIGURE 18-4 The dash display on a Chevrolet showing that an object is being detected at the front and left front of the vehicle.

TECH TIP

Check for Repainted Bumpers

The ultrasonic sensors embedded in the bumper are sensitive to paint thickness because the paint covers the sensors. If the system does not seem to be responding to objects, and if the bumper has been repainted, measure the paint thickness using a nonferrous paint thickness gauge. The maximum allowable paint thickness is 6 mils (0.006 inch or 0.15 millimeter).

by the control module, the red lamp flashes and the system is disabled. Follow service information diagnostic procedures because the parking-assist module cannot usually be accessed using a scan tool.

SELF-PARKING Self-parking vehicles, also called *automatic parking vehicles*, use the camera(s) and control the electric power steering to guide the vehicle into a parking space. The driver may or may not have to add anything in many advanced systems, whereas the driver must control the throttle and the brakes in early systems. ● SEE FIGURE 18-5.

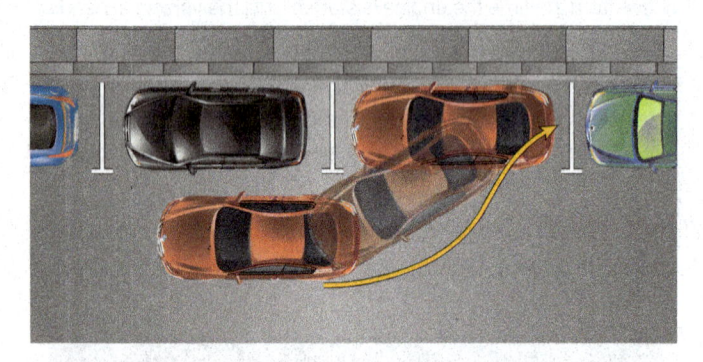

FIGURE 18-5 A self-parking-capable vehicle is able to parallel park or enter into a parking spot with little, or no input from the driver.

LANE DEPARTURE WARNING

PARTS AND OPERATION The **lane departure warning system (LDWS)** uses cameras to detect if the vehicle is crossing over lane marking lines on the pavement. Some systems use two cameras, one mounted on each outside rearview mirror. Some systems use infrared sensors located under the front bumper to monitor the lane markings on the road surface. The system names also vary according to vehicle manufacturers, including the following:

- Honda/Acura: Lane Keep Assist System (LKAS)
- Toyota/Lexus: Lane Monitoring System (LMS)
- General Motors: Lane Departure Warning (LDW)
- Ford: Lane Departure Warning (LDW)
- Nissan/Infiniti: Lane Departure Prevention (LDP) System

If the cameras detect that the vehicle is starting to cross over a lane dividing line, a warning chime sounds or a vibrating mechanism mounted in the driver's seat cushion is triggered on the side where the departure is being detected. This warning does not occur if the turn signal is on in the same direction as detected. ● SEE FIGURE 18-6.

DIAGNOSIS AND SERVICE Before attempting to service or repair an LDWS fault, check service information for an explanation on how the system is supposed to work. If the system is not working as designed, perform a visual inspection of the sensors or cameras, checking for damage from road debris or evidence of body damage, which could affect the sensors. After a visual inspection, follow the vehicle manufacturer's recommended diagnosis procedures to locate and repair the fault in the system.

CAUTION: Do not clean the camera lenses using any harsh cleaning agents. Just clean the lens using a mild soap and water to avoid and prevent possible damage to the camera lens coating.

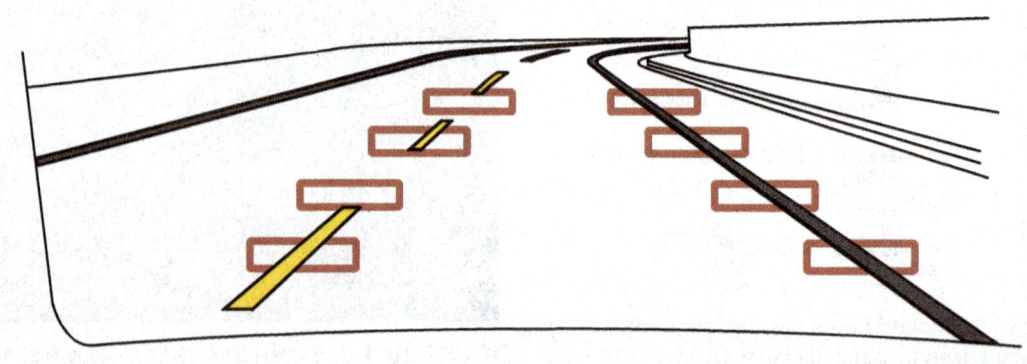

FIGURE 18-6 A lane departure warning system often uses cameras to sense the road lines and warns the driver if the vehicle is not staying within the lane, unless the turn signal is on.

LANE KEEP ASSIST

PURPOSE AND FUNCTION The purpose of **lane keep assist (LKA)**, also called *lane keep assist system (LKAS)*, is not only to warn the driver if the vehicle is moving out of the lane of traffic, but when there is no response from the driver, to also automatically use the electric power steering system to steer the vehicle back into the lane. ● **SEE FIGURE 18-7**.

PARTS AND OPERATION Most lane keep assist systems use a camera mounted in front of the inside rearview mirror with a clear view of the road ahead. A typical LKAS is able to monitor the road about 160 feet (50 m) ahead, and at vehicle speeds above 40 MPH (60 km/h) with the camera observing a 40-degree view ahead of the vehicle. The camera can detect the lane marking, which includes the center line; lane separation lines; and the right-side painted line, often called the fog line; because it helps drivers see the right side of the road under poor or in foggy visibility. When the camera detects that the vehicle is starting to get close to either lane marking, the vehicle performs the following functions:

1. It warns the driver by a warning sound, and/or lights the LKA symbol on the dash. In some vehicles, the warning includes vibrating the steering wheel in an attempt to get the driver's attention.
2. If the warnings do not result in corrective action by the driver, the LKAS uses the electric power steering to steer the vehicle back into the lane between the two lane markings.

ADAPTIVE CRUISE CONTROL

PURPOSE AND FUNCTION **Adaptive cruise control (ACC)**, also called *radar cruise control*, gives the driver more control over the vehicle by keeping an assured clear distance behind the vehicle in front. If the vehicle in front slows, the ACC detects the slowing vehicle and automatically reduces the speed of the vehicle to keep a safe distance. If the vehicle speeds up, the ACC also allows the vehicle to increase to the preset speed. This makes driving in congested areas easier and less tiring.

TERMINOLOGY Depending on the manufacturer, adaptive cruise control is also referred to as the following:

- Adaptive cruise control (Audi, Ford, General Motors, and Hyundai)
- Dynamic cruise control (BMW, Toyota/Lexus)
- Active cruise control (Mini Cooper, BMW)
- Autonomous cruise control (Mercedes)

It uses forward-looking radar to sense the distance to the vehicle in front and maintains an assured clear distance. This type of cruise control system works within the following conditions:

- At speeds from 20 to 100 MPH (30 to 161 km/h).
- Designed to detect objects as far away as 500 feet (150 m).
- The cruise control system is able to sense both distance and relative speed. ● **SEE FIGURE 18-8**.

FIGURE 18-7 Lane keep assist systems not only warn the driver that the vehicle is not staying within the lane of traffic, but will also use the electric power steering to actually move the steering wheel to bring the vehicle back into the lane. This action can startle a driver if the driver has never experienced the vehicle taking control of the steering before.

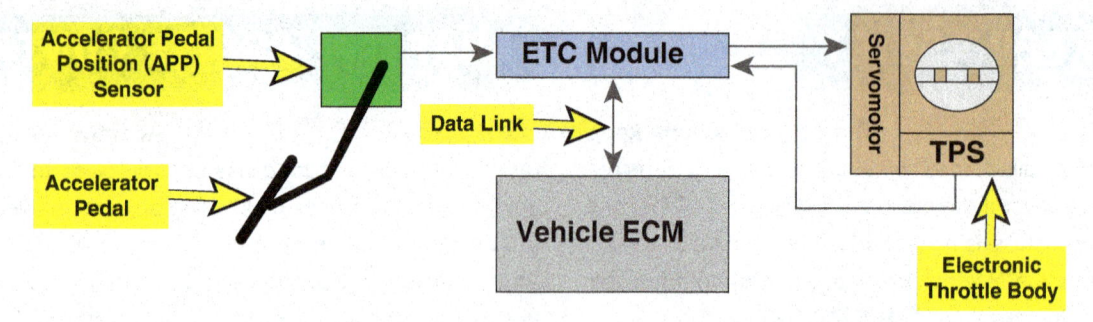

FIGURE 18-8 Adaptive cruise control can use radar to determine the distance of another vehicle in front. The control unit checks the driver's selected speed and sets the distance between the vehicles to determine what action is needed. The PCM then can operate the throttle or the brakes through the antilock brake/electronic stability control system to slow the vehicle, if needed, to maintain the set distance.

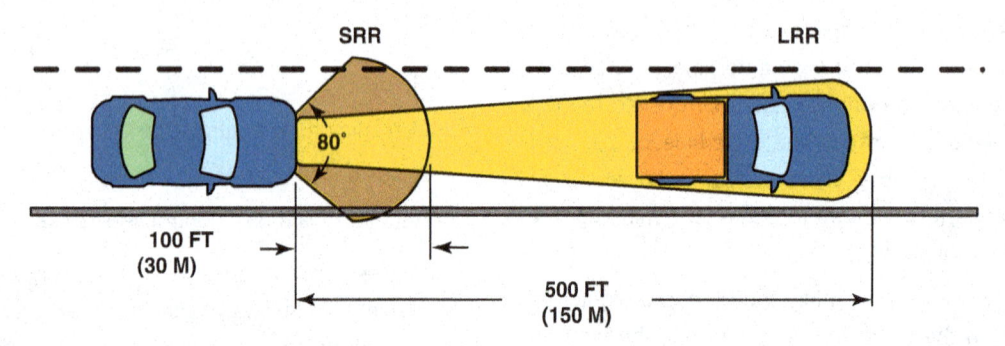

FIGURE 18-9 Most radar cruise control systems use radar, both long and short range. Some systems use optical or infrared cameras to detect objects.

PARTS AND OPERATION Radar cruise control systems use long-range radar (LRR) to detect faraway objects in front of the moving vehicle. Some systems use a short-range radar (SRR) and/or infrared (IR) or optical cameras to detect when the distance between the moving vehicle and another vehicle in front is reduced. ● **SEE FIGURE 18-9**.

The radar frequencies include the following:

- 76 to 77 GHz (long-range radar)
- 24 GHz (short-range radar)

DIAGNOSIS AND SERVICE If the radar cruise control is not working properly, begin by making sure the sensor, which is usually behind the grille on most vehicles, is not covered. The system does not operate if the system is covered by heavy mud, ice, or snow. Additionally, some aftermarket vehicle front covers obstruct the sensor view. If the sensor is replaced, some systems require a realignment using special tools. Always refer to the manufacturer's service information for specific instructions.

Case Study

The Case of the Inoperative Radar Cruise Control

The driver of a Lexus NX 300h hybrid electric vehicle experienced a situation where the radar cruise control stopped working due to ice on the sensor after driving through light snow showers. When the front was checked, it was discovered that ice had accumulated on the front grille. Using an ice scraper brush, the grille was cleaned, restoring the proper operation of the radar cruise control. ● SEE FIGURE 18-10.

Summary:
- **Complaint**—Radar cruise stopped working and a message appeared to clean the sensor.
- **Cause**—Ice buildup on the grille.
- **Correction**—Cleaning the front of the grille, using a brush, restored the proper operation of the radar cruise control.

Frequently Asked Question

What Is Intelligent Speed Advice (ISA)?

Intelligent Speed Advice (ISA) uses a sign recognition camera or a navigation system (GPS) to determine the speed limit, which is used to warn the driver of the posted speed limit. Some ISA systems automatically limit the speed of the vehicle by limiting engine power to prevent the vehicle from accelerating past the current speed limit unless overridden. The European New Car Assessment Program (Euro NCAP) is a European car safety performance assessment program which is awarding vehicle manufacturers if their vehicle is equipped with this system.

FIGURE 18-10 (a) A dash warning message appeared when the cruise control stopped working. (b) The front of a Lexus hybrid shows some ice buildup that was enough to block the radar signals needed for the radar cruise control to work.

REAR CROSS-TRAFFIC WARNING (RCTW)

PURPOSE A **rear cross-traffic warning (RCTW)** system sounds an audible warning when a vehicle is crossing at the rear while backing. Some vehicles are capable of automatically braking to avoid a collision.

PARTS AND OPERATION Rear cross-traffic alert is used to warn the driver when backing from a parking space if there is a vehicle approaching from either side. The system uses radar sensors that are installed on both sides of the vehicle near the rear bumper. These sensors are able to detect vehicles approaching from the left or right side of the vehicle. These sensors activate when the vehicle is placed in reverse and can detect vehicles from up to 65 feet (20 m) on either side. The system is usually designed to function under the following conditions:

- When the vehicle is in reverse and your speed is less than 5 MPH (8 km/h)
- The system is designed to detect other vehicles approaching between 5 and 18 MPH (8 to 29 km/h).

If a vehicle is detected, the system will sound a warning and often flash the side mirror indicators. Rear cross-traffic alert may not work if one of the rear sensors is blocked or during heavy rain or snow.

● SEE FIGURES 18-11 AND 18-12.

EV AND HEV DRIVER ASSIST SYSTEMS   **257**

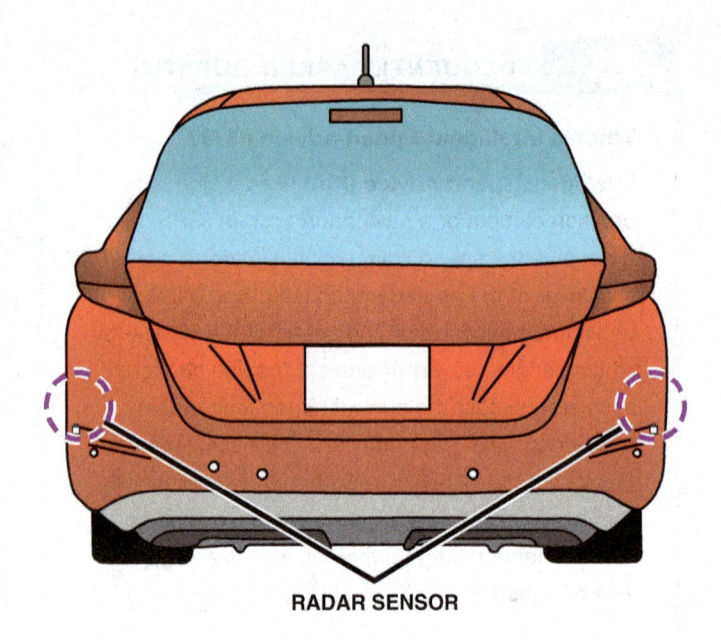

FIGURE 18-11 Rear cross-traffic warning systems use radar sensors at the rear corners of the vehicle, which are able to detect a moving vehicle approaching from the sides.

FIGURE 18-12 If a vehicle is approaching from the side when the gear selector is in reverse, a warning is sounded.

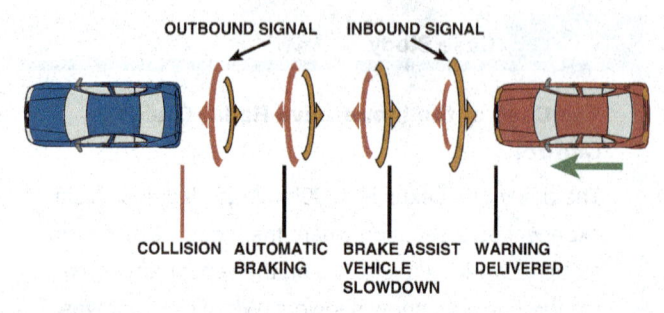

FIGURE 18-13 Sensors are used to detect when the distance is closing fast enough that a collision may be possible, and the system intervenes to automatically apply the brakes if needed.

If the warnings are ignored, the automatic braking system will intervene and either provide brake assist or apply the brakes autonomously (by itself) to achieve maximum braking in an effort to avoid a collision. ● **SEE FIGURE 18-13**.

PRE-COLLISION SYSTEM

PURPOSE The purpose of a pre-collision system is to monitor the road ahead and prepare to avoid a collision, and to protect the driver and passengers. A pre-collision or a collision avoidance system uses the following systems:

1. The long-range and short-range radar or detection systems used by a radar cruise control system to detect objects in front of the vehicle
2. Antilock brake system (ABS)
3. Adaptive (radar) cruise control
4. Brake assist system

TERMINOLOGY Pre-collision systems can be called by various names, depending on the make of the vehicle. Some include the following:

- Ford/Lincoln: Collision Warning with Brake Support
- Honda/Acura: Collision Mitigation Brake System (CMBS)
- Mercedes-Benz: Pre-Safe or Attention Assist
- Toyota/Lexus: Pre-Collision System (PCS) or Advanced Pre-Collision System (APCS)
- General Motors: Pre-Collision System (PCS)
- Volvo: Collision Warning with Brake Support or Collision Warning with Brake Assist Operation

The system functions by monitoring objects in front of the vehicle and can act to avoid a collision by the following actions:

AUTOMATIC EMERGENCY BRAKING

PURPOSE AND FUNCTION An **automatic emergency braking (AEB)** system intervenes and automatically applies the brakes if needed. Automatic braking is often part of a safety package that includes radar cruise control, and will apply the brakes in the event of a possible collision. Sensors such as radar, sonar, and/or cameras are used, depending on the system to detect the distance to another object. The controller, usually an antilock braking system (ABS) controller, then issues a warning if a collision is possible. This warning can include one or more of the following:

1. A buzzer
2. A warning light flashing on the dash
3. A vibration of the driver's seat

- Sounds an alarm
- Flashes a warning lamp
- Applies the brakes and brings the vehicle to a full stop (if needed)

If the driver does not react, the following actions are performed by the vehicle:

1. Applies the brakes in full force to reduce vehicle speed as much as possible.
2. Closes all windows and the sunroof to prevent the occupants from being ejected from the vehicle.
3. Moves the seats to an upright position.
4. Raises the headrest (if electrically powered).
5. Pretensions the seat belts.
6. Airbags and seat belt tensioners function as designed during the collision. ● SEE FIGURE 18-14.

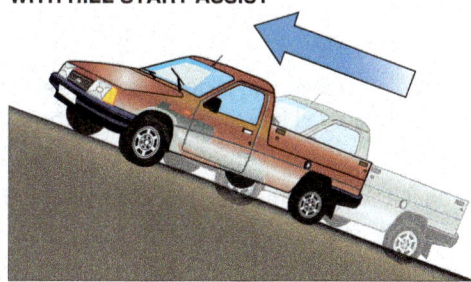

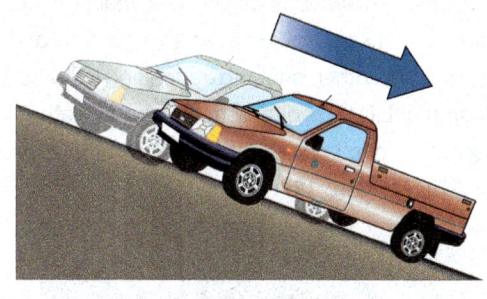

FIGURE 18-14 A pre-collision system is designed to prevent a collision first, and interacts to prepare for a collision, if needed.

CAMERAS

PURPOSE AND FUNCTION Cameras are used to replace the human eye. Cameras are able to recognize objects better than radar. While radar can detect objects, the camera is used to recognize objects.

PARTS AND OPERATION The light that reflects off an object in front of the lens passes through the lens and is collected at a focal

Case Study

The Case of the Tesla Model Y

The owner of a Tesla Model Y was given a bright yellow flyer (standard printer paper size) when registering to attend a car show, and told us to put it on the dash. Almost immediately, the vehicle started acting up. When the accelerator pedal was depressed, the vehicle would keep trying to stop by applying the brakes in short bursts over and over. The only thing that changed was that yellow flyer on the dash. The driver removed the flyer from the dash and the vehicle was able to function normally. It was dark out, and the bright yellow flyer was reflecting onto the front windshield, essentially creating a hologram in the front of the vehicle. This likely caused the front facing camera to see an object in front and the collision warning system was activated.

Summary:
- **Complaint**—When the accelerator pedal was depressed, the vehicle would keep trying to stop by applying the brakes in short bursts.
- **Cause**—A bright yellow flyer was placed on top of the dash which created a refection that fooled the front facing camera.
- **Correction**—The flyer was removed from the dash, which restored proper vehicle operation.

point. The light then passes to a Charge-Coupled Device (CCD). A CCD is a device for the movement of electrical charge, for conversion into a digital value. In a CCD image sensor, pixels are represented by metal-oxide-semiconductors (MOS) capacitors. These capacitors allow the conversion of incoming photons into electron charges at the semiconductor-oxide interface. ● SEE FIGURE 18-15.

The calculation uses the image and vehicle speed to determine how close and rapid it is approaching so the controller can command corrective action. The controller calculates the distance to impact based on the size of the object in the field of view (over multiple frames).

As the object gets closer to impact, the vehicle implements a corrective action. The calculation uses the object's size as it appears in the field of view times the vehicle's speed to determine the time to impact.

DIAGNOSIS The diagnosis of the camera system begins by reading the DTCs. The operation of the camera can be affected by heavy rain, snow, or an accumulation of ice or mud. Before making any repairs, it is important to verify the lens of the camera is free of anything that obstructs its view. Calibration of the

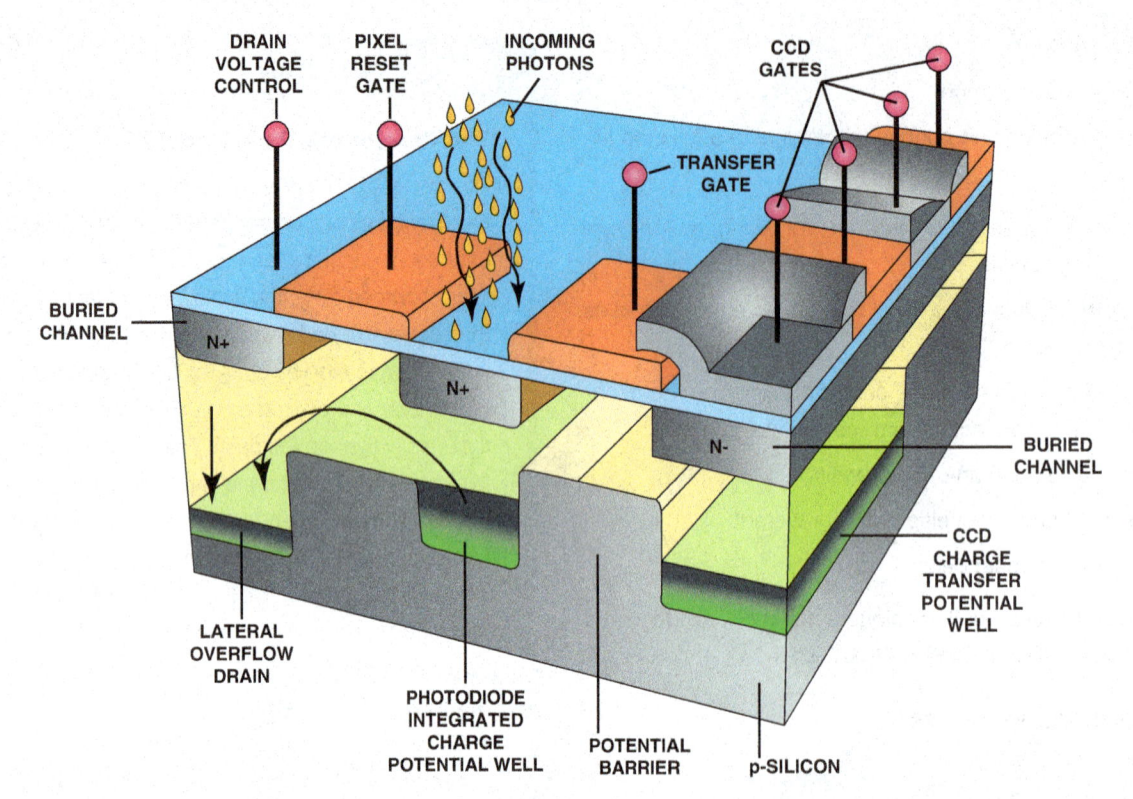

FIGURE 18-15 A charge coupled device (CCD) is an integrated circuit on a silicon surface forming light-sensitive elements called pixels. The light photons generate a charge that can be used by electronics and turned into a digital copy of the image on the device.

camera is required when one or more cameras are replaced or a mounting component, such as a windshield, bumper cover, mirror, or door, is replaced.

LIDAR SYSTEMS

DEFINITION LiDAR means **Light Detection and Ranging** or *Light Imaging, Detection, And Ranging*. LiDAR systems emit light pulses that are reflected off of objects and return for interpretation. LiDAR systems are able to create 3-D images at 300 yards (300 m), which is a lot further than a camera is able to detect objects. LiDAR is used to not only detect an object, but also to recognize an object, like what a camera is able to do. These systems are used to measure the distance, location, and relative speed of nearby objects, and to confirm and validate the data from the other onboard radar and camera sensors. The operation of LiDAR is diminished by bad weather. The light pulses reflect off of rain or snow, making the object difficult to define. ● **SEE FIGURE 18-16**.

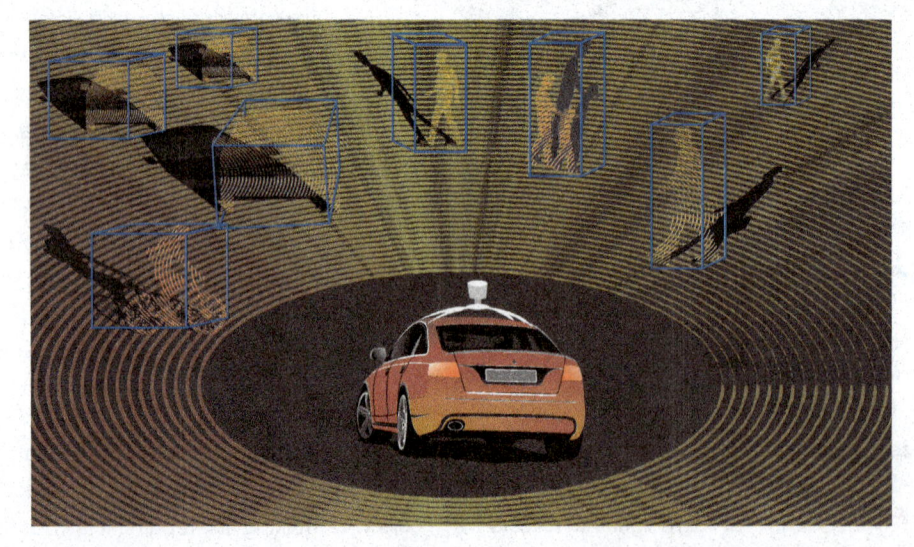

FIGURE 18-16 LiDAR is a detection system that uses light from a laser to create a picture of the surrounding area.

PARTS AND OPERATION LiDAR is usually seen on prototype autonomous vehicles that use a rotating object on the roof so that the laser light from the sensor can view all objects surrounding the vehicle. This type of sensor is very expensive and not practical for most vehicles that have to be driven into garages or car washes. The latest LiDAR system uses solid-state (not moving) sensors that are capable of detecting objects surrounding the vehicle. There are two different wave lengths used in LiDAR systems including 905 nanometers or 1,550 nanometers. A nanometer is a metric unit of length equal to one billionth of a meter (0.000000001 m).

DIAGNOSIS AND CALIBRATION LiDAR systems are capable of self-diagnosis and store a DTC when it determines there is a failure. The trouble code is accessible via a diagnostic scan tool. The calibration of the system is performed in a static manner using targets that are positioned according to the vehicle-specific instructions. A static calibration is used because multiple sensors are calibrated at the same time. Refer to the manufacturer's service information for specific information.

DRIVER ASSIST DIAGNOSIS

VIN DECODER To identify what ADAS a vehicle is equipped with, use the vehicle identification number (VIN), or the regular production order (RPO), for vehicles built by General Motors. There are many online VIN decoders available, including one on the National Highways Traffic Safety Administration (NHTSA) website. Visit https://vpic.nhtsa.dot.gov/decoder/ At this site, enter the VIN and select "decode." The results will show all of the ADAS used on that specified vehicle.

DIAGNOSTIC STEPS Similar to troubleshooting any other system or fault, the steps in the diagnostic procedure include the following:

- **STEP 1** Verify the customer concern. Check the customer concern and determine that it is a true fault, and not a misunderstanding, on how the system is supposed to work.
- **STEP 2** Perform a visual inspection. Check for any physical faults that could affect the operation of the advanced driver assist system, such as road debris and/or minor collision damage.
- **STEP 3** Check for any stored or pending diagnostic trouble codes. Check all modules by performing a full module scan to check for faults in all of the modules.
- **STEP 4** Check service information for the specified procedure to follow to service or repair the verified fault.
- **STEP 5** Perform the specified procedure and static calibrations of the sensors as needed.
- **STEP 6** Perform the specified dynamic calibration of the sensors as needed.
- **STEP 7** Test drive the vehicle under the same operating conditions that were used to verify the fault to verify the repair.
- **STEP 8** Clear all advanced driver assist system-related diagnostic trouble codes (DTCs) and return the vehicle to the customer.

CAMERA AND RADAR SENSOR CALIBRATION

CAMERA CALIBRATION Calibration of the camera is required when one or more cameras are replaced on a mounting component, such as a windshield, bumper cover, mirror, or door. The calibration is an in-shop, static process. Large patterned mats are placed around the vehicle at specific locations and the scan tool is used to initiate the process. ● **SEE FIGURE 18-17**.

TYPICAL PROCEDURE Some camera systems require a specific target so that the camera can be calibrated. Some vehicles that do not require a special target, a factory, or factory-level scan tool imitate the learning process. They will often use lines that are taped to the floor around the vehicle to use as a target. ● **SEE FIGURE 18-18**.

Some systems also require that the vehicle be driven at slow speeds under specific operating conditions to complete the learning. This process is used to do the final accurate calibrations. Refer to service information for specific diagnostic and calibration information for the vehicle being serviced.

RADAR CALIBRATION Calibration of the radar is required anytime the unit is replaced or reinstalled. In many cases, the calibration procedure must be performed anytime a grille or fascia is removed or replaced. The calibration process may be static (in the shop), or dynamic (on the road), or a combination of the two. The static process involves the use of a scan tool and an aiming procedure. The aiming procedure requires manufacturer-specific targets. ● **SEE FIGURES 18-19 AND 18-20**.

Check service information for specific diagnostic and calibration information for the vehicle being serviced.

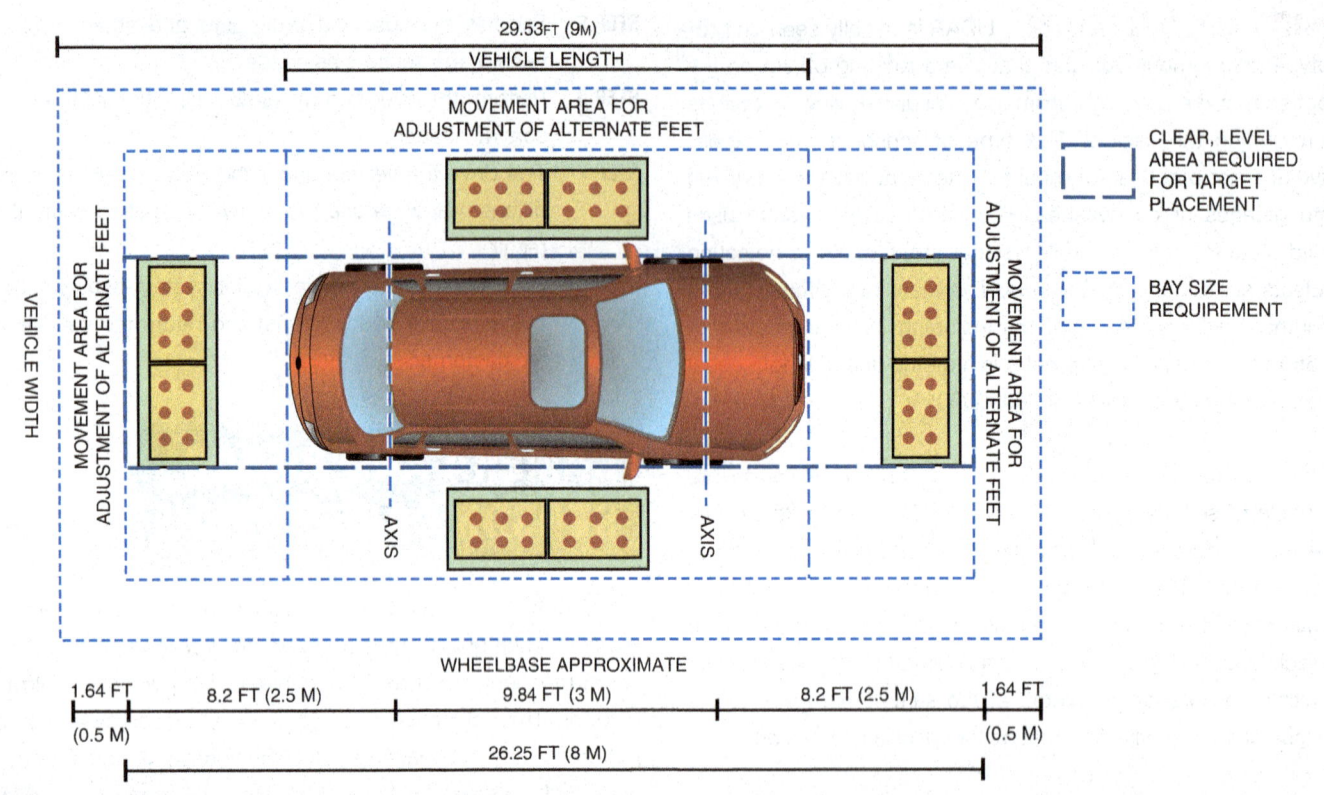

FIGURE 18-17 A typical camera calibration shop requirement to be used to calibrate the cameras on a vehicle equipped with advance driver assist systems. The area around the vehicle must be open and free from objects or windows that could affect the camera calibration.

FIGURE 18-18 A typical target setup required to calibrate the camera on a vehicle equipped with an advanced driver assist system. Always follow the specified calibration procedure for the vehicle being serviced.

FIGURE 18-19 Before the radar sensor can be calibrated, the target must be installed at a very precise location at the front of the vehicle. The measurements involved include finding the exact center of the vehicle often using a special tool as shown.

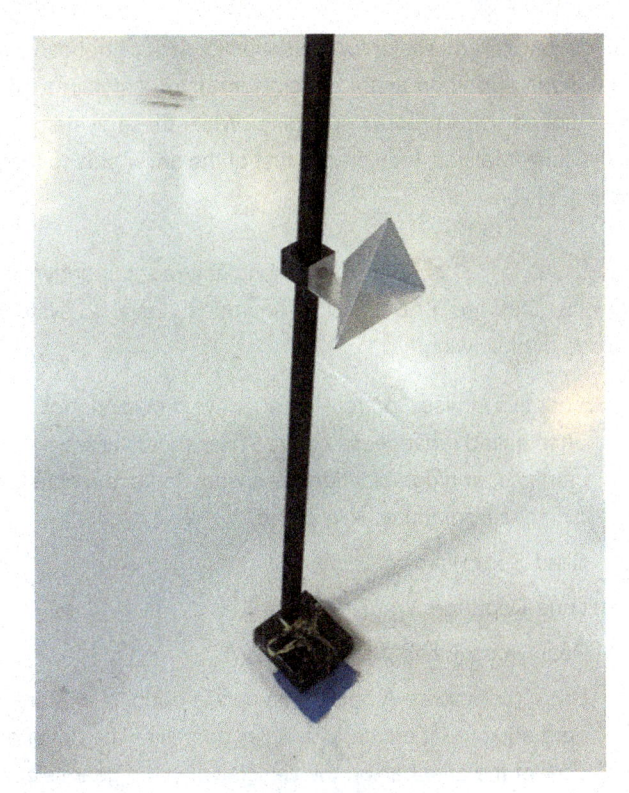

FIGURE 18-20 A typical radar target being placed in the specified position after careful measurements from the centerline of the vehicle and the exact distance from the front and at the specified height.

AUTONOMOUS VEHICLE OPERATION

DEFINITION Automotive Engineers (SAE) defines an autonomous vehicle (AV) as a vehicle that uses an automated driving system that monitors the driving environment and makes navigation decisions without driver input.

HISTORY The autonomous automobile finds its roots in da Vinci's Self-Propelled Cart of the 1500s. Technology used in an aircraft autopilot, and cruise control, provided the basis for early test vehicles. Throughout the 1970s and 1980s, advances were made in camera and computer technology that allowed unmanned vehicles to travel short distances in defined areas at slow speeds. Technology from the MQ-1 Predator aircraft in the 1990s allowed for the first use of radar and thermal imaging in test vehicles. In 2015, Tesla downloaded "Autopilot" software to all Model S vehicles, giving them a first-of-a-kind hands-free driving for highway and freeway driving.

BENEFITS Autonomous vehicles may have major advantages that nonautonomous vehicles do not offer. The vehicle-to-vehicle communications of autonomous vehicles should result in fewer traffic collisions. The precise driving and navigation technology of the vehicle allows for increased roadway capacity and reduced congestion and makes driving easier for people with certain disabilities. Autonomous vehicles can potentially reduce insurance costs and allow for an increase in speed limits and in occupant productivity because of the precise nature of the operating systems.

CONCERNS The transition to autonomous vehicles creates some major concerns, including the following:

- There are concerns about the resistance of drivers of a non-autonomous vehicle to give up control of the vehicle to a computer.
- There are also concerns as to how well the hardware functions are related to cybersecurity and the loss of privacy.
- There are concerns about managing the transitions between automated control to driver control and the assignment of liability when errors occur.
- Possible failure of one or more sensors or operating systems or by weather conditions affecting sensor readings.
- In tests, some passengers in self-driving vehicles suffered from motion sickness.

LEVELS OF AUTOMATION

SAE DEFINITIONS SAE International, who establishes standards for the automotive industry, has created a standard (J3016) that classifies the vehicle capabilities into five levels. SAE J3016 has been formally adopted by the United States Department of Transportation (DOT) as the reference for defining the five levels of automation. ● **SEE CHART 18-1 AND FIGURE 18-21**.

As the vehicle transitions from no automation to partial automation, and then to full automation, numerous systems are needed to complete the tasks that are otherwise completed by the driver. The systems used are determined by the manufacturer and the level of automation desired.

LEVEL 0 SYSTEMS Level 0 systems do not include any assistance to the driver, who is in total and continuous control of the vehicle at all times. However, because most fatal accidents are due to driver errors, the emphasis is on safety systems that take the driver out of the control. Fatal accidents are often due to one or more of the following:

- Distracted driving—This could be due to others in the vehicle talking or behaving in such a manner that distracts the driver. Texting while driving is also a major cause of accidents caused by distracted driving.

SAE LEVEL	VEHICLE CAPABILITIES
Level 0	No automation: The driver is in complete and total control of the vehicle at all times.
Level 1	Driver assistance: The driver is in control of the vehicle but has help with maintaining speed and assured clear distance between vehicles by way of radar cruise control.
Level 2	Partial automaton: The vehicle is capable of maintaining speed and distance between other vehicles and also accelerates, brakes, and turns to follow the road. Requires the driver to have their hands on the wheel.
Level 3	Conditional automation: The vehicle is capable of driving itself under most driving conditions. The driver is free to keep hands off the steering wheel and can look at other things, such as a video, while the vehicle drives itself.
Level 4	High automation: The vehicle is capable of driving itself under most driving conditions, but the driver may need to intervene in case of a situation that the automated system cannot handle.
Level 5	Full automation: The vehicle is able to handle all functions without the need for the driver to intervene under all conditions.

CHART 18-1 The SAE J3016 levels of automated vehicle capabilities.

- Impaired driving—According to the National Highway Traffic Safety Administration (NHTSA), more than 10,000 people die in alcohol-impaired driving crashes each year.

LEVEL 1 SYSTEMS

Level 1 systems use cruise control to help maintain a constant vehicle speed, which makes driving at highway speeds easier for the driver. Cruise control can also be used in suburban areas to help the driver maintain a constant speed to help avoid speeding. While these systems do not reduce fatalities, they are the first of the driver aids to make driving easier.

LEVEL 2 SYSTEMS

Many manufacturers currently offer vehicles that are SAE Level 2 equipped. Level 2 systems include the following:

- Adaptive Cruise Control—An adaptive cruise control, often called *radar cruise control*, uses radar, lasers, cameras, or a combination of sensors, to keep a constant distance from the vehicle ahead.
- Blind-Spot Warning (BSW)
- Lane-Departure Warning
- Rear Cross-Traffic Warning (RCTW)
- Backup Camera—A backup camera is optional or standard equipment on many vehicles and gives the driver a view of the area behind the vehicle when the gear selector is in reverse.
- Forward-Collision Warning (FCW)
- Automatic Emergency Braking (AEB)
- Self-Parking

The driver may or may not have to add any input in many advanced systems, whereas the driver must control the throttle and the brakes in early systems. Many of the Level 2 systems are grouped together and are commonly referred to Advanced Driver Assist system (ADAS). These

LEVEL	NAME	WHO IS DRIVING?	WHO IS MONITORING?	WHO INTERVENES?
0	NO AUTOMATION	driver	driver	driver
1	DRIVER ASSIST	driver + system	driver	driver
2	PARTIAL AUTOMATION	system + driver	driver	driver
3	CONDITIONAL AUTOMATION	system	system	driver
4	HIGH AUTOMATION	system	system	system + driver
5	FULL AUTOMATION	system	system	system

FIGURE 18-21 A graphic example of who is driving and monitoring the conditions, and who can intervene if a situation requires evasive action.

systems are currently standard or optional equipment and their operation and service procedures are available from service information.

LEVELS 3, 4, OR 5 SYSTEMS Autonomous vehicles that are capable of Level 3, 4, or 5 are equipped with radar, LiDAR, and cameras to detect objects surrounding the vehicle. In addition, these vehicles need to be in communication with other vehicles. The other systems need to be able to act and react to traffic and road conditions. If all vehicles were at Level 5 automation, this could result in the following advantages:

- A decrease in accidents and death on the highways.
- Reduced congestion because vehicles can be driven close together, therefore allowing roads to carry more traffic faster.
- Because a driver does not need to get into or out of a vehicle, vehicles can be self-parked close to each other, which frees parking spaces and reduces the need for additional parking, especially in urban areas.

COMPUTER POWER NEEDED Data processing needs to increase exponentially in self-driving Level 5 autonomous vehicles. To interpret and process all this digital information from sensors, onboard vehicle systems, and the cloud to hold all of the data, the vehicle needs to have sufficient computing power. The architecture used in automobile electronics is traditionally made up of individual electronic control units, and these can be improved and enhanced for autonomous driving.

ARTIFICIAL INTELLIGENCE (AI)

The automotive industry is working to develop **artificial intelligence (AI)** systems for the transportation industry, including automated and autonomous driving systems for passenger cars, commercial trucks, and industrial applications. Artificial intelligence is machine learning accomplished through programming and training that allows the computer to react much like a human. It enables vehicles to understand their environment and to process sensor and camera data. It is estimated that these computers are capable of 30 million deep-learning operations per second and require a bandwidth that supports 1 GB per second of data transfer. ● **SEE FIGURE 18-22**.

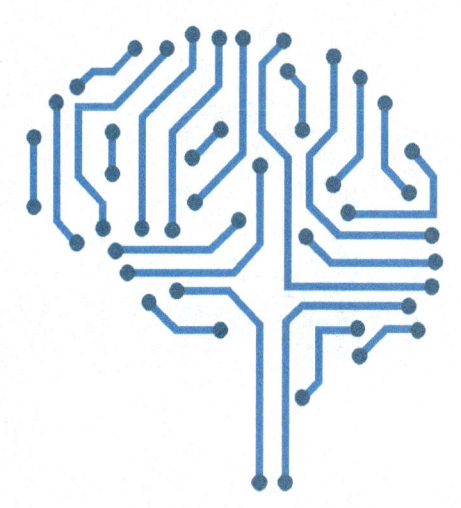

FIGURE 18-22 Artificial intelligence includes the hardware and the software needed to make judgments based on the input from sensors and knowledge of the surrounding environment.

DEDICATED SHORT-RANGE COMMUNICATION (DSRC)

PURPOSE AND FUNCTION Dedicated short-range communication (DSRC) is used for vehicle-to-vehicle communication, as well as the vehicle to the infrastructure. It uses a 5.9 GHz frequency and 75 MHz bandwidth to transmit critical information like speed, location, direction, and traffic. DSRC is an open-source network with low latency, which allows it to transmit messages in milliseconds. The operating range of the system is approximately 1,000 feet (300 meters).

PARTS AND OPERATION DSRC is supported by a network of roadside equipment and onboard equipment mounted in the vehicle that allows for communication to occur safely and without interference from other forms of communication. The transmitters and receivers operate on protocols that are defined by IEEE 802.11p and IEEE 1609 for vehicular communication. ● **SEE FIGURE 18-23**.

DIAGNOSIS AND CALIBRATION Diagnosis of the DSRC systems involves testing hardware, as well as signal strength. The hardware has self-diagnostic capabilities and the ability to store fault codes. This information is accessible with a diagnostic scan tool. Repairs are not made to the hardware; instead, it is replaced. The software is upgradeable by the manufacturer or the service technician. The signal strength is measured with specific equipment designed to measure the frequency of DSRC devices.

FIGURE 18-23 Dedicated short-range communication (DSRC) is used for vehicle-to-vehicle communication to help prevent accidents and makes it safer for everyone.

SUMMARY

1. The advanced driver assist systems are designed as a driver aid and are not intended to replace the driver.
2. The blind spot monitor (BSM) is a vehicle-based sensor device that detects other vehicles located to the side and rear of the vehicle.
3. The parking-assist system is used to help drivers avoid contact with another object while moving slowly.
4. Self-parking vehicles, also called automatic parking vehicles, use the camera(s) and control the electric power steering to guide the vehicle into a parking space.
5. The lane departure warning system (LDWS) uses cameras to detect if the vehicle is crossing over lane marking lines on the pavement.
6. The purpose of lane keep assist (LKA), also called lane keep assist system (LKAS), is not only to warn the driver if the vehicle is moving out of the lane of traffic, but when no response, to also automatically use the electric power steering system to steer the vehicle back into the lane.
7. Adaptive cruise control (ACC), also called radar cruise control, gives the driver more control over the vehicle by keeping an assured clear distance behind the vehicle in front.
8. A rear cross-traffic warning (RCTW) system sounds an audible warning when a vehicle is crossing at the rear while backing. Some vehicles are capable of automatically braking to avoid a collision.
9. An automatic emergency braking (AEB) system intervenes and automatically applies the brakes if needed.
10. The purpose and function of a pre-collision system is to monitor the road ahead, prepare to avoid a collision, and to protect the driver and passengers.
11. To identify what ADAS a vehicle is equipped with, use the vehicle identification number (VIN), or the regular production order (RPO) for vehicles built by General Motors.
12. The ADAS diagnosis includes eight steps to find and correct the root cause of the problem and to be properly calibrate the radar and cameras.

REVIEW QUESTIONS

1. Parking-assist systems use what type of sensor?
2. What is the difference between a lane departure warning and a lane keep assist?
3. What type of sensors are used in automatic emergency braking and pre-collision control systems?
4. What is the purpose and function of advanced driver assist systems?
5. When is the calibration of a camera on an autonomous vehicle required?

CHAPTER QUIZ

1. What is not a function of advanced driver assist systems?
   a. Self-drive capability
   b. Take the load off the driver
   c. Help the driver avoid a collision if a vehicle in front of them stops quickly
   d. Alert the driver of a potential issue

2. Blind spot monitor (BSM) warnings can be _____.
   a. visual
   b. audible
   c. vibrating (tactile)
   d. Any of the above

3. Self-parking vehicles use _____ and control the _____ to control the vehicle into a parking space.
   a. radar; throttle
   b. camera; electric power steering
   c. sonic sensor; brakes
   d. sadar; electric power steering

4. The purpose of lane keep assist (LKA) is _____.
   a. to warn the driver if moving out of a lane
   b. used with adaptive cruise control to self-drive the vehicle without driver input or control
   c. to use the electric power steering to keep the vehicle within the lane
   d. Both a and c

5. Rear cross-traffic alert is used to warn the driver when backing out from a parking space if there is a vehicle approaching from either side. The system uses _____ installed on both sides of the vehicle near the rear bumper.
   a. sonar
   b. ultrasonic
   c. radar
   d. cameras

6. A parking-assist system works to warn the driver if the vehicle is getting close to an object. What type of object *cannot* be detected by most systems?
   a. Objects larger than 3 inches (8 cm) wide
   b. Objects larger than 10 inches (25 cm) high
   c. Objects underneath the vehicle
   d. Any of the above

7. Calibrating radar and cameras involves all of the following *except* _____.
   a. factory or factory-level scan tool
   b. special targets set at precisely specified location around the vehicle
   c. both static and dynamic calibrations are required
   d. driving the vehicle in a circle 10 times to calibrate the cameras

8. LiDAR systems are capable of _____.
   a. creating 3-D images at 300 yards
   b. recognizing an object
   c. measuring distance, location, and speed
   d. All of the above

9. Calibrating radar and cameras involves all of the following *except* _____.
   a. Factory or factory-level scan tool
   b. Special targets set at precisely specified location around the vehicle
   c. Both static (stationary and dynamic (moving) calibration is required
   d. Driving the vehicle in a circle 10 times to calibrate the cameras

10. Dedicated short-range communication (DSRC) systems are capable of _____.
    a. Creating 3-D images at 300 yards
    b. Recognizing an object
    c. Measuring distance, location, and speed
    d. allows it to transmit messages in milliseconds

Chapter 19
FUEL CELLS AND ADVANCED TECHNOLOGIES

LEARNING OBJECTIVES

After studying this chapter the reader should be able to:

- Explain how a fuel cell generates electricity and list advantages and disadvantages of fuel cells.
- List the types of fuel cells and vehicle systems that use them.
- Explain how ultracapacitors and transaxle work in fuel-cell hybrid vehicles.
- Discuss the use of hydraulic pressure as an energy source.
- Describe the HCCI combustion process.
- Discuss alternative electricity sources.

KEY TERMS

Electrolysis 269
Energy carrier 269
Fuel cell 269
Fuel-cell hybrid vehicle (FCHV) 270
Fuel-cell stack 270
Fuel-cell vehicle (FCV) 270
Homogeneous charge compression ignition (HCCI) 279
Low-grade heat 274
Membrane electrode assembly (MEA) 270
Polymer electrolyte fuel cell (PEFC) 270
Proton exchange membrane (PEM) 270
Specific energy 269
Ultracapacitor 277

FUEL-CELL TECHNOLOGY

BACKGROUND A **fuel cell** is an electrochemical device in which the chemical energy of hydrogen and oxygen is converted into electrical energy. The principle of the fuel cell was first discovered in 1639 by Sir William Grove, a Welsh physician. In the 1950s, National Aeronautics and Space Administration (NASA) put this principle to work in building devices for powering space exploration vehicles. Fuel cells are being developed to power homes and vehicles while producing low or zero emissions. ● **SEE FIGURE 19-1**.

PARTS AND OPERATION The chemical reaction in a fuel cell is the opposite of **electrolysis**. Electrolysis is the process in which electrical current is passed through water in order to break it into its components, hydrogen and oxygen. While energy is required to bring about electrolysis, this same energy can be retrieved by allowing hydrogen and oxygen to reunite in a fuel cell. While hydrogen can be used as a fuel, it is *not* an energy source. Instead, hydrogen is only an **energy carrier**, as energy must be expended to generate the hydrogen and store it so it can be used as a fuel.

HYDROGEN-POWERED BATTERY A fuel cell is a hydrogen-powered battery. Hydrogen is an excellent fuel because it has a very high **specific energy** when compared to an equivalent amount of fossil fuel. One kilogram (kg) of hydrogen has three times the energy content as one kilogram of gasoline. Hydrogen is the most common element on earth, but it does not exist by itself in nature. Hydrogen is 14 times lighter than air.

HYDROGEN SOURCES Hydrogen is a low-carbon, nontoxic fuel that is domestically produced from local resources. This is because its natural tendency is to react with oxygen in the atmosphere to form water (H_2O). Hydrogen is also found in many other compounds, such as natural gas or crude oil. In order to store hydrogen for use as a fuel, different processes must be undertaken to separate it from these materials. For example, hydrogen can be produced from water using an electric current to separate the hydrogen from the oxygen using a process called electrolysis. ● **SEE FIGURE 19-2**.

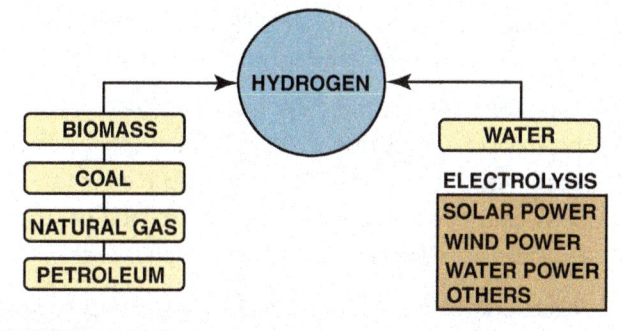

FIGURE 19-2 Hydrogen does not exist by itself in nature. Energy must be expended to separate it from other, more complex materials.

ADVANTAGES OF A FUEL CELL A fuel cell can be used to move a vehicle by generating electricity to power electric drive motors, as well as powering the remainder of the electrical system of the vehicle. Advantages include the following:

- Because they are powered by hydrogen and oxygen, fuel cells by themselves do not generate carbon emissions, such as CO_2. Instead, their only emissions are water vapor and heat, and this makes the fuel cell an ideal candidate for a ZEV (zero-emission vehicle).

- A fuel cell is also much more energy-efficient than a typical internal combustion engine (ICE). While a vehicle powered

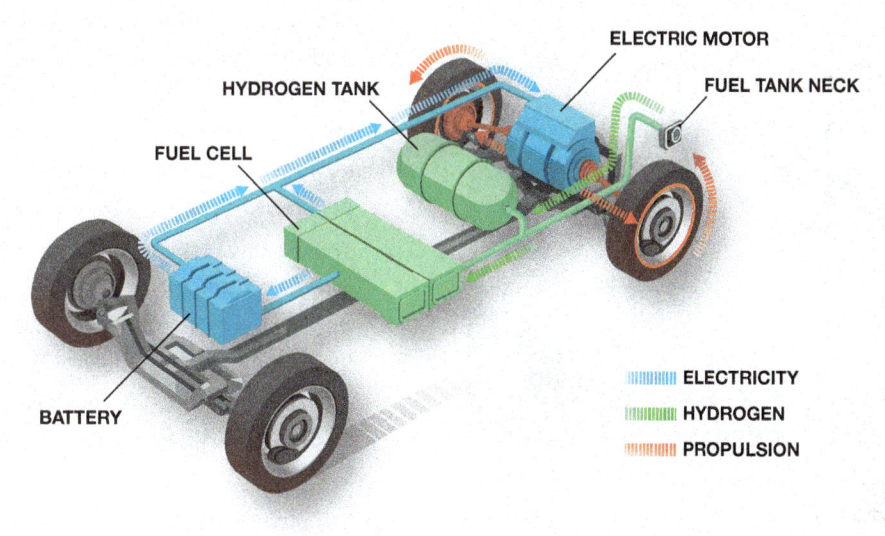

FIGURE 19-1 A fuel cell vehicle uses a fuel cell and a high-voltage battery to provide electrical power to the electric drive motor.

by an ICE is anywhere from 15% to 20% efficient, a fuel-cell vehicle can achieve efficiencies upward of 40%.

- Fuel cells have very few moving parts and have the potential to be very reliable. Vehicle manufacturers have spent many years and millions of dollars in order to develop a low-cost, durable, and compact fuel cell that operates satisfactorily under all driving conditions.

A **fuel-cell vehicle (FCV)** uses the fuel cell as its only source of power, whereas a **fuel-cell hybrid vehicle (FCHV)** also has an electrical storage device that can be used to power the vehicle. Most new designs of fuel-cell vehicles are now based on a hybrid configuration due to the significant increase in efficiency and driveability that can be achieved with this approach. ● **SEE FIGURE 19-3.**

DISADVANTAGES OF FUEL CELLS
While major automobile manufacturers continue to build demonstration vehicles and work on improving fuel-cell system design, no vehicle powered by a fuel cell has been placed into mass production. There are a number of disadvantages of fuel cells, including:

- High cost
- Lack of refueling infrastructure
- Safety perception
- Insufficient vehicle range
- Lack of durability
- Cold weather starting problems
- Insufficient power density

All of these problems are being actively addressed by researchers, and significant improvements are being made. Once cost and performance levels meet that of current vehicles, fuel cells may be adopted as a mainstream technology.

FIGURE 19-3 The Toyota FCHV is based on the Highlander platform and uses much of Toyota Hybrid Synergy Drive (HSD) technology in its design.

FUEL-CELL TYPES
There are a number of different types of fuel cells, and these are differentiated by the type of electrolyte that is used in their design. Some electrolytes operate best at room temperature, whereas others are made to operate at up to 1600°F (871°C).

The fuel-cell design that is best suited for automotive applications is the **Proton Exchange Membrane (PEM)**. A PEM fuel cell must have hydrogen for it to operate, and this may be stored on the vehicle or generated, as needed, from another type of fuel. There are several types of fuel cells, and except for the PEM type, however, most of the others are most suitable for use as power-generating units.

● **SEE CHART 19-1** for a comparison of the types of fuel cells and their most common uses.

PEM FUEL CELL OPERATION
The Proton Exchange Membrane fuel cell is also known as a **Polymer Electrolyte Fuel Cell (PEFC)**. The PEM fuel cell is known for its lightweight and compact design, as well as its ability to operate at ambient temperatures.

This means that a PEM fuel cell can start quickly and produce full power without an extensive warm-up period. The PEM is a simple design based on a membrane that is coated on both sides with a catalyst, such as platinum or palladium.

- There are two electrodes, one located on each side of the membrane. These are responsible for distributing hydrogen and oxygen over the membrane surface, removing waste heat, and providing a path for electrical current flow.
- The part of the PEM fuel cell that contains the membrane, catalyst coatings, and electrodes is known as the **Membrane Electrode Assembly (MEA)**.
- The negative electrode (anode) has hydrogen gas directed to it, while oxygen is sent to the positive electrode (cathode). Hydrogen is sent to the negative electrode as H_2 molecules, which break apart into H ions (protons) in the presence of the catalyst. The electrons (e) from the H atoms are sent through the external circuit, generating electricity that can be used to perform work.
- These same electrons are then sent to the positive electrode, where they rejoin the H ions that have passed through the membrane and have reacted with oxygen in the presence of the catalyst. This creates H_2O and waste heat, which are the only emissions from a PEM fuel cell.
  ● **SEE FIGURE 19-4.**

FUEL-CELL STACKS
A single fuel cell by itself is not particularly useful, as it generates less than 1 volt of electrical potential. It is more common for hundreds of fuel cells to be built together in a **fuel-cell stack**. In this arrangement, the

	FUEL-CELL TYPES			
	PEM (POLYMER ELECTROLYTE MEMBRANE)	**PAFC (PHOSPHORIC ACID FUEL CELL)**	**MCFC (MOLTEN CARBONATE FUEL CELL)**	**SOFC (SOLID OXIDE FUEL CELL)**
Electrolyte	Sulfonic acid in polymer	Orthophosphoric acid	Li and K carbonates	Yttrium-stabilized zirconia
Fuel	Natural gas, hydrogen, methanol	Natural gas, hydrogen	Natural gas, synthetic gas	Natural gas, synthetic gas
Operating Temp. (°F) (°C)	176–212°F 80–100°C	360–410°F 180–210°C	1100–1300°F 600–700°C	1200–3300°F 650–1800°C
Electric Efficiency	30% to 40%	40%	43% to 44%	50% to 60%
Manufacturers	Avista, Ballard, Energy Partners, H-Power, International, Plug Power	ONSI Corp.	Fuel Cell Energy, IHI, Hitachi, Siemens	Honeywell, Siemens-Westinghouse, Ceramic
Applications	Vehicles, portable power units, small stationary power units	Stationary power units	Industrial and institutional power units	Stationary power units, military vehicles

CHART 19-1

Types and details of fuel cells, including those most suitable to stationary power generation rather than for use in a vehicle.

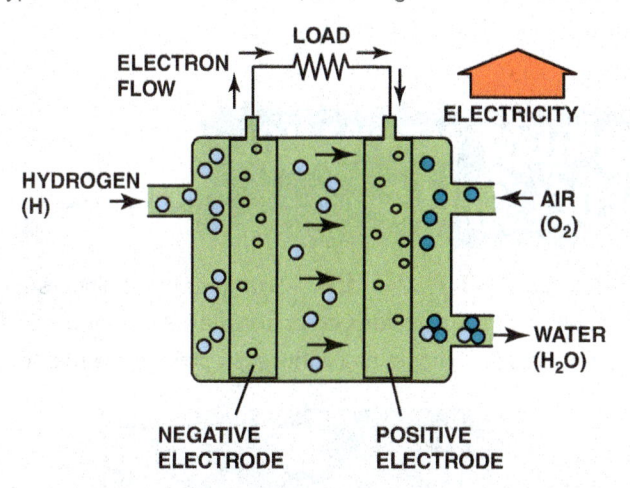

FIGURE 19-4 The polymer electrolyte membrane only allows H^+ ions (protons) to pass through it. This means that electrons must follow the external circuit and pass through the load to perform work.

TECH TIP

CO Poisons the PEM Fuel-Cell Catalyst

Purity of the fuel gas is critical with PEM fuel cells. If more than 10 parts per million (PPM) of carbon monoxide is present in the hydrogen stream being fed to the PEM anode, the catalyst is gradually poisoned and the fuel cell is eventually disabled. This means that the purity must be "five nines" (99.999% pure). This is a major concern in vehicles where hydrogen is generated by reforming hydrocarbons, such as gasoline, because it is difficult to remove all CO from the hydrogen during the reforming process. In these applications, some means of hydrogen purification must be used to prevent CO poisoning of the catalyst.

fuel cells are connected in series so that total voltage of the stack is the sum of the individual cell voltages. The fuel cells are placed end-to-end in the stack, much like slices in a loaf of bread. Automotive fuel-cell stacks contain upward of 400 cells in their construction. ● **SEE FIGURE 19-5**.

The total voltage of the fuel-cell stack is determined by the number of individual cells incorporated into the assembly. The current-producing ability of the stack, however, is dependent on the surface area of the electrodes. Since output of the fuel-cell stack is related to both voltage and current (voltage × current = power), increasing the number of cells or increasing the surface area of the cells increases power output. Some fuel-cell vehicles use more than one stack, depending on power output requirements and space limitations.

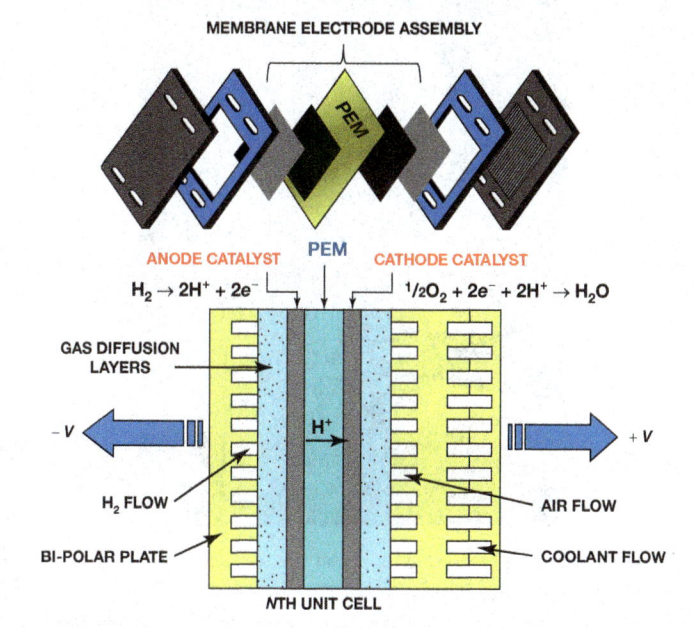

Anode catalyst: $H_2 \rightarrow 2H^+ + 2e^-$
Cathode catalyst: $1/2 O_2 + 2e^- + 2H^+ \rightarrow H_2O$

FIGURE 19-5 A fuel-cell stack is made up of hundreds of individual cells connected in series.

FUEL CELLS AND ADVANCED TECHNOLOGIES

REFUELING WITH HYDROGEN

FUELING PROCEDURE Hydrogen is a compressed gas that is stored aboveground at the station. Most hydrogen stations have fuel delivered by a tanker truck, although some stations make their fuel onsite. Like CNG, hydrogen is normally sold by the kilogram (2.2 lb). Filling a vehicle takes just minutes and, to obtain extended driving ranges in fuel-cell electric vehicles (FCEVs), the hydrogen needs to be filled at high pressures. Filling up with hydrogen is very similar to putting propane in a barbeque tank. Just clamp the nozzle onto the receptacle. When the seal is tight, the dispenser pushes high-pressure, gaseous hydrogen into the tank. When the tank is full, the dispenser stops and then the nozzle can be disconnected. To find a hydrogen station, visit the U.S. Department of Energy website: https://www.afdc.energy.gov/stations/#/find/nearest ● **SEE FIGURE 19-6**.

PRESSURES USED The two most commonly used pressures at hydrogen filling stations include:

- H35 = 35 MPa (5,000 PSI)
- H70 = 70 MPa (10,000 PSI)

The higher the pressure, the more hydrogen can be added to the onboard storage tank(s). The speed of hydrogen fueling is directly related to the amount of cooling that the dispenser allows to offset the heat of compression. The three temperatures that are used to supply hydrogen include the following:

- T40 station H_2 @ −40°C (−40°F)
- T30 station H_2 @ −30°C (−22°F)
- T20 station H_2 @ −20°C (−4°F)

SAE J2601 SAE International-created standard J2601 is the standard for hydrogen-fueling protocol of hydrogen fuel-cell electric vehicles (FCEVs). This standard is used worldwide for hydrogen-fueling stations. The standard J2601 fueling protocol uses a simple control in which the dispenser fuels until the target pressure is reached, based on initial start conditions, giving a consistent hydrogen fueling. Therefore, a H70-T40 (10,000 PSI at −40°F) fueling dispenser enables this fast-fueling by providing hydrogen fuel to the fuel-cell vehicle in usually less than 3 minutes.

DIRECT METHANOL FUEL CELLS

PURPOSE AND FUNCTION High-pressure cylinders are one method of storing hydrogen onboard a vehicle for use in a fuel cell. This is a simple and lightweight storage method, but

FIGURE 19–6 (a) A hydrogen fueling station located at a Shell gasoline station in Los Angeles, CA. (b) The door on the side is opened to show the fill nozzle with shut-off valve. The hydrogen at this station is made on the roof of the dispenser using water and electricity. An electrical current separates the hydrogen from the oxygen in the water, then compresses the hydrogen, which is then sent to a storage tank, also on the roof.

often does not provide sufficient vehicle driving range. Another approach has been to fuel a modified PEM fuel cell with liquid methanol instead of hydrogen gas. ● SEE FIGURE 19-7.

OPERATION Methanol is most often produced from natural gas and has the chemical formula CH_3OH. It has a higher-energy density than gaseous hydrogen because it exists in a liquid state at normal temperatures, and is easier to handle since no compressor or other high-pressure equipment is needed. This means that a fuel-cell vehicle can be refueled with a liquid instead of high-pressure gas, which makes the refueling process simpler and produces a greater vehicle driving range. ● SEE FIGURE 19-8.

DISADVANTAGES Unfortunately, direct methanol fuel cells suffer from a number of problems, not the least of which is the corrosive nature of methanol itself. This means that methanol cannot be stored in existing tanks and, thus, requires a separate infrastructure for handling and storage. Another problem is "fuel crossover," in which methanol makes its way across the membrane assembly and diminishes performance of the cell. Direct methanol fuel cells also require much greater amounts of catalyst in their construction, which leads to higher costs. These challenges are leading researchers to look for alternative electrolyte materials and catalysts to lower cost and improve cell performance.

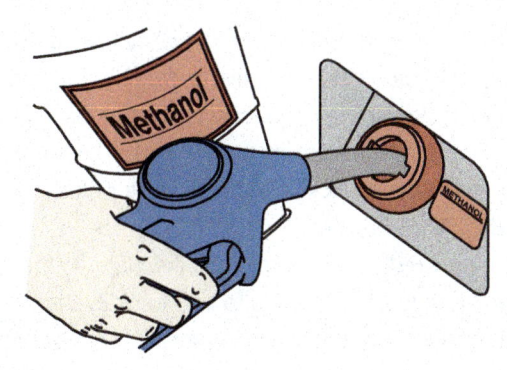

FIGURE 19-8 A direct methanol fuel cell can be refueled similar to a gasoline-powered vehicle.

NOTE: Direct methanol fuel cells are not likely to see service in automotive applications. However, they are well suited for low-power applications, such as cell phones or laptop computers.

FUEL-CELL VEHICLE SYSTEMS

FUEL-CELL HUMIDIFIERS Water management inside a PEM fuel cell is critical. Too much water can prevent oxygen from making contact with the positive electrode; too little water can allow the electrolyte to dry out and lower its conductivity. The amount of water and where it resides in the fuel cell is also critical in determining at how low a temperature the fuel

FREQUENTLY ASKED QUESTION

What Is the Role of the Humidifier in a PEM Fuel Cell?

The polymer electrolyte membrane assembly in a PEM fuel cell acts as a conductor of positive ions and as a gas separator. However, it can perform these functions effectively only if it is kept moist. A fuel-cell vehicle uses an air compressor to supply air to the positive electrodes of each cell, and this air is sometimes sent through a humidifier first to increase its moisture content. The humid air then comes in contact with the membrane assembly and keeps the electrolyte damp and functioning correctly.

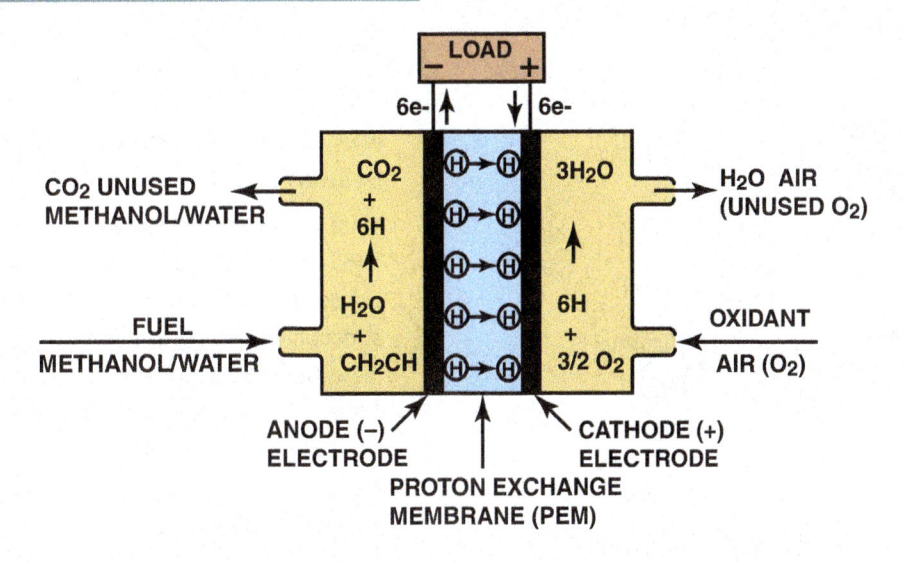

FIGURE 19-7 A direct methanol fuel cell uses a methanol/water solution for fuel instead of hydrogen gas.

cell starts, because water freezing in the fuel cell can prevent it from starting. The role of the humidifier is to achieve a balance where it is providing sufficient moisture to the fuel cell by recycling water that is evaporating at the cathode. The humidifier is located in the air line leading to the cathode of the fuel-cell stack. ● **SEE FIGURE 19-9**.

Some newer PEM designs manage the water in the cells in such a way that there is no need to pre-humidify the incoming reactant gases. This eliminates the need for the humidifier assembly and makes the system simpler overall.

FUEL-CELL COOLING SYSTEMS Heat is generated by the fuel cell during normal operation. Excess heat can lead to a breakdown of the polymer electrolyte membrane, so a liquid cooling system must be utilized to remove waste heat from the fuel-cell stack. One of the major challenges for engineers in this regard is the fact that the heat generated by the fuel cell is classified as **low-grade heat**. This means that there is only a small difference between the temperature of the coolant and that of the ambient air. Heat transfers very slowly under these conditions, so heat exchangers with a much larger surface area must be used. ● **SEE FIGURE 19-10**.

In some cases, heat exchangers may be placed in other areas of the vehicle when available space at the front of the engine compartment is insufficient. In the case of Toyota FCHV, an auxiliary heat exchanger is located underneath the vehicle to increase the cooling system heat-rejection capacity. ● **SEE FIGURE 19-11**.

An electric water pump and a fan drive motor are used to enable operation of the fuel-cell cooling system. These and other support devices use electrical power that is generated by the fuel cell and, therefore, tend to decrease the overall efficiency of the vehicle.

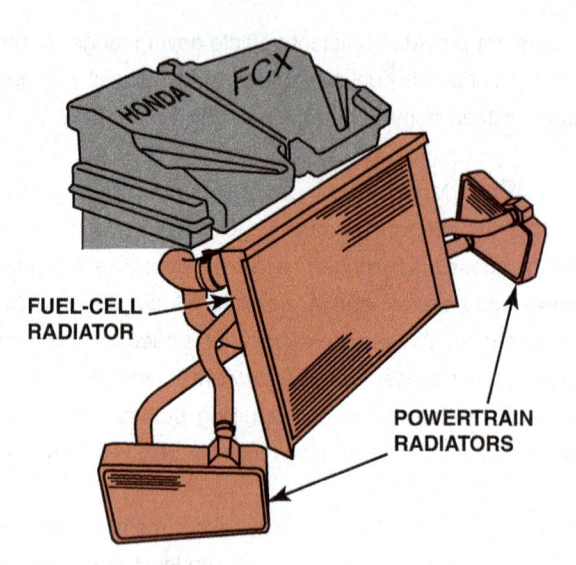

FIGURE 19-10 The Honda FCX uses one large radiator for cooling the fuel cell, and two smaller ones on either side for cooling drivetrain components.

FIGURE 19-11 Space is limited at the front of the Toyota FCHV engine compartment, so an auxiliary heat exchanger is located under the vehicle to help cool the fuel-cell stack.

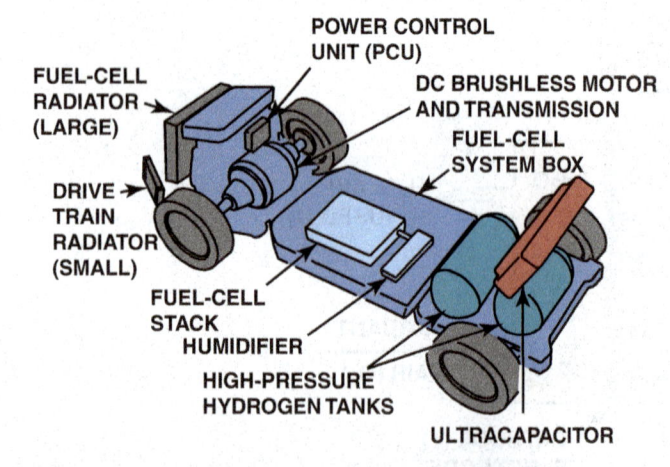

FIGURE 19-9 Powertrain layout in a Honda FCX fuel-cell vehicle. Note the use of a humidifier behind the fuel-cell stack to maintain moisture levels in the membrane electrode assemblies.

> **? FREQUENTLY ASKED QUESTION**
>
> **When Is Methanol Considered to Be a "Carbon-Neutral" Fuel?**
>
> Most of the methanol in the world is produced by reforming natural gas. Natural gas is a hydrocarbon, but does not increase the carbon content of our atmosphere as long as it remains in reservoirs below the surface. However, natural gas that is used as a fuel causes extra carbon to be released into the atmosphere, which is said to contribute to global warming. Natural gas is not a carbon-neutral fuel, and neither is methanol that is made from natural gas.

AIR SUPPLY PUMPS Air must be supplied to the fuel-cell stack at the proper pressure and flow rate to enable proper performance under all driving conditions. This function is performed by an onboard air supply pump that compresses atmospheric air and supplies it to the fuel-cell positive electrode (cathode). This pump is often driven by a high-voltage electric drive motor.

FUEL-CELL HYBRID VEHICLES

PURPOSE AND FUNCTION Hybridization tends to increase efficiency in vehicles with conventional drivetrains, as energy that was once lost during braking, and otherwise normal operation is instead stored for later use in a high-voltage battery. This same advantage can be gained by applying the hybrid design concept to fuel-cell vehicles. Whereas the fuel cell is the only power source in a fuel-cell vehicle, the fuel-cell hybrid vehicle relies on both the fuel cell and an electrical storage device for motive power. Driveability is also enhanced with this design, as the electrical storage device is able to supply energy immediately to the drive motors and overcome any "throttle lag" on the part of the fuel cell.

SECONDARY BATTERIES All hybrid vehicle designs require a means of storing electrical energy that is generated during regenerative braking and other applications. In most FCHV designs, a high-voltage nickel-metal hydride (NiMH) battery pack is used as a secondary battery. This is most often located near the back of the vehicle, either under or behind the rear passenger seat. ● **SEE FIGURE 19-12**.

The secondary battery is built similar to a fuel-cell stack, because it is made up of many low-voltage cells connected in series to build a high-voltage battery.

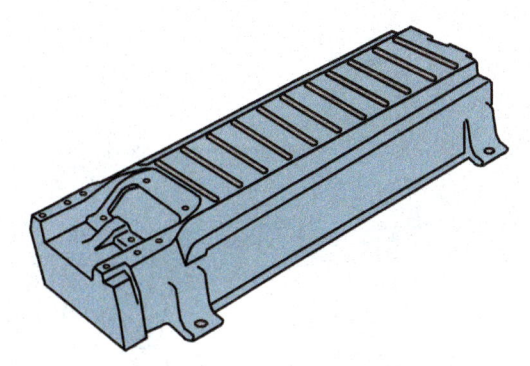

FIGURE 19-12 The secondary battery in a fuel-cell hybrid vehicle is made up of many individual cells connected in series, much like a fuel-cell stack.

HYDROGEN STORAGE

PURPOSE AND FUNCTION One of the issues with fuel-cell hybrid vehicles is how to store sufficient hydrogen onboard to allow for reasonable vehicle range. Modern drivers have grown accustomed to having a minimum of 300 miles between refueling stops, a goal that is extremely difficult to achieve when fueling the vehicle with hydrogen. Hydrogen has very high energy content on a pound-for-pound basis, but its energy density is less than that of conventional liquid fuels. This is because gaseous hydrogen, even at high pressure, has a very low physical density (mass per unit volume). ● **SEE FIGURE 19-13**.

A number of methods of hydrogen storage are being considered for use in fuel-cell hybrid vehicles. These include high-pressure compressed gas, liquefied hydrogen, and solid storage in metal hydrides. Efficient hydrogen storage is one of the technical issues that must be solved in order for fuel cells to be adopted for vehicle applications. Much research is being conducted to solve the issue of onboard hydrogen storage.

HIGH-PRESSURE COMPRESSED GAS Most current fuel-cell hybrid vehicles use compressed hydrogen that is stored in tanks as a high-pressure gas. This approach is the

FIGURE 19-13 A photo showing the hydrogen storage tanks underneath a Toyota Mirai fuel-cell vehicle. This vehicle uses two carbon-fiber-reinforced fuel tanks.

FUEL CELLS AND ADVANCED TECHNOLOGIES

least complex of all the storage possibilities, but also has the least energy density. Multiple small storage tanks are often used rather than one large tank in order to fit them into unused areas of the vehicle. One drawback with this approach is that only cylinders can be used to store gases at the required pressures. This creates a good deal of unused space around the outside of the cylinders and leads to further reductions in hydrogen storage capacity. It is common for a pressure of 5,000 PSI (350 bar) to be used. ● SEE FIGURE 19-14.

Many newer systems use pressures as high as 10,000 PSI (700 bar) to increase the range of the fuel cell-powered vehicle. The tanks used for compressed hydrogen storage are typically made with an aluminum liner wrapped in several layers of carbon fiber and an external coating of fiberglass. In order to refuel the compressed hydrogen storage tanks, a special high-pressure fitting is installed in place of the filler neck used for conventional vehicles. ● SEE FIGURE 19-15.

There is also a special electrical connector that is used to enable communication between the vehicle and the filling station during the refueling process. ● SEE FIGURE 19-16.

The filling station utilizes a special coupler to connect to the vehicle high-pressure refueling fitting. The coupler is placed on the vehicle fitting, and a lever on the coupler is rotated to seal and lock it into place.

LIQUID HYDROGEN Hydrogen can be liquefied in an effort to increase its energy density, but this requires that it be stored in cryogenic tanks at −423°F (−253°C). This increases vehicle range, but impacts overall efficiency, as a great deal of energy is required to liquefy the hydrogen, and a certain amount of the liquid hydrogen "boils off" while in storage.

One liter of liquid hydrogen has only one-fourth the energy content of 1 liter of gasoline. ● SEE FIGURE 19-17.

FIGURE 19-14 The Toyota FCHV uses high-pressure storage tanks that are rated at 350 bar. This is the equivalent of 5,000 pounds per square inch.

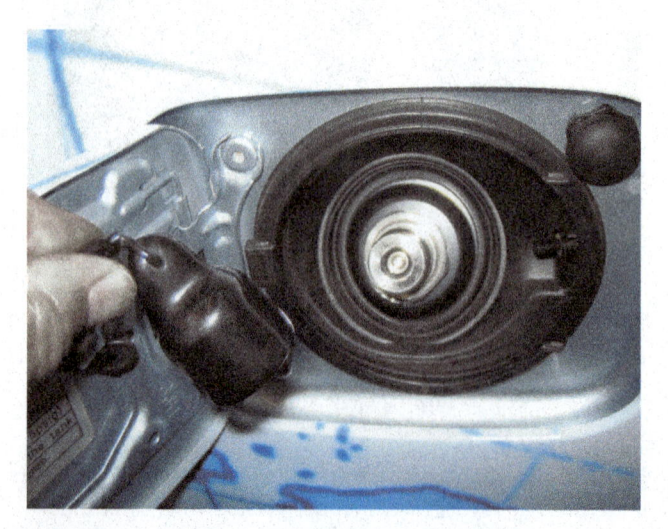

FIGURE 19-15 The high-pressure fitting used to refuel a fuel-cell hybrid vehicle.

FIGURE 19-16 Note that high-pressure hydrogen storage tanks must be replaced in 2031.

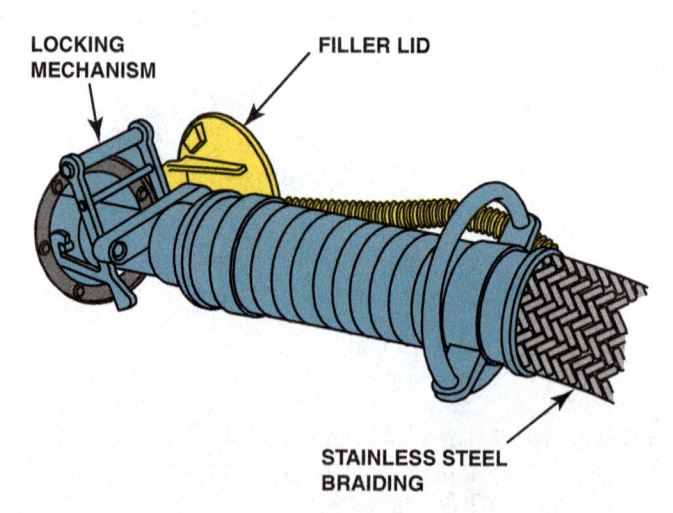

FIGURE 19-17 Refueling a vehicle with liquid hydrogen.

SOLID STORAGE OF HYDROGEN
One method discovered to store hydrogen in solid form is as a metal hydride, similar to how a NiMH battery works.

A demonstration vehicle features a lightweight fiber-wrapped storage tank under the body that stores about 6.6 pounds (3.3 kg) of hydrogen as a metal hydride at low pressure. The vehicle can travel almost 200 miles with this amount of fuel.

- One kilogram of hydrogen is equal to 1 gallon of gasoline.
- Three gallons of water generates 1 kilogram of hydrogen.

A metal hydride is formed when gaseous hydrogen molecules disassociate into individual hydrogen atoms and bond with the metal atoms in the storage tank. This process uses powdered metallic alloys capable of rapidly absorbing hydrogen to make this occur.

ULTRACAPACITORS

PURPOSE AND FUNCTION
An alternative to storing electrical energy in batteries is to use ultracapacitors. A capacitor is best known as an electrical device that blocks DC, but allows AC to pass. However, a capacitor can also be used to store electrical energy, and it is able to do this without a chemical reaction. Instead, a capacitor stores electrical energy using the principle of electrostatic attraction between positive and negative charges.

PARTS AND OPERATION
Ultracapacitors are built very different from conventional capacitors. **Ultracapacitor** cells are based on double-layer technology, in which two activated carbon electrodes are immersed in an organic electrolyte. The electrodes have a very large surface area and are separated by a membrane that allows ions to migrate, but prevents the electrodes from touching. ● SEE FIGURE 19-18.

Charging and discharging occurs as ions move within the electrolyte, but no chemical reaction takes place. Ultracapacitors can charge and discharge quickly and efficiently, making them especially suited for electric-assist applications in fuel-cell hybrid vehicles.

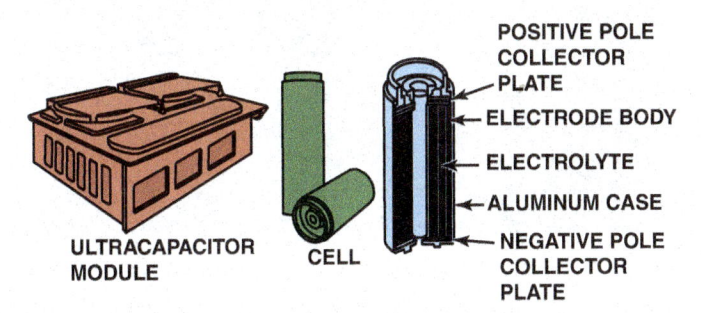

FIGURE 19-18 The Honda ultracapacitor module and construction of the individual cells.

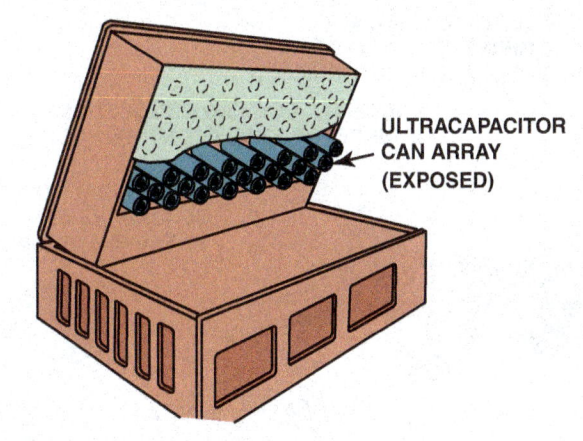

FIGURE 19-19 An ultracapacitor can be used in place of a high-voltage battery in a hybrid electric vehicle. This example is from the Honda FCX fuel-cell hybrid vehicle.

Ultracapacitors that are used in fuel-cell hybrid vehicles are made up of multiple cylindrical cells connected in parallel.
● SEE FIGURE 19-19.

This results in the total capacitance being the sum of the values of each individual cell. For example, ten 1.0-farad capacitors connected in parallel have a total capacitance of 10.0 farads. Greater capacitance means greater electrical storage ability, and this contributes to greater assist for the electric motors in a fuel-cell hybrid vehicle.

ADVANTAGES
Ultracapacitors have excellent cycle life, meaning that they can be fully charged and discharged many times without degrading their performance. They are also able to operate over a wide temperature range and are not affected by low temperatures to the same degree as many battery technologies.

DISADVANTAGES
The one major downside of ultracapacitors is a lack of specific energy, which means that they are best suited for sudden bursts of energy, as opposed to prolonged discharge cycles. Research is being conducted to improve this and other aspects of ultracapacitor performance.

FUEL-CELL VEHICLE TRANSAXLES

PURPOSE AND FUNCTION
Some fuel-cell hybrid vehicles use a single electric drive motor and a transaxle to direct power to the vehicle. It is also possible to use wheel motors to drive individual wheels. While this approach adds a significant amount of unsprung weight to the chassis, it allows for greater control of the torque being applied to each individual wheel.
● SEE FIGURE 19-20.

FUEL CELLS AND ADVANCED TECHNOLOGIES

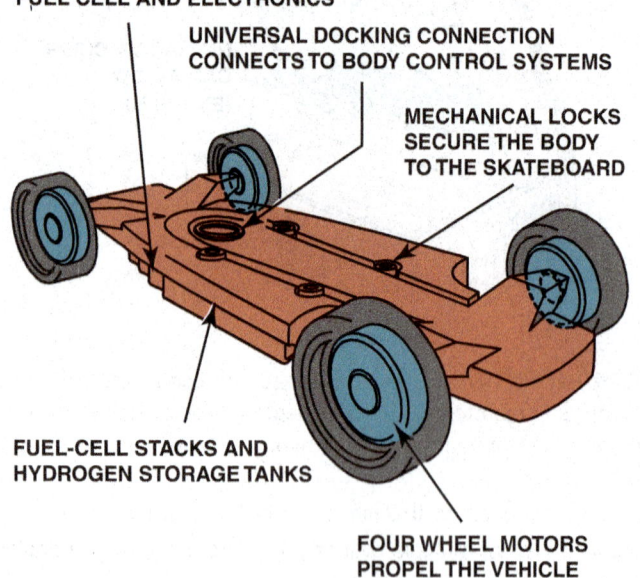

FIGURE 19-20 The General Motors "Skateboard" concept uses a fuel-cell propulsion system with wheel motors at all four corners.

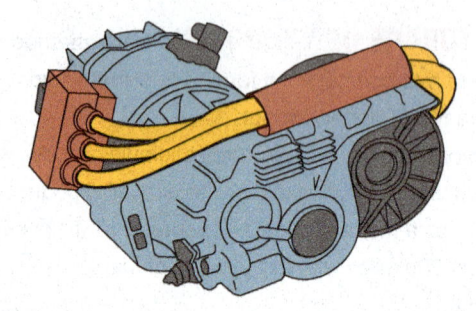

FIGURE 19-21 The electric drive motor and transaxle assembly from a Toyota FCHV. Note the three orange cables, indicating that this motor is powered by high-voltage three-phase alternating current.

Aside from the hydrogen-fueling system, fuel-cell hybrid vehicles are effectively pure electric vehicles in that their drivetrain is electrically driven. Electric motors work very well for automotive applications because they produce high torque at low RPMs and are able to maintain a consistent power output throughout their entire RPM range. This is in contrast to vehicles powered by ICEs, which produce very little torque at low RPMs and have a narrow range where significant horsepower is produced.

ICE-powered vehicles require complex transmissions with multiple speed ranges in order to accelerate the vehicle quickly and maximize the efficiency of the ICE. Fuel-cell hybrid vehicles use electric drive motors that require only a simple reduction in their final drive and a differential to send power to the drive wheels. No gear shifting is required and mechanisms, such as torque converters and clutches, are done away with completely. A reverse gear is not required either, as the electric drive motor is simply powered in the opposite direction. The transaxles used in fuel-cell hybrid vehicles are extremely simple with few moving parts, making them extremely durable, quiet, and reliable. ● SEE FIGURE 19-21.

FUEL-CELL TRACTION MOTORS

Much of the technology behind the electric drive motors being used in fuel-cell vehicles was developed during the early days of the California ZEV mandate. This was a period when battery-powered electric vehicles were being built by the major vehicle manufacturers in an effort to meet a legislated quota in the state of California. The ZEV mandate rules were eventually relaxed to allow other types of vehicles to be substituted for credit, but the technology that had been developed for pure electric vehicles was now put to work in these other vehicle designs.

The electric traction motors used in fuel-cell hybrid vehicles are very similar to those being used in current hybrid electric vehicles. The typical drive motor is based on an AC synchronous design, which is sometimes referred to as a DC brushless motor. This design is very reliable, as it does not use a commutator or brushes, but instead has a three-phase stator and a permanent magnet rotor. ● SEE FIGURE 19-22.

An electronic controller (inverter) is used to generate the three-phase high-voltage AC required by the motor. While the motor itself is very simple, the electronics required to power and control it are complex.

Some fuel-cell hybrid vehicles use a single electric drive motor and a transaxle to direct power to the vehicle. It is also possible to use wheel motors to drive individual wheels. While

FIGURE 19-22 Drive motors in fuel-cell hybrid vehicles often use stator assemblies similar to ones found in Toyota hybrid electric vehicles. The rotor turns inside the stator and has permanent magnets on its outer circumference.

this approach adds a significant amount of unsprung weight to the chassis, it allows for greater control of the torque being applied to each individual wheel.

FUEL-CELL POWER CONTROL UNITS
The drivetrain of a fuel-cell hybrid vehicle is controlled by a power control unit (PCU), which controls fuel-cell output and directs the flow of electricity between the various components. One of the functions of the PCU is to act as an inverter, which changes direct current from the fuel-cell stack into three-phase alternating current for use in the vehicle drive motor(s). ● SEE FIGURE 19-23.

Power to and from the secondary battery is directed through the power control unit, which is also responsible for

- Maintaining the state of charge of the battery pack and
- Controlling and directing the output of the fuel-cell stack.
  ● SEE FIGURE 19-24.

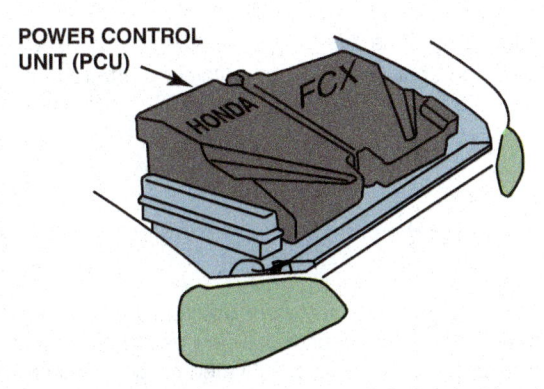

FIGURE 19-23 The power control unit (PCU) on a Honda FCX fuel-cell hybrid vehicle is located under the hood.

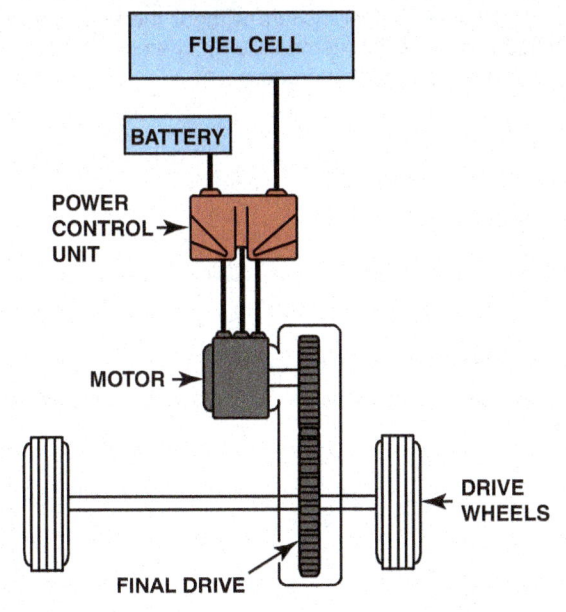

FIGURE 19-24 Toyota's FCHV uses a power control unit that directs electrical energy flow between the fuel cell, battery, and drive motor.

During regenerative braking, the electric drive motor acts as a generator and converts kinetic (moving) energy of the vehicle into electricity for recharging the high-voltage battery pack. The PCU must take the three-phase power from the motor (generator) and convert (or rectify) this into DC voltage to be sent to the battery. DC power from the fuel cell is also processed through the PCU for recharging the battery pack.

A DC-to-DC converter is used in hybrid electric vehicles for converting the high voltage from the secondary battery pack into the 12 volts required for the remainder of the vehicle electrical system. Depending on the vehicle, 42 volts may also be required to operate accessories, such as the electric-assist power steering. In fuel-cell hybrid vehicles, the DC-to-DC converter function may be built into the PCU, giving it full responsibility for power distribution.

HCCI

TERMINOLOGY
Homogeneous Charge Compression Ignition (HCCI) is a combustion process. HCCI is the combustion of a very lean gasoline air–fuel mixture without the use of a spark ignition. It is a low-temperature, chemically controlled (flameless) combustion process. ● SEE FIGURE 19-25.

HCCI combustion is difficult to control and extremely sensitive to changes in temperature, pressure, and fuel type. While the challenges of HCCI are difficult, the advantages include having a gasoline engine being able to deliver 80% of diesel efficiency (a 20% increase in fuel economy) for 50% of the cost. A diesel engine using HCCI can deliver gasoline-like emissions. Spark and injection timing are no longer a factor, as they are in a conventional port-fuel injection system.

FUTURE OF HCCI
While much research and development needs to be performed using this combustion process, it has been shown to give excellent performance from idle to mid-load, and from ambient to warm operating temperatures, as well as cold start and run capability. Because the engine operates only in HCCI mode at light throttle settings, such as during cruise conditions at highway speeds, engineers need to improve the transition in and out of the HCCI mode. Work is also being done on piston and combustion chamber shape to reduce combustion noise and vibration that is created during operation in the HCCI operating mode.

Ongoing research is focusing on improving fuel economy under real-world operating conditions, as well as controlling costs.

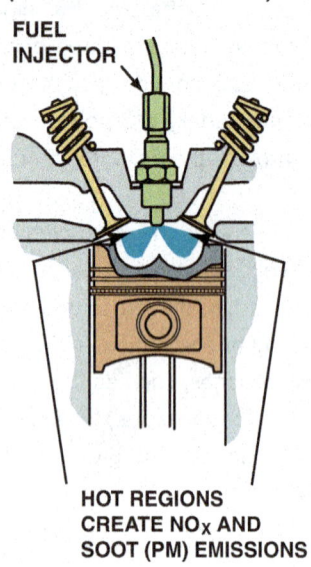

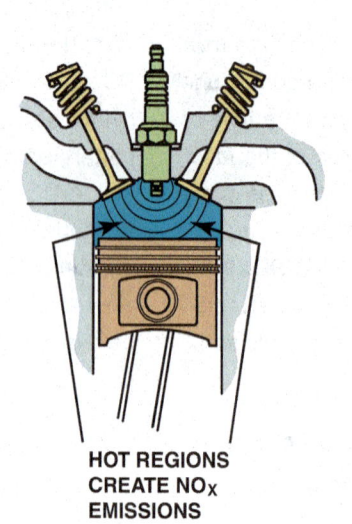

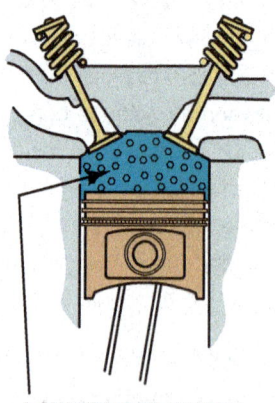

FIGURE 19-25 Both diesel and conventional gasoline engines create exhaust emissions due to high peak temperatures created in the combustion chamber. The lower combustion temperatures during HCCI operation result in high efficiency with reduced emissions.

SUMMARY

1. Fuel cell is an electrochemical device in which the chemical energy of hydrogen and oxygen is converted into electrical energy.
2. A fuel-cell vehicle (FCV) uses the fuel cell as its only source of power, whereas a fuel-cell hybrid vehicle (FCHV) also has an electrical storage device that can be used to power the vehicle.
3. The higher the pressure, the more hydrogen can be added to the onboard storage tank(s). The speed of hydrogen fueling is directly related to the amount of cooling that the dispenser allows to offset the heat of compression.
4. Ultracapacitors are built very different from conventional capacitors. Ultracapacitor cells are based on double-layer technology, in which two activated carbon electrodes are immersed in an organic electrolyte.
5. Homogeneous Charge Compression Ignition (HCCI) is a combustion process. HCCI is the combustion of a very lean gasoline air–fuel mixture without the use of a spark ignition. It is a low-temperature, chemically controlled (flameless) combustion process.

REVIEW QUESTIONS

1. How does a fuel cell work?
2. What are the advantages and disadvantages of fuel cells?
3. How is hydrogen produced?
4. How does an ultracapacitor work?
5. What are the advantages and disadvantages of using hydrogen?

CHAPTER QUIZ

1. A fuel cell produces electricity from _____.
   a. gasoline/oxygen
   b. nitrogen/hydrogen
   c. hydrogen/oxygen
   d. water/oxygen

2. What are the by-products (emissions) from a fuel cell?
   a. water vapor
   b. CO
   c. CO_2
   d. Nonmethane hydrocarbon

3. Which type of fuel cell is the most likely to be used to power vehicles?
   a. PAFC
   b. MCFC
   c. PEM
   d. SOFC

4. Which liquid fuel could be used to directly power a fuel cell?
   a. Methanol
   b. Biodiesel
   c. Ethanol
   d. Unleaded gasoline

5. Which is not a function of an ultracapacitor?
   a. Can pass AC
   b. Can be charged with DC
   c. Discharges DC
   d. Can pass DC

6. The commonly used pressures at hydrogen filling stations include_____
   a. H35
   b. H70
   c. H93
   d. Either a or b

7. Hydrogen storage tanks are usually constructed from _____.
   a. steel
   b. aluminum
   c. carbon fiber
   d. Both b and c

8. HCCI is a process that eliminates what parts or components in a gasoline engine?
   a. Fuel tank
   b. Battery
   c. Fuel injectors
   d. Ignition system

9. Hydrogen can be produced from _____
   a. water
   b. natural gas
   c. crude oil
   d. Any of the above

10. What does H70-T40 mean when describing a hydrogen filling station?
    a. The type of hydrogen
    b. The temperature and pressure rating
    c. The size of the storage tank
    d. The estimated time needed to fill the tank

Chapter 20
FIRST RESPONDER PROCEDURES

LEARNING OBJECTIVES

After studying this chapter, the reader should be able to:

- Follow first responder standard operating procedures.
- Identify electric and hybrid electric vehicles.
- Safely depower a hybrid electric vehicle.
- Safely handle spills from a hybrid electric vehicle.
- Discuss first responder issues with electric and hybrid electric vehicles.

KEY TERMS

Cut lines 288
Double cut method 288
Hazardous materials (hazmat) 288
Hot stick 285
Incidents 283
International Fire Service Training Association (IFSTA) 288
National Fire Academy (NFA) 288
National Fire Protection Association (NFPA) 288
Personal protective equipment (PPE) 288
Standard operating guidelines (SOG) 283
Standard operating procedures (SOP) 283

EV AND HEV FIRST RESPONDER PROCEDURES

REASONS FOR CONCERN Everyone is used to the sound of an internal combustion engine and can tell when a vehicle is running, while electric vehicles and many hybrid electric vehicles do not make a sound. It can be difficult for first responders to tell if the vehicle is safe to approach and before performing an extrication of the people in the vehicle.

INCIDENTS Incidents involving an electric or hybrid electric vehicle (HEV) could include the following:

1. Vehicle crash
2. Fire
3. Crash and fire
4. Submerged or partially submerged vehicle

SOP/SOG Whenever first responders approach an incident, they do not know for sure what they will find or how to handle the situation. The best approach for first responders is to follow **standard operating procedures (SOP)** also called **standard operating guidelines (SOG)**. SOP/SOG procedures and guidelines are used to ensure that everyone in the department perform common tasks in a specific manner.

SAE recommended practice (RP) standard J2990 addresses the potential hazards grouped into three categories:

1. Chemical
2. Electrical
3. Thermal

Other incidents may occur from secondary events such as garage fires and floods. Nickel-metal hydride (NiMH) and lithium ion (Li-ion) batteries used for vehicle propulsion power and the standard operating procedures specify that human life should be considered the highest priority over any property damage. Standard operating procedures also include the use of the proper personal protection equipment (PPE) including:

- Protective clothing including helmet with a face shield
- Self-contained breathing apparatus (SCBA)
- High-voltage gloves, including leather protective gloves over the rubber insulated gloves
- Have insulated tools available, if possible, in the event that tools are needed. ● **SEE FIGURE 20-1**.

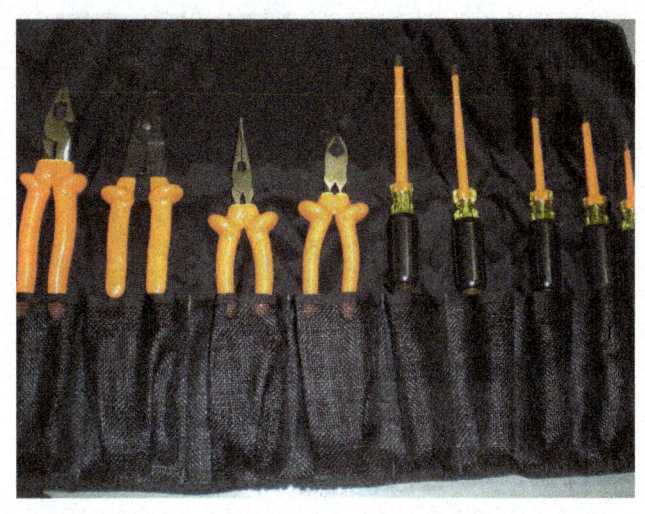

FIGURE 20-1 Insulated tools should be used, if possible, when tools are needed to free an occupant or perform removal of battery cables of a hybrid electric vehicle.

VISUAL ANALYSIS When approaching the scene of an incident, the first consideration is always the safety of people including:

- Occupants of the vehicle
- First responders
- Others in the area

If the initial visual evaluation of the scene indicates that a hybrid electric vehicle may be involved, check the vehicle to confirm that it is a hybrid.

IDENTIFYING AN EV OR HYBRID VEHICLE To confirm whether a vehicle is a hybrid, look for the word "HYBRID" on the rear, front, or side of the vehicle. Many electric and hybrid electric vehicles look the same or at least similar to a gasoline powered vehicle, especially if it has been involved in a collision. ● **SEE FIGURES 20-2 AND 20-3**.

FIGURE 20-2 Often the identification of a hybrid or electric vehicle is small, such as on the side of this Lexus RX450h.

FIRST RESPONDER PROCEDURES **283**

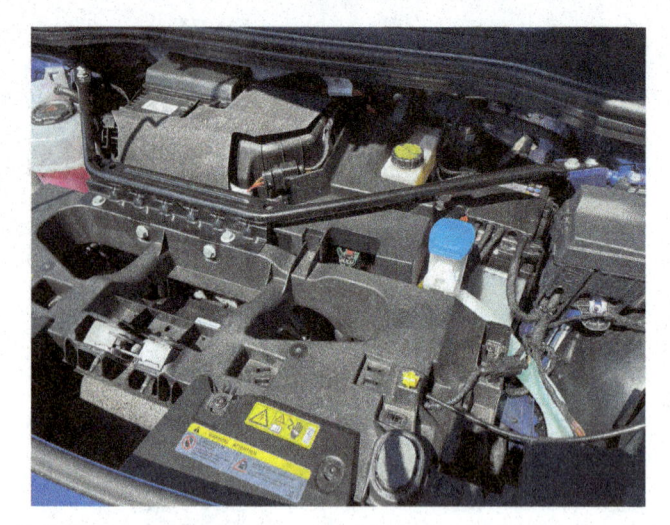

FIGURE 20-3 The under-hood view of a VW ID4 electric vehicle. At first, it appears to be the same as many conventional vehicles with the master cylinder reservoir and the 12-volt battery near the bulkhead and the other plastic covered components toward the front.

EV AND HEV ITEMS TO CHECK

ORANGE CABLES
Orange cables under the hood, or orange shielding bolted to the underside of the vehicle indicates that the vehicle is a hybrid electric vehicle. If a hybrid badge or label is not visible (due to damage, for example), the presence of orange cables under the hood or orange shielding under the vehicle would also identify the vehicle as an HEV. Electrical energy flows between the high-voltage battery module and the motor through either two or three heavy-duty orange cables. In some hybrid vehicles, high-voltage cables also deliver current to the air-conditioning (A/C) compressor (if equipped). The high-voltage cables are routed under the vehicle between the battery box and the engine compartment inside sturdy orange plastic protective shields. ● **SEE FIGURE 20-4.**

> ### ⚠ WARNING
>
> Failure to properly shut down the high-voltage system before first responder procedures are performed could result in serious injury or death from electrical shock. To prevent serious injury or death, DO NOT touch high-voltage harnesses or components without wearing appropriate PPE.

❓ FREQUENTLY ASKED QUESTION

What Do the Colors of Cables Mean?

Hybrid electric vehicles are equipped with plastic conduit to cover and protect the electrical cables. This plastic conduit is color coded to help identify the potential risk. The colors and their meanings are as follows:

- **Black**—12-volt cable. Not a shock hazard but can power airbags and pretensioners.
- **Red**—12 volts
- **Blue**—42 volts. Not a shock hazard but could maintain an arc if the circuit is opened. Blue is used for some electric power steering systems and mild hybrid vehicles, such as a belt-alternator starter (BAS) system. ● **SEE FIGURE 20-5**.
- **Yellow**—42 volts. Not a shock hazard but could maintain an arc if the circuit is opened (cut). Usually used for electric power steering.
- **Orange**—Identifies a circuit that has 60 volts or higher. Shock hazard could cause severe burns or death.

FIGURE 20-4 A hybrid electric vehicle can often be identified by looking for orange-colored cables under the hood, as well as other markings on the engine cover.

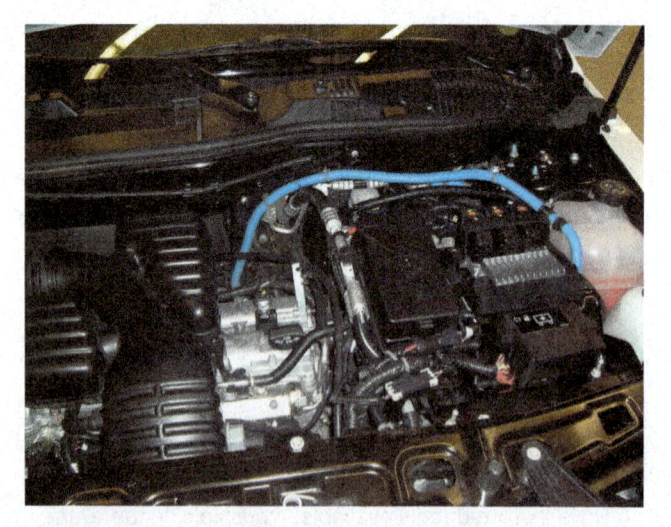

FIGURE 20-5 Blue cables under the hood of a General Motors mild-hybrid electric vehicle.

12-VOLT AUXILIARY BATTERY Most 12-volt auxiliary batteries used in many electric and hybrid electric vehicles are hidden from view, often under black plastic panels. The locations of a conventional lead-acid 12-volt battery generally include the following:

- Under the hood (i.e., Nissan Leaf, Chevrolet Bolt, VW ID4, Mustang Mach E)
- In the trunk (i.e., Toyota/ Lexus HEVs, Chevrolet Volt)

The first responders should check their guidelines as soon as possible after identifying the make and model of vehicle. In electric and hybrid electric vehicles, this battery also provides power to the high-voltage battery control systems. Disconnecting or cutting the negative cables to the battery may be necessary in some emergency situations.

HIGH-VOLTAGE BATTERY The electric motor is powered by a high-voltage battery module. The high-voltage battery modules are in plastic containers, which are then placed in a sturdy metal box. ● **SEE FIGURE 20-6**.

All components inside the battery box are completely insulated and isolated from the vehicle body. For maximum safety, the high-voltage battery box is positioned directly behind the seat-backs or under the rear seat where it is well-protected from potential damage in a collision. ● **SEE FIGURE 20-7**.

FIGURE 20-6 A Toyota Highlander hybrid battery pack located under the rear seat.

NOTE: Small quantities of a highly alkaline liquid electrolyte, which is corrosive to human tissue, are used in the manufacture of the nickel-metal hydride (NiMH) battery cells. However, in the finished cells, electrolyte is absorbed into the battery separator and sealed in a metal case, and any leakage would be extremely rare. The electrolyte is nonflammable, nonexplosive, and creates no hazardous fumes or vapors in normal operating conditions.

? FREQUENTLY ASKED QUESTION

How Can the Battery Be Disconnected If It Is Under the Vehicle?

Some vehicles have the 12-volt auxiliary battery under the vehicle or behind panels that have to be removed to gain access to the battery terminals or cable. In these cases, the vehicle manufacturer specifies that the correct procedure to follow to depower the high-voltage circuit is to remove a fuse or relay. Instead of trying to locate a fuse that may not be readily seen as being the correct one to remove, the suggested approach is to remove all fuses and relays. Many hybrid electric vehicles use more than one fuse panel or relay center. It is best to check the first responder vehicle information to be sure. This way the 12-volt power is removed from the high-voltage controller and the high voltage is retained in the battery pack.

FIRST RESPONDER SAFETY

HOT STICK Whenever approaching a hybrid electric vehicle, one option that can be used by first responders is the **hot stick**. A hot stick is a long tool used to pull high-voltage lines away from buildings or vehicles. ● **SEE FIGURE 20-8**.

This may or may not be available to first responders and could be used to move orange cables out of the way to get access to an occupant.

SHEPHERD'S HOOK Some vehicle manufacturers specify that a long pole with a large loop on one end be used to grab a person and remove them from high voltage. This tool is commonly referred to as a shepherd's hook and is made from non-electrical-conducting fiberglass.

AIRBAGS AND TENSIONERS All hybrids have front airbags and front seat belt pretensioners. Most hybrid electric vehicles also have side airbags for front-seat occupants, and many are equipped with side curtain airbags as well. These

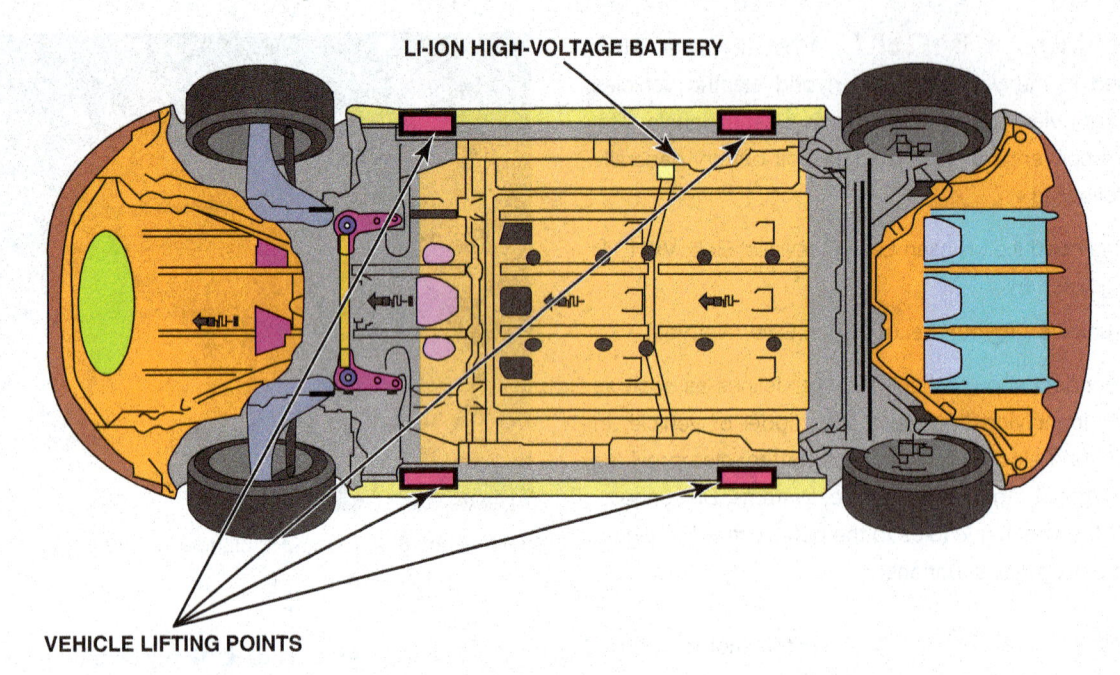

FIGURE 20-7 Under view of a typical electric vehicle showing the location of the high-voltage battery and the recommended, lifting points.

systems all use pyrotechnic devices with a deactivation time (after 12-volt power is disconnected) of up to 3 minutes. To reduce the risk of injury during the deactivation period, the following steps are recommended:

- Keep out of the path of an undeployed front airbag, and do not cut into the center of the steering wheel or dashboard where the front airbags are stored.
- Do not cut into the rear (C) pillar where the side curtain inflator is stored. ● SEE FIGURE 20-9.

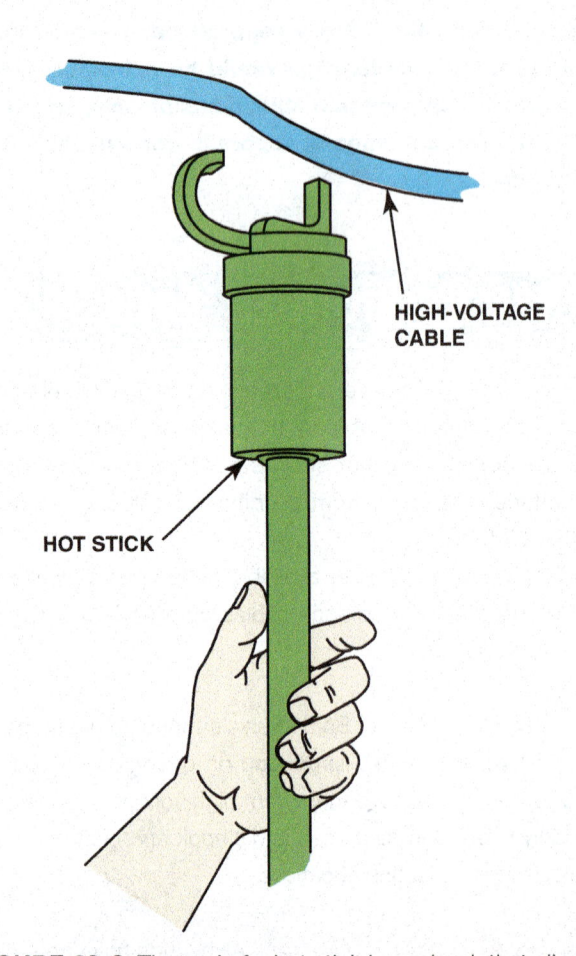

FIGURE 20-8 The end of a hot stick has a hook that allows first responders to grab and move high-voltage cables without being shocked because the pole is made from fiberglass, which is an insulator.

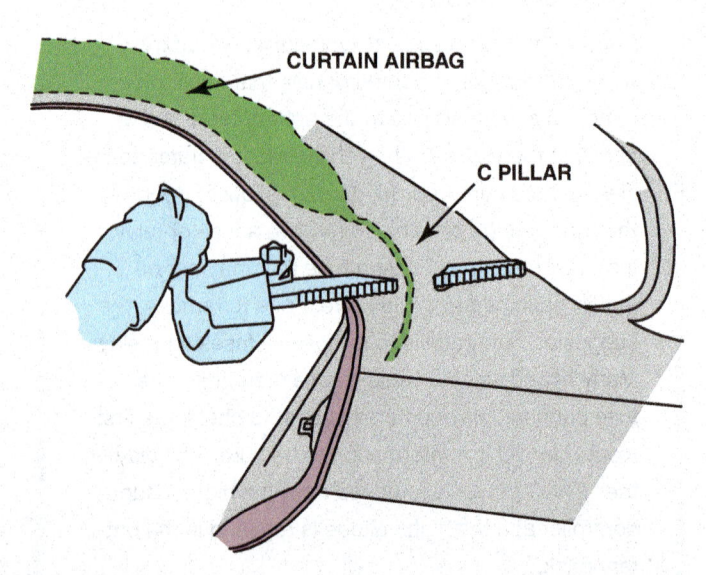

FIGURE 20-9 Use caution when cutting roof pillars because the curtain airbags could be deployed.

286 CHAPTER 20

> **WARNING**
>
> Extreme heat (320°F to 356°F [160°C to 180°C]) can cause unintended airbag inflation. Follow recommended procedures to avoid possible injury from a deploying airbag or inflator.

ELECTRIC SHOCK POTENTIAL

LOCATIONS OF SHOCK HAZARDS Unprotected contact with any electrically charged ("hot" or "live") high-voltage component can cause serious injury or death. However, receiving an electric shock from a hybrid vehicle is highly unlikely because of the following:

1. Contact with the battery module or other components inside the battery box can occur only if the box is damaged and the contents are exposed, or the box is opened without following proper precautions.
2. Contact with any electric motor or device that has high voltage, such as the air-conditioning compressor that operates using high voltage and is identified by having orange electrical conduit.
3. The high-voltage cables can be easily identified by their distinctive orange color, and contact with them can be avoided.
4. The system main relays (SMRs) disconnect power from the cables the moment the ignition is turned off.

DANGEROUS CONDITIONS The high-voltage (orange) cables can be hot whenever:

- The ignition switch is on.
- The engine has been turned off by the auto idle-stop feature.
- The air conditioner is on in vehicles that use an electric drive A/C compressor.

NOTE: The only condition common to all three situations in which the cables can be "hot" is that the ignition is on. Therefore, when the ignition switch is off, electric current cannot flow into the high-voltage cables because the system main relays that control the high voltage are turned off when the ignition is off.

EMERGENCY RESPONSE

FOLLOW STANDARD OPERATING PROCEDURES (SOP) On arrival, emergency responders should follow standard operating procedures (SOP) for vehicle incidents. Standard operating procedures usually include the following steps:

STEP 1   Identify the vehicle as soon as possible to determine if it is an electric or a hybrid electric vehicle.

STEP 2   Disable the vehicle by performing the following:
- Remove the ignition key or fob.
- Move the key or fob at least 15 feet away from the vehicle in case it is a smart key that can keep the vehicle powered up if near the vehicle.
- Verify that the "READY" light is off (if equipped).
- Place the transmission in PARK or Neutral.
- Approach the vehicle from the side; avoid walking in the front or rear of the vehicle if possible.

STEP 3   Stabilize the vehicle. Chock the wheels and set the parking brake if possible.

CAUTION: Do not place cribbing (blocks) under the high-voltage power cables, exhaust system, or fuel system.

STEP 4   Access the occupants. Use normal removal procedures as required such as:
- Pull the steering column forward and away from the occupant.
- Cut the front pillar.
- Remove (peel) the roof.
- Door removal/displacement. Doors can be removed by conventional rescue devices such as hand, electric, and hydraulic tools.
- Dashboard displacement.
- Rescue lift airbags. Responders should not place cribbing or rescue lift airbags under the high-voltage power cables, exhaust system, or fuel system.

STEP 5   Turn the ignition off. Turning the ignition off and moving the key or key fob away from the vehicle will disable the high-voltage system.

STEP 6   Disconnect or cut the 12-volt battery cables.

FREQUENTLY ASKED QUESTION

What Are Cut Lines?

Cut lines are dashed or dotted lines printed on yellow tape that is wrapped around the positive and/or negative 12-volt battery cables showing the first responder where the cable should be cut to disable the 12-volt electrical system. Only some hybrid electric vehicles have these cut lines marked on the battery cables. The **double cut method** is preferred using insulated cutters. A double cut method means that after making the first cut on a battery cable, then move about 2 inches and make another cut so cables will not make contact if jarred. When the 12 volts are cut, the high-voltage system is depowered and no high voltage should be in any of the orange cables except at the battery pack itself. ● SEE FIGURE 20-10.

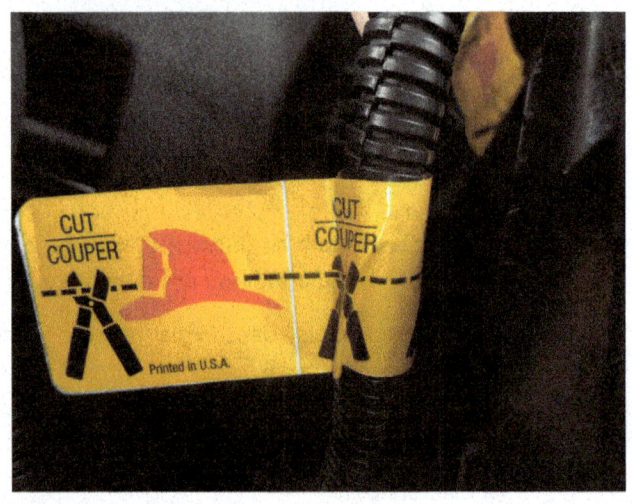

FIGURE 20-10 The dotted lines on the battery cables indicate where first responders should cut the 12-volt battery cables, which will depower the high-voltage system.

FIRE

FOLLOW SOP/SOG Approach and extinguish a fire using proper vehicle firefighting practices as recommended by **National Fire Protection Association (NFPA)**, **International Fire Service Training Association (IFSTA)**, or the **National Fire Academy (NFA)**. Water (or foam if available) has been proven to be a suitable extinguishing agent. Perform a fast, aggressive fire attack. Use large amounts of water. Attack teams may not be able to identify the vehicle as being a hybrid until the fire has been knocked down and overhaul operations have commenced. A dry powder or CO_2 fire extinguisher can also be used if water is not readily available.

NOTE: If a fire occurs in the high-voltage battery pack, the incident commander will have to decide whether to pursue an offensive or defensive attack.

OFFENSIVE FIRE ATTACK Flooding the high-voltage battery pack, located in the cargo area, with large amounts of water at a safe distance will effectively control the HV battery pack fire by cooling the adjacent NiMH battery modules to a point below their ignition temperature. Any remaining modules that are not extinguished by the water will burn themselves out.

DEFENSIVE FIRE ATTACK If the decision has been made to fight the fire using a defensive attack, the fire attack crew should pull back a safe distance and allow the NiMH battery modules to burn out. During this defensive operation, fire crews may utilize a water stream or fog pattern to protect exposures or to control the path of smoke.

HAZMAT ISSUES

HAZARDOUS MATERIALS (HAZMAT) Hybrid vehicles contain the same common automotive fluids used in other vehicles. These fluids and chemicals may be considered **hazardous materials (hazmat)**.

12-VOLT AUXILIARY BATTERY Conventional 12-volt batteries used in hybrid electric vehicles are lead–acid type. If a 12-volt battery is damaged, liquid electrolyte could spill. This mild sulfuric acid solution can be neutralized using baking soda. Most 12-volt auxiliary batteries used in many electric and hybrid electric vehicles are hidden from view, often under black plaster panels. These batteries can be located under the hood (Bolt, VW ID4, Mustang Mach E) or in the rear passenger compartments areas such as in Toyota/ Lexus HEVs.

The first responders should check their guidelines as soon as possible after identifying the make and model of vehicle.

HIGH-VOLTAGE (HV) BATTERIES The high-voltage NiMH battery electrolyte is a caustic alkaline (pH 13.5) that is corrosive to human tissues. The electrolyte, however, is absorbed in the separator material and will not normally spill or leak out even if a battery module is cracked. A catastrophic crash that would breach both the metal battery pack case and the plastic battery module would be a rare occurrence. Similar to using baking soda to neutralize a lead–acid battery electrolyte spill, a diluted boric acid solution or vinegar is used to neutralize a NiMH battery electrolyte spill. Handle NiMH electrolyte spills using the following **personal protective equipment (PPE)**:

- Splash shield or safety goggles
- Rubber, latex, or nitrile gloves
- Apron suitable for alkaline materials
- Rubber boots

Neutralize NiMH electrolyte using a boric acid solution or vinegar: boric acid solution—5.5 ounces of boric acid to 1 gallon of water (800 grams boric acid to 20 liters water).

SUBMERGED VEHICLES

If a hybrid electric vehicle is submerged, the system main (high-voltage) relays cut off high voltage to all systems except the batteries themselves. The relays are opened by the circuit that monitors any electrical connection between the high-voltage system and the body (ground). ● **SEE FIGURE 20-11**.

Therefore, there should not be a shock hazard involving a submerged hybrid electric vehicle. Treat a submerged hybrid electric vehicle as a normal incident. It will not usually be known if the vehicle is a hybrid electric vehicle until it has been removed from the water. Perform the following steps to handle a hybrid electric vehicle that is fully or partially submerged in water:

STEP 1 Remove the occupants.
STEP 2 Remove vehicle from the water.
STEP 3 Drain water from the vehicle if possible.

NOTE: There is no risk of electric shock from touching the body or the framework of the vehicle whether in or out of the water.

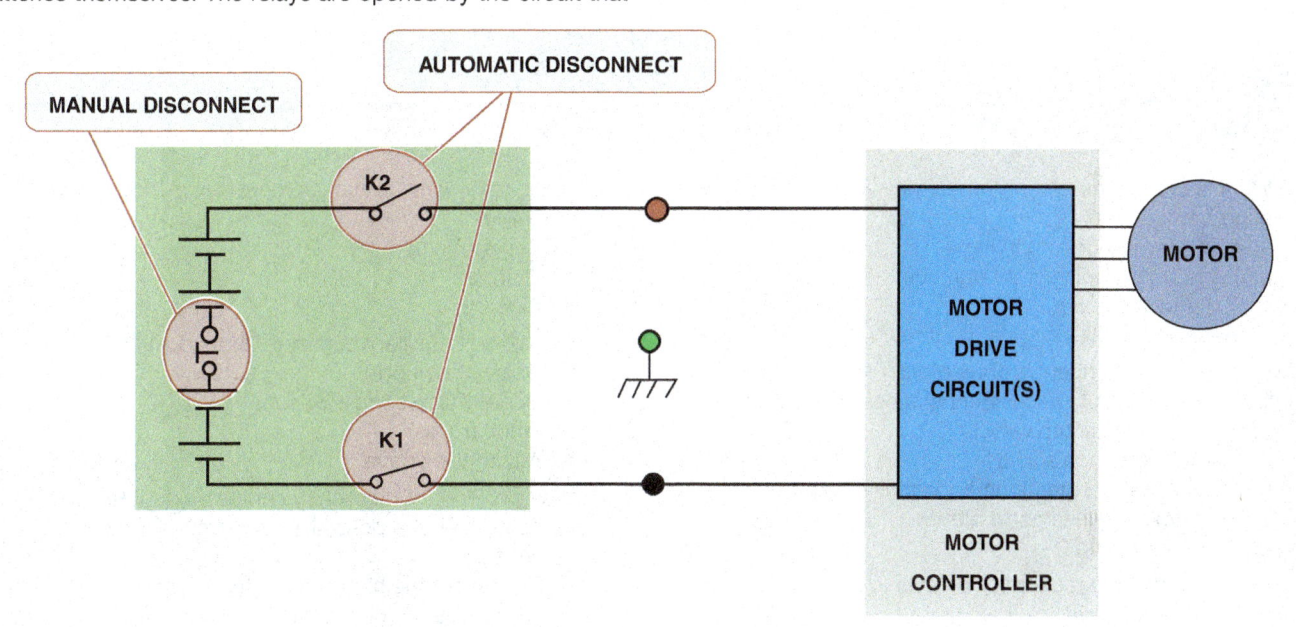

FIGURE 20-11 In the event of a collision or submersion, the system main relays will disconnect the high-voltage. None of the high-voltage is connected to chassis ground.

SUMMARY

1. Any incident involving an electric or hybrid electric vehicle should be treated following standard operating procedures (SOP).
2. Identification of the hybrid electric vehicle includes:
   - Emblems
   - Orange cables
3. The wiring conduit colors and their meanings are as follows:
   - Black—12 volts
   - Red—12 volts
   - Yellow—42 volts
   - Blue—42 volts
   - Orange—60 volts or higher
4. To depower the high-voltage system, the 12-volt auxiliary battery must be disconnected. Use the double cut method for best results.
5. Cut lines are often marked on the 12-volt battery cable to indicate where they should be cut to disable the 12-volt system, which in turn depowers the high-voltage system.
6. The location of the high-voltage battery and 12-volt battery can vary according to make, model, and year of vehicle or behind the rear seat. The 12-volt auxiliary battery can be located either under the hood or in the trunk area.

7. The steps involved in the event of an incident with a hybrid electric vehicle include:
Step 1—Identify the vehicle.
Step 2—Disable the vehicle.
Step 3—Stabilize the vehicle.
Step 4—Access the occupants.
Step 5—Turn off the ignition.
Step 6—Disconnect or cut the 12-volt battery cables.

8. In the event of a fire with a hybrid electric vehicle, follow standard operating procedures.

9. Most hybrid electric vehicles do not create any hazardous materials that are not commonly found in any other incident involving conventional vehicles.

REVIEW QUESTIONS

1. What is the meaning of the various colors of wiring?
2. What steps should be followed when dealing with an incident involving a hybrid electric vehicle?
3. Why should a first responder "double cut" the 12-volt power cable?
4. What is the difference between an offensive and defensive first responder attack?
5. Why does a vehicle submerged in water NOT represent a shock risk to first responders?

CHAPTER QUIZ

1. What is the highest priority when following standard operating procedures?
   a. Save or protect human life
   b. Protect the vehicle from damage
   c. Extinguish the fire
   d. Rescue animals

2. What personal protective equipment (PPE) should be used when responding to an incident that could involve an electric or a hybrid electric vehicle?
   a. Helmet with face shield
   b. Self-contained breathing apparatus (SCBA)
   c. High-voltage linesman's gloves
   d. All of the above

3. How would a first responder be able to identify an electric or hybrid electric vehicle?
   a. Emblems on the front, side, or rear of the vehicle
   b. Orange-colored cables
   c. Blue-colored cables
   d. Both a and b

4. A fire involving a hybrid electric vehicle should be extinguished using _____.
   a. water or a fire extinguisher
   b. large amounts of water only
   c. dry chemical fire extinguisher only
   d. CO_2 fire extinguisher only

5. What is the color of the cables for the 12-volt auxiliary battery?
   a. Blue
   b. Yellow
   c. Red or black
   d. Orange

6. What color wires or cables represent a shock hazard?
   a. Yellow
   b. Red or black
   c. Orange
   d. Blue

7. The 12-volt auxiliary battery is located where?
   a. Under the hood
   b. Under the second-row seat
   c. In the trunk
   d. Any of the above

8. Why should 12-volt battery cables be double cut?
   a. To prevent the possibility of the cut ends coming in contact
   b. To prevent the high voltage from arcing
   c. To be sure the circuit has been cut
   d. All of the above

9. If the electrolyte from a high-voltage battery is spilled, what should be used to neutralize it?
   a. Baking soda
   b. Vinegar or boric acid
   c. Water
   d. CO_2

10. The high-voltage system will be shut off if the_____.
    a. ignition is turned off
    b. air bags deploy
    c. vehicle becomes submerged
    d. Any of the above

appendix
SAMPLE HYBRID/ELECTRIC VEHICLE SPECIALIST (L3) ASE-TYPE CERTIFICATION TEST

CONTENT AREA	QUESTIONS IN THE TEST	PERCENTAGE OF THE TEST
A. Battery System	11	25%
B. Internal Combustion Engine	6	13%
C. Drive Systems	9	20%
D. Power Electronics	13	29%
E. Hybrid Supporting Systems	6	13%
TOTAL	45	100%

A. BATTERY SYSTEM

1. Hybrid electric vehicle manufacturers specify that high-voltage (HV) protective gloves be worn that meet what specification?
   a. SAE J1930
   b. UL 1140-A
   c. ANSI class "0"
   d. OSHA Standard 1000

2. What rating should a DMM have to be safely used on a hybrid electric or electric vehicle?
   a. CAT III
   b. SAE J1930
   c. 10 megohm
   d. UL 1100

3. Using a scan tool, what PID indicates that a HV battery pack is degraded?
   a. Internal resistance
   b. State-of-charge (SOC)
   c. Battery block voltage
   d. All of the above

4. At what state-of-charge does the ICE start to charge the HV battery on most hybrid electric vehicles (HEVs)?
   a. 30%
   b. 40%
   c. 50%
   d. 60%

5. When diagnosing HV battery pack concerns, what scan tool data is one of the first to check?
   a. State-of-charge (SOC)
   b. Internal resistance
   c. External resistance
   d. Electrolyte level

6. What tool or type of meter should be used to check for voltage leaks/loss of isolation?
   a. A CAT III DMM
   b. An insulation tester
   c. An ohmmeter
   d. A high impedance voltmeter

7. A HV battery pack has been removed from the vehicle. The connecting straps (connectors) for some of the modules are found to be corroded. Technician A says that the connectors should be replaced. Technician B says that the battery modules should all be checked for state-of-charge to see that they are all within specifications. Which technician is correct?
   a. Technician A only
   b. Technician B only
   c. Both Technicians A and B
   d. Neither Technician A nor B

8. HV battery packs are cooled using _____.
   a. a separate cooling system with the coolant circulated by an electric-operated pump
   b. cabin or outside airflow moved by an electric blower
   c. the ICE cooling system to circulate coolant around the HV battery module assembly
   d. Either a or b

9. If the HV battery pack becomes degraded, what symptom may the driver experience?
   a. A warning light on the dash
   b. Reduced fuel economy
   c. The ICE runs all or most of the time
   d. Any or all of the above

10. The internal resistance of a HEV battery is being checked using a scan tool. What is normal internal resistance?
    a. 15 to 40 milliohms
    b. 1.5 to 5.0 ohms
    c. 3 to 7 ohms
    d. 10 to 15 ohms
11. A HV battery pack is being diagnosed using a scan tool. A diagnostic trouble code can be set if there is _____ or more difference in voltage between battery blocks.
    a. 2.2
    b. 1.2
    c. 0.3
    d. 0.1

B. INTERNAL COMBUSTION ENGINE

12. How is the idle stop function disabled to allow the ICE to run at all times?
    a. Push a button on the dash on most HEVs
    b. Follow a prescribed procedure
    c. Turn on the heater
    d. Open all doors
13. The viscosity of engine oil specified for use in a HEV is usually SAE _____.
    a. 0W-20
    b. 0W-30
    c. 5W-30
    d. 10W-40
14. If the torque displayed on a scan tool indicates that the motor/generator that is attached to the ICE is showing "positive torque." This means that the _____.
    a. ICE is being driven by the motor/generator (crank mode)
    b. ICE is powering the motor/generator (run mode)
    c. motor generator is charging the HV battery
    d. motor/generator is supplying electrical energy to the traction motor
15. The ICE does not start (nothing happens when the starting button or ignition key is engaged). What is the most likely cause?
    a. The ICE fuel tank is empty
    b. The auxiliary 12-volt battery is discharged or defective
    c. The electric fuel pump for the ICE is defective
    d. The HV battery pack is discharged below 50% SOC
16. A scan tool is needed to _____.
    a. check the SOC of the auxiliary 12-volt battery
    b. check the oil level in the ICE
    c. crank the engine at normal cranking speed to perform a compression test
    d. All of the above
17. The ICE cooling system uses _____.
    a. the same coolant as used in liquid cooled electronic cooling system
    b. pure (100%) antifreeze to provide long-term corrosion resistance
    c. an ICE or electric-powered water pump
    d. Both a and c

C. DRIVE SYSTEMS

18. What is needed to safely remove and/or install a permanent magnet rotor?
    a. HV gloves
    b. A special holder/installer
    c. Insulated tools (wrenches and pliers)
    d. All of the above
19. Hybrid electric vehicle (HEV) diagnostic trouble codes _____.
    a. are global (generic) codes only (P0XXX)
    b. can include letters such as P0A30
    c. often can pin down the fault
    d. Both b and c
20. An insulation (isolation) tester applies _____ to test for continuity between the high-voltage cable and the chassis ground.
    a. a high voltage pulse
    b. a high amperage current supplied at 12 volts
    c. a resistance between the two components being tested
    d. a low voltage (about 2 volts) and a low current (about 0.5 A)
21. What data would be an indication of where a noise or shudder from the drivetrain may be located?
    a. A low HV battery SOC
    b. An auxiliary battery fault code
    c. An insulation/isolation fault DTC for the traction motor
    d. A fault code (DTC) for a failed resolver
22. If there is a stored diagnostic trouble code (DTC) for a loss of insulation, where should the technician first check?
    a. At the HV disconnect plug
    b. At the location stated in the DTC description
    c. At the closest location to the chassis ground connection
    d. At the closest location to the HV battery
23. What type of lubricant is used in most HEV transmissions?
    a. POE dielectric fluid
    b. Usually ATF of the specified type
    c. POA engine oil
    d. Silicone grease
24. A diagnostic trouble code (DTC) has been set for motor-rotor position sensor (resolver) fault. Technician A says that this part is a replaceable part if defective. Technician B says that it is part of the traction motor assembly and is replaced as an assembly. Which technician is correct?
    a. Technician A only
    b. Technician B only
    c. Both Technicians A and B
    d. Neither Technician A nor B
25. A cover is being removed from a HV component such as the inverter/converter. What is the purpose of the two-wire connector that is disconnected in order to remove the cover?
    a. It is used to set a diagnostic trouble code if the cover is removed
    b. Used to shut off the HV system and discharge the capacitors to avoid personal injury
    c. Used to trigger the dash warning lamp for overheat of the inverter/converter
    d. Used a ground connection so the cover is properly grounded

26. The parking pawl on most hybrid electric vehicles (HEVs) _____.
    a. is mechanically applied using a cable
    b. is not used but instead uses an electromagnet to keep the vehicle from rolling when parked
    c. uses an electric motor to move the parking pawl into position
    d. uses the traction motor to keep the vehicle from moving when parked

D. POWER ELECTRONICS

27. The internal resistance of the HV battery modules _____.
    a. can be determined by using a scan tool
    b. can be measured using an ohmmeter after removing the modules from the battery pack
    c. has to be determined using a special HV tester
    d. can be calculated from using the current draw of the traction motor and the HV battery SOC

28. The ICE does not stop running when warm and at idle speed. What could be the cause?
    a. Any problem with the ICE MAF sensor
    b. A low SOC of the HV voltage battery
    c. A fault with the HV battery
    d. Either b or c

29. When working on a hybrid electric vehicle (HEV), what type of meter leads should be used with the DMM?
    a. Leads with alligator clips
    b. CAT III rated leads
    c. DOT-approved leads
    d. SAE-approved leads

30. A factory-level aftermarket scan tool was used to retrieve two diagnostic trouble codes (DTCs). There were a P0A80 and P3006. These codes mean _____.
    a. the P0A30 is a false code because it has a letter instead of all numbers
    b. the P3006 is a factory DTC
    c. both codes could be retrieved using a global (generic) scan tool (code reader)
    d. the P0A30 is a factory code

31. The master warning lamp on the dash is on. There are many DTCs set and the driver stated that the vehicle had run out of gas when the warning light came on. What is the best approach to fix this problem?
    a. Preform a circuit check of the HV system checking for loss of insulation
    b. Disconnect the HV battery service plug and check the system for damage related to the HV system and electronic drive system
    c. Clear the codes and verify that they do not return
    d. Check the ICE fluids and restore to proper level

32. Before disconnecting the HV service plug, what should be done?
    a. Wear HV gloves
    b. Disconnect the 12-volt auxiliary battery or specified fuse/relay
    c. Check service information to determine how to gain access to the HV plug
    d. All of the above

33. The start button is pushed and the dash lights up but the vehicle does not move and the ready to move light is not on. What is the most likely cause?
    a. A weak (low charge) 12-volt auxiliary battery
    b. The driver did not depress the brake pedal and the system is in the accessory mode
    c. A discharged HV battery pack
    d. A fault with the ignition on switch

34. What is used to conduct heat from the inverter–converter to the area where the coolant flows?
    a. Heat conductive grease
    b. Engine oil
    c. ATF
    d. Silicone grease

35. A hybrid electric vehicle (HEV) has been in an accident. The service technician wants to check to make sure that the high-voltage (HV) cables have not been hurt or have lost their electrical isolation (insulation). How is this test performed?
    a. Disconnect both cables at both ends and measure the resistance between the two cables. It should be more than 10k ohms
    b. Remove the service plug and allow the capacitors to discharge and then measure the voltage between the two terminals
    c. After removing the HV cable from the vehicle, measure the resistance and they should be less than 0.1 ohm per foot of length
    d. Use an insulator tester and after disconnecting the HV cable, connect one tester lead to the terminal of the cable and the other to a good chassis ground. The results should be greater than one million ohms

36. The 12-volt auxiliary battery has been charged and even replaced several times due to low charge. The voltage of the battery as shown on a scan tool display and a DMM shows 11.2 volts. What is the most likely cause?
    a. A too small auxiliary battery
    b. A defective DC/DC converter
    c. A defective alternator
    d. A defective inverter

37. Where are the high-voltage capacitors located?
    a. Under the HV battery pack on most HEVs
    b. Inside the inverter/converter compartment
    c. Usually attached to the ICE and they share the ICE cooling system
    d. Under the vehicle between the HV battery and the ICE

38. The AC/DC inverter cooling pump is being replaced because it stopped functioning. What type of coolant should be used when refilling the system?
    a. Premixed universal coolant only
    b. The coolant that is recommended
    c. Blue coolant that has a dielectric additive included
    d. Any of the above

39. The system main relays (SMR) may trip and disable the vehicle if what occurs?
    a. An airbag deploys
    b. The vehicle is submerged in water
    c. The system detects a fault in the insulation (isolation) between the HV system and the chassis ground
    d. Any of the above

E. HYBRID SUPPORTING SYSTEMS

40. How should HV gloves be tested before each use?
    a. Visual inspection for any tears or openings
    b. Roll the glove up to trap air and see if the air leaks
    c. Use a voltmeter and check the resistance of the rubber (should be greater than 10k ohms)
    d. Both a and b

41. The owner complained that while driving on a mountainous area, the HV battery display read at the top of the scale. About the same time, the brake pedal became harder to depress and more force was required to slow the vehicle. What is the most likely cause?
    a. Normal operation
    b. A fault with the master cylinder
    c. A HV battery SOC fault that caused the regenerative braking system to default to normal hydraulic brakes
    d. Driver error

42. Before the brakes are serviced on many hybrid electric vehicles, what precaution(s) are often needed to be performed?
    a. The brake hydraulic system needs to be placed in service mode
    b. The brake pedal needs to be depressed at least 30 times to discharge the accumulator
    c. The HV served plug should be removed and placed in a safe location away from the vehicle
    d. All of the above

43. Many hybrid electric vehicle diagnostic trouble codes also include "subcodes." What is the purpose of the subcodes?
    a. They help the service technician pin down the location of the fault
    b. They are used only for engineers and not to be used by a service technician
    c. They list the voltage of the HV battery when the fault occurred
    d. They refer to the area in service information where the details of the system are explained

44. The wiring to the electric power steering has yellow conduit which indicates _____.
    a. dangerous high voltage (lower than orange cable but still fatal)
    b. 12-volt circuit
    c. 42-volt circuit
    d. 60-volt circuit

45. The A/C compressor on a hybrid electric vehicle has failed and has to be replaced. What precautions are needed to be taken?
    a. Use PAG refrigerant oil
    b. Use the specified non-electrical conductive refrigerant oil
    c. Replace the HV cable to the compressor
    d. Use a high-volume vacuum pump during the evacuation process.

ANSWERS

1. c	13. a	25. b	37. b
2. a	14. a	26. c	38. b
3. d	15. b	27. a	39. d
4. c	16. c	28. d	40. d
5. a	17. a	29. b	41. a
6. b	18. b	30. b	42. a
7. c	19. d	31. c	43. a
8. d	20. a	32. d	44. c
9. d	21. c	33. b	45. b
10. a	22. b	34. a	
11. c	23. b	35. d	
12. b	24. a	36. b	

GLOSSARY

AC coupling AC coupling position is selected, a capacitor is placed into the meter lead circuit, which effectively blocks all DC voltage signals, but allows the AC portion of the signal to pass and be displayed.

AC induction motor (ACIM) An AC induction motor is also known as an AC asynchronous motor, or AC induction motor (ACIM), because it allows a certain amount of slip between the rotor and the changing magnetic field in the stator. The term asynchronous means that the speed of the motor is not necessarily related to the frequency of the current flowing through the stator windings.

Acoustic vehicle alerting system (AVAS) Creates the sound whenever the vehicle is traveling at low speed. The U.S. National Highway Traffic Safety Administration (NHTSA) requires the device to emit warning sounds when travelling at speeds less than 19 MPH (30 km/h)

Active balancing Active balancing is achieved when energy is drawn from the most charged cell and transferred to the least charged cells, usually through DC–DC converters.

Active grille shutters (AGS) Active grille shutters (AGS) are designed to remain to decrease the aerodynamic drag by forcing the air to flow underneath the vehicle when closed. Only when there is a need for cooling do the active grill shutters open to allow air to flow through heat exchangers. They are used in all types of vehicle to help improve fuel economy.

Adaptive cruise control (ACC) Adaptive cruise control (ACC), also called radar cruise control, gives the driver more control over the vehicle by keeping an assured clear distance behind the vehicle in front.

Advanced driver assist systems (ADAS) Various vehicle systems that provide help to the driver.

Alternating current (AC) Electric charge in alternating current (AC) changes direction periodically. The voltage in AC circuits also periodically reverses because the current changes direction.

Always Be Charging (ABC) The saying that many owners of electric vehicle mention when discussing charging at home. Due to the vehicle itself needing to keep the systems functional and within a temperature range, many owners simply keep their EV connected to the charging station when at home.

American National Standards Institute (ANSI) American National Standards Institute (ANSI) is a private, nonprofit organization that administers and coordinates the U.S. voluntary standardization and conformity assessment system.

American Society for Testing and Materials (ASTM) American Society for Testing and Materials.

Armature The armature, made up of many conductors, is installed inside this strong magnetic field, with very little clearance between the armature and the field coils.

Artificial intelligence (AI) AI is machine learning accomplished through programming and training that allows the computer to react much like a human.

Atkinson cycle The Atkinson cycle engine is an engine that uses a late closing intake valve to reduce compression pressures and an extended power stroke event.

Automatic emergency braking (AEB) An automatic emergency braking (AEB) system intervenes and automatically applies the brakes if needed. Automatic braking is often part of a safety package that includes radar cruise control, and will apply the brakes in the event of a possible collision.

Battery control module (BCM) The battery control module (BCM) is responsible for controlling the operation of the high-voltage battery based on the requests from the hybrid control module.

Battery density Battery density refers to the amount of energy in kilowatt-hours (kWh) that a battery can store per kilogram of mass (kWh per kilograms) or volume (kWh per liter) of volume. The higher the number, the higher the energy density of the battery.

Battery electric vehicle (BEV) A battery electric vehicle (BEV), also called an electric vehicle (EV), uses a high-voltage battery pack to supply electrical energy to an electric motor(s) to propel the vehicle under all driving conditions.

Battery management system (BMS) The battery management system (BMS) is an electronic system that manages cells in a battery pack. The BMS monitors and controls the state of charge (SOC), state of health (SOH), state of function (SOF), temperature, and load balancing/individual cell efficiency.

Belt alternator starter (BAS) The belt alternator starter (BAS) system was the most common early stop–start system. The BAS system was the least expensive system that can be used and still claim that the vehicle is a hybrid.

Blind spot monitor (BSM) The blind spot monitor (BSM) is a vehicle-based sensor device that detects other vehicles located to the side and rear of the vehicle.

BNC connector A BNC connector, which is a miniature standard coaxial cable connector. BNC is an international standard that is used in the electronics industry.

Body control module (BCM) The body control module (BCM) monitors the operation of the climate control system as well as the driver's door switch and driver's seat belt.

Boost converters Boost converters are used to enhance high-voltage systems that operate on a lower high-voltage battery. The boost converter boosts the nominal voltage output by the battery to as much as 500 volts to meet increased electrical demand based on the load.

Brushless motors Brushless motors, which use permanent magnet rotors, produce high starting torque and are typically over 90% efficient.

Cabin filter A cabin filter is used to remove particulate matter and to prevent clogging of the vehicle's evaporator.

Carbohydrates All life-forms are able to collect, store, and use energy from their environment. In carbon-based biology, the basic energy storage compounds are in carbohydrates, where the carbon atoms are linked by single bonds into a chain.

Carbon (C) Most of the energy used in the world has been generated by burning organic fuel that contains carbon (abbreviated C). An economy that uses only carbon-based fuels is often referred to as a carbon-based society. Carbon is formed from materials that were once alive on the earth.

Carbon footprint The carbon footprint includes energy-related emissions from human activities, including heat, light, power, refrigeration, and all transport-related emissions from vehicles, freight, and distribution.

Category three (CAT III) A category three (CAT III) certified digital multimeter (DMM) is required for making measurements on these high-voltage systems.

Cathode ray tube (CRT) An analog scope uses a cathode ray tube (CRT) similar to a television screen to display voltage patterns. The scope screen displays the electrical signal constantly.

Channel Scopes are available that allow the viewing of more than one sensor or event at the same time on the display. The number of events, which require leads for each, is called a channel. A channel is an input to a scope.

Column-mounted electric power steering (C-EPS) Column-mounted electric power steering (C-EPS) has sensors and the assist motor located inside the vehicle so they are not exposed to the heat and outside elements as is the rack-mounted system.

Commutator The classic DC motor uses a rotating armature in the form of an electromagnet with two poles. A rotary switch called a commutator reverses the direction of the electric current twice every cycle, to flow through the armature so that the poles of the electromagnet push and pull against the permanent magnets on the outside of the motor.

Controller Area Network (CAN) Robert Bosch Corporation developed the Controller Area Network (CAN) protocol, which was called CAN 1.2, in 1993. The CAN protocol was approved by the Environmental Protection Agency (EPA) for 2003 and newer vehicle diagnostics, and became a legal requirement for all vehicles by 2008.

Current clamp A current clamp (also called an amp clamp) is an electrical probe with jaws that open to allow the clamping around an electrical conductor. The probe measures the magnetic field created by the current flow and converts it into a waveform on the scope. It can be used with a scope to measure AC or DC current in a circuit without disconnecting any wires or components.

Cut lines Places marked on low-voltage electrical cable in a hybrid electric vehicle that should/can be cut by a first responder to disable the high-voltage circuits.

DC-to-DC converters DC-to-DC converters are electronic devices used to transform DC voltage from one level of DC voltage to another higher or lower-level voltage.

DC coupling DC coupling is the most used position on a scope because it allows the scope to display both alternating current (AC) voltage signals and direct current (DC) voltage signals present in the circuit. The AC part of the signal will ride on top of the DC component.

DCFC (DC Fast Charge) Level 3 chargers are often called a DCFC (DC Fast Charge) or DC Quick Charge (DCQC).

Destination charging Hotels and motels often provide charging stations known as destination charging. Hotels are adding chargers to their properties to help attract EV drivers traveling on long trips.

Digital multimeter (DMM) A digital multimeter is capable of measuring electrical current, resistance, and voltage.

Digital storage oscilloscope (DSO) A digital scope takes samples of the signals that can be stopped or stored and is therefore called a digital storage oscilloscope, or DSO.

Direct current (DC) Direct current (DC), the electric charge (current) only flows in one direction.

Dog mode Dog mode (also called pet mode) is a climate control feature in Tesla and some other electric vehicles that leaves the air conditioning or heater on when owners leave their pets in their car. It is accessed through the climate-control settings by selecting "Dog" under the "Keep Climate On" settings.

Double cut method A double cut method means that after making the first cut on a battery cable, then move about 2 inches and make another cut so cables will not make contact if jarred. When the 12 volts are cut, the high-voltage system is depowered and no high voltage should be in any of the orange cables except at the battery pack itself.

Duty cycle Duty cycle refers to the percentage of on-time of the signal during one complete cycle. As on-time increases, the amount of time the signal is off decreases and is usually measured in percentage.

Electric auxiliary pump In order to adapt a conventional automatic transmission to a hybrid powertrain, an electric auxiliary pump is used to maintain fluid pressure in the transmission during internal combustion engine (ICE) idle stop.

Electric power steering (EPS) All HEV and EV vehicles use electric power steering (EPS) systems, which is also called electric power-assisted steering (EPAS).

Electric power-assisted steering (EPAS) Electric power steering takes the place of hydraulic components that were previously used by using an electric motor to provide power assist effort.

Electric vehicle (EV) An electric vehicle (EV) uses a high-voltage battery pack to supply electrical energy to an electric motor(s) to propel the vehicle under all driving conditions.

Electric vehicle supply equipment (EVSE) Electric vehicle supply equipment (EVSE) supplies electricity supplies electricity to charge an electric vehicle (EV). The primary function of a plug-in vehicle charging station is to provide electrical safety for the operator and to address the risks of fire and electric shock.

Electrical Distribution System (EDS) The Electrical Distribution System (EDS) is to provide the electrical conduction path through the battery pack.

Electrolysis The process where electric current is passed through water in order to break it into hydrogen and oxygen gas.

Electromagnetic induction The creation of a voltage in a conductor by a moving magnetic field is called electromagnetic induction.

Electromagnetic parking sensors (EPS) Electromagnetic parking sensors (EPS) detect when a vehicle is moving slowly and toward an object.

Electromagnetism The creation of a magnetic field by the use of an electrical current.

Energy carrier Any medium that is utilized to store or transport energy. For example, hydrogen is an energy carrier because energy must be used to generate hydrogen gas that is used as a fuel.

Energy Energy is defined as the ability to do work.

Energy-Efficiency Ratio (EER) Energy-Efficiency Ratio (EER) is a value representing the relative electrical efficiency of cooling equipment in the cooling season. EER is calculated by dividing cooling capacity (in British thermal units per hour [Btu/h]) by the power input (in watts or W). The higher the EER, the less electricity the equipment uses to cool the same amount of air. A unit with an EER of 7 costs about twice as much to operate as one with an EER of 14.

Engine control module (ECM) The engine control module (ECM) is responsible for all engine control systems when the engine is running.

EV range The size or capacity of the battery pack used determines how far that the vehicle can travel without using the ICE, commonly called the EV range.

External trigger An external trigger is when the waveform starts when a signal is received from another external source, rather than from the signal pickup lead.

Flux lines Magnetic lines of force.

Frequency Frequency is the number of cycles per second measured in hertz.

Fuel cell A fuel cell is an electrochemical device in which the chemical energy of hydrogen and oxygen is converted into electrical energy.

Fuel-cell hybrid vehicle (FCHV) A vehicle that uses a fuel cell to create electricity and also uses an electrical storage device such as a high-voltage battery that can be used to power the vehicle.

Fuel-cell stack A collection of individual fuel cells "stacked" end-to-end, similar to slices of bread.

Fuel-cell vehicle (FCV) A vehicle that is powered directly from the electrical power generated by a fuel cell.

Geothermal energy Geothermal energy is energy derived from the heat of the earth. The earth's core is approximately 4,000 miles from the surface and is so hot that it is molten. Temperatures are believed to be at least 9000°F (5000°C). A well is drilled and the earth's core heats water into steam that drives a turbine to drive an AC generator to produce electricity.

Geothermal heat pump (GHP) Geothermal can be used in cold weather to warm the interior of a building and can be used in warm weather cool the inside of a building using a geothermal heat pump (GHP) system.

Graticule A typical scope face usually has 8 or 10 grids vertically (up and down) and 10 grids horizontally (left to right). The transparent scale (grid), used for reference measurements, is called a graticule. This arrangement is commonly 8 × 10 or 10 × 10 divisions.

Greenhouse gases (GHG) Greenhouse gases (GHG) are those gases in our atmosphere that, if in too great a concentration, can prevent heat from escaping the surface, leading to an increase in the temperature on earth. In a nursery greenhouse, the glass panes are painted white to reflect the heat back into the greenhouse.

Guess-O-Meter (GOM) The dash display that shows the miles per kWh is often called a Guess-O-Meter (GOM) because it is often not accurate.

Guobiao standard (GB or GB/T) The Chinese national standard. BYD and other Chinese companies use this standard connector, as well as Mahindra and Tata electric vehicles.

Haptic actuator A vibration is often created in the steering wheel or the driver's seat called a haptic actuator. The vibration is created by using a DC motor with a weight that is out of balance. When the motor rotates, a vibration is created.

Hazardous materials (hazmat) Chemicals or fluids that may be considered to be hazardous.

Hertz Frequency is the number of cycles per second measured in hertz.

High voltage (HV) High-voltage (HV) circuits that if touched with an unprotected hand could cause serious burns or even death.

Homogeneous-Charge Compression Ignition (HCCI) A low-temperature combustion process that involves air–fuel mixtures being burned without the use of spark ignition.

Hot stick A hot stick is a long tool used to pull high-voltage lines away from buildings or vehicles.

human–machine interface (HMI) The human–machine interface (HMI) was very basic in the past because the vehicles were equipped with most of the following to let the driver know what the vehicle (the machine) was doing: Speedometer; Fuel level gauge (HV battery charge level); Outside air temperature; Tire pressures; Instrument panel/dashboard warning icons.

Hybrid control module The electronic module that controls the hybrid drive unit.

Hybrid electric vehicles (HEV) Hybrid electric vehicles (HEV) are vehicles that have two sources of propulsion either with an electric motor supplied energy from the high-voltage battery or an internal combustion engine (ICE).

Hydraulic impulse storage accumulator A hydraulic impulse storage accumulator is used to provide fluid pressure as the internal combustion engine (ICE) restarts after the idle stop mode.

Hydroelectricity Hydroelectricity is defined as converting the energy of flowing water into the mechanical energy of a turbine to turn a hydroelectric generator to generate electricity.

Incidents A possible hazardous condition such as an automobile accident.

Inertia Inertia is the resistance of an object to change its state of motion.

Insulated-gate bipolar transistors (IGBTs) The current flow through the motor/generator ECU is controlled by six insulated-gate bipolar transistors (IGBTs). Three of these transistors control the voltage side of the circuit and are called positive or high-side IGBTs. The other three transistors are negative or low-side IGBTs because they are on the negative (ground) side of the stator's coils.

Intelligent Speed Advice (ISA) Intelligent Speed Advice (ISA) uses a sign recognition camera or a navigation system (GPS) to determine the speed limit, which is used to warn the driver of the posted speed limit.

Interior permanent magnets (IPMs) Brushless permanent magnet motors use two designs of rotors In one type, the permanent magnets are housed inside the outer shell of the rotor and are called interior permanent magnets (IPMs).

Internal combustion engine (ICE) The internal combustion engine (ICE) used in a hybrid vehicle can be either gasoline or diesel, although only gasoline-powered engines are currently used in hybrid vehicles.

International Electrotechnical Commission (IEC) The International Electrotechnical Commission (IEC) has several categories of voltage standards for meter and meter leads. These categories are ratings for over-voltage protection and are rated CAT I, CAT II, CAT III, and CAT IV. The higher the category (CAT) rating of the meter, the greater the level of protection to the technician when measuring high-energy voltage. Under each category there are various voltage ratings.

International Fire Service Training Association (IFSTA) Approach and extinguish a fire using proper vehicle firefighting practices as recommended by International Fire Service Training Association (IFSTA).

Inverters Inverters are electronic devices that can turn DC (direct current) to AC (alternating current). It is also responsible for controlling speed and torque for electric motors.

Irradiance The term used to define the amount of solar radiation is irradiance. The solar irradiance at the earth's surface varies greatly depending on factors such as:

- Latitude
- Time of day
- Time of year
- Cloud cover
- Haze

Joule One joule is defined being the energy transferred to an object by the mechanical work of moving it a distance of 1 meter against a force of 1 newton. 1 Nm (newton-meter) = 1 Joule.

Kilowatt (kW) Kilowatt (kW) is a measure of electrical power.

kilowatt-hours (kWh) kWh is a unit of energy. Battery capacity is measured in kilowatt-hours (kWh). A kilowatt is 1,000 watts and a watt is a volt times an ampere, which is a measurement of electrical power. The higher the kWh rating of the battery, the more electrical energy it can store.

Kinetic energy The energy of a moving object that has mass.

kWh/100 mi The EPA also expresses an EV's energy consumption in terms of the number of kilowatts per hour needed to run the vehicle for 100 miles shortened to kWh/100 mi. For example, a Tesla Model 3 usually uses about 28 kW per 100 miles.

Lane departure warning system (LDWS) Lane departure warning system (LDWS) uses cameras to detect if the vehicle is crossing over lane marking lines on the pavement.

Lane keep assist (LKA) Lane keep assist (LKA), also called lane keep assist system (LKAS), is not only to warn the driver if the vehicle is moving out of the lane of traffic, but when there is no response from the driver, to also automatically use the electric power steering system to steer the vehicle back into the lane.

Lenz's law An induced current move so that its magnetic field opposes the motion that induced the current. This principle is called Lenz's law. The relative motion between a conductor and a magnetic field is opposed by the magnetic field of the current it has induced.

Light Detection and Ranging (LiDAR) A type of sensor used in advanced driver assist systems that use lasers to detect objects.

Liquid-cooled condensers (LCC) Liquid-cooled condensers (LCC) exchange heat by removing heat from one fluid and transferring it to another fluid. A liquid-cooled condenser is a heat exchanger that removes heat from refrigerant vapor and transfers it to the liquid running through it.

Lithium iron phosphate (LiFePO$_4$) Lithium iron phosphate (LiFePO$_4$) is a type of battery chemistry that is stable at higher temperatures and does not contain cobalt, which is in limited supply world-wide.

Load test Most automotive starting and charging testers use a carbon pile to create an electrical load on the battery. The amount of the load is determined by the original CCA rating of the battery, which should be at least 75% charged before performing a load test.

Locksmith ID The shop or service technician must be a registered vehicle security professional and have a locksmith ID number in order to obtain the security codes or key specific information must be reentered during the process.

Loss of Isolation (LOI) When the ground fault system detects high voltage leaking to ground, it sets a diagnostic trouble code that includes the location of the fault. This type of fault is called a loss of insulation/isolation (LOI).

Low-grade heat A fuel cell must have a much larger heat exchanger because its coolant temperature typically runs very close to that of the surrounding air. This is known as low-grade heat.

Medium hybrid A hybrid electric vehicle design that utilizes "medium" voltage levels (between 50 and 200 volts). Medium hybrids use regenerative braking and idle stop but are not capable of starting the vehicle from a stop using electric mode.

Megohm A megohm is defined as a unit of resistance, equal to one million ohms MΩ using an uppercase M and an abbreviation meg.

Membrane Electrode Assembly (MEA) The part of the PEM fuel cell that contains the membrane, catalyst coatings, and electrodes.

Micro hybrid A term used to describe belt alternator starter (BAS) and other mild hybrid systems.

Mild hybrid A hybrid electric vehicle design that uses regenerative braking and idle stop but cannot propel the vehicle in electric-only mode. A mild hybrid drive typically operates below 50 volts.

Miles per hour (MPH) Level 2 charging adds about 25 miles of Range Per hour (RPH), labeled as miles per hour (MPH) on the dash display of a Nissan Leaf.

Milliohm Milliohm (plural milliohms) is defined as one thousandth of an ohm, abbreviated as mΩ with a lowercase m. In other words, this is a resistance value that is less than 1 ohm.

MPGe To help consumers compare the energy consumption of electric vehicles with those that run on fossil fuel, the EPA created a miles-per-gallon measurement, called MPGe. This is calculated based on a conversion factor of 33.705 kilowatt-hours of electricity equaling one gallon of gasoline. Therefore, a battery that has a capacity of 100 kWh is equal to the energy of about three gallons of gasoline.

National Automotive Service Task Force (NASTF) The National Automotive Service Task Force (NASTF) is a cooperative effort of the automotive service industry, the tool industry, and the original equipment manufacturers to ensure that automotive professionals employed outside of the OEMs have all the information, training, and tools they need to diagnose and repair modern automobiles.

National Electric Code (NEC) The National Electric Code (NEC) is derived from the National Fire Protection Agency. The NEC codes are the standards to which buildings and equipment must meet minimum regulatory safety requirements in order to be safe enough for the general public to install and use. The NEC requires any charging station to be NRTL certified in order to be installed anywhere in the United States. In most places, installing an EVSE requires a building permit.

National Electrical Manufacturers Association (NEMA) The standards established by the National Electrical Manufacturers Association (NEMA) define a product, process, or procedure with terminology, construction, dimensions, and performance ratings. The NEMA 14 devices are four-wire grounding devices (2 hot terminals, a neutral and a ground) from 15 to 60 amperes with a voltage rating of 250 volts. Both the NEMA 14-30 and 14-50 are in common residential use and either may also be used for home charging of electric vehicles.

National Fire Academy (NFA) An organization devoted to fire fighter training.

National Fire Protection Association (NFPA) An association to identify areas of need for training materials and foster the development and validation of training materials for the fire service and related areas.

Nationally Recognized Testing Laboratory (NRTL) Most charging station manufacturers send samples to a Nationally Recognized Testing Laboratory (NRTL), such as Intertek (ETL mark) or Underwriter's Laboratory (UL mark) for testing of their device for safety.

Nickel, cobalt, and aluminum (NCA) Nickel, cobalt, and aluminum (NCA) cathode material results in a long battery life and faster charging capability compared to some other types of battery chemistry.

Nickel, manganese, and cobalt (NMC) A NMC battery uses a combination of nickel, manganese, and cobalt (NMC) for the cathode material. This cathode material results in slightly lower energy, but is less volatile and can withstand variation in temperature.

Nickel-metal hydride (NiMH) Most current production HEVs use nickel-metal hydride (NiMH) battery technology for the high-voltage battery. Nickel-metal hydride (NiMH) batteries have a positive electrode made of nickel hydroxide. The negative electrode is unique, in that it is a hydrogen-absorbing alloy, also known as a metal hydride. The electrolyte is an alkaline, usually potassium hydroxide. The nominal voltage of an NiMH battery cell is 1.2 volts.

Noise-reducing tire The purpose of a noise-reducing tire is to eliminate noise in the 130 to 240 Hz range that would be normally covered up by normal engine noise in a vehicle with an internal combustion engine. The noise reduction is accomplished by adding acoustical foam to the inside of a tire.

Occupational Safety and Health Administration (OSHA) The Occupational Safety and Health Administration (OSHA) requirements specify that the HV gloves get inspected every six months by a qualified glove inspection laboratory.

One-pedal driving One-pedal driving means that for normal driving, the driver only needs to use the accelerator pedal to accelerate and decelerate.

Oscilloscope An oscilloscope (usually called a scope) is a visual voltmeter with a timer that shows when a voltage changes.

Ozone Ozone is composed of three atoms of oxygen and is abbreviated O_3. Ozone occurs naturally in the atmosphere and can be detected by smell after a thunderstorm. Ozone has a strong clean smell, and in high concentrations it can be a lung and respiratory irritant. Ozone can be created by lightning, which breaks the molecular structure of oxygen (O_2) into atoms (O), which then combine back into oxygen or combine to create ozone.

Ozone-depleting substances (ODS) Depletion of the earth's upper ozone layer due to the release of man-made chemicals threatens human health and damages plant life. Certain man-made chemicals used in refrigeration, air conditioning, fire and explosion prevention, and as solvents can trigger reactions in the atmosphere that destroy the ozone layer. Ozone-depleting substances (ODS) include chlorofluorocarbons (CFCs), hydrochlorofluorocarbons (HCFCs), halons, and methyl bromide.

Parking-assist system A system that include sensor and or cameras to assist the driver while parking.

Passive balancing Passive balancing is achieved by having energy drawn from the most charged cell and dissipated as heat, usually through resistors. Passive balancing allows the stack to act as if every cell has the same capacity as the weakest cell. Using a relatively low current, it drains a small amount of energy from high SOC cells during the charging cycle so that all cells charge to their maximum state-of-charge (SOC).

Personal protective equipment (PPE) Equipment such as safety glasses and high-voltage gloves are to be worn to help protect the service technician from personal injury when working on vehicles.

Phone as a Key (PAAK) Many hybrid electric and electric vehicles, as well as some regular (ICE) vehicles can be controlled using a smart phone application (app). This control of the vehicle, including remote start from the smart phone, is referred to as Phone as a Key (PAAK).

Photovoltaics (PV) Photovoltaics (PV) is defined as the production of electric current at the interface of two semiconductor materials, which causes them to absorb photons of light and release electrons to produce electricity.

Plug-in hybrid electric vehicle (PHEV) A plug-in hybrid electric vehicle (PHEV) is a vehicle that is designed to be plugged into an electrical outlet at home, at work, or when traveling to charge the batteries. By charging the batteries in the vehicle, it can operate using electric power alone (stealth mode) for a longer time, thereby reducing the use of the internal combustion engine (ICE).

Polymer electrolyte fuel cell (PEFC) Another term for Proton Exchange Membrane fuel cell. (See definition for PEM.)

Positive temperature coefficient (PTC) It refers to the tendency of a conductor to increase its electrical resistance as its temperature increases. PTC heaters convert electrical energy into heat, and this is used to boost heat to the passenger compartment.

Pouch cell Pouch design HV battery uses laminated architecture in a bag referred to as pouch cell. It is light and cost-effective, but exposure to humidity and high temperature can shorten its life.

Power Power is defined as the rate of doing work or the rate at which work is being done.

Power steering control module (PSCM) The power steering control module (PSCM) and the power steering motor are serviced as an assembly and are serviced separately from the steering column assembly.

Pressure transducer A pressure transducer can be used in the low- and/ or high-pressure refrigerant line. The transducer converts the system pressure into an electrical signal that allows the ECM to monitor pressure.

Proton Exchange Membrane (PEM) Proton Exchange Membrane fuel cell. A low-temperature fuel cell known for fast starts and relatively simple construction.

PTC heaters Positive temperature coefficient (PTC) refers to the tendency of a conductor to increase its electrical resistance as its temperature increases. PTC heaters convert electrical energy into heat, and this is used to boost heat to the passenger compartment.

Public Charging Stations (PCS) Public Charging Stations (PCS) are available at many locations and most commercial Level 2 charging stations.

Pulse train A DC voltage that turns on and off in a series of pulses is called a pulse train. Pulse trains differ from an AC signal in that they do not go below zero. An alternating voltage goes above and below zero voltage.

Pulse width Pulse width is a measure of the actual on-time measured in milliseconds. Fuel injectors are usually controlled by varying the pulse width.

Pulse-width modulation (PWM) As on-time increases, the amount of time the signal is off decreases and is usually measured in percentage and can be measured in degrees.

Pumping losses Pumping losses refer to the energy required to overcome the restriction in the intake system to fill the cylinders with air during the intake stroke.

Range Range is how far an electric vehicle can travel on a full battery charge.

Range anxiety Range anxiety is a feeling that many drivers experience when driving an electric vehicle because they fear running out of electric battery energy before they reach their destination. This condition is very common, but according to studies, this feeling lasts about two weeks after first getting an electric vehicle.

Range per hour (RPH) Level 2 charging adds about 25 miles of range per hour (RPH), labeled as miles per hour (MPH) on the dash display of a Nissan Leaf.

Rear cross-traffic warning (RCTW) Rear cross-traffic warning (RCTW) system sounds an audible warning when a vehicle is crossing at the rear while backing. Some vehicles are capable of automatically braking to avoid a collision.

Regeneration The process where electrical energy is directed to and recharges the high-voltage battery. This process is called regeneration, regen, or simply "reclaiming energy."

Resolver Most electric motors use an internal sensor to detect rotor position, speed, and direction that is called a resolver or encoder. The resolver consists of an AC generator or excitation coil and two AC pickup coils or detection coils. The resolver is triggered by a rotating iron egg-shaped wheel that is attached to the rotor.

Right-hand rule Magnetic flux cylinders have direction, just as the flux lines surrounding a bar magnet have direction. Most automotive circuits use the conventional theory of current flow (+ to –), and therefore the right-hand rule is used to determine the direction of the magnetic flux lines.

Rotor In an electric motor, the rotating part (usually on the inside) is called the rotor, and the stationary part is called the stator.

SAE Combo Charging System (CCS) The SAE Combo Charging System (CCS) is a DC Fast Charging (DCFC) connector standard used by BMW, Ford, GM, VW, and other vehicle manufacturers.

SAE J2534 SAE J2534 is a standard for communications between a computer and a vehicle. The original standard was introduced in February of 2002, and was identified as version 02.02. The EPA and CARB regulations require all automakers to provide a J2534 service to everyone in the United States for reflashing emission-related controllers.

Scroll compressor The scroll compressor is a highly efficient and durable design, with very good noise, vibration, and harshness (NVH) characteristics. This is because it is a balanced unit that uses an orbiting motion rather than sliding to compress the gases. It also has very low power consumption relative to other compressor designs, making it especially attractive for hybrid applications.

Self-parking Self-parking vehicles, also called automatic parking vehicles, use the camera(s) and control the electric power steering to guide the vehicle into a parking space. The driver may or may not have to add anything in many advanced systems, whereas the driver must control the throttle and the brakes in early systems.

Sequestration The process of storing carbon dioxide underground is called sequestration.

SLI battery A battery used for starting, lighting, and ignition.

Smog Smog is a term used to describe a condition that looks like smoke and/or fog.

Snubbers Snubbers are capacitors and resistors arranged in a circuit to control the high-voltage surges that can occur when circuits containing coils are switched on and off. Snubbers are also called flyback, freewheeling, suppressor, or catch diodes.

Solar cell A photovoltaic cell, also called a solar cell, is made from semiconductor materials. In a solar cell, a thin semiconductor wafer is used to form an electric field, positive on one side and negative on the other. When light strikes the solar cell, electrons are loosened from the atoms in the semiconductor material N-type and P-type silicon wafers. With electrical conductors attached to the positive and negative sides, an electrical circuit is formed so the electrons can develop an electric current to turn on a light bulb.

Specific energy The energy content of a battery relative to the mass of the battery. Specific energy is measured in watt-hours per kilogram (W-h/kg).

Squirrel-cage rotor A squirrel-cage rotor is composed of parallel thick copper or aluminum conductors connected to a ring of the same material at the ends. As the stator magnetic field rotates, the field interacts with the magnetic field established by the magnetic poles of the rotor, causing the rotor to turn at nearly the speed of the rotating stator magnetic field.

Standard operating guidelines (SOG) Procedures and guidelines are used to ensure that everyone in the department perform common tasks in a specific manner.

Standard operating procedures (SOP) Procedures and guidelines are used to ensure that everyone in the department perform common tasks in a specific manner.

State-of-charge (SOC) The state-of-charge (SOC) is the percentage of the available capacity that can be stored in a battery. A battery that has a state of charge of 100% is fully charged.

Stator In an electric motor, the rotating part (usually on the inside) is called the rotor, and the stationary part is called the stator.

Steering position sensor (SPS) The PSCM uses the steering position sensor (SPS) to determine the steering system on-center position.

Steering shaft torque sensor The steering shaft torque sensor and the steering wheel position sensor are not serviced separately from each other or from the steering column assembly.

Stratosphere The earth's upper atmosphere. Most of the earth's ozone is located in the stratosphere.

Strong hybrid Another term for "full hybrid" (see definition for full hybrid).

Surface permanent magnets (SPMs) Brushless motors, which use permanent magnet rotors, produce high starting torque and are typically over 90% efficient. One type uses the permanent magnets are mounted on the outside surface of the rotor. These are called surface permanent magnets (SPMs).

System main relays (SMRs) System main relays (SMRs) are heavy duty relays that control the high-voltage circuit between the battery and the other components of the high-voltage system. SMRs are often referred to as contactors. Depending on the design of the battery control system, the battery will contain one to three SMRs.

Thermal storage material (TSM) Thermal storage material (TSM), also called phase change material (PCM) evaporator, has a wax chamber in the tank end or between the tubes. The cold insulation case is placed between refrigerant tubes, which extracts cold energy during the air-conditioning cycle.

Time base Setting the time base means setting how much time will be displayed in each block called a division.

Time-of-use (TOU) A time-of-use (TOU) electric rate plan is needed to achieve the largest savings for charging. A TOU plan offers lower electric rates during off-peak periods (usually 11 PM until 5 AM), with higher rates for using electricity during high-demand times. Because most EVs are parked at home overnight, TOU rates are a wise choice for most EV owners.

Torque Torque is the term used to describe a rotating force that may or may not result in motion. Torque is measured as the amount of force multiplied by the length of the lever through which it acts. If a one-foot-long wrench is used to apply 10 pounds of force to the end of the wrench to turn a bolt, then 10 pound-feet of torque is being applied.

Transmission control module (TCM) The electric control module that is used to control the operation and shift or an automatic transmission.

Trigger level Trigger level is the voltage that must be detected by the scope before the pattern will be displayed. A scope will start displaying a voltage signal only when it is triggered or is told to start. The trigger level must be set to start the display. If the pattern starts at 1 volt, the trace will begin displaying on the left side of the screen after the trace has reached 1 volt.

Trigger slope The trigger slope is the voltage direction that a waveform must have in order to start the display. Most often, the trigger to start a waveform display is taken from the signal itself. Besides trigger voltage level, most scopes can be adjusted to trigger only when the voltage rises past the trigger level voltage. This is called a positive slope.

Ultracapacitor An ultracapacitor delivers a quick burst of energy during peak power demands. Some models use an ultracapacitor to help restart the engine.

Ultrasonic object sensors Ultrasonic object sensors are used to measure the distances to nearby objects and are built into the fender, and front and rear bumper assembly. The sensors send out acoustic pulses, and a control unit measures the return interval of each reflected signal, calculating object distances.

Ultraviolet (UV) radiation Ultraviolet (UV) radiation is divided into three. The designations include:

- Designation "A," abbreviated UVA, is not absorbed by the ozone layer and generally is not damaging to biological organisms.
- Designation "B," abbreviated UVB, is only partially absorbed by the ozone layer and can cause damage to biological organisms.
- Designation "C," abbreviated UVC, is almost completely absorbed by the ozone layer and represents little, if any, health concerns.

Variable valve timing (VVT) Variable valve timing (VVT) involves the use of electric and hydraulic actuators that are used to change the timing of the camshaft(s) in relation to the crankshaft. Variable valve timing, also called variable cam timing (VCT), allows the valves to be operated at different points in the combustion cycle to improve performance.

Volatile organic compounds (VOC) Volatile organic compounds (VOC) are gases emitted by paints, solvents, aerosol sprays, cleaners, glues, permanent markers, pesticides, and fuels.

Watt Electric power is the rate at which electrical energy is transferred by an electric circuit. The SI unit of power is the watt.

Watt's law Watt's law describes the relationship between power (P), voltage (E), and current (I). The relationship among power voltage and current can be expressed by the formula $P = I \times E$ and its derivatives $P/E = I$ and $P/I = E$.

Watt-hour The watt-hour is a unit of energy equal to a power of one watt operating for one hour. 1 watt-hour equals 3,600 joules. The kilowatt hour is a unit of energy equal to 1,000 watt-hours, or 3.6 megajoules.

Wind power Wind power is the generation of electricity using air flow through wind turbines, which are mechanically powered generators driven by a large turbine blade.

Wind farms Wind farms are an array of many individual wind turbines that are connected to the electric power transmission network gird. Onshore and offshore wind farms are an inexpensive source of electricity, competitive with coal or gas plants.

Wireless power transfer (WPT) Wireless power transfer (WPT) uses electromagnetic induction (magnetic resonance) between the transmitting pad on the ground and a receiving pad attached for the underside of the vehicle. Wireless charging allows the vehicle to be simply driven over the transmission pad and after a communication "handshake," electrical energy is transmitted from the transmission pad to the receiving pad and then converted from AC to DC to charge the high-voltage battery.

Work Force exerted over a distance.

Work place charging (WPC) Work place charging (WPC) is very popular because the vehicle owner can charge their vehicle while at work and usually for free.

Worldwide harmonized Light vehicles Test Procedure (WLTP) In the United States the Environmental Protection Agency (EPA) estimates of electric vehicle range, while in Europe electric vehicle range uses the Worldwide harmonized Light vehicles Test Procedure (WLTP).

Zero-emission vehicles (ZEVs) Electric vehicles that use battery power alone to propel the vehicle are called zero-emission vehicles (ZEVs).

INDEX

A

Absorbed glass mat (AGM) battery, 104
AC asynchronous motor. *See* AC induction motor (ACIM)
A/C components
    belt-driven compressor, 217
    compressor oil, 217–218
    compressors, 215–216
    condensers, 218–219
    electrically powered compressor, 217
    evaporators, 219
    expansion devices, 219
    subcooling condensers, 219
    thermal storage during idle stop, 221
    three high-voltage wires, 217
    two high-voltage wires, 217
AC coupling, 68
Acid rain, 32–33
AC induction motor (ACIM), 146
Acoustic vehicle alerting system (AVAS), 10
AC synchronous motor, 146–147
Adaptive cruise control (ACC)
    diagnosis and service, 256–257
    parts and operation, 256
    purpose and function, 255
    terminology, 255
Advanced driver assist systems (ADAS)
    antilock brake system, 251
    electronic power steering, 251
    electronic throttle control (ETC) system, 251
    foundation of, 251
    purpose, 251
Airbags and tensioners, 285–286
Air-conditioning system. *See also* A/C components
    A/C mode, 214
    airflow, 214
    defrost mode, 214
    operation, 213–214
    service, 61, 220
Alkaline batteries. *See* Nickel-metal hydride (NiMH) battery
Alternating current (DC) electricity
    definition, 91
    generation, 91–92
    waveforms, 92
Alternative out-of-vehicle HV battery service
    internal resistance, 135
    procedure, 134–135
    state-of-charge, 135
Always Be Charging (ABC), 169

American National Standards Institute (ANSI), 4
American Society for Testing and Materials (ASTM), 4
Ampere hour, 105
Antilock braking system (ABS), 190, 251
Application programming interface (API), 98
Armature, 145
Artificial intelligence (AI) systems, 265
Atkinson cycle
    background, 38
    engines, 38
    operation, 38
Automatic emergency braking (AEB) system, 258
Automatic parking vehicles. *See* Self-parking vehicles
Automation levels, 263–265
    Level 1 and 2 systems, 264
    Level 3, 4, or 5 systems, 265
    Level 0 systems, 263–264
    SAE definitions, 263
Autonomous vehicle (AV) operation, 263
Auxiliary battery
    discharged, 103
    testing and service, 62
Auxiliary components, 113–114
Auxiliary water pump diagnosis, 211

B

Batteries. *See also* Auxiliary battery
    absorbed glass mat, 104
    capacity *vs.* vehicle mileage, 129–130
    degradation rate, 136
    high-voltage, 120
    hydrogen-powered, 269
    inspection and testing, 137–138
    lead-acid, 122
    lithium-ion high-voltage, 123–124
    nickel-metal hydride, 120–123
    normal operation, 136
    passive and active cell balancing, 136
    service safety precautions, 105–106
    12-volt, 103
    valve-regulated lead-acid, 104
Battery control module (BCM), 130
    current sensors, 130
    HV disconnect, 131
    System Main Relays, 130
    temperature sensors, 130–131
    voltage block monitoring circuits, 130
Battery density, 126

Battery electric vehicles (BEVs), 15, 166. *See also* Battery capacity
Battery management system (BMS), 131
Battery works
   charging state, 104
   discharging state, 103
   fully discharged state, 103–104
   principle involved, 103
Belt alternator starter (BAS) system, 110–111
Belt-driven compressor, 217
Blind spot monitor (BSM)
   function and terminology, 252
   parts and operation, 252–253
Body control module (BCM), 112
Boost converters, 155–156
Brake pedal position (BPP) sensor, 193
Braking system service, 59–60
Brushless motors
   AC induction motor, 146
   AC synchronous motor, 146–147
   electric motor torque, 148
   operation, 147–148
   permanent magnet motors, 147
   types, 146

C

Cabin cooling. *See* Air-conditioning system
California Air Resources Board (CARB), 15
Cameras, 259
   calibration, 261
Capacitors
   construction, 92–93
   in converters, 151–152
   definition, 92
   farad rating, 153
   operation, 93–94, 151–152
   precautions, 151
   principles, 151
   snubbers, 153
   spike suppression, 94
Carbohydrates, 28
Carbon-based fuels, 28
Carbon footprint
   definition, 33
   reduction, 34
Carbon-neutral fuel, 274
Catch diodes. *See* Snubbers
Cathode ray tube (CRT), 66
CAT III digital multimeter, 7
CGS (Centimeter Gram Second) measuring system, 80
CHAdeMO, 169
Channels, 70
Charge-Coupled Device (CCD), 259

Charging battery
   AGM, 109
   procedure, 108
   timing, 109
Chevrolet Bolt drive unit, 246
Coke bottle resonance, 63
Cold-cranking amperes (CCA), 105
Cold-weather concerns, 166
Colors of cables checking, 284
Column-mounted electric power steering (C-EPS), 200
Combustion, 37
Communications, 96–97
   CAN bus, 97
Commutator, 146
Compartment heating system
   auxiliary water pump diagnosis, 211
   electric engine water pump, 210
   failure mode, 211
   heat mode, 210
   modes of operation, 212
   parts and operation, 209–210
   principles, 209
Compression stroke, 37
Compression test, 52
Compressors, 215–216
   belt-driven, 217
   electrically powered, 217
   oil, 217–218
Computing power vehicles, 265
Condensers, 218. *See also* Capacitors
   liquid-cooled, 223–225
Conductance testing, battery, 108
Controller Area Network (CAN) protocol
   bus communication, 97
   class A, B, and C, 97–98
   features, 97
Converters, 153–155
   boost, 155
   capacitors in, 151–152
   DC-to-DC, 153–155
   mild hybrids, 115
   replacement of, 159–161
Coolant dye leak testing, 48–49
Coolant heat storage system
   operational modes, 49–50
   parts and operation, 212
   purpose, 49, 212
   retaining heat, 49
Cooling system service, 59
Cooling system testing
   coolant dye leak testing, 48–49
   pressure testing, 48

scan tool, 47–48
visual inspection, 48
Cranking amperes, 105
Current clamps, 71
Current sensors, 130
Cylinder leakage test, 53–54
Cylindrical NiMH battery, 122

D

Data recording, 72
DC coupling, 68
DCFC (DC Fast Charge), 169
DC Quick Charge (DCQC), 169
DC-to-DC converters, 153–155
testing, 157
Dedicated short-range communication (DSRC), 265–266
Department of Transportation (DOT), 263
Depowering high-voltage system, 9
Destination charging, 173
Diagnosis procedures, 63
Dielectric insulating material, 151
Digital multimeter (DMM), 7
Digital storage oscilloscope (DSO), 66. *See also* Oscilloscope
accessories, 71–72
current clamps, 71
data recording, 72
line characteristics, 72
pressure transducers, 71
vacuum transducer, 72
waveform analysis, 72–73
Direct current (DC) electricity
definition, 90
generation, 90
waveform, 90
Direct-drive electric power steering (D-EPS) system, 200
Direct methanol fuel cells
disadvantages, 273
operation, 273
purpose and function, 272–273
Discharged auxiliary battery, 103
Dog mode, 225
Double overhead camshaft (DOHC) engines, 42
Driver assist diagnosis
diagnostic steps, 261
vin decoder, 261
Driver assist systems. *See* Advanced driver assist systems (ADASs)
Dual-voltage electrical system, 120
Duty cycle, 68

E

Eight channel scope, 70
Electrical Distribution System (EDS)
isolation testing, 132
purpose, 131–132
state-of-charge management, 132
Electrically powered compressor, 217
Electrical measurements
megohms, 96
milliohms, 96
Electrical power, 81–82
Electric auxiliary pump, 230
Electric engine water pump, 210
Electric machine, 41
Electric motor control
electronic cooling system, 151
generator mode, 149
insulated-gate bipolar transistors, 149–150
motor mode, 148–149
principles, 148
resolver, 150–151
temperature sensors, 151
Electric motor stator testing, 157
Electric motor torque, 148
Electric power-assisted steering (EPAS), 200
Electric power steering (EPS)
advantages, 200
control unit, 201
diagnostic procedure, 204–205
diagnostic trouble codes (DTCs), 205
fault detection, 203
inputs and outputs, 202
motor types, 201
parts and operation, 201–204
power steering control module, 203
steering shaft torque sensor, 203
steering wheel position sensor, 203
terminology, 200
types/designs, 200–201
Electric shock potential, 3, 287
Electric vehicle (EV), 15
advantages of, 23–24
battery capacity, 166
battery heating, 129
charging cost, 167
cold-weather concerns, 166
disadvantages of, 24
driving, 17–18
electric motors and ICEs, 16
equivalent economy, 129
front-wheel-drive, 25
history, 15
hot-weather concerns, 166
increasing speed of, 24
kilowatts per 100 miles, 167
lifting process, 58
maintenance, 18–20
owning and charging, 172–174

Electric vehicle (EV) (*continued*)
   purchasing price, 18
   range, 166
   routine service procedures, 57–63
Electric vehicles (EV) transmissions
   acceleration *vs.* top speed, 245
   Chevrolet Bolt drive unit, 246
   Ford Mustang Mach-E, 245
   Nissan LEAF, 246–247
   single speed gearing, 245
   two-speed gearing, 248
Electric vehicle supply equipment (EVSE)
   hard wired, 180
   home level 2 charging, 181–182
   location, 180, 181
   National Electrical Manufacturers Association, 179–180
   National Electric Code, 180
   Nationally Recognized Testing Laboratory, 180
   permits, 180–181
   purpose and function, 179
   SAE J1772 standard charger plug, 182–184
   Underwriter's Laboratory (UL mark), 180
   wattage, 182
Electrohydraulic power steering (EHPS), 204
Electrolyte, 120–121
Electromagnetic induction, 94
   definition, 143
   principles, 143
   voltage strength, 143–144
Electromagnetic parking sensors (EPS), 253
Electromagnetism, 94
   coil conductor, 143
   creation of, 142
   definition, 142
   electromagnets, 143
   field interaction, 142
   motor principle, 142–143
   principles, 142
   right-hand rule, 142
   straight conductor, 142
Electromagnets, 143
Electronically controlled continuously variable transmission (eCVT), 243
Electronically erasable programmable read only memory (EEPROM), 98
Electronically variable transmission (EVT), 232
Electronic cooling system
   construction, 127
   diagnostic steps, 157
   heat effects on electrical/electronic system, 126–127
   internal combustion engine, 157
   need for, 126, 156–157

Electronic medical devices, 2
Electronic power steering (EPS), 251
Electronic throttle control (ETC) system, 251
Emergency response, 287
Encoder. *See* Resolver
Energy
   carrier, 269
   definition, 79
   forms of, 79
   goethermal, 85–87
   recirculation, 239
   solar electric generation, 82–83
   units, 79–80
Energy efficiency ratio (EER), 87
Engine control module (ECM), 112, 116
Engine coolant temperature (ECT) sensor, 47
Engine cooling system, 46
Engine fundamentals, 37–38
Environmental concerns, 28–32
Environmental Protection Agency (EPA), 15, 32, 129
European New Car Assessment Program (Euro NCAP), 257
EV and HEV items to check
   high-voltage battery, 285
   orange cables, 284
   12-volt auxiliary battery, 285
EV and HEV module communications
   CAN bus communication, 97
   CAN class A, B, and C, 97–98
   CAN features, 97
EV heating
   electrical resistance heating, 221
   heated seats and steering wheel, 220–221
   PTC heaters, 221–222
   range, 220
EV range, 164
Exhaust stroke, 38
Extended range electric vehicle (EREV), 165

F

Farad rating, 153
Fire
   defensive attack, 288
   offensive attack, 288
   SOP/SOG, 288
First responder procedures
   EV and HEV items to check, 284–285
   identifying EV/hybrid vehicle, 283–284
   incidents, 283
   SOP/SOG, 283
   visual analysis, 283
First responder safety
   airbags and tensioners, 285–286
   hot stick, 285

shepherd's hook, 285
Five-stroke cycle, 38
Flux lines, 142
Flyback. *See* Snubbers
Force, 189–190
Ford escape precautions, 196
Ford/Lincoln 10R80 MHT
    components, 234–235
    description, 234
    service procedures, 235–236
Ford Mustang Mach-E, 245
Fossil fuels reduction, 28
Four channel scope, 70
Four-stroke cycle operation, 37–38
Freewheeling. *See* Snubbers
Frequency, 68
Front-wheel-drive (FWD) vehicle, 229
Fuel-cell stack, 270–271
Fuel cell technology
    advantages of, 269–270
    air supply pumps, 275
    background, 269
    carbon-neutral fuel, 274
    cooling systems, 274
    definition, 269
    direct methanol, 272–273
    disadvantages of, 270
    homogeneous charge compression ignition, 279–280
    humidifiers, 273–274
    hybridization, 275
    hydrogen-powered battery, 269
    hydrogen sources, 269
    hydrogen storage, 275–277
    parts and operation, 269
    Polymer Electrolyte Fuel Cell, 270
    power control units, 279
    refueling with hydrogen, 272
    stack, 270–271
    traction motors, 278–279
    transaxles, 277–278
    types of, 270, 271
    ultracapacitors, 277
Fuel economy, non-high voltage components, 57
Full hybrid electric vehicle, 20

G

General Motors parallel hybrid truck (PHT)
    description, 231
    operation, 231–232
    service, 232
Geothermal energy, 85–87
Geothermal heat pump (GHP) system, 87
Global (generic) diagnostic trouble codes, 157

Graticule, 66
Greenhouse gases (GHG), 29
Ground-level ozone, 30
Guess-O-Meter (GOM), 129
Guobiao standard (GB/T), 170, 172

H

Haptic actuator, 252
Hard wired, 180
Hazardous materials (hazmat) issues, 288
    high-voltage (HV) batteries, 288–289
    12-volt auxiliary battery, 288
Health and environmental concerns, 32
    acid rain, 32–33
    carbohydrates, 28
    carbon-based fuels, 28
    carbon footprint, 33–34
    chemistry of carbon-based emissions, 28–29
    fossil fuels reduction, 28
    greenhouse gases, 29
Heat/cool HV batteries
    heating methods, 129
    need for, 128
    service of, 128–129
Heating, ventilation, and air-conditioning (HVAC) system, 220–221
Heat pump
    liquid-cooled condenser (LCC), 223–225
    parts and operation, 222
    purpose and function, 222
Heavy-duty starter, 112–113
HEV ICE cooling system, 46–47
    engine (ICE) cooling, 46
    thermostats, 47
HEV/PHEV maintenance items, 57
High-pressure compressed gas, 275–276
High-voltage (HV) batteries
    air filter, 60
    checking process, 285
    cooling and heating system, 128–129
    electric motor requirements, 120
    purpose and function, 120
High-voltage battery monitor
    scan data test procedure, 133–134
    state-of-charge, 133
High-voltage cables, 116
High-voltage glove photo sequence, 11–12
High-voltage tools and equipment
    CAT III digital multimeter, 7
    depowering high-voltage system, 9
    hoisting, 9
    insulated hand tools, 7–8
    meg-ohm meter (insulation tester), 7
    safety interlock system, 8–9

Home level 2 charging, 181–182, 186
Homogeneous Charge Compression Ignition (HCCI), 279–280
Horse power, 80–81
Hot stick, 285
Hot-weather concerns, 166
Human–machine interface (HMI)
   communication methods, 251–252
   definition, 251
Hybrid and electric vehicle safety
   caution, 2
   electric shock potential, 3
   high-voltage circuits, 2
   high-voltage tools and equipment, 7–8
   medical devices, 2
   personal protective equipment (PPE), 4–6
   safe working environment, 3
Hybrid control module, 116
Hybrid electric rear drive axle, 244
Hybrid electric vehicle (HEV), 15. See also Electric vehicle (EV)
   driving, 16–17
   fuel cell technology, 275
   high-voltage battery monitor, 133–134
   history of, 15–16
   ICE cooling system, 46–47
   levels of, 20
   maintenance, 18–20
   maintenance mode, 57–58
   medium, 20
   micro, 20
   mild, 20
   powertrain classifications, 20–22
   purchasing price, 18
   routine service procedures, 57–63
   strong, 20
Hybrid electric vehicle (HEV) transmissions
   classifications, 230
   electric auxiliary pump, 230
   hydraulic impulse storage accumulator, 231
Hybrid engine design
   offset crankshaft, 41–42
   piston pin offset, 40–41
Hybrid engine run mode
   operating procedure, 51–52
   purpose, 50–51
Hybrid engine system
   coolant heat storage system, 49–50
   cooling system testing, 47–49
   HEV ICE cooling system, 46–47
   run mode, 50–52
   testing, 52–54
   variable valve timing, 42–46
Hybrid engine testing
   compression test, 52
   cylinder leakage test, 53–54
Hybrid internal combustion engines, 37
   Atkinson cycle, 38–39
   differences, 37
   engine fundamentals, 37–38
Hybrid Synergy Drive (HSD), 127
Hydraulic impulse storage accumulator, 231
Hydroelectricity
   definition, 84
   economic impact, 84
Hydrogen-powered battery, 269
Hydrogen storage
   high-pressure compressed gas, 275–276
   liquid, 276
   purpose and function, 275
   solid, 277

I

ICE (internal combustion engine) cooling system
   basic operation, 208
   engine cooling, 208
   thermostat, 208–209
   water pump, 208
ICE vehicle mileage, 129
Incidents, 283
Induced voltage, 94, 143
Induction, 143
Inertia, 189–190
Instrument cluster warning messages, 57
Insulated-gate bipolar transistors (IGBTs), 95–96, 149–150
Insulated hand tools, 7–8
Intake stroke, 37
Integrated Drive Module (iDM), 244
Intelligent battery sensor module, 112
Intelligent Speed Advice (ISA), 257
Interior permanent magnets (IPMs), 147
Intermittent Blower Motor, 215
Internal combustion engines (ICE), 15, 37
International Electrotechnical Commission (IEC), 7
International Fire Service Training Association (IFSTA), 288
Inverters, 155, 159–161
Isolation testing
   EDS, 132
   loss of, 158

J

JIS (Japanese Industrial Standard), 105–106
Joule, 79

K

Kilowatt (kW), 81, 92, 129
Kilowatt-hour (kWh), 81, 129, 164
Kinetic energy, 189

L

Lane departure warning system (LDWS), 254
Lane keep assist (LKA), 255
Laws of thermodynamics, 79
Lead–acid batteries, 122
Lenz's law, 144
Level 1 charging
    20-ampere circuit, 167–168
    precautions using, 168
Level 2 charging
    higher voltage system, 168–169
    on-board chargers, 169
Level 3 charging
    DC fast charging, 169
    electrical connectors, 169–172
LiDAR systems, 260–261
    definition, 259
    diagnosis and calibration, 261
    parts and operation, 261
Light Detection and Ranging, 260
Light Imaging, Detection, And Ranging, 260
Line characteristics, 72
Liquid-cooled condenser (LCC), 223–225
Liquid hydrogen storage, 276
Lithium-ion high-voltage batteries
    advantages, 123–124
    cathode material, 125–126
    construction, 123
    cylindrical, 124
    description, 123
    designs, 124–125
    disadvantages, 124
    operation, 123
    pouch type, 124
    prismatic hard case, 124
    repair, 134
    types of, 125–126
    uses, 123
Lithium iron phosphate (LiFePO$_4$), 125
Load testing, battery, 107
Locked rotor current, 147
Locked rotor torque (LRT), 147
Locksmith ID number, 99
Low-grade heat, 274

M

Magnetic force
    electromagnetic induction, 94
    electromagnetism, 94
    magnetism, 94
Manual transmission equipped vehicles, 112
Mass, 189–190
Medium hybrid electric vehicle, 20
Meg-ohm meter (insulation tester), 7
Megohms, 96
Membrane Electrode Assembly (MEA), 270
Micro hybrids
    auxiliary components, 113–114
    batteries, 113
    body control module, 112
    electric vehicle, 20
    engine control module, 112
    heavy-duty starter, 112–113
    intelligent battery sensor module, 112
    manual transmission equipped vehicles, 112
    operation, 112
    parts involved, 112
    transmission control module, 112
    ultracapacitors, 113
Mild hybrids
    battery, 115
    diagnosis and testing, 117
    electric motor, 115–116
    electric vehicle, 20
    engine control module, 116
    high-voltage cables, 116
    hybrid control module, 116
    inverter/converter, 116
    parts and operation, 115–116
    terminology, 115
    transmission control module, 116
Miles-per-gallon measurement, 129
Miles per hour (MPH), 169
Milliohms, 96
MKS (Meter Kilogram Second) measuring system, 80
Module reprogramming
    off-board, 100
    on-board, 100
    programming hardware, 98–99
    purpose, 98
    remote, 100
    SAE J2534 standard, 98
    vehicle security professional—locksmith ID, 99
Motor control
    examples, 94–95
    insulated-gate bipolar transistors, 95–96
    principles, 94
Motors. *See also* Electric motor control
    brushless, 146–148
    DC motor, 146
    examples, 148–149
    global (generic) diagnostic trouble codes, 157
    operation, 145
    power, 144
MPGe, 129
Mustang Mach E, 174, 194, 229, 245, 285, 288

N

National Automotive Service Task Force (NASTF), 99
National Electrical Manufacturers Association (NEMA), 179–180
National Electric Code (NEC), 180
National Fire Academy (NFA), 288
National Fire Protection Association (NFPA), 288
National Highway Traffic Safety Administration (NHTSA), 10
Nationally Recognized Testing Laboratory (NRTL), 180
Newton-meters (N-m), 80
Nickel, cobalt, and aluminum (NCA), 125
Nickel, manganese, and cobalt (NMC), 125
Nickel-metal hydride (NiMH) battery
   advantages/disadvantages, 122
   charging/discharging operations, 121
   cylindrical, 122
   description and operation, 120
   designs, 122
   electrolyte, 120–121
   prismatic, 122
   series connection, 122–123
   uses, 120
Nissan LEAF, 246–247
Noise-reducing tires, 61–62
Non-high voltage components, 57

O

Occupational Safety and Health Administration (OSHA), 4
Off-board programming, 100
Offset crankshaft, 41–42
Oil and filter service, 58–59
On-board reprogramming, 100
One-pedal driving, 18
   advantages, 195
   definition, 194
   examples, 194–195
One-, two-, and three-motor hybrid system, 22–23
Open circuit battery voltage test, 107
Orifice tube (OT), 218–219
Original equipment manufacturers (OEMs), 134
Oscilloscope
   AC coupling, 68
   channels, 70
   DC coupling, 68
   definition, 66
   display grid, 66–67
   leads, 71
   measuring auxiliary battery voltage, 71
   on-time and off-time, 69
   pulse trains, 68–69
   setting time base, 67
   setup photo sequence, 74–75
   triggers, 70
   types of, 66
   volts per division, 67
Owning and charging EV
   cost, 174
   locating station, 173–174
   Public Charging Stations, 173
   work place charging, 173
Ozone
   definition, 30
   ground-level, 30
   upper-level, 30
   vehicles and, 30
Ozone-depleting substances (ODS), 30

P

Parallel hybrid powertrain, 20–21
Parallel hybrid truck (PHT), 231–232
Parallel regenerative braking systems, 191–193
Parking-assist system, 253–254
   diagnosis, 253–254
   electromagnetic parking sensors, 253
   function and components, 253
   operation, 253
   self-parking vehicles, 254
   ultrasonic object sensors, 253
Permanent magnet motors, 147
Personal protective equipment (PPE), 283, 288–289
   eye protection, 4
   fire extinguishers, 6
   high-voltage gloves, 4–5
   insulated rubber mats and blankets, 5–6
   insulated shoes/boots, 5
   leather protectors, 5
   personal protection equipment, 6
   shop uniform, 5
Pet mode. *See* Dog mode
Phase change material (PCM). *See* Thermal storage material (TSM)
Phone as a Key (PAAK), 15
Photovoltaics (PV), 82, 184
   operation, 82–83
pH SCALE, 32–33
Pinion-mounted electric power steering system (P-EPS) system, 200–201
Piston pin offset, 40–41
Plug-in hybrid electric vehicle (PHEV), 15, 165
   battery capacity, 164
   charging, 165
   examples, 164–165
   identifying, 164
   terminology, 164
Polymer Electrolyte Fuel Cell (PEFC), 270
Positive/high-side IGBTs, 95

Positive temperature coefficient (PTC), 213
Pouch cell, 125
Pound-feet (lb-ft), 80
Power, 80
   electrical, 81–82
   horse, 80–81
   wind, 83
Power drive unit (PDU), 94–95
Power output (watts)
   background, 92
   formulas, 92
Power steering control module (PSCM), 203
Power stroke, 38
Pre-charge resistor, 155
Pre-collision system, 258–259
Pressure transducers, 71
Preventative maintenance. See Routine service procedures
Prismatic NiMH battery, 122
Programming software, 99
Prony brakes, 81
Proton Exchange Membrane (PEM), 270
PTC heaters, 213
Public Charging Stations (PCS), 173
Pulse trains
   definition, 68
   duty cycle, 68
   frequency, 68
   pulse width, 68
   signal, 69
Pulse width, 68
Pulse-width modulation (PWM), 68

R

Rack-and-pinion electric power steering (R-EPS) system, 200
Radar calibration, 261–263
Radar cruise control. See Adaptive cruise control
Range, 166
Range anxiety, 167
   driving electric vehicle, 18
Range per hour (RPH), 169
Rear cross-traffic warning (RCTW) system
   parts and operation, 257–258
   purpose, 257
Rear-wheel-drive (RWD) applications, 229
Rebooting digital display, 251
Reclaiming energy. See Regeneration
Refueling with hydrogen
   fueling procedure, 272
   pressures used, 272
   SAE J2601, 272
Regeneration, 190
Regenerative braking systems
   benefits of, 191

   components, 193–194
   deceleration rates, 195
   Ford escape precautions, 196
   friction, 190
   inertia, force, and mass, 189–190
   limitations of, 190
   one-pedal driving, 194–195
   parallel, 191–193
   series, 191
   servicing, 195–197
   transferring energy back to motor, 190
   types of, 191
   unique master cylinders, 195–196
Relative motion, 94, 143
Remote programming, 100
Reserve capacity, batteries, 105
Resolver, 150–151
Revolutions per minute (RPM), 68
Right-hand rule, 142
Rotor, 145
Routine service procedures
   air-conditioning service, 61
   auxiliary battery testing and service, 62
   braking system service, 59–60
   cooling system service, 59
   customer perception, 57
   diagnosis procedures, 63
   engine maintenance, 59
   high-voltage battery air filter, 60
   instrument cluster warning messages, 57
   noise-reducing tires, 61–62
   non-high voltage components, 57
   oil and filter service, 58–59
   steering system service, 62–63
   tire service, 61

S

SAE Combo Charging System (CCS), 169
SAE J2601, hydrogen-fueling protocol, 272
SAE J2534 standard, 98
SAE J1772 standard charger plug, 182–184
Safety interlock system
   local interlock, 8–9
   purpose and function, 8
Sample hybrid/electric vehicle specialist (L3) ASE-type certification test, 291–294
Scope. See Oscilloscope
Sealed valve-regulated (SVR)/sealed lead-acid (SLA). See Valve-regulated lead-acid (VRLA) batteries
Self-parking vehicles, 254
Senseless DC motor design, 147
Sequestration, 34
Series hybrid powertrain, 20–21

Series-parallel hybrid powertrain, 21–22
Series regenerative braking systems, 191
Servicing regenerative braking systems, 195–197
Shepherd's hook, 285
Shock hazards, 287
Single channel scope, 70
SI units (International System of Units), 79–80
SLI battery, 103
Smog. *See* Ozone
Snubbers, 153
Solar cell. *See* Photovoltaics (PV)
Solar electric generation
   photovoltaics, 82
   sun, 82
Solid hydrogen storage, 277
Solid-state battery, 126
Squirrel-cage rotor, 146
Standard operating procedures (SOP)/standard operating
      guidelines (SOG), 283, 287
State-of-charge (SOC), 173
   management, 132
Stator, 145
Steering shaft torque sensor, 201–202, 203
Steering system service, 62–63
Steering wheel position sensor, 203
Stop-start systems
   BAS system, 110–111
   definition, 110
   diagnosis, 114–115
   micro hybrids, 112–114
   mild hybrids, 115–117
Stratosphere, 31
Strong hybrid electric vehicle, 20
Submerged vehicles, 289
Suppressor. *See* Snubbers
Surface permanent magnets (SPMs), 147
System main relays (SMRs), 3, 130

T

Temperature sensors, 130–131, 151
Terminal voltage test, 107
Tesla, 194, 221, 223, 225
Tesla HV batteries, 124, 129
Tesla Supercharger, 170, 171
Thermal storage material (TSM), 220
Thermostatic expansion valve (TXV), 218, 219
Thermostats, 47
36-48 volt battery
   construction and design, 109–110
   diagnosis and testing, 110
   purpose and function, 109
Three-motor hybrid systems, 22–23
Time-of-use (TOU), 172

Tire service, 61
Top dead center (TDC), 38
Torque, 80
Torque delivery, 230
Torque Sensor Signal, 201
Toyota hybrid eCVT transmissions, 243
Toyota/Lexus power-split system
   applications, 236
   construction, 241–243
   deceleration and braking, 240
   description, 236–237
   full-throttle acceleration and high-speed cruise, 238–240
   light acceleration, 238
   normal driving, 238
   operation, 237–240
   service procedures, 243
   vehicle stopped, 237–238
Traction battery, 103
Transmission adaptive pressure (TAP) values, 232
Transmission control module (TCM), 112, 116
Transmissions/transaxles
   adaptive cruise control, 255–257
   advanced driver assist systems, 251
   artificial intelligence (AI) systems, 265
   automatic emergency braking (AEB) system, 258
   automation levels, 263–265
   autonomous vehicle, 263
   blind spot monitor, 252–253
   computing power vehicles, 265
   configurations, 229
   dedicated short-range communication, 265–266
   diagnosing hybrid, 244–245
   driver assist diagnosis, 261
   electric vehicles, 245–248
   Ford/Lincoln 10R80 MHT, 235–236
   human–machine interface, 251–252
   hybrid electric rear drive axle, 244
   hybrid electric vehicle, 230–231
   lane departure warning system, 254
   lane keep assist, 255
   LiDAR systems, 260–261
   multiple speed, 230
   parallel hybrid truck (PHT), 231–232
   parking-assist system, 253–254
   powertrain configuration, 229
   pre-collision system, 258–259
   principles, 230
   purpose and function, 229
   rear cross-traffic warning (RCTW) system, 257–258
   torque delivery, 230
   Toyota hybrid eCVT, 243
   Toyota/Lexus power-split, 236–243
   two-mode hybrid transmission, 232–234

Triggers
- external, 70
- level, 70
- slope, 70
- using, 71

12-volt auxiliary battery checking, 285

12-volt battery
- ampere hour, 105
- charging, 108–109
- cold-cranking amperes, 105
- conductance testing, 108
- cranking amperes, 105
- discharged auxiliary battery, 103
- importance of, 103
- Japanese Industrial Standard, 105–106
- load testing, 107
- purpose and function, 103
- ratings, 105
- reserve capacity, 105
- voltage test, 106–107

Two channel scope, 70

Two-mode hybrid transmission
- components, 232
- description, 232
- first mode of operation, 232–233
- second mode of operation, 233–234
- two-mode service, 234

Two-motor hybrid systems, 22–23

Two-speed gearing transmission, 248

U

Ultracapacitors, 113, 277

Ultrasonic object sensors, 253

Ultraviolet (UV) radiation
- intensity of, 31
- ozone control of UVB irradiance, 31
- types of, 31

Underwriter's Laboratory (UL mark), 180

Unique master cylinders, 195–196

Upper-level ozone, 30

V

Vacuum transducer, 72

Valve-regulated lead-acid (VRLA) batteries, 104

Vane phaser system, 43–45

Variable cam timing (VCT), 41

Variable valve timing (VVT)
- camshaft phasers, 43
- diagnosis of, 45–46
- parts and operation, 43
- purpose of, 42
- spline phaser system operation, 43
- systems, 42
- vane phaser system, 43–45

Vehicle security professional—locksmith ID, 99

Voltage block monitoring circuits, 130

Voltage regulator, 153

Voltage test, battery, 106–107

Voltmeter with clock, 66

Volts per division *(V/div)*, 67

VW ID4, 284

W

Watt, 82, 92

Watt-hour, 81

Watt's law, 82

Waveform analysis, 72–73
- data recording, 72
- line characteristics, 72

Wind farms, 83–84

Wind power, 83

Wireless power transfer (WPT)
- charging standards, 184
- measurements, 185
- working process, 184

Woods Dual Power, 15

Work, 80

Work place charging (WPC), 173

Worldwide harmonized Light vehicles Test Procedure (WLTP), 129

Wound rotor, 146

Z

Zero-emission vehicles (ZEVs), 166